Introduction to Applied Psychology

W. Larry Gregory
New Mexico State University

W. Jeffrey Burroughs
Clemson University

Scott, Foresman and Company
Glenview, Illinois   Boston   London

Library of Congress Cataloging-in-Publication Data

Gregory, W. Larry.
    Introduction to applied psychology / W. Larry Gregory, W. Jeffrey
Burroughs.
        p.   cm.
    Bibliography: p.
    Includes index.
    ISBN 0-673-18739-X
    1. Psychology, Applied.   I. Burroughs, W. Jeffrey.   II. Title.
BF636.G66 1989
158--dc19   88-23982
                                                                            CIP

1 2 3 4 5 6-RRC-94 93 92 91 90 89

Preface

Increasingly, psychologists are obtaining employment in nontraditional settings. Many undergraduate students, however, are unaware of the kind of work psychologists do outside of mental health clinics and child development settings. This text, oriented toward college sophomores, is designed to educate students about the wide variety of positions psychologists fill in governmental, industrial, educational, and social-service settings. The introductory chapter is followed by a methodology chapter emphasizing research tools used in applied settings. A series of chapters then describes various areas of applied psychology. Students are given information on the nature of the applied area in question and on employment settings and work activities. Each chapter features a section designed to help students discover the variety of work activities and settings open to psychologists in different applied areas. Each chapter also describes various applications so that readers are able to see psychological principles making an impact on everyday problems.

The introductory chapter explains the purpose of the book, includes a historical note to provide a context for the material that follows, and then discusses some of the forces in society and within the field of psychology that are driving an overall trend toward applications. The relationship between basic research and applications is described, and the organization of the book is summarized in a section called "Mapping the Territory." In many ways the introductory chapter is a displaced preface that presents the "why" and "how" of the book in more extended form.

The second chapter covers basic research design and analysis techniques and stresses ways in which these techniques are implemented in applied settings. The topic of evaluation is so important that a special evaluation section has been included in an appendix so that students can gain an in-depth understanding of the issues and techniques involved.

The balance of the book is organized into three major sections: Psychology in Business and Industrial Settings (engineering psychology, industrial/organizational psychology, organizational development, applied cognitive psychology, and consumer psychology); Psychology in Community Settings (clinical psychology, community psychology, health psychology, applied social psychology, psychology and the law, and applied environmental psychology); and Psychology and Human Development (psychology in educational settings, sports psychology, and applied developmental psychology). The "Mapping the Territory" section in Chapter 1 describes each of these chapters in more detail.

This book is designed to be used in a sophomore-level course that covers the applied areas in psychology. In our experience such a course appeals both to majors who need an understanding of career options in psychology and to nonmajors who desire insight into various applied work settings. The content of applied psychology courses varies considerably from school to school. This text will be of most use in a course that surveys the various areas of applied psychology. A strength of the book is its broad coverage—areas of psychology not frequently considered in applied texts are described in detail here. It should be noted that some courses in applied psychology are actually adjustment courses that emphasize self-help topics. This text is not an adjustment text.

Many people contributed time and effort to this book, and we would like to acknowledge their support. First, thanks to our authors; their expertise in their various disciplines is the strength of this book, and their patience with us as editors made it possible to produce a cohesive and accessible survey of the field. Our academic reviewers included Scott Geller, Virginia Polytechnic University; Douglas Johnson, the University of Arkansas; Robert Lueger, Marquette University; William Roe, Phoenix College; and Robert Vance, The Ohio State University. Scott Hardy, psychology editor at Scott, Foresman, saw the need for a book in applied psychology and has given us constant support. Rebecca Strehlow, our developmental editor, challenged assumptions and helped shape the text. Her patience and professional competence are deeply appreciated. Kay Bartolo, project editor at Scott, Foresman, supervised production. Finally, we express deep thanks to our families for patience, love, and support.

W. L. G.
Las Cruces, New Mexico

W. J. B.
Clemson, South Carolina

Contents

Part 1

Today's Psychological Research

1 Applied Psychology: An Introduction

W. Jeffrey Burroughs
Clemson University

W. Larry Gregory
New Mexico State University

Psychology is a science in the process of transforming itself. A significant aspect of that transformation is stronger emphasis on the *application* of psychological principles and research findings to the solution of everyday problems. In this book, specialists in 16 areas of applied psychology tell what they do and how they do it. The result is a comprehensive survey of the many dynamic fields within the larger discipline.

This introductory chapter has four purposes. First, it will tell you why we undertook the project. Second, it will sketch the historical background of applied psychology in order to provide a meaningful context for the material in the chapters that follow. Third, the chapter will analyze the reasons for the current intense interest in applied psychology and for its greatly expanded role in today's world. Fourth, it will outline the text's organization to provide direction for your study.

A Displaced Preface: Genesis of This Book

If you are like most students, the preface is the part of the book you skip over on your way to the assigned reading. But we believe that knowing why and how we put this text together will give purpose and direction to your study. That is the reason why we have included additional introductory material here in Chapter 1.

Some people, including some students in the discipline, think that being a psychologist means engaging in individual counseling or conducting group therapy sessions, as in the photograph. The fact is that applied psychology covers the full range of human activity—from product design to affirmative-action employment practices.

Picture a student going to see a professor in a psychology department to find out about careers in the field. Maybe you have even been in this situation yourself. Frequently students visiting their instructors to talk about employment opportunities in psychology do not have a clear picture of their career options. All too often this realization comes toward the end of their college years. For many, being a psychologist means being a clinician.

The unfortunate fact is that, even after completing an introductory psychology class (and in many cases after taking more advanced coursework), you may know very little about the profession of psychology. This book is for you. You will learn about the exciting strides that psychologists are making toward the solution of critical, everyday problems, and you will discover the many employment possibilities available in the expanding and emerging field of applied psychology.

Historical Context

So what's new? Haven't psychologists always been concerned with everyday problems? The answer is yes — and no. Application does have a long and distinguished pedigree in the history of psychology. To cite just a few examples, Walter Dill Scott published books on advertising in 1903 (*The Theory of Advertising*) and 1908 (*Psychology of Advertising*). Also published in 1903 was Edward K. Thorndike's *Educational Psychology,* an application of psychology to the educational process. In 1908 Hugo Munsterberg produced *On the Witness Stand,* an application of psychology to the field of law, followed in 1915 by *Psychology: General and Applied,* the first text that systematically applied psychological principles and research findings to a series of everyday problems.

In 1917 the first issue of the *Journal of Applied Psychology* appeared, with G. Stanly Hall (the first president of the American Psychological Association) as editor. As Goldstein and Kasner (1987) have noted, the definition of the scope of the journal sounds suprisingly modern. Areas such as the application of psychology to law, business, diagnosis of mental disorders, education, industry, the environment, and sports are all mentioned. In fact, many of the areas that make up the contents of *our* book were identified 50 years ago!

Despite these encouraging beginnings, however, progress in applied psychology has been uneven, and concern for applied problems has not always been strong. In various disciplines within psychology, applications research has sometimes been seen as an inferior endeavor to that of formulating theory. The field has at times favored basic science over applied science and regarded those who were successful in theory more highly than it did those who were successful in applications. Today, however, forces are at work to raise the stature of applied psychology. Some of these influences will be considered in the next section.

The Trend toward Applications

What are some of the factors pushing psychology in the direction of applications? First, psychologists have found, both in the past and currently, that solutions to many of society's problems require an understanding of psychological principles. As social problems have become more obvious and pressing, psychologists have responded with solutions. Second, just as many adults seem to go through "midlife crises" during which they evaluate and reassess the direction of their lives, the field of psychology, as it enters middle age, seems to be examining its goals and questioning the relevance of research that has been pursued.

Many psychologists have changed the direction of their work so that it will have greater impact on human problems. Some have come to believe that successful application is, in many respects, the ultimate test of the usefulness of their theories. Applications, then, can strengthen and enrich the development of theories. Each of these points is considered in the sections that follow.

Meeting Society's Needs

One of the reasons applied psychologists are in demand is that the expertise of many is highly valued in the marketplace. The reason for this success is that their work has increasingly been responsive to problems that exist in society.

The work patterns of factory operatives like these women in a Detroit sparkplug factory, c. 1912, were the focus of studies by pioneer industrial/organizational psychologists. The applications of their research were expected to increase worker efficiency and productivity, but, unfortunately, the process of "scientific management," as it was called, too often resulted in lowered worker morale and motivation.

In understanding what types of problems have been addressed, it is useful to look at some areas of psychology that have been historically prominent in applications and then at those in which psychology has been applied to more recent societal problems.

Historically Prominent Areas of Application. The titles of the books cited in the "Historical Context" section indicate that applied psychology has historically addressed problems present in society. For example, individuals working in the area of **industrial/organizational psychology** in the early 1900s were addressing management's desires to improve job performance. In an activity called **scientific management,** psychologists observed workers to discover how tasks could be performed with the least expenditure of time and effort. Although these methods improved efficiency, they gradually were recognized as creating inhumane practices that actually lowered worker motivation. The rise of labor unions in the 1930s led management to again turn to industrial/organizational psychologists to help understand the dynamics of human relationships among workers and between workers and management. Industrial/organizational psychologists demonstrated to management that worker satisfaction affected productivity. More recently, in the face of sagging American productivity and foreign competition, industrial/organizational psychologists have again been consulted to help improve worker motivation and satisfaction.

    Clinical psychology has also filled needs present in society. The large number of psychiatric casualties resulting from World War II increased the need for clinical services. In 1944, the U.S. Army established a training program for clinical psychologists so that these needs could be met. After the war, the Veterans Administration was responsible for providing psychological services for a large number of disabled veterans. As more training programs were established to provide clinicians to care for these individuals, the number of clinical psychologists increased dramatically. Ever since this highly active period at the close of World War II, the demand for clinical services in all sectors of society has continued to grow. Clinical psychology has responded to these needs by expanding and diversifying.

    A third area that has served needs in society is **consumer psychology.** Scott's (1903, 1908) early observations on advertising pointed to the possibilities of using psychological techniques to sell commercial products. These possibilities began to be realized when behavioral psychologist John B. Watson went to work for the J. Walter Thompson advertising company in 1920. Watson was very successful in applying behavioral techniques to the marketing of products. Among other things, he created an advertising campaign for Johnson's Baby Powder that was aimed at young, inexperienced mothers. The ads stressed the product's effectiveness in increasing cleanliness and reducing the chance of infection. Watson also developed spokesperson endorsements for Pond's Cold Cream, employing the then-reigning queens of Spain and Romania to provide testimonial endorsements for the new product. Producers intensified their efforts to understand the dynamics of consumer behavior in the 1950s with the result that scientific

This photograph was taken just after the two battle-weary Marines had come in after two days of combat on Eniwetok in the Pacific. The fact that thousands of veterans became "psychiatric casualties" as the result of their experiences in World War II accelerated the development of clinical psychology and required the training of large numbers of clinical psychologists in the 1940s and 1950s.

methods of product marketing were introduced. By devising marketing strategies, companies were able to produce and sell goods and services for which demand had already been determined. Research in consumer psychology developed so that corporations could make more informed marketing decisions. Today, computers make possible the acquisition and sophisticated analysis of a wide range of information on consumer behavior.

Finally, applied psychologists have historically filled needs in educational settings. In 1886 Lightner Witmer founded the first psychological clinic in the United States at the University of Pennsylvania. Most of his work was with "problem students" who were referred by schools in the Philadelphia area. In the early 1900s tests were developed to identify students who needed special educational attention. The role of school psychologist was identified in 1915 when Arnold Gesell was hired by the State of Connecticut to " . . . make mental examination of backward and defective children in rural, village, and urban schools, and to devise methods for their better care in the public schools" (Connecticut Special Education Association, 1936, p. v). The need for diagnostic and therapeutic services for school children has increased. Federal legislation passed in the 1970s requires that all children, regardless of any handicapping condition, receive a free and appropriate education. Such a mandate has created a great and continuing demand for applied psychological services in educational settings.

Recent Areas of Application. As society's needs have changed, new opportunities for applied psychologists have emerged. Several examples will help you see how psychologists have responded to these changes. For example, the increased use of high-technology control systems in such places as nuclear power plants and jet aircraft has stimulated a need for practicioners in **engineering psychology.** These scientists develop person-machine interfaces that allow humans to operate equipment safely and as efficiently as possible. The establishment of megacorporations and the flood of mergers and takeovers in the 1980s has produced a need for specialists in **organizational development** to facilitate these transitions and to diagnose and solve problems caused by growth and change. As society has recognized the need to protect and preserve the environment, individuals involved in **environmental psychology** have worked to identify those aspects of environment that people value and to understand the effects of environment on behavior. Finally, as scientists have increasingly recognized the effects of psychological stress on the health of individuals, practicioners in health psychology have investigated the psychological causes of physical illness. These examples serve to show the flexibility of applied psychology in response to changing social needs.

Making Psychology Relevant

In many areas of psychology that have traditionally emphasized laboratory research, there has been a growing recognition that the theories and methods used may not have great generalizability outside controlled laboratory settings. Such concerns have led many psychologists to focus on the **external validity** of their experiments. Experiments are said to be externally valid when it is possible to generalize their results to settings and problems encountered in everyday life. Psychologists have referred to these everyday problems as real-world problems, in contrast to problems posed and solved solely in what might be called a "laboratory world." When the authors in this text refer to real-world problems or real-world psychology, they are concerned about the external validity of research in the field.

Supporting and Enriching Theory

Other psychologists have noticed an additional common pattern in the results of laboratory experiments. For example, a theory is proposed to account for a body of experimental results. As subsequent experimental work is performed, additional findings will be presented. Some of these findings will support the original theory and some will call for revisions. Often, as more studies are done, the theoretical issues involved become more and more focused. Researchers obtaining different results with only small variations in their procedures find that support is available for both sides of many theoretical arguments. Additional qualifying factors are introduced in order to explain these small discrepancies. Rather than eliciting a powerful theory that has broad applicability, psychologists focus on minute theoretical differences that have effects only under highly controlled laboratory conditions. Some psychologists (for example, Baddeley, 1981) have called for attention to theories that matter—theories that illuminate problems in the real world. A concern for applications can reveal problems in theories that in turn can lead to higher-quality theories.

Basic Research and Applied Psychology

A major theme in this book is the relationship between basic research in psychology and applications of psychology to the real world. As has been mentioned already, these different focal points in psychology have often been at odds. Yet it is clear that they need to fit together in a symbiotic relationship: applications without theory may be ill-conceived, costly, and time-consuming; theory without applications may be irrelevant. Kurt Lewin made the interdependence of the two very clear. In *Field Theory in Social Science,* published in 1951, he stated:

> The greatest handicap of applied psychology has been the fact that, without proper theoretical help, it had to follow the costly, inefficient, and limited method of trial and error. Many psychologists working today in an applied field are keenly aware of the need for close cooperation between theoretical and applied psychology. This can be accomplished in psychology, as it has been accomplished in physics, if the theorist does not look toward applied problems with highbrow aversion or with a fear of social problems, and if the applied psychologist realizes that there is nothing so practical as a good theory. (p. 169)

In the area of applied social psychology, Cialdini (1980) proposed a *full-cycle model* to describe the interaction between theory and application. This model is helpful because it is general enough to be used in a variety of applied areas. According to the model, research ideas and problems come from observations of behavior in everyday experience. Based on these observations in naturally occurring settings, a research hypothesis is advanced. The hypothesis is then rigorously tested under controlled conditions in a laboratory setting. If the hypothesis is successful, field experiments in naturalistic settings follow. Based on the results of these tests, the initial explanation may be modified and returned to a laboratory setting for further refinement. This cycling back and forth between highly controlled laboratory settings and externally valid field settings produces an explanation of behavior that is both theoretically strong and relevant to an actual problem in the real world. Such an explanation of behavior will move toward the fulfullment of Lewin's promise of a "practical theory."

Regrettably, not all research in applied psychology satisfies the dual requirements of valid theory and relevant application. But such research is certainly an ideal to be pursued. As you proceed through the chapters, evaluate the research projects you read about in terms of theory and application. Strong research in applied psychology will give attention to both.

Mapping the Territory

For a long time there has been a need for a book that focuses on what psychologists *do* rather than on theories and ideas. Of course in describing what psychologists do, it is essential to learn about the tools they use—their methods and theories. But our focus is different from that found in most texts. Rather than simply presenting a body of theory and research, the authors of *Introduction to Applied Psychology* communicate a sense of what it is like to work as psychologists in fields ranging from engineering to law to sports. In each chapter you will find a section entitled "What Do _____ Psychologists Do?", in which the authors describe their work in a particular area of applied psychology. They explain the types of activities performed as well as the settings in which they work. As you read, you will discover the wide variety of activities and work settings open to psychologists in different areas of application. Examples and case studies further develop the presentation; typically the theoretical background is described and applied areas of research investigated. Each of the chapters encourages students to synthesize their own ideas of a particular area of applied psychology.

Before setting out to explore the territory, it is important that students have some background in the techniques psychologists use to gather evidence to test their research ideas. Chapter 2 of Part I describes methods used in designing such tests as well as statistical techniques used in evaluating results. It is particularly important for psychologists active in applied settings to evaluate their work. Otherwise, they may repeat, at substantial cost, a program that has no positive application for the parties involved. The chapter on methodology generally addresses evaluation; in addition Appendix A, "An Introduction to Program Evaluation," gives more specific information on this important process.

Part II covers applications of psychology in business and industrial settings. This segment contains information on some of the oldest (industrial/organizational and consumer psychology) and newest (applied cognitive psychology and organizational development) areas of application. Applications of psychology in business share a strong requirement of cost-effectiveness—if the applications proposed do not favorably affect the financial bottom line of an organization, they will probably be rejected. Individuals working in these areas of applications must continually meet the challenge to make psychology fiscally responsible.

Part III focuses on the role of psychology in community settings. The first three chapters of this section (clinical, community, and health psychology), investigate applications of psychology to promote physical and mental health. While these areas share a common goal, their approaches differ. Clinical psychologists have traditionally emphasized treatment of individuals experiencing mental health difficulties; community psychologists have focused on the prevention of mental and social problems by developing community-wide interventions to promote wellness; and health psychologists have investigated behavioral factors associated with physical illness. The remaining three chapters in Part III (applied social, legal, and environmental psychology), deal with the improvement of society in general. Applied social psychology employs theories of social behavior developed by social psychologists in the solution of social problems. The chapter on psychology and the legal process describes psychology's traditional expert-witness role (testimony on the mental condition of defendants) and also covers newer research into processes in the legal system such as judgments of witness credibility and jury decision making. Finally, the chapter on environmental psychology describes how the built and the natural environment influence behavior and, in turn, how behavior can influence the environment.

Part IV, the last segment of the text, looks at applications of psychology to human development. Educational and school psychology are described in the chapter on psychology in educational settings. Applications of psychology to sports and motor development is the topic of the next chapter. The final chapter 16, covers a relatively new area, applied developmental psychology, in which theoretical insights from the area of developmental psychology are applied across the human life span.

The overall picture of applied psychology that emerges is extremely diverse. Although such diversity may cause problems for you as a student trying to master a body of material, it will at the same time suggest the exciting possibilities open to those who may choose to get more training in psychology. Several fields described here currently provide strong professional opportunities to individuals with psychological training; others are very new and are just emerging as areas of promise. The overall goal in preparing this book has been to inform and excite you about the dynamic areas of applications in psychology.

Glossary

clinical psychology   A field in applied psychology that concentrates on the diagnosis and treatment of mental and behavioral disorders.

consumer psychology   A field in applied psychology that studies the psychological processes underlying the acquisition, consumption, and disposition of goods, services, and ideas.

engineering psychology   A field in applied psychology that focuses on the interrelationships between humans and machines.

environmental psychology   A field in applied psychology that focuses on the interrelationships between people and the built and natural environment.

external validity   The extent to which the results of an experiment can be generalized beyond the conditions represented in the research.

full-cycle model   A model of applied research in which a researcher identifies a social phenomenon that exists in everyday experience, and then cycles back and forth between highly controlled laboratory experiments and externally valid field settings to develop a powerful and applicable explanation of social behavior.

industrial/organizational psychology   A field in applied psychology that focuses on the relationships between people and their work.

scientific management   An early approach to industrial/organizational psychology that emphasized time-and-motion studies in order to develop highly efficient, albeit sometimes inhumane, methods of performing jobs.

2 / Research Methods Used in Applied Settings

David Martin
New Mexico State University

A drunken man was searching for something under a street light. When asked what he was looking for, he said that he had dropped his keys and couldn't find them. He pointed to a place a half-block away and said, "I lost them over there."

"Well, why aren't you looking for them over there?" he was asked.

"It will be easier to find them under the light," he answered.

Psychologists working in applied settings sometimes think that laboratory researchers follow the same strategy as the drunk. The accusation is that these investigators choose research topics on the basis of ease of enlightenment rather than on the practical importance of the subject.

Research done solely because of intellectual curiosity, with no eye toward eventual application, is called **pure** or **basic research.** Those who do pure research argue that the findings that go into building the scientific body of knowledge should be as uncontaminated as possible. This means that the data should undergo exhaustive examination with the cleanest experimental methods available before being added to the structure. "Cleanest methods" require careful manipulation of one variable or at the most a few variables, while controlling all other variables.

Applied psychologists, on the other hand, feel that this type of research is often unrealistic. In the real world many variables change in combination. In addition, when working in applied settings, a researcher usually does not have the luxury of doing perfectly clean research. There are many reasons why this is true.

First, if the problem is a brand-new subject of research, there may be no extablished methods for investigating it. Second, the resources available for finding an answer may be quite modest. Investigator's salary, salaries of research participants, equipment and computer costs, and other expenses all must be considered. Given these conditions, it may not be cost-effective to expend the resources necessary for a large-scale, completely controlled experiment. Third, in applied settings the time for finding a solution is usually limited. The research is typically part of an ongoing project having certain deadlines. If the "best answer" has not been found by the deadline, then perhaps the "best guess" will have to do.

To applied researchers these limiting conditions can, at times, be frustrating. It may seem to them that most of their time is spent putting out fires instead of functioning as scientists. Yet the rewards can also be great. Besides the gratification that comes from contributing to the body of scientific knowledge, applied researchers can also derive satisfaction out of seeing a final product as the successful culmination of their efforts.

From this point-counterpoint argument emerge two positions that seem to have little overlap. In actuality, these positions lie at opposite ends of a continuum, with the approaches of most psychologists falling somewhere in between. Applied researchers usually *do* attempt to make some scientific contribution, and most basic researchers *do* try to choose potentially important research topics. However, it is important to recognize that the continuum exists, because the research methods discussed in this chapter relate directly to the researcher's position on it.

This chapter is divided into four sections, each devoted to an essential stage in the research process. For each stage, the typical approach used by a basic researcher is compared and contrasted with the approach used by an applied researcher. This comparison will help you understand some differences in methodology between the two approaches.

Getting a Research Idea

The first step in doing any type of research is to find something to investigate. Basic researchers sometimes have a difficult time doing this successfully. It may seem that coming up with an idea would be no problem. After all, everyone observes human behavior every day, and interesting questions come to mind: What is the best way to break a habit? Do children who are punished do better in school? Are good-looking people happier in life? How can we get people to use their seatbelts? The list is endless.

The first problem is that some of the questions are very difficult to define operationally. That is, the operations that will be most effective in investigating the question are not at all obvious. Second, some questions are concerned with such a large chunk of knowledge that one research study and sometimes one whole research career will barely make a dent in them. Third is the very practical consideration of fitting the research into the body of knowledge. A researcher could spend a career constructing a certain building block for the body of knowledge. However, if this block does not fit into the current structure in a systematic way and is not compatible with the blocks being formed by other investigators, the contribution certainly will not be recognized as valuable and could be lost.

For these reasons, most basic researchers actually get their ideas from studying other people's research. They keep up with the body of knowledge by reading the professional literature, usually in a fairly well-defined area. When they come upon a subject that interests them and feel they have a unique, creative approach, they may attempt to solve the problem. As their careers advance, the research itself will generate additional avenues of investigation to be pursued.

Many applied researchers are critical of the type of research this approach can lead to. Some believe that the original observations that led to the research paradigm and defined the probem is often forgotten by basic researchers. The investigators eventually get "paradigmatic tunnel vision" and end up investigating easily researchable and intellectually intriguing, but relatively unimportant, side issues. They forget the original problem that was of more importance, but which was more difficult to solve.

Applied psychologists, on the other hand, typically have no difficulty finding research problems; the problems find them. In developing a product, be it a machine, a training program, a personnel selection test, or an organizational structure, practical questions arise. Some of these questions concern human behavior and are assigned to the applied psychologists on the product development team. These psychologists must try to find answers as efficiently as possible.

The real creative activity for applied psychologists is not so much in teasing out subtle theoretical distinctions, but in finding ways to manipulate variables and measure behaviors within real-world settings. These researchers have to deal with practical constraints imposed by economic, ethical, and political considerations. They will be forced to make compromises and at the same time find sound answers. After discovering those answers, researchers must also communicate them to the other members of the design team in such a way that the team has confidence in the conclusions.

Because of the nature of the research setting, applied psychologists tend to need a broader outlook on psychology than do basic researchers. They need to have some familiarity with a number of areas rather than specialized knowledge of a narrowly defined area. Beyond this they must also have some knowledge of economics, engineering, law, medicine, and sometimes other disciplines. A psychologist in an applied setting may be asked to do such diverse tasks as evaluating, suggesting, and defending personnel selection tests; recommending an office layout; designing a training program; recommending a new organizational structure; and even counseling employees. For this reason, the applied psychologist must maintain breadth at some sacrifice in depth.

Finding Out What Has Been Done

In some respects both types of researchers must determine what has already been done in order to keep from duplicating it or repeating the errors of previous investigators. However, some might also argue that this knowledge can be counterproductive in that it can limit consideration of alternative approaches to the research problem.

For basic researchers, the major purpose for this investigation is to assess the present state of the body of knowledge. This allows them to determine what their potential contribution might be and how it will fit into the structure. In this respect, experimental psychology is a little different from some branches of science such as physics. In general, there are two types of physicists — theoretical and applied. Theoretical physicists are the architects for the body of knowledge, while applied physicists construct the building blocks. Basic researchers in psychology do both tasks. They assess and design the body of knowledge and also do the research to form the building blocks.

The job of finding out what has been done is relatively easy for a basic researcher. Concurrent with a tremendous increase in the volume of scientific literature has come a comparable growth in the information systems available for searching through this literature. Both manual and automated systems can be used.

The manual systems include library filing-card catalogs that enable investigators to find books and other larger sources. The subject or author index of *Psychological Abstracts* is useful for locating journal articles that describe basic research. Printed in this publication is an abstract of each article that has appeared in the most frequently used psychology journals during a particular time period. Thus it is possible to find out if any research was published on a given subject or by a given author during any desired period of time.

After locating several recent articles on the topic of interest, one may proceed to the reference sections of these articles to "tree backward" through the literature. It is also possible to "tree forward" by using the *Scientific Citation Index.* This resource lists articles that cite a specific article. Thus after identifying an early key article that any author working in a particular area would cite, a researcher can find this article in the *Index* and determine which later articles have made reference to it.

While it is possible to do a good literature search manually, the big breakthrough in recent years has been the general availability of computerized search systems. These systems accept either key subject terms or authors' names and limit the area of search to articles that meet the specific requirement, thus automatically reducing manual search. They also can supply printouts of all the abstracts that meet the specifications. Interaction with the retrieval programs of on-line systems can further limit or expand the sphere of search and allows screen display of the abstracts found. The most widely used literature base for these automated systems is still *Psychological Abstracts,* but others, such as military technical reports, are available.

For applied psychologists, on the other hand, the real purpose of finding out what has been done is not so much to make sure that the right investigation will be undertaken, but rather to keep from having to do it at all. Because research requires time and resources and because there are a lot more questions than answers, applied psychologists want to do original research only when absolutely necessary. If they can find an answer in somebody else's work (sometimes even if the answer only approximates the one they need), then they can save the research resources for another project.

The basic problem for applied researchers is the lack of a good literature base and a searching system for the kinds of problems they are interested in. There are certainly logical reasons why this situation differs from that for basic research. For basic researchers, the final product is the literature base, where the body of knowledge is stored. For applied researchers, the final product is an answer to a limited question generated by a particular project. The recording of that answer for posterity is, at most, a by-product of the research. To be sure, if the original question generalizes to other projects or advances theory applicable to other projects, a record of the outcome can be of importance. Unfortunately, in the press of finding answers to other new problems, the recording of the old findings often gets lost in the shuffle.

In other cases a record of research results is made but does not become publicly available. Answers to questions that enhance an organization's competitive advantage are often treated as classified information within the organization. This proprietary information may not become available in the public domain for a number of years. Obviously, this situation makes the applied psychologist's job more difficult.

Even given this situation, applied researchers can often get some idea of what has been done. For some problems there are company or industry standards. These are sometimes documented in handbook form and spell out in some detail answers to recurring questions. For example, some very large companies publish documents specifying company procedures for doing such things as formatting a document, naming and coding parts, or developing a training program.

An example of industry's standards is mentioned in Chapter 3. Engineering psychologists working on the design of military systems have available a number of government documents detailing the military specifications for systems design in the human-factors area. In most cases the engineering psychologist does not have to conduct an experiment to determine the size of a dial or the shape of a knob. These specifications, based on previous research, are contained in such documents.

Another source of information for applied psychologists are colleagues who do similar jobs in other organizations. These informal contacts provide information difficult to document but valuable and widely used. Even in cases where colleagues have no ready-made answers, they may have dealt with similar problems and be willing to provide some insight into the techniques used to solve them.

Finally, the basic research literature may be useful, although less so than might be imagined. For example, this writer was once hired as a consultant to try to determine a set of coding principles. These principles would guide employees of a large company whose job it was to construct the codes and abbreviations used throughout the company. At first it appeared that the voluminous psychological literature on memory for nonsense syllables would provide a good database for this project. Unfortunately, because the nonsense syllables in these experiments were never used to represent something the way an abbreviation or code does, this database from the basic research literature was not very useful.

What can sometimes prove most useful from the basic literature is theory. While the research designs and experimental paradigms are often so narrow that they do not generalize to the real world, the theoretical structure holding the data together sometimes does. And even when the theory does not make very clear-cut predictions in the real-world situation, it can, at least, help to identify the important dimensions that must be taken into consideration in solving the problem.

Ideally, in the future, applied psychologists will come to a greater realization of the importance of creating and maintaining an applied research literature and a retrieval system. Until this happens, finding out what has been done will continue to be difficult for researchers working in applied settings.

Designing Research

Basic researchers like to design experiments having unambiguous outcomes. In general, they wish to manipulate as few variables as possible, have as much control over other variables as possible, and be able to make a causal statement at the conclusion: manipulating variable A caused a change in behavior X.

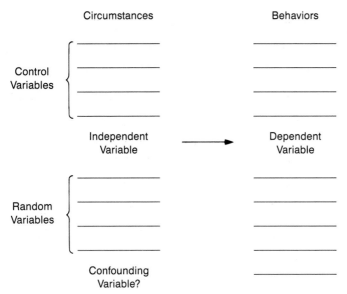

FIGURE 2.1 A schematic representation of the design of a simple single-variable experiment.

Figure 2.1 shows an ideal experiment that a basic researcher attempts to design. The object for all experimentally oriented scientists is to relate the set of circumstances on the left side of the figure to the behaviors on the right. In order to do this, a basic researcher usually chooses one circumstance to manipulate, calling it the **independent variable.** At least two levels of the independent variable must be represented in the experiment. The levels of the independent variable are the different conditions an experimenter manipulates. One, or more than one, of the behaviors is then chosen as the **dependent variable** and is measured while the independent variable is being manipulated.

For example, suppose an experimenter is interested in people's ability to learn words based on how frequently those words occur in their language. A list of 10 high-frequency words and a similar list of low-frequency words could be constructed and shown to subjects. The high- and low-frequency word lists constitute two levels of the independent variable. The number of trials required to learn the list perfectly could be measured. If word frequency has an effect on learning, one would expect the number of learning trials to be greater for one of the lists. So far, so good.

What should an experimenter do with the other circumstances that have been conveniently ignored? In general, a basic researcher would like to control them, to turn them into control variables. If it is possible to control a circumstance, then it cannot possibly change with the levels of the independent variable and cause a problem. For example, an investigator might find that, on the average, high-frequency words have fewer letters than low-frequency words. If there was no control for word length, it is possible that this circumstance could become a **confounding variable.** A confounding variable is one that changes systematically with the levels of the independent variable. Any change in the dependent variable that is attributed to the manipulation of the independent variable could instead be due to the confounding variable. In the example, a difference in trials needed to learn the lists might be due to word length rather than to word frequency. To ensure that word length does not become a confounding variable, an experimenter could make it a control variable. For example, only seven-letter words might be used.

Thus, in order to draw precise conclusions from an experiment, it would seem that an experimenter should manipulate one variable and control all others. One problem that immediately arises is that all variables cannot be controlled: cloning human subjects is forbidden; time will not stand still for the most talented experimenter; two objects cannot occupy the same point in space. In other words, experimenters could not make all the other circumstances into control variables if they wanted to. Should they want to?

Suppose all circumstances other than the independent variable could be controlled. How might the conclusion read? Word frequency has an effect on learning . . . when 7-letter words are used, and lists are 10 words long, and 30-second trials are used, and 21-year-old males with blue eyes and IQs of 110 are tested at 3:17 on Tuesday afternoons in New Mexico, and so on. The obvious problem is that by controlling all variables one produces a unique set of circumstances. While the conclusion can be very precise, it is true only for this unique set.

In general, basic researchers opt for precision rather than generality. Applied researchers are biased the other way. However, even basic researchers must put some generalizability into their experiments. They do this by including random variables in the design. Random variables are allowed to seek their own level, within the constraint that true random selection is taking place. An experimenter's confidence in this procedure lies in the fact that for any random process having a large number of instances, the statistical likelihood of bias is small. Thus it is unlikely that a random variable will be systematically related to the independent variable. For example, if 50 subjects are randomly chosen to form two groups, it is unlikely that 50 highly intelligent people will end up in one condition of an experiment and 50 very unintelligent people will end up in the other.

This is certainly an oversimplification of a basic researcher's task in choosing an experimental design. In fact, these investigators often use designs with many different conditions rather than the two mentioned earlier. Also several independent variables are often incorporated into an experiment, rather than just the single independent variable described. However, the simple design proposed offers a starting point for comparing the designs of applied researchers.

Applied researchers like to design research so that it resembles the real world as much as possible. In general, they wish to allow variables that naturally change together to do so, to use realistic levels of these variables, to take multiple measures of behavior, and, for practical reasons, to use as few subjects as possible. The section that follows describes methods that most resemble the simple experimental design (single variable) and progressively moves toward less empirically based techniques.

Multiple-Variable Designs

At times it is possible for applied psychologist to use the experimental approach; however, they are usually concerned with the effects of many variables rather than just one or two. Unfortunately, they typically cannot do many small experiments, manipulating one variable in each. A major problem with this approach is that important **interaction effects** are lost. An interaction between two independent variables occurs when the effect of one independent variable depends on the level of the other independent variable that is being considered. For example, in the word-frequency experiment described earlier in the chapter, suppose both word frequency and speed of presentation of the words are manipulated. It may turn out that the effect of word frequency on number of trials to learn the list of words depends on the level of presentation speed considered. Perhaps when the list is presented rapidly, low-frequency words are much harder to learn than high-frequency words. When words are presented more slowly, these word-frequency effects are much less pronounced.

One cannot predict the way two independent variables will interact without doing a multiple-variable experiment that manipulates both simultaneously. The top section of Figure 2.2 shows the effect of two independent variables when they are manipulated in two separate single-variable experiments. The bottom section shows several possible outcomes of manipulating the two variables simultaneously. Each of these outcomes could occur and still be consistent with the results of the single-variable experiments graphed in the top section of the figure. Without actually performing the multiple-variable experiment, information about the way two variables will interact cannot be obtained.

It is, of course, possible to combine many variables within one experiment, with each level of one variable combined with every level of the other variables. Statistical tests are also available for analyzing these effects and interactions. However, a practical problem with such designs is that the experiment can get far too large. To determine how many combinations of conditions must be present, the number of levels of each variable are multiplied. For example, in Figure 2.2 you saw that for two variables with two levels each, four combinations were needed. If we wished to have a group of 10 subjects exposed to each combination, 40 subjects would have been required.

Now suppose that an applied engineering psychologist is designing an aircraft cockpit. Perhaps there are four possible altimeter designs, five possible instrument configurations, three different altitude indicator displays, two different joystick locations, and five different joystick designs. Designing an experiment

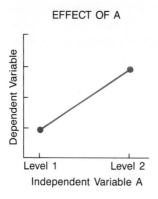

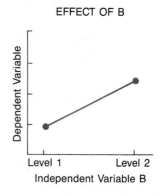

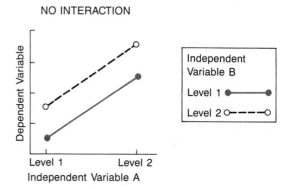

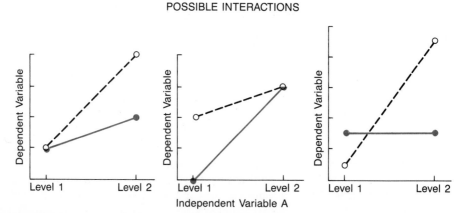

FIGURE 2.2 The top two graphs show the individual effects of independent variables *A* and *B*. The lower graphs show how these effects combine assuming *no* interaction, and three ways they could combine if they *do* interact.

combining all variables at all levels with 10 subjects in each group would require $4 \times 5 \times 3 \times 2 \times 5 \times 10 = 6000$ subjects. Obviously, these designs can quickly become impractical.

Recently developed designs allow applied experimenters to do this type of research without having to represent every combination. These designs, variously called **response surface methodologies** or **incomplete block designs,** permit testing only certain critical combinations of variables and levels. The statistics employed, then, allow the designer to infer the combinations that produce the best performance. Unfortunately, these techniques are, as yet, not widely used by applied psychologists. Instead, most experimenters design a number of smaller experiments using the combinations of what they believe to be the critical variables. Because of this they cannot evaluate the possible interactions between the variables represented in different experiments. They hope that these interactions are nonexistent or unimportant. They are usually right; sometimes they are wrong.

Correlational Designs

Applied psychologists are typically less concerned with establishing a casual connection between an independent and dependent variable than are basic researchers. Often determining whether there is a relationship between variables is good enough. For this reason, **correlational designs** can be used.

A concrete example will illustrate the difference between the experimental designs discussed in the preceding sections and correlational designs. A researcher might wish to know whether there is a relationship between managerial style, such as authoritarian or democratic, and managerial success. To perform an experiment it would be necessary to turn managerial style into an independent variable by gaining control over it. For instance, managers could be randomly assigned to two groups. One group could be trained to act in an authoritarian manner and the other trained to be democratic. Comparing the results achieved by managers in the two groups, a researcher could determine if differences in managerial style caused differences in success rates.

Far more typically, a researcher would choose a correlational design in which an independent variable is not manipulated. Using this design, a group of managers could be identified and the place of each on a scale from authoritarian to democratic could be determined by using some test. Then some measure of managerial success would be taken, perhaps a numerical rating by each manager's supervisor. The two quantities could then be plotted as shown in Figure 2.3. Each dot on this scatterplot represents one manager's two scores.

A statistical operation could then be performed to compute a correlation coefficient. This is a number between 0 and 1 with a + or − sign attached. A 0 indicates no relationship at all between the variables. A 1 indicates a perfect relationship (or a straight line on a scatterplot). The numbers between show the strength of the relationship. Minus numbers indicate that the relationship is negative. That is, as one variable increases the other decreases. Positive numbers indicate that the variables increase together.

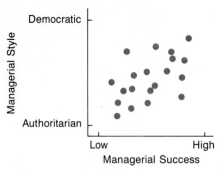

FIGURE 2.3 A scatterplot (entirely fictitious) showing the relationship between managerial style and success for 20 managers.

It is very important to note that from simple correlational data it is possible to say something about one variable being *related* to a second variable; it is not possible to say that the change in one variable *caused* the change in the other. In the example, the managerial style may not have caused the success. Some third variable may have caused both the style and success. Perhaps more intelligent managers have chosen to be more democratic and these managers have also been more successful. Alternatively the third causal variable could be a personality trait, socioeconomic class, amount of schooling, or some other unknown variable.

The basic problem is that in a correlational design nothing is being independently manipulated. Since neither variable is under the researcher's independent control, other circumstances are free to change with it. In fact, in most cases both variables are subject-controlled behaviors and can be considered dependent variables. Thus it is only when an experimental design is used that one can conclude that a change in one variable caused a change in the other.

Regression Designs

A **regression design** is, in some respects, similar to correlation and in other respects similar to experimentation. It is similar to correlation in that an investigator is concerned with the strength of a relationship between variables. It is similar to experimentation in that there is a dependent variable and one or more independent, or at least predictor, variables.

Basically an experimental design helps answer the question: Is there a causal relationship between two variables? A correlational design asks: Is there any kind of relationship and how strong is the relationship; how well can we predict the value of one variable from the value of the other? A regression approach asks a further question: Can a simple rule be formulated for predicting one variable from the other, and, if so, how good is the rule? Usually a linear rule is sufficient to describe the relationship, and linear regression is used. A linear rule means that as the independent or predictor variable increases by one unit, the dependent variable always increases by a constant amount.

Shirtsleeves, a smile, the appearance of friendly interest—these may be indicators of a "democratic" managerial style. Is such an approach the key to managerial success? An experimental research design can establish a *causal connection* between the two variables—style and success. A correlational research design, on the other hand, can only determine the *relationship*—positive or negative—between the two variables.

Regression designs are important because applied psychologists often wish to predict. For example, the personnel psychologist has a test that is supposed to measure success on the job. Of course, it is important that those scoring high or low on the test perform in significantly different ways on the job, that is, that the score be highly related to job performance. But what the psychologist really wishes to know in this case is, given a particular test score for this applicant, how well is he or she likely to perform on the job? An answer to this question requires a knowledge of the shape and orientation of the function or rule relating the independent variable to the dependent variable. Regression allows this to be determined and also tells the psychologist how well the rule predicts.

High-speed computers have greatly increased the usefulness of regression designs by providing rapid analysis of complex multiple-regression research. With multiple regression, more than one independent variable is used as a predictor. Suppose that for each applicant a personnel psychologist has several test scores available as well as a high-school grade point average, an interview rating, and three letters of recommendation. In hiring an employee, what weight should be given to each of these items? And given the proper weighting, how well can we expect the employee who is hired to do on the job? Multiple regression can answer these questions.

Of course, the answers are important in terms of productivity. They also can serve to ensure that the organization is not discriminating against applicants on the basis of nonrelevant factors such as ethnic origin, sex, or age. The personnel psychologist may have to defend the hiring practices of the organization in court. In order to do this, credible evidence must exist to show that the items considered in hiring decisions are related to job performance. Multiple-regression techniques can provide this type of evidence.

Factor-Analysis Designs

An additional type of design that resembles correlation is **factor analysis.** When a researcher is faced with a multitude of items that measure various aspects of behavior, factor analysis can help find the underlying factors or dimensions that are related to the behavior.

For example, suppose Dr. A., a Detroit-based consumer psychologist, was interested in making sure that the automobiles her company manufactures appeal to a broad market. She might wish to determine the factors that underline the public's image of a car. To do this, she could set up pairs of contrasting adjectives such as fast/slow, big/small, costly/economical, reliable/unreliable, and so on, and ask a large sample of people to rate many different cars on these scales.

The technique of factor analysis would allow Dr. A. to determine which of the items clustered together. The idea is that items highly correlated with one another form a cluster. Items in the cluster can be considered to represent the same underlying factor. A researcher must then examine the type of items making up a cluster to determine how to label any particular factor. In this way Dr. A. might discover that there are only five or six perceived dimensions underlying a person's perception of an automobile. It would then be possible to determine how each of the company's cars is perceived in each of these categories. Perhaps the company would wish to design an advertising campaign for a particular car to emphasize or de-emphasize one of the factors.

Because the mathematical operations involved in factor analysis are quite complex and cumbersome, our description here is highly simplified. While not quite technically correct, at this point it may be helpful to think of factor analysis as a way of taking a large number of variables and determining which are highly correlated with one another. Those that are highly correlated are assumed to measure a single underlying concept. Fortunately, even though mathematically complex, today's computers make the technique accessible to many more investigators than in the past. Factor analysis can be particularly useful for applied psychologists working in the areas of consumer psychology, personnel selection, and construction of surveys and questionnaires.

Quasi-experimental Designs

In recent years there has been a greater realization that some simple, well-controlled experimental designs do not work well in applied field settings. The major features of laboratory research, such as random assignment, physical isolation of subjects, and short duration of the experiment, are often not present in applied settings. Yet a researcher would still like to make as strong a causal statement as possible. For this purpose, a **quasi-experimental** design is sometimes appropriate.

Earlier in this chapter, when a simple model of an experiment was being discussed, the set of circumstances was partitioned into three categories of variables: independent, control, and random. In quasi-experimental designs there is still an independent variable, and even in applied settings it is possible to control some variables. However, assigning subjects to the levels of the independent variable in a truly random way often cannot be done. A quasi-experiment is based on comparing nonequivalent groups that differ from each other in ways other than just the levels of the independent variable. Any difference in the dependent variable that could be attributed to the independent variable could also be due to other dimensions or nonequivalence. Quasi-experimental designs attempt to rule out these other potentially confounding effects.

To illustrate one type of quasi-experimental design, imagine that you are in charge of designing training programs for an insurance company. Videodisc technology now makes it possible to train new claim adjusters using an interactive videodisc system rather than human trainers. You would like to determine whether the training is as effective with the new system. The problem is that

Questions over the relative merits of interactive videodisc instruction and traditional training with a live teacher could be resolved by using a quasi-experimental research design.

you need the answer in six weeks and you have only one training class that will receive instruction during this time period. This class is not large enough to randomly assign half to each of two groups.

You decide to use an untreated control group design with pretest and posttest. To do this you give the new class the standard pretest that all classes take. They then receive the videodisc instruction and take the standard posttest. At this point, by comparing the pretest scores with the posttest scores, you could determine how much the participants have learned. But what you really want to know is how they compare to a class receiving traditional instruction.

For this comparison you decide to use the class from the previous six weeks. Comparing the scores from the posttest for the two groups, you discover that the videodisc group scored an average of 83 compared to the traditional group's 89. In a typical experiment with randomized groups such a result would be interpreted as an indication that the videodisc condition was inferior.

However, there is no reason to expect the two groups to be equivalent. They were recruited at a different time of year, by a different recruiter, from a different region of the country. And, since both groups took the pretest, you can compare the groups on both pretest and posttest as shown in Figure 2.4. The figure shows that, in fact, the videodisc group learned more than did the traditional group. A statistical test would be calculated to determine if this effect was more likely due to chance or was a significant effect. The point is that one can draw causal conclusions using this design even though the groups were not randomly chosen.

A second class of quasi-experimental designs consists of interrupted time-series designs. To illustrate this design, suppose that a researcher working for the Australian Road Research Board was attempting to evaluate the effects of a new law requiring the use of seatbelts in cars and an associated promotional campaign. For five years immediately before the change, the percentage of drivers wearing seatbelts has been determined. The researcher has now collected similar data for the three years since the new law went into effect. Figure 2.5 shows what might be found (while these are not the exact data, they approximate real findings). Such evidence would offer pretty good support for the argument that the law caused a change in behavior.

FIGURE 2.4 Hypothetical results of an untreated control group design with pretest and posttest.

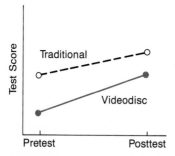

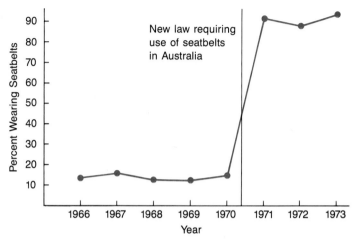

FIGURE 2.5 Result illustrating an interrupted time-series design.

Such a design is not perfect. Perhaps some other historical event occurred to influence the wearing of seatbelts, such as cheaper insurance rates for those who use them. But it is possible to evaluate these potential confounding variables. It may also be possible to add a nonequivalent group to strengthen the result. For example, the percentage of people in the United States wearing seatbelts during these years could be determined. If there was no corresponding increase at the critical time in the U.S., the conclusion would be strengthened.

There are many additional quasi-experimental designs available. However, most of them are some variant or combination of nonequivalent control group and interrupted time-series designs. The recent advances in these designs and in the associated statistics for analyzing the results of these quasi-experiments have given applied psychologists an additional set of tools for doing causal research in field settings.

Single-Case and Small-N Designs

In some applied settings, such as clinical mental health, medical, and other milieus in which psychologists work with individuals, large-group designs are not possible or appropriate. They are not possible because of the limited number of individuals who have a particular problem or who qualify to be subjects in the research. They are not appropriate because researchers wish to have some flexibility about when to impose the particular levels of the independent variable and what those levels will be. And some researchers would argue that large-group designs are seldom appropriate because they tell us about the behavior of some nonexistent "average," person rather than about the behavior of real individuals.

Single-case and **small-*N* designs** are similar to interrupted time-series designs discussed in the last section. The most classic type is an ABA design, where

A stands for one level of the independent variable, which is usually "no treatment," and B stands for a second level, which is usually "treatment." Typically, A is in effect for a period of time during which repeated dependent variable measurements are taken. Once a researcher is satisfied that a stable baseline is present, then the treatment is imposed. If the treatment is effective, the behavior being measured will show an obvious shift to a different level. The B condition will be continued until a new stable state is achieved. Finally, in order to demonstrate in another way the effectiveness of the treatment in B, the researcher then removes the treatment, and the behavior is expected to return to the A (no treatment) baseline level.

Suppose you are a psychologist working in medicine and are confronted with a patient having symptoms of *anorexia nervosa*. This is a disorder in which the patient has a compulsion to become as skinny as possible and eats very little or nothing at all, sometimes to a life-threatening extent. You devise a program in which you provide feedback in addition to reinforcement for eating. This consists of presenting the patient with a daily record of calories consumed and number of mouthfuls eaten at each meal. The dependent variable is calorie intake, which is measured by observing food portions eaten at each meal.

Figure 2.6 shows data from this type of experiment based on results reported by Agras, Barlow, Chapin, Abel, and Leitenberg (1974). In this case the researchers were not satisfied with simply recovering the baseline (they also probably wanted to end the experiment with the patient under treatment). Thus they expanded the design to ABAB. A visual inspection of the data makes a very strong case for the effectiveness of the treatment. Indeed, researchers using single-case designs seldom do any statistical analysis of their data. They feel that if they have

FIGURE 2.6 An ABAB single-case design. Adapted from "Behavior Modification of Anorexia Nervosa" by W. S. Agras, D. H. Barlow, H. N. Chapin, M. D. Abel, and H. Leitenberg, 1974, *Archives of General Psychiatry, 30* (3), p. 283. Copyright 1974, American Medical Association.

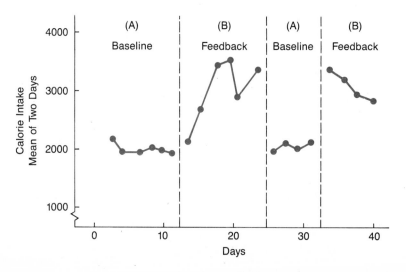

achieved proper control of the potentially confounding extraneous variables, then any important experimental effects will be readily apparent to the eye.

An example of a small-*N* experiment in an industrial setting is one reported by Hermann, de Montes, Dominguez, Montes, and Hopkins (1973). These investigators were interested in decreasing the instances of tardiness among factory workers. The company had unsuccessfully attempted to control the problem with yearly bonuses awarded to punctual workers. Twelve workers with chronic tardiness problems were identified: six formed the control group and six the treatment group. After eliminating the overall yearly bonus for those in the treatment group, a cash voucher was given every day they were on time. The controls received no daily bonus.

Figure 2.7 shows the results. The upper graph shows the percentage of instances of tardiness for the control group. This group is not necessary for the basic design, but it certainly provides additional support for the conclusion. The lower graph shows what happens as the treatment is repeatedly administered. The design is **ABABAB**. Although there was some decrease in the baseline throughout the experiment, the effects of the daily incentive program are quite

FIGURE 2.7 An ABABAB small-*N* design showing the effect of a daily bonus system for punctuality. From J. A. Hermann, A. I. de Montes, B. Dominguez, F. Montes, and B. L. Hopkins, (1973) "Effects of Bonuses for Punctuality on the Tardiness of Industrial Workers," *Journal of Applied Behavioral Analysis, 6,* p. 567. Copyright 1973 by the Society for the Experimental Analysis of Behavior, Inc.

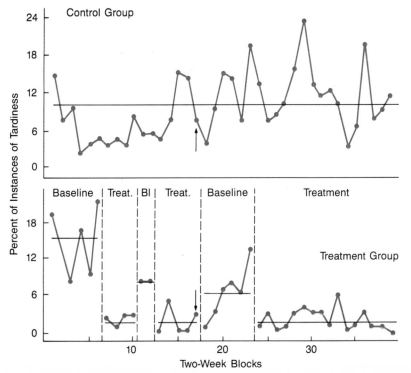

Punch in—cash in. The results of a small-*N* experiment determined that an effective means of reducing worker tardiness was to give cash vouchers daily for on-time arrival. This reward system replaced end-of-year bonuses for punctuality. In this case, research suggested that instant gratification was a better motivator than the delayed payoff had been.

apparent. A final interesting highlight: If a worker under the incentive program had earned a bonus every day, these bonuses would have added up to the same amount of money contained in the former yearly bonus. The new successful program cost the company no additional money!

There are potential drawbacks to single-case designs. Sometimes in field settings, where good control of extraneous variables cannot be achieved, baseline variability is a problem. In this case it can be difficult to detect clear-cut experimental effects because of the variability. A second problem can occur when there is an increasing or decreasing baseline, for example, when a patient is deteriorating at the time of treatment. A third problem concerns a nonrecoverable baseline. For example, small-*N* designs are difficult to use when the treatment consists of some permanent change such as learning. People generally do not "unlearn" when returned to the original baseline condition.

Even given these limitations, single-case and small-*N* designs now offer an alternative to large-group experimental designs. Applied researchers, such as those in medical, clinical, community, educational, and industrial settings, have found them to be a useful tool.

Observational Techniques

Under this general heading are a number of what are usually considered quite diverse research strategies. These include **case studies, naturalistic observation, activity-sampling techniques, process analysis,** and **critical-incident techniques.** Each of these techniques has at least two common characteristics: (1) the observation or data collection is done in, or relatively close to, the real-world setting and (2) the researcher has little or no control over the variables of critical interest.

Case Studies

A case study is a very detailed account of the behavior and events that happened to a single individual or during a single incident. Case-study reports made up the overwhelming majority of the database for clinical psychology during the first half of this century.

On one end of a continuum are the case studies in which a researcher has some control over the variables of interest. For example, a therapist might try a new therapeutic technique and then determine how the patient's behaviors or thoughts have changed. In some respects, case studies at this end of the continuum appear similar to single-case baseline designs. However, a researcher usually does not repeatedly measure a single aspect of behavior. Instead, a pattern of behaviors is usually observed. In addition, and perhaps most critically, no baseline is either established or recovered. At best this type of case study is an AB design, a type very difficult to interpret.

At the other end of the continuum are case studies that use nothing more than naturalistic observation. In this case, the researcher does not intervene into the setting but just observes the natural flow of events. Usually, detailed records are kept of the behaviors and events under observation. The researcher then attempts to find consistent patterns that relate behaviors and events to one another.

A problem with this type of case study is that even if it is done perfectly, the data are at best correlational. In natural settings, circumstances are related to one another and change together so that it is difficult, and usually impossible, to attribute a change in behavior to a single circumstance. One can say that variables are related, but saying that one variable caused another variable to change is virtually impossible.

In addition to these basic design problems, case studies are often plagued with procedural difficulties. How should a researcher select what to observe? Obviously, all events and behaviors cannot be observed over a long period of time. For example, in one study of a pilot's eye movements during flight, only 160 minutes of recording were taken, but this consisted of 76,800 frames of photography that required many months for analysis (Fitts, Jones, & Milton, 1950). Imagine the work that would be required to analyze everything an individual does, not just a small subset of behaviors such as eye movements. And imagine an observation period lasting years rather than hours. Obviously, the researcher must select what to observe and when. Potentially, a great deal of bias can enter into this selection process.

How can a researcher quantify the observations? Even when ongoing recordings are made of behavior, the best that can be done is usually to count behaviors. Quantifying behaviors is quite difficult. And in the usual case study, good recording is not even done. Typically, researchers recall events and behaviors from memory. Such data are highly subject to bias.

Much of the research done by applied psychologists depends upon skillful observational techniques. A researcher must judiciously select what to observe and when to observe, then accurately recall and quantify events and behaviors. Observers must constantly guard against influencing the behaviors they are studying. Sometimes this means disguising their identities.

Finally, how can observers be sure that they are not influencing the behaviors being observed? At the naturalistic observation end of the continuum, an observer wants to be unobtrusive. However, this is seldom possible. Do you think that the factory supervisor will behave in a usual manner while being followed all day by an official-looking observer carrying a clipboard? Watchers can certainly influence the behaviors they are watching — how much so is difficult to determine.

Activity-Sampling Techniques

Applied psychologists working in industrial and educational settings often wish to know what people do with their time. The information may be needed as part of task analysis prior to developing a training program; to restructure the task in order to improve efficiency; to determine what skills a task requires so that the appropriate employees will be selected; or just as a means of comparing various industrial or educational systems. An activity-sampling technique allows a researcher to find out what people do in a systematic way.

Basically, a researcher defines a time interval, and at these predetermined times an observer records exactly what the person being observed is doing. By establishing categories of activity that define the task being performed, it is possible to count the number of times and for how long the person engaged in a particular type of activity and determine the percentage of the total time spent on each type.

Process Analysis

Process analysis refers to techniques for recording the various steps involved in a process. Doing a process analysis could be a first step in redesigning the sequencing of steps, redistributing the steps across people or machines, or changing a workplace arrangement or machine design.

One classic form of process analysis, time-and-motion analysis, describes the actions performed in an industrial process and the time required to perform each action. The use of a flow diagram that shows the locations and sequencing of the operations in a manufacturing process is another. These techniques are used to analyze work situations that are repetitive and standardized.

When operations and the relationship between operations are statistical in nature, a technique called link analysis is sometimes used. Link analysis is used primarily when designing the layout of workspace arrangements for operators and machines, or in planning the layout of displays. A link is formed when any two locations in the workspace or on the display panel are used in sequence. A location consists of a machine, a human, a source of information, or an instrument. A link has a number attached to it indicating the frequency with which it is used (e.g., how many times does the secretary move from the copier to the desk?) and the importance of the link.

In doing a link analysis, a schematic link diagram is made with the various locations identified. If the analysis is of an existing workspace or display, the locations can be put on the diagram at their present physical locations. Links are then drawn between locations, and each link is marked with a number between one and nine that reflects its relative importance and frequency of use. The locations can then be moved about on the diagram so that, in general, links are made as short as possible and as few links cross each other as possible. Higher-value links receive priority. If done properly, a link analysis helps the researcher to design workspaces or instrument panels that are more efficient.

Critical-Incident Techniques

A critical-incident technique can be useful in analyzing infrequently occurring events such as accidents. A researcher who is interested in the causes of aircraft accidents might put observers on many aircraft for many years and never observe an accident (to say nothing of the difficulty in recovering the data after an accident). Traditional research techniques are essentially useless for such situations.

However, Fitts and Jones (1947) were able to investigate 460 "pilot errors" using a critical-incident technique. They asked pilots if they had made, or had seen anyone else make, "an error in reading or interpreting an aircraft instrument, detecting a signal, or understanding instructions." From these incidents they classified 227 of the experiences as shown in Table 2.1. The nice thing about such a classification scheme is that it implies solutions to the problems that lead to the critical incidents. In fact, a number of changes were made in the design of aircraft instruments based upon this research.

TABLE 2.1

Classification of Pilot-Errors Based on Critical-Incident Analysis

Type of Error	Number of Errors
I. Multirevolution instrument errors:	
A. Errors involving instruments with two or more pointers, e.g., misreading the altimeter by 1,000 feet, the clock by 1 hour, etc.	40
B. Errors involving instruments with rotating dials observed through a "window," e.g., misreading the tachometer by 1,000 rpm, the air-speed meter by 100 mph.	8
II. Reversal errors, e.g., reversals in interpreting the direction of bank shown by a flight indicator, reversals in interpreting direction from compasses, etc.	47
III. Legibility errors:	
A. Instrument markings difficult or impossible to read because of improper lighting, dirt, grease, worn markings, vibration, or obstructions.	32
B. Parallax: Difficulty in reading an instrument because of the angle at which it is viewed.	5
IV. Substitution errors:	
A. Mistaking one instrument for another, e.g., confusing manifold-pressure gauge with tachometer, clock with air-speed meter, etc.	24
B. Confusing which engine is referred to by an instrument.	6
C. Difficulty in locating an instrument because of unfamiliar arrangement of instruments.	6
V. Using an instrument that is inoperative, i.e., reading an instrument which is not working or is working incorrectly.	25
VI. Scale interpretation errors, i.e., errors in interpolating between scale markers or in interpreting a numbered graduation correctly.	15
VII. Signal interpretation errors: Failure to notice a warning light in the aircraft, or confusing one warning light with another.	5

The advantage of the critical-incident technique is that it can be used where other techniques are useless. However, there are also problems associated with its use. The technique does rely on the accuracy of the respondent's memories. If there are consistent memory errors, recording a large number of incidents does not correct this problem. Second, while it is possible to get frequencies, as shown in the table, a researcher cannot be very confident that these frequencies are highly related to the actual frequency of errors. Some incidents may be easier to remember, and the incidents reported certainly depend upon who is asked to do the remembering.

Certain weaknesses are inherent in each of the observational techniques that have been discussed. Nevertheless, these techniques can provide information in situations that are difficult or impossible to investigate using more conventional experimental methods. In many cases, the answers that the observational techniques provide are adequate for making a recommendation and are certainly better than a guess based on no data. In other cases these techniques can suggest which aspects of a problem are important enough to warrant further study by more rigorous methods.

Analysis of Results

Most basic researchers are not interested in an experimental result unless it can be shown to be statistically significant. This is because they would like to generalize from their experimental sample to a larger population, often all adult humans. Thus they use an **inferential statistical test** to determine if what they have discovered about the sample is true about the population. If the statistical test is significant at the .01 level, then there is less than one chance in 100 that the difference found in the experiment could be due to chance variation in sampling from the population. In other words, it is highly likely that there are two populations of scores out there, one for each of the levels of the independent variable.

In contrast, sometimes applied psychologists do not even care about statistical tests. This is particularly true if they are testing the entire population rather than a sample. For example, two office layouts are compared, using as subjects all the employees who work in the office. In this case, no inference is being made to any larger population of office workers, although it can be argued that an inference is in fact being made from a sample of behaviors to a population of behaviors.

At other times applied psychologists may be comparing two equally costly alternatives. All they have to do is recommend one over the other, and they have limited funds to investigate the problem. In this case, they may use up whatever funds are available, find out which alternative looks better at that point, and recommend it regardless of statistical significance.

When applied psychologists do use statistical tests, they often want to know more than whether or not a statistically significant effect has been determined. There is a saying among applied researchers, "A difference is a difference only if it makes a difference." Even tiny differences due to an independent variable can be statistically significant if enough data are collected.

What the applied psychologist would rather know is the size of the effect. Statistical tests are available for determining this. Rather than saying that an independent variable makes a difference, these tests show how much of the total variability in the dependent variable can be attributed to the manipulation of the independent variable. For example, research might disclose that the speed of responding differs when information is displayed in two different ways on the screen of a computer. However, if that difference accounted for less than 2% of the variability in speed, one might not be too concerned about which way the information is displayed.

In addition to wanting to know the size of the effect, applied researchers often wish to know the functional relationship between an independent variable and an effect. This issue was discussed under the topic of regression earlier in this chapter. Imagine a designer trying to determine how intense to make a warning light on an instrument panel so that it will generate a response within two seconds. It does not help much simply to know that the intensity of a warning light makes a difference in response speed. The key information is the func-

In a research laboratory of the U.S. Air Force's Aerospace Medical Division, a subject's psychomotor abilities (how much he can do and how fast he can do it) are tested by means of the Purdue Pegboard, one of many devices developed by psychologists to provide objective evidence of human skills.

tional relationship between intensity and response speed, which will allow prediction of how fast an operator is likely to respond to a warning light of a particular intensity. A simple one-variable, two-level experiment followed by an inferential statistical test will not answer the question.

Thus basic researchers and applied researchers often analyze their results in different ways. Basic researchers are usually attempting to test theories that apply to large populations and wish to add this information to the scientific body of knowledge. An inferential statistical test that allows them to infer whether a difference is due to population differences or due to chance is often sufficient to choose between competing theories. On the other hand, the analysis of applied researchers often focuses on different concerns. Depending on the situation, they might pose these questions: Is there any difference in the sample itself? How much of the overall variability in behavior is due to the independent variable? What is the functional relationship between this variable and the behavior?

Conclusion

This chapter was designed to give you a sense of the way applied psychological researchers go about their business. It covered the major research methods used in the field of applied psychology. The differences between basic and applied researchers have been intentionally overdrawn, but the fact is that these two somewhat artificially distinct positions really define a continuum of approaches. Different researchers would place themselves at different points on the continuum depending upon their interests. Furthermore, the same researcher might be found at several places depending upon the topics being investigated. It is important to have this variety of research methods available in psychology because applied psychologists work in so many different settings.

Glossary

activity sampling techniques   An observational research technique to systematically discover what activities individuals are pursuing. A time interval is established and at these predetermined times the researcher records what the person being observed is doing. The percentage of time spent on various activities can be ascertained.

basic research   Research aimed at building scientific knowledge rather than at formulating applications.

case study   An intensive investigation and analysis of a single individual.

confounding variable   A variable that co-varies with the independent variable in an experiment. If positive results are achieved, it will not be clear whether they are due to the independent variable or to the confounding variable.

correlational design   A research design that allows for investigation of how related two variables are.

critical incident technique   An observational research technique by which reports of infrequent incidents are gathered and analyzed. Often used to analyze the causes of accidents.

dependent variable   The variable that is expected to change when the independent variable is manipulated.

factor analysis   A statistical technique used to cluster sets of variables together in order to discover underlying commonalities.

incomplete block design   Analysis of variance design that allows a researcher to test only certain critical combinations of variables and levels of those variables without the necessity of running subjects in all of the various conditions.

independent variable   A variable that is manipulated by the experimenter.

interaction effects   When two (or more) independent variables are manipulated in the same experiment, an interaction occurs when the effects of one independent variable on the dependent variable change depending on what level of the other independent variable is being considered.

naturalistic observation   The study of subjects in their natural environments without interference from the investigator.

process analysis   An observational research technique for recording and analyzing the various steps involved in a process.

pure research   See basic research.

quasi-experimental design   An experimental design that does not randomly assign subjects to conditions and instead compares nonequivalent groups to each other. The designs are structured to remove these weaknesses.

regression design   A research design that allows the prediction of one variable from another variable (or group of variables).

response surface methodologies   A research methodology that allows investigators to contrast selected combinations of variables without the need of running large numbers of subjects in all possible conditions.

single-case design   A research method where the behavior of a single subject is studied using an ABA design where A is a nonintervention condition of baseline observations and B is an intervention condition where some change of interest is made. The baseline conditions are contrasted with the intervention condition.

small-N design   Design similar to single-case designs where a limited number of subjects are investigated. See single-case design.

Part 2

Psychology in Business and Industrial Settings

3 / Engineering Psychology

David Martin
New Mexico State University

In an age of supertechnology, such as that required for the development and operation of nuclear power plants, the role of engineering psychologists has been to provide information that will assist designers in creating systems that fully accommodate human skills *and* human limitations.

Imagine that you are the pilot of an aircraft approaching the runway for a landing. One of your final actions is to reach for the control that will change your flap angle in order to slow the plane. As you reach for this control and pull, you have a vague sense that something is amiss, but it still comes as a shock to you when you put the plane down in a belly landing. Later you learn that you accidentally activated the control to raise the landing gear rather than one to change the flaps. Is this "human error"?

Imagine that you are the operator of a nuclear power plant. You have spent many days and months in training, but when you finally hear the warning signal telling you that an automatic valve has malfunctioned, your heart speeds up a little. You determine that you must mechanically override the bad valve. Assuming that the red-colored valve is the radioactively "hot" one, you calmly override the system and close it down. Several minutes later you notice that the temperature readings are unusual and the core is heating up. By the time you call your supervisor things are getting worse and you have a potential disaster on your hands. Later you learn that the original problem was in the warning system, not the valve, and that in fact you compounded the problem because the red valve was the "cold" one, not the "hot" one. Is this "human error"?

These incidents are real. They are only two examples of the multitude of things that can go wrong in a complex human/machine system. As the world becomes increasingly sophisticated technologically, more people have to contend with these complex mechanisms. These systems can frustrate or delight, increase or decrease efficiency—in some cases they can even kill. The easy answer to problems—really no answer at all—is to blame bad system performance on the human. However, labeling a problem "human error" is nothing more than scapegoating. It does not deal with the underlying cause of the problem, nor explain how the problem can be avoided in the future.

It would seem that since psychology is the study of human behavior, psychologists should be able to determine how humans will generally behave when interacting with a human/machine system and also how the system should be designed to maximize performance given human limitations. Fortunately, one branch of psychology has begun to investigate these questions. This relatively new area is called *engineering psychology.*

What Is Engineering Psychology?

Basically, an engineering psychologist is concerned with specifying the capacities and limitations of the human in a human/machine/environment system so that the system can be operated safely, efficiently, and pleasurably. One of the strengths of engineering psychology is that the human is studied within the context of a system. In traditional experimental psychology researchers often investigate human behavior outside of the context of any system simply because it is interesting. Engineering psychologists, on the other hand, usually consider the human to be embedded in a system context. Figure 3.1 shows a simple, general model for human/machine/environment systems. The components of such systems—machines and humans—interact. That is, as one facet of the system changes, the characteristics of other components change, causing the performance requirements for the human to be quite different.

One of the first things you may notice is that the system forms a circle rather than a straight line. That is, the output of the human component is the input of the machine component and vice versa. As an arbitrary starting point in this circle, consider the input to the human. Stimulus energy is picked up by the human sensors. This energy may come from the output of a machine such as the reading on a speedometer, the text on a computer screen, or the sound of a warning alarm in a power plant. Alternatively, the stimulus energy may come from the environment and indicate the condition of the human/machine system within this environment. The view of the roadway through a windshield and the feel of a rolling ship are examples of this stimulus energy. Figure 3-1 illustrates the five traditional senses, although certainly others could be involved, such as the vestibular system, which indicates linear acceleration and angular rotation, and the proprioceptive system, which indicates the position of muscles and joints.

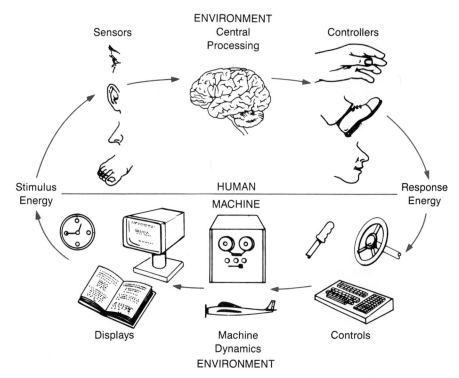

FIGURE 3.1 A general model of human/machine/environment systems.

The sensors convert the stimulus energy into neural information, and the nerves convey the information to the human central-processing mechanism, considered to be located mainly in the brain. At this point, some form of central processing occurs, such as encoding, deciding, thinking, and retrieving or storing information. When an engineering psychologist studies central processing functions, such work often overlaps with the area of applied cognitive psychology (see Chapter 6). Some of the most interesting and sophisticated problems in engineering psychology today are concerned with central-processing issues, such as: How should information be displayed in order to aid decision making? At what rate can a human being process information before an overload condition exists?

After the information has been centrally processed, the output is again conveyed down neural pathways to controllers. Again a number of possibilities exist for the control of the machine. Traditionally this control has been accomplished using the hands, fingers, and feet. Present technology also allows the possibility of vocal control, in which an operator actually speaks to a machine. It has been suggested that in the future it may even be possible to control a machine by using the physiological output of the brain itself. At this point in the system the human output, that is, a form of physical energy, becomes the machine input.

The response energy from the human must be transmitted in some way to the machine. The machine's controls might consist of levers, wheels, keyboards, or any other device that would allow the machine to receive information. Obviously one of the important decisions an engineering psychologist must make is choosing a machine control compatible with the human controller.

The information fed into the control must then be transmitted to the machine by some means such as a direct mechanical linkage, hydraulic linkage, or electronic linkage. The machine's response depends upon the particular machine dynamics involved. If the machine is a vehicle, the response may be a particular change in orientation, which may be very rapid (such as in a sports car), or very slow (such as in an ocean liner). If the machine is a computer, a sequence of keystrokes may be converted by the machine dynamics into a command to print out the results of a complex operation. Quantitatively specifying machine dynamics is an engineering task in which engineering psychologists may play a key role. Such a task can be difficult and time-consuming, since there are as many specifications as there are numerous and varied machines.

If the human is to achieve some measure of control over the machine, the machine output must be displayed in some way to the human operator. These displays can take many forms, from written text to dials to sophisticated electronic displays such as those found in modern aircraft. Again, much of the work of engineering psychologists has focused on designing the machine displays to be compatible with human sensors and central-processing mechanisms. The display completes the human/machine circle and illustrates that the system shown in Figure 3.1 is a closed-loop system. A system is a closed loop if the human has some ongoing means of control over the machine. That is, the machine must feed information back to the human, who then must take appropriate action to maintain control of the system. In an open-loop system, once a process is initiated, it continues through to completion without any ongoing human control.

Figure 3.1 also illustrates that the human/machine system exists within a particular environment. This environment may change the operating characteristics of the machine and/or the human. For example, an aircraft may respond quite differently in the presence of a wind shear than it will in calm air. A human will also respond in a particular way while attempting to weld underwater at a depth of 200 feet. Environmental conditions an engineering psychologist might have to take into account include temperature, lighting and noise conditions, vibration, the presence of toxic materials, and even weightlessness. When considering even less exotic environments, the engineering psychologist might still have to take into account the organizational environment in which the system exists (see Chapter 5) or the architectural environment in which the system must operate (see Chapter 13).

What Do Engineering Psychologists Do?

In many respects engineering psychologists are like engineers. In designing their applications, they include the human operator as an engineering component of a system. While treating people as components might at first seem inhumane, it is the best way to design a machine that will allow humans to realize maximum benefit from the machine.

Note that while the two examples cited at the beginning of this chapter dealt with systems that, due to improper design, had safety problems, two other criteria were also mentioned as being important to the engineering psychologist: efficiency and pleasure. Particularly in industrial settings (see Chapter 4), the system designer is concerned with designing a system to maximize efficiency and performance. A system that can produce more widgets or fewer widget rejects is more cost-effective than alternative systems. And if that system can be designed so that operators derive satisfaction from working with it, operators will be easier to hire and train and will probably be less likely to quit.

Some systems, particularly consumer systems, have pleasure or operator-enjoyment as primary goals. Video games, for instance, are designed to maximize operator enjoyment. The designer who can provide more enjoyment sells more systems and thereby enjoys greater success.

Job Activities

How do engineering psychologists go about designing human/machine/environment systems? The answer to this question depends a great deal upon the particular job setting. A few engineering psychologists work in university or research institute settings doing basic research. Their findings, which usually have an applied orientation, provide the basic body of knowledge that other engineering psychologists and human-factors specialists use in applied settings. This research activity is extremely important, especially as it relates to rapidly changing technology. For example, just as the answers to design questions concerning mechanical dials were being found, it became possible to display information in a dynamic way on a cathode-ray tube. As the technology changed, the questions changed, and the old answers became obsolete. The research arm of applied psychology has to provide answers to new and basic questions. However, this chapter will emphasize the role of engineering psychologists, who apply this body of knowledge to real-world systems.

Unfortunately, some application-oriented experimental psychologists face situations in which systems have been largely completed prior to asking human-factors questions. These engineering psychologists may be able to recommend only that the display panel be painted a different color, a toggle switch be turned over, or that rubberized flooring be used so that the operator does not slip. These changes would probably be only minor improvements in system performance at best. Bringing engineering psychologists in at the tail end of systems design may be better than not bringing them in at all, but it drastically reduces the scope and value of their participation.

A more effective way to use engineering psychologists is to involve them early in the system-design process. Figure 3.2 shows the usual steps that must be taken during systems design.

Defining Objectives.   The first thing that is needed is a statement of the objectives for the system. These objectives are usually phrased in terms of inputs to the system and required outputs. Objectives may define an acceptable range of

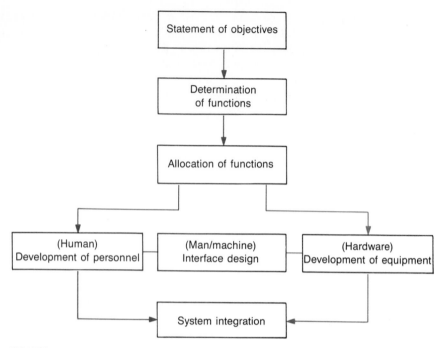

FIGURE 3.2 The usual stages of system design.

inputs and outputs and set time relationships. Sometimes an objective may be more political than industrial or scientific. For example, the United States government's decision to put a man on the moon was primarily a political move in the space race with the U.S.S.R. Even in industrial settings, the objectives may be political and are often established by high-level committees. However, even at this point, the engineering psychologist may have some impact that will later make a difference in the system design.

Definition and Allocation of System Functions. The second step is to define the functions of the system. In other words, what activities must the system perform? At this point the designers must be careful not to be so specific that design options become limited. For example, a function of the moon landing was to gather rock and soil samples. During the determination of functions it would not have been necessary to know whether a human or a robot would be collecting these samples. Nor would it have been necessary to know how a human or a robot would move around on the moon's surface, only that locomotion was a required function.

Once the functions have been defined, they must somehow be allocated to humans or to machines. In order to know how to divide functions, the engineering psychologist must be aware of the advantages and disadvantages of using humans and machines for various activities. In the 1950s Paul Fitts, one of the fathers of engineering psychology, listed the functions that were best accomplished by humans and machines. The list, which came to be known as "Fitts' List" is shown in Table 3.1. Today these decisions about using humans or machines are usually made in a much more sophisticated way, by using either reference handbooks containing compilations of human-factors specifications or computer simulations of large-scale person/machine systems. Such sources of information permit a number of design decisions to be made without the necessity of carrying out new experiments for each new project.

It is obviously important for the engineering psychologist to make recommendations concerning the allocation of functions in the systems-design process. Engineers typically have little training in human-factors considerations and allocate functions according to tradition, costs, or their best guesses. Even at this

TABLE 3.1

Comparing the Advantages of Humans and Machines: The Fitts List

Function	Machine	Human
Speed	Much superior.	Lag 1 second.
Power	Consistent at any level. Large, constant standard forces.	2.0hp for about 10 seconds 0.5hp for a few minutes 0.2hp for continuous work over a day.
Consistency	Ideal for: routine; repetition; precision.	Not reliable: should be monitored by machine.
Complex activities	Multi-channel	Single-channel.
Memory	Best for literal reproduction and short term storage.	Large store, multiple access. Better for principles and strategies.
Reasoning	Good deductive.	Good inductive.
Computation	Fast, accurate. Poor at error correction.	Slow, subject to error. Good at error correction.
Input sensitivity	Some outside human senses, e.g., radioactivity.	Wide energy range (10^{12}) and variety of stimuli dealt with by one unit; e.g., eye deals with relative location, movement and color. Good at pattern detection. Can detect signals in high noise levels.
	Can be designed to be insensitive to extraneous stimuli.	Affected by heat, cold, noise and vibration (exceeding known limits).
Overload reliability	Sudden breakdown.	Graceful degradation.
Intelligence	None.	Can deal with unpredicted and unpredictable, can anticipate.
Manipulative abilities	Specific.	Great versatility.

stage, organizational or political considerations can enter into decisions. Most of the systems designers for the moon landing felt that the mission could have been accomplished much more easily without humans along. Almost all of the scientific experiments performed could have been carried out by machines. Eliminating humans would have removed the need for complex life-support systems and allowed the payload to be smaller. However, certain people at high levels of government felt that, for political reasons, it was important to have an American set foot on the moon.

Another example illustrating how organizational factors can influence function allocation involves personnel in England's Royal Mint. The mint was having problems with the high number of defective coins getting by their inspectors.

The 20th century has seen manufacturing move from labor-intensive to robotic. In this photograph of a plant in Salisbury, North Carolina, it appears that a single human finger is controlling the entire operation. Engineering psychologists sometimes discover that a recommendation reducing human participation in a job process may be vetoed because it is considered to be politically or socially undesirable.

The engineering psychologist consulted to correct the problem determined that the function of spotting defects in coins could be done more accurately and efficiently by machines than by humans. However, because the Royal Mint employed many high-seniority human inspectors, the decision was made to continue this less efficient method of inspection. The engineering psychologist's recommendations could only deal with ways to make human inspectors more accurate. In this case, social considerations were the determining factor in function allocation.

Design and Personnel Development. Once the system functions have been allocated to machines or humans, engineers begin to develop the equipment necessary for the system. It is important at this point for the engineering psychologist to work closely with the equipment engineers, particularly with respect to the design of displays and controls. If the engineer works independently, the engineering psychologist may later be confronted with hardware design that is difficult to reverse. For example, toward the end of the systems-design process the engineer might come to the human-factors specialist to determine the size of the dial face or the shape of a dial pointer. If consulted earlier in the process, when the only constraint was that quantitative information be displayed to the operator, the human-factors specialist might have recommended that a digitial counter be used rather than a dial.

Development of personnel will also be taking place at this time. This task can be accomplished by the engineering psychologist, although it is sometimes assigned to an industrial psychologist. The first thing that must be determined is what the operator of the system must do. This requires a task analysis. If the system is brand-new, the engineering psychologist must imagine the logical sequence of steps an operator will go through and chart these in a flow diagram. Later, after the hardware has been developed, it is usually possible to validate such a task analysis by simulating the operator's task. If the system under development is similar to an existing system, it might also be possible to do a task analysis by observing the operator of the old system, by interviewing the operator, and by reviewing operation manuals for the system.

As a result of a task analysis, the engineering psychologist identifies subtasks an operator must perform and the skill level required to perform them. At this point the subtasks must be allocated to the personnel in the system. This step is usually called **job specification,** in that the job for each operator is being defined. In the military, this step is sometimes called the development of personnel subsystems. The designer will usually group subtasks that require similar skills and training in order to specify a job for a particular operator.

When job specification is done in enough detail, it is possible to determine criteria by which operators will be selected. These criteria often include such things as educational level, prior job experience, physical strength, and so on. From the job specification and the task analysis it is also possible to design the appropriate training programs for the system operators. Providing criteria for personnel selection and guiding the development of training programs are the work of industrial/organizational psychologists, described in Chapter 4.

Systems Integration and Evaluation. During the "development of personnel" stage, the engineering psychologist must continue to work on the human/machine interface design. For example, it is pretty difficult to design a particular work station until the number of operators using that station and their various jobs are defined. The final system integration, to a large degree, will be dependent upon the success of the engineering psychologist in coordinating hardware development and personnel development while also designing the human/machine interface for the system. If the engineering psychologist has been a part of the systems-design process since the beginning, this job will not be too difficult. However, if the engineering psychologist is not involved until this point, the job of designing the human/machine interface may be difficult, if not impossible. How does one work out the interface for a system that requires an operator to have three arms, four legs, and two heads!

Particularly when the system under consideration includes complex and sophisticated hardware, it is important for the systems designer to consider the maintenance of the system as well as its operation. Some engineering psychologists are experts in the area of maintainability; they are concerned with designing systems that can be efficiently maintained. The maintenance of a complex system is no small consideration. For example, the cost of maintaining B-52 bombers over the decades since they were introduced has far exceeded the original purchase price of the aircraft. Maintenance is usually a labor-intensive operation, making cost-effectiveness an important consideration.

An evaluator looks on as two soldiers of the Seventh Infantry Division prepare to engage targets. By law, weapons systems involving human operators must be evaluated according to specifications developed by human-factors specialists. In the field, the performance of soldiers and equipment is rated in a mock-combat situation.

Once a system has been designed, a prototype of the system is typically built. Then testing and evaluation of the system can begin. Up to this point the systems designers have worked with paper-and-pencil versions of the system or small-scale mock-ups, and have used their knowledge of human factors to create an effective system. However, when things do not work out as planned, testing and evaluation must find any faults that still exist. An engineering psychologist will probably be involved in this process, typically not the same one who worked on the system design since that person could be biased in his or her judgments. At this point only fine tuning may be required to match the system to the capabilities and limitations of the operators. Especially in the case of military systems, a detailed set of specifications is available to aid the engineering psychologist in testing and evaluating the system. In fact, it is a federal requirement that all U.S. military weapons systems involving human operators be evaluated from a human-factors viewpoint.

Work Settings

Engineering psychologists may be found working in a variety of settings; here three are reviewed: government, academic, and industrial.

Individuals in government settings may work for federal, state, or local agencies or for the military, often in research and development laboratories. Here they may pursue projects designed to solve human-factors problems in the agency to which they are assigned. As an example of this type of work setting, we have already referred to the stringent person/machine systems work conducted by the military. When such work is completed, it will typically be described in technical reports published by the governmental agency itself.

Individuals working in government settings may also be involved in monitoring investigators working outside the agency on a contract basis, such as individuals at universities or independent research organizations. This technical supervision ensures that the goals of the agency are met. Finally, psychologists working in government agencies may be responsible for determining future research directions for the agency. When directions are established, the agency will circulate requests to researchers asking for their proposals and competitive bids for specific pieces of research. While the exact proportions of laboratory and field studies, contract monitoring, and the writing of requests for research proposals and bids may vary between jobs, individuals in government settings will typically work in several of these areas.

In academic settings, engineering psychologists will be deeply involved in class instruction. Most individuals will teach two or three courses (but sometimes as many as four) during a semester, in addition to working with students on individual research projects. Psychology departments vary in the emphasis placed on research versus teaching. In departments where there is a graduate program, less course instruction and more research are typically expected. In addition, as graduate students progress through their courses of study, they perform master's and doctoral research that is closely supervised by faculty committees.

Particularly in the area of engineering psychology, the equipment needed to accomplish meaningful experimental work is very expensive. As a result, a large percentage of a college professor's research time must be spent in writing grant proposals and responding to requests from government and industry for quotations for research to be performed. Obtaining such funding is an ongoing problem. Of course, when research is completed, the results must be communicated to others. College professors who are engineering psychologists report the results of their work in technical reports and articles in scholarly journals.

A third employment setting for engineering psychologists is in industrial organizations. Just as government organizations such as the military need the input of experts to make the fit between humans and machines more comfortable and productive, private organizations must solve similar problems. Particularly in areas of high technology, where humans must interact with computers in order to operate complex systems, engineering psychologists must monitor the balancing of demands and user needs. A central difference between government work and employment in the private sector is the demand for clear profitability. In addition to being scientifically competent, the interventions of engineering psychologists must be financially beneficial to a corporation. Many times potentially useful projects may not be pursued because they are inconsistent with the mission of a company or because they lack potential for profitability.

What's in the Name?

As with many fledgling disciplines, those who work with human/machine/environment systems have not always agreed on the label for their profession. Figure 3.3 illustrates one way of characterizing the terms in common use. Regardless of training and experience, those who are concerned with human/machine problems can be said to be working in the general area of human factors (the shaded area of Figure 3.3). At least in the U.S., this term is widely accepted. For instance, the major professional association to which people working in this area belong is called the Human Factors Society.

In Europe and internationally, a widely accepted term for the general field of human factors is **ergonomics.** Meaning literally "the scientific study of work," the term may capture the difference in emphasis in these countries. Ergonomists in Europe are more likely to be interested in industrial work settings than are human-factors specialists in the U.S. For example, because work physiology is a major emphasis in Europe, physiologists make up a large segment of ergonomists. In the U.S. only a small percentage of the Human Factors Society members call themselves physiologists. Most of the engineers would call themselves human-factors engineers and have been trained in industrial engineering programs. The emphasis in these programs is usually on the actual design of equipment for human use. The term *human engineering* has also been used to refer to the activity performed by human-factors engineers.

The psychologists who work in the human-factors area are usually called engineering psychologists. In fact, Division 21 of the American Psychological

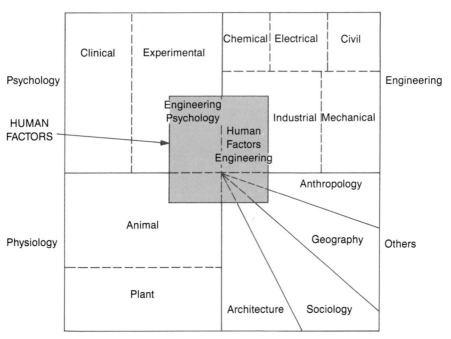

FIGURE 3.3 The relationship of various fields to human factors and engineering psychology.

Association is called the Society of Applied Experimental Engineering Psychologists. Unlike engineers, who come from educational programs that prepare students for entry-level positions with a bachelor's degree, most engineering psychologists are trained in graduate schools to at least a master's degree level. These psychologists could have received their education from one of the 16-or-so programs offering formal programs in engineering psychology (Koch, 1980). However, some of them could have attended more traditional experimental psychology programs, then learned some engineering psychology skills through on-the-job training.

Figure 3.3 illustrates that a few human-factors specialists also come from other social and biological sciences. Those concerned with designing systems that fit the physical dimensions of the operator are working in the area of **anthropometry** and could have been trained in physical anthropology. Some of the people who deal with urban systems and transportation systems are geographers. When the system has an effect upon large groups of people, a sociologist may be involved. Finally, if the system includes environmental design such as workplace layout, an architect could be the human-factors specialist (see Chapter 13).

As is typical of applied settings, in the human-factors area the borders defining academic disciplines often become unrecognizably blurred and the human-factors specialist is difficult to pigeonhole. Solutions to real-world problems often require interdisciplinary approaches that defy precise labeling.

Research and Applications

The foregoing discussion probably gave you a sense of the way in which engineering psychologists approach problems. The next section will provide examples of the types of decisions engineering psychologists must make in the systems-design process. Then, to help you see how contributions of an engineering psychologist are integrated into the development of a new product, a case study will be presented.

Types of Design Decisions

The process of design is a sequence of decisions. Here you will consider some of the most important points in the design process at which an engineering psychologist might provide input. As this material is presented, you will also look at some data that are available to aid the human-factors specialist. Of necessity, the principles presented here are quite simple. You should not be misled into thinking that all design decisions can be made by using common sense. The case study discussed in the next section will illustrate the complexity of an actual systems-design project.

Display Considerations.   One of the decisions that has to be made in designing any system is how information about the machine or the environment should be displayed to the human. Should the information be presented visually, aurally, or through some other sense modality? In order to answer this question, the designer has to consider other questions. How loaded are the various sense modalities already? At what rate must information be presented? Should access to the information be independent of the directional orientation of the sense organ? For example, a buzzer might be used for a warning signal because the aural channel has little load, the information has only two states (warning/no warning), and the human cannot be "hearing in the wrong direction."

Other questions to be answered in choosing a display are: Is static or dynamic information being presented? Is the information being used in an analog or digital form? To illustrate this last question, consider Figure 3.4. The dial on the left that resembles a clock face is an example of an analog display. The counter shown on the right is a digital display. A plus sign in the figure indicates that the type of display is recommended for the particular function shown on the left. A minus sign indicates that the display is not recommended, and a zero indicates a neutral position. Note, for example, that a moving pointer analog display is good for check readings, while a digital display is not. Perhaps this explains why some people hate digital watches. They do not really want to know exactly what time it is (a quantitative reading). They want to know, Is it time yet?, or Is this class halfway over? These questions imply a check-reading function, for which a moving pointer display is recommended.

In addition to choosing a type of display, the engineering psychologist must be sure that the display is designed to maximize information accuracy. Various

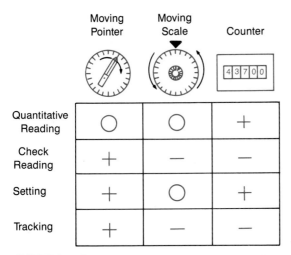

FIGURE 3.4 Recommended uses for three types of displays. From *Man-made Engineering* by A. Chapanis, 1965, Belmont, CA: Wadsworth, p. 42.

handbooks specify the recommended levels for the size of numbers on a dial, the number of major and minor index markings, the color and style of the pointer, and so on. Similar recommendations are listed for digital displays and for displays using other sensory modalities.

For example, the left side of Figure 3.5 shows a control similar to one found on many machines such as room heaters. Which way do you turn the knob to increase the heat? The same control loses its mystery by the simple relabeling shown on the right. The information is now displayed using a fixed scale and moving pointer. Note that this redesign required no change in the machine mechanics.

You can see that a moving-scale fixed-pointer display receives a neutral or negative recommendation for all functions. The problem with this type of display is that people expect a display to indicate an increase with a movement in the clockwise direction. They also expect scales to be marked with higher readings on the clockwise side of lower readings. One of these expectancies must obviously be violated with a moving-scale display.

With the increasing use of computer driven cathode-ray-tube displays, a whole new set of questions faces systems designers. In some respects their decisions are easier to make because the display options are software-controlled, and changes are relatively easy to make by simply rewriting computer programs. But the decisons can also be more difficult to make because research to evaluate the large number of options has not been done. Now that computers and microprocessors may also provide synthesized speech as stimulus energy, the research has fallen even farther behind the technological possibilities.

To illustrate the kind of work that has been done on static (unchanging) pictorial displays, consider the standard symbols shown in Figure 3.6. Shown in the figure are four versions of symbols representing each category of public information.

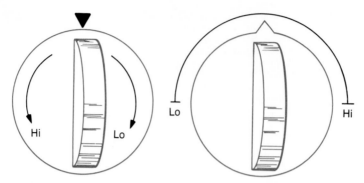

FIGURE 3.5 By changing the ambiguous moving-scale fixed-pointer knob shown on the left to a moving-pointer fixed-scale display, the ambiguity is resolved. From *Man-made Engineering*, by A. Chapanis, 1965, CA: Wadsworth, pp. 45 and 46.

Mackett-Stout and Dewar (1981) investigated the effectiveness of these symbols using four measures: errors in picking out the correct symbol when the symbols were presented in a very brief, poorly visible presentation; distance at which a symbol is recognized; accuracy of interpreting the meaning of each symbol; and rated degree of correspondence between each symbol and its meaning. They then combine these measures to determine the overall efficiency index shown

FIGURE 3.6 Symbols that have been used to represent each of eight categories of public information. Above each symbol is its efficiency index. From "Evaluation of Symbolic Information Signs" by J. Mackett-Stout and R. Dewar, 1981, *Human Factors*, 23 (2), p. 142.

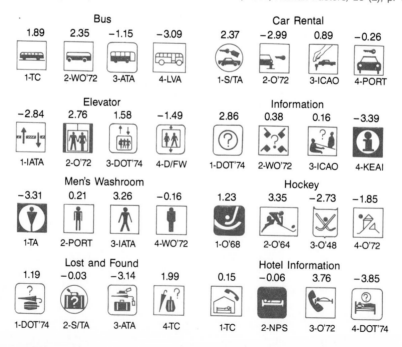

above each symbol. Large positive numbers indicate good efficiency. Systems designers can use this index to recommend the appropriate symbol for a particular application.

Control Considerations. A control is used to convey information from the human to a machine or system. At the present time controls are nearly always manual, or operated mechanically by some part of the body. In the future, however, it may become practical for a human to communicate with a machine by speaking to it or even by having a sensing device send the machine brainwave information.

Basically, controls can be defined along three dimensions. The discrete versus continuous dimension for controls is similar to the digital versus analog dimensions for displays. A discrete control, such as a light switch, can take on only a finite number of states. A continuous control, such as volume control on a radio, is infinitely adjustable. A second control dimension is defined by linear versus rotary controls. An obvious example is turning on an appliance by pushing a button, versus rotating a knob. The third dimension is defined by the number of spatial dimensions in which a control operates. A push button is one-dimensional while an aircraft joystick, which can be moved forward and backward as well as side-to-side, is two-dimensional. Three-dimensional controls are also possible, although infrequently used.

Engineering psychologists have devoted much attention to the design and positioning of machine controls. The reasons are obvious: safe and efficient functioning of equipment depends on correct and expeditious handling of knobs, switches, levers, and buttons. Appropriate design can be a life-and-death matter, for example in the cockpit of an aircraft, in the control room of a submarine, or, as in the photo, in a location where radiation must be controlled.

One example of research into controls is investigation into the shape of rotary knobs. A large number of studies have been conducted to formulate recommendations based on the function the knob will serve. For example, it is recommended that knobs attached to a control requiring multiple turns for adjustment be round in shape with many shallow grooves. Knobs attached to controls requiring fine adjustment of less than one turn should have fewer, deep grooves or be triangular or even square in shape.

In some cases the errors that could be caused by misidentification of a control are so serious that shape-coded controls are recommended. This is especially true when the eyes are busily engaged in another activity and the control must be identified on the basis of touch alone. Figure 3.7 illustrates the type of shape-coded controls that are used on many aircraft today. These controls have helped to decrease the type of error mentioned at the beginning of this chapter, when the pilot accidentally raised the landing gear rather than adjusting the flaps.

When people manipulate a control, they have certain expectations about the effect this will have on the machine. For example, people in general would

FIGURE 3.7 Shape-coded aircraft controls. From *Human Engineering Guide to Equipment Design* by C. T. Morgan, J. S. Cook, A. Chapanis, and M. W. Lund, 1963, New York: McGraw-Hill, p. 258.

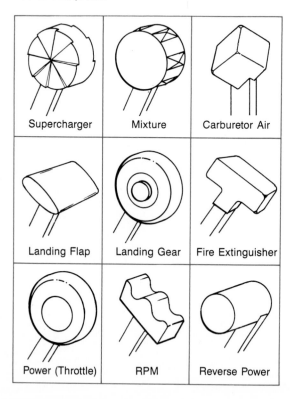

Supercharger	Mixture	Carburetor Air
Landing Flap	Landing Gear	Fire Extinguisher
Power (Throttle)	RPM	Reverse Power

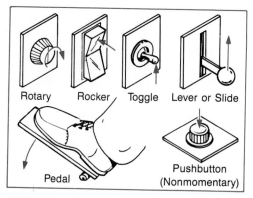

FIGURE 3.8 Typical control response stereotypes for equipment to turn on, the output to increase, or motion forward, clockwise, up, or to the right.

expect the control actions shown in Figure 3.8 to result in something being turned on, increasing, or moving forward, clockwise, or to the right. These expectations are called *population stereotypes*. Some of these stereotypes appear to be universal in that they are consistent across cultures. Other stereotypes differ depending upon the culture. At the moment I am writing this chapter, I am sitting in my temporary office in Australia. On the wall is a rocker switch that controls whether the lights are on. To switch them on, I must push the bottom of the switch, opposite to what is shown in Figure 3.8. Switches are consistently installed this way in Australia, thus forming a population stereotype different from the one in North America. Figure 3.9 shows the population stereotypes relating the direction of movements of controls to display indicated movements. How consistent these stereotypes are can be determined by asking a large number of people to grasp the knob or lever and move the display indicator in a particular direction. You have experienced the strength of a stereotype if you have ever changed from an American- to a Japanese-made car and tried to adjust the radio

FIGURE 3.9 Direction of control movement recommended for a particular change in display indicator. From *Human Engineering Guide to Equipment Design* by C. T. Morgan, J. S. Cook, A. Chapanis, and M. W. Lund, 1963, New York: McGraw-Hill, p. 255.

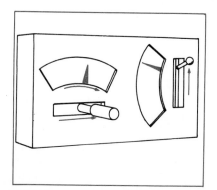
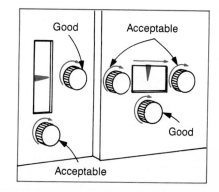

volume. In this case your tendency to reach for the left knob rather than the right one is just a nuisance, but you can imagine situations in which violating a population stereotype could be fatal.

A final control recommendation that must be considered is the control/display (C/D) ratio. In this case, the concern is not the direction of movement but the relationship between the size of control movement and display movement. For example, a tuner knob on a radio could be designed to go from one end of the range to the other in half a turn or in ten turns. The farther the control has to be moved to cause a particular change in the display, the higher the C/D ratio. High C/D ratios lead to long travel times, but shorter fine-adjustment times. Low ratios lead to short travel times but long fine-adjustment times. Low ratios lead to short travel times but long fine-adjustment times. The engineering psychologist should recommend C/D ratios for a system that are as close as possible to the optimum ratio for that system.

Anthropometric Considerations. The system or environment being designed should, of course, fit the physical dimensions and strength limitations of the humans interacting with it. Engineering anthropometry is the scientific discipline that studies the measurement of the body's physical capabilities and limitations with the goal of optimizing human/machine interactions. It may seem to you that determining these quantities should be pretty straightforward. Just get out a trusty tape measure and measure a number of potential users. However, a number of questions must be considered. How large a sample of people should be measured to represent the population of users? What is the population of users? What method of measurement is best? Once you have good measurements, should you design the system for the average user? What proportion of users must the system fit?

Usually it is impossible to measure the entire population of system users. With the exception of custom-built systems, such as when the Mercury space capsule was designed for seven specific astronauts, the population is too large, so a sample must be taken for measurement. In some cases this work has already been done. A number of sources list many measurements that have been taken in the past. Figure 3.10 illustrates a typical set of body dimensions. How useful would these data be if you were attempting to design an automobile for a major car manufacturer?

One problem that you would quickly discover is that even if this sample is good, the population is wrong. These measurements were taken for 1967 Air Force flying personnel. The Air Force has certain minimum and maximum requirements on height and weight that would eliminate extremes on certain of these dimensions. The 1967 population of flying personnel also excluded over half of the adult population, namely women. Surely women will be driving the car.

In this day of multinational corporations, you would also expect to sell cars in Latin America, Europe, and Asia where average body dimensions vary considerably from those found in the United States. In addition, average body measurements change a bit over the years. Even for a limited population such as Air Force males, it has been found that there was an average growth in height of

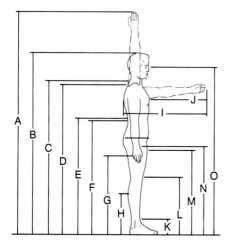

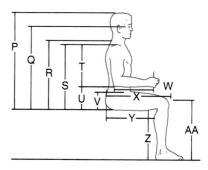

Key to figure	Dimension	5th* Percentile	95th* Percentile
A	Overhead reach	78.6	87.6
B	Stature	65.9	73.9
C	Cervical height	56.1	63.7
D	Shoulder height	53.4	60.9
E	Elbow height	41.3	47.3
F	Waist height	38.9	45.0
G	Knuckle height	27.7	32.4
H	Calf height	12.6	15.5
I	Depth of reach		
	one arm	20.2	26.8
	both arms	19.2	24.5
J	Functional reach	29.1	34.3
K	Ankle height	4.7	6.2
L	Kneecap height (top)	17.1	22.4
M	Crotch height	30.8	36.2
N	Wrist height	31.6	36.7
O	Eye height	60.8	68.6
P	Sitting height	34.7	38.8
Q	Eye height, sitting	30.0	33.9
R	Mid-shoulder height	23.7	27.3
S	Shoulder height	22.2	25.9
T	Shoulder-elbow length	13.1	15.3
U	Elbow rest height	8.2	11.6
V	Thigh clearance height	5.6	7.4
W	Elbow-grip length	12.8	14.9
X	Buttock-knee length	22.1	25.6
Y	Buttock-popliteal length	18.2	21.5
Z	Popliteal height	15.8	18.7
AA	Knee height	20.4	23.6

*1967 Air Force officer flying personnel

FIGURE 3.10 Tabular format for presentation of anthropometric percentile data. From *Engineering Anthropometry Methods* by J. A. Roebuck, Jr., H. E. Kroemer, and W. G. Thomson, 1975, New York: John Wiley & Sons. Reproduced by permission.

.0032 in. per year from 1955 to 1975 (Roebuck, Kroemer, & Thomson, 1975). At this point the measurements in the figure do not seem especially useful, and we have not even considered such factors as the ages of the population and disabled individuals.

There are many techniques for measuring the physical characteristics of the body. In terms of linear dimensions, you can use a fairly, simple instrument, such as an **anthropometer.** These devices consist of long rods marked off in gradations and filled with one or two perpendicular branches. The pointed branches can be aligned with body parts so that the distance of the part from the floor or from other body parts can be determined. For measuring smaller distances various calipers, compasses, and tapes are useful.

For determining the position of the body in space and body contours, there are grid boards on which the body can be traced or a shadow cast. Another device is a template equipped with rods running perpendicularly through a board; these are pushed against the body and measurements taken. Recently, photographic methods have been used in combination with grids of various kinds for measuring body dimensions.

Anthropometric measurements are also taken to determine the dimensions of the body during motion and the strength capabilities of the body in various positions. A number of instruments called **goniometers** have been inverted for measuring body angles. In this way the extent that the body can be flexed in certain directions can be determined. To measure the strength of the body in various positions, a variety of mechanical, hydraulic, or pneumatic **dynamometers** have been developed. Basically these instruments provide a specific resistance and measure the force the body can exert when it squeezes, pushes, or pulls against resistance.

Once the population of users is determined and appropriate measurements have been taken or found in tables, how should these measurements be used to design the system? The measurements will probably be listed for many more precentiles than are shown in Figure 3.10. A percentile specifies the proportion of the population that falls at or below a given measurement. For example, we would know from Figure 3.10 that if we placed a control 78.6 in. above the floor, 96% of the population could reach it while standing flat footed, and 4% cannot reach that high. At 87.6 in., only 6% of the population could reach the control (those at the 95th percentile and above). So whom should the system be designed for?

Unfortunately there is no simple answer to this question. One strategy would be to design the system for the 50th-percentile "average" person. A problem with this approach is that in fact no person is average, that is, nobody is at the 50th-percentile level on all dimensions. Figure 3.11 shows the percentile level for each of twelve body dimensions for three sample individuals. Person 1 appears to be near the 50th-percentile level on several dimensions but is above the 80th on one and below the 20th on two others. The perfect 50th-percentile person would be represented by a flat line at 50. The variability shown in the figure is quite typical of people. If one expands the concept of the "average person" to include

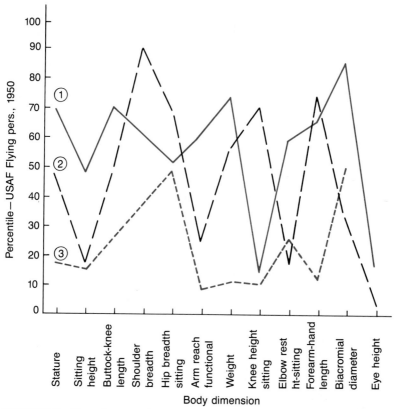

FIGURE 3.11 Three lines, each representing one person, showing the percentiles for each of twelve body dimensions. From *Engineering Anthropometry Methods* by J. A. Roebuck, Jr., H. E. Kroemer, and W. G. Thomson, 1975, New York: John Wiley & Sons. Reproduced by permission.

the 15 percentage points above and below the midpoint for each dimension, one may think that it is beginning to represent all people. In fact, it would still represent exactly no one. This has been documented by Daniels (1952) in an analysis of only ten dimensions for over 4,000 flying personnel. Out of 4,000 measured, no single person fell into the middle percentiles (33–66) on all dimensions!

More typically, rather than designing for the 50th-percentile person, the engineering psychologist would attempt to include the 5th through 95th percentiles on each dimension. An obvious strategy, particularly on critical dimensions, is to provide an adjustment for the user such as adjustable seats or steering wheels. If all dimensions are infinitely adjustable, the users can custom-fit the system to themselves. However, adjustment is expensive to build in, and systems must accomodate individuals at the extremes of the dimensions, so this strategy is not practical for many design situations. Compromises have to be made.

From this discussion you can begin to appreciate the problems encountered by the human-factors specialists doing engineering anthropometry. What may at first have appeared to be a simple matter of taking several measurements and confidently recommending numbers is really a much more complex process.

In the future, additional sophisticated tools will be available to the engineering anthropometrist. Advances in computer graphics and mathematical modeling techniques now make it possible to display on a computer a graphic, three-dimensional figure in a workspace, dress that figure in clothes of specified thickness, and have the figure move around, reaching for controls. Then by changing a few computer inputs, the specifications of the figure or the workspace can be changed and the effects can be evaluated. In the future it should also be possible for the computer to observe and evaluate a sample of humans and update its own measurement tables. These advances should make the job of designing systems and environments to meet human physical specifications easier and more effective.

In the final part of the chapter many of the design considerations discussed in this section and the systems-design process described in the first section will be illustrated using a case study. This case study should give you a feel for the actual role of the engineering psychologist in a real-world applied setting.

Case Study: Developing the Kodak Disc Camera

If someone asked you to list the human factors variables involved in developing a new camera, you could come up with a number of items. However, you would still be amazed at the amount of engineering psychology work that went into the development of the Eastman Kodak Company's Disc Camera℠. Over a period of several years, members of Kodak's Human Factors Section conducted more than 50 experiments using over 2,000 subjects in an effort to maximize both human performance with and human preference for the new camera.

The aim was to create a relatively innovative design that would win broad acceptance from consumers, because millions of cameras were to be manufactured for distribution prior to the first sale of the first camera. A major mistake in design could have been financially disastrous to the company. This section will examine several of the human-factors research efforts that led to the Disc Camera.

In many respects the Disc Camera development is a classic case, from a human-factors point of view. Human-factors specialists were involved in design decisions from the very beginning and also helped refine the product as later design decisions were made. Initially the company had several goals in mind for the new camera (Faulkner, Rice, & Heron, 1983). First, the camera was to be smaller than other cameras and, if necessary, was to have a different shape. Second, it was expected that the design would take advantage of technological advances in lenses and film speed to provide expanded capabilities. These features would influence the way people take pictures and allow them to photograph in situations where they had not commonly used cameras in the past. The third goal was to transfer as many decisions as possible from the photographer to the camera.

Starting with these goals, human-factors specialists were asked to help define the system parameters or dimensions, that is, such factors as flash capability, shutter speed, near-focus limit, and so on. Too often in system development an engineer sets these parameters and human-factors people have to work within them.

Choosing System Parameters. In an effort to help with choosing system parameters, Faulkner and Rice (1982) first attempted to define how and where amateur photographers use and misuse their cameras. Kodak operates a special photofinishing laboratory for the evaluation of new equipment, materials, and procedures. The lab offers services to all company employees at reduced rates. While the film is being processed, a print evaluation is done. Data are collected concerning both camera usage and picture quality.

Usage information consists of 20 factors describing the conditions under which each picture was taken, such as camera-to-subject distance, source of illumination, and so on. Picture quality is an evaluation of more than 20 problems such as underexposure, camera shake, poor focus, or finger over the lens. Two basic classes of situations cause poor picture quality. The first kind occurs when the photographer attempts to take a picture that is beyond the capabilities of the camera and film. These problems can sometimes be corrected by extending the camera's capabilities. The second group of problems result from the photographer's incorrect decisions or incorrect actions, for example, forgetting to turn over the flipflash, failure to focus, and so on. This class of problems can sometimes be corrected by placing the decision or action within the camera rather than with the operator.

Kodak developed a database with full picture-quality descriptions of over 40,000 color prints. From the usage and print-quality information, it was possible for researchers to develop a *system utilization space,* in this case a photographic utilization space. A typical utilization space is illustrated in Figure 3.12.

FIGURE 3.12 A typical photographic utilization space showing the frequency of camera usage as a function of distance and lighting. From "Human Factors, Photographic Space, and Disc Photography" by T. W. Faulkner and T. M. Rice. Proceedings of the Human Factors Society, 26th Annual Meeting, 1982. Copyright 1982 by the Human Factors Society, Inc.

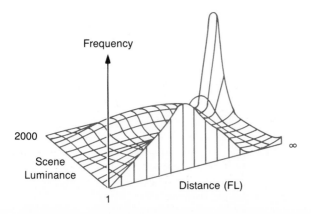

This is a three-dimensional map showing the frequency with which people take pictures at a particular distance under a particular lighting condition. For instance, you can see that one of the humps indicates that a lot of pictures are taken at long distances in bright light. Many of these pictures are of landscapes.

This utilization space is different for each camera, and some of the space will lie outside of any camera's capabilities. When a picture is taken outside of the camera's capabilities, picture quality is degraded. The researchers wanted to design the new camera in such a way that the frequency of degraded pictures was minimized. To do this, they examined the utilization spaces for cameras using 110mm-size and 135mm-size film. Then, taking into account the expected extended capabilities of the new camera, they projected a Disc Camera utilization space.

Next researchers developed what is termed a *system coverage map*. This is a diagram, similar to that shown in Figure 3.13, that defines the area in which acceptable pictures can be taken with a given camera. It is bounded by one line that delineates the closest distance at which focus is acceptable, a second line that delineates acceptable lighting with no flash, and a third line related to lighting with a flash. A set of equations was worked out that relate system parameters to coverage space. For example, increasing the aperture of the lens (as in going from f4 to f2.8) will increase the flash range (R max), lower the minimum ambient luminance (B min), and place the near-focus limit (Rc) at a greater distance. The first two changes provide increases in coverage, but the third produces a decrease.

Given the utilization space projected for the Disc Camera and the coverage space defined by the equations, the researchers were able to superimpose the two and determine what set of system parameters would maximize the proportion of picture-taking attempts within the system coverage space. In this way, they could be assured that as few unacceptable pictures would be taken as pos-

FIGURE 3.13 A system coverage map showing the area in which distance and lighting are adequate for taking acceptable pictures. From "Human Factors, Photographic Space, and Disc Photography" by T. W. Faulkner and T. M. Rice. *Proceedings of the Human Factors Society, 26th Annual Meeting,* 1982. Copyright 1982 by the Human Factors Society, Inc.

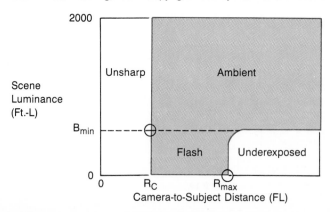

sible, at least those that were unacceptable due to the photographer's operating the camera beyond its capabilities.

Performance Analysis.   Now that fewer unacceptable pictures were likely to be taken due to the camera's design, what about the pictures that are unacceptable due to the photographer's actions, such as when a stray finger gets in the way of the lens or the flash? Caplan (1982) attempted to evaluate this dimension.

Nine styrene models having different camera configurations were tested. The cameras differed in terms of shutter release location, whether there was a cover/handle, and so on. (See Figure 3.14 which shows a selection of configurations.) A representative group of 48 camera users simulated using the cameras by taking six horizontal and one vertical "picture" of the experimenter. The subjects were told that the experiment was an attempt to find out how easy the cameras were to hold steady. Finger blockage was not mentioned to the subjects, although the experimenter actually recorded the amount, if any, of the lens or flash covered by a finger.

Three models were found to be least vulnerable to the problem of "finger over the lens." Vulnerability to "finger over the flash" was about nine times greater for the poorest camera compared to the best. The results for each camera were then weighted by using the photographic space data gathered previously. Of particular importance in the weighting were the relative frequency of horizontal versus vertical pictures taken by users (a large majority of amateur pictures are horizontally oriented), the amount of lens or flash blockage acceptable, and the percent of pictures requiring a flash. These weighting data along with the experimental results allowed the researchers to give each camera a number that reflected the relative total degrades. Caplan reported that the worst model would probably produce almost 14 times as many degraded pictures as the best, certainly an important consideration.

FIGURE 3.14   The nine camera models rated for preference.

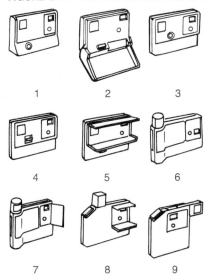

Preference analysis. While it is desirable to design a camera that will take good pictures, the camera will not be a commercial success unless people like it. The final set of experiments determined people's preference for various camera configurations (Faulkner, Rice, & Heron, 1983).

These investigators reported three preference experiments that moved progressively from broad questions such as "Is a vertical or horizontal orientation better?" to more refined questions, for example, "Which cover/handle is preferred?" Following is a review of the second experiment to illustrate a general methodology used in preference experiments.

First, a lifelike stryene model of each camera configuration was constructed. Subjects were Kodak employees who were matched to demographic data of the potential market of camera users. The subjects were individually tested with the experimenter first demonstrating each model and pointing out key features such as the lens, viewfinder, shutter release, and flash. After each camera had been demonstrated and placed on a table, the subject was asked to pick up each model and take a picture with it. Comments made by the subjects were recorded.

Next, subjects rated the cameras by indicating one of five categories for each; the top two categories indicated a positive attitude, the middle neutral, and the bottom two negative. They then ranked the cameras in order of preference.

The nine camera models tested are shown in Figure 3.14. You can see that the cameras differ with regard to type and location of flash module, type of lens cover, type and location of shutter release, and location of viewfinder. The results of the category rating procedure are shown in Figure 3.15. Table 3.2 shows the results of the ranking data. You will note that the two methods give very similar results. After looking at these results it may seem that you now know the answer to the original question, "Which camera model is preferred?" However, there are two additional questions that are important, "Do different groups of

FIGURE 3.15 Category scaling results from camera preference experiment. From "The Influence of Camera Configuration on Preference" by T. W. Faulkner, T. M. Rice, and W. K. Heron, 1983, *Human Factors,* 25 (2), p. 132.

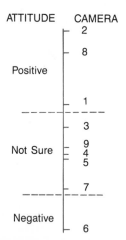

TABLE 3.2

Rank-Order Scaling of Camera Models in the Camera Preference Experiment

Camera Model	Mean Rank	Statistical Significance (p ⩽ 0.05)
2	3.1	Higher than Cameras 1, 3, 5, 9, 4, 7, 6
8	3.9	Higher than Cameras 4, 7, 6
1	4.8	Higher than Camera 6
3	4.9	
5	5.2	
9	5.3	
4	5.4	
7	5.9	
6	6.5	

From "The Influence of Camera Configuration on Preference" by T. W. Faulkner, T. M. Rice, and W. K. Heron, 1983, Human Factors, 25 (2), p. 133.

people like different models?" and "What features of the camera are most preferred over all models?" The first question is important if you wish to market the camera to a wide range of people. The second question is important if you wish to make minor adjustments in design while retaining the desirable features.

Two mathematical techniques permit researchers to answer these questions. The details of these techniques are too complex to go into here. However, they are similar to the methodology of factor analysis and multiple regression that was discussed in Chapter 2. The first technique is called **cluster analysis.** It was used to divide subjects into groups or clusters based on their rank-order scores. The comments the subjects made were also grouped into the appropriate clusters and were compared to verify that people expressing similar views were being grouped into the same cluster. Three clusters best fit the data. These are shown in Table 3.3, with the mean rank for each model listed for each cluster.

The three clusters are obviously quite different from one another and give us information that the average rankings did not. For example, we can see that Model 9 was the most preferred model by Cluster C but the least preferred by Cluster A. The middle ranking for Model 9 shown in Table 3.2 is due to averaging across very strong preferences for two quite different groups.

The second technique used is called **multidimensional scaling.** It is a way of determining what dimensions underlie the preferences of each cluster. The mathematical operations order each of the camera models along several unnamed dimensions. The researcher must then examine the models and each subject's comments to determine what each dimension represents. The two dimensions that appeared important to the 22 people in Cluster A were a dislike of models with a pop-up flash and a preference for cameras with lens covers. Together these dimensions accounted for 70% of the variance in the ranking data.

Three dimensions appeared important to the 17 people in Cluster B. These were: holding steadiness, holding comfort, and resistance to covering the lens or flash with the finger. Together these dimensions accounted for 72% of the

TABLE 3.3

Three-Cluster Breakdown of Rank-Order Scaling in the Camera Preference Experiment

Cluster A (22 subjects)			Cluster B (17 subjects)			Cluster C (24 subjects)		
Camera Model	Mean Rank	Statistical Significance ($p \leqslant 0.05$)	Camera Model	Mean Rank	Statistical Significance ($p \leqslant 0.05$)	Camera Model	Mean Rank	Statistical Significance ($p \leqslant 0.05$)
2	1.8	Higher than Cameras 1, 4, 8, 7, 6, 9	2	3.2	Higher than Cameras 1, 3, 4, 5	9	2.8	Higher than Cameras 5, 6, 7
5	3.3	Higher than Cameras 7, 6, 9	8	3.4	Higher than Cameras 3, 4, 5	8	2.9	Higher than Cameras 5, 6, 7
3	4.2	Higher than Cameras 6, 9	7	3.4	Higher than Cameras 4, 5	1	4.1	Higher than Cameras 6, 7
1	4.5	Higher than Cameras 6, 9	6	3.8	Higher than Cameras 4, 5	2	4.1	Higher than Cameras 6, 7
4	4.5	Higher than Cameras 6, 9	9	5.2		3	4.6	Higher than Cameras 6, 7
8	5.3	Higher than Camera 9	1	6.2		4	5.2	Higher than Camera 7
7	5.9		3	6.3		5	5.9	
6	7.3		4	6.8		6	7.6	
9	8.1		5	6.8		7	7.8	

From "The Influence of Camera Configuration on Preference by T. W. Faulkner, T. M. Rice, and W. K. Heron, 1983, Human Factors, 25 (2), p. 134.

variance. Nearly all of the reactions of the 24 people in Cluster C concerned the single dimension of shutter-release location. This dimension by itself accounted for 48% of the variance.

From the cluster analysis and the multidimensional scaling it became clear that there were difficulties in finding one model most preferred by all people. One group liked the cover/handle on Camera 2 because it provided protection for the lens, shutter release, and viewfinder. A second group liked the cover/handle because it improved ease of holding. However, a third group did not like it. Altogether, about 60% like cover/handles and about 40% preferred models without a handle of any kind.

The obvious solution to this dilemma was to market two different designs. If you look at Disc Cameras for sale today, you will find one that looks something like Camera 2 and a second that resembles Cameras 1 and 3. This research was considered important by the company, and the engineering psychologists obviously had a large effect on the final designs chosen.

This case history exemplifies the type of systems-design work in which human-factors specialists were used appropriately. They were brought into the design process at the very beginning and helped to determine some of the system parameters based upon historical usage data. They were then allowed to make recommendations during the ongoing systems-design process. These recommendations were based upon experimental work that investigated both the user's performance characteristics and the user's preferences.

Conclusion

This chapter described the systems approach that engineering psychologists take in their work and showed how this approach emphasizes the interaction of humans and machines within particular environments. In the design of a human/machine system, you saw that the engineering psychologist provides the human-factors input basic to almost all phases of the design process. You learned about the settings where engineering psychologists work and how engineering psychology relates to similar jobs identified by different titles in different geographical areas.

The chapter showed how the research of engineering psychologists provided information concerning different types of design decisions and identified optimal types of displays used to present information from machines to human operators. You learned about the design of control mechanisms that human operators use to communicate information to machines and reviewed research performed in the area of engineering anthropometry to measure physical capabilities and limitations so that human/machine interactions can be optimized. Finally, a case study of the development of the Kodak Disc Camera was presented to show how the various techniques used by engineering psychologists in the systems-design process fit together.

The purpose of this chapter has been to give you a greater appreciation for the roles played by engineering psychologists. Few people have even heard of this profession. Yet engineering psychologists, and human-factors specialists in general, have the potential of making human interactions with machines safer, more productive, and more pleasant.

Glossary

anthropometer A class of devices having a long rod marked off in gradations and having one or two perpendicular branches. The pointed branches can be aligned with body parts so that the distance of the part from the floor or from other body parts can be determined.

cluster analysis A statistical technique used to divide subjects into groups or clusters based on some measure of association between the items. In the present chapter, cluster analysis was used to combine groups of survey respondents according to their preference rankings for different camera prototypes.

dynamometer An instrument designed to measure the strength of the body in various positions by providing a resistance and measuring the force the body can exert when it squeezes, pushes, or pulls against this resistance.

engineering anthropometry   The scientific discipline that studies the measurement of the body's physical capabilities and limitations with the goal of optimizing human/machine interactions.

ergonomics   A term for the general field of engineering psychology used in Europe and internationally.

goniometer   A class of instruments used for measuring body angles. With these devices the extent that the body can be flexed in certain directions can be determined.

job specification   Defining the tasks that must be accomplished in order to perform a particular job. Often the skills and training required to perform the job are also specified.

multidimensional scaling   As used in the present chapter, a statistical technique to determine what dimensions underlie the preferences people express. The mathematical operations ordered each of the camera models along several unnamed dimensions. The researchers then examined the models and each subject's comments to determine what each dimension represented.

population stereotypes   Expectations held by people when they manipulate a control device about the effect that the manipulation will have on a machine.

4 Industrial and Organizational Psychology

Peter Dorfman
New Mexico State University

Greg Rush works as an automobile mechanic after school. Upon graduation, he wants to work for General Motors. Although his skills are good, Greg worries that he will not be able to pass the company's pre-employment tests.

Sharon Cooper was trained as a nurse. She has been out of the workforce for 17 years while she raised her three children. Now that she wants to return to her former career, she is unsure of the best method to regain her skills.

Bill Adams has been the lead design engineer in a high-tech firm for six years. He is upset upon learning that he has been passed over for promotion to a managerial position. Although he doesn't want to leave the company, Bill feels that he will have no other alternative if his leadership skills are ignored.

Josh Brady's latest performance appraisal was a real shock. He believes the mediocre performance ratings are very unfair. Although he can appeal the ratings, he knows that his boss might really take it out on him in the future.

Carmen Martinez is the chairperson of a university department. She is new on the job and doesn't want to antagonize the faculty. At the same time, she knows that several faculty members have not been teaching up to their ability. She is worried that if she puts pressure on these instructors, she will be perceived as the "typical female boss."

Isabel Reitman has just received her law degree and has been hired by a prestigious law firm. Recently she heard that the firm has a poor reputation for promoting women.

Wendy Smith is a superachiever on the job. Her work constantly receives rave reviews: "Reports are error-free and filed before the due date. Her coworkers however, seem to resent her success. One even suggested that she slow down so that they wouldn't look so bad.

All these people have problems that relate to their relationship with work organizations. Greg is concerned about the entry requirements when applying for a job. Sharon must regain her nursing skills through retraining. Bill needs to make a decision regarding his future with the firm. Josh is angry about his performance appraisal. Carmen is concerned about the most appropriate leadership style. Isabel is worried about job discrimination, and Wendy's colleagues seem to resent her achievement. The problems of these individuals introduce you to industrial/organizational psychology.

What Is Industrial/Organizational Psychology?

Suppose you become an industrial/organizational (I/O) psychologist and someone at a party asks what you do for a living. Your reply will likely bring on a variety of facial expressions that range from blank stares to looks of, "Ah— you're one of those shrinks who help people with problems." It may be easy to dispel the belief that you are a psychiatrist or clinical psychologist, but it is difficult to give an adequate explanation of the role of an I/O psychologist, primarily because the scope of I/O psychology is so wide. As the rest of this chapter will show, I/O psychologists work in a variety of settings that include business, government, academia, and private consulting firms. Their activities may include helping organizations to select and train employees, measure their job performance, and determine appropriate compensatory systems. Industrial/organizational psychologists may also address problems in work organizations related to providing appropriate leadership, motivating employees, and coordinating diverse work groups. Underlying most efforts are the goals of improving worker productivity, job satisfaction, motivation, and job commitment.

I/O psychology itself can be defined as the scientific study of people in work organizations. These organizations include both goods-producing industries, such as automobile manufacturing and coal mining, and service organizations such as universities, hospitals, and banks. It is important to point out that I/O psychologists seek to *understand* people in organizations and then *apply* this knowledge to resolve problems of human behavior at work (Howell & Dipboye, 1986). Thus I/O psychology is both scientific and practical. The scientific side seeks to advance knowledge about people at work, and the practical (or professional) side is concerned with the application of knowledge to solve real problems in the work world (Muchinsky, 1987).

I/O psychology can be viewed as both a science and a profession. Its primary emphasis as a science is understanding people in work activities through research. Conversely, the emphasis of psychology as a profession lies in the application of knowledge to solve practical problems. The two faces of I/O psychology should be viewed as the two sides of a coin—each is vital to the integrity of the other. For instance, as a scientific endeavor a research psychologist might determine, through careful and systematic study, that a new technique is superior to older techniques to train supervisiors. A practitioner of I/O psychology, such as a training director who actually provides such training within an organization, ideally

The information being presented to these workers as well as the design of the equipment they will operate may have been shaped by the recommendations of industrial/organizational psychologists.

would use the knowledge generated by the scientific arm of the field. I/O psychologists understand and have a firm commitment to the interdependent roles of research and practice.

If one looks at the history of I/O psychology from 1900 to the present, one can see major changes in the scope, focus, and complexity of the field. The scope has broadened beyond belief. Today I/O psychology addresses most aspects of organizational life — from interests in individuals to groups to organizations. One aspect of the increased complexity of the field is obvious; because many aspects of organizational life are related to each other, it is difficult to separate them and study each aspect independently. For example, the amount of pay people receive may influence their job satisfaction, and job satisfaction, in turn, influences attendance and productivity. Complexity of the field affects the profession at other levels as well. The Civil Rights Act of 1964 has had a major influence on the work of I/O psychologists. This law and many others affect the selection, placement, training, and appraisal of people at work.

Specialty Areas

Another indication of complexity is the development of subfields in industrial and organizational psychology. The two main subareas are industrial (often called personnel) and organizational psychology. To a lesser extent, engineering psychology, industrial relations, consumer psychology, organizational development, and vocational psychology may also be considered as subfields. We will concentrate on the first two areas mentioned.

The first, personnel psychology, includes activities related to the selection and placement of people in organizations, the training of these individuals to perform up to job standards, and the subsequent measurement of their job performance. Historically, personnel activities have been the focus of the discipline of I/O psychology since these activities help managemnt solve problems and improve organizational efficiency. This part of the field of I/O is said to have a strong orientation to individual differences. Since people differ from each other in abilities, interests, and skills, knowledge about these differences can predict who will be a successful employee or who needs further training.

The focus of organizational psychology, the second major specialty area within I/O psychology, is on the process by which individuals adjust to their job, coworkers, supervisors, and the organization as a whole. Organizational psychologists are concerned with people and their job attitudes (e.g., how committed are they?), their work motivation (e.g., how much intensity and effort do they put forth on a task?), their job satisfaction (e.g., do they have a positive attitude toward what they do?), their leadership behavior (e.g., are they effective leaders?), and their interaction with the organization as a system (e.g., does the organizational atmosphere foster individual growth?).

It might be useful to point out some similarities and differences between the two specialty areas within I/O psychology. Often in the area of personnel psychology, decisions that the organization makes in its efforts to select, train, and evaluate personnel are considered. In the organizational subarea the focus is largely on how decisions will affect individual workers. Personnel psychology has an applied orientation, whereas organizational psychology is often primarily concerned with theoretical development. However, although the focus of organizational psychologists may be on developing theories of leadership, motivation, and job satisfaction, ultimately, they wish to apply these theories to solve management problems.

However, few fields of scientific inquiry are neatly divided, and I/O psychology is no exception; that is, the goals of both subareas are really very similar — to understand the work behavior of people in organizations and to apply this knowledge to solve real-world problems. Also, both specialty areas are concerned with the organization's impact on employee turnover, absenteeism, motivation, job satisfaction, and productivity.

One final point with regard to the somewhat arbitrary division of I/O psychology. The field of engineering psychology is sometimes included as a third, albeit small, subspecialty within I/O psychology. Engineering psychology is concerned with the design of machines, systems, and work environments to match the capabilities and limitations of human beings. Since Chapter 3 was devoted to this topic, there is no need to discuss it here. Also not included are the subareas of industrial relations, consumer, and vocational psychology.

Related Disciplines

You may think at this point that I/O psychology seems to cover just about every aspect related to people in work situations. Is there anything that it does not consider? The answer is yes, although I/O psychology seems to be expanding into areas that were once considered as outside its primary focus. The personnel specialty area of I/O psychology is closely related to the field of personnel management. I/O psychologists and personnel managers share the same interests in selection, training, performance appraisal, and job analysis. Not typically included within I/O psychology are personnel management issues of wage and salary administration, industrial/labor relations, employee benefits and services, and labor and compensation law (Cascio, 1987).

Organizational psychology is almost redundant with the organizational behavior section of management sciences (Rowland & Ferris, 1982). Both concentrate on job satisfaction, motivation, leadership, communication, and organizational development. However, the field of management sciences (taught in schools of business administration) concerns many areas not typically the focus of I/O psychologists, including business and policy planning, industrial and labor relations, health-care management, managerial consultation, macroorganizational theory, and production-operations management.

In summary, personnel management and industrial psychology share common interests and are applications-oriented, whereas organizational behavior and organizational psychology have close ties and are frequently theoretically oriented. All of these fields, however, have the common goals of understanding people in organizations and improving the use of human resources in these entities. It should be pointed out that other disciplines also contribute to the understanding of people at work. The literature on work behavior is scattered across several areas of the social sciences including sociology, labor economics, industrial engineering, and political science.

What Do Industrial/Organizational Psychologists Do?

There are a number of reasons why an individual would want to work as an I/O psychologist. All indicators point to a bright future for the field. I/O psychologists are reasonably well paid for their efforts, particularly when compared to many other specialty areas within psychology; they have a high rate of employment (almost 100%) even for newly graduated students. Their jobs are usually commensurate with their training (i.e., they do what they are trained to do) and most often they can work in the employment settings of their choice. Today there are more than 2,800 industrial/organizational psychologists.

Job Activities

Most I/O psychologists find their jobs fascinating. To see why, consider an organization of which you are now a member, perhaps your university. It is composed of individuals and groups of people, has a defined structure with designated leaders, and has functions that need to be carried out and coordinated in order to accomplish the goals of the organization. Now think of the really interesting aspects of your organization. Do you notice how informal groups or cliques form with their own standards of behavior (good and bad), or how quickly the grapevine transmits information (often only partially correct), or how frustrated you become when rewards are given to the wrong people (apple-polishers), or how you seem to lack motivation or drive (particularly in the middle of the semester), or how you know you can do the job after graduating (but someone else was selected and hired)? All of these things — group norms, communication patterns, job frustration, motivation, and selection — are interesting objects of study for the I/O psychologist.

Besides being a fascinating job, there is another bright aspect to the field. As an I/O psychologist, you can have a positive impact on the lives of many individuals at work. For instance, if you are a practitioner working for a company, you can develop interviewing procedures that are fair, train supervisors in giving recognition to employees, or set up worthwhile management-development programs. All of these are meaningful endeavors that can have a positive impact on people's lives.

The best way to describe the job of an I/O psychologist is to discuss the goals and job-related activities that interest I/O psychologists. These interests and activities include improving job satisfaction and motivation, hiring job applicants who will prove to be successful, training individuals in specific skills, implementing management-development programs, designing objective performance appraisal and compensation systems, determining qualities of successful leaders, and resolving conflicts between labor and management.

Work Settings

I/O psychologists are employed in four major settings: business and industry, consulting firms and research organizations, government, and academia. As can be seen in Figure 4.1, approximately one fourth of all I/O psychologists work in business and industry, and another fourth in consulting organizations. About a third work in university settings, and the rest are spaced out among the remaining job settings.

You may not be aware of the number of I/O psychologists nor the range of their jobs within business and industry. Simply looking at an organizational chart and searching for the job title "I/O psychologist" is misleading. Although you might find "staff psychologist," more often than not the titles of I/O psychologists will reflect their job functions, such as director of personnel research, coordinator of training, supervisor of test development and evaluation, or vice president for human resources (See Table 4.1). You will find that psychologists are employed in virtually all sectors of business and industry, and the scope of job responsibilities is equally as broad. I/O psychologists may design tests and other means to select those individuals who are most likely to succeed at work; plan training programs to ensure high levels of skills among employees; develop sophisticated performance appraisal systems; plot compensation systems aimed

FIGURE 4.1   Work settings of industrial/organizational psychologists.

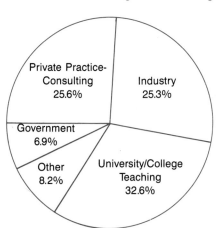

TABLE 4.1

Places of Employment and Job Titles of Selected Industrial Psychologists

Bell Telephone Laboratories
  Business Systems Supervisor
City Government
  Assistant Personnel Director
Columbia Broadcasting System
  Director of Compensation
Continental Oil
  Director of Advertising
Dow Chemical
  Manager of Consumer Research
Executronics
  Vice President
General Dynamics
  Head of Human Factors Laboratory
General Electric
  Senior Staff Specialist
Harcourt Brace Jovanovich
  Executive Editor of Test Department
International Multifoods
  Director of Management Development
McGraw-Hill
  Regional Manager
Metropolitan Life Insurance
  Staff Psychologist
Port Authority of New York and New Jersey
  Supervisor of Test Development and Evaluation
Procter & Gamble
  Personnel Research Psychologist
Reynolds Metals
  Manager of Personnel Research
Sears, Roebuck
  National Director of Training and Development
Self-Employed
  Management Consultant
Standard Oil
  Manager of Psychological Services
State Department of Health and Welfare
  Program Planner, Bureau of Research and Training
Texas Instruments
  Personnel Director of Worldwide Operations
U.S. Naval Personnel Research and Development Center
  Research Engineering Psychologist
U.S. Steel
  Staff Supervisor of Testing and Counseling
Westinghouse Electric
  Manager of Employee Relations
Weyerhauser
  Industrial Psychologist
Xerox
  Manager of Information and Planning Services

From *Psychology and Industry Today, 4th ed. (p. 17) by D. P. Schultz and S. E. Schultz, 1986, New York: Macmillan.*

at motivating employees; or engage in long-term research programs designed to assess the effectiveness of management career planning. Almost always, those I/O psychologists who apply psychological techniques and principles to improve situations at work are responsible for evaluating the usefulness of their activities.

Many firms do not employ full-time psychologists simply because they are neither large enough nor sufficiently aware of the range of job activities and skills of an I/O specialist. Consulting firms are often approached when people problems that require an outside expert arise. These consulting companies may be large (e.g., Psychological Corporation, Science Research Associates, Dunlapp and Associates, Personnel Decisions Research Institute) with many employees, but most are small firms employing a few I/O psychologists. Many psychologists are not associated with firms, but operate as free-lance consultants in private practice. Generally, the consulting firm will contract to perform a specific activity such as evaluating executives for promotion or developing and administering tests. At other times, it may engage in process consultation — assisting managers to diagnose and treat problems that exist in the organization. These problems may be relatively ambiguous (such as poor morale and bad communication) or they may be more concrete (such as rectifying problems with a particular training program).

The United States government provides a third work setting for I/O psychologists. Work activities in government are as diverse and broad as those in business and consulting organizations. I/O psychologists are employed in numerous federal agencies including the U.S. Office of Personnel Management, Equal Employment Opportunity Commission, Office of Naval Research, U.S. Army Research Institute for the Behavioral and Social Sciences and Air Force Human Resources Laboratory.

In addition, the many research institutes and organizations largely funded by private industry and government agencies provide a fourth work setting for I/O psychology. Examples include the Educational Testing Services (ETS), American Institutes for Research (AIR), and Life Insurance Marketing and Research Association (LIMRA). Individuals who work in these organizations typically are involved in relatively long-term research programs with an orientation to develop and to apply I/O psychology to relatively complex problems. Examples of research that has been conducted in these settings include developing a human relations training program for police officers, validating job selection tests for the government, and improving the effectiveness of interviews as personnel selection procedures. Results of these activities have often led to important developments within the field.

Finally, I/O psychologists are employed in colleges and universities. As you might expect, most I/O psychologists in academia reside within psychology departments; however, schools of business also employ a large number. Faculty in academic settings are required to teach, to conduct research, and to serve the university. Whereas the research conducted in business, government, and consulting organizations is often controlled from top levels in the organization, I/O psychologists in academia are generally free to select any topic of interest for their research efforts.

Research and Applications

The information in the preceding section should have oriented you to this dynamic field. The real excitement comes in considering the ways research helps solve problems in the workplace. The goal of the rest of this chapter is to give you a perspective on the field as a whole by describing a *limited* number of areas. The scope of I/O psychology is so diverse, with so much information available, that complete coverage of even the selected topics in so short a space would be impossible.

Personnel Psychology

The introduction to this chapter identified I/O psychology as being concerned with the following "personnel" activities: employee staffing (including recruitment and employee selection), personnel training and development, job analysis, and performance appraisal. This section will briefly examine the process by which organizations recruit individuals and the choice process by which individuals, in turn, select organizations. The major emphasis is on the process by which organizations select people and place them in jobs. Other important personnel topics, including employee training and performance appraisal, will

Although you won't see industrial/organizational psychologists at that all-important job interview, chances are good that they have made important contributions to the development of effective recruiting, selection, training, and development procedures of the organization interviewing you.

not be considered in detail because of space limitations. However, by the end of the chapter, you should have a grasp of the major concerns of I/O psychologists and of their contributions to the "personnel" functions in organizations. The following "personnel problem" can serve as an example to show how these topics form an important and intertwined system of activities. Suppose that your mother-in-law wanted to expand her small car-repair facility into a large-scale automobile dealership and repair operation. You have been asked to gear up and run the company. Assume that she has secured the necessary financial capital and your initial responsibility is to staff the organization. Where do you start? After studying all the available books concerning automobile dealerships, you decide that the job positions of sales manager, salespersons, service manager, finance and insurance manager, service technicians, and parts and body repair personnel are required for the expanded service. These people will also need to be trained and their job performance assessed to ensure quality work. All of these functions require a thorough understanding of each job.

Job Descriptions and Job Analysis.   All organizations need explicit descriptions of what people are expected to do in their jobs. Standard job descriptions are published in the Dictionary of Occupational Titles (DOT), a publication of the Department of Labor listing over 20,000 jobs. Figure 4.2 contains an example of the DOT information for mechanic and car salesperson. Besides the general picture or "blueprint" of the job, the DOT also specifies the characteristics and traits that are required by jobholders. Personal qualities like numerical and verbal ability, level of intelligence, and motor coordination may all be specified.

However, to describe a job in detail and to describe the job as it actually exists in an organization, it may be important to conduct a **job analysis.** The purpose of the job analysis is to provide information about the job in sufficient detail so that personnel functions can be carried out in a logical manner. As was suggested earlier, it makes little sense to select people for a job before knowing the skills and abilities (or educational background and experience) required to successfully perform the job. Moreover, designing a training program requires a thorough understanding and descriptions of the specific tasks required in the job. Both of these aspects of the job—task requirements and people requirements—are necessary elements to explicitly define any job (Cascio, 1987). Industrial/organizational psychologists believe that job analysis forms the backbone of all personnel functions.

Many procedures have been developed to conduct a job analysis (Levine, 1983; McCormick, 1979). Although trained specialists should conduct the project, many people in the organization play significant roles in the procedure. The job analyst might use one of several standardized procedures, such as those presented in the U.S. Department of Labor Handbook for Analyzing Jobs, or the standardized measure called The Position Analysis Questionnaire. The job analyst might observe people performing their jobs, interview them, or interview their supervisors. Alternatively, the analyst might develop a questionnaire for job incumbents to specify which tasks they perform, how often they perform them, and how important the tasks are to job success. Sometimes job analysts will

273.353-010 SALESPERSON, AUTOMOBILES (ret. tr.) salesperson, cars.

Sells new or used automobiles on premises of automobile agency: Explains features and demonstrates operation of car in showroom or on road. Suggests optional equipment for customer to purchase. Computes and quotes sales price, including tax, trade-in allowance, license fee, and discount, and requirements for financing payment of car on credit. Performs other duties as described under SALESPERSON (ret. tr.; whole, tr.). May be designated as SALESPERSON, NEW CARS (ret. tr.); SALESPERSON, USED CARS (ret. tr.).

620.261-010 AUTOMOBILE MECHANIC (auto. ser.) garage mechanic.

Repairs and overhauls automobiles, buses, trucks, and other automotive vehicles: Examines vehicle and discusses with customer or AUTOMOBILE-REPAIR-SERVICE ESTIMATOR (auto. ser.): AUTOMOBILE TESTER (auto. ser.); or BUS INSPECTOR (auto. ser.) nature and extent of damage or malfunction. Plans work procedure, using cha r ts, technical manuals, and experience. Raises vehicle, using hydraulic jack or hoist, to gain access to mechanical units bolted to underside of vehicle. Removes unit, such as engine, transmission, or differential, using wrenches and hoist. Disassembles unit and inspects parts for wear, using micrometers, calipers, and thickness gages. Repairs or replaces parts, such as pistons, rods, gears, valves, and bearings, using mechanic's handtools. Overhauls or replaces carburetors, blowers, generators, distributors, starters, and pumps. Rebuilds parts, such as crankshafts and cylinder blocks, using lathes, shapers, drill presses, and welding equipment. Rewires ignition system, lights, and instrument panel. Relines and adjusts brakes, alines front end, repairs or replaces shock absorbers, and solders leaks in radiator. Mends damaged body and fenders by hammering out or filling in dents and welding broken parts. Replaces and adjusts headlights, and installs and repairs accessories, such as radios, heaters, mirrors, and windshield wipers. May be designated according to specialty as AUTOMOBILE MECHANIC, MOTOR (auto. ser.); BUS MECHANIC (auto. ser.): DIFFERENTIAL REPAIRER (auto. ser.): ENGINE-REPAIR MECHANIC. BUS (auto. ser.); FOREIGN-CAR MECHANIC (auto. ser .): TRUCK MECHANIC (auto. ser.). When working in service station may be designated AUTOMOBILE-SERVICE-STATION MECHANIC (auto. ser .). Additional titles: COMPRESSOR MECHANIC. BUS (auto. ser.); DRIVE-SHAFT-AND-STEERING-POST REPAIRER (auto. ser.): ENGINE-HEAD REPAIR (auto. ser.): MOTOR ASSEMBLER (auto. ser.).

FIGURE 4.2 Examples of entries in the *Dictionary of Occupational Titles.*

perform the job themselves and gain personal experience, or ask job incumbents to keep diaries of their daily activities. An increasingly popular technique is to have job incumbents describe critical incidents that have occurred on the job and then use these incidents to develop a list of behaviors critical for job success. Contemporary researchers, such as Ben Schneider and Neal Schmitt (1986), have suggested that the job analysis should also convey information about the psychological rewards that accompany each job, such as challenge and variety. With the job analysis information at hand, you are now ready to proceed to the second step in staffing your new organization, that of recruiting employees.

Recruitment. Organizations seek out people who they hope will prove to be valuable employees. Obviously, people in turn seek out good jobs in good organizations. Too often organizations forget the importance of applicant decisions in the process. The two-way matching process is the crux of recruiting activity. What applicants want in jobs must be a prime concern. Then an organization must set up both internal recruiting processes (to interest current employees in openings) and external recruiting (to seek out and attract capable individuals from the outside labor market).

What makes a good job? Why would an individual want to seek out and work for one company rather than another? Obviously, there will be huge differences between individuals as to what they want out of a job. The amount of pay is certainly a major concern and is often rated as the most important factor in considering which job to accept. Consider the remark of Samual Gompers, ex-president of the American Federation of Labor (AFL), "A job's a job; if it doesn't pay enough, it's a lousy job." Yet few people today would suggest that pay is the only important factor. Interesting and meaningful content, congenial coworkers, advancement opportunities, job security, and participation in job-related decisions all influence workers' perceptions of the desirability of their jobs (Jurgensen, 1978). Later in the chapter the factors that determine "quality of worklife" will be addressed.

Returning to the automobile dealership scenario, assume that you have considered all of these aspects of the jobs. Before the recruiting activity begins, organizations should develop a human resource plan. The most basic plan would specify the number and the kind of people that are needed, their skills and abilities, and a time framework to indicate when they are needed.

Before recruiting from outside the organization, an organization would be advised to start an internal search process. In addition to improving the morale and motivation of those already employed, internal recruiting can also reduce costs associated with filling jobs. Personnel from inside the organization will not have to go through the socialization process since they already know the organization. External recruiting is an appropriate strategy in filling positions for which current employees do not possess appropriate skills or training. Numerous strategies have been developed to successfully recruit new employees. Among the recruitment sources used by companies are employee referrals, newspaper advertisements, community agencies, private employment agencies, career conferences or job fairs, college and university placement services, professional societies, and labor unions. Two major factors that need to be considered when choosing a particular source are (1) the cost of the process and (2) the time from the contact to actually getting the people "on board."

To further complicate recruiting decisions, it has been shown that various recruitment techniques result in differing success rates (Taylor & Schmidt, 1983). For example, one bank tracked their "quit rates" after one year and found that employee referrals were much better than newspaper ads and hiring agencies in securing individuals who would remain with the organization. In fact, had the company used their best sources, it would have saved over $180,000 (Gannon, 1971). Other studies have also supported the effectiveness of employee referrals and direct applications over newspaper ads and employment agencies (Decker & Cornelius, 1979). However, the exclusive use of employee referrals may create problems including the inbreeding of attitudes, potential favoritism and kick-backs to supervisors, and the absence of minority recruiting if the workforce is homogeneous and white (Mangum, 1982).

Being able to portray the organization in a favorable light is a reasonable goal when designing a recruitment strategy. Certainly, the organization must look reasonably attractive, or there won't be many applicants. Yet recent evidence suggests that a more realistic portrayal of the organization (what it is really like) may reduce potential disillusionment and disappointment of many new employees. People ususally have unrealistic expectations about organizations (Wanous, 1980), and problems arise when these expectations are not fulfilled. What can be done about this problem? It turns out that the interview situation provides a good opportunity to present a realistic view of the job. John Wanous (1980), who developed the idea of a **realistic job preview** (RJP) found that job attitudes and long-term survival rates in the organization were improved with this procedure. Research suggests that RJPs may reduce job turnover by approximately 10% (McEvoy & Cascio, 1985).

One can assume that both organizations and individuals make choices during the recruitment process. Just as organizations "prospect" for the right people, prospective employees seek out the right organizations. Consider the various approaches that organizations use to select employees from the pool of job applicants.

Employee Selection. The selection problem in organizations would be simple if all people were alike; organizations could choose people randomly. A moment's reflection tells one, however, that people are different in many respects — in appearance, background, education, training, experience, interests, and abilities. "The scope [of the employee selection process] is broad and includes decisions affecting hiring, promoting, transferring, demoting, terminating, and classifying". (Grant, 1980 p. 369). Obviously, it is not an easy task to fulfill all these requirements. One way to illustrate the difficulty involved when choosing among individuals would be to consider the following selection problems.

1. A baseball team is in last place and next year's draft is approaching. Two players will be up for grabs. One hits with power but strikes out fairly often. The other hits for a higher batting average, is a good fielder, but hits mostly singles.
2. An interviewer for a medical school has only one remaining opening for next year's class. One of the applicants is black, comes from a broken home, put herself through college, and has a 3.5 grade point average. The other is a male applicant, white, has a higher medical aptitude test score, and has a slightly higher grade point average.
3. A department store opens in a city where unemployment is high. After placing a help wanted ad in the newspaper, 2,000 people line up outside the personnel office to try to get one of the 60 available jobs.

Although the specific requirements for the slots in each of these three cases are different, there are many common elements. As Robert Guion (1981) notes, first, that bringing a new member into an organization — or retraining, retiring, or firing an old member — involves a choice. It may be a choice between qualified people with different characteristics (as with the baseball players). Second, the choice is based upon human judgment — the judgment of one person or a small group of people. The interviewer from the medical school may make the decision alone or may need to meet with the dean or the selection committee. Third, predicted task performance influences a choice. Organizations try to predict how well the job will be performed based on individual differences between people. The department store chain will likely use standardized tests to predict which applicant will have the highest likelihood of job success. Fourth, the data (on which to make the decision) are often haphazard. Often, judgments and predictions are made on information that is very subjective such as hunches, gut feelings, and "off the cuff" recommendations from others. Fifth, the choice has a public relations component. If the medical school selects the white applicant, it may be accused of being insensitive to the needs and problems of the black community. If it selects the black applicant, it may be accused of reverse discrimination.

Imagine that the person responsible for making selection decisions in an organization had the characteristics of Superman — able to tell if an applicant was honest, dependable, sociable, intelligent, experienced, and knowledgeable simply by looking at the person. Good selection decisions would be a snap; people who were willing and able to do a good job would be selected, and unqualified or unwilling applicants would be turned away. Although some job interviewers have professed to have such skills, for most mortals the selection decision is difficult. Why? Because the prediction of how a person will perform in the future is based on less than adequate information. Therefore organizations often use a combination of sources (e.g., interviews, application blanks, tests) in the hope that additional information will result in good selection decisions. I/O psychologists consider these sources as alternative predictors of job performance, and through them try to assess the person's motivation, experience and training, and aptitude.

Employment Interviewing.   Virtually every major organization in the United States uses the interview as a method to select people (Latham, Saari, Pursell, & Campion, 1980). Various people in the organization may have responsibility for meeting face to face with the applicant. In addition to the people in the organization whose full-time job is recruiting and interviewing, the line manager will almost always interview the prospective applicant. Besides helping to select the right job candidate, the interview is a useful information and communication device. That is, the interviewer can describe the job in detail, who the applicant will be working with, the working conditions, the salary arrangements, the promotional opportunities, and company policies. In turn, the applicant can ask questions about the job and the working conditions. As might be expected, the interviewer generally emphasizes the postive aspects of the job in order to sell the firm. However, as was mentioned previously, if the interviewer is not reasonably candid about the job, unrealistic expectations may develop that can lead to job dissatisfaction and disillusionment (Wanous, 1981).

What do interviewers actually do? They try to size up the candidate and determine whether the individual will fit within the organization and become a productive employee. Questions asked by the interviewer are intended to assess an applicant's level of motivation as well as ability and skill related to the job in question and reveal something about the individual's personality. All in all, the interviewer will try to predict the person's chances of success on the job and determine whether or not the individual's personal style meshes with the organization's style. Usually, the interviewer will make a global assessment and recommendation about the applicant.

As you can see from the preceding discussion, the interviewer has a difficult task. How good are interviewers in assessing people? Hundreds of studies have been conducted to answer this question (Arvey & Campion, 1982). Unfortunately, almost all the evidence suggests that the interview process is a notoriously poor procedure for predicting an individual's performance. It is extremely vulnerable to personal biases, whims, and gut feelings of the interviewer. Consider the following facts: (1) The judgments of two or more interviewers about the same applicant often differ markedly, yet each interviewer is likely to be confident in his or her prediction (Webster, 1964). (2) First impressions are critical—biases are usually formed early in the interview, and interviewers will probe for information that confirms their initial impressions (Peters & Terborg, 1975). (3) Nonverbal behaviors such as facial expressions and gestures have an impact on the final evaluations (Imada & Hakel, 1977). (4) Interviewers tend to develop their own stereotype of a good applicant and accept people who match this stereotype (Webster, 1982). (5) Women may be at a disadvantage in the interview, particularly for jobs that are dominated by males (Terborg & Ilgen, 1977). Even so-called facts may be unreliable. As you might expect, people also have a tendency to inflate their previous work experience and salary. No wonder that the interview is so often unreliable and invalid as a predictor of job success.

However, several recent projects by I/O psychologists demonstrate that a carefully constructed interview can be very valuable. Frank Landy helped a large metropolitan police force design a group interview procedure that proved to be successful in predicting the job performance of patrol officers. In another study, Gary Latham (and colleagues) developed a structured interview based on a thorough job analysis to predict the job performance of hourly employees and supervisors. Impressive interviewing results were also obtained by Richard Arvey. He helped a large specialty-foods firm develop a set of structured questions to determine who would most likely succeed as retail sales clerks/cashiers. In all cases, questions asked of the candidates were based on a thorough analysis of the job.

It is safe to say that the interview will be part of the employee selection process for a long time to come. So while it may be possible to assess interpersonal confidence, motivation, and intelligence by an interview, you should realize that the simplicity of the procedure is very deceiving. What can be done to improve the interview process so that it will meet your needs? Fortunately, the following suggestions should have a positive impact on the succcess of any interview.

The interviewer should plan for the interview and structure the interview so that the same critical questions are asked of all candidates. The questions should be job-relevant. Many of the typical biases and problems of the interview can be reduced if training is provided for the interviewers. Finally, it would be very useful to obtain follow-up data about the adequacy and validity of the recommendations made by specific interviewers. A recent study conducted in a large energy corporation confirms that some interviewers are much better than others in selecting individuals who will become successful employees (Dougherty, Ebort, & Callender, 1986). These and many other worthwhile suggestions can be found in a handbook developed by the American Association of Personnel Administrators, 1979. Table 4.2, developed by researcher Milt Hakel, also serves as a useful guide. The time and energy put forth in developing a quality interview procedure will pay off. Interviewing is both an art and a science; it deserves careful consideration in the selection process.

Application Blanks and Biographical Data.   As with the interview, use of application blanks and résumés (AB&R) is almost universal. One can quickly learn about a person's education, experience, previous employment, and training through the AB&R. Other relevant personal information may also be obtained. Often the interviewing process begins with the interviewer reviewing both the application blank and résumé. The logic behind the use of the AB&R is very straightforward—individuals who have had particular job experiences in the past will have the ability to perform them in the future (Owens, 1976). People who have shown a pattern of lifelong successful endeavors and prior achievement are considered good risks by organizations.

One major purpose of the application blank is determining whether the applicant meets minimum training and education requirements. A major issue now being debated in the courts and professional organizations concerns the usefulness and possible discriminatory impact of minimal educational requirements for some jobs. It seems reasonable to require a certain educational achievement level for jobs such as architect, as presumably an architect should have a degree in the discipline. Yet, what about the often-seen requirements for a high school diploma? Is it really necessary? If the requirement for a high-school diploma has a negative impact on minority groups and if challenged in the courts, the organization must prove that such a requirement is a valid indicator of future job performance. This is no easy task!

As a last comment regarding biographical information, some companies have developed standardized questionnaires known as weighted application blanks (WAB) and biographical information blanks (BIB). Both the WAB and BIB ask for information that is found in the usual application blank (e.g., previous work

TABLE 4.2

Guide for Use in Evaluating Selection Interviewer Applicants

Opening

Give a warm, friendly greeting—smile.

Names are important—yours and the applicant's. Pronounce it correctly and use first and last names consistently. Tell the applicant what to call you and then ask the applicant for his or her preferred form of address.

Talk briefly about yourself (your position in the company and then your personal background, hobbies, interests, etc.) to put the applicant at ease so that she or he might reciprocate with personal information.

Ask the applicant about hobbies, activities, or some other topic that you believe will be of interest to "break the ice."

Structuring the Interview

State the purpose of interview: "The purpose of this interview is to discuss your qualifications and to see whether they match the skills needed to work as a selection interviewer. First, let's talk about your work experience and next your education and training. Then I will give you a preview of what the interviewer's job is really like. Finally, there will be a chance to ask about anything you want. How's that?

Since you plan to take notes, mention this to the applicant: "By the way, I will be taking some notes during the interview so that I don't miss any pertinent information that may come from our discussion. Okay?"

Work Experience: Most Relevant Job

Use this comprehensive opening question: "Let's talk about your work experience. How about starting with the job that you feel gave you the best preparation for working as a selection interviewer. Tell me all about the job: how you got it, why you chose it, your actual job duties, what you learned on the job, the hours and your attendance record, the pay, why you left (or are leaving), and things like that."

Probe and follow up to cover each of these items thoroughly: how the applicant got the job, reasons for choosing it, job duties, etc.

Summarize the major facts and findings from the applicant's most relevant job. For example: "Let me summarize what we have covered to make sure that I've got it right. You worked as a _____ where most of your time was spent doing _____ and _____, and you used these skills, _____ and _____. You chose the job because of _____ and your reasons for leaving it are _____ and _____. Anything else to add?"

Other Work Experience

If time is available, discuss other jobs the applicant has held that might be pertinent. Get a brief overview of each job the applicant has held. Emphasize jobs held in the last five years or less, since older experience is less likely to be relevant for your decision.

Ask the work experience questions you specifically prepared for this applicant when you planned the interview.

Summarize your major findings about all jobs. When the summary is satisfactory to the applicant, go on to discuss education and training.

Education and Training

Use this question to start the discussion: "Now let's talk about your education and training—schools, courses, likes and dislikes, things like that. Let's start with this: What did you learn in school that might be helpful for you in working as a selection interviewer?

Probe to get specific answers to these questions: "What training have you had in interviewing techniques? What courses have you had in psychology or personnel management?" and so on.

TABLE 4.2   cont.

Ask the education and training questions you specifically prepared for this applicant when you planned the interview.

Summarize the applicant's education and training, just as you summarized work experience. When the applicant is satisfied with your summary, go on to discuss the Job Preview List.

Job Preview List

Introduce the Job Preview List: "As a selection interviewer, you have many responsibilities and duties. Here is a list of some major factors."

Give the applicant the Job Preview List. Discuss it point by point. Be sure that you describe the job realistically. Don't "paint a rosy picture."

Selection Interviewer Job Preview List

1. Conduct screening and final evaluation interviews with all applicants for nonexempt factory and clerical positions.
2. Administer and score screening tests and weighted application blanks.
3. Maintain records and compile reports on all applicants for Affirmative Action purposes.
   .
   .
   .
10. Recommended two candidates for each position for interviews by the hiring manager.

Applicant's Questions

Turn the interview over to the applicant: "As I mentioned at the start, you would have a chance to ask anything you would like. We've just had a short preview of what the job would be like, but here is a chance to ask anything you want about the company, training, and so on."

Respond fully and frankly to all of the applicant's questions, and note any further information that the applicant volunteers that will aid you in making your evaluation.

Closing the Interview

Conclude with a warm, friendly close—smile.
Outline the next steps in the decision process.
Tell the applicant when to expect a decision.
Thank the applicant.

After the Interview

Take time to write summary notes immediately. Describe the applicant's behavior and the impressions he or she created. Cite facts and specific incidents from the interview or from the person's work or educational history.

Wait a day and then complete the Evaluation Form.

From "Employment Interviewing" by Milton D. Hakel. In K. M. Rowland & G. R. Ferris (Eds.), Personnel Management *(pp. 149·151). Boston: Allyn and Bacon, 1982.*

history and education). In addition BIBs include questions that tap into a person's experiences and background, including interests, opinions, attitudes, hobbies, and early life experiences. In contrast to the usual use of an application blank, WABs and BIBS are "objectively scored." The goal for an I/O psychologist is to determine if an item such as years of education or years of work experience relates to sucess on the job. For example, in one company, petroleum engineers who scored high on BIB items that reflected favorable self-impressions, professional orientation, drive, and general adjustment have a high likelihood of success within their organization. Although BIBs have proven to be useful in helping to select job applicants (Reilly & Chao, 1982), they have serious drawbacks in that some questions may have a possible discriminatory impact on minority groups.

Recommendations and Reference Checks. Managers often obtain reference checks before hiring individuals from other organizations. These reference checks may be obtained by phone, by letter, or by face-to-face conversation. Similar to the logic behind the application blank and résumé, the information obtained from a reference check or letter of recommendation assumes that past behavior is the best predictor of future behavior. Here, the information is based upon the opinion of others rather than on the applicant's statement of what he or she did in the past as on the application blanks. Wayne Cascio suggests that recommendations and reference checks can be used to confirm and verify past employment and educational history, evaluate interpersonal competence, evaluate the preformance record, and, finally, see if the person would hypothetically be rehired by previous employers (1987). A significant question concerns whether reference checks are worth the time and money. They may be, if the person providing the information is open, candid, and competent to make the evaluation. On the other hand, many consider written letters of recommendation to be almost worthless since these letters are generally favorable. Also, it is difficult to compare job candidates unless the letters follow the same format. Nevertheless, as an initial screening device, letters of recommendation may help to separate the average from the truly exceptional.

Tests.

> A personnel manager, learning that one of his best workers had scored very low on a test that eventually would be used in selecting future employees, nearly discharged the worker; ... "The tests really opened our eyes about her. Why she's worked here for several years, does good work, gets along well with others. That test shows how she had us fooled!" (Lyman, 1963, p. 2).

Since World War I, industrial psychologists have had a large impact on the development and use of tests for the purpose of employee selection. Although over 60% of large organizations (employing over 25,000 individuals) use tests to help screen potential employees, the use of tests in smaller organizations is relatively limited, especially compared to the use of application blanks and interviews (Tenopyr, 1980). Most of you are no doubt aware of the considerable controversy generated by the use of IQ tests in schools. The use of tests in employment situations is similarly a hotly debated issue. In fact, because of legal challenges and philosophical issues, the use of standardized tests for the selection and placement of individuals at work has decreased in the recent past (Doverspike, Barrett, & Alexander, 1985).

Perhaps it would be worthwhile to consider the controversy over testing. Most people would not consider it unreasonabe to take a test in order to be licensed as a doctor or a lawyer. Almost everybody is willing to take an exam in order to get a driver's license or a typing test in order to get a job as a typist. However, there is considerable ill will generated among job applicants when asked to take personality, interest, or aptitude tests that don't seem on the face of it to be related to the job. Whatever the reasons, today there seems to be a "war on testing" (Lerner, 1979, 1980). Numerous critics point out that tests unfairly discriminate against minority groups, that they rarely predict what they are supposed to, and that it is somehow un-American to let large testing agencies, (e.g., Educational Testing Service) decide the fate of so many people (*American Psychologist,* October, 1981). On the other side of the debate, psychologists often point out that if care is exercised in the construction and use of tests, they increase the fairness and efficency of selection. As Mary Tenopyr, past president of the Industrial/Organizational division of the American Psychological Association, points out, tests have been shown to be among the most valid and fair measures of selecting people for jobs. Numerous studies confirm her beliefs regarding the usefulness of carefully constructed tests.

The logic behind the use of tests for selecting employees is very simple. Since people differ in many ways and since these differences may be related to job performance, it is valuable to develop this information, select people, and assign them to jobs according to their individual differences. This is really nothing new; Plato long ago suggested that testing is a reasonable process since "no two persons are born exactly alike but each differs from each in natural endowments, one being suited for one occupation and another for another. . . . It follows that all things will be produced in superior quantity and quality, and with greater ease when each man works at a single occupation in accordance with his natural gifts."

A test can be defined as any systematic procedure used for obtaining information about an individual's behavior, characteristics, or traits. One way to distinguish between the different types of tests is to classify them according to content; do they measure mental ability, mechanical and spatial ability, perceptual and motor ability, personality and interests, or actual samples of work performed in a specific job? Tests that measure mental abilities such as verbal fluency, memory, or numerical ability have been shown to predict job performance in many settings (Ghiselli, 1965). This is particularly true when the job requires complex decision making or reasoning. One recent conclusion concerning these types of tests is that they may be valid predictors of job performance for most jobs (Schmidt, Hunter & Outerbridge, 1981). However, the use of cognitive ability tests has been legally challenged when test score differences between majority and minority candidates result in few minority applicants being hired. It is unjustifiable and illegal to use a test of mental ability to select individuals if test scores reveal minority-majority differences and the tests are not predictive of job performance. It must be remembered that intelligence is only one determinant of job performance and that other factors such as motivation, good coworkers, supervisors, and equipment are also critically important.

For many blue-collar jobs, the use of mechanical ability and perceptual/motor ability tests has proven fruitful. Mechanical ability tests contain many questions that assess the knowledge of tools and their uses as well as measure the ability to manipulate spatial relationships. Perceptual/motor tests tap into a wide variety of motor skills including finger dexterity, manual dexterity, and reaction time.

Most managers are convinced that an individual's personality and interests will have a large influence on his or her job performance, hence the logic in developing tests to measure such human characteristics. Perhaps people who show certain personality and interest patterns will be more motivated to perform particular jobs, and/or be more successful because of a particular personality style. For instance, outgoing, lively, enthusiastic, sociable, and dominant people are considered most likely to succeed in sales jobs. Personality tests and interest inventories may involve structured (i.e., objective type) questions, whereby individuals respond to the accuracy or descriptiveness of certain attributes. A response to a statement such as "I am very serious about my life" illustrates this point. Other personality tests use unstructured stimulus material such as the projective tests of Rorschach (the inkblot test) to measure personality traits. Interest inventories such as the Strong-Campbell Interest Inventory (SCII) compare the subject's interests to those of people employed in various occupations. These interest inventories have a better history in predicting job choice than job success.

In general, the use of personality and interest tests have had a dismal history in employment selection. Almost all research studies have found that personality measures particularly have been unrelated or very weakly related to job performance. Yet carefully constructed personality tests that measure job-related traits can be appropriate in specific situations. Standard Oil of New Jersey (SONJ) was successful in developing a personality test that through the years has proved worthwhile in predicting management success. Similarly, certain scales of the California Psychological Inventory (e.g., Tolerance and Achievement via Independence) were found to be useful in predicting leadership and suitability of police officers. Although there still exists considerable controversy about the usefulness of personality tests, one needs to consider the ill will generated when job applicants are required to take such tests, and organizations should carefully consider whether or not the use of personality tests is advisable.

In contrast to personality tests, work-sample tests directly measure important work related skills and behaviors. These tests require people to perform job operations in a controlled, but realistic, situation. In a sense, they can be thought of as minisamples of a person's skill in performing a particular job. For instance, what better way to select mechanics than to set up a work station with actual equipment, have people perform all the critical job operations, and then score their performance? Work samples should be thought of as achievement tests that measure what a person knows as a result of specific training and experiences.

Written work-sample tests (often called job knowedge tests) are quite similar in concept to the performance work sample just described. Here, however, paper-and-pencil tests can be used to measure the job applicant's factual

The value and appropriateness of personality tests in screening job applicants is controversial, but no fault has been found in sampling work skills. The service manager can best assess the ability of this prospective employee by observing performance at an actual work station.

knowledge about a particular skill, for example, repair of diesel engines or refrigeration equipment. The theory underlying work samples and job knowledge tests is that the best predictor of future performance is often a measure of a person's knowledge or skill at performing elements of the job in question. Because a good work sample should reflect a point to point correspondence between the work-sample element and the job performance element (Asher & Sciarrino, 1974), constructing, administering, and scoring these tests is not an easy task.

Assessment of Selection Techniques.　Recall that the underlying rationale in the selection process is that since people differ in their ability, motivation, and interpersonal competence (among many other things), information about these characteristics can predict who among the applicants is likely to be the most effective and least likely to quit or be absent. A valid selection procedure can result in the saving of enormous sums of money. One insurance company reported that it costs $31,600 to replace one salesperson (Flamholtz, 1974) and as much as $185,000 for a sales manager (Hinrichs, 1980). Even more startling is the fact that the U.S. Navy has estimated that it costs $1.5 million to train a competent fighter pilot (Wanous, 1980). No wonder that a faulty selection procedure can be catastrophic for an organization.

It is not enough to assume that because a test looks as if it should measure the ability in question and as if it should be predictive of future job success, it really does. First one needs to determine if a test (or any other predictor) is reliable—will it get the same measurements consistently over time? If a test measures something reliably, then consider the issue of validity—does the test (or any other predictor) measure what it is supposed to measure? If we think of weighing ourselves on the bathroom scale as a "test" of weight, do we get consistent measurements (the issue of reliability) and do the numbers on the scale truly reflect the number of pounds a person weighs (the issue of validity)?

Establishing the validity of a measure is a difficult, yet vital, process. It is vital for two reasons. First, it is good business practice to ensure that the selection procedures used are identifying and selecting applicants who will be the most competent to do their jobs. By examining Figure 4.3, you will see a chart indicating the likelihood that an individual will succeed on a job (chances out of 100) if a particular score on the test is achieved. One obvious conclusion from this chart is that the higher the score on the ability test, the higher the likelihood of success. Perhaps a more subtle conclusion from the chart concerns the fact that many people who have moderate or low test scores would also succeed.

Industrial psychologists are currently developing procedures, called **utility analyses,** designed to estimate the economic and productivity gains associated with the use of valid selection procedures (Cascio, 1987b). An exciting new development in the testing area concerns the demonstration, through research, that ability tests that are valid predictors of job success in one situation may gener-

FIGURE 4.3 Example of an expectancy chart. The chart shows the relation between scores made on the Purdue Mechanical Adaptability Test and rated success of maintenance employees in an artificial ice plant. From *Industrial Psychology*, 7th edition, by E. J. McCormick and D. R. Ilgen, 1980. Englewood Cliffs, NJ: Prentice-Hall, p. 137.

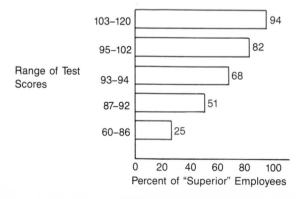

alize across different employment situations (Hunter & Hunter, 1984). Conventional wisdom of I/O psychologists for many years suggested that tests must be validated for each job in each new situation (or company and geographic location). Thus, for example, tests that were developed and validated to select police officers in one geographical location could not be assumed to be valid in another geographical location. Consider the savings in time and effort if the same test for selecting police officers in New York could be used in Chicago or Honolulu without the necessity of separate development and validation procedures.

A second reason for being concerned about a test's validity relates to the issue of employee discrimination. The question is, is it fair to use a selection procedure (e.g., test) that has the impact of excluding a large percentage of minority applicants for jobs? Most people would assume that it is not fair to do this, particularly if the test is worthless in selecting good people. However, what if the test is good at selecting the most qualified, and yet it still excludes a large proportion of minority applicants or women? The laws regarding testing and employee discrimination are clear in this respect. If a test, or any other selection procedure, has a negative impact on "protected" minority groups (or women), it must be job-related or "of business necessity" to be considered nondiscriminatory. That is, the procedure must predict job performance—those who score highest in the test must also be the best employees, and, conversely, those who fail the test should also be unable to perform the job. We will return to this issue at the end of the chapter since I/O psychologists have been at the forefront of the testing and employee discrimination issue.

Managerial Selection.   The selection of new managers is somewhat different from other types of employee selection. The following questions reflect the increased complexity and difficulty in selecting higher-level personnel: Can one adequately define the total job responsibilities of the managerial position? Is it possible to determine and measure management success? What predictors should give a good indication of the likelihood of future managerial success?

Conducting a job analysis for a management position is often more difficult than conducting one for a nonmanagement position, simply because managing is a more complex job activity. Consider that a manager may have supervisory, financial, sales, customer relations, and record-keeping responsibilities. The issue of determining and measuring managerial success is even more difficult than the first problem of defining the management position. Since the effective manager optimizes human, material, and financial resources, the organization is left with the problem of measuring each of these. The measurement issue is not trivial, since it is essential to measure and define success in order to look for those specific things that will predict managerial effectiveness.

The final issue to be considered is determining predictors that can be used to forecast management success. The variety of measures now being used for managerial selection is extensive. Supervisor recommendations, based on past performance, are often used in promoting people and selecting managers. However, a superior performance in a technical job does not necessarily mean that a person is suited for a management-level position. The use of seniority within unionized companies is another way to select managers and is often used to promote hourly workers to the entry level of management.

Recently, there has been a trend to assess potential managers by requiring job candidates to perform actual behaviors required on the job. This can be accomplished at an assessment center. Candidates meet for several days and take part in exercises designed to reveal managerial behaviors essential for job success. The program usually includes business games, leaderless group discussions, and decision-making exercises, used by multiple evaluators to rate the candidates' work motivation, interpersonal skills, intellectual ability, and administrative skills. Assessment centers are becoming big business—most large corporations favor them. Although the centers have their critics, they have consistently been shown to be a useful tool in predicting the future success of potential managers (Klimosky & Brickner, 1987).

Before considering the subarea of organizational psychology, let's return to the example of staffing the automobile dealership. By now you have been introduced to the importance of conducting a job analysis. In order to hire the right people, it is important to understand the variety of tasks and the performance standards that will be required of each employee. When one assesses each

Supervisors like this airline reservations manager are responsible for developing skills and attitudes that will enhance the organization's performance and the employee's feeling of accomplishment and self-worth. Managers at every level and in every occupational context face the same challenge: how to establish good working relationships with those they supervise. The insights provided by industrial/organizational psychologists can help in the process.

job candidate, one must make sure that the selection procedure reveals important, job-related characteristics of the applicant's ability, experience, training, and motivation. That is, in the interview, one asks job-related questions. One looks for job-relevant experience and education given on the application blank. One develops work sample tasks or other tests to ensure that the applicant can do the work or has the ability to learn the job. Obviously, hiring a good work force is just the first element in effective management. Employees need to be trained, their performance assessed, and rewards given for effective performance. Training, performance appraisal, and compensation are as important to organizational success as is effective employee selection.

Organizational Psychology

Industrial/organizational psychologists have had a continuing interest in the "people variables" that contribute to organizational success. In their popular book *In Search of Excellence,* Peters and Waterman (1982) found one common link among successful organizations—a committed and motivated workforce. More likely than not, employees exerted 110% effort, liked their work, got along well with coworkers, and strove to accomplish challenging goals. Leaders developed policies that encouraged, rather than discouraged, high motivation and productivity. These "people variables" (worker motivation, job satisfaction, groups, organizational climate, and leadership) have been the focus of organizational researchers for years. You will now look at an important area of organizational research—group behavior and leadership processes. Realize again that these topics only sample the area of organizational psychology and are intended to give you a feeling for the type of research and application that is conducted in this area.

Nature and Function of Groups. People in organizations spend a large percentage of their time interacting with others, and this interaction often takes place in group situations. Much of the enjoyment of a job stems from the friendships formed while working with others. Organizational researchers have studied group processes in prescribed work groups such as departments, project teams, and quality circles as well as in emergent groups such as informal cliques and friendships (cf. Aldefer, 1987; Friedlander, 1987; Pearce & David, 1983). It is important to know how groups function since organizations are increasingly turning toward groups to help get things done. Quality circles, semiautonomous work groups, project teams, and management task forces are popular group structures used by organizations (Hackman, 1987).

Groups have tremendous influence on the attitudes and behaviors of group members. Consider the informal cliques that exist in high school and college; students in the clique dress and talk alike, and often exhibit similar levels of academic performance. Of course, groups in work organizations have a similar impact on group members. If you visit a large organization, you might notice that male executives wear suits, mid-level managers wear ties and jackets, and lower-level managers wear ties (no jackets). Similar informal differentiation might be found among female managers.

On a less superficial level, work groups also have an impact on the behaviors, attitudes, and performance of members. For instance, a cohesive work group might develop informal norms that specify how hard individuals should work—thus holding down the level of productivity of individual members. Such a norm could be a major problem in implementing a financial incentive plan to improve performance. In fact, a group may have as much impact on a person's job behavior and performance as either the policies of the company or the person's natural ability or motivation. Indeed, membership in certain groups may be highly coveted. Group membership exposes one to the rewards that other group members can offer, such as friendship, security, and fun as well, as to the sanctions (verbal threats, physical punishment, ostracism) that may occur for noncompliance with group standards.

Social psychologists for a long time have been interested in group processes, particularly their origin, impact, and effect on individuals. Industrial/organizational psychologists have been similarly interested in several questions: What types of groups exist? Why do they form? How is an individual's behavior different when working alone as contrasted to working in a group? From a scientific perspective, we would like to know what tasks, organizations, and people variables influence group processes. From a practical standpoint, we need to consider when groups are more effective than individuals, when they are less effective, and what techniques are available to improve group performance.

First consider what a group is and what it is not. A group is a small number of people who interact with one another such that the behavior of each person influences the others (Shaw, 1976). Often the group members interact over a fairly long time period, have common interests, and perceive themselves to be mutually dependent to attain desired goals. Thus strangers traveling on a bus should not be considered a group, but if they become stranded in a snowstorm, a group as defined by Shaw will develop. In this situation the goal is survival; people will take on different responsibilities, leaders will emerge, and behavior will be regulated by group norms.

Organizational researchers distinguish between formal and informal groups. *Formal* denotes a task-oriented subgroup that has been recognized as part of an organization's structure. For instance, committees, task forces, and departments are formal groups established by the organization to accomplish specific objectives. The organization will specify the composition of the group, specific duties and responsibilities for each individual, authority structure, and communication channels. Each group will appear as a complete segment on the company's organizational chart.

In contrast, *informal* groups emerge and develop apart from the formal plan. Some are based on individual friendships. People with common interests, backgrounds, and attitudes are likely to form informal groups. They may arrive at work together and take breaks together, thus satisfying social needs (including those for self-esteem and affiliation). Another type of informal group, often referred to as an instrumental group, will emerge to help accomplish and fulfill job tasks and goals.

Frequent job-related interaction among individuals will result in an elaborate network that does not appear on the organizational chart, yet supplements the formal work groups. For instance, people soon learn to rely on specific individuals to help them in their jobs, with the result that formal communication channels in an organization are often bypassed by this grapevine or network. Or, projects may get completed because an informal task group of committed people may work outside the formal group responsible for the project. These informal groups — friendship and instrumental — often regulate the social and task behaviors of group members. This takes place because of unwritten rules and guidelines about ideal or accepted behaviors of group members. These standards of conduct are called **work norms.** To understand why groups have such a large impact on members' behaviors, let's look at the concept of norms in greater detail.

Work Norms. If you visited an organization and watched a work group for several weeks, you would notice certain regularities and consistent patterns of behaviors. A time to begin work (as opposed to simply being at work), when to quit work, how hard to work, how to respond to supervisor's requests, and how to dress are constants that group members adhere to and rarely violate. Work norms not only specify the proper conduct of the work group; they also enable each member to predict the behavior of others, thus producing a sense of security.

As you might expect, the norm that often counts the most in group behavior concerns job performance — how much effort, intensity, and output are expected from each member. Individuals who go all out to make performance records are often told by other group members that "this isn't the way it is done around here" and they had better "get with the program" (i.e., slow down). Conversely, individuals who loaf will often be told by other members that they aren't working up to the levels expected by the group. In both cases, the group clearly knows what is expected of each person and will enforce compliance with the norm. Terry Mitchell (1982) describes the work norms he encountered as a college student while employed in the Department of Motor Vehicles. His job was to paint lines on the streets. Although work started at 8:00 A.M., it was rare for the trucks to leave the yard before 9:00 A.M., and work stopped at 3:00 P.M. in order for workers to report back and clean up before the 4:00 P.M. quitting time. He estimated that he worked an average of four hours a day. Terry's graph of the range of acceptable behaviors that represented a norm are shown in Figure 4.4. Notice that the time spent on the street created more intense feelings than the appropriate time to leave the yard.

Groups have a number of ways to encourage compliance. On the positive side, group members can praise people and suggest that what they are doing is correct. They can also reward people by giving out the plums of the job to those who comply. In contrast, negative sanctions may be effectively imposed on individuals who violate the norm. Usually the process of enforcing the norm begins with increased communication, verbal and nonverbal, as to both correct and deviant behaviors. If behavior is not corrected, verbal threats, harassment, and perhaps even physical abuse may follow.

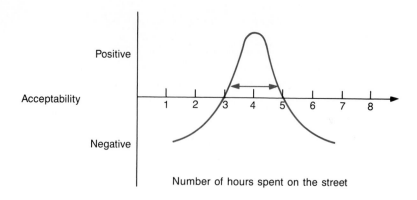

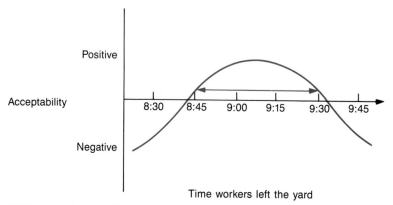

FIGURE 4.4 Acceptability of norms to group members. Curves in the figure show how acceptable various behaviors are to group members. From *People in Organizations: Understanding Their Behavior* by T. R. Mitchell, 1978, New York: McGraw-Hill, p. 239.

In connection with the concept of norms, it might be worthwhile to discuss the Hawthorne studies (Roethlisberger & Dixon, 1939) which led to the human relations philosophy of management. These studies provide good examples of norms that operate to reduce job output and the pay of workers. In one of the studies called the Bank Wiring Room Study, a member of the research team observed 14 men assemble electrical switches. The work group consisted of 9 people who wired the terminals, 3 solderers, and 2 inspectors. Extensive records were kept of the activities and job performance of the work group. It was very apparent that the work group itself decided on the number of units to be produced in one day. Although the company set a standard (called a bogey) that was 914 wiring connections per hour, or 7,312 terminals per day, the workers openly discussed their own productivity norms of 6,600 terminals per day, quite a bit below the company-set quota. From interviews with the worker, it was also apparent that the work performance could be considerably higher; furthermore, greater output would of course mean higher wages.

The reason for restriction of output was not hard to understand, however. The workers were concerned that if the group constantly exceeded the standard, the company would change it—perhaps not an unreasonable explanation.

> INTERVIEWER: You say there is no incentive to turn out more work. If all of you did more work, wouldn't you make more money?
> WIREMAN: No, we wouldn't. They told us that down there one time. You know, the supervisors came around and told us that very thing, that if we turned out more work we could make more money, but we can't see it that way. Probably what would happen is that our bogey would be raised, and then we would just be turning out more work for the same money. I can't see that. (Roethlisberger & Dixon, 1939, p. 418)

The groups had a not-so-subtle means to enforce these production norms. Group disapproval ranged from verbal abuse, calling the high achiever "slave," "runt," or "cyclone," to physical punishment in the form of a (hostile) game in which the individual would be smacked in the arm (called binging). Another interesting part of this study concerns the two cliques that formed within the group of 14 people. Both had a social norm that regulated their own group— one group fooled around more, whereas the other group was more serious and considered themselves superior. Also, four workers who were not part of either group often bore the brunt of the petty antagonism and abuse from both cliques.

From the examples cited, you might at this time be overly pessimistic and wrongly conclude that group norms always restrict output. Often, highly cohesive groups adopt a norm of excellence—consider the teams who win the Super Bowl or the World Series. Players are fond of talking about putting out 110% effort all the time. Norms of high production are found in many such groups. In an interesting study, Dale Johnson (1974) worked as part of a maintenance crew cleaning food-processing equipment. Actually, he was also a researcher, using a technique called participant observation. The norms that developed on the job encouraged careful and speedy work. Negative sanctions were applied by the group when workers were slow or sloppy. As an interesting development, the company changed its policy regarding an employee's "right" to relax at the end of the day, if they completed their assigned work. Foremen were required to assign extra tasks to those who finished early. Guess what? Surprise! Surprise! A new production norm developed whereby workers restricted their output and paced themselves so that their regular tasks would fill up the normal eight-hour day.

Work Roles.   A **work role** reflects the pattern of activities that identifies a person's job—what they do at work as well as how they should do it. Thus roles specify the appropriate behaviors, attitudes, and beliefs expected of individuals who occupy particular positions in the organization. The role of a department chairperson in a university, for example, consists of both a formal and informal job description that specifies the behaviors expected of a person holding that position. Roles, however, are often not clear-cut. Who specifies the appropriate behaviors, the individual occupying the position, or other people who frequently

Work roles: they are the specifiers of behaviors on the job. The relationships among workers are largely determined by each one's concept of his "place" in the organization. Problems arise when roles are cloudily defined or hazily understood or when conflicting elements, such as a supervisor's need to support and to criticize an employee, come into play.

interact with the individual? The concept of a role set helps us answer this question. A role set is the group of people (plus written information like job descriptions and policy manuals) that communicate role expectations to an individual. For example, the department chairperson's role set would consist of other faculty members, deans, students, and secretaries, as well as written material, that help define the job.

One problem associated with work roles is that the actual behaviors expected for each role may be ambiguous. For example, what behaviors are expected of new teachers in their first university positions? Role ambiguity can result when we are not sure of what we are supposed to do or how to do it. Engineers and other professionals often experience role ambiguity after being promoted to management. The research literature indicates that those who experience role ambiguity have more stress and tension and lower job satisfaction (Pearce, 1981). Furthermore, job performance may suffer, moral problems may appear, and individuals are more likely to leave the organization when faced with high levels of role ambiguity. Let's face it, most people want to know what they are supposed to do in a job and how they should go about doing it. Sometimes, however, knowing exactly what one is expected to do creates another and equally serious problem — role conflict.

A first-level supervisor often experiences role conflict. Here the person is torn between the expectations of management (act like management — support company policy, be efficient, and reduce costs) and the expectations of those he or she supervises (act for the workers — go to bat for them when management/labor conflicts arise). While these lead people are supposed to identify with management, their education and training make them feel closer to those they supervise (Sasser & Leonard, 1980). Clearly, the first-line supervisor has an extremely difficult role to fill.

As a second example of role conflict, many women now play the role of "worker" as well as "wife" and "mother". The percentage of women in the work force has grown steadily during the last three decades, and the trend is expected to continue (Bureau of Labor Statistics, 1980). About 37% of corporate management and administrative jobs are held by women, up from 24% a decade ago. More than one third of the 70,000 MBAs graduating each year are women, compared with 25% twenty years ago ("Corporate Women," 1987). Career responsibilities, including heavy workloads during the day (and perhaps in the evening) as well as travel, conflict with the duties and responsibilities traditionally associated with raising children. Unfortunately, although husbands will acknowledge the importance of extra income, many expect their working wives to maintain all family responsibilities.

As with role ambiguity, high levels of role conflict will present problems in the organization. People with excessive amounts of role conflict will be less satisfied and show higher levels of anxiety and tension than will people with low levels of role conflict. It is generally impossible to reduce all role conflict, but organizations should be aware that excessive levels will have a negative impact on the effectiveness of the worker and, consequently, on the organization.

Status.   Like roles and norms, status will help determine what is expected of individuals in job or social situations. **Group status** here refers to the rank or worth of a group member as determined by other group members. Activities, behaviors, and characteristics valued by the group confer high status; conversely, an absence of valued behaviors means lower status. Factors influencing status, include personality (warm and friendly), birth factors (race, national origin, family name), employment type, (physician, architect, business executive), and success within a specific job (full professor, president of a company). Certain symbols may reinforce a person's status. An executive's standing may be enhanced by a walnut desk and a plush carpet. The student's ski lift tickets or brand-name jeans, the physician's white coat, and the shoulder patches of military personnel all may serve to identify status.

In general, a group will be most effective when its members agree on the relative status of each person (status consensus) (Collins & Goetzkown, 1964). Even so, a group that is unanimous with regard to each individual's rank may have problems if the individual members always defer to people with higher status. If communication is stifled because of these status differences, groups that must solve complex problems will be at a disadvantage.

Group Processes—The Individual as a Group Member. Managers often have strong feelings as to whether decisions made by a group are superior to those made by a manager working alone. Those who believe in synergy (working together to achieve an effect greater than the combined inputs of individuals alone) fall on one side of the argument. The other side is represented by those who suggest that a camel is the result of a committee trying to design a horse.

People in groups act differently than individuals working alone (Mitchell, 1982). A phenomenon called the **social facilitation effect,** for example, the mere presence of another person, can alter people's perceptions, heighten their motivation, and enhance their performance. However, there is also a problem called **social loafing** that can reduce motivation (Latane, Williams & Harkins, 1979). In situations where an individual's level of effort cannot be measured, for example, in a tug-of-war, people work with less intensity than when working alone. Another characteristic of group processes concerns a well-known problem of one or two people dominating the group. This is fine if the leaders are the brightest and most creative people in the group, but it is a problem if it is simply the loudest or most domineering who take over. Of course, high-status individuals inevitably play a larger part in the decisions of the group.

In highly cohesive groups characterized by strong interpersonal attraction, a phenomenon called **groupthink** can produce disastrous results. Irving Janis describes groupthink as a mode of thinking that degrades decision making in highly cohesive groups such as President Kennedy's crisis center for the Bay of Pigs invasion of Cuba in 1961. Critical evaluation of alternative solutions was stifled by the self-imposed need for cohesion, appearance of conformity, and, in general, playing ball with the leader. In a similar vein, groupthink logic seemed to play a part in the disastrous decision to launch the space shuttle *Challenger* that exploded on takeoff. Many engineers and other technical experts recommended against the launch; their pleas were ignored by groups of managers higher up in the organization. Table 4.3 summarizes the points Janis (1972) suggests as symptoms of groupthink.

Strategies to Enhance the Effectiveness of Group Decision Making. There exists a great deal of research literature on the processes by which groups make decisions and on techniques that will enhance decision-making effectiveness. Perhaps one of the best summaries of the advantages and disadvantages of group decision making is suggested by Maier and shown in Table 4.4. As you can see, pluses and minuses can be expected when groups make decisions. For example, groups generate a greater number of alternative approaches to a problem—a plus—but often compromise with less than effective solutions—a minus.

Two organizational scientists, Richard Hackman and Jay Morris, have developed a model of group processes that not only illuminates the nature of group behavior, but also provides prescriptions as to how to improve group effectiveness. These researchers suggest that overall effectiveness of an organizational work group depends on the level of *effort* the group members expend to carry

TABLE 4.3

Characteristics of Groups Suffering from Groupthink

1. An illusion of invulnerability, shared by most or all the members which creates excessive optimism and encourages taking extreme risks.
2. Collective efforts to rationalize in order to discount warnings which might lead the members to reconsider their assumptions before they recommit themselves to their past policy decisions.
3. An unquestioned belief in the group's inherent morality, inclining the members to ignore the ethical or moral consequences of their decisions.
4. Direct pressure on any member who expresses strong arguments against any of the group's stereotypes, illusions, or commitments, making clear that this type of dissent is contrary to what is expected of all loyal members.
5. Self-censorship of deviations from the apparent group consensus, reflecting each member's inclination to minimize to himself the importance of his doubts and counterarguments.
6. A shared illusion of unanimity concerning judgments conforming to the majority view (partly resulting from self-censorship of deviations, augmented by the false assumption that silence means consent).
7. The emergence of self-appointed mindguards—members who protect the group from adverse information that might shatter their shared complacency about the effectiveness and morality of their decisions.

From Victims of Groupthink *(pp. 197–198) by I. Janis, 1972, Boston: Houghton Mifflin.*

out the tasks, the amount of *knowledge and skill* the members bring to bear on the task, and the appropriateness of the *performance strategies* used in decision making. By examining one part of Hackman's model in Figure 4.5, focus on those conditions that will foster hard work on a group task (Hackman, 1987). Notice that "social loafing," a problem discussed earlier, needs to be minimized by members' shared commitment to the team. Also, group effectiveness will be enhanced if the organizational reward system provides challenging objectives and reinforces their achievement.

In sum, keys to successful group problem-solving include motivated members, appropriate use of available skills and knowledge, and effective problem-solving strategies. Often, the group leader or manager implements the decision

TABLE 4.4

Assets and Liabilities in Group Problem Solving

Group Assets	Group Liabilities
Greater sum total of knowledge and information.	Social pressure.
Greater number of approaches to a problem.	Tendency to reach a consensus before all good solutions are considered.
Participation in problem solving increases acceptance.	Individual domination.
Better comprehension of the decision.	Conflicting secondary goal: Winning the argument.

Adapted from N. R. F Maier, "Assets and Liabilities in Group Problem Solving. The Need for an Integrative Function," *Psychological Review* 74 (1967), 239–49.

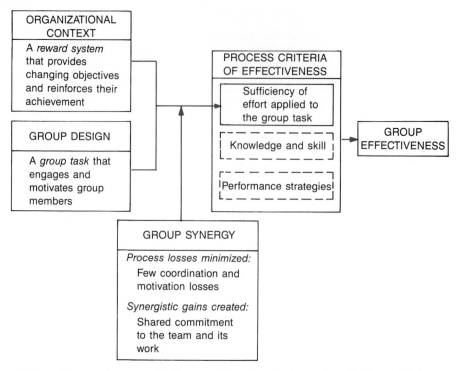

FIGURE 4.5 Keys to group effectiveness. From J. R. Hackman, "The Design of Work Teams" in *Handbook of Organizational Behavior,* edited by J. W. Lorsch, 1987, Englewood Cliffs, NJ: Prentice-Hall, p. 325.

or suggestion offered by the group. The implementation issue brings up an important problem faced by supervisors. When should subordinates participate in decisions and how much participation is optimal? The next section on leadership processes in organizations will suggest answers to those questions.

Leadership Processes in Organizations. The quality of leadership present in complex organizations must be considered a key factor in organizational success. Consider how strong leadership by Thomas J. Watson at IBM, Steve Jobs at Apple Computer, or Lee Iacocca at Chrysler Corporation shaped norms, values, and vision at each of these firms (Bass, 1985). Clearly, the leader can influence the morale, satisfaction, commitment, and productivity of organization members. Who are most likely to assume positions of leadership? What traits and abilities increase the likelihood that individuals will emerge as leaders? How can leadership effectiveness be measured? What actions and behaviors by leaders will lead to supermotivated subordinates? Are the traits and behaviors important for leadership success in one situation (for example, head of a volunteer charity) similar to those important in other situations (for example, director of a state government agency)? These questions, not all of which can be answered here, are representative of the interests of I/O psychologists working in this area.

Defining leadership has been a particularly perplexing problem. Common to all definitions of leadership is the notion of *influence*—the process of affecting the activities of an organized group in its tasks of goal setting and goal achievement (Stogdill, 1950). If you think of any organization in which you have worked, most likely it was the manager or supervisor (holding a formal position of leadership) who assigned people to specific tasks, controlled their pay, provided performance feedback, set the group goals, and resolved conflicts among the group members. The leader's ability to influence group behavior may stem from personal power (attractiveness, charisma, or expertise) or position power (authority vested in the individual by the organization).

Although leadership processes may not be completely understood, they make up one of the topics most studied by I/O psychologists. A central question that has been investigated is whether decisions are best if they are made autocratically by a leader or democratically, with participation from subordinates. A second major concern has been on a leader's behavior. Under what circumstances is it better to focus on the task by providing structure and direction for subordinates or to focus on group relationships by being considerate and supportive. Since more than 4,500 articles and books were cited in just one recent leadership text (Bass, 1981), by necessity, this chapter looks at only one aspect of leadership in detail—that of subordinate participation in decison making.

Leaders may make decisions alone or they may share in the process with subordinates, peers, or supervisors. The term *participation* is typically applied when subordinates share in the decision-making process with supervisors. Gary Yukl suggests that there are four distinct levels of participation. These are autocratic decisions (no influence by subordinates); consultation (subordinates opinions are solicited, but the decision is made solely by the supervisor); joint decisions (both supervisors and subordinates make a group decision); and delegation (subordinates alone are given responsibility and authority for making decisions).

Which level is optimal? When should one decision process be used rather than another? It is clear that employees' participation usually results in their greater satisfaction and motivation. Yet there is a down side for too much participation, particularly in situations where time is critical. Supervisors may be perceived as weak, ineffective, or not on top of things if every decision requires group input. Fortunately, some recommendations can be made as to the appropriate mix. Victor Vroom and Arthur Jago (1988) have developed a situational model of decision participation that instructs leaders on how to choose the appropriate degree of employee participation. Leaders are instructed to ask a series of questions about the specific situation in which a decision is to be made.

One question, for example, asks the leader if he or she has sufficient information to make a high-quality decision. Another question asks if the leader was to make the decision without subordinate input, is it reasonably certain that the subordinates would be committed to the decision? A third question considers employee development; it asks how important is it to maximize the opportunities for subordinate development. Based on a total of 12 questions such as those presented above, the leader chooses the optimal level of subordinate participation — one that will likely maximize decision quality, subordinate development, and commitment to the decision. Perhaps a specific example will help clarify the process. What if you had recently installed new diagnostic machines in the automobile service department, yet the expected productivity has not been up to that expected? The first-line supervisors reporting to you have differing views about the likely source of the problem. Vroom and Jago, presenting a problem almost identical to this one, suggest (based on their model) that the supervisors make the decision after sharing the problem with subordinates in a group meeting and eliciting their ideas and suggestions.

New and exciting theories of leadership have been developed in the 1980s. Fred Fiedler's cognitive resource theory (Fiedler & Garcia, 1987) attempts to explain conditions under which a leader's intelligence or technical competence will enhance follower performance. As might be expected, he finds that intelligent leaders make high-quality decisions and plans; however, this holds true only under conditions of low stress. A leader's experience, rather than intelligence, contributes to performance under conditions of high stress. For Fiedler, under low stress, leaders use their intelligence but not their experience; under high stress, leaders use their experience but not their intelligence.

Other new leadership theories have focused on the charismatic aspects of leadership. Charismatic leaders are able to inspire followers to perform well beyond the call of duty. A charismatic leader will develop a vision and a mission for the future, create positive images in the minds of followers, set challenging goals for the followers to achieve, and show confidence and respect for followers (House & Singh, 1987). As might be expected, followers of charismatic leaders express high commitment, devotion, and loyalty to the leader. Robert House conducted an intriguing study of the charismatic characteristics of former presidents of the United States. As part of the study, historians classified 12 presidents as either being charismatic or noncharismatic leaders. All charismatic presidents were either reelected or assassinated during their first term whereas only one of the six noncharismatics was reelected. In addition, the charismatic leaders exhibited personality patterns, as reflected in their inaugural addresses, that reflected a high need for both achievement and power.

In extending the charismatic concept to work and military organizations, Gary Yukl and David Van Fleet describe charismatic (or inspirational leaders in their terms) as those who stimulate enthusiasm among followers and build subordinates' confidence in their ability to successfully perform assignments (Yukl & Van Fleet, 1982). Based on the seminal leadership work by James MacGregor Burns (1978), Bernard Bass has developed a theory of "transformational and transactional leadership" (1985). Consistent with the concept of charismatic leadership, the *transformational leader* motivates people to perform at higher levels than they ever thought possible. The extremely high motivational level of followers is hypothesized to exist because the transformational leader is able to inspire subordinates while providing them with individualized consideration and intellectual stimulation. In contrast, the *transactional leader* achieves his or her influence in the workplace by providing support and direction to employees, exchanging rewards for satisfactory performance, and in general helping employees to get what they want from their jobs. According to the theory, the transactional leader may be a competent supervisor, but will not engender the passion for superperformance that is generated by the transformational leader. Who are these transformational leaders? George Patton of the Third Army, Thomas J. Watson at IBM, Lee Iacocca at Chrysler Corporation, and Steve Jobs at Apple Computer exhibited transformational leadership. You might have guessed that many leaders have both transformational and transactional characteristics — Franklin D. Roosevelt provides one such example. Before leaving the discussion of leadership, it is important to note that what was presented here was only a selective and somewhat superficial look at today's leadership research and theory. The field continues to excite I/O researchers and many important questions about leadership still remain unanswered.

Critical Issues Facing the Work Force

Today organizations are facing a number of problems that defy easy solution. Managers frequently want answers to the questions that involve trade-offs, such as these: How can we improve productivity and at the same time pay our workers a "living wage"? Can we restructure jobs to make them more rewarding without huge capital expenditures? Can affirmative action be implemented without reverse discrimination? How can I motivate workers, strongly encourage them to come to work on time, and yet seem like a participative manager? Even though the answers are not simple, industrial psychologists have studied these issues and often can help develop solutions. This chapter concludes with a brief discussion of four critical issues facing the work force.

Critical Issue: Improving Productivity.   The failure of U.S. productivity to improve in the 1960s and 1970s was a well-documented and frightening phenomenon. Contrast the huge productivity growth in Japan (7.5%) to that of the United States (2.1%) during the years 1950 to 1978 (U.S. Bureau of Labor Statistics). Since improvement of productivity is vital to the standard of living in the United States, it is no surprise that attention has been focused on the reasons for and solutions to the productivity dilemma.

Numerous culprits for the decline in productivity growth rate have been identified. These include people factors (changing work habits and values of the U.S. work force) as well as technology factors (a slowdown in capital spending, and research and development activities). Fortunately, the negative trend in productivity growth seems to have been reversed in the mid 1980s. The reasons for this are not so clear. While new technology — automation, robots, and computers —

A visual aid like this "Quality Train" graphically underscores the importance of team work and job pride, but supervisors have to use a variety of techniques in motivating and guiding both new and old employees.

have undoubtedly increased the level of productivity, some of that increase may be due to the people factor—better management, and employees working harder, smarter, and longer. Some important efforts have included increased spending for capital improvements, investments in research and development leading to technological advancements, decreased government-influenced inflation, decreased oil prices, and a greater awareness by management and unions of the value of productivity improvements (Cascio, 1986).

Managerial methods to spur people on to higher performance levels have varied considerably and sometimes seem very humorous. For instance, before bankruptcy, managers of the giant W. T. Grant retail store would be hit in the face with custard pies if they didn't meet their quotas. "Other 'negative incentives' consisted of store managers having their ties cut in half, being forced to run around the store backwards, and pushing peanuts with their noses" (Karlins, 1981, p. 5). In contrast, one sales manager at IBM dreamed up an innovative attempt to reward successful employees. He rented a sports stadium for an evening. "After work, his salesmen ran onto the stadium's field through the players' tunnel. As each emerged, the electronic scoreboard beamed his name to the assembled crowd. Executives from corporate headquarters, employees from other offices, and family and friends were present, cheering loudly"(Peters & Waterman, Jr., 1982, p. xxiv).

A recent review of psychological approaches to productivity improvement (Katzell & Guzzo, 1983) provides insight into the variety of approaches that can be used to improve productivity. One impressive finding (among 207 experiments conducted since 1971), is that 87% of the studies reported an improvement in at least one concrete measure of productivity. Such measures include output, quality, costs, turnover, absenteeism, or accidents. Training seemed to be the most successful and frequently used motivational technique.

Training is defined as the systematic acquisition of skills, rules, concepts, or attitudes that result in improved performance on the job (Goldstein, 1986). Employee training may be very specific, as in the case of teaching a telephone operator to handle long-distance calls, or it may be less concrete, as in training a manager to accept a leadership role. Most organizations have a firm commitment to training. A Carnegie Foundation report (1985) indicated that organizations spend more than $40 billion a year on programs that range from basic skills training, such as reading, to executive development programs. When properly designed and evaluated, training efforts can have a substantial effect on productivity.

Three other motivational practices have been widely adopted in industry: (1) performance-based compensation systems; (2) goal setting combined with positive reinforcement; and (3) job redesign. Each of these has been the object of study by industrial/organizational psychologists:

Compensation Systems.   Pay systems that are based on an individual performance are an old, yet potent, means to improve productivity. Since the 1930s, survey after survey has found that piece-rate incentive systems (the more you produce, the more you make) often yield large productivity gains. One survey of 2,500 incentive systems indicated that productivity per worker was 63% higher for workers paid on an incentive basis than for workers paid on an hourly basis (Cherrington, 1982). Individual incentive plans typically increase job performance by at least 30%. Group incentive plans are also valuable, particularly when jobs are interdependent and require cooperation among the workers. Group incentives (based on group output), profit sharing (bonuses calculated on the company's profits), and the Scanlon Plan (reduction of labor costs) are successful because individuals see concrete pay advantages for working hard. In 1982 employees of Lincoln Electric received an average bonus check of $15,400. not surprisingly, workers at this plant eagerly boasted of their commitment to high productivity.

Goal Setting.   The motivational strategy of goal setting has a high potential for increasing productivity. The reason for setting goals is straightforward. When goals are specific and challenging, employees will understand where to focus their efforts and expend their energy. A literature review by Ed Locke found that the processes of goal setting yield productivity increases averaging 18%. In fact, goal setting is a crucial feature of Management by Objectives — a very popular management technique used in organizations. If goals are directed to important aspects of performance, quality and quantity of production often increase. This may seem like common sense, but organizations and individuals often do not set goals that are measurable and therefore have trouble rewarding successful achievement. When good performance is rewarded through raises, promotions, and personal recognition, employees feel that their extra efforts pay off.

Automation and Work Redesign. Automation and work redesign modify the nature of the way work is accomplished, On the technical side, automation will continue to have a huge impact on productivity. Robots, minicomputers, computerized manufacturing, and automated office equipment are technological innovations that affect the jobs of millions of workers. Obviously, the nature of work changes when a plant becomes automated. Those workers not displaced by new technology may monitor the automated equipment rather than performing the job by hand. In addition, monitoring may require less skill than before, and it is often a less interesting job. On the brighter side, high technology has created skilled jobs necessary in the design and maintenance of new equipment. Human resource needs also change with automation. For instance, secretaries are now being hired based on their familiarity with word processors and personal computers. Further, managers need training in the use of personal computers (a traumatic experience for those people not raised in the computer generation). Although job displacement is inevitable with automation, people will always be involved in the use of any automated system—even if it is only in the design, installation, and maintenance of these systems.

Job redesign efforts also aim to increase production and make jobs more satisfying. Jobs may be changed to include more challenge and responsibility, to require a greater variety of skills, or to provide more independence and autonomy for the worker. On the other hand, entire systems of work activities can be altered—physical equipment, work schedules, and job rewards. The goal of these efforts is to enhance the motivation of employees. Each of the three approaches to motivation—pay for performance, goal setting, and job redesign—has built-in potential for productivity improvement. The challenge to management is to realize this potential.

Critical Issue: Improving Quality of Work Life. J. Richard Hackman thinks that we need to ask the question, What kind of life do we want to create for the people who do the productive work of this society? (Hackman, 1982, p. 385). This question addresses a traditional concern of industrial/organizational psychologists, how to define health, well-being, and job satisfaction of employees. The concept of "quality of work life" (QWL) is very broad and refers to the total relationship between a worker, his or her job, and the work environment. At a basic level, QWL refers to whether people are treated well, paid a living wage, work in a pleasant and safe environment, and are able to exert control over their work. Ed Lawler suggests, "A high QWL exists when jobs are enriched, democratic supervision is practiced, and employees are involved in their work" (1982, p. 486). Although this may seem to be common sense, it is easy to find management philosophies directly in contrast to concern for QWL. For instance, the former Chief of Naval Operations, Elmo (Bud) Zumwalt, once suggested that the Navy assumes that everyone below the rank of commander is immature. This statement reflects an attitude clearly in contrast to the QWL concept.

Projects to improve QWL are varied. They include activities that modify individual jobs, change the nature of work groups, and even influence the organizational structure itself. Beginning at the individual job level, job enlargement and job enrichment programs are designed to provide workers with more challenging and meaningful work. For job enlargement, workers perform a greater variety and number of tasks. For job enrichment, workers are given more responsibility and autonomy, and are allowed greater self-direction regarding how the job is done. A garment worker, for instance, might be responsible for several separate operations, check product quality, schedule the work, and deal directly with customers in situations where goods are returned.

At the group level, two innovative QWL activities—quality circles (QC) and semiautonomous work groups are increasing in popularity. The Japanese credit much of their success to quality-control circles. Members of a work group meet voluntarily to identify, discuss, and recommend solutions to production and quality problems. Members are first trained in group problem-solving techniques, industrial engineering processes, and quality-control procedures. Numerous

Japanese firms attribute some of their success in producing highly regarded goods to the "quality circle" idea. Groups of workers voluntarily get together to identify problems and recommend solutions. The concept has spread to the United States. In the photograph, a group of managers at the Boise, Idaho, plant of Hewlett-Packard are shown at a QC meeting to find solutions for a problem with document flow.

American companies that have adopted the QC concept include General Motors, Ford, Westinghouse, RCA, and General Electric, among many others. Properly implemented, QCs can result in increased productivity, better attendance, lower absenteeism, and higher self-esteem of workers. Critics point out that the positive evidence for the success of QC's is generally anecdotal, based on less than rigorous evaluation methods, and may be nothing more than a short-lived effect related to the newness of the program. However, recent studies conducted by I/O psychologists point to convincing evidence of success for QCs (Barrick & Alexander, 1987).

In the case of semiautonomous work groups (often referred to as self-managed work groups), a team of workers will make decisions that are typically handled by supervisors. The team may decide on daily work assignments and production schedules to best meet management productivity goals. In some cases, they may be responsible for selecting and training new employees and for terminating those people whose performance is unsatisfactory. Also, radical changes may be made in the design of jobs. For instance, in contrast to the typical assembly line, Volvo's Kalmar automobile plant in Sweden is designed so that cars move along work stations where each group of workers completes a large segment of work (such as installing the engine or cooling system). The job changes at the Gaines pet food plant in the United States are often cited as another successful effort to create autonomous work groups. Here, teams of workers are responsible for a complete segment of the production cycle, such as packing and storing products. These efforts at Volvo and at Gaines seem to have the desired effect of improving worker satisfaction. However, the Gaines example also boasts of improved productivity and lower absenteeism, while productivity at the Volvo plant remains disappointing.

From the discussion so far, you might correctly assume that there are many positive outcomes, and perhaps some costs, associated with QWL programs. Increasing productivity, job satisfaction, improved quality, and reduction in turnover and absenteeism are commonly noted in the literature. Ed Lawler has even made the controversial suggestion that the government consider legislation to mandate that employers be concerned with QWL (1982). The following is a balanced summary of the research evidence on work redesign, which we would also expect to be generally true for almost all QWL programs (Hackman, 1982).

1. Work redesign, when competently executed in appropriate organizational circumstances, generally increases the work satisfaction and motivation of employees as jobs are enriched.
2. The quality of the product or service provided generally improves.
3. The quantity of work done sometimes increases, sometimes is unchanged, and sometimes even decreases. (Decreases in quantity might be noticed as people worked especially hard on their enriched jobs to produce work of especially high quality).
4. Findings regarding employee attendance at work—absenteeism and turnover—are not clear.

One must also consider potential and significant "costs" before undertaking any QWL activity. First, QWL efforts are hard to implement successfully. They require considerable time, commitment, and financial investments. Increased wages, training costs, and facility costs associated with job redesign must also be considered. It may be wise to remember that QWL efforts may fail because they are seen by workers as gimmicks rather than as fundamental changes. Because I/O psychologists are trained in understanding human motivation and job satisfaction, they are frequently involved in the design, implementation, and evaluation of QWL programs.

Critical Issues: Attendance and Turnover.   All organizations want their members to show up on time every day and remain in the organization as long as they make a positive contribution. Unwarranted absenteeism, tardiness, and unwanted turnover cost American industry huge amounts of money. Some estimates suggest that approximately 500 million workdays are lost each year at a cost between $10 and $25 billion. Consider the fact that unwarranted absenteeism at General Motors costs the company about $1 billion per year (Deitch & Dilts, 1981). Further, for most organizations, including GM, measures of productivity are adversely affected by absenteeism. It's no wonder that absenteeism is considered a major problem.

As with any issue that concerns employee motivation, however, the causes of absenteeism and turnover are complex and evade easy or simplistic solutions. However, organizations can reduce their absenteeism and control turnover. To do so, they need to first distinguish voluntary absenteeism (going fishing) from involuntary absenteeism (illness or family problems). The organization probably has little control over some situations, particularly when people may not be able to come to work due to health, family, or transportation problems. Also, organizations have little control over the economy, which (not surprisingly) has a large influence over the absenteeism rate. When times are tough, people tend to come to work for fear of being laid off.

What options are available to reduce absenteeism? Few I/O psychologists would debate the point that the more an individual is satisfied with his or her job, the less likely he or she will be to take unwarranted absences and risk getting fired. Yet the link between job satisfaction and attendance is far from perfect. Frank Landy (1985) suggests that because this link is so tenuous, efforts to increase satisfaction with the hope of improving attendance is simply wishful thinking.

Instead, some companies have provided positive incentives for punctuality and good attendance. Perhaps you have heard about lotteries or cash bonuses awarded to individuals who maintain perfect attendance for a certain period. Most companies, however, try to reduce absenteeism through company rules and policies that explicitly define acceptable and nonacceptable absences. Policies should be clearly understood, easily administered, and fair to all. Both positive and negative procedures working together may be the best solution to the absenteeism problem. For instance, researchers found that attendance in a large manufacturing firm was dramatically improved by instituting nonmonetary privileges for good and improving attendance, and warnings and negative sanctions for excessive absenteeism and declining attendance.

Whereas absenteeism is typically viewed as a totally undesirable phenomenon, employee turnover has both positive and negative consequences for the organization, the individual, and society. Turnover is functional when it has positive consequences and dysfunctional when negative consequences result. Organizations care most about voluntary turnover that is dysfunctional (a good employee who quits). The high cost of turnover is well documented. For instance, recall that one competent fighter pilot costs the Navy approximately $1.5 million to replace. The costs of replacing a store manager at a large department store chain may easily approach $10,000. Even the cost of replacing a bank teller may reach several thousand dollars.

Consider why these costs are so high. There are direct costs such as recruiting, selection, and training of new employees plus severance pay for those who leave involuntarily. Indirect costs include the loss of productivity prior to separation, loss during the time the position is vacant, and a possible decrease in customer relationships and/or in the reputation of the organization. Other negative consequences of turnover besides costs are also apparent. If the person who quits was a high performer, others may have to pick up the slack and work harder. Individuals who leave may be negatively affected particularly if they lose seniority and other perquisites. They also may experience stress in changing jobs and moving to a new location. Society may also lose. For instance, high turnover may result in a plant remaining idle because of a lack of trained operators.

Yet as Bill Mobley (an expert in turnover research) notes (1982), the turnover process may yield positive consequences. Replacements can bring new strategies, unique ideas and experiences, and technological knowledge that can serve as catalysts for organizational growth. There are also the advantages of getting rid of poor performers and replacing them with better employees. Those who produce poor quality work and are frequently absent have an impact reaching far beyond their low-level work. The departure of management-level personnel allows others to move up the career ladder and creates perceptions of individual growth within the company.

What can be done to reduce unwanted turnover? Like absenteeism, a significant indicator of labor turnover is the state of the economy — a rise in unemployment is correlated with reduction in quitting. But it is important to determine *which* individuals are most likely to leave certain employers. Demographic analysis suggests that, in general, younger workers are more likely to leave than older workers and short-term employees are more likely to depart than those with longer service. Of most interest to industrial/organizational psychologists are individual variables like job satisfaction, organizational commitment, expectations of finding other jobs, and intentions to quit. As you might expect, each of these factors is consistently related to turnover.

Satisfied, committed, highly paid, and high-performing individuals are less likely to think of quitting and therefore less likely to search for a new job or actually quit (Cotton & Tuttle, 1986). The availability of other employment is, of course, related to the likelihood of that person's looking for new employment. A simple yet potentially effective method to predict whether a specific person is likely to leave is simply to ask that person about his or her intention to quit or stay.

Richard Steers and Thomas Stone make the following suggestions to manage the turnover process: (1) Present a realistic job preview during the interview so that job expectations are clarified. (2) Reward good employee performances and clarify what is expected of all individuals. (3) Monitor employee attitudes and improve job satisfaction and commitment wherever possible. (4) Attend to possible nonwork factors such as a lack of day-care facilities that may result in unwanted turnover. Monitor employee attitudes on a regular basis.

Critical Issue: Discrimination In The Workplace. Wayne Cascio in his excellent book, *Applied Psychology and Personnel Management*, suggests that sweeping civil rights legislation enacted in the 1960s and 1970s, combined with increasing motivation of individuals and companies to rectify unfair employment, makes the legal aspects of employment the dominant issue of personnel management today. This was not always so. As recently as 25 years ago, supervisors, personnel directors, and others responsible for employment decisions rarely took the time to consider whether a personnel decision had a discriminatory impact on a particular sex, race, or age group. It was not uncommon to see help-wanted ads that specified "men only," "no colored wanted," or "wanted, experienced director – 30 to 45 years old." Indeed, the situation was bleak. One personnel representative of Southern Bell in 1962 testified before the United States Civil Rights Commission and indicated that blacks were not hired as operators

Since the mid-1960s, affirmative action to eradicate and redress job discrimination has been an important component of organizational life. Industrial/organizational psychologists have been involved in pertinent research such as determining the validity of certain tests and studying the discriminatory impact of some types of employee selection procedures.

or mechanical employees because "local traditions and customs have not changed to the point that we feel it is the thing to do in our company at this time." Obviously, things have changed, yet the problems of discrimination will continue to be an issue for the foreseeable future.

The United States government has employed a comprehensive approach, using the legislative, executive, and judicial branches to eradicate unfair discrimination in the workplace. Several pieces of legislation have had major impact on the personnel policies of organizations. The Age Discrimination in Employment Act of 1967 protects individuals over 40 years of age. Handicapped individuals are protected by the Vocational Rehabilitation Act of 1973. However, one piece of legislation stands out in importance. Title VII of the 1964 Civil Rights Act (and the 1972 amendment) prohibits discrimination in employment on the basis of race, color, religion, sex, or national origin. The 1964 act created a federal agency called the Equal Employment Opportunity Commission (EEOC) to enforce and promote the law. At first the commission's powers were limited, but in 1972 EEOC was given power to initiate litigation (lawsuits) against offending businesses if conciliatory efforts fail to rectify the problem. Coverage of Title VII now includes private companies that regularly employ more than 15 individuals, educational institutions, unions with 15 or more members, and federal, state, and local governments. EEOC is a busy agency. It processes approximately 70,000 complaints and may be involved in approximately 500 class action lawsuits annually.

Today all aspects of the employment relationship are subject to guarantees of equal employment opportunity. This means that recruiting, decisions to hire an employee, training, and compensation must all be nondiscriminatory. Simply put, only in extremely rare circumstances can an employer use a person's race, color, sex, national origin, or religion as factors to be considered in employment decisions. Racial discrimination is never tolerated. Thus while it is legitimate to select females for female roles in the movies, airlines cannot refuse to hire male stewards just because business*men* prefer young and attractive women. Gender would be considered to be a "bona fide occupational qualification" for casting films, but not for jobs with the airlines.

The executive branch of the United States government also has made significant contributions to eradicate employee discrimination. Through executive orders, all Presidents of the United States since Franklin D. Roosevelt have issued directives prohibiting discrimination. For instance, Executive Order 11246, issued in 1965 by President Johnson, prohibited discrimination by federal contractors and subcontractors on the basis of race, color, religion, or national origin. A later order also prohibited sex discrimination as well. The Office of Federal Contract Compliance Programs enforces the executive orders and ensures that contractors meet affirmative action requirements. This powerful agency may cancel present contracts, bar future bids, and even advise the Department of Justice to institute criminal proceedings upon noncompliance with rules and regulations. Companies with more than $50,000 worth of business must regularly develop and report affirmative action plans to enhance employment opportunities of women and minority groups.

To complete the last prong of the comprehensive effort to eradicate employee discrimination, it is necessary to consider how judicial decisions have clarified (or in some cases confused) the interpretation of the law. In general, the courts have been consistent in the following regard. First, *results* or *consequences* of employment decisions are as important as an *intention* to discriminate. Second, the EEOC guidelines on employee selection procedures should be followed in determining whether unfair discrimination has occurred. Third, the procedure in a discrimination case should progress through several stages. In general, the plaintiff (person who files a suit) initially must demonstrate that the employment decision had a discriminatory impact. After the plaintiff demonstrates discrimination through a *prima facie* violation (meaning that evidence is sufficient to establish a fact, unless rebutted), the defendant must demonstrate that the employment practice was job-related or is a business necessity.

Griggs v. *Duke Power Company* (1971) has been a landmark discrimination case. Employees had to have a high school diploma (or pass an intelligence and a mechanical aptitude test) to advance beyond the very lowest paying jobs. Specifically, the problem occurred when workers without high school diplomas took the tests in the hope of promotion. Although the standards in scoring the tests were applied equally to whites and blacks, the consequences of the testing was that blacks were disqualified at a substantially higher rate than whites. Yet, neither the high school requirement nor the passing of the tests was shown to be significantly related to job performance. The Supreme Court ruled in favor of Griggs, and the message from the Court became clear. Discriminatory intent did not have to be shown; rather, the effects or consequences of employment decisions would be the deciding criterion in discrimination cases. If an employment decision has a negative impact on an individual because of his or her race, sex, color, national origin, or religion, the employer must bear the burden of proof that the employment practice has an important relationship to the success of the organization.

The requirement that tests must be job-related resulted in a flurry of activity for I/O psychologists. A particularly important aspect of these efforts was to determine if the test (or any other selection procedure) was biased against minority groups. These activities continue to be an important area of work for I/O psychologists.

Since determining the validity of an employment test is no easy task, many employers have dropped employment testing altogether in hopes of avoiding expensive litigation. This "end run" will likely prove inefficient and ineffective — inefficient because many employment tests are the most reliable and valid means to fairly select people for jobs, and ineffective because *all* personnel selection practices can be "called on the carpet" for unfair discrimination. Consider the case of *Weiner* v. *County of Oakland* (1976). The courts looked askance at the questions asked Mrs. Weiner during her interview. Clearly, the courts indicated, it is not job-related to ask whether her husband approved of her working or whether her family would suffer if dinner wasn't served on time. Yet these and other obviously discriminatory questions were asked during her interview. Look at Table 4.5 for a list of questions to avoid asking during an interview.

As with most far-reaching pieces of legislation (and with associated government agencies that monitor and enforce the legislation), Title VII of the Civil Rights Act and EEOC have been subject to much controversy. Criticism abounds over the quality of the leadership of EEOC, the lack of a consistent and coherent policy, the perceived incompetence of some agency personnel, and long delays in investigating cases. However, the job of EEOC has not been made any easier by unwarranted and trivial claims. In one case a man filed over 100 charges of discrimination claiming he was a victim because he was a Transylvanian and a vampire. Also, since people tend to blame the situation rather than themselves for failure, it is easier for them to suppose that they had been discriminated against than to accept blame for negative occurrences. Thus failure on the job may be attributed to discrimination, but individual incompetence could be the key to the personnel decision. Nevertheless, overwhelming evidence suggests that although blacks and females have made significant strides in the workplace, they continue to be underrepresented in managerial and high-paying positions and overrepresented in service positions. The effects of hundreds of years of discrimination cannot be wiped out in five years.

What role do I/O psychologists play in eliminating the problem of discrimination? One contribution has been in trying to identify precisely what discrimination is. This is more difficult to do than one might expect. Employment selection procedures are, by design, meant to discriminate, that is, to identify and select the most qualified individuals. Most I/O psychologists would agree that discrimination occurs whenever minorities have an equal chance for success on the job but do not have an equal probability of being hired. This view might not satisfy everyone, since a test (or any selection procedure) that results in lower scores by minorities would not be discriminatory by this definition if it could be shown to be job-related.

Industrial/organizational psychologists are engaged in a variety of endeavors related to discrimination issues. Many statistical models of test fairness have been developed by psychologists. Extensive research studies investigating possi-

---

TABLE 4.5

Examples of Questions to Avoid in Interview Situations

1. Information regarding arrests.

2. Information regarding citizenship.

3. Information regarding spouse's salary, children, child-care arrangements, or dependents.

4. Overgeneral information (e.g., "Do you have any handicaps?"), which might highlight health conditions unrelated to job performance.

5. Marital status of the applicant.

6. Military discharge information.

7. Information related to pregnancy.

8. Whether the applicant owns or rents a home.

From Psychology of Work Behavior *3rd edition, (p. 115), by F. J. Landy, 1985, Homewood, IL: Dorsey Press.*

ble test bias and unfair discrimination were undertaken in the 1960s and 1970s. Psychologists have testified in the courts as to the validity and discriminatory impact of various selection procedures. As a result of these efforts, many poor employment procedures have been identified and improved. For instance, work-sample tests less discriminatory than traditional paper-and-pencil tests have been developed. In a similar manner, I/O psychologists have investigated the possible discriminatory impact of poor performance appraisals, inappropriate job analysis methods, and training designs that may screen out minorities. In each case, the overriding goal has been to develop fair procedures that are job-related.

Conclusion

The future of I/O psychology is intertwined with the changes in the nature of work. You are no doubt aware that major changes in the nature of work have occurred since the Industrial Revolution. What was predominantly a rural society has become urban and highly industrialized. Huge organizations now produce the goods and services that form the economic base of our society. Specialized jobs require professional managers to coordinate diverse activity among workers. Technological change and automation have further changed the nature of work.

Major changes in the nature of the work force have also taken place. Consider the following examples: (1) Some experts have predicted that 75% of the work force in the future will need computer skills to perform their job. (2) Engineering skills learned at the university are often obsolete within five years of graduation. (3) Women now constitute 42% of the labor force, up from 28% in 1947. (4) Quality of work life has become an important job concern; younger workers are more educated and demand better, more interesting, and more meaningful jobs. All of these changes have had an impact on the profession and science of I/O psychology and constitute critical issues facing the field. Problems noted in the previous section, such as improving productivity, improving the quality of work life, decreasing absenteeism and turnover, and implementing nondiscriminatory hiring and advancement practices, are currently topics of extreme interest both to management and to I/O psychologists.

The contributions of I/O psychology should be considered in relation to the goals and objectives of the discipline. I/O psychologists desire to increase the performance, effectiveness, and productivity of people at work while simultaneously enhancing worker satisfaction, job involvement, and health. The profession believes that knowledge about human behavior gained through experience and research can best meet these objectives. What will the future bring? Many people believe that the United States is at the crossroads. Clark Kerr, in his book *Work in America: The Decade Ahead* (1979), asks, "Will the work situation be positive, characterized by high productivity and satisfied, well-paid and motivated workers, or will the future be bleak: resources running out, conflict and confrontation between workers, corporations, and government?" Perhaps both trends may occur simultaneously. However, the outcomes may be influenced by, and certainly will have an impact on, I/O psychology.

This chapter has defined I/O psychology in a number of ways. It has considered various specialty areas within the field and noted similarities and differences between these areas and related disciplines. In the section titled "What Do I/O Psychologists Do?" the job activities and work settings of I/O psychologists were reviewed. In the section on research and application, representative aspects of personnel and organizational psychology were described. In the personnel area, the importance of job analysis as a basis for other personnel activities was emphasized. Techniques of employee recruitment were next considered as a second step in the staffing process. Predictors such as interviews, application blanks, recommendations, and tests that are used to select employees were then reviewed, and various ways to assess the effectiveness of these measures were considered. In a second section on organizational psychology, the impact of group behavior in the workplace was evaluated. Explicit consideration was given to the effects of group processes on performance and decision making. Next, leadership processes in organizations were described. Finally, a series of critical problems facing industrial organizations today were presented, together with research that has tried to address these problems.

Glossary

Equal Employment Opportunify Commission (EEOC) The government agency charged with enforcing and promoting laws against discrimination in the workplace.

groupthink A destructive pattern of group decision making where a group becomes so concerned with maintaining consensus and solidarity that it does not evaluate alternative courses of action realistically.

group status The perceived rank or relative worth of group members as determined by other group members.

job analysis An evaluation of the activities and tasks that must be performed on a job and the knowledge, skills, and abilities that are necessary to perform them.

realistic job preview Presentation of realistic job information designed to inform job applicants about the true nature of work in an organization.

social facilitation Improved performance on well-learned tasks in the presence of others.

social loafing The observation that the efforts of a group at a task where all efforts are added together and all members participate together (for example a tug-of-war) is less than the sum of the efforts of individuals when measured separately.

utility analysis A statistical technique designed to estimate the economic and productivity gains associated with valid selection procedures.

work norms A series of social rules that specify work-related behaviors that group members adhere to.

work role The pattern of activities that identifies a person's job.

5 Organizational Development

George T. Brennan
Massachusetts Mutual Life Insurance Company

Joe Gabbert
Need Data Central

In 1978, a computer wizard left his secure job at a large well-established computer firm to develop and market his own design for a microcomputer for personal or business use. With the knowledge of design and production he had developed in his previous job, this whiz set up a new business with a small group of friends and respected coworkers. The group clicked immediately, working creatively to transform the new design into a working product. The computer was efficient, easy to program and use, cheap to produce and market. Within a year it was selling well, and within three years sales had more than tripled. Although our computer wizard found himself wealthy and successful, as president of the company, he was faced with a thorny new problem. The small group of friendly coworkers had turned into a large, complex organization of engineers, production managers, assembly workers, programmers, marketing specialists, accountants, sales representatives, and so on. The president missed the small, cohesive

The organization. It looms over the lives of millions of people. Helping it to operate more effectively and with greater human satisfaction is the goal of organizational development psychologists.

group that had started the ball rolling. But sales and profits were up, everyone's expectations were optimistic, and employee morale was very high.

Suddenly, nationwide economic problems had a major effect on the business; the company's sales leveled off and began to drop. The president had to lay off employees, cut comfortable expense accounts, and begin to look more closely at the organization's efficiency. Problems seemed to pop up like monsters in a video game; unit managers began to squabble, sales representatives' competitiveness became cutthroat, production quality began to lag, and assembly workers began a union-organizing effort. People at all levels were complaining that the company was not such a great place to work anymore.

The president was in a quandary. Faced with the challenge of responding to the ever changing computer market in order to keep the business alive and well, he also had to find the key to restoring morale and togetherness in the organization. His intense involvement with the business side of the company had made it hard for him to see the whole organizational picture—to grasp the meaning of sudden organizational growth, then cutback, for his employees, and to conceptualize ways of renewing the optimistic spirit of the early days. What he needed was some outside help to turn the organization around.

What did he do? Just what thousands of other presidents, directors, and managers have done. He turned to an organization development (OD) consultant. An OD consultant is a professional, often from outside the organization, who is an expert in how people work together; how to identify organizational problems; and how to stimulate and improve organizational functioning.

This chapter serves as an introduction to organization development, an area of growing professional interest that draws on theory and research from a wide variety of social science disciplines, including organizational psychology, sociology, education, and management science. The chapter includes a brief review of the history of OD, a current definition, OD values and assumptions, typical OD approaches and techniques, and case examples. Finally, there is a concluding section on current and future trends.

What Is Organizational Development?

As an area of applied theory and practice, organization development has a fairly short history. Most observers point to the work of social psychologist Kurt Lewin and his associates in the late 1940s and 1950s as marking the beginning of activities that have come to be known as organization development. Actually, even earlier experiments such as the Hawthorne studies (Roethlisberger & Dickson, 1939) provided initial attention to how persons and organizations interact (Chapter 4 covered I/O psychology). More recently, new theories and techniques have led to many different approaches to OD and increasing efforts to standardize its application and improve quality control.

Lewin (1951) developed a **field theory of social psychology** that focused on understanding human behavior by simultaneously considering both individual characteristics and the social and physical environments of the individual. This approach led Lewin to studies of individual attitudes and of person-to-person interactions in small-group settings. Lewin found that the patterns and processes of group discussions dramatically affected attitudes and behavior, and that group-based discussions of feelings and interpersonal relations could lead to increased self-awareness and sensitivity to others. The developing application of Lewin's group training techniques became known as *sensitivity training* or *T-group training.*

French and Bell (1972) describe how, in the 1950s, Lewin's colleagues began to apply his group techniques to complex organizations such as Union Carbide and Esso Standard Oil Corporation. It was in these successful pioneering efforts that the expanded application of Lewin's work found both systematic direction and a name: organization development. It was found that by working with groups of people within the same organization, interpersonal relations and teamwork throughout the entity could be improved. Consequently, the organization's work was more effective.

During the same time period, survey research and feedback techniques were also used to develop organizations. This approach, used by Rensis Likert, Floyd Mann, and others at the University of Michigan, involved the administration of a questionnaire on organizational functioning to members of a company or department. The results of the questionnaire were summarized and fed back to managers and staff for use in problem solving. Thus structured process allowed participants to learn about their organizational problems and to work together to solve them. The technique helped educate people about organizational processes, and improved their teamwork and problem solving. Survey feedback proved to be an effective early approach that has continued in popularity.

These and other early applications of Lewin's ideas led to the rapid development and refinement of organization development approaches in the 1960s, culminating in Beckhard's (1969) definition of OD.

> *Organization development is an effort (1) planned, (2) organization-wide, and (3) managed from the top, to (4) increase organization effectiveness and health through (5) planned interventions in the organizations "processes," using behavioral-science knowledge* (Beckhard, 1969, p. 9).

While there have been numerous attempts to readjust the perceived boundaries of the field (Goad, 1979; Schein, 1985), Beckhard's summary still holds as one of the most widely accepted definitions.

OD: A Systematic Improvement Effort Gets People Involved.   According to Beckhard, an OD program involves a planned, systematic effort to diagnose an organization's strengths and weaknesses and implement a strategic plan for improvement. Basically, this process is a structured problem-solving effort that pulls leaders and staff together in group meetings to learn about their organization and improve the way in which they work together. A systematic process ensures that the right people are involved and that the right issues are addressed at the right time. Scientific methods and the results of research studies are also introduced to confirm the effectiveness of diagnostic methods and group processes.

Another characteristic of OD efforts is that, ideally, they are conducted organization-wide rather than with isolated individuals or groups. Experience has shown that organizational problems often permeate the entire structure. For example, even localized problems in part of a computer company's warehouse can have dramatic effects on other departments if they strain customer relations, reduce sales, and alter production schedules. Improvements in such a situation require contributions from people in different departments to correct difficulties; a professional OD effort would involve such people as needed to uncover the problems and coordinate efforts to solve them.

Because OD efforts are organization-wide and can involve so many different people, it is important for them to be managed from the top. Top management and the managers of affected departments must be involved with and committed to the improvement process. Such involvement has a variety of positive benefits. First of all, management support shows staff that the effort is important and worthy of their attention. Second, as managers solicit staff ideas and encourage participation, people in the organization feel appreciated and respected. This generally improves their morale and helps get management and staff working together as a team to correct the difficulties they share. Finally, the more leaders in an OD project learn about their organizations and people, the better prepared they will be to handle similar problems that may develop in the future.

As Beckhard stresses in his definition, the goals of an OD program are twofold: to make organizations more effective in the ways they conduct their business, and to make them healthier environments for the people who work in them. Unfortunately, in many organizations today these twin concerns for productivity and people get out of balance, usually with work and profits taking precedence over people. Designers of OD programs strive to bring them into balance, understanding their complementary nature. Organizations need healthy, motivated people to get their work done, and people need successful, productive organizations to keep them employed.

With these two goals in mind, it is important for OD consultants to have some understanding of the characteristics of effective, healthy organizations. To this end, numerous definitions and models have been proposed, and extensive research on organizational processes has been conducted by those in the field. Table 5.1 lists some of the characteristics of healthy organizations as described by Douglas McGregor (1960). Using these characteristics, consultants are better able to diagnose problems and teach their clients how to improve ways of operating.

In completing Beckhard's definition of OD, it is important to note that OD consultants help make organizations more effective and healthy by means of skillfully planned interventions incorporating behavioral science knowledge and techniques. Effective OD consultants understand the strengths and weaknesses of different types of organizations and can help people examine what they are

TABLE 5.1

McGregor's Characteristics of Effective Work Teams

1. The "atmosphere" tends to be informal, comfortable, relaxed. There are no obvious tensions. It is a working atmosphere in which people are involved and interested. There are no signs of boredom.

2. There is a lot of discussion in which virtually everyone participates, but it remains pertinent to the task of the group. If the discussion gets off the subject, someone will bring it back in short order.

3. The task or the objective of the group is well understood and accepted by the members. There will have been free discussion of the objective at some point, until it was formulated in such a way that the members of the group could commit themselves to it.

4. The members listen to each other! The discussion does not have the quality of jumping from one idea to another unrelated one. Every idea is given a hearing. People do not appear to be afraid of being foolish by putting forth a creative thought even if it seems fairly extreme.

5. There is disagreement. The group is comfortable with this and shows no signs of having to avoid conflict or to keep everything on a plane of sweetness and light. Disagreements are not suppressed or overriden by premature group action. The reasons are carefully examined, and the group seeks to resolve them rather than to dominate the dissenter.

   On the other hand, there is no "tyranny of the minority." Individuals who disagree do not appear to be trying to dominate the group or to express hostility. Their disagreement is an expression of a genuine difference of opinion, and they expect a hearing in order that a solution may be found.

   Sometimes there are basic disagreements which cannot be resolved. The group finds it possible to live with them, accepting them but not permitting them to block its efforts. Under some conditions, action will be deferred to permit further study of an issue between the members. On other occasions, where the disagreement cannot be resolved and action is necessary, it will be taken but with open caution and recognition that the action may be subject to later reconsideration.

6. Most decisions are reached by a kind of consensus in which it is clear that everybody is in general agreement and willing to go along. However, there is little tendency for individuals who oppose the action to keep their opposition private and thus let an apparent consensus mask real disagreement. Formal voting is at a minimum; the group does not accept a simple majority as a proper basis for action.

7. Criticism is frequent, frank, and relatively comfortable. There is little evidence of personal attack, either openly or in a hidden fashion. The criticism has a constructive flavor in that it is oriented toward removing an obstacle that faces the group and prevents it from getting the job done.

8. People are free in expressing their feelings as well as their ideas both on the problem and on the group's operation. There is little pussyfooting, there are few "hidden agendas." Everybody appears to know quite well how everybody else feels about any matter under discussion.

9. When action is taken, clear assignments are made and accepted.

10. The chairman of the group does not dominate it, nor on the contrary, does the group defer unduly to him or her. In fact, as one observes the activity, it is clear that the leadership shifts from time to time, depending on the circumstances. Different members, because of their knowledge or experience, are in a position at various times to act as "resources" for the group. The members utilize them in this fashion and they occupy leadership roles while they are thus being used. There is little evidence of a struggle for power as the group operates. The issue is not who controls, but how to get the job done.

TABLE 5.1 cont.

11. The group is self-conscious about its own operations. Frequently, it will stop to examine how well it is doing or what may be interfering with its operation. The problem may be a matter or procedure, or it may be an individual whose behavior is interfering with the accomplishment of the group's objectives. Whatever it is, it gets open discussion until a solution is found.

From The Human Side of Enterprise *(pp. 232–235) by Douglas McGregor, 1960, New York: McGraw-Hill.*

doing in a way that will help them make positive changes. In this manner, the skills and tasks of an OD consultant are similar to those of a therapist or teacher. They are different, however, in that OD consultants focus on work-related rather than personal-growth issues, and they rely heavily on management-science theory and research to structure their interventions. Representative of this type of information is theory and research in such areas as leadership and decision making, conflict management, strategic planning and goal setting, and organization design.

Later in this chapter, several types of OD interventions will be described and a case presented that illustrates their use in real-life situations. In addition, the skill and knowledge areas needed by OD consultants will be articulated in greater detail.

What Do Organizational Development Professionals Do?

Now that you have some understanding of what organization development is, it is appropriate to look at some of the activities that OD professionals engage in by returning to the problems of the computer-wizard-turned-company-president. Imagine for a moment that you are an OD professional. What would you do if the computer wizard called and discussed his dilemma? How would you proceed to help his company become more effective and healthy? What processes and techniques would you use? What additional resources, if any, might you need to get the job done?

Job Activities

If you are like most OD professionals, you would use a consulting process similar to that depicted in Figure 5.1 to guide your efforts. You would approach each step carefully, working closely with the computer wizard and others in the firm to make sure you correctly understood their situation and were helping them make reasonable progress with their problems. You would also exercise patience, understanding that change can be difficult and that a typical OD effort can take months or even years to realize all its goals.

Step 1: Entry and Contracting. After discussing the computer wizard's problems in general over the phone, you schedule a meeting to go over the problems in

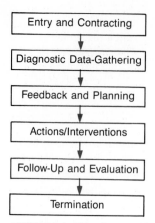

FIGURE 5.1 The diagram shows steps in a typical OD consulting process.

depth and determine whether or not you could really be helpful to him and his company. Your decisions would be as open and honest as possible so that you could understand his situation and he could learn about you and your work. If things go as expected, you then build a "contract" with each other to include the following items: (1) the overall goals of the OD program (e.g., improve production quality, reduce staff dissatisfaction, increase company sales, etc.), (2) ways in which progress would be evaluated, (3) your role as a consultant, (4) your expectations of his role in the change process, (5) potential methods to be used, (6) approximate time frames and costs, and (7) next steps for moving ahead.

Through this process you are striving to build a constructive, helping relationship based on mutual trust and collaboration, and a shared understanding of OD concepts and practices. You need to develop the same type of relationship with others in the company (e.g. department heads, staff, etc.) Beginning to work with others in the company may be difficult, however. People are sometimes reluctant to work with OD consultants for fear that these specialists will blame them for the company's problems. To this end, you and the computer wizard would schedule meetings with groups of managers and staff to explain your contract, educate them about OD, and as much as possible allay their fears.

Step 2: Diagnostic Data-Gathering. Once a contract has been written and the cooperation of appropriate people enlisted, you proceed to diagnose the company's problems. Working from the perceived problems of the client as discussed in your meetings with him and others, it is wise to prepare an in-depth diagnosis to make sure you address causes rather than just symptoms of problems. To this end, you would work with the computer wizard and his people to collect data about the strengths and weaknesses of the organization. An important issue here would be the identification of what parts of the organization were in trouble and their interrelationship with other parts of the total system. Such data gathering should explore a variety of functions of the organization. You would be guided in where to look for organizational problems by your ideas about what

An initial priority for organizational development psychologists is establishing a relationship of mutual trust and respect with management and staff. Often the very presence of an "outsider" causes anxiety. Staff members worry, Is the consultant being brought in as a "cover" for management—to fix blame, make unwanted changes, even fire some of them?

constitutes an effective organization and by the initial problems at hand. In this way you would function similarly to a physician who diagnoses physical ailments based on a patient's presenting problems.

A variety of diagnostic methods are available to you in this situation, again depending upon the identified problems. Included here would be (1) standardized questionnaires, (2) individual and group interviews, (3) company performance data, and (4) personal observation of meetings.

Interviews and personal observation of meetings are generally useful ways to proceed because they allow the consultant to build greater trust and rapport with participants and to discuss organizational problems in greater detail and with greater sensitivity. However, data from interviews and observation tend to be less objective than measures such as standardized questionnaires, which some clients consider more convincing. For these reasons, many consultants use a variety of data-collection techniques simultaneously in order to develop a well-rounded picture of an organization's strengths and weaknesses.

Step 3: Feedback and Planning. Once your data have been gathered, you are ready to present the results to your client. You work with the computer wizard and his people to plan any needed changes. At this point, the data are examined in relation to the presenting problems and goals established in step 1. Your goal is to work collaboratively with members of the organization to decide what changes should be made and to set specific improvement objectives that will meet their needs and expectations. What is needed most to make the improvements work is the mutual commitment of people inside the computer company.

Most likely, during this phase you would be scheduling a series of feedback and planning sessions with relevant members of the computer company. Your purpose is to discuss the data and engage these employees in a creative problem-solving process to formulate plans to improve the organization. Representatives of the various groups should come to understand their particular roles in strengthening the company and articulate specific improvement objectives and next steps for their units. Typically these objectives concern the way work is structured, the strategic directions of the firm, the ways departments interrelate, supervisor-subordinate relations, company policies, and employee benefits. Whatever specific changes may be called for, however, essentials of the process are that it (1) incorporate sound problem-solving techniques, (2) involve those whose participation is needed to make the changes work, and (3) result in a manageable number of clearly articulated, achievable goals and objectives.

During this stage of the process, OD consultants may take the opportunity to educate their clients as well as solve problems. Such sessions include presentations and discussions of organizational theory in conjunction with the graphic presentation of data summaries. In addition, consultants use such meetings to improve the human relations and group discussion skills of participants. For example, T-group techniques might be used to encourage productive interaction and model effective leadership behavior for clients. Generally, the skills participants learn in these problem-solving sessions transfer to work meetings as well.

Whatever adjustments are made in feedback and planning sessions, consultants need to be aware of the difficulties of introducing organizational change at this stage of the consulting process. As discussed earlier, organizational change is difficult and requires the finesse of experienced consultants and managers. This is particularly so during this initial stage of the OD process, when people are often made aware of their own contributions to organizational problems for the first time. Any feedback should be constructive and timely so that people do not become defensive and resist changes. Participants should also be assured that management will not punish them for past mistakes. They must be effectively encouraged to jump in and work together to make the future more productive and enjoyable.

Step 4: Actions/Interventions. After improvement goals have been established, the next step for you and the computer wizard would be to begin the process of working on them. This process, which could take from a few weeks to a few years depending upon the problems to be addressed, would typically include a combination of (1) "interventions" by you or other consultants and (2) "actions" by members of the company itself.

For example, you as the OD consultant might intervene by conducting a series of workshops with managers and staff to improve management-staff relations. You might also work regularly with the computer wizard and his key managers to improve their teamwork and decision making. Meanwhile, other specialists might be brought in to help the company develop a new product line and improve warehousing procedures.

In addition to your interventions, various departments might take their own actions to help turn the company around. For example, sales might work to tap new customer markets while manufacturing units develop employee incentive plans to improve productivity and morale.

Generally, activities in this stage of the consulting process go well if the previous stages have been conducted successfully. Problems here usually result from improper diagnosis, failure to include key people or groups, not focusing improvement efforts on achievable goals, or failure to anticipate the consequences of proposed actions. Critical to the action/intervention stage is another factor, coordination of effort. As stated earlier, actions taken in one department can have ramifications throughout the company. Thus interventions in various parts of the firm need to be coordinated so that changes result in overall improvement and do not produce new problems.

For example, suppose the sales department begins to improve the firm's market share as a result of your intervention. The production units and shipping department should be informed so that they can gear up their efforts to meet the increased demand. Otherwise, the company will find itself with a large group of eager customers and no way to deliver on their orders. A few months of situations like this could set the company back further than it was before. Not only will customers be lost, but the frustration of sales personnel may lead to turnover and lowered morale.

In order to facilitate coordination of effort, most OD consultants meet regularly with the company's top management team and/or interdisciplinary groups of department managers and staff to review progress on OD goals. Such meetings help keep people informed of changes in different units and broaden their perspective on implementation issues. Production staff hear about the unique difficulties of shipping personnel, and shipping personnel can be exposed to the customer relations issues that surface among salespeople. Because of such communication, coordination meetings generally enhance the overall spirit, teamwork, and morale in the entire company. People feel closer to each other and better understand each other's unique work problems.

Step 5: Follow-up and Evaluation.   During this stage of the consulting process, your primary objective would be to monitor the improvement activities instituted earlier, to make sure they were progressing and having the desired impacts on the computer company. Many OD efforts begin with positive intentions and show improvements during the initial stages of implementation when spirit is high. Unfortunately, it is easy for efforts to stall as interventions proceed. Sometimes unforeseen difficulties emerge that get in the way. Other times, staff return to the bad habits that originally got them into trouble.

As a professional OD consultant, you would collect evaluation data regularly to help monitor your progress. You also meet periodically with the com-

One of the values of enlisting the services of OD consultants is that their professional activities—observing, interviewing, gathering groups for conferences—help to break down the barriers between individuals and departments.

puter wizard and others to help them adjust their efforts as needed. Such evaluation data would also help you and the computer company determine when the project should be terminated or returned to the diagnostic and planning stages for further activity.

Evaluating OD activities can be a complicated task given the number of uncontrollable variables involved in the research process and the difficulty of measuring OD goal areas such as employee morale and teamwork. Because of this, evaluation may often be sidestepped by consultants. Follow-up and evaluation are critical, however, because they help reinforce needed changes and give OD efforts a greater chance to succeed. Consultants need to learn appropriate research techniques and work with clients during the entry and planning stages of their work to institute evaluation as a regular part of the consultation process.

Step 6: Termination. The ending of a consultative assignment varies from project to project. Termination may mean an OD consultant's leaving the company altogether or simply stopping this project and beginning something new. For example, our computer wizard might be so pleased with your problem-solving work in his microcomputer division that he invites you to help his new product-line division (e.g., robotics) get started on the right foot. Thus you might write another contract with his new vice-president for robotics and begin the consulting process over again.

During the termination process, a critical goal would be to make sure the wizard and his staff learned from their successes and failures with the effort. The ending of projects is generally a time of reflection, and consultants as well as clients need to take advantage of these opportunities for learning. To this end, most consultants schedule a close-out conference with key individuals and groups from the client organization. During these sessions they review the organizational issues addressed during the project and discuss how progress was made or not made by those involved. If done well, individuals develop keen insight into their behavior from such meetings and internalize the OD process so that they can apply it to future organizational problems.

Conclusions about the Consulting Process. While the consulting process depicted in Figure 5.1 and discussed above appears to be quite simple and neat, it is rarely implemented in such careful order. For example, clients sometimes have predetermined notions about what they want OD consultants to do and hire them hoping to reinforce their agenda. In other situations, the problems encountered are so complex that continual diagnosing and replanning are needed as the intervention proceeds. In still others, politics and other factors cause projects to be terminated abruptly, only to be restarted later when conditions improve.

Whatever complications crop up during an OD project, however, professional consultants generally use the process described here to guide their efforts. Even though they may be implementing a specific intervention technique (for example T-group training) or working through organizational politics, knowledge of the overall process helps them put these activities into proper perspective. In addition, it helps them include important consulting activities such as diagnosing, goal setting, and follow-up to improve the quality of their efforts.

Work Settings

Thus far in this chapter, a general overview of the theory and practice of OD has been provided. As you can see, the job can be exciting and challenging for someone who likes working with people and having an impact on society by improving organizations. But what about career opportunities in the field?

Surprisingly, even in economically troubled times, there typically are good job opportunities available for people trained in OD and related fields. Organizations are increasingly "management-minded" and realize that the improvement of productivity is critical, especially in today's competitive market. Although technological innovations will certainly help, improvements in management and teamwork are critical to the productivity-improvement effort. Thus specialists in these areas who can influence the corporate (or government) "bottom line" are valuable commodities in the marketplace.

Positions in organization development generally fall into two major categories: internal and external consulting. Internal consultants are those hired by private- or public-sector firms to operate within the organizational structure itself. They typically work for the office of the director, or within a personnel or human resource development staff office. In some cases they operate as experienced line managers who contribute to special OD efforts part-time as needed. Whatever the case, internal consultants are an integral part of the organizational culture and have as their principal clients the departments and offices within the organization. Their OD efforts typically include both organization-wide and unit-specific improvement activities.

External consultants, on the other hand, work independently or through a consulting firm to deliver OD services. Their clients typically include a variety of organizations interested in whatever special skills they have to offer. A number of external consultants come from the academic ranks, providing services part-time in conjunction with their university teaching and research. However, increasing numbers of consultants have struck out on their own to develop private consulting practices or to form small consulting firms.

Because of competitiveness in the consulting business, most external practitioners specialize in terms of specific industries (e.g., health care, government agencies, data processing) or specific intervention techniques (e.g., survey feedback, strategic planning, multinational expansions). In addition, most use management development training programs as a way of exposing potential clients to their skills and services. In this way, executives and managers can learn more about what a consultant can offer them before sitting down to explore a contract for OD services.

Whether an OD specialist is functioning as an external or internal consultant, many of the same skills and experiences are required. A study by Warrick and Donovan (1979) identified 40 major skills needed by OD practitioners categorized under four headings: (1) knowledge skills, (2) consulting skills, (3) conceptual skills, and (4) human skills.

1. *Knowledge Skills.* Because OD is such an eclectic field, OD consultants need a knowledge base in a variety of professional disciplines. In addition to their knowledge of OD theories and practices, they need to be familiar with such areas as organization theory, group behavior, learning, motivation, management, business (e.g., accounting, budgeting, etc.), and training technology. In addition, they need to be familiar with current social issues and future trends as they affect organizations.

2. *Consulting Skills.* In order to act on their knowledge base, successful OD practitioners need a variety of consulting skills. These range from the dynamic skills of organizational diagnosis, team building, and conflict resolution to the more mundane but critical skills of proposal writing, marketing programs and ideas, and report writing. Organizations often decide to go or not to go with an OD program on the basis of the impression left by proposals, marketing presentations, and reports. Unless such efforts are concise and useful, the best of consulting interventions can be short-circuited.

3. *Conceptual Skills.* Since OD programs often result in significant changes in organizations, it is important that consultants be able to

think through their actions carefully and anticipate the potential far-reaching impacts of their work. To this end, they should have developed a sound philosophical base regarding human behavior as well as a big-picture sense of organizations in terms of both internal and external dynamics. Specifically, consultants need to appreciate the complex relationships between individuals and between groups within organizations. Furthermore, it is important for them to see an organization within its context—the role the company fills in relation to its suppliers, customers, and competitors. OD consultants also must be skilled in communicating abstract theories and models in ways that are meaningful to a wide range of people, not just to those trained in academic circles. Finally, OD practitioners must be able to innovate, to devise new ways to respond to complex situations, stimulating creativity among those involved in the process.

4. *Human Skills.* Probably most important to an OD consultant are skills related to working with people. The human skills of a professional show clients what to expect from an OD effort in terms of teamwork, caring for people and production, and creating environments for open communication. Effective demonstration of these skills is critical to the success of a client-consultant relationship. Also, OD specialists need human skills such as being a good listener, showing a willingness to confront and take risks, and conducting oneself with integrity. In addition, it is helpful for consultants to be flexible in order to cope with stressful, frustrating situations.

Research and Applications

The intervention techniques used in OD are termed **programmatic interventions** because they seek to exert their effect on organizations as a whole and in some systematic way. Because of the eclectic problem-solving nature of organization development, consultants typically use a variety of intervention techniques in their work. However, certain programmatic interventions have become strongly associated with the practice of OD. This section is devoted to a few of the most popular and useful of these. Descriptions of others can be found in the chapter references.

Programmatic interventions generally consist of a prescribed set of structured activities used in conjunction with the consulting process to help an organization improve its functioning. As a general rule, they are targeted to specific parts of the organization (e.g., individuals, groups, two or more groups, total organization), and specific organizational processes (e.g., leadership, communication, planning, decision making, role definition, etc.). Depending upon the particular approach used, the consultant functions as a trainer, group facilitator, coach/advisor, peacemaker, problem solver, or combination of the above.

Participants in sessions led by organizational development consultants acquire interpersonal skills that carry over to their day-to-day work meetings. The result may be the kind of dynamic interaction of a work team implicit in the photograph.

Team Building

One of the most popular and effective OD interventions used today is called *team building*. This technique is designed to enhance the effectiveness of what many theorists believe to be the most important building block of organizations: the work group. Generally everyone in an organization has to coordinate his or her efforts with others. Teamwork or team spirit is just as important to work groups as they are to college sports teams. People want to feel happy and secure with their superiors and peers, and confident that they are accomplishing their goals as productively as possible. Such teamwork is especially important for management teams because their decisions and actions have a major influence on organizational performance.

Unfortunately, many management teams and work groups do not interact successfully. Either the teams are fraught with conflict among individuals, or there is confusion over what people are trying to accomplish. Team-building interventions consist of group meetings with a consultant designed to address these issues. Generally, the aims of these sessions are to (1) clarify group goals and individual role expectations; (2) examine and improve group interpersonal relationships; and (3) allow group members to practice improved ways of working together. Such meetings are often preceded by diagnostic interviews to help the consultant uncover what the most important group issues are. The group session(s) can then be tailored to the group's most pressing improvement needs.

A variety of activities can be included in such team-building sessions. Sometimes consultants deliver presentations on feedback skills, group decision-making procedures, and conflict-resolution techniques to educate participants and help them develop insight into their behavior. At others they administer and interpret standardized questionnaires to help people learn about their interpersonal work styles and improve communication with one another. In still other sessions, consultants guide group discussions on critical issues facing the team, helping participants explore the nuances of problems and plan for the future. Whatever approach is used, however, team-building efforts are designed to be thought-provoking, action-oriented, and improvement-facilitating. Ideally, people leave with the sense of direction and enthusiasm that will carry over to their daily work.

It is important to note that team-building interventions are useful for healthy as well as unhealthy work groups. Healthy teams often schedule such sessions off-site once or twice a year to get away and relax, rekindle their enthusiasm for working together, and plan for the future. A third-party consultant adds fresh ideas to their discussions and can serve as a "process consultant," observing and pointing out strengths and weaknesses in group behavior that might have gone unnoticed. Team-building sessions are also especially helpful for new groups just getting started or for those undergoing a transition in leadership. The structured activities and discussions allow people to know one another quickly and often prevent problems from developing.

Survey Feedback

As mentioned earlier, **survey feedback** and development programs are currently very popular. Growing from early work at the University of Michigan, they involve the administration of a questionnaire to members of an organization in order to collect data on their functioning. These data are then summarized and fed back to the people who generated the data, with the purpose of helping them diagnose their strengths and weaknesses and develop plans for improvement.

The data collection instruments used in survey feedback efforts vary in their focus, complexity, and standardization. Some focus on employee perceptions and attitudes while others explore observable organizational behaviors and work-production processes. Generally, the instruments developed are complex, including questions covering a variety of theory-based issues related to organizational effectiveness. In some cases, however, consultants develop a few open-ended or tailor-made questions to explore specific issues of known importance to the organization. Whatever particular methods are selected, consultants have a responsibility to use sound data collection techniques and add as much scientific rigor to their results as the situation will allow.

From a process perspective, survey feedback efforts can be very effective in helping link large organizations together "top to bottom." As organizations increase in size, communication becomes more difficult, especially between top management and lower-level staff. During the process of a survey feedback effort, lower-level staff get the opportunity to confidentially let management know what's on their minds. Their individual comments are summarized and fed back to top and middle-level managers for problem solving. In addition, it is customary for all staff members to discuss the data in work-group sessions once top management has had the opportunity to look at the initial reports. Plans can then be made at all levels of the organization for taking corrective action, both on company-wide and work group-specific issues.

Staff can also get involved as needed in the implementation of changes, either within their work groups or as representatives to company-wide task forces.

Conflict Resolution

Frequently, OD consultants are asked to mediate conflict situations within organizations. The problem can be between two individuals, leader and subordinates, or two departments that must work together. Such **conflict resolution** situations are generally very sensitive and potentially explosive, and require all the psychological skills a consultant can draw upon. A third-party peacemaker must be especially skilled in the process of contract building, diagnosis, intervention, and follow-up, being able to help those involved get at the roots of real versus perceived problems, and move at a pace that is constructive given the level of tension established.

One of the most demanding roles of an organizational development professional is that of negotiator. The application of psychological principles to the process of conflict identification and resolution has become a pivotal function of individuals in the field. While strikes are the most obvious and dramatic evidence of relationships gone wrong, conflict of varying kind and degree besets many organizations both public and private.

After the consultant has had the opportunity to meet independently with those involved, a series of problem-solving meetings is generally scheduled. During those meetings the focus is upon getting to know one another better, finding constructive ways to communicate and resolve conflicts, and discussing in depth the points at issue. The consultant acts as teacher, discussion facilitator, and referee during these sessions. Participants are helped to learn about the nature of organizational conflict, to keep their discussions moving constructively, and to control the level of tension in the room. It is very important for consultants to be objective in their behavior and sensitive to the feelings of participants during this process. Positive communication techniques and feedback-sharing help immensely in this regard. Such techniques not only help resolve the conflicts at hand but constitute a model for ways to prevent debilitating conflict in the future.

Strategic Planning

A very popular issue today, given the competitiveness of the business environment, is the issue of **strategic planning.** Many companies are struggling to maintain a niche in the marketplace and keep a few steps ahead of the competition. Furthermore, one of the frequent causes of business failure is poor planning and management. Problem-plagued businesses do not tend to think ahead to accurately predict future conditions in their business environment that can affect their operations. For example, many people have attributed the recent problems of the American auto industry to this very organizational weakness. They claim that U.S. executives neglected to plan early enough for increasing gasoline prices and consumer interest in smaller cars. Because of this, the overall economy has suffered and these manufacturers are now forced to play catch-up with Japanese competitors.

Strategic planning interventions are designed to help top managers overcome these difficulties by exploring environmental trends and company needs five to ten years down the road. Data are generally collected in advance on a variety of business and organizational issues by members of different departments within the firm. Those data are then used by top managers to conduct problem-solving and goal-setting sessions. These sessions in turn result in long-range and short-range strategic goals for the firm, which are passed down to relevant parts of the organization for refinement and implementation.

If conducted well, strategic planning efforts can provide several beneficial effects to organizations. First, they help organization members to focus on the importance of their work in the larger financial sense and to become more goal-directed in their activities. Also, they structure the participation of departmental staff in organization-wide efforts and thus help link the total organization in the same way as survey feedback efforts. Finally, they help top managers make the most of their human resources. Strategic planning can help managers explore both financial and personal issues as they look to the future. The goal is not only to be in the right product and market areas, but to have everyone in the business working together effectively as a closely knit team.

Structural Interventions

The final type of programmatic efforts to be covered in this section are those referred to by French, Bell, and Zawacki (1983) as structural interventions. These are activities designed to improve organizational effectiveness and health through changes in the technology of work, work-flow process, and/or the ways organizations are divided into subunits and managed. Three common structural interventions are termed **organization design, sociotechnical systems,** and **job enrichment and enlargement.**

Organization design interventions are conducted to help companies design the structural characteristics of new divisions or reorganize their old operations. OD consultants assist in the process of examining the tasks to be done, the preferred breakdown and composition of work groups, and the necessary processes, procedures, and linkages between work groups needed to effectively run the organization. In addition, the OD consultant works carefully with the managers and staff affected to make sure the transition to the new organizational structure is a smooth one. Changes of this magnitude affect a number of people. Thus individuals must be consulted and regularly involved to avoid needless mistakes and develop enthusiasm for the effort. OD consultants, with their knowledge of organizational change dynamics, are invaluable in this regard.

Another type of structural intervention, particularly useful in manufacturing industries, is the sociotechnical systems intervention, developed by the Tavistock Institute in London, England. Using the sociotechnical systems approach, OD consultants work with manufacturing units to help them develop a better "fit" between equipment and technologies used and social relationships among the workers involved. For example, sometimes workers' jobs are structured in ways that create isolation and dysfunctional competition among them. Sociotechnical systems interventions attempt to pull workers and management together to explore alternative ways of using equipment and organizing tasks to prevent such problems. In many cases, working conditions and morale can be improved without changing the fundamentals of equipment or the basic structural design of the firm. Rather, the change is made by adjusting work-flow processes and the ways employees interact in relation to the equipment at hand.

Closely related to work with sociotechnical systems are interventions known as job enrichment and job enlargement. In these efforts OD consultants work with managers and staff in problem-solving sessions to redesign staff jobs so that they are more rewarding and motivating. This might mean redefining them by the addition of more relevant and interesting tasks or giving individuals a larger role in planning and controlling their work. Whatever the case, the OD consultant is used to help design jobs that are more productive for the corporation and satisfying to workers.

Case Study of an Office in Transition

In order to better understand the consulting process in action and the use of specific intervention techniques along the way, a case study will be presented. The case involves a state government office of approximately 60 individuals responsible for the financial and programmatic oversight of a variety of social service programs. An OD consultant was originally called in to help the newly appointed Director of Social Services work more effectively with her top management team of four individuals. After only a few weeks in office, the director sensed that her key managers were resistant to her ideas for improving the organization and were undermining her leadership efforts with lower-level staff.

To begin the effort, the OD consultant and director met for approximately three hours to discuss the presenting problems and agree on a course of action. Given the circumstances, both thought that a team-building program would be a good place to begin, but they sensed that it might be difficult to get the necessary commitment of others. To this end, the director agreed to speak with the top managers on her own to express her concerns and let them know she wanted to solve the problems she perceived in a collaborative, unbiased way with the help of a third-party consultant. These sessions went reasonably well, so the consultant was brought in to a weekly management meeting to explain the process of team building and schedule diagnostic interviews with each of those involved.

The diagnostic interviews raised some interesting data and helped the participants feel more comfortable with the process and the consultant. After two weeks the data were fed back to the group at a two-day management team-building session. First of all, it was apparent that the managers were having difficulty accepting their new leader, given the enjoyable working relationship they had had with the director who had just retired. The new director exacerbated these difficulties by frequently criticizing office procedures and suggesting operational changes. Even though individuals agreed that some of these changes would be helpful, the group was reluctant to go along for fear of betraying the previous director and hurting his reputation in the state. Furthermore, a number of the suggested changes were not based on a correct understanding of current work procedures, and some were communicated abruptly and condescendingly during staff briefings and in other public settings.

During the session, the consultant structured discussions so that both sides of the emerging conflict could air their views and get to know one another more positively. As a result, the director apologized for being abrasive and pushing changes too fast. She agreed to improve her communication style, step back, and, with the help of her managers, to get to know the office personnel better. On the other hand, the managers acknowledged that their "grieving" for the previous director was inappropriate and that they needed to give the new person a chance. Also, they recognized the need for improvements in each of their departments and agreed to proceed if changes were approached carefully with the involvement of staff. Finally, the entire group realized that their weekly management meetings were not being conducted as efficiently and productively as they could be. Changes were needed in the agenda and in the way that group problem-solving discussions were handled.

The session ended with an action plan to be worked on by the group during the next six to twelve months. First of all, the consultant would come back to run a one-day workshop on effective meeting skills and sit in on weekly management meetings periodically to offer the group feedback on their behavior. Once a month, the group would review their progress using a group behavior check-list provided by the consultant. In addition, the director would enroll in a one-week communication lab to work on her style. Second, the director would sys-tematically visit each of the departments with her managers to meet the staff and learn about their work, withholding evaluative judgments unless major problems were uncovered. Concurrently, she would meet periodically with each of the managers individually to learn their ideas for office improvements and exchange views on management styles. Following these meetings, the group would reconvene with the consultant to discuss what they had learned and determine how to proceed with any improvement efforts indicated.

Eight months later the group reconvened for a two-day weekend retreat. Based on their individual efforts and periodic feedback from the consultant, the group was working better and everyone felt pleased with their progress. However, they all agreed that changes were needed in their operations, some more fundamental than others. After considerable deliberation the group agreed on two major changes based on the data they had collected: (1) increased automa-tion of financial management practices and (2) improved services to the local program offices for which they had oversight responsibility.

Since these changes would have a major impact on staff in the office, it was decided that the time had come for them to get involved in the OD effort. Management first informed the staff of the rationale for the proposed changes and got their reactions. In order to get more honest feedback, the consultant was used to collect anonymous data from the staff via group interviews. Data were collected not only about employee reactions to the changes themselves, but also about their ideas for how best to proceed with improving the organization. Next, the data from these interviews were consolidated and presented to manage-ment, along with a brief discussion on how the organization change was to be implemented.

As a result of the feedback session, managers agreed to go ahead with the changes, working through the departments affected to make sure that staff were involved appropriately. A contract for new automated equipment was put out for bid with specifications developed by staff from two of the departments. In addition, staff from all of the program oversight departments attended a course on customer relations. After this, each department developed customer-service goals based on what they had learned. Finally, a cross-functional steering com-mittee was established. Composed of several representatives from each depart-ment, this committee helped define problems that the staff perceived in the changes and increased coordination among staff where needed.

During this stage of the effort, the OD consultant's role shifted from diag-noser and intervener to evaluator. Baseline data were collected from a combina-tion of (1) office productivity measures, (2) an employee attitude survey, and (3) a service feedback questionnaire developed for local program personnel. Follow-up measures were then collected periodically to help the office evaluate its progress and take corrective action as needed.

This looks like one of those fully functioning teams that constitute the building blocks of successful organizations. Interventions by organizational development consultants often have the teaching of team-building techniques as a high priority.

After one year of steady progress, an agreement was reached to terminate the consulting effort. A half-day close-out conference was held during which the consultant, director, and management team reviewed their progress over the past two years and reflected on strengths and weaknesses in their behavior during the effort. Even though the formal consulting relationship ended at this time, an agreement was reached to call on the consultant as needed in the future for advice and assistance. All in all, everyone felt that the effort had been a slow, but steady, success. The organization was clearly in better shape, and all employees had learned more about themselves and had improved their management skills in the process.

The Future of Organizational Development

Looking towards the future, it is apparent that there will continue to be an important place for OD consultants in the organizational world. Managers are increasingly aware of people-management issues and the need for opening channels of communication with employees. However, as managers become more sophisticated, the field of OD will also have to evolve and improve. For example, environmental changes in technology, world economics, lifestyles, and so on have already begun to have an impact on the work of consultants. Because of trends in these areas, efforts are increasingly focusing on such issues as the "people-ware" side of computer changes, productivity improvement, cross-cultural business relations, and the problems of two-career families. Undoubtedly, the 1990s and beyond will bring added changes to our culture. Thus the work of OD consultants will require further adjustments. The issues addressed in diagnostic efforts will be different, and the overall change process will have to be refined to more effectively help organizations improve.

One particularly important trend that OD consultants need to be aware of is the emergence of the field known as human resources development, or HRD. Increasingly, large organizations are concerned with the overall recruitment, development, and use of their human resources. Rather than maintaining a traditional personnel department devoted to recruiting, testing, and placement, organizations are creating HRD departments to study a variety of management functions with the goal of improving the organization's overall effectiveness and health. As such multidisciplinary groups are formed, OD consultants will increasingly find themselves working with other HRD specialists from within the organization.

According to the American Society for Training and Development (see McLagen & Bedrick, 1983), HRD units employ professionals to carry out the following types of roles:

1. *Training and Development.* Identifying, assessing, and, through the design and implementation of planned learning programs, helping develop the competencies of managers and staff to perform their current or future responsibilities.

2. *Union/Labor Relations.* Helping ensure effective and healthy union-organization relationships and negotiations.

3. *Employee Assistance.* Providing confidential problem-solving counseling (and preventive workshops) to employees in the areas of career development, alcohol/drug abuse, and work/life difficulties.

4. *Compensation/Benefits.* Assuring that pay systems and benefit packages (e.g., health insurance and retirement programs) are fair, consistent, and motivating.

5. *Personnel Research and Information Systems.* Assuring a personnel database for legal, research, and other purposes.

6. *Selection and Staffing.* Matching people and their career needs and capabilities with the jobs and career paths afforded by the organization.

7. *Human Resources Planning.* Determining the organization's major human resource needs, strategies, and philosophies, laying the groundwork for HRD activities in the near and distant future.

8. *Organization/Job Design.* Defining how tasks, authority, and systems will be organized and integrated across organizational units and in individual jobs to promote organizational effectiveness and health.

9. *Organization Development.* Assuring working relationships between and within units in an organization and helping groups initiate and manage change more effectively.

The emergence of HRD has a number of implications for aspiring OD professionals, some more positive than others. On the positive side, the increasing numbers of professionals in these areas offer broadened career options for psychologists. Individuals who may not have the training and experience to work in OD with upper-level managers can begin to get some of the experience they will need by filling training and other positions in HRD departments. In addition, seasoned OD professionals who are ready for a change can shift to other areas, such as human resource planning or employee counseling, that may be of more interest to them.

Expanding HRD units also offer a host of internal resources that OD specialists can draw upon during their efforts. This is particularly so for external consultants who can use the internal specialists' knowledge of corporate culture to ensure the relevancy of their interventions. In addition, the skills of various HRD professionals can be extremely useful in key stages of the consulting process. For example, the skills of personnel research specialists can be very helpful during the diagnostic phase of an OD effort. Other skill areas may be needed more during the intervention phase, when training, job design or counseling activities are indicated. By using the knowledge of internal HRD resources, the OD professional can speed up the effort and make it more cost-efficient. In addition, such use reinforces the utility of emerging HRD departments to line managers and increases the chances that they will use them in the future to increase the effectiveness of their units.

However, the emergence of HRD does present OD professionals with new challenges. First and foremost are the needs for interdependence and coordination of effort. OD professionals hired as external consultants by line managers will have to coordinate their efforts with those of the in-house HRD staff, who may already be involved in development work with the same department. Obviously, in organizations with established HRD units, OD professionals will no longer be able to work totally on their own. Rather, they will need to support and coordinate closely with HRD staff to avoid confusion for clients and potential duplication of effort.

Increased interdependence among professionals will undoubtedly create its own challenges. OD and HRD specialists will encounter problems over roles and boundaries. Where does OD end and HRD begin, and vice versa? Do some positions carry more status than others, and how does one manage the feelings of those who perceive that their job status is lower than that of others? When should OD and HRD professionals work together and when should they operate independently? Faced with these questions, OD consultants may be looking at a whole new client system — themselves. Odds are that this group of hard-nosed problem-solvers will find a way to work through whatever emerges, that is, if they don't find a way to prevent such problems from occurring in the first place.

Conclusion

This chapter has presented an introduction to organization development. Emerging from early efforts in sensitivity training and survey feedback, OD has evolved into an eclectic set of problem-solving interventions intended to improve organizational effectiveness and health. We defined OD as a change effort that is planned, organization-wide, managed from the top, and designed to increase organizational effectiveness and health.

To illustrate the type of work OD professionals do, a representative model of the consulting process was presented together with a variety of programmatic interventions: team-building programs, survey feedback efforts, conflict resolution interventions, strategic planning activities, and structural interventions.

In order to clarify practical applications of the consulting process, a case study of an OD project with a government agency was discussed. The case pointed out the long-term nature of typical OD consultations as well as the needs for flexibility and follow-up on the part of the consultant. In addition, the case study showed the value of working "top to bottom" in an OD consultation. By beginning with the top management team of the office before moving down to staff, the consultant created a more positive environment for change.

The chapter concluded with a discussion of future trends in the field of organization development. Students should look very closely at the emerging field known as Human Resources Development. HRD specialists play a number of roles similar to those of OD consultants, and there are usually more positions available for entry-level personnel in HRD than in OD. Furthermore, the HRD field is an exciting one that is growing in popularity in both the private and public sectors today.

Glossary

conflict resolution   An organizational change technique where a third party peacemaker intervenes in an organizational conflict.

field theory of social psychology   Lewin's theory asserting that the behavior of an individual is a function of what the theory terms the life space that includes both person and environmental forces.

job enlargement   Increasing the complexity of a job by loading it horizontally and giving a worker a wider variety of tasks to perform.

job enrichment   Increasing the complexity of a job by loading it vertically and giving a worker increased responsibility for the operations involved in performing the job.

organization design   An organizational change technique where the structure of the organization is altered. Analyses include task examination, structuring of work groups, and identification of the necessary processes, procedures, and linkages between work groups needed to effectively run the organization.

programmatic interventions   An intervention that seeks to change an entire organization in some systematic way.

sociotechnical systems   An organizational change technique that requires restructuring of the technology involved in a production process so that individuals and work groups feel more responsible for their work.

strategic planning   An organizational change technique designed to analyze and plan for business trends in the future — typically in the next 5 to 10 years.

survey feedback   An organizational change technique in which questionnaires are first administered to organization members to evaluate their functioning. These data are then fed back to members of the organization to diagnose problems and plan improvements.

team building   An organizational change technique used to enhance coordination and effectiveness within work groups.

6 / Applied Cognitive Psychology

Kenneth R. Paap
New Mexico State University

A relatively new and exciting field of application to develop in psychology is applied cognitive psychology. The field applies cognitive principles to seek solutions to real-world problems. Not only has applied cognitive psychology become a dynamic applied field in its own right, but it has at the same time enriched traditional cognitive psychology considerably.

What Is Applied Cognitive Psychology?

To understand applied cognitive psychology, it is necessary to first understand something about cognitive psychology generally. Defining cognitive psychology is a lot like defining charisma. Although a precise definition of "cognitive" is elusive, psychologists label their colleagues as cognitive or not with the ease of people saying who has charisma and who has not. One reason for this difficulty in definition is that cognitive psychology involves considerably more than the study of the intellect. In addition to basic issues concerning perception, learning, and memory, it extends to neuropsychological problems such as dyslexia and aphasia, clinical problems such as depression, and social problems such as stereotyping. It might be said that cognitive psychologists are mostly concerned with human behavior, yet some of the most exciting work in the area asks if chimpanzees can acquire language, discriminate intention from accident, and appreciate the difference between liars and truthtellers (Premack & Woodruff, 1978).

Cognitive Psychology as Information Processing

Because cognitive psychology covers such a wide range of content areas, it is sometimes equated with the **information-processing** approach to the study of behavior. This is probably the best way to define cognitive psychology, but in doing so one should avoid the assumption of any particular information-processing model and also be aware that exceptions will not be uncommon. A psycholinguist influenced by Noam Chomsky (1980), a developmental psychologist influenced by Jean Piaget (1971), or an ecological psychologist influenced by J.J. Gibson (1979) may well regard themselves as cognitive psychologists while strongly denying that they use the information-processing approach.

Information processing takes its name from its fundamental assumption: behavior can best be understood by analyzing the flow of information from the time it arrives as input to one of the sense organs until it results in an overt response or is stored for future use. The information-processing approach was developed by psychologists who believed that an understanding of complex behavior could not be achieved by simply searching for the rules that bound stimuli to responses. They rejected the idea that an everyday task, such as carrying on a conversation, could be understood in any real sense without specifying the

This chapter was written when the author was a Research Fellow at Birkbeck College, University of London. I would like to thank my colleagues at Birkbeck for their support, particularly Max Coltheart and Glyn Humphreys.

The information-processing system of these students learning sign language at the Model Secondary School for the Deaf in Washington, D.C., substitutes visual for auditory stimuli.

nature of the mental events that intervene between the sound-wave patterns reaching a listener's ear and an eventual response made as listener becomes speaker.

Psychologists who adopted the information-processing approach directed much of their effort toward understanding how information is represented and processed in the brain. Although information-processing models are becoming increasingly influenced by neuropsychology (e.g., Johnson, Partridge, & Lopez, 1983), the theories developed by cognitive psychologists are rarely meant to be literal models of neural functioning. Instead they tend to be more abstract models that describe hypothetical structures and processes in general terms, structures that could be implemented as a neural network in a human brain or as a computer circuit in a robot brain.

It will be helpful to examine in somewhat more detail what it means to say that cognitive psychologists are interested in the way information is represented and processed. Read the word shown in Figure 6.1. Many characteristics of the human information-processor are suggested by this simple demonstration. Consider the different types of information that became available when you looked at the word *butter*. One type is conceptual information. The stimuli impinging on the back of the retina lead to the construction of a perception that you could describe in terms of which parts were figure and which were background, what lines and curves were present, and how they were organized relative to one another. Thus the perceptual processes produced an interpretation of the word

BUTTER

FIGURE 6.1 Different memory structures and mental processes are evident even when simple decisions about simple stimuli are made.

butter that was different from the two-dimensional mosaic of stimulated receptors in the eye, but which corresponded fairly closely to the input.

In addition to seeing a perception, the stimulus is also recognized and comprehended as an English word. This suggests that the information represented in a visual code can be transformed to a more abstract semantic (meaning) code. The semantic codes that permit humans to comprehend words must be part of a **long-term memory** that contains a knowledge of language, often referred to as **semantic memory.** The way information is represented and organized in semantic memory has captured the attention of many cognitive psychologists. Retrieval times may reveal some of this organization. For example, it takes you longer to agree that butter is something that can be eaten than to verify that it is yellow. This may signify something about the way this information has been stored.

Suppose instead of answering questions about butter in general, you are asked whether you have any in your refrigerator right now. Some cognitive psychologists feel that this type of information is stored in a different kind of long-term memory called **episodic memory.** This kind of storage contains information about events that are part of personal experience tied to specific places and particular times. In answering the last question, does it matter how many other things besides butter are in the refrigerator? For most people it doesn't, and this suggests that it is not necessary to search through one's memory of refrigerator contents one item at a time looking for butter.

In contrast, retrieval processes from **short-term memory** seem to follow a step-by-step approach. Imagine that you are going to pick up several specific items at the grocery store. As you are busily rehearsing the items, someone asks if butter is one of them. The longer the list of items you're holding in short-term memory, the longer it will take for you to determine the answer. Searching through short-term memory seems to be a serial comparison operation where the target item, butter in this case, is compared to each item in memory until a match is found or the list is exhausted.

Not only are retrieval processes for short- and long-term memory sometimes different but the structure of the information also seems different. Information in short-term memory seems to be in an acoustic code, compared to the semantic codes in long-term memory that provide information about meaning. This is consistent with the finding that confusion errors in short-term memory tend to be acoustic (recalling *pen* when the word was really *pin*) while those in long-term memory tend to be semantic (recalling *pen* when the word was really *ink*).

Information does not simply flow upstream from the less abstract visual codes to the more abstract acoustic and semantic codes, but also feeds back and can, for example, determine what is seen. Because the sequence BUTTER is familiar to most readers while 13 UTTER is not, the beginning of the stimulus in Figure 6.1 is seen as a letter and not as a number. Since the stimulus is consistent with either organization, it must be the case that the expectations derived from stored knowledge of the world can influence the construction of perceptions. This works to the delight of artists and to the chagrin of a court system that must rely on eyewitness testimony.

Another process that cognitive psychologists have been traditionally interested in is that of **attention.** Selective attention permits directing a limited supply of processing resources (mental effort) to the part of the total environment of current interest. Suppose there are two conversations going on at the same time and you are dividing your attention between them. By selecting the more interesting one and focusing all your attention in that direction, you will be able to comprehend more of the attended conversation. Of course, you will be aware of even less of the content of the unattended conversation. Cognitive psychologists are interested in where and how attention affects the flow of information processing. It is also known that some things require deliberate attention while others do not. Cognitive psychologists are interested in the development of automatic processes that permit experts to perform complex tasks with little effort or do several things at the same time.

Past and Present Approaches to Application

Interest in applied cognitive psychology has increased in part because of dissatisfaction with the approaches of mainstream cognitive psychology. As a result, to appreciate applied cognitive psychology some historical perspective is useful. The development of cognitive psychology in the late 1960s was, in part, a reaction to the theoretical and methodological constraints of traditional stimulus-response psychology. Alan Baddeley (1981), in his paper on the psychology of everyday life, suggests that cognitive psychology can be identified with a willingness to discuss theories that are not specified in formal and minute detail and to examine evidence collected with less rigor than that gathered in highly controlled and artificial laboratory conditions. Although this observation holds true in general, it seems only fair to point out that thousands of laboratory studies were conducted in the 1970s that, in retrospect, were more and more specific tests of the specifics of the cognitive models introduced in the 1960s.

The consequence of having so many cognitive psychologists thrashing away at the same problems came to the author's personal awareness at a national convention at the end of the last decade. In a postconvention conversation, Dominic Massaro, one of the early proponents of information processing (Massaro, 1975), asked what I thought the overall theme of the meetings had been. We looked at each other, nodded, simultaneously sighed, and announced that "everyone is right." Subtle differences in the laboratory conditions could dramatically influence the results in most of the experiments performed, and so there was support for both sides of most issues that cognitive psychologists held close to their hearts. Rather than developing powerful theories with broad applicability, cognitive psychology became enmeshed and preoccupied with theoretical details.

Why was cognitive psychology failing to meet the expectation of its earlier promise? Despite their original intentions, researchers rarely studied the psychology of the rich and complex behavior that makes up everyday life. As Alan Baddeley would put it, too much time was being spent on studying behavior that was easy to investigate instead of that which was important to study. The time was ripe for cognitive psychology to apply its principles to real problems. Don Norman, another of the early proponents of the information-processing approach to cognitive psychology, concluded that attempting to apply theories to real-world phenomena reveals the pitfalls in the theories and leads to improved theoretical understanding (Norman, 1976). He believes that it is essential to the further growth of cognitive psychology for researchers to cycle back and forth between theory and application.

Many other cognitive psychologists share the convictions and hopes expressed by Norman. Wayne Shebilske, a cognitive psychologist interested in learning processes, feels that cycling between theory and application has already produced theoretical advances in his work. For example, his applied goal in developing lesson plans that improve reading instruction (cf. Shebilske & Fisher, in press) led him to study long passages of prose in textbooks. This decision turned out to be crucial from a theoretical point of view. An important issue in research on reading is the extent that time to process text is influenced by higher-level

Children like those in this reading class may be the ultimate beneficiaries of the research of applied cognitive psychologists who have been testing theories about reading. One study disclosed that perceived importance of ideas has a significant effect on time taken to process text.

variables such as perceived importance of ideas, as opposed to lower-order variables such as word frequency. In an applications-oriented experiment using long passages of prose, Shebilske found that the "importance" of an idea has a significant effect that had never been detected in earlier theory-oriented studies using shorter passages. The example shows the importance of testing theories in true-to-life settings rather than relying solely on laboratory materials.

Recently Norman (1981a) wrote that "cognitive engineering [his term for applied cognitive psychology] is a new discipline, so new that it doesn't exist, but it ought to" (p. 150). Since applied cognitive psychology is an emerging discipline, relatively few projects have gone the whole way from theory to application. As Shebilske puts it, "My work is going from theory toward application, but it has not yet arrived. No book adopts our typography; no classroom uses our lesson plan; and no baseball team employs our program during spring training." Nonetheless, an increasing number of cognitive psychologists are moving to applied topics, and the perspective they bring to their work is interesting and distinctive. In the following section the role of the applied cognitive psychologist in the workplace will be considered.

What Do Applied Cognitive Psychologists Do?

Since the field of applied cognitive psychology is new and interdisciplinary, the type of work done by applied cognitive psychologists is varied and as a result is difficult to describe precisely. Many applied cognitive psychologists hold academic appointments in psychology departments and at the same time are affiliated with nonacademic research organizations that bring together scientists from many different fields. For example, Don Norman, whose work is described later in the chapter, is a professor in the psychology department at the University of California at San Diego and also director of the Institute of Cognitive Science at that university. Similarly, the author of this chapter holds joint appointments in the Department of Psychology and the Computing Research Laboratory at New Mexico State University. If the idea of combining teaching with research is appealing, then an academic position in applied cognitive would be an attractive career goal. The current demand for applied cognitive psychologists in academic settings is good relative to several other nonclinical areas in psychology; a Ph.D. is a prerequisite for these positions.

Many applied cognitive psychologists are also working in industry or for government agencies. Employers usually do not distinguish between students trained in applied cognitive and those in engineering psychology. Thus an applied cognitive psychologist may work in a human-factors group involved in product testing and product development. As a member of a development team, the applied cognitive psychologist would be expected to ensure that products will be easy to learn and to use. The psychologist is likely to construct typical tasks typical users must perform and observe what happens when people use a prototype of the product being developed. Features that cause trouble can be identified and modified. Some experiments directly pit one version of a product against alternative versions so that results can be used to decide on the final design of the product. Other experiments may seek to test more general factors that facilitate human performance. Industry supports this type of research despite the fact that the new knowledge may not be applicable for many years. When this chapter's author worked in a software human-factors group at IBM, most of the psychologists spent about two thirds of their time on more immediate product development and testing projects and about one third on theoretical work for long-range planning. This mix is likely to vary considerably from one work setting to the next, but most applied cognitive jobs in industry would involve some combination of both activities.

Applied cognitive psychologists also work in private consulting and research companies such as Bolt, Beranek, & Newman or Perceptronics. In these settings, job activities are similar to those performed in house by psychologists working for large corporations. Consulting firms will typically negotiate a contract with another company or the government for each piece of research to be performed.

Research and Applications

Simply summarizing the achievements of cognitive psychology in different applied areas cannot communicate the exciting dimensions of the field. To convey a more complete picture of the interplay between theory and application, the remainder of the chapter takes an in-depth look at several projects. Each project was selected because it illustrates the application of a major principle derived from the core areas of information-processing theory. Each project was conducted by individuals who would clearly be labeled cognitive psychologists, thereby sharpening distinctions between applied cognitive psychology and the allied field of engineering psychology. Finally, these projects provide good examples of the sophistication needed to construct models useful in the real world. Although a reading of the primary sources would show that the theories and methods are more complicated than presented here, they are described in sufficient detail for you to appreciate what cognitive psychologists do.

Photointerpretation: Schemas and Top-Down Processing in Scene Perception

The work of Irving Biederman and his associates at the State University of New York at Buffalo on the perception of real-world pictures or scenes provides an excellent example of how cognitive psychology can be applied outside the laboratory, and of how this application can advance a basic understanding of perception (Biederman, 1981; Biederman, Mezzanotte, Rabinowitz, Francolini, & Plude, 1981; Biederman, Mezzanotte, & Rabinowitz, 1982). This work investigates factors that influence understanding of scenes when an observer is presented with a novel scene for a very short time. Individuals engage in what may be termed photointerpretation—a generic term used here to refer to any task that involves the need to make judgments about large numbers of real-world scenes. Applications would include everyone from the intelligence officer who scans thousands of photos beamed back from a satellite, to the historian looking through thousands of old newspaper photos, to the TV director who must monitor several camera angles simultaneously.

Perceiving and Comprehending a Scene. Viewers scan scenes in a series of fast hops called **saccades** and relatively longer pauses termed **fixations.** Owing to a mechanism called saccadic suppression, an observer is functionally blind when the eye is moving during saccades. Accordingly, the scene is perceived on the basis of the image that stimulates the retina during each fixation. During this time the observer is fixated on some specific location in the scene for about a quarter of a second (250 msec). Thus the perceived continuity experienced as a scene is scanned is constructed from the contents of several successive fixations.

Continuous scene perception involves the integration of information picked up during each fixation. As a result it is theoretically important to determine what information is acquired from a single fixation and how it is acquired. The importance of studying the single fixation can be more fully appreciated when one realizes that scenes can be comprehended even when they are displayed for only 150 msec (Biederman, 1972). That is about one seventh of a second and quite a bit shorter than the duration of a typical fixation.

Although the problem of what can be seen in a single glance has been a topic of intensive study since the inception of cognitive psychology (cf. Neisser, 1967), the vast majority of these efforts have used either verbal stimuli (e.g., letters, digits, words) or isolated objects. Research in scene perception was not ignored, but most investigators were interested in the order of fixations or in how information from one fixation is integrated with the next. Thus earlier investigators had discovered that when a picture is presented the eye will move from its initial position to a new region that is interesting, unexpected, or important (Loftus & Mackworth, 1978; Yarbus, 1967), but only recently has it been understood how the eye "knows" what is interesting, important, or unexpected on the basis of the first glance.

Perceiving a scene involves more than recognizing the creatures and objects in the scene. For example, it is not sufficient to say that a scene consists of a chair, a person, a desk, and a typewriter. In order to fully comprehend a scene, the relationships between things must be appreciated and cognitively represented. Accordingly, in addition to recognizing the elements pictured, perceiving the scene would involve knowing that the person is seated on the chair, that the chair is in front of the desk, that the typewriter is on the desk, and that, perhaps, the person is typing.

Even more information is available if the scene's setting is familiar to the perceiver. This may lead to the activation of what has been termed a **schema.** Schemas are learned through experience, and in this case may specify the typical organization for a particular type of setting. Schemas are the parts of knowledge of the world that apply to particular settings and permit the generation of expectations about the objects that are likely to be in those settings as well as the relations that should hold among those objects.

Viewing the scene described earlier may lead to the activation of the "office" schema; the perceiver would know that he or she was looking at an office rather than at a concert, a restaurant, or a zoo. The "office" schema is likely to become activated since it fulfills the expectation that offices will contain typewriters, desks, and people (but not violins, menus, or monkeys). It also fulfills the expectation that the person would be seated on the chair and that the typewriter would be placed on the desk, rather than the reverse arrangement.

Bottom-Up Processing.   Scene perception can be analyzed as a set of cognitive processes. A useful understanding of scene perception requires that one know how these processes are related to one another. One intuitive approach is to assume that the processes taken place sequentially, starting from the most basic operations and building to the most complex. This is often referred to as **bottom-up processing,** a sample model of which is depicted in Figure 6.2. In comprehending a line drawing of a real-world scene, one might assume that the most basic process is Feature Detection. The scene is of a large number of lines and curves that occur in various locations, intersect with one another at various angles, and have various orientations. If the first stage of processing involves the detection of these elementary features, the second stage might involve organizing the features into surfaces that belong to single objects, then determining the physical relations among those objects. In Figure 6.2 this second stage is termed Physical Parsing and Arrangement. In the parsing stage, the image is divided into components. As a result of this process, one can determine how many objects are displayed and which ones are on top of or in front of the others.

The third stage, Object Recognition, involves assigning meaning to each of the components that were parsed and arranged in the previous stage. It is at

FIGURE 6.2   Example of a pure bottom-up model for scene recognition.

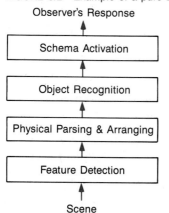

this stage that the observer would know that the object on the left is a type-writer while the one on the right is a telephone.

Finally, the bottom-up model assumes that the highest level of processing, Schema Activation, would occur last. This seems very intuitive — how could one know that the scene was an office unless one had already recognized that the scene contained the right objects?

In summary, the bottom-up account of scene perception holds that a schema is activated only after Physical Parsing and Arrngement and Object Recognition is complete. Biederman (1972) tested this prediction by investigating the effects of different types of distortions or violations in pictures on an observer's ability to find a target object in a briefly displayed scene. First the task and the types of violations that were used will be considered. Once this has been understood, the logic of the test will become clear.

Detecting Objects in Scenes That Contain Violations. Each trial began with the presentation of the name of the target, (e.g., sofa). This indicated to the subject the necessity of reaching a decision as to whether or not the upcoming scene contained a sofa. The target name was followed by a blank screen with only a small dot in the center, which served as a fixation point. Once the subject was fixated, the scene was presented for 150 msec and immediately followed by a location cue and a visual mask. The location cue was a dot that indicated the true location of the target, given that a target had been presented. Location cues were presented whether or not a target was actually present. The visual mask was a scrambled image that terminated the observer's visual memory of the scene and ensured that performance would be based only on the amount of information that could be extracted from the picture in 150 msec. The subject was to state, as rapidly as possible, whether the target had or had not occurred in the scene.

Some of the scenes contained violations while others were normal. For purposes of this analysis, the violations can be classified into two categories: physical violations and schema violations. *Physical violations* consist of "out-of-order" physical elements. Support and interposition violations are most common. Most objects need support, since gravity prohibits them from flying or floating. A scene violates the support relation if there is an object that does not appear to be resting on a surface. The "Goodyear" sofa in Figure 6.3 violates the support relation.

Interposition reflects the constraint that most objects will visually obscure the contours of objects that are behind them. An interposition violation occurs whenever a background object appears to pass through a foreground object. In Figure 6.3, visibility of the part of the building obstructed by the fire hydrant would constitute an interposition violation.

Schema violations reflect constraints imposed by a particular schema on what objects should appear in visual scenes and where they should be located. In Figure 6.3, the sofa violates not only the physical relation of support, but also the schema relation of probability since it is unlikely that one would find a sofa in a street scene. A second schema violation, that of position, is said to

FIGURE 6.3 The sofa in this scene provides an example of both a physical violation (support) and a schema violation (probability). From "Scene Perception: Detecting and Judging Objects Undergoing Relational Violations" by I. Biederman, R. J. Mezzanotte, & J. C. Rabinowitz in *Cognitive Psychology,* 14(2), p. 152.

occur if an object that belongs in a schema is placed in a location where it is unlikely to occur. If the fire hydrant in Figure 6.3 were on top of the mailbox, that would constitute a position violation.

Physical and schema violations should have different effects on the target-detection task. Recall that this task required the subject to decide if the target object was or was not in the scene. According to the bottom-up model shown in Figure 6.2, the information necessary to make that decision becomes available when the Object Recognition stage is complete. Thus performance should be influenced only by processing that occurs at the Object Recognition stage or the stages that come before it.

According to the bottom-up model, physical violations should be quite disruptive to the task of recognizing objects, while schema violations should have little or no effect. The model assumes that objects are recognized only after the physical parsing and arranging is complete. If the scene contains a physical violation, it should take longer to parse the scene (to determine where one object ends and another begins) or to arrange the scene (to determine the spatial relations between the objects). Furthermore, if the physical violation is severe enough and the duration of the scene is brief enough, it may even be impossible to complete this processing. Consequently, the physical violations of support and interposition should increase the likelihood that a target will be missed entirely or, if detected, will take longer to recognize. On the other hand, the schema violations of probability and position should not have an adverse effect, since schemas are not activated until after objects have already been recognized.

Two types of errors can occur in the target-detection task. A "miss" occurs when the target is actually presented in the scene, but the subject incorrectly responds "no." A "false alarm" occurs when the target is not presented and the subject incorrectly responds "yes." For several reasons, only the miss rate will be discussed. First, in Biederman's studies, the percentage of misses was more than twice as great as the percentage of false alarms. Second, from a practical standpoint, a false alarm is less serious than a miss. If subjects performing a photointerpretation task think they see a target, they will stop and take a second look. This should lead to the correction of a false alarm. In contrast, if subjects miss a target that is really there, it is unlikely that they will interrupt their scans to double-check a scene that has already been fixated. Thus a miss is much less likely to be corrected than is a false alarm.

As noted above, the bottom-up model for scene perception predicts that physical violations should be more disruptive than schema violations. A good measure of disruption in the target-detection task is how much the miss rate increases when a scene contains a specific type of violation compared to when the scene is normal. However, contrary to the predictions of the bottom-up model, there is a tendency for schema violations to be more disruptive than physical violations! The schema violations of position and probability increase the miss rate by about 9%, versus only 5% for the physical violation of support. The physical violation of interposition actually leads to a small (about 3%) *decrease* in the miss rate.

Another good measure of disruption is the increase in the time it takes to make a correct response when violations are present. The predictions from the bottom-up model are not supported by such reaction-time data either. Interposition and position violations have little or no effect on the time it takes to make a correct response. A schema violation, probability, slowed decision time by about 18 msec while the physical violation of support actually speeded decision time by about the same amount.

An Alternative Theory: Top-Down Processing. The results of the target-detection task suggest that the bottom-up model is wrong. Physical violations were not more disruptive than schema violations. If anything, the opposite seems to be true. This suggests that schema activation can take place much earlier than was thought possible. Biederman and his colleagues (Biederman et al., 1982) devised a new task, violation detection, to test the possibility that schema activation could actually occur before or at the same time as the processing of physical relations and the recognizing of individual objects.

The sequence of events in the violation-detection task is identical to that for the object-detection task. The trial starts with the name of a target object, indicating which object in the upcoming scene may be undergoing a particular type of violation. For example, some subjects had to decide if the target object violated the position relation. Thus, as soon as the scene was presented, they would have to decide if the target was in a likely place (correct) or an unlikely place (position violation).

It should be clear that schema activation must occur in order for a subject to detect either probability or position violations. The schema represents knowledge about a particular setting. For example, the "street" schema is the repository of expectations concerning what objects are likely to be found in a street and where they should be in relation to each other. Thus one cannot accurately judge that a hydrant doesn't belong on top of a mailbox until the "street" schema has been activated and information is retrieved about the appropriate locations for hydrants and mailboxes.

The results show that schema activation occurs most of the time even when scenes are displayed for only 150 msec. The schema violations of support and probability are correctly detected about 90% of the time. It is also informative to examine the mean reaction times necessary to detect each type of violation. Probability violations were detected the fastest, followed by support, position, and interposition violations. These results are consistent with those obtained in the object-detection task and confirm a new hypothesis that schema activation is an early process in scene perception. The results clearly do not support the bottom-up model; this account would have predicted that the physical violations of support and interposition would have been detected much sooner than the schema violations of position and probability.

On the basis of his experiments, Biederman concludes that the bottom-up model is wrong and that some type of processing, termed **top-down processing,** is needed to account for scene perception. Figure 6.4 shows one possible top-down model that could be used to account for how scenes are perceived. A comparison of Figures 6.2 and 6.4 reveal several differences between the two types of models. Perhaps the most important distinction is that top-down models assume that the earlier activation of higher, more abstract stages of processing can influence the lower levels of processing.

The dotted lines in Figure 6.4 show some potential pathways for top-down processing. Pathway A suggests that the early activation of a particular schema may sometimes facilitate the recognition of individual objects. The presence of this pathway would account for how schema violations could disrupt performance in the target-detection task. Pathways B and C suggest that the physical parsing and arranging of the scene may sometimes be facilitated by the earlier recognition of some objects or the activation of a particular schema. If you look again at the street scene shown in Figure 6.3, you may infer that the perceptual system finds it easier to decide where one object begins and the other ends, or which object is in front of another, if it already knows that the physical relations must fit the "street" schema.

Another difference between the two types of models shown in Figures 6.2 and 6.4 concerns the assumptions about the timing and order of processes. The strict bottom-up model shown in Figure 6.2 assumes a serial order where all the processing at one stage is completed before the next stage begins. Top-down

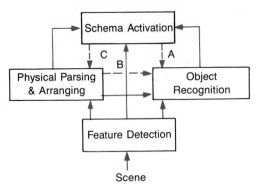

FIGURE 6.4 Example of a model for scene perception that involves top-down processing. Top-down effects are shown as dashed pathways.

models usually assume that some stages occur simultaneously. The specific version shown in Figure 6.4 suggests that Physical Parsing and Arranging, Object Recognition, and Schema Activation can all start to take place at the same time, as soon as input becomes available from the feature-detection process. For example, the solid line that directly links Feature Detection to Schema Activation suggests that schemas can be activated on the basis of feature information alone and that it will not always be necessary to first determine the physical relations or identify individual objects.

Biederman, Mezzanotte, and Rabinowitz (1982) suggest that it may be possible sometimes to recognize a scene (activate a schema) before any individual object is correctly identified. Such data would provide experimental evidence for the direct link between feature detection and schema activation. The existence of the link would account for the fact that schema violations are no harder, and sometimes easier, to detect than physical violations.

In summary, it is apparent that Biederman's decision to study the perception of real-word scenes, as opposed to collections of unrelated objects, has led to some exciting theoretical discoveries. Scenes that contain many objects in a complex array of relationships can be comprehended in a single glance. This suggests that some theories of perception may have overemphasized the importance of eye movement and locomotion in the observer's ability to perceive complex scenes (e.g., Gibson, 1979). Not only can scenes be comprehended in a single glance, but it is also clear that the activation of schemas is an integral part of the perceptual process (i.e., scene perception is a top-down process) and not simply the last stage (i.e., scene perception is not a bottom-up process). The early involvement of schema activation means that knowledge of the world influences one's ability to recognize individual objects and to determine the physical relations in the scene. These discoveries, together with a systematic investigation of their limitations, permit one to apply theory to the improvement of photointerpretation. This is the topic of the final part of this section.

Representative Application: Photointerpretation. One of the most important contributions that cognitive psychologists can make in applied settings is to provide guidelines for the design of new products or systems. Sound theory, rather than intuition, is likely to be the best predictor both of features that should be included in a product or system because they facilitate performance and of those that should be avoided because they will interfere with performance. The development of a new and complex product can be a very expensive process. Accordingly, it becomes very costly to build several versions of the product so that one can be tested against the others to determine which design is best. A good cognitive psychologist should be able to determine in advance that some potential designs are doomed to failure and to suggest how old barriers might be breached.

One obstacle that confronts people engaged in some forms of photointerpretation is the saccadic barrier. The saccadic barrier refers to the fact that as an observer scans a scene, he or she is likely to make only three fixations per second. However, Biederman (1981) suggests that the brain may have the capacity for processing visual information two to three times faster than the eye can feed it in. Thus one way to crack the saccadic barrier and increase the speed of photointerpretation is to present information at extremely rapid rates. For this reason it may be highly practical to design a system for presenting information frame by frame at rates higher than the eye can process. Such a system would allow a large number of images to be rapidly searched for a particular type of information. The operator would be able to control the presentation rate so that frames of potential interest could be "frozen" and looked at more carefully.

The target-detection task that Biederman developed permitted him to investigate three stimulus characteristics that should limit performance in a high-speed system. He found that observers were more likely to miss a target if it was (1) more distant from the fixation point, (2) smaller, and (3) better camouflaged. More important, the experiment also reveals how these stimulus characteristics interact with one another and how they are influenced by the observer's expectations. Would a target that would be difficult to detect in its usual position in an appropriate setting stick out like a sore thumb if it were placed in an unlikely setting? Based on the earlier discussion of the target-detection task, you should anticipate that the "sore thumb" hypothesis is not a good one. A schema violation makes it harder, not easier, to detect the target. Thus, all other things being equal, it would be easier to conceal a missile in Times Square than in a military installation.

Based on their experiment, Biederman and his colleagues were able to develop recommendations for the design of high-speed information displays. Since images at different distances from the eye appear larger or smaller, these guidelines are formulated in a standardized way so that they can be used for systems that project images of various sizes and that have operators at various distances from the image. To give a feeling for the guidelines Biederman and his colleagues recommend, if images are at arm's length and the images are displayed for only

150 msec, observers can detect targets that are at least 2.5 inches in size and that are not more than 4.5 inches from the area of the image that was fixated.

The recommendations to the designers of high-speed information displays are clear. The saccadic barrier can be breached if the operator's primary goal is simply to comprehend the gist or topic of each scene. The barrier can also be exceeded if target detection is important, but targets must be large and in their expected locations. Slower rates of presentation will still be needed if the specific targets that need to be detected are small and sometimes appear in unexpected locations or settings.

Human Computer Interaction: Errors in Response Selection and Execution

The greatest source of difficulty in many real-world tasks is the selection and execution of the appropriate response. A user interacting with a computer system provides an excellent example of a task that consists mostly of trying to select the right response at the right time. Don Norman of the University of California, San Diego, has pioneered the use of error analysis both as a means

Does it seem that floor workers in stock and commodity exchanges do several things at once? Their swift and accurate perception of scenes activates schemas and subschemas of appropriate responses that appear to be almost simultaneous.

to construct a theoretical framework for understanding how people perform multiple or complex tasks and as a way to establish design guidelines minimizing the incidence of error or the effect of an error, once committed (Norman, 1981a,b,c, 1982). One of Norman's colleagues, Gary Perlman, has used Norman's guidelines to develop a new computer-operating system called MENUNIX.

First the general model Norman developed to account for errors in complex tasks and the types of everyday slips of action that led to its construction will be described. Then features of MENUNIX that represent applications of the theory will be presented to demonstrate how applications can follow from theory in this area.

Action Sequences. Norman conceptualizes human performance in terms of **action sequences.** For example, there is an action sequence that determines your driving performance as you make your daily drive from work or school to home. Action sequences are controlled by a set of schemas. In order for you to understand how schemas can control actions, it will be necessary to expand the definition of *schema* that was used in discussing Biederman's work on scene perception. In scene perception, the sensory and semantic aspects of schemas were considered. Schemas, when activated, specify what objects are likely to be present and where they are likely to be relative to other objects. Schemas also may have a motor component consisting of a set of procedures that directs the flow of motor activity. Simply stated, the motor component specifies the appropriate course of action to take whenever you find yourself in a given situation.

Norman assumes that two things determine whether or not the action specified in the motor component of a schema will be triggered. First, actions will be triggered only if the appropriate conditions have been satisfied. For example, as you drive home you must make a right turn from Shannon onto Chamizal. Thus you probably have a Shannon-at-Chamizal schema that specifies what objects are likely to be there and where they are likely to be. This schema also has a motor component that specifies the motor activities leading to a right turn. That action will be taken only if there is a reasonable match between what you see and the sensory-semantic component of your Shannon-at-Chamizal schema.

A reasonable match between the environment and the triggering conditions is not sufficient to actually trigger the action. The schema must also have a sufficiently high level of activation. Activation levels are determined by intentions. If you intend to drive home, this intent highly activates what might be termed the "drive-home super schema," together with all of the lower-level schemas associated with it. This interaction betweeen schemas can be seen in Figure 6.5. If a high level of intention (e.g., an intention to drive home) activates all of the relevant subschemas (e.g., for avoiding obstacles, maintaining speed, braking properly, making the correct turns), and if all of these schemas have well-defined triggering conditions, then all of the required schemas will be triggered as their conditions are satisfied by the environment. Thus the activity that leads to a right turn when the conditions of the Shannon-at-Chamizal schema are satisfied will be triggered only if a previous intention has led to the activation of that schema.

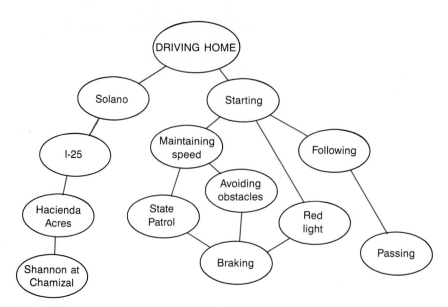

FIGURE 6.5 A partial representation of schemas involved in traveling a familiar route. The intention to drive home activates the appropriate superschema and all the relevant subschema. It also inhibits (not shown) related, but incompatible, schemas, such as those associated with driving to the store.

Causes of Action Slips.   The model for action sequences suggests that there are three fundamental causes of errors or **action slips.** Recall that the model assumes that an intention sets loose a number of related schemas, each with an activation value and a set of trigger conditions. The motor component of a schema is carried out whenever the combination of its activation value and a good match to its trigger conditions reaches a sufficient level. Within this theoretical framework an error can occur because of (1) faulty selection of an intention, (2) faulty activation of schemas, and (3) faulty triggering of schemas.

Since intention is equated with the highest-level schema in an action sequence, the first class of error can be thought of as the selection of a wrong "parent" schema, which will activate a host of unwanted "child" schemas that are just waiting to be triggered. This often results in what may be called *mode errors.* actions that would have been absolutely correct if they had only been performed in the appropriate situation. Two of the mode errors reported by Norman involve an executive who picks up the phone and says "Come in" and the secretary who tries to throw the immovable carriage of a new electronic typewriter. Mode errors involve the flawless execution of an action sequence that, unfortunately, is appropriate for some other circumstance. Since a mode error is caused by the misclassification of the situation, it is likely to occur when the inappropriate situation is very similar to that which is appropriate.

A different type of error is illustrated by the driver who stopped his car and intended to release his seatbelt, but unbuckled his watchband instead. This new type of error was also made by the hostess who put the cake in the refrigerator and popped the salad into the oven. Norman calls these *description errors* and suggests that they, too, are caused primarily by the faulty selection of an intention. They are called description errors rather than mode errors because the intention was incompletely or ambiguously described. Thus, in formulating his intention, the driver did not specify *what* was to be released. The hostess correctly specified the relevant objects (cake and salad) and functions (baking and cooling), but the ordering was improper. The same problem is illustrated by another example from Norman's collection of action slips. An angler in a rowboat in the middle of a lake cleaned a fish and then proceeded to throw the filet overboard and save the bones. In general, description errors are most likely to occur when different actions have similar descriptions (putting things in ovens and putting things in refrigerators) or when different actions are triggered by objects with similar descriptions (e.g., the intrinsic fishiness of the part you want to keep and the part you want to throw away).

The second major set of errors is caused by the faulty activation of schemas. An inappropriate action may occur if an irrelevant schema becomes too highly activated. Conversely, a required action may fail to occur if the activation level in a relevant schema is too low.

Unintentional activation can lead to an action slip despite the fact that the initial situation was correctly classified (no mode error) and all of the correct actions were specified (no description error). One way this can happen is if behavior is captured by a well-formed habit. Schemas associated with habits are likely to seize control of a less familiar action sequence whenever there is a partial overlap between the intended and the habitual action. This is termed a *capture error.* A famous example, attributed to William James, involves the person who is much more used to taking off his clothes to go to bed than to change for a formal dinner. Thus, as he starts to take off his work clothes, he becomes captured by the highly activated habitual schema and finds himself in bed instead of at the dinner table. Another example, described by Norman, involves an ardent card player who counts the pages of a manuscript as they emerge from the copy machine " . . . . 8, 9, 10, jack, queen, king." For newcomers to Britain, driving sometimes seems to be one long series of capture errors, as they look the wrong way at intersections and often turn into oncoming lanes of traffic. A distinctive characteristic of the capture error is that there is nothing in the external environment that contributes to the unintentional activation of the wrong schema.

What have been termed *data-driven errors* are in many ways the reverse of a capture errors. In this case some aspect of the environment is so salient that it leads to the spontaneous activation of an inappropriate schema and the triggering of an unintended act. Consider a colleague who claims to frequently jump into any open elevator and to pull into any empty parking space. Another good example comes from the unfortunate person who borrowed money to operate the soda vending machine, but instead popped the coins into the candy machine that was encountered first.

Failure to perform an appropriate action can sometimes be traced to a loss of activation in a relevant schema, either through decay over time or through interference from intervening actions. Amazingly, a loss of activation at the very highest level of an action sequence seems quite common. Almost everyone has had the experience of purposefully walking to a room only to forget what they intended to do. In addition to forgetting an intention, loss of activation can lead to a failure to trigger an important subschema (forgetting to put water in the coffee pot) or to a repetition of the same schema twice (starting the already running car).

The third general class of action slips is caused by the faulty triggering of action schemas. The error is not caused by the fact that the wrong schemas are active; rather it is caused by failing to trigger them at the right time. *Triggering failures* are errors often caused by competition between two action schemas that are simultaneously activated. Peter often uses a red light as an opportunity to activate his "smoking" schema, while continuing to maintain his general "driving" schema (and more particularly the "red light" subschema). Both completing schemas are "waiting" for a change in the environment: the "smoking" schema is waiting for the lighter to pop out and the "red light" schemas is waiting for a green light. Peter insists tht the click of the lighter is often enough to trigger the schema that leads to depressing the accelerator while the light is still red!

Finally, many action slips will be caused by thoughts unintentionally triggering actions, that is, invoking schemas only meant to be thought, not executed. For example, Norman reports the case of a jogger whose thoughts were focused primarily on counting steps to himself, but who also planned to say hello to a woman down the road. When they were about to cross paths, the woman smiled, said "Good morning," and received a cheery "Thirty-three" in reply. Thoughts may also trigger an inappropriate action when the *result* of the action can be substituted for the action itself. This sounds like doubletalk, but consider this example from a computer operating system. Norman notes that in order to terminate a running program in a particular system you must press the break key. This produces the desired result of stopping the program and also displays the percent symbol (%). Users who become very familiar with this system frequently report typing "%" (the desired result), rather than the break key (the action that leads to the desired result). Because of their design, computer systems frequently offer golden opportunities for this type of error.

Representative Application: The Design of the MENUNIX Operating System. Computer users are often provided with operating systems that have hundreds of available programs, each with many options. This is a mixed blessing, since these riches can make it difficult for novice users to find the programs they need and for experts to get to and use the programs they want. Furthermore, large, complex operating systems are likely to enhance the probability and impact of errors. These problems can be minimized by designing "friendly" interfaces between the human user and existing operating systems. This was

Perlman's goal in developing the interface called MENUNIX. His efforts were guided both by Norman's recent theory on action sequences and by other long-established principles in cognitive psychology.

MENUNIX takes its name, in part, from the word menu. Like the menu in a restaurant, MENUNIX displays a set of options from which users must make selections. This reduces user memory load, since one only has to *recognize* the command that produces the desired action instead of having to recall it. A friendly computer system is like the teacher who gives multiple-choice tests (students only have to recognize the right answer) rather than difficult essay exams (students have to retrieve information from memory). This is especially important since computers are very particular and will not accept close approximations of the right command. Suppose you want to use the computer as a word processor and rewrite the first draft of a paper. You may correctly recall that you need to use the edit program to accomplish this task, but fail to recall whether the specific command is "ed," "edit," "editor," or even "modify." Having a menu permits you to simply recognize the command that fits your intention.

One potential problem with the menu approach is the need for the user to scan through several hundred options looking for the one that is needed. The overall menu must be divided into small menus that permit users to quickly look in the right place. Organizing programs into minimenus of options that have common functions is one step in the right direction. Although this seems like

Operating computers involves a multitude of action choices. The menu approach of a friendly system like MENUNIX offers users a choice of hierarchically arranged options.

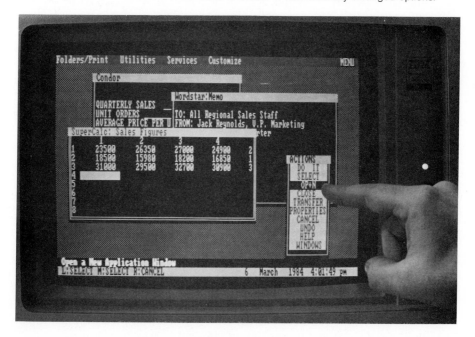

an obvious thing to do, in systems that have been developed over a long period, it is not uncommon to find that programs are organized according to where they were written rather than according to their functions.

Not only does MENUNIX use functional categories to organize its menus, it also organizes them hierarchically. Early and very influential work in cognitive psychology has shown that learning and memory are facilitated when material is placed in hierarchical categories (Miller, 1956; Mandler, 1967). Thus the highest level of MENUNIX has a menu listing various general collections of programs. First the user must indicate an interest: playing computer games, writing a program, composing a manuscript, and so on. For example, if composing a manuscript is selected, the menu that appears lists the programs used in writing: editing, finding spelling errors, looking up words in the dictionary, and various types of style analyses. Selecting the editing option will drop the user into the next lower level of the hierarchy, and the new menu will provide a new set of options: insert new material, delete old material, or move material from one place to another. The hierarchical organization always places the user close to the options likely to be needed. Because the programs at each level are functionally related and of cognitively manageable size, users are reminded of old programs and can easily discover new ones.

Several design features of MENUNIX guard against mode errors. Recall that mode errors occur when a person misclassifies a situation and takes an action that is not appropriate for the current circumstances. Computer users may believe they are at one level of a command hierarchy when, in fact, they are at another. One way of coping with mode errors is to reduce their impact. This can be accomplished by *not* allowing permissible responses at one level to trigger disastrous results at another level.

To clarify what this means, consider what might happen if the system is not designed with mode errors in mind. Suppose you think you are in the "insert new material" mode at the very lowest level of the hierarchy and wish to insert the word *edit* in one particular location in a manuscript. If you have made a mode error and are actually at a higher level, typing the word *edit* will be interpreted as a command that leads to destroying the entire manuscript, and then destroying the ability to use the normal procedure for undoing things you should not have done.

MENUNIX protects users by always providing feedback when new modes are entered. One especially useful type of feedback is called a *prompt*. Prompts ask users for specific information needed to run procedures on the computer. This often permits users to catch budding mode errors, since the prompt will ask for something that does not make sense to the user who thinks he or she is in some other mode. For example, if a user wants to copy information in the computer's memory from one location to another, the "c" key should be pressed to initiate the "copy" command. This first produces the prompt, "files to be copied?" and then the prompt "destination?". The user is provided with a clear idea of what response is required at any time. This reduces the possibility of supplying the right information at the wrong time.

In order to call up a particular file from the computer's memory, many systems make use of what are termed *selectors* — single letters or numbers that are shorthand for the name of the entire file. Mnemonic (first-letter) selectors such as "c" for *copy* or "d" for *debugger* work well for the fairly permanent collections that reside in the program menu, but can't be used to select options from the more temporary file menu, since new files are continually added and deleted. Consequently, files that share the same first letter will often be placed in the same directory, and one doesn't want the added burden of having to scan the directory simply to avoid duplication of the selector. In situations like this, some systems assign letter selectors to files in alphabetical order as the files are added to the directory. However, this scheme is likely to result in data-driven errors. For example, when a user wants a file named "paper" that happens to have been assigned to the selector letter "c," the name could activate the letter "p," and the competing activation will slow the correct response or lead to the incorrect response. This type of error is much less likely to occur in MENUNIX, since files are assigned and then accessed by number selectors. Since the response set (numbers) is from a different domain than the file names (letters), activation caused by the letters of a file name will not interfere with the selection of the correct response.

Recall that activation errors are not always data-driven (caused by stimuli in the external environment), but are sometimes caused by a well-learned action sequence *capturing* a more unusual sequence. Such capture errors occur when schemas shared by both sequences are triggered. Norman illustrates the potential for capture errors with the following example. Consider a user, Professor G., who is in the edit mode and composing a scholarly paper. In a fit of caution she may decide to momentarily interrupt the composing process to transfer what has already been written from temporary memory to a permanent file. To do this she types ":w." The "w" stands for the command, "write to a file." On another rare occasion she may have entered the edit mode to reread and possibly modify a paper written earlier, but decides that no changes are necessary. Accordingly, the professor simply wants to get out of the edit mode so that she can move on to a new task. To do this she must type ":q." The "q" stands for the command "quit the editor".

In contrast to the two cases just set forth, it is much more common to perform both the "w" and "q" commands at the same time. That is, one usually does not quit the edit mode until some changes have been made to the text that should be saved. Thus users form the habit of both writing to a file and quitting the editor with the unitized action sequence ":wq." Consequently, the well-learned action sequence ":wq" is likely to capture and override either the ":w" or ":q" sequences. For example, it is not unusual for users who wish simply to write to the file and continue editing (intending to ":w") to find themselves out of the edit mode and back to a higher level in the command hierarchy as a result of having typed ":wq."

One way to avoid this type of capture error is to avoid overlapping sequences. In fact, new versions of the system just described replace the sequence ":wq" with the command "ZZ". The capture error should be eliminated, since the simple and fairly rare commands of ":w" and ":q" are no longer components of the more common "ZZ" command.

Norman has an excellent idea for avoiding capture errors, and that is to catch them when they are about to occur by having the system flag the critical-choice point where the unusual path must be taken. Computers can force human to monitor the feedback at the appropriate level by waving flags as the critical-choice point is reached. All that is required to build such features into an operating system is a number of prompts that force users to declare an overall intention (particularly when the intention is an unusual one that departs from a normal procedure), as well as knowledge on the designer's part of the critical places at which errors are likely to occur.

Many computer systems breed description errors. Recall that these errors occur when an insufficient specification of the intended action leads to an erroneous act closely related to the desired one. Description errors are likely to occur when it is difficult, at a quick glance, to distinguish one command from another. MENUNIX reduces the probability of desription errors by using single characters to select options, and by always displaying the program menu to the left and the file menu to the right. This avoids the description errors that commonly occur in another system where, at a given moment in time, it is possible to produce three different actions depending upon whether a key is typed in lowercase or uppercase, or as a control key.

The action produced by a particular command is also more readily comprehended in MENUNIX than in many other systems, since each item on the menu consists of both the single character that is used to select the command and a two- or three-word phrase that describes its function. Many systems use only single words, and often these are abbreviated in inconsistent ways that make them very difficult to decode.

Norman provides a good example of how description errors are likely to occur when the name of a command is ambiguous and the obvious hypothesis for its use leads to disaster. For instance, in order to "clean house" and easily delete unwanted files, a special command, termed DSW, was added to a particular system to handle this unusual problem. DSW simply goes through the files one at a time asking the user to respond and indicate whether the file should be kept or not. Users must respond either "yes" or "no" to each file name. The name DSW supplies absolutely no clue as to what the command does, so problems can arise in understanding what a "yes" or "no" response will actually do. Users who do not know the specifics of the command are likely to guess on the basis of an analogy to similar command sequences. In these other command sequences "yes" means "yes I want to keep that file." In DSW "yes" means "yes I want to erase that file" and it is possible that novice users will keep the files they wish to delete and destroy forever all of the files they really intended to keep.

Description errors such as this are likely to occur when the command structure lacks consistency, that is, when the same approach that leads to the attainment of one goal does not work to reach a very similar goal. Norman cautions that a user who lacks some knowledge about how to achieve one operation is likely to try to derive the appropriate sequence of steps by anology to a similar operation that *is* fully understood. This common and very powerful method of human thought can prove disastrous when it is applied to a computer situation.

In summary, many principles derived from cognitive theory have been applied to the design of MENUNIX in order to make it one of the more friendly interfaces between person and computer. Perlman views MENUNIX as part of a continuing project in his study of user-interface design issues. Although a systematic evaluation of the successes and failures of MENUNIX is yet to be made, novices seem to benefit particularly from the hierarchical structure that introduces them to programs as they need them and from the fact that explicit prompts for information must be supplied. Features that experts seem to appreciate include speed and accuracy, since most command sequences consist of only a few keystrokes. Experts also seem to benefit from the many reminders that help prevent the types of action slips discussed by Norman.

Conclusion

Most cognitive psychologists use the information-processing approach in their research. This approach emphasizes the importance of understanding how information is represented and processed in the human brain. Specifically, Chapter 6 looked at the storage and retrieval processes involved in long- and short-term memory and at attention — the process of directing mental effort to the most pressing aspects of the environment. An analysis of reasons why cognitive psychologists have gotten involved in applications led into a discussion of jobs and job settings of applied cognitive psychologists.

In order to better understand the relationship between theory and research in applied cognitive psychology, two specific research programs were studied.

The first described the work of Irving Biederman and his colleagues on the perception of real-world scenes. You learned about bottom-up and top-down processing and saw how top-down processing provides a better account of results in experiments where scenes are presented at extremely rapid rates. You then learned about the applied problem of photointerpretation, noting how the theories and tasks that had been developed to study scene perception were used to develop guidelines for the design of high-speed information display systems.

The second example reviewed a general model that Don Norman has developed to account for errors in complex tasks. It described a number of errors or slips of action that are the basis of the model. As you saw, the MENUNIX computer operating system, developed by one of Norman's colleagues, Gary Perlman, utilized Norman's guidelines in its error-preventing design. Specific features of MENUNIX that correct the action errors noted by Norman were described.

In both examples, it is important to note that when cognitive psychologists apply their models to real-world situations, they not only contribute to the solution of important problems but also advance the theoretical understanding of human performance. Such an approach seems to hold great promise for the future of cognitive psychology.

Glossary

action slips   Schema-related errors in action.

attention   The processes by which we perceive information selectively.

bottom-up processing   According to this theory, the processing of information takes place sequentially, starting from the most basic operations (for example, feature detection) and building to the most complex (for example, schema activation).

episodic memory   Memory for particular events in a person's experience.

fixations   The pauses made by the eye as it scans an image.

information processing   A general theoretical perspective that emphasizes how information is perceived, organized, represented, and processed in the brain.

long-term memory   A memory store of very large size and indefinite duration.

saccades   The movements made by the eye as it progresses from fixation to fixation as it scans an image.

schema   A set of cognitions gathered from past experience that structure one's knowledge of settings, actions, and persons. They permit human beings to generate expectations about what settings, actions, and persons are likely to be and are used to filter and help interpret additional information.

semantic memory   The part of memory that contains one's knowledge of words and concepts.

short-term memory   A memory store of short duration and limited size that holds recently encountered information.

top-down processing   According to this theory, the processing of information does not occur in sequence from the most basic to most complex operations. Rather, schemas are activated early in the process and subsequently influence the other stages of information processing.

7 / Consumer Psychology

John C. Mowen
Oklahoma State University

When Coca-Cola reformulated its main product, the new, sweeter drink was introduced with a flourish of publicity. Consumer reaction was immediate and strong—"What have you done with my Coke?". As company officials later acknowledged, consumer loyalty to traditional Coke was stronger than anticipated. To satisfy consumer demands, original Coke was reintroduced under the name Coca-Cola Classic. What prompted the initial reformulation? Was consumer response a surprise? Had Coca-Cola intended to produce two Cokes from the beginning? These are questions related to perceptions of a product—one of the provinces of consumer psychology.

More generally, the consumer psychologist studies psychological processes underlying the acquisition, consumption, and disposition of goods, services, and ideas. This applied field of study borrows concepts and theories from all branches of psychology. Only in a society of abundance could such a discipline emerge. Indeed, consumer psychology and its closely related discipline, consumer behavior, are mere babes in longevity. The first textbook in the field was published in 1967, and not until 1974 was there a journal devoted to the study of the consumer process—the *Journal of Consumer Research.*

Consumer psychologists are interested in finding solutions to real-world problems. For example, investigators over the past ten years have examined such problem areas as the effects of inflation on consumption (Katona, 1975), the impact of deceptive advertising on adults (Armstrong, Gurol, & Russ, 1979), the general effect of advertising on children (Goldberg & Gorn, 1978), and the use of psychological concepts to encourage the conservation of energy and water.

Not all the individuals doing research in such areas would call themselves consumer psychologists. Social, environmental, experimental, and even physiological psychologists do research on consumer psychology issues. In fact, the investigations carried out by economists, marketers, and sociologists fit within the consumer psychology field.

What Is Consumer Psychology?

One way of introducing you to consumer psychology is to discuss the consumer buying process. Some 95% of the articles written on consumer psychology focus on one or more of the factors that influence consumer buying, so this model provides a good overview of the field. Figure 7.1 depicts a model of the buying process that is an amalgam of several previously developed approaches. The model pictures five major areas of study: consumer inputs, information reception, memory systems, decision making, and personal factors. Each of these will be discussed and research presented to illustrate the function of each area in the buying process.

Consumer Inputs

Consumer inputs are the various stimuli intended to influence consumer behavior. Several general classes of such stimuli may be identified.

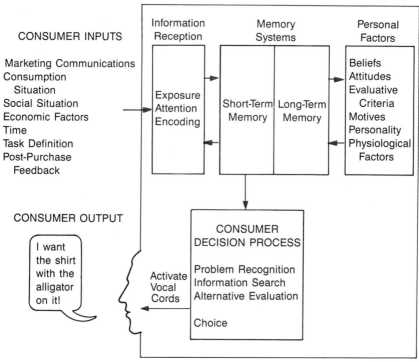

FIGURE 7.1 The diagram displays a model of consumer behavior.

Marketing Appeals. Marketing-oriented inputs are the television and radio commercials, magazine ads, billboards and so forth on which companies spend billions of dollars every year. Also included are product packaging and sales messages of people such as used-car dealers engaged in the personal selling of products and services.

As one would expect, a great deal of effort has gone into developing messages that appeal to consumers. In business, these marketing-oriented inputs are resources for those developing promotional strategies. Research in promotion asks such questions as, How do you gain the consumer's attention? what makes a message effective? or, how can we persuade the consumer to chose our product? Based upon the answers to such questions, promotional material is designed to optimize its impact on the consumer.

Consumption Situation. The consumption situation is a second type of consumer input. Four general situational factors have been identified as influencing consumption. These are physical surroundings, social surroundings, time, and task definition.

Relatively little attention has been given to studying how physical surroundings influence buying behavior. However, even casual observation of the layout of restaurants, shopping malls, and supermarkets indicates that arrangement and appearance have an impact on behavior. One case study found that moving an appetizer-deli section from the back of a grocery store to a heavy traffic area

Does this display of soap attract customers and convince them to buy? Consumer psychologists are interested in all the factors that go into buying decisions—layout, positioning, sound, color, crowds, and many more.

increased its sales by 350%. Areas of study include the influence of the physical layout on mood, shopping patterns, store image, and buying interest. Other physical factors that need more systematic investigation include the influence of music, color, and crowds on buying behavior. Such variables may have potent effects on purchasing behavior. For example, one study found that music judged as pleasurable increased the likelihood that individuals would select a product if the music was played while the product was examined. In contrast, if disliked music was played, individuals would avoid selecting the product with which the music was paired.

The social situation also has a major impact on buying behavior. Studies in this area, predominantly by social psychologists and sociologists, focus on how the presence and perceived expectations of other people influence consumption.

One study performed by Venkatesan (1966) found that the opinions of others dramatically influenced the selection of clothing. The study was modeled after the classic social psychological study of conformity performed by Asch (1956). In the Asch study, individuals were asked to state which of three unequal lines was closest in length to a fourth line. When the test individuals did the task alone, they were inevitably accurate. However, if a number of other people first did the task and chose an incorrect line, a pervasive tendency existed for the test individuals to agree with the group, even when the group was obviously wrong.

Venkatesan replicated the Asch study, but this time the task involved selecting a business suit. Not surprisingly, the subjects preferred the garment chosen by the individuals in the group, even though all suits were identical. Interviews indicated that many of the respondents actually changed their perceptions of the suits after learning of others' preferences.

The study of time, the third situational factor affecting consumer decisions, has been gaining popularity. The rise in the number of fast-food restaurants over the past 20 years is partially explained by a lack of time available for more traditional meals. In addition, with the increase of discretionary time in society, it has become important to learn how people use their leisure hours and how those choices affect their product purchases.

The fourth and final type of consumption situation involves task definition. The type and quality of product bought often depend on the reason for the purchase. If the purchase is a gift, shoppers may act very differently than they do when buying for themselves. The study of gift giving is likely to become increasingly important. One reason is that many department stores earn over 50% of their profits during the Christmas season, when gift giving is the predominant purchase motivation.

Among the situational factors affecting consumer decisions is time. New social patterns in which more people are working longer hours and also spending more time in leisure activities has resulted in a tremendous increase in the number of fast-food restaurants.

Economic Factors.   Economic factors make up the third type of inputs to consumer decisions. In the 1970s a major area of study was the impact of inflation on consumption. Consumers adapted slowly to the knowledge that prices were spiraling upwards in a seemingly endless fashion. Consequently, individuals bought goods as a hedge against inflation and simultaneously saved less of their income. After all, why save when the money will be worth less next year?

During the recession of 1981–1982, a new phenomenon emerged — disinflation. The prices of houses fell, interest rates surged, and people began saving again. For business, short-term implications of these changes in consumption were dramatic. Consumers became discouraged, stopped spending, and the economy went into a severe recession.

A final consumer input is the feedback of the outcomes of previous purchases. Consumer behaviorists have focused on identifying the factors that influence a consumer's satisfaction or dissatisfaction with a purchase. One of the most consistent findings is that consumers are dissatisfied if the product fails to perform as they expected. Thus the experience gained from using a product will provide feedback to a consumer, thereby acting as another type of input for future buying decisions.

Information Reception

A second component of the model of consumer behavior is information reception. Experimental and cognitive psychologists tend to focus on this aspect of the consumption process. Information reception refers to the factors that influence whether the consumer chooses to expose himself to certain stimuli — particularly marketing-oriented inputs — and whether the consumer will pay attention to such stimuli.

In order for consumers to receive a message about a product, they must be exposed to the message. The problem for an advertiser is that consumers can anticipate the reception of messages and choose not to be exposed to them. One outcome of this selection process can be seen during very popular television shows. Workers at the water departments of cities have noted that during commercials of the Super Bowl, the water in storage tanks is rapidly drained. Of course the reason is that viewers are selective and choose commercial time, rather than game time, to go to the bathroom.

Getting the consumer to attend to a message has problems similar to that of exposure. Consumers may engage in selective attention in order to limit the amount of information that they have to process. Perhaps you have experienced this phenomenon at a party. You are interacting with one person but would much rather be talking to a member of the opposite sex nearby. You probably pay more attention to that person while nodding in agreement to every word spoken by the person with whom you are ostensibly interacting.

The problem addressed by many consumer psychologists concerns how to create messages that will engage the consumer's attention. One finding is directly related to this problem. It has been suggested that two types of attention exist — voluntary and involuntary.

Voluntary attention allocates mental effort to current goals and plans. Thus a consumer interested in buying a car with good gas mileage will generally pay attention to such information. In this case, then, a readiness exists to process information concerning auto gas mileage. Advertisers attempt to take advantage of such voluntary attention processes by determining the goals and plans of consumers who form their target market. They then gear their advertising so that the messages and images created tap into these goals and plans.

Involuntary attention is a response to stimuli that are not a part of the plans and goals of the consumer. For example, events that depart from expectations will tend to catch an individual's notice. A novel advertisement, a big price reduction, or even loud music are things that may occur unexpectedly and attract a consumer. Hunger or fatigue are other types of stimuli causing involuntary attention.

It should be noted that both voluntary and involuntary attention are processes that result in active involvement of the thought processes of a consumer. Evidence exists, however, that consumers can learn about the environment without such active information processing. Called **low-involvement learning,** the process seems to result in a consumer's learning about products without consciously allocating thought processes to the stimuli.

Krugman (1965) suggested that much of television advertising has its effects through such a low-involvement process. One aspect of low-involvement learning is reminiscent of the charges leveled by Vance Packard that the media were composed of "hidden persuaders." Krugman has suggested that consumer defenses are lowered when this type of learning occurs. Thus messages are received relatively uncritically. The tendency to analyze persuasive messages is lowered, and consumers may later buy products for reasons that have not been well thought through.

Consumer psychologists are also interested in the measurement of attention. In particular, they would like to know which aspects of messages tend to attract attention and on which parts of a single message consumers focus. A number of types of instruments have been developed to assess attention. Currently, devices designed to measure pupil dilation and to track eye movements are popular. It has been shown that pupils grow larger when information processing is occurring. Because information processing is an indication of attention, a change in pupil size indicates that a consumer is focusing on a stimulus.

The idea that pupil size is related to attention has anecdotal support. Individuals have reported that shrewd traders of goods, especially in the Middle and Far East, watch the eyes of prospective buyers. When the pupils of the customer's eyes enlarge, it is supposed to indicate interest in the item on which they are focusing. It is rumored that when merchants see the "big" eyes, they will bargain much harder.

Individuals in the print advertising area are also interested in determining on which parts of their ads consumers focus. Elaborate eye-tracking devices have been developed to identify exactly which features of an ad capture the consumer's attention.

Memory Systems

Memory systems play a key role in the model of consumer behavior. Generally, one can say that the consumer psychologist borrows the theories and techniques developed by the cognitive psychologist and applies them to consumer problems. Memory can be defined as the process of encoding, storing, and retrieving information.

While a number of views exist as to how memory operates, one commonly held perspective is that it consists of two types of storage: short term, which is associated with active thought process, and long term, where information is permanently held. (This subject was discussed in Chapter 6.) Short-term memory is viewed as having limited storage capacity, roughly seven plus or minus two pieces of information. On the other hand, long-term memory appears to have an unlimited storage capacity. However, it takes substantial effort to place information into long-term memory and then to retrieve it at a later time.

Consumer psychologists are particularly interested in learning how consumers place information received about a product into long-term memory. The consumer is bombarded with hundreds of messages every day about products. Some of the messages are attended to and then stored, while others are ignored and never placed into long-term memory. One finding is that repeated messages have a greater likelihood of being encoded (Sawyer, 1974).

Other research by cognitive psychologists has shown that changes in context can affect the ability of people to retrieve information from long-term memory. It is likely that the same phenomenon operates in the consumer area. That is, when consumers view advertisements, they see the product in a certain type of package, perhaps associated with a particular celebrity endorser, and being used with particular other products. If these images are also used in the store, they may increase the likelihood that the advertisement will be recalled and the product purchased. The Mr. Whipple commercials for Charmin ™ tissue are a case in point. The commercials are highly effective in gaining attention. Through the use of displays and packaging containing Mr. Whipple's picture and admonition, "Don't squeeze the Charmin," the ad is instantly brought back to mind.

Consumer Decision Making

Identifying how consumers make decisions about the products they buy has received perhaps more attention from consumer psychologists over the past several years than any other topic. Generally, a consumer is viewed as going through a series of steps in the decision process. These steps are *problem recognition, information search, alternative evaluation,* and *product choice.*

Problem recognition occurs when the individual perceives that a difference exists between a *desired state* and an *actual state.* The analysis of problem recognition then focuses naturally on factors that influence actual and desired states. Dissatisfaction with the actual state could develop when a product gets old or out of style. It could also result from running out of a product, like gasoline.

Marketing specialists rate "reference group influence" as a major factor in the buying decisions of teenagers.

In addition, circumstances could change. A person could graduate from college, have a child, or inherit a fortune. Any of these things can make consumers dissatisfied with what they have.

The desired state is influenced by such things as the need for novelty, reference group influence, marketing efforts, and making other purchases. For example, buying a house may produce a need for new furniture. The desired state of affairs has changed.

Once a problem is identified, a consumer will go through a search process to identify a set of products that will potentially remedy the problem. Actually, two types of search exist. Internal search refers to a search of long-term memory for products that may solve the problem. External search involves looking through newspapers and magazines, talking to friends, and visiting retailers.

Alternative evaluation refers to the process of evaluating the various brands of a product that would seem to solve the identified problem. A number of models of alternative evaluation have been developed. Social psychologists have in particular been involved in this area because of its close relation to attitude formation and change.

The evaluation of a brand may be viewed as a process in which a consumer rates the brand on a number of attributes, at the same time assessing the importance of the various attributes. Attributes are the various features of a product in which a consumer may be interested. For example, consumers shopping for a car are interested in such attributes as handling, gas mileage, price, styling, and so forth. Not all attributes carry the same weight. A macho 19-year-old may consider power extremely important in a car, while his grandfather might rate the importance of gas mileage very highly.

In this evaluation process an attitude towards the brand is formed. One way to measure attitude is by having consumers rate a product's standing in each category and then multiply each rating by the importance of the attribute. For the consumer psychologist, then, attitude is the sum of all of the importance ratings multiplied by the belief ratings.

The final step in the consumer decision process is brand choice. Currently, many psychologists consider the choice process to involve the application of what are called **heuristics** (*Heuristic* means "helping to discover or learn."). Psychologists apply the term to the thought process by which people choose among alternatives. The idea that consumers use heuristics comes from the recognition that active memory is limited and that as a consequence consumers cannot cognitively process the thousands of pieces of information they may have about a set of competing products.

A number of different types of heuristics have been proposed as devices used by consumers in different situations. For example, it has been suggested that in low-involvement choice situations consumers may use a choice heuristic labeled "affect referral." This means choosing a brand the buyer feels best about. The idea is that because a purchase is not particularly important, consumers choose not to think deeply about it and make an expeditious selection based on a general "feeling."

Another type of choice heuristic is the lexicographic aproach in which consumers are assumed to have first ordered the attributes in terms of their importance. Alternatives are compared on the most important attribute, and the brand with the highest rating on that attribute is then chosen. If a tie between two brands occurs, the next most important attribute is used. The process continues until only one brand remains. Research by Wright (1975) has shown that consumers using the lexicographic approach tend to process information more accurately than if they use a number of other choice heuristics.

Personal Factors

A separate category of factors are personal qualities that make each person unique, best viewed as general response tendencies housed in long-term memory. In this group are such concepts as personality, beliefs, motives, attitudes, and the evaluative criteria that an individual uses to compare products. Physiological states are another personal factor that influences purchase decisions. Thus hunger, thirst, and fatigue may well affect the types of products a consumer buys.

These personal factors influence all of the other processes discussed so far. For example, attitudes toward a particular television show influence whether or not a person will watch it. Such selective exposure results in either seeing or not seeing commercials shown during the course of the show. In a similar way, basic motivating factors influence whether or not people attend to stimuli. McClelland (1956) has found that individuals are motivated by three main factors — the need for achievement, power, and affiliation. Companies advertising products that appeal to individuals having a high need for affiliation often show groups of individuals having fun while using the product. Commercials of soft-drink manufacturers frequently use such a strategy. Their target market is predominantly young people who are highly motivated by the need to be liked by others, the need for affiliation.

In assessing the influence of personal factors in the consumer behavior area, psychologists have gradually moved away from using traditional measures found in the psychological literature. The personality scales of clinical psychology are particularly avoided. Their focus on personality disorders appears to contribute little to the understanding of consumption.

During the 1950s, constructs borrowed from Freud's psychoanalytic theory were very popular with consumer psychologists and supported what was called motivational research. The idea was to embed in television and print advertising various symbols that appealed to consumers' unconscious motivations. Motivational researchers also interpreted why consumers act as they do: for women adding an egg to a cake mix symbolizes an effort to achieve motherhood; people dislike prunes because they are reminiscent of old people; a man buys a convertible as a substitute mistress.

The Freudian approach to consumer behavior is generally held in ill-repute today; however, one ocasionally hears of charges that companies embed pictures of various parts of the human anatomy in the ice cubes found in liquor commercials. Indeed, a game which can bring titters at a cocktail party is to closely scrutinize the ice cubes in the print ads of liquor manufacturers for assorted bosoms and other anatomical parts.

Currently, the personality research done by consumer psychologists focuses on identifying specific sets of attitudes, opinions, and interests that predict liking and preference for certain products. Called psychographics, the approach involves the detailed study of consumers who either like or dislike a product. The characteristics of consumers who like the product are used to develop a profile of the target market of the firm. Based upon the profile, strategies for the development of advertisements, new products, pricing, and distribution can be identified.

An example of psychographics may be found in a study by Sadalla and Burroughs (1981). These researchers investigated the eating preferences of individuals and how these preferences related to their opinions, interests, and activities. They classified foods into five categories—vegetarian, gourmet, health, fast, and synthetic. (Synthetic foods are high-technology items like processed bacon, instant eggs, instant breakfast drinks, and highly processed cheese snacks.) They then identified individuals whose food preferences could be classified as falling into one of the five categories. These same individuals then rated themselves on a variety of characteristics. In addition, another group of subjects described what they thought vegetarians, gourmets, high-techers, and so on would be like.

The results were surprising. The way people rated themselves was in close agreement with the way others rated them. Vegetarians were seen as noncompetitive, sexual, and liking crafts and folk dancing. Gourmets were perceived as using drugs, living alone, and liberal. Their hobbies were glamour sports and gambling. Fast-food devotees were religious, logical, conservative, and polyester. They seemed to have no favorite hobbies, and their preferred food was fast-food hamburgers.

The above information can be extremely useful to a firm. For example, the study indicated that a person who really likes synthetic food (e.g., bacony nuggets) also is logical, religious, and conservative. This information can be used in developing advertisements and packaging.

In summary, this model of the consumer buying process has explored the nature of the questions consumer psychologists generally ask. But what do consumer psychologists do on the job and where do they work? These questions are considered in the next section.

What Do Consumer Psychologists Do?

Consumer psychologists working in different settings may perform very different tasks on a day-to-day basis, but they share a common belief in the importance of marketing as organizations exchange goods and services for consumers' money. Within business organizations, marketing ensures that products appropriate to the needs or wants of some group of consumers are produced and sold efficiently. The primary role of research in marketing is to provide information that allows consumers and products to be matched effectively. The activities of consumer psychologists can be considered within the marketing framework.

Job Activities

In accomplishing their work, consumer psychologists are sensitive to a number of factors that affect the marketing process. The technological explosion that began after World War II and seems to gain speed daily has resulted in a vast number of new products to be established in the marketplace. Consumer psychologists seek to provide management with information concerning what attributes new products should have in order to be successful. To do this, information about consumer preferences for particular product ideas is sought as well as broader information about consumer values and attitudes.

In addition to the introduction of new products, rapidly changing market conditions also require constant product reformulation and improvement. Consumer psychologists are responsible for assuring that product "improvements" will be perceived as such by consumers and that reformulations of products will be acceptable (remember the New Coke story).

Accompanying the increase in the introducton of new products has been an increase in **segmentation** as a marketing strategy. Marketers realize that consumers are not all alike and that selling the same product to all individuals will not be as efficient as identifying a particular group of consumers and targeting advertising and product promotion to that group. Furthermore, by identifying the needs and desires of subgroups of the population, it is possible to develop specific products to cater to the specialized needs of these segments. Given this marketing strategy, a major responsibility of the consumer psychologist is to identify these marketing segments by considering the needs, wishes, desires, attitudes, and lifestyles of consumers.

In recent years the consumer protection movement has gained strength. This growth is reflected in an increase in the activities of private consumer groups and governmental regulatory agencies such as the Federal Trade Commission, the Federal Communications Commission, and the Food and Drug Administration. In all of these groups consumer psychologists bear responsibility for discovering how various products and the marketing appeals used to sell them are perceived by consumers. When gaps exist between consumer perceptions of products and what the products can actually deliver, legislative control may be appropriate to protect consumers. Consumer psychologists may be involved in determining the public's reaction to proposed legislation. In order to further protect and inform consumers, various sources of consumer information are available such as unit pricing, nutritional labeling, and energy conservation labeling. Consumer reaction to these sources of information, also critical to an assessment of their effectiveness, is the domain of consumer psychologists

Work Settings

Consumer psychologists may be found working in academic, industrial, and governmental settings. Academic positions in consumer psychology are typically found within the marketing departments of business schools in universities. An individual in such a position would typically teach at the graduate and/or undergraduate level and perform research to develop or refine marketing principles and buyer behavior. In addition, consumer psychologists in academic positions may consult with industrial organizations on problems in which they have special expertise. Such consulting is useful because it requires teachers to confront real-world research problems and allows them to gain valuable experience that can then be shared with students.

A second area where consumer psychologists may be employed is in industrial settings. Here the research is undertaken primarily to fulfill corporate objectives by ultimately providing some monetary payoff to the organization. Industrial settings employing consumer psychologists are quite varied, ranging from companies marketing consumer products to advertising agencies to survey research firms. Representative activities of psychologists working for corporations producing consumer goods would include the following: tracking the performance of existing brands, identifying market segments that are important to the product in question, testing reformulations of these products as they are modified over time, and aiding in the development of new products.

Psychologists working for advertising agencies are involved in developing and testing the persuasive communications that the agency prepares for its clients. Since media space is extremely expensive, many agencies feel that the costs of pretesting are warranted and thoroughly evaluate potential advertising messages

GREAT BED R

DAILY NEWS

The insights and techniques developed by consumer psychologists can be applied to fundraising efforts of public-service organizations such as foundations for medical research, as well as to strictly commercial ventures.

to make sure they will appeal to the targeted consumer groups. Consumer psychologists working in the industrial area might also work in a market research firm. Such firms typically provide services to clients that larger manufacturing corporations would provide in-house. Market research firms design and conduct surveys, perform experiments, and analyze data on a consulting basis. Psychologists operating in this environment typically divide their time between several different projects for different clients.

Consumer psychologists also find employment in government agencies and nonprofit organizations. The consumer movement has caused an increased demand for consumer information and education, and as a result a limited number of psychologists are employed by government agencies to aid in the development, dissemination, and evaluation of this type of material. An additional area of employment for consumer psychologists is in nonprofit organizations. As these institutions have begun to use marketing techniques to increase their fundraising efficency, a new area of application has opened to consumer psychologists.

Research and Applications

This section of the chapter focuses in more depth on three separate areas of recent work in consumer psychology. The first section will discuss work indicating that brain lateralization may influence buying behaviors. The second reviews the research on the effects of advertising on children. The third section talks about some fascinating studies on how norms can be used to make consumers say yes.

Split Brains: A Psychological Delicacy

The idea that hemispheres of the human brain are somewhat specialized has been known for many years. Sensations from the left side of the body, the left ear, and the left field of view go to the right side of the brain. Conversely, sensations from the right side of the body go to the left hemisphere of the brain. The two hemispheres are almost identical and are connected by fibers called the *corpus callosum.* In effect the corpus callosum allows the two sides of the brain to communicate.

Much of the research on brain lateralization has been performed on individuals who for some reason have had their corpus callosum severed. In most respects these individuals appear normal. In only highly specialized tasks do anomalies in behavior appear.

Lindzay and Norman (1977) discussed one such example. Mr. X., whose corpus callosum has been cut, is given the task of identifying a common object, say a pair of scissors. But first a mask is placed over each of his eyes so that either his left or right field of vision is blocked. If the scissors are placed into his left hand and his left field of vision is blocked, he can identify the scissors. However, if the scissors are placed into the same hand and his right field of vision is blocked, Mr. X. cannot identify what is in his hand.

This peculiar finding occurs because in most cases the speech center is found in the left hemisphere of the brain. Thus if the image of the scissors is blocked from the left brain, either by placing the scissors in the left hand or by covering the right visual field, the speech center does not have access to the information that scissors are present.

Interestingly, if the right visual field is blocked and scissors are shown to the person, he will be able to pick up with his left hand another pair of scissors, even though he cannot identify them verbally. Researchers have concluded from this that the right hemisphere, while nonverbal, is able to carry out some symbolic information processing (Hansen, 1981).

The research on brain lateralization has largely been performed on patients suffering from extreme cases of epilepsy. Hansen (1981) reported that such cases have been successfully treated by cutting through the corpus callosum, thereby disconnecting the brain halves. As a result of this procedure, a seizure will be less likely to spread from one side of the brain to another. Other research has been conducted in U.S.S.R. (Deglin, 1976). There, investigators have done electroconvulsive therapy in which one side of the brain is momentarily put out of function by an electric shock. The researchers then studied the behavior of patients with only half of the brain functioning.

A number of individuals have discussed the differences between left- and right-brain-dominated processes. The left hemisphere appears to dominate speech, arithmetic, and symbolic information handling. The left brain seems more logical, causal, pictorial, and argumentative (Ornstein, 1971). In contrast, right-brain processes are more diffuse, spatial, intuitive, and musical. Right-brain-dominated people tend to be more influenced by spatial, imaginative impressions (Lundsgaard, 1978).

Bogen (1977) argued that the brain lateralization phenomenon may account for many of the dichotomies in human behavior described by philosophers and psychologists. Thus Maslow talked of the rational versus the intuitive, Hilgaard of the realistic versus the intuitive, Hobbes of the directed versus the free, and Freud of the secondary versus the primary. In each case, the first descriptor matches the left-brain functioning and the second matches right-brain functioning. In summary, it appears that in normal individuals neither hemisphere monopolizes the handling of different types of information. Rather, it appears to be a matter of relative dominance (Hansen, 1981).

The work done in consumer psychology on brain lateralization has been limited and much of it is speculative. Nonetheless, the potential contributions of the research area are substantial. The areas of application are in attention, memory, choice, and individual differences.

Hansen (1981) wrote the first major article in the consumer psychology literature dealing with brain lateralization. He speculated that the phenomenon may be involved in attention processes. Referring to the work by Broadbent (1977), Hansen suggested that the right brain may participate in an early stage of attention in which incoming information is globally analyzed. The process occurs without the conscious use of psychic energy to analyze the stimulus. In contrast, left-brain processes may be required to verify exactly what the stimulus is. This verification process requires involvement on the part of the consumer. These concepts suggested to Hansen the idea that trademarks, brand names, and so forth could have their impact through right-brain functioning.

Closely related to attention is the role of involvement and the use of right-brain versus left-brain processing. Krugman (1965) suggested that consumers processed information differently depending upon their involvement with the product. In 1977, Krugman went a step further to suggest that low-involvement situations resulted in right-brain processing and that high-involvement situations activated left-brain processing.

The limited research available on the role of involvement in consumer behavior is generally consistent with the Krugman suggestion. For example, it appears that in low-involvement situations consumers seem not to form attitudes about a product prior to buying it. This finding is consistent with right-brain functioning. Because the left brain has not been involved in the decision process, conscious consideration of the product would not have taken place and as a consequence no attitude has been formed.

From these concepts the idea emerges that the media through which a message is transmitted should match the involvement of the consumer. Thus when consumers are highly motivated to make a correct product choice, they are likely to be in a left-brain processing mode. As such, the media choice should be one in which complex messages are easily transmitted, such as a magazine. In contrast, when product involvement is low, as in the case of toilet tissue, it may be best to use a highly pictorial medium that produces repetition of the message and complements a low-motivation buying decision. Television has been suggested by Krugman as such a medium.

Whether the right or left brain is activated may also influence choice behavior. Olshavsky and Granbois (1979) found that in many purchases an active decision process never really occurred. Consumers in many situations seem to buy a product without giving any thought to the purchase. These unthinking purchases seem to occur frequently where brand loyalty exists. Such behavior is consistent with right-brain functioning in that only simple recognition of an alternative is involved.

Also related to choice behavior is the work by Zajonc (1980). A social psychologist, in the past 15 years Zajonc has shown in numerous contexts that mere exposure to a stimulus can increase liking for the object. The idea is that being exposed to something on numerous occasions results in a positive reaction to it. In a 1980 study Zajonc showed that subjects did not even have to be aware of the exposure for the increased liking to occur.

Hansen (1981) proposed that these findings are also consistent with right-brain functioning. The mere exposure effect seems to occur in low-involvement situations and to result from repeated visual or auditory contact with the object in question. The extension of Zajonc's work to consumer behavior and advertising is direct. By repeatedly showing the product on television, the consumer may come to perceive the product more favorably without being aware of it, because awareness occurs in the left brain.

Finally, emotional conditioning may occur in a similar manner. Some authors have suggested that emotional appeals to buy a product are effective in low-involvement situations. By linking a product to a popular celebrity, to an effective emotional appeal, or to some other positive product, the right brain may become activated and later influence choice without conscious awareness.

The possibility that individual differences may exist in hemispheral dominance has large implications for advertising. Lindzay and Norman (1977) speculated that individuals may be more or less right- or left-brain dominated. To the extent that their proposal is true, advertisers would have to match the type of appeal, not only to the medium, but also to a target market that is either right- or left-brained.

An observation that the author has made is relevant to this idea. A number of programs sponsored by the federal government to persuade people to stop smoking, use seatbelts, and so forth tend to rely on left-brain messages. That is, the advertisement is loaded with good reasons not to smoke, litter, or take drugs. One would expect this type of informational appeal because the originators of the programs are thoughtful people who are probably left-brain-dominated. However, it may be that a large segment of their target market is right-brain-oriented. Such individuals may be more intuitive and pictorial, and not likely to be influenced by complex, logical messages. The result may be messages that are never attended to and processed by the individuals for whom they were developed.

Children and Advertising

Research in the sciences and in particular in the social sciences has some type of value structure underlying it. The fact that personal values influence researchers' work, however, does not mean that these individuals are somehow biased. Values generally influence science through their impact on the topics chosen for study.

In consumer psychology one can identify three general approaches to the field. In one a researcher tries to develop information on the consumption process in order to assist manufacturers in their marketing efforts. The value system here

In studying TV advertising directed at children, researchers may investigate the extent to which youngsters understand advertisements, the degree to which commercials influence their product preferences, and the role this kind of advertising plays in child-parent relationships.

is "pro business." The second approach involves investigating consumption in order to test the generality of theories developed in other areas of psychology. One might call this an "academic" value system. A third type of researcher is interested in the consumption process in order to develop laws and regulations that may be promulgated to protect the consumer from big business and generally to improve the quality of life. The value system represented might be labeled "pro regulation." Research focusing on the impact of television commercials on children has been derived partially from the third value structure.

The idea that psychological research can be used to develop laws and regulations is relatively new. The area is called "public policy." In children's advertising the focus has been on identifying the extent that children understand advertisements, that advertisements influence children's product preferences, and that commercials cause friction between children and their parents.

The Case Against Children's Ads.   A variety of charges have been leveled against children's advertising. Some have compared children's ads to Nazi propaganda methods. However, such name-calling is generally ineffective. The more potent criticisms are highly specific. One is that children simply are exposed to too many ads. Estimates are that the average child sees 20,000 commercials per year, 1,000 of which are on Saturday morning (Action for Children Television, 1977). In these ads the major type of product seen by children tends to be highly sugared food which may carry long-term risks to dental health.

A second general criticism is that children under 8 are very trusting of commercials. Thus ads are viewed as shaping children's desires for products, irrespective of the merits of the product. The ads may also confuse children, take advantage of their misunderstanding, and contribute to the development of poor decision-making skills by focusing on irrelevant product attributes. Disappointment, irritation and conflict with parents may result when children's TV-induced desires are not fulfilled.

A third criticism of television concerns its possible effects on intellectual and emotional development. Marie Winn (1977), a major proponent of this view, argued that television alters a child's brain functioning. Linking the problem to hemispheric lateralization, she stated that television overdevelops the rights hemisphere while retarding the growth of the verbal and logical left-hemisphere skills. Winn attributed the lowered scores of today's children on standardized tests to the effects of television. Recent evidence revealing that children who spend the most hours watching T.V. also have the poorest reading skills would seem to support Winn's position. She further charged that it dulls a child's enthusiasm for real life, noting that a boy who had gone through a devastating tornado said, "Man, it was just like something on TV."

At a broader level, children's advertising, as well as advertising in general, is charged with the crime of creating materialism among television viewers. Even worse, some have argued that advertising can play on the natural fears of susceptible groups. For example, among children it is very important to be liked by their peers. Promoting a toy by creating the belief that not having it will mean not having friends would play on such a fear.

In 1974 the Federal Trade Commission proposed a voluntary ban on premium advertising to children. The proposal was based on the idea that free gifts may focus children's attention on factors not relevant to the product. In particular, cereal premiums were believed to lead to preferences for cereals heavily laden with sugar.

Partly in response to the increased activism of the FTC, the advertising industry countered the criticisms in 1974. Their response was a natural one because over $20 billion annually was being spent on children. The industry made the following three arguments:

1. Advertisements teach kids how to make buying decisions.
2. Critics of ads are in the minority—only 18% of Americans favored the elimination of commercials in children's programs.
3. No evidence existed for the harmful effects of advertising to children.

Research on Children's Advertising.   Research on the effects of advertising on children was sparse prior to 1970. During the 1950s the public was generally apathetic concerning children and television. Indeed, at that time the medium was new and the fears of its misuse not prevalent. In an early study, McNeal (1964) found that as children grew older a general dislike and mistrust of television advertising occurred. In the early 1960s, 50% of the 5-year-olds and 75% of the 9-year-olds reported negative feelings towards TV commercials. Part of the tendency toward negativity may be caused by the increased understanding of the purpose of commercials. For example, it has been found that older children have a greater understanding of what a commercial is and can more easily discriminate program material from ads than younger children can.

The 1974 proposal by the FTC to ban premium advertising did spur some research. Shimp, Dyer, and Divita (1976) performed a study to test the effects of premiums on children. In the study, children were exposed to commercials that contained 10 to 15 seconds of a premium offer. The results revealed that the children could recall no more product information when the premium was included in the commercial than when it was absent. Based in part on this study, the FTC dropped the proposed guideline in 1977, stating that no research was available supporting their original contentions.

Interestingly, two years later Miller and Busch (1979) published an article that indicated that premiums do have an impact on children. These authors used breakfast cereals as the product and tested three different ad formats. In the first an announcer talked about the cereal; in the second Mr. Magic, a local television personality, endorsed the cereal; finally, the third commercial used a format identical to the first two except that the last 6 seconds of the ad was devoted to a presentation of the premium offer—a free comic book.

The result revealed that when the children were given a chance to select a brand of cereal from among four choices, they tended to choose the advertised cereal more often when the premium offer was made. This outcome occurred without any apparent changes in attitudes or recall about the cereals. It appears, then, that although children may not remember more information about a product for which a premium has been offered, nonetheless their preferences for the product are strengthened by the offer of a premium.

In addition to examining the effects of the use of premiums in children's advertising, consumer psychologists have done research on the more general effects of television advertising on children. Robertson, Rossiter, and Gleason (1979) performed a study examining the effects of commercials on children's perception of over-the-counter drugs. The study was motivated in part because 19 states had asked for a ban on advertising of proprietary drugs between the time periods of 6:00 A.M. and 9:00 P.M. The study used boys and girls in the third, fifth, and seventh grades. The researchers asked the children a long series of questions about their views on medicines and also about their television-viewing habits.

The general finding was that young children have a high regard for pharmaceutical drugs. Older children, however, had attitudes about the same as their parents. The results of the Robinson study also showed some weak relationships between exposure to ads for medicines and illness experience, illness anxiety, a belief in the efficacy of medicine, intent to take medicine, and the self-administration of medicine. Little evidence existed in the study that the exposure to the pharmaceutical advertisements caused the children to intend to take remedies, have a greater illness experience, and so on. When other factors were taken into consideration, using medicine was not related to commercial exposure. These results showed that parental actions and a child's illness experience were the dominant factors in explaining attitudes toward medicine.

A number of studies, however, have found evidence that seeing ads on television influences the behavior of children. Robertson and Rossiter (1976) found in a survey study that heavy TV viewers at Christmas experienced more disappointment over not receiving toys than did light TV viewers. Poulos (1975) in an experimental study found that TV commercials influenced food preferences. Another author found that exposure to commercials resulted in children attempting to influence their parents to buy the product. Atkin (1975) found that a paper-and-pencil measure of "materialism" correlated to a small but significant degree with TV exposure.

Goldberg and Gorn (1978) investigated the influence of commercials on childrens' desires to play with particular playmates. The children saw a commercial advertising a certain toy. The child was then given the choice of playing with a boy described as very "nice" or a boy described as "not so nice" but who had the toy in his possession. Sixty-four percent of the children preferred playing with the "not-so-nice" boy. Seventy percent of a control group preferred playing with the "nice" boy.

Other researchers have looked at the incidental learning that results from watching television commercials. Such incidental learning may subtly influence the values and beliefs of children. Atkin and Miller (1975) found that girls who watched commercials in which girl models played with racing car sets believed it was O.K. for girls to do so and felt an increased desire for the toys.

While the research into the effects of commercials on children is mixed, most parents of young children will vouch for the attention-gaining ability of commercials. A young child can be playing happily with toys and completely ignore the television. Then an advertisement comes on and the child's attention is immediately focused on it. Goldberg and Gorn (1978) argued that a number of factors may help to increase the effectiveness of commercials. In particular, rapid action, upbeat music, quick cuts, and product close-ups all have strong attention-getting abilities. In addition, the use of attractive child models may through observational learning have a strong impact on preschoolers.

Criticisms of Research. A number of criticisms have been leveled at the research in the area of children's advertising. Miller and Busch (1979) noted that there has been too much reliance on paper-and-pencil tests, surveys, and oral statements. They felt that efforts should focus more on behavioral changes.

Donohue, Henke, and Donohue (1980) made a similar point. They noted that children less than 7 or 8 years old have little competence with language. That is, their ability to verbalize their thoughts into sentences, to label abstract concepts, and to use an adequate vocabulary is limited. In addition, young children are generally shy when in the presence of strangers. Thus getting information from them verbally or in writing is very difficult.

These authors, however, point out that although young children have limited verbal abilities, it does not mean that no understanding is present. Children are able to perceive and understand many things that they cannot express in words, especially social and personal matters. Based on these ideas, Donohue et al. (1980) argued that some nonverbal approaches would be more appropriate for use with children less than 8 years old.

Donohue et al. constructed an experiment in which the dependent variables were represented by pictures drawn by professional artists. Also created were figures of men, women, boys, and girls whom the children could use to represent members of their family. The children were shown an animated commercial for cereal that they had not seen before. The researcher then assessed the children's understanding of the commercials by having the children manipulate the figures to respond to the investigator's questions.

Their findings revealed that the kids understood the intent of the commercial at a younger age than previously reported. Children 3 to 6 years old knew that the purpose of the animated commercial was to make them want to purchase a product, even though no mention of a product purchase was made. They also understood the idea of audience segmentation, that is, they knew for whom the commercials were intended, as well as the preferences of the other members of the family.

A Theoretical View. The strongest finding to emerge from the research on the effects of children's advertising is that younger children appear more strongly influenced by the commercials. Roedder (1981) summarized much of this research, saying that older children (as opposed to younger ones) pay less attention to advertising, can more easily discriminate between programs and commercials, understand better the persuasive intent of advertising, and believe it to be less truthful.

Age-related differences in responses are normally explained by citing Piaget's theory of cognitive development. Children are viewed as moving through a series of stages, each characterized by different cognitive structures used for perceiving and handling information. For example, children from 2 to 7, who are usually in the *preoperational stage,* tend to focus only on the dominant dimensions of a stimulus. Children at the *concrete operational* stage (typically 8 to 11 years) are more cognitively differentiated but are unable to think abstractly about ideas.

Roedder (1981) suggested that the Piagetian research has not lived up to its promise, noting that some studies have failed to confirm its predictions. More damaging is the fact that the theory does not explain how or why children process information. Roedder suggested that information-processing theory may be a better approach because it provides a more detailed description of cognitive functioning. (Note that the information-processing approach is the basis for the section on memory functions mentioned earlier in the chapter.) From such a perspective an adult's or child's cognitive functioning is viewed as consisting of short-term memory, with a limited storage capacity, that must transfer information to long-term memory before it decays.

Roedder (1981) divided children into three groups on the basis of their information-processing abilities. Strategic processors are ages 10 or 11 and older. They are able to spontaneously use strategies to store and retrieve information. They tend to focus on the central characteristics of the message and ignore the peripheral message content that may convey social beliefs. Cued processors, aged 6 to 9, reveal deficiencies in understanding of commercials. At this age level, children are capable of using storage and retrieval strategies, but only when prompted to do so. Thus children need to be reminded in some way that product-relevant information is different from the more peripheral social information. Children under 6 are characterized as limited processors. Even with help they are unable to distinguish the pertinent from the peripheral in commercials.

In Roedder's view, no special regulatory effort is needed to assist strategic processors. They are able to understand the persuasive content of messages. Cued processors, however, require educational efforts to facilitate message understanding. Such education could take the form of teaching the children how to recognize the central aspects of product apppeals. The instruction could occur in the public school system or at home. Roedder argued that special regulatory effort is required to control commercial information targeted to limited processors. These are the children for whom premiums and social appeals are especially effective.

Necessity for Research. The investigation of the effects of advertising on children is a "natural" for consumer psychologists. The sheer number of hours that children spend in front of the TV set almost demands extensive research of the subject. Research on how television transmits values, influences family harmony, and affects the intellectual ability of children is crucial. While government regulation had fallen in disfavor at the time this chapter was written, researchers should continue their investigations on whether some type of regulatory activity is appropriate for commercials aimed at children under 9.

A useful alternative to regulation has been providing public-service announcements to inform children of good eating habits and other values generally considered desirable. A second approach is to actually incorporate value training in TV programming. Goldberg, Gorn, and Gibon (1978), in a controlled experiment, found that the cartoon show *Fat Albert*, starring Bill Cosby, was particularly effective in changing children's short-term preferences for highly sugared snack and breakfast foods. The show begins with a warning from Cosby: "If you're not careful, you may learn something before it's done." Goldberg et al. used an episode called "Junk Food" that focused on the value of eating fruits and vegetables as opposed to sugared snacks. Exposure to the show resulted in children chosing fewer sugared snack and cereal foods than children in a control group.

Perhaps the way to handle the "children's advertising problem" is to encourage a greater amount of program responsibility among producers and directors.

Getting the Consumer to Say Yes

While no legislation has been passed that specifically limits advertising to children, laws have been enacted to protect the general consumer against unscrupulous business practices. The earliest of these laws was the Pure Food Act, partly in response to Upton Sinclair's book, *The Jungle*, which exposed the unsanitary conditions of the Chicago meatpacking houses in the early part of this century. The year 1966 saw the passage of the Highway Safety Act, instigated in part by Ralph Nader's book, *Unsafe at Any Speed*. This Act established the National Highway Traffic Safety Administration, now responsible for enforcing many of the product recalls by automobile manufacturers. Other laws passed during the last 20 years help ensure "truth-in-lending," fair reporting of credit, and standards for consumer product warranties. The Federal Trade Commission (FTC) is a major defender of the consumer, particularly in regard to business practices limiting competition or involving deception in advertising.

While earlier laws were generally concerned with consumer safety issues, more recently efforts have been turned to less life-threatening problem areas. (Note, however, that it was not until 1972 that the Consumer Product Safety Commission was formed.) The FTC in particular has been active in such areas. For example, it has attempted to restrain advertisers from making misleading claims and demonstrations. In one case Geritol was forced to note that the "tired feeling" it claimed to eliminate could be caused by many factors (e.g., a lack of sleep) on which the potion has no impact. Similarly purported cures for baldness must now indicate that the condition is usually hereditary.

The FTC has also acted against misleading demonstrations. In one case a company showed that one of its shaving creams could shave sandpaper. The commercial was removed after it was learned that the sandpaper was really sand on a Plexiglas mock-up. Similarly, a leading soup maker once put marbles in the bottom of a bowl in order to make the vegetables protrude through the soup.

In the personal selling area, some common unscrupulous tactics include the **bait-and-switch** and the **low ball.** Both of these are based on the consumer's greed.

In bait-and-switch, the retailer advertises a product at a very low price in order to get consumers into the store. However, the retailer usually has no intention of selling the advertised product. The idea is to lure the customer in so that another, higher-priced product can be sold.

At least two versions of low ball exist. In one a service is advertised at a very low price in order to get the consumer into the shop — say for a lube job on a car. The work is performed as advertised, but mysteriously the mechanic finds something else seriously wrong with the car, like a failing transmission.

A second type of low ball occurs when a customer is buying a product such as an automobile. A salesperson offers the customer the car at a much lower price than the competition's. The customer becomes excited and agrees to purchase the car. The salesperson then mentions that the sales manager will have to approve the deal. The salesperson goes to the lounge, drinks some coffee, returns, and states that the sales manager turned it down and the best that they could do would be "so-and-so." This price would be higher than the competition's. By this time the buyer has become committed to the car and will oftentimes take it at the higher price.

A Psychological Perspective.   Social psychologists have long been interested in investigating factors that induce people to conform to the wishes of others. The Asch studies mentioned earlier in the chapter are examples. More recently psychologists have investigated how norms can be used to influence others. Two such norms are the desire for self-consistency and the need to reciprocate favors from others.

The idea that most individuals like to be self-consistent in their actions and thoughts is exemplified in a compliance technique labeled the **foot-in-the-door** approach. Named after the saying that good salespeople can always make a sale if they can just get a foot in the door, the technique uses a two-step approach. Step one: Get your foot in the door by asking the target to do something so innocuous that most find it hard to refuse. In the first study of the foot-in-the-door, Freedman and Fraser (1966) first asked homeowners to place a small sign in their windows supporting safe driving. The request was small and almost everyone complied. Step two: After getting the individual to comply to the first request, ask for what you wanted all along. The second request of Freedman and Fraser was for the homeowner to place a large, unattractive billboard promoting auto safety on their front lawn. In comparison to a control group who had not received the innocuous request first, the foot-in-the-door group was significantly more likely to comply with the critical request.

A salesperson can employ a variety of psychological principles in devising ways to get into a prospective customer's home. The foot-in-the-door technique involves making an innocuous request the homeowner finds it hard to refuse, such as, "Let me demonstrate this on your hall carpet."

A series of studies has shown that the foot-in-the-door technique works because after complying with the first request, the individual develops the self-perception that this is the proper thing to do, that it does not "hurt" to do it. Thus, when a second similar, but larger, request is made, a predisposition already exists to say yes. Studies have shown the foot-in-the-door technique increases the likelihood of people donating blood, contributing to charity, completing marketing surveys, or signing up for medical plans. Furthermore, the technique seems to be effective even when the two requests are separated in time and made by two different people.

Note that the low-ball technique is based upon a very similar principle. After making the commitment to buy a car, an individual quickly develops a self-perception of owning it, riding in it, and showing it off to friends. Even discovering that the price is much higher than expected does not reverse the commitment; the buyer acepts the "new" price.

The foot-in-the-door technique is based upon the norm that people should be consistent in their actions. Recognition of this norm can give unscrupulous individuals power over the unsuspecting public. A second psychological principle — the norm of **reciprocity** — also can be used illicitly. Indeed, it has a long history of use and abuse.

The rule of reciprocity says that one good deed deserves another. If a friend or even a stranger does you a favor, you are obligated to reciprocate in kind. Reciprocity is so widespread that sociologists have concluded that all human societies have subscribed to the rule. In fact, anthropologists have argued that reciprocity is what makes us human. Certainly, following the norm has benefits that are undeniable. It allows for the division of labor, creates interdependencies among loved ones, and helps create a climate for trade and the exchange of goods.

Because of its power, the norm of reciprocity can be abused. Many travelers going through airports have been exposed to this tactic by the Hare Krishna, an Eastern religious cult. When the Krishnas arrived in the United States in the late 1960s, they engaged in fundraising by requesting donations from strangers. However, their strange dress, chants, and so forth resulted in poor results. Then a solution to the problem was found. Instead of simply accosting a stranger with a request for funds, why not give him something first?

The tactic was successfully tried on the author of this chapter in 1977. Returning from an interview for a job I had to change planes at Chicago's O'Hare Airport. Dashing through the terminal, I suddenly was confronted by an attractive woman dressed in weird clothing. She pressed a flower in my hand and said, "This is a gift for you!" After waiting for a moment to let her feigned benevolence soak in, she than asked for a donation for her religious group. Of course, I immediately reached for my billfold, succumbing to her duplicity.

Hare Krishnas and similar solicitors use the norm of reciprocity—giving passersby flowers is supposed to make them feel obliged to give something in return, like money.

After getting my ticket for the plane and waiting for it to arrive, I thought back on the experience. With the flower's fragrance still in my nose, I realized that I had been duped by the norm of reciprocity. What was worse, the week before I had just completed a study investigating its use. I was humbled—a researcher supposedly possessing a fundamental understanding of the principle had been taken in.

Actually, the use of the norm of reciprocity can be seen almost daily. Indeed, the old saying, "Scratch my back and I'll scratch yours." exemplifies its use. Providing samples of a product to potential buyers and entertaining a client at an expensive lunch are common ploys in business. Inviting a boat owner to an elaborate dinner may be motivated by the hope of borrowing the vessel for a vacation trip.

More recently, social psychologists have found that the norm of reciprocity can be created without even giving up anything. The technique, first identified by Robert Cialdini and his colleagues, has been labeled the **door-in-the-face.** The approach is the mirror image of the foot-in-the-door. The requester asks a person to do something so outrageous that most people would never do it. Never intending for the person to say yes to the first request, the requester then makes the critical, second request, which is always a less demanding version of the first.

An early experimental test of the door-in-the-face was performed by Cialdini and Ascani (1976). In the study, people were called on the phone and asked if they would donate blood. In the control condition, they were asked only if they would donate a pint of blood as a part of the campus blood drive. In the "door" condition, they were first asked if they would pledge to give a pint of blood once every 2 months for a period of at least 3 years. When people refused, the experimenter would ask if they would donate a single unit of blood. About 18% more people complied when the extreme request was made first.

What happens in the door-in-the-face? By getting the target to say no to the first request, the experimenter sets up a situation in which a concession can be offered. The experimenter graciously accepts the negative response and responds with a much smaller second request, in the process making it seem as though something has been given up. Of course, in reality nothing whatsoever was given up. But by creating the illusion of a concession, the requester sets up an obligation on the part of the target to reciprocate by also making a concession. The only concession possible is to say yes to the second request.

The door-in-the-face has been used successfully in research studies to increase the percentage of people willing to chaperone juvenile delinquents to the zoo, to observe traffic at intersections, to distribute information for an organization, and to complete marketing research surveys.

Conclusion

This chapter first presented an overview of consumer psychology by discussing a model of the consumer decision process. The model sees consumer decisions as having five major influences. Consumer inputs are such things as advertisements, physical and social surroundings, and economic factors that influence the buying of products. Information reception refers to the factors that determine whether or not a consumer attends to a message. Memory systems encode, store, and retrieve information received by the consumer. Consumer decision-making refers to the process of deciding what and when to buy. Activated by a perceived discrepancy between an actual and ideal state, the decision usually involves a search for information, evaluation of alternative brands, and choice. The last factor influencing decisions is the consumer's own personal characteristics. Such things as consumer attitudes, personality, and motives will influence other elements of the consumer decision process.

The second section portrayed the consumer psychologist on the job and described activities that might be undertaken and settings in which consumer psychologists function.

Finally, the chapter considered in detail three areas of current interest to consumer psychologists — brain lateralization, children's advertising, and consumer compliance techniques. These topics were selected because of their relevance and because they illustrate the types of research questions that dominate research in the field. Readers should note, however, that numerous other areas of consumer psychology are creating excitement among researchers. Briefly, some of the questions being posed are these: What causes rumors about products and companies to start and how can misinformation be prevented? Do consumers develop counterarguments to advertising messages, and, if so, how do these influence purchase decisions? Do consumers attempt to determine the motivations of companies, product endorsers, and themselves and, if so, how do such attributions affect consumption decisions? How do members of a family influence consumption?

Glossary

bait and switch   A sales technique whereby a retailer advertises a product at an artificially low price in order to bring customers into the store. Once the customer is in the store, another, higher-priced product is substituted.

door-in-the-face compliance technique   A compliance technique whereby a person is first presented with a very large request that is typically declined. The first request is followed by a smaller, more reasonable request that the individual typically will accept.

foot-in-the-door compliance technique   A compliance technique whereby an individual is first induced to comply with a small, innocuous request and then presented with a second, larger request. After complying with the first request, individuals are likely to act consistently and comply with the second request.

heuristics   A rule-of-thumb that allows for an efficient search for the solution to a problem.

low ball   A sales technique through which a consumer is committed to a product or service at a low price. The retailer then adds on extra cost (termed "throwing the low ball") either by raising the price of the item or finding additional reasons to charge the consumer.

low-involvement learning Learning about consumer products without consciously allocating thought process to the products.

marketing segmentation A marketing strategy by which subgroups of the population are identified and targeted for advertising and promotion of a particular product.

reciprocity norm A social norm that encourages individuals to reciprocate favors.

Part 3

Psychology in Community Settings

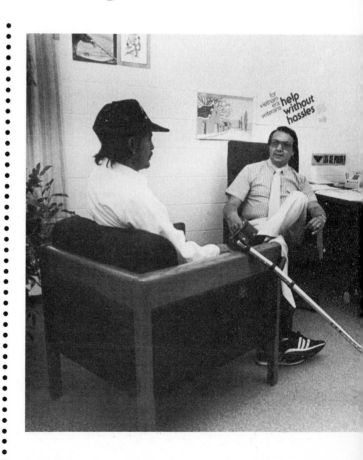

8 / Clinical Psychology

George Chartier
Arizona State University

Current enrollment in doctoral degree programs in psychology at several hundred universities in the United States and Canada is about 20,000 with the largest single group of students (approximately one third) specializing in clinical psychology. Similarly, clinical psychology programs are very popular among the more than 10,000 working at the master's degree in the discipline. The appeal of graduate study in clinical psychology is such that clinical training programs commonly receive 20 applications annually for each available opening, and this ratio climbs as high as 100 to 1 at the most prominent universities. Clinical psychologists also make up the single largest group (about 46%) within the membership of the American Psychological Association (APA) (Howard et al., 1986), the national organization of psychologists in the United States, which has grown rapidly in recent years to a 1985 membership of more than 66,996 (Stapp, Tucker, & VandenBos, 1985).

It is clear, then, that clinical psychology is an enormously attractive educational and professional field, despite the fact that it is primarily a phenomenon of the twentieth century and, indeed, did not really "explode" until after World War II. How can one account for this remarkable growth and popularity? What is clinical psychology? What do clinical psychologists do? How, where, and with whom? As you shall see, these are complex and difficult questions. This chapter provides answers to questions about this exciting and diverse field.

What Is Clinical Psychology?

Given the rapid growth and dynamic, expansive nature of clinical psychology, it is perhaps not surprising to find that the field is not clearly defined in the eyes of the public (and, to a lesser extent, among clinical psychologists themselves). Nevertheless, a combination of the definitions offered by Goldenberg (1973) and Korchin (1976) seems appropriate:

> *Clinical psychology is the branch of psychology dedicated to understanding and improving the lot of individuals in distress, using the best knowledge and techniques available, while striving through research to increase the knowledge and sharpen the techniques needed for improved intervention in the future.*

A number of features of this definition are useful in understanding the field and the functions of clinical psychologists:

1. Clinical psychologists share with their nonclinical colleagues a foundation in basic psychology and a primary concern with the understanding of behavior.
2. Efforts at understanding behavior include the assessment of abilities, deficits, and personal characteristics of individuals through a variety of tests, observation, and other informational sources.

The author has drawn on the work of Bernstein and Nietzel (1980) in several sections of this chapter.

3. Clinical psychologists intervene to help people who are in need through a variety of direct (e.g., psychotherapy) or indirect (e.g., community mental health programs) means.

4. Clinicians conduct research on human behavior, with particular emphasis on applying research to practical problems in assessment and intervention.

5. A clinical attitude prevails, in that the clinical psychologist seeks to apply general principles and abstract research findings to the understanding and treatment of the individual case.

Although the general characteristics of the field are well established, professional journals and convention meetings reflect a very active and continuing debate on specific directions the field should take. For example, questions involve the role of practitioners holding degrees at less than the docotoral level, the relevance of existing criteria for licensure or certification, the value of clinical assessment and therapy, the prevention of psychological dysfunctions, and the provision of services to subgroups of society who do not ordinarily receive them.

Most of all, perhaps, the field continues to grapple with what has been termed the scientist-practitioner controversy that began as far back as 1896. The main issue may be captured in this question: How can the clinical psychologist operate as a scientist who requires convincing empirical evidence to guide treatment and other clinical decisions and at the same time provide services to people in immediate need for whom little or no such evidence is available? Some clinical (and some nonclinical) psychologists feel strongly that the two roles are incompatible, and that clinical students should be trained in, and later function in, one area or the other. An outgrowth of this line of thought and argument is training programs that have been designed to produce individuals who will function primarily as practitioners (Korman, 1976). On the other hand, many clinicians endorse the more moderate position that the scientist-practitioner model should continue to dominate, but with persistent efforts at improvement, in the hope that both laboratory knowledge and consulting-room experiences can further enrich the field.

Although the assessment and treatment aspects certainly would fit with the popular public stereotype of clinical psychology, other features of the field are not nearly as well known. Most clinical psychologists are trained in the science of human behavior and the technology of its application to the problems of individuals. Though not all clinicians remain engaged in all aspects of the field, it is the combination of research, assessment, and intervention, all oriented toward understanding human behavior and alleviating the distress of individuals, that gives clinical psychology its status as a unique discipline (Bernstein & Nietzel, 1980).

What Do Clinical Psychologists Do?

Because the professional activities of clinical psychologists range so widely and are expanding so rapidly, the examples to follow cannot be considered exhaustive. Clinical psychologists vary considerably in the extent to which they engage in these activities, though it is probably accurate to say that the majority function to some degree in several of the broad categories in the normal course of their professional duties.

Job Activities

This section will present six common job activities of clinical psychologists. The activities of assessment, treatment, research, teaching, consultation, and administration will be considered.

Assessment. Generally, assessment refers to the gathering and interpretation of information about people. The data may focus on behavior, mood, self-image, intellectual abilities, perceptions, preferences, or other characteristics. The clinical psychologist may use assessment data for a wide variety of purposes. In clinical *service* contexts the data may be employed to arrive at formal diagnoses, to assist in deciding on appropriate treatment plans, to aid in predicting prognosis, to provide descriptions of personality characteristics, to guide vocational or educational choices, to assist in child custody and other legal decisions, to provide evidence of treatment effectiveness, and so on. In clinical *research* contexts, assessment data may be used in several ways, for example, to select research subjects with particular characteristics (e.g., social anxiety), to measure the correlation among two or more variables, or to measure the effects of one or more therapeutic methods. The ways in which clinical psychologists use assessment data seem almost limitless.

Before attending a conference like this, a clinical psychologist will probably have interviewed, tested, and observed the patient under consideration.

The means and methods of assessment are also tremendously diverse and numerous, and only a small sampling can be offered here. Assessment devices most frequently employed can be categorized as either interviews, tests, or observations.

In interviews, the most commonly used procedure, a skilled clinician attends not only to what the person says but how he or she responds to questions and comments. For example, a tendency to change the subject at certain points or to show nonverbal signs of emotion inconsistent with the content of the problem under discussion is likely to influence the interpretation of a clinician. Interviewers differ not only in level of skill, but also in theoretical orientation, which influences the kind of information they will look for and obtain. Interviews also vary in the degree to which they are structured, ranging from almost no consistent outline to guides consisting of specific, predetermined areas of clinical inquiry. Although a clinical interview does not follow a prescribed course, vast amounts of information can be obtained from it, and its importance in the practice of clinical psychology is unquestioned.

Tests lend more structure to assessment in that they usually involve a set of standard stimuli to which a person is asked to respond. Responses usually are compared to the responses of others with known characteristics who have taken the test. There are literally hundreds of psychological tests in various formats and for various purposes. Personality inventories are illustrated by the Minnesota Multiphasic Personality Inventory (MMPI), a paper-and-pencil test on which a person is asked to indicate whether each of 566 items does or does not apply to him or her. Responses are easily and reliably scored, and may be compared to statistical norms to facilitate interpretation.

Projective techniques, such as the well-known Rorschach inkblots, are designed to be vague and ambiguous enough not to elicit predictable or "socially acceptable" responses. The idea is that ambiguity allows interpretation of the stimuli to be determined primarily by unconscious processes and therefore to reflect true attitudes, motivations, conflicts, and the like. Intelligence tests such as the Wechsler Intelligence Scale for Children (WISC) and the Stanford-Binet test provide measures of various aspects of intellectual functioning. They are often used in predicting performance in academic settings and in the diagnosis of mental retardation. Prominent among instruments for diagnosing organic brain dysfunction is the Halstead-Reitan, a battery of tests that assess behavioral disturbances caused by brain damage. Clinical psychologists also often use a variety of other special-purpose measures, such as specific tests for depression, social anxiety, assertiveness, phobic fears, sex guilt, or marital satisfaction, to name but a few.

Information gathered through *observation* is often extremely useful. Typically, the clinician uses such methods to evaluate specific problematic behaviors in specific, well-defined situations. Behaviors may be sampled directly through observation and recording of target responses in home, school, or hospital settings. The observer may be the clinician, other trained personnel, or significant others (e.g., parents, spouses, or friends) whose cooperation is enlisted. More commonly, patients are asked to record and report on their own behavior or emotional reactions in certain real-life situations. Alternately, the clinician may observe the patient in contrived situations designed to simulate actual conditions. For example, patients may be asked to role-play a variety of threatening situations, or a parent and child may be assigned a "task" so that their modes of interaction can be assessed.

It is important to note that all methods of assessment are not perfectly reliable and valid, and some less so than others. Psychological assessment is a complex process in which a clinician attempts to develop a "working image" (Sundberg & Tyler, 1962) of the person being assessed, in much the same way that a researcher generates a "working hypothesis" of the nature and function of certain variables of interest. The "image" part of this term serves as a reminder that a clinician's impression is always partial and limited. The "working" part of the term indicates that a clinician forms hypotheses about a person, defines them in ways that can be tested, and revises them as new evidence becomes available.

Treatment.   Psychological treatment (or intervention, to use a more generic term) refers to attempts to alleviate distress. The particular treatment methods chosen by clinical psychologists often reflect their theoretical allegiance and assumptions. There are dozens of schools of therapy, each with its group of proponents advocating procedures ranging from radical approaches such as nude encounter groups or forced solitary confinement to more traditional client-therapist interactions in which a client's childhood experiences or current concerns are explored conversationally. Although impossible to describe all approaches, two major theoretical positions, **insight therapy** and **behavior therapy,** can be identified. While it is informative and convenient to make these distinctions, recognize that variants of each often blur the distinctions between them.

Insight therapy include psychoanalytic, humanistic, and existential treatment. While there are significant differences among them, all share the general assumption that suffering results from a person's inadequate understanding of what motivates his or her behavior, particularly when different needs and drives are in conflict. The emphasis in insight therapy, then, is on uncovering the causes — both historical and current — of disordered behavior, and not on altering the behavior directly. The assumption is that increased awareness, or insight, of causal relationships will lead individuals to better control over and improvement in their functioning. Therapists of different theoretical bents attempt to facilitate such insights in different ways, ranging from free association and dream interpretation in psychoanalysis, to nondirective reflection of feelings in Carl Rogers' client-centered therapy, to the often directive confrontation of current needs in Fritz Perls' Gestalt therapy. In addition to their relative lack of emphasis on the dysfunctional behavior itself, insight therapies derive from the work of practitioners who have, for the most part, operated outside the scientific mainstream of clinical psychology.

Behavior therapy, in contrast, is closely allied to experimental psychology in the development of therapeutic methods and insistence on proof of their effectiveness. The numerous variants within the broad category of behavior therapy embody the assumption that disordered behavior (whether directly observable or not) is most effectively treated by direct means. Hence behavior therapists attempt to help people unlearn maladaptive responses and/or learn new ones in the face of current circumstances and with relatively little attention to historically distant life events. The kinds of responses targeted for alteration may be emotional, cognitive, physiological, or motor behaviors. A variety of learning theories and principles underlie many different therapeutic approaches, including classical conditioning (e.g., systematic desensitization), operant conditioning (e.g., token economies) and social learning theory (e.g., modeling). These therapeutic approaches will be described in detail later in the chapter.

More recently, cognitive-behavioral methods based on these and other theories have been developed to modify directly such "private events" as self-defeating thoughts, perceptions, and judgments. These therapies strive to teach individuals to think in different ways so that they can feel better (thoughts are related to emotions) and function more appropriately (thoughts are related to actions). The feeling of gaining control over one's life enhances adjustment.

To what extent are insight versus behavorial approaches reflected in the therapeutic activities of clinicians? In a recent study, Smith (1982) found that the largest percentage (about 41%) of therapists surveyed identified themselves as **eclectic** in orientation. The term has at least two meanings: (1) some clinicians view themselves as employing concepts and techniques from more than one theoretical system in the treatment of a given patient; (2) some clinicians select a particular treatment method for a particular patient, depending on the patient's unique set of needs and problems. Although it is not clear which of these meanings most accurately describes the way most clinicians view themselves, the survey findings do indicate that a substantial (and growing) percentage of practitioners are neither wedded to a single theoretical view nor completely consistent in their application of treatment to their patients.

The kinds of problems treated by clinical psychologists are also quite varied. A partial list of such difficulties include infantile autism, depression, anxiety, schizophrenia and other psychoses, marital dissatisfaction, antisocial behavior, tics, obsessions, compulsions, drug and alcohol abuse, obesity, sexual dysfunction, low self-esteem, subassertiveness, paranoid ideas, bedwetting, social withdrawal, hyperactivity, phobic fears, learning disorders, explosive rage, interpersonal ineffectiveness, and so on in a seemingly endless stream of difficulties that vary in severity and duration as well as kind. Because patient complaints are frequently very complex and often involve a combination of biological and social as well as psychological factors, it is common for clinical psychologists to refer cases to other professionals like physicians, psychiatrists, or social workers for adjunctive care. Sometimes clinical psychologists participate in multidisciplinary treatment teams to care for certain patients. Some clinical psychologists also specialize in certain problem areas, such as disorders of children and youth, or problems of sexual orientation and function, or in certain treatment modalities, such as cognitive-behavioral therapy. Special mention might be made of problems encountered in behavioral medicine, a new area of specialization that focuses on physical diseases produced or worsened by psychological factors. Clinical psychologists may supplement medical therapies for persons afflicted with coronary diseases, asthma, diabetes, ulcers, essential hypertension, and other physical problems, generally through interventions designed to reduce anxiety and regulate emotional arousal.

Therapeutic interventions also differ widely in their goals, ranging from attempted solutions to quite specific situational problems (such as a fear of flying) to plans for a complete analysis and reorganization of a patient's personality, or any point between these two extremes. Treatment may take the form of the traditional one-on-one therapy, but it is now also common for a clinician to work with groups of people ranging from married couples and family groups to office coworkers, hospital ward residents, or even the members of an entire community. The intervention may be direct, as when the clinician is in face-to-face contact with the identified patient or patients, or indirect, as in the case of dealing with a troubled child through contact with the parents. Indirect interventions may also include an emphasis on prevention, as when community-oriented clinical psychologists assist, for example, in the development of programs in schools, nursing homes, and neighborhood centers with the intent of increasing psychological well-being before problems surface.

One may surmise at this point that clinical psychologists serve everyone, and, indeed, it is difficult to think of exceptions to this statement. Their clientele is made up of all age groups, both genders, and all socioeconomic levels. The clinical contact may be arranged voluntarily by the patient, the patient's family, or a legal or social service agency, or may occur as a result of the clinician's involvement in a hospital, school, work setting, or community. People may be seen on an outpatient basis or as inpatients in institutions or service facilities. Treatment contacts may vary in frequency from one time only to one or more times per week to once a month or so. The fees patients pay for clinical services may range from zero (as in the case of free clinics and programs funded by governments or other third parties) to modest sums (as in the case of sliding scales based upon patient income) to the very substantial amounts charged to those able to pay. Treatment sessions may be highly organized and focused on a specific problem, totally spontaneous, or somewhere in between, and may vary between the extremes of commonplace exchange and intense emotional drama.

Research.   Because clinical psychology is usually associated in the layperson's mind with testing and therapy, many are surprised to learn of the strong research orientation of the field. In fact, most clinical psychologists are trained to do research, and this activity distinguishes them most clearly from the other mental health professions. Some writers in the field argue that it is in the research arena that clinical psychologists have made and will continue to make their most important contributions. Support for this viewpoint may be drawn, for example, from the Joint Commission on Mental Illness and Health (1961) which, after commenting on the rather poor quality of earlier research on mental health, noted that "emphasis today is placed increasingly on sophisticated research designs, on highly specialized techniques and instruments, and on complex statistical procedures for data analysis. Psychologists are likely to have had the requisite training and experience for this type of research and this fact helps to account for their prominent position in this field" (p. 199).

Clinical research is conducted in an extremely wide variety of topical areas, with research on the effectiveness of treatment methods having become more and more popular in recent years. Other targets of clinical research include test construction and validation, perceptual processes, genetic influences, brain-behavior relationships, drug effects, aging, group dynamics, interpersonal processes, communication and language, personality, cultural influences and social issues, program evaluation, and of course the entire spectrum of psychological disorders.

The kinds of research methods employed are also diverse, and several will be illustrated in a subsequent section. The case study and the more scientifically valid single-subject method report on the functioning of a particular individual. Such studies increase understanding of particular problems and suggest worthwhile treatment strategies. Experimental designs and correlational designs are used to study groups of people, the first under controlled laboratory conditions so that the effects of specific manipulated variables can be determined convincingly, and the second under more or less uncontrolled conditions to see whether variables naturally "go together" in people. From the clinician's point of view, data drawn from experimental and correlational studies, whether produced by fellow clinicians or other psychologists, develop general principles that guide clinical practice.

Clinical research may also vary in the degree of representativeness of the phenomenon under study. For example, research on depression might use subjects who are indeed judged to be "naturally" clinically depressed or college students who score high on a depression test but who are apparently functioning reasonably well. In addition, the psychological treatment that research subjects receive might be identical or dissimilar to actual therapy. As research departs from actual treatment, it becomes an analogue of the real-life process. Decisions between analogical and real-life research must be based on cost, convenience, accessibility of subjects, availability of assistants and space, and the degree to which a researcher believes that the opportunities for advancing knowledge afforded by one approach outweigh those afforded by another.

Clinical research reports appear monthly or bimonthly in dozens of professional journals. Some of these present a broad spectrum of topics; others focus on a specific approach or problems. In addition, clinical psychologists present research at local, regional, and national conventions, and write books and book chapters incorporating research findings. They also prepare grant proposals for submission to the National Institute of Mental Health and other government and private funding sources for financial support of their research activities.

Even this brief summary should make it clear that clinical psychology's involvement in research is exceptionally diverse and intense. At the same time it should be noted that most clinical psychologists choose careers in psychotherapy or other areas of clinical practice once they complete the research requirements of their graduate program. As a result, the majority of clinical research is produced by a minority of clinical psychologists. This state of affairs and other influences have recently led some persons in the field to question the viability and relevance of the scientist-practitioner model of training, which strives to equip the clinician to function as both researcher and practitioner, and to which most training programs subscribe to one degree or another. The issue continues to be debated, often heatedly, and alternative models of training have emerged in recent years, as will be mentioned in a later section.

Teaching. Clinical psychologists spend a significant amount of their time in teaching and other educational activities. This is particularly true of those who hold full-time or part-time positions in colleges and universities, where they often teach undergraduate and graduate courses in such areas as abnormal psychology, clinical psychology, applied psychology, personality, psychological testing, research design, psychotherapy, behavior therapy, clinical assessment, statistics, and such special-topic courses or seminars as those in schizophrenia, depression, child psychopathology, marriage and family therapy, and cognitive behavior therapy. The number of courses taught usually range from two to four per term for full-time faculty to an occasional course or two for those with part-time appointments whose primary professional activities lie elsewhere.

The supervision of graduate students and psychology interns in clinical practicum contexts is another important teaching function of clinical psychologists. Such practica usually involve a student who is seeing one or more patients under the direct supervision of the more experienced clinician. The supervision is often an intense, one-on-one series of regular meetings in which the two parties work toward the development of the student's in-therapy skills as well as the conceptualization and implementation of a treatment plan. Small groups of students and their supervisor may also meet together to discuss cases. A variety of aids are employed, including audio- or videotaping and unobtrusive live observation of student-patient sessions. The details of practicum supervision vary from one clinician to another, but usually include attempts to combine theoretical principles and research evidence acquired earlier in the student's graduate preparation with the experience and guidance of the clinical supervisor. A practicum supervisor is ultimately responsible for a case and cannot permit students to make serious errors; at the same time, students must have some degree of freedom of thought and action in order to become competent clinicians. It should be noted that the patient is aware of and consents to the supervisory arrangement, and that confidentiality is respected by all parties concerned.

Clinical psychologists also supervise research efforts of many kinds, including undergraduate honors and graduate master's theses, and doctoral dissertation projects, as well as a variety of independent studies. The process is often lengthy and uneven as a supervisor helps a student sharpen the research idea, develop the design and methodology, plan the implementation, statistically analyze the data, and interpret and discuss the results. In this role also, the clinical psychologist has the difficult task of guiding the novice researcher without being so directive that the student learns little except how to follow instructions.

Clinical psychologists also operate in a variety of other contexts. They may teach regular-length or short-series courses or workshops to special groups such as police officers, medical students, parents of children with special needs or problems, and hospital nursing staffs as part of their in-service training. They may offer workshops to the general public on such topics as stress management, self-control, coping with depression, and child management. Such workshops are often viewed as having preventive and/or therapeutic aspects as well as educational value. Clinical psychologists may also perform educational services through invited addresses to civic groups and academic communities, newspaper and popular magazine articles, and appearances on radio and television productions.

Consultation.   Consultation involves attempts to provide assistance and advice to individuals or organizations on a wide variety of problems. In consulting, a clinician usually draws upon his or her expertise in assessment, treatment, and/or research. Consultation may be temporary and irregular (i.e., on special cases only), continuing but on a part-time basis, or a full-time endeavor as an individual enterprise or as a member of a psychological consulting firm. While often very lucrative, consultation sometimes is given for little or no pay as a service, for example to the community or the profession itself. Consultation may be on applied (i.e., assessment and treatment) or research issues, or on a combination of both.

It is convenient to discuss consultation in terms of a dimension ranging from a single-case focus to an organizational focus. To illustrate the former, clinicians may be asked by fellow clinicians or the staff of a facility to assist in the diagnosis, assessment, and/or treatment planning of a particularly difficult patient. This kind of consultation often brings a consultant into direct contact with the patient and is usually precipitated by the consultant's acknowledged expertise with such patients or with special assessment or treatment techniques. In such cases a consultant may assume direct responsibility for the case or offer advice on how to handle the case. In the realm of research, a clinician may be consulted for advice on design and procedure by an investigator planning a research study. Informal consultation here includes requests for advice on how to locate appropriate services for a particular patient, how to choose among graduate programs in psychology, where to find certain books and research articles, and so forth.

Something of a middle ground between the single-focus and the organizational dimension occurs when a clinician consults on a continuing basis with members of a mental health agency, hospital or medical school, rehabilitation facility, corrections or penal institution, business or industrial concern, or social service agency on a number of specific problems associated with patients, residents, employees, or clients. In such instances the advice and counsel of the consultant, since it is shared simultaneously with a number of persons, may be expected to have much greater positive influence than that obtained by consulting on one case at a time with one person at a time. Put another way, the impact of the consultations may pyramid downward, from the consultant to the immediate staff members and then to a number of persons with whom the staff members deal on a daily basis.

Clinical psychologists sometimes engage in organizational development work (see Chapter 5). Organizational consultation focuses not on specific single cases, but on those structures or functions of organizations that are problematic. Take, for example, a mental health center or other organization. The flow and patterning of contacts among and between staff and clientele may generate psychological discomfort, reflected in such behaviors as interpersonal conflict, complaints, high rates of staff turnover, and absenteeism. Consultants may spend considerable time observing the system and interviewing personnel and clients in order to pinpoint difficulties and recommend changes designed to reduce the problems. In another instance, a consultant might have the task of assisting a director or administrator in developing new methods or programs such as establishment of criteria for the selection of new employees, guidelines for assigning personnel to various jobs within the organization, or ways of increasing awareness and communication between management and employees.

Formal training in consultation skills is only rarely required by a clinical psychologist's graduate program, and may or may not be available as an elective. Most consultants appear to depend on their clinical and interpersonal skills, in combination with their grounding in research, assessment, treatment, and basic behavioral principles, to serve them in this role.

Administration.   Clinical psychologists often find themselves planning, organizing, and controlling the operations of organizations to which they belong. In academic settings, such administrative roles may include being a member or chair of personnel and budget committees, director of a counseling or treatment clinic, director of a clinical psychology training program, head of a department of psychology, director of a research center, member or chair of various university-level committees, or dean of a college. In clinical or research settings, administrative positions might include director of specialized treatment programs, director or chief of psychology in hospitals, medical schools and community mental health centers, director of internship training, director of research or research training, principal investigator on grant-supported research projects, or member or head of various administrative committees. In business and industry, clinical psychologists occupy such positions as head of a consulting firm or testing center, personnel manager, director of research and development, and a variety of other middle-management and executive-level posts.

It is assumed that, in order to perform the myriad duties embodied in administrative roles, individuals must have specific administrative skills and training. Again, most clinical psychology programs do not require training in this area, though it is usually available as an option somewhere in the university for the graduate student with such career interests. In general, it would appear that the psychologist's training and experience is both a help (e.g., increased sensitivity to individual differences) and a hindrance (e.g., conflict between helping and controlling roles) in administrative work (Sundberg, Tyler, & Taplin, 1973).

At this point it is worth repeating that not all clinical psychologists are involved in all six kinds of the activities described above. It is probably fair to say, however, that most clinicians do engage in several of these functions in the course of a typical week. Indeed, the opportunity to perform in a number of different professional capacities is, to many clinicians, undoubtedly one of the most appealing and satisfying features of the field.

One way of estimating how clinicians distribute their time is reported by Garfield and Kurtz (1976), who asked 855 members and fellows of the Division of Clinical Psychology of APA to indicate the percentage of time spent in various functions. The results are shown in Table 8.1. Notice that clinicians, on the average, spend more time in service delivery (assessment and treatment) than in research, a trend that causes dismay among those in the field who value the strong research contributions of clinical psychologists. Increase in national and societal concern with underserved populations over the past 20 years is at least partially responsible for this trend. Governmental efforts to provide access to clinical services for the poor, the aged, abused children, and minority groups, has changed the job market for clinicians toward service delivery. Furthermore, within service functions there is substantially more involvement in treatment activities than in assessment. The discrepancy may not be as large as it appears, however. The survey respondents seem likely to have had formal assessment activities (e.g., testing, diagnostic interviews) in mind, whereas in a very real sense a clinician engages in informal assessment more or less continuously in the course of treatment activities. Finally, it is interesting to note that clinical psychologists spend slightly more than half of their time in functions clearly and directly related to their training (assessment, treatment, research), but not much less time in activities for which they are likely to have received little formal preparation (teaching, consultation, administration).

TABLE 8.1

Percentage of Time Devoted to Designated Activities

Activity	%
Assessment	9.8
Treatment	31.8
Research	10.8
Teaching	24.3
Consultation	5.2
Administration	13.2
Other	4.8

Note: N = 855.

Work Settings

Just as it may be said that clinical psychologists serve everyone, so may it be said that they are (almost) everywhere. Furthermore, the settings in which they function are expanding at what appears to be an ever-increasing rate. Many of these settings have already been explicitly mentioned or implied, but it is also informative to examine the concentrations of clinicians in particular categories of work settings, as revealed by two surveys conducted by Garfield and Kurtz (1976) and Stapp and Fulcher (1981). Although the two surveys differed somewhat in the way that questions were asked, it is nevertheless possible to discern the general pattern of employment settings. As shown in Table 8.2, the largest percentage of clinical psychologists is employed in human-service settings (mental health centers, hospitals, clinics, medical schools), and the trend appears to be increasing. Private practice (including individual and professional group practice) is currently the second most popular professional setting, having succeeded academic settings in the five years between the surveys. It may be noted that the "other" category, which makes up a substantial percentage of respondents in both surveys, includes consulting firms, private and government research organizations, business and industry, criminal justice systems, military service, other government agencies, and nonprofit organizations.

Other features of employment in the field include an unemployment rate of only 1.0 to 1.5% overall, even for very recent doctorate recipients (Fulcher & Stapp, 1981). While salary data are difficult to summarize, it is generally the case that earnings are highest in private practice, consulting firms, and business or industry (Stapp & Fulcher, 1981). Clinical psychologists are also highly inclined to be employed full time through combining two or more part-time positions (Fulcher & Stapp, 1981), or to hold a second, part-time position in addition to their primary full-time employment (Stapp & Fulcher, 1981).

To summarize, the field of clinical psychology offers exceptional opportunities to engage in a wide variety of professional activities in an unusually broad array of settings. Yet it was only a relatively short time ago that clinical psychologists were found almost exclusively in universities or in child-guidance clinics, where a great deal of time was spent in intelligence testing. In the past 20 years the field has skyrocketed into the diverse, dynamic entity that has been described.

TABLE 8.2

Primary Employment Settings

Setting	(N = 855)	(N = 1,192)
Human service settings	35.0%	39.2%
Private practice	23.3%	28.9%
Academic	29.0%	22.7%
Other	12.7%	9.2%

Research and Application

This section will focus on three kinds of clinical research: the case study, single-subject experimental research, and programmatic efforts to develop a therapeutic strategy through the use of experimental research designs. The reader may consult Chapter 2 in this book on the merits and disadvantages inherent in each of these approaches to research. Also, it should be noted that these are but three of the multitude of research designs employed by clinical as well as nonclinical psychologists and that the studies cited are but a handful of those that have appeared in dozens of journals in recent years.

A Clinical Case Study

Leventhal's (1968) report represents an interesting combination of two seemingly incompatible treatment approaches. Basically, he began therapy with an 18-year-old female college student whose main problems centered on extreme dependence on her mother, an inability to make decisions, high anxiety and hesitancy in her approach to life, and pronounced difficulty in dating and making friends. Leventhal began with a **client-centered approach,** on the assumption that this approach to therapy, involving an unconditionally warm, accepting, empathic, and nondirective therapist, would both win the patient's trust and permit her to explore her own feelings and future directions. Several months later the patient had made some limited improvement, at which point the therapist felt that she was struggling to reveal her most secret thoughts and conflicts but was unable to do so. The difficulty seemed to focus on sex, including any talk whatsoever about sexual matters or even using words related to sex. The patient then related her strict and puritanical background and associated fears and guilt, although she was still unable to discuss her sexual inhibitions. She insisted that she would not tolerate talk about the subject and continued over the next several months to struggle to describe her ambivalent feelings about sex and the sexual thoughts that were so disturbing to her.

The therapist felt that this inability to deal with sexual material was a real barrier to the client's therapy and to her growth. He therefore persuaded her to join in an attempt at **systematic desensitization,** a behavior therapy based on the learning principle of counterconditioning (Wolpe, 1958). In systematic desensitization, counterconditioning principles are usually applied by teaching the patient to gradually perform a relaxation response, or other nonanxious response, as a substitute for the anxiety response elicited by problematic stimuli (in this case, sex-related words). Accordingly, Leventhal and the patient constructed a list of sex-related words in a carefully graded hierarchy of least to most disturbing to her. Beginning with the least disturbing, the patient read the word to herself, wrote it, spoke it aloud, and heard it repeated by the therapist. If the client became disturbed or upset, the process was stopped until she could relax again. This process was repeated until the entire list was completed. The therapist immediately and strongly reinforced successful completion of each part of the sequence through verbal praise. As a result of this counterconditioning, the client was able to substitute a relaxed response to the sex-related words for the previous anxious response. The procedure, which took nine sessions, was strikingly successful in reducing the patient's sex anxiety, both during the therapy and in the patient's natural environment. The patient was now able to respond much more freely and openly to the client-centered approach. At the end of therapy she seemed to have made very substantial progress in her self-concept and in her ability to live effectively and independently.

As this is a case study, it is not, strictly speaking, a research effort. From a clinical treatment perspective it is clear that the therapy worked, but from a scientific perspective it is not clear why it worked. A number of explanations are possible. For example, the patient might have improved without therapy, this particular therapist might have been effective regardless of the methods he used, or only one of the forms of therapy might really have been needed to cause improvement. Nevertheless, the study is of value in suggesting ways of combining different treatment modalities that may be useful in other clinical applications and in future research on therapeutic strategies. Also, it is interesting to note that the particular techniques are theoretically quite different and presumably incompatible. In the client-centered approach, a therapist's nondirective stance within an atmosphere of unconditional warmth, empathy, and genuineness develops a patient's own potential for self-actualization and responsible decision-making. In contrast, the systematic-desensitization approach involves a direct, therapist-controlled and administered focus on the removal of anxiety symptoms. Apparently neither the therapist nor the patient in the case study just given had much difficulty in alternating among the quite divergent roles required by the combination of humanistic and behavior therapies. This observation both suggests that different brands of therapy might not be as incompatible as their theoretical foundations would indicate and illustrates the now-common tendency of therapists to approach clinical work in an eclectic manner.

Single-Subject Clinical Research

Single-subject research, unlike case studies, involves *controlled* investigation of single cases. In clinical applications, the main purpose of this research is to confirm experimentally that changes in the behavior of individuals are in fact a function of the therapeutic procedures designed to produce these changes. The following research by Reisinger (1972) illustrates the typical use of a single-subject approach to a clinical problem.

The patient, a 20-year-old woman who had been in a state hospital for six years, had shown no appreciable response to previous therapy efforts. Variously diagnosed as borderline psychotic, hysteric, and "anxiety-depressive," she was described as fearful, withdrawn, self-rejecting, and depressed. Her behavior included frequent crying and infrequent verbalization usually involving fear, personal injury, and death. Taking a Skinnerian, or operant conditioning, point of view, Reisinger attempted to modify the patient's depressed behavior by providing positive reinforcement for appropriate responses (smiling), and by applying response costs, or penalties, for inappropriate responses (crying). The treatment approach was based on the behavioral theory that depression is caused, at least in part, by reduced levels of positive reinforcement and may be alleviated by increases in behavior that is likely to be reinforced by others in one's life (e.g., Lewinsohn, Weinstein, & Shaw, 1968).

The treatment program was implemented by ward aides trained in the use of behavior-modification procedures, specifically, a **token economy.** During a 2-week *baseline* (nonintervention) period, the patient was observed 3 times per day for a maximum of 2 hours each time. These observations showed smiling to be at zero frequency and crying episodes (of 5 to 30 minutes duration) at approximately 29 per week. At the conclusion of the baseline period, the patient was informed that smiling would result in receipt of tokens and that crying would result in loss of tokens. The tokens were poker chips redeemable for desired items or privileges. During the ensuing 6-week *treatment* phase, the patient was observed as before and was given a token without comment if she smiled or was approached when she cried and simply told, "You will be fined one token for crying." At the end of this phase the patient was smiling much more often (27 times per week) and crying much less (2 times per week), practically the reverse of the rates shown in baseline. A 2-week *extinction* phase was then implemented in order to determine the effects of the prior treatment. Token rewards and fines were terminated, and, as expected, smiling decreased (to a low of 11 resposes per week) and crying increased (to 9 episodes per week).

While these changes provided some evidence for the controlling power of the treatment procedures, Reisinger next instituted a *reversal* phase in order to demonstrate that power more convincingly. During the next two weeks, the treatment contingencies were reversed such that smiling resulted in token fines and crying resulted in token rewards. As expected, the patient's rate of smiling went down to 3 responses per week and her rate of crying went up to 18 episodes per week. The extinction and reversal phases thus showed that the treatment procedures were effective in causing changes in the patient's behavior.

Next, the original *treatment* contingencies were reinstated for a 4-week period and this time included social reinforcement (praise) along with token reinforcement for smiling. The final week of this phase indicated that smiling increased to 23 responses and crying decreased to 2 episodes. Finally, in a 4-week *fading* phase, token reinforcement for smiling was eliminated but social praise was continued, and crying was ignored rather than fined. The purpose of fading was to determine if the positive changes could be maintained under conditions more similar to ordinary nonhospital living. The final week of this phase showed virtually the same high rates of smiling and low rates of crying that existed at the end of the last treatment phase.

The patient was discharged soon after the fading phase. A 14-month follow-up indicated that she continued to function in the community (for the first time in six years), with no apparent need for additional treatment.

The therapeutic methods employed in the above example illustrate a few of the many **contingency management techniques** derived from operant conditioning

Techniques of operant conditioning were used to treat these two autistic boys. The food they are receiving is positive reinforcement for playing ball with each other.

principles and applied to clinical problems (see O'Leary & Wilson, 1975, for a complete account). The basic premise of operant conditioning is simply stated. Behavior is learned and strengthened as a result of its consequences. Since its sudden and sharp rise in popularity some 20 years ago, the contingency-management approach has opened up exciting new vistas for clinical psychologists and probably has been applied to a broader range of problems than any other behavioral/social learning method. Part of the reason for this is flexibility. Contingency management is suitable for a wide variety of dysfunctional behaviors in young children, adolescents, and adults. It can be tailored to the particular needs and problems of individuals or applied to the common difficulties of small and large groups. It can be used in the therapy room, in homes, in schools, and in hospitals. Because the principles of contingency management are relatively easy to learn, subdoctoral staff, friends, parents, teachers, and peers can be trained in its practice, thereby broadening the field of therapeutic agents and, in many cases, reducing the economic cost of treatment. It can even be employed by individuals wishing to modify their own behavior in the interest of achieving greater self-control (see Kanfer, 1975).

Perhaps the most remarkable feature of the huge research literature on contingency management is the consistency with which it finds such methods to be effective in altering specific behaviors in desired directions (Bernstein & Nietzel, 1980). There is a serious question, however, of the extent to which such changes are durable and generalizable. Many clinical researchers in the field believe that the key to maintaining improved behaviors over time and in natural settings is the continued reinforcement of those behaviors by significant others. Kanfer

(1975), however, is among those writers who suggest that most patients ultimately must take responsibility for maintaining their changed behavior and that contingency-management programs would do well to incorporate training in self-reinforcement and other self-management procedures. Alternately, Bandura (1977) emphasizes that treatment strategies are effective to the extent that they promote the patient's sense of **self-efficacy,** that is, the expectation that one is indeed capable of behaviors that produce positive outcomes. How then may one account for the apparent success of the treatment described in the example of the crying woman? The data available supports the assertion that the treatment was effective in altering significant behavior patterns, but they do not permit one to determine whether the patient's posthospital functioning was a result of continued external reinforcement, unplanned changes in self-reinforcement tendencies, increased self-efficacy expectations, or some other process. Research on these and related questions is among the principal goals in the field at this time.

Finally, it may be noted that the use of single-subject methodology is strongly identified with behavior modification research, which attempts to experimentally isolate the effective ingredients of treatment from other factors acting on the patient simultaneously. However, as Leitenberg (1973) points out, single-subject methodology is a useful strategy for examining the ongoing effects of other psychotherapeutic interventions as well, including techniques such as dream analysis or free associations involved in the "insight" therapies described earlier in the chapter. Generally speaking, any therapy research that includes an objectively measurable response (for example, the number of maladaptive responses in free association), an objective administration of treatment, and the possibility of a withdrawal (or reversal) condition can use such designs to find out what works and what does not.

Programmatic Clinical Research: Modeling Therapies

This section will summarize the work of Albert Bandura and his colleagues in developing, through a series of related experiments, a set of treatment strategies based upon the observation of live or symbolic models as therapeutic agents. Like the single-subject experimentation discussed above, research into such **modeling therapies** uses controlled experiments that permit verification of functional relationships between relevant variables. However, unlike single-subject research methods, the experimental designs employed have used large numbers of subjects assigned to various experimental conditions. Although the summary that follows will not include all of the relevant research, it will attempt to illustrate the kind of progress that can be made through systematic, sustained efforts at treatment program development.

Modeling, or observational learning, is a most important feature of social learning theory. According to Bandura (1969), "virtually all learning phenomena resulting from direct experiences can occur on a vicarious basis through observation of other persons' behavior and its consequence for them" (p. 118). In many cases, learning through observation is much more effective and rapid than learning through direct trial-and-error experience. Observation of competent models makes it unnecessary, for example, for drivers to suffer accidents before learning the meaning of traffic signals, and models appear to be required for the development of such important and sophisticated behaviors as human language. Bandura (1969) theorizes that modeling effects are influenced by four major factors — attentional processes, retentional processes, motor reproductive abilities, and incentive or motivational processes — that determine the degree of learning and/or the probability that the modeled behavior will be imitated. He also proposes that observing the behavior of others, either in actuality or symbolically (as in films), can have three effects in addition to developing *new* behaviors such as speech. Observing a model can *facilitate* the performance of similar responses already present in the repertoire of the observer, or it can *inhibit* imitative behavior if the model suffers negative consequences of a particular act. Modeling can also lead to the *disinhibition* of behaviors that the observer has avoided because of fear and anxiety, and in the process promote the vicarious and direct extinction of the fear. The disinhibiting effects are the focus of the research to be described. More specifically, Bandura (1971) proposes that extinction of fears, inhibitions, and other avoidance behaviors may be attained by exposing fearful observers to models who engage in threatening activities without experienceing any negative consequences for their behavior. It is further assumed that such extinction of fear will reduce defensive behavior (i.e., promote approach behavior) in the formerly fearful observers.

The studies to be described were designed with the dual purpose of developing effective modeling therapies and investigating theoretical issues. All employed basically the same experimental design. Subjects were first given an avoidance-behavior test in which they were asked to perform threatening activities to the extent that they were able to do so, for example, to get as close to a feared (but confined) animal as their anxieties would allow. Those subjects who displayed sufficiently strong avoidance were then assigned to one or another of the various treatment conditions. Following treatment, the subjects were again administered the behavior-avoidance test with the same feared object. In addition, posttreatment assessment included a behavior-avoidance test with a different feared object, in order to measure the generalization of treatment effects to stimuli other than those encountered in treatment. Also, these same assessment procedures were repeated one month after treatment in order to determine how well the treatment effects were maintained.

The first study in the series (Bandura, Grusec, & Menlove, 1967) examined the effectiveness of graduated live modeling in reducing strong avoidance behavior of long duration, as well as the possibility that inducing positive emotions may enhance vicarious extinction. Graduated modeling refers to modeling activities that move from least threatening to most threatening, with the aim of provoking minimal anxiety throughout the treatment process and allowing subjects to observe their responses.

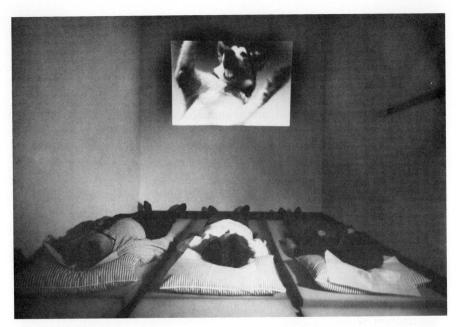

One of the Bandura studies on overcoming phobias examined the effectiveness of graduated modeling in reducing avoidance behavior. In addition to live demonstrations, the study on dog phobias involved the use of brief film clips, such as the one shown here.

Children who were exceptionally fearful of dogs were assigned to one of four conditions. In the *model + positive context* treatment condition, the children first were placed in a party atmosphere to make them feel happy and relaxed (hence presumably less fearful). They were then exposed to live peer models who fearlessly interacted with a dog, beginning with such behaviors as petting and feeding it from outside its pen, then walking it around the room on a leash, and, in the latter sessions, climbing into the pen with it and continuing positive interactions with it. Treatment consisted of eight 10-minute sessions in all, held over the period of only 4 days. The modeling sequences themselves lasted only 3 minutes per session.

Children in the *model + neutral context* treatment condition were treated identically, except that there was no attempt to induce a positive emotional state through a party atmosphere. In a *dog + positive context* control condition, a third group of children observed the dog in the party context but with no model present so that the effects of exposure to the threatening animal itself could be measured. A fourth group of children in the *positive context* control conditon participated in the party activities but were exposed to neither the dog nor to the models, in order to examine the effects of induced positive emotion and repeated behavioral assessments.

The children's fear of dogs was then reassessed by means of the graded avoidance-behavior test, in which they were asked to approach the dog, feed it, remain alone with it in the room, and, most difficult of all, to climb into the playpen with it and pet it while alone. This same test was also conducted with different, unfamiliar dogs, and the tests were repeated with both animals 30 days following the completion of the treatment program. Figure 8.1 illustrates the effectiveness of these treatment procedures. It is quite clear that the modeling treatments produced generalized and stable vicarious extinction of avoidance behavior. The two groups of children who had observed the peer model interact fearlessly with the dog showed significantly greater approach behavior toward both the dog used in treatment and an unfamiliar dog than did children in the two control conditions. It is also clear that the party atmosphere had little effect on the favorable results. Furthermore, 67% of the children in the modeling conditions were able to perform the most threatening behavior (remaining alone in the room confined with the dog in the pen), whereas few of the children in the control conditions were able to do so.

The second study, by Bandura and Menlove (1968), was designed primarily to assess the effects of multiple modeling. The reasoning was based in the experimental literature, which suggests that the amount of extinction of fear should be partly determined by the variety of modeling stimuli that are neutralized. For example, if the objective was to reduce fear of spiders, showing models interacting with a number of different types of spider would increase the effectiveness of the treatment. The study also examined the effectiveness of presenting the models using brief film clips, a method that could be implemented conveniently and economically.

The subjects, again dog-phobic children, were assigned to one of three groups. Children in the *single model* condition viewed a series of eight 3-minute films that depicted a fearless model in the same progressively more threatening interactions with a dog as in the experiment described above. In the *multiple*

FIGURE 8.1 · Mean dog-approach scores achieved by children in each of the treatment conditions in the three different periods of assessment. From "Factors Determining Vicarious Extinction of Avoidance Behavior" by A. Bandura, J. R. Grusec, and F. L. Menlove, 1967, *Journal of Personality and Social Psychology, 8,* p. 21.

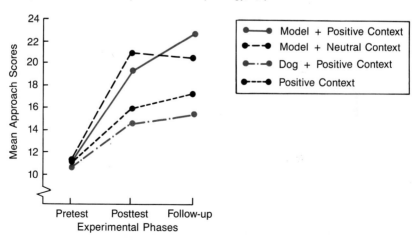

model condition, the films included models of both sexes and various ages interacting with a number of dogs who were progressively larger and more fearsome. Children in the *control* group saw films that were entertaining but contained no dogs. As in the preceding experiment, the children's actual avoidance behaviors were assessed before treatment, immediately after treatment and 30 days later.

As shown in Figure 8.2, the two modeling conditions were more effective than the control in increasing the children's ability to interact with a dog at the end of the treatment. Further, children who received the multiple-modeling treatment continued to improve upon follow-up. Children in the multiple-modeling group were also twice as likely as those in the single-model condition to perform the terminal behavior in the follow-up assessment—that of remaining alone in a room confined in the pen with a dog. Finally, the effectiveness of the filmed multiple-modeling treatment was further tested by providing it to children in the control group (who had not changed in their avoidance behavior) after the experiment was completed. These children subsequently showed increases in dog-approach behavior that were comparable to those achieved by children in the original multiple-modeling group.

In another, extensive study, Bandura, Blanchard, and Ritter (1969) compared the relative effectiveness of three treatment methods in producing not only behavioral changes, but also changes in emotions and attitudes. In this study the investigators worked with adolescents and adults whose severe snake phobias caused most of them to avoid occupational and recreational activities that might conceivably bring them into contact with snakes. All subjects were evaluated

FIGURE 8.2 Median dog-approach scores achieved by children who received either single-model or multiple-model treatments, or who participated in a control condition. From "Factors Determining Vicarious Extinction of Avoidance Behavior through Symbolic Modeling" by A. Bandura and F. L. Menlove, 1968, *Journal of Personality and Social Psychology, 8,* p. 102.

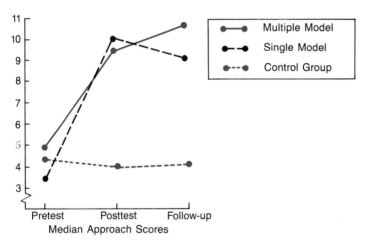

before and after various treatments to measure their emotions, attitudes, and behaviors toward snakes. One group of subjects was exposed to **participant modeling,** a procedure in which subjects witnessed a live model interacting with a large king snake and then were guided into physical contact with the reptile. Participant modeling included several elements designed to reduce fears and behavioral inhibitions: modeling of effective performance and fearless behavior; physical guidance in performing these same behaviors; and social reinforcement for the subject's efforts.

A second group of subjects received **symbolic modeling** treatment that consisted of a 35-minute film showing children and adults in progressively more threatening interactions with a snake. These symbolic-modeling subjects also had been taught, early in treatment, a method of inducing and maintaining deep relaxation through their exposure to the film. Furthermore, they were allowed to stop the film if it became too anxiety-provoking, return to their state of deep relaxation, and review the threatening segment of the film.

In a third condition, *systematic desensitization,* described earlier in the chapter, was used. As before, subjects in this condition were provided with a graded hierarchy of stimuli to elicit the fear, in this case, 34 written descriptions of situations in which subjects interacted with snakes in some way. The situations were arranged in progressively more threatening order, ranging from looking at pictures of snakes to handling live snakes. Subjects were initially put in a state of deep relaxation and then asked to imagine each of the situations. Each situation was followed by a period of deep relaxation and situations were repeated as necessary until they could be imagined without serious discomfort. As in the previous example with sex-related words, subjects substituted a relaxed response for their previously anxious one. Systematic desensitization is widely recognized as effective treatment for phobias such as fear of animals and provides a standard against which to compare the effectiveness of modeling treatments. Subjects in a fourth group, a *control* condition, received no specific treatments and participated only in the evaluations of their reactions to snakes.

After treatment, all subjects were reassessed on the same measures taken before treatment. The behavorial test was conducted with snakes obviously different from those used in treatment and consisted of a graded series of tasks ranging from looking at a caged snake from a distance to actually holding a snake. Immediately before and during the performance of each task, subjects were asked to rate the intensity of their fear on a 10-point scale in order to provide measures of anticipatory and performance anxiety. In addition, their attitudes toward snakes were assessed on two scales administered immediately before and immediately after the two (pretreatment and posttreatment) behavioral tests.

As shown in Figure 8.3, participant modeling produced the most effective reduction in avoidance of snakes, symbolic modeling and desensitization produced substantial but less powerful effects, and control subjects remained unchanged. The power of the modeling plus participation treatment was particularly clear; 92% of the subjects were able to perform the most aversive of the behavorial approach tasks — holding a snake on their laps! Another finding was

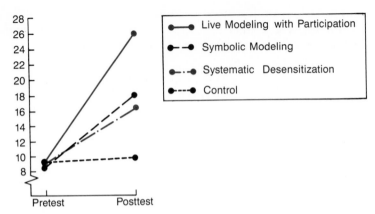

FIGURE 8.3 Mean number of snake-approach responses performed by subjects before and after receiving different treatments. From "The Relative Efficacy of Desensitization and Modeling Approaches for Inducing Behavioral, Affective, and Attitudinal Changes" by A. Bandura, E. B. Blanchard, and B. Ritter, 1969, *Journal of Personality and Social Psychology, 5,* p. 183.

that both modeling treatments produced marked decreases in anxiety both be-fore and during interaction with the snakes. In contrast, systematic desensitiza-tion caused reductions in anxiety only during interaction with snakes and to a lesser degree than the modeling procedures. Also, both the symbolic modeling and desensitization treatments resulted in more favorable attitudes toward snakes, but the live modeling with particpation was the most powerful in this area as well. Finally, subjects in the participant-modeling group reported that their suc-cess in overcoming the phobia had increased their confidence in dealing effec-tively with other fearful events in their lives. This confidence extended beyond nonsocial anxieties like fear of snakes to include additional confidence in social interaction. This latter finding marks an early stage in the development of self-efficacy theory, an approach that has been pursued in subsequent research and is described more fully in the next study to be considered.

Bandura, Adams, and Beyer (1977) tested the theory that psychological treat-ment methods exert their influence by changing what they have termed a per-son's **self-efficacy** expectations. A self-efficacy expectation is how strongly a person believes that he or she can successfully engage in some behavior. Ac-cording to self-efficacy theory, therapies (like participant modeling) that require clients to actually execute behaviors are the most influential source of efficacy information because they provide direct, actual experiences of personal mastery (or failure). The resulting expectations determine how strong and how persis-tent a client's efforts toward therapeutic change will be.

The subjects used in the study were adult snake phobics who anxiously avoided a wide range of social, recreational, and vocational activities where they might conceivably encounter a snake, and who suffered from nightmares and intrusive thoughts about reptiles. Subjects in the *participant-modeling* treatment group received much the same treatment as the corresponding group in the

In treating snake phobias, clinical psychologists emphasized participant modeling by setting up a hierarchy of tasks that brought phobics into progressively closer interaction with reptiles.

preceding experiment, except that the modeling component was de-emphasized in order to reduce overlap with the other treatment condition. Subjects proceeded through a hierarchy of tasks that brought them into closer and closer interaction with a snake. The duration of treatment varied considerably with the individual case and ranged from 40 minutes to 7 hours, with a median time of 90 minutes to successfully complete the most aversive task in the hierarchy. Subjects in a second *modeling* condition observed the therapist perform the same graduated set of activities and for the same length of time as each subject's matched counterpart in the participant-modeling condition. As the modeling treatment involved vicarious experience only, it was predicted to be less effective in altering both self-efficacy expectations and avoidance behavior than the performance-based participant modeling procedures. *Control* group subjects were simply administered the assessment procedures.

Self-efficacy expectations were assessed at various points before and after treatment, and consisted of ratings of (a) whether the subjects could perform each of the 29 tasks in the graded hierarchy and (b) the subjects' degrees of confidence in their ability to do so. Behavioral-approach tests were also conducted before and after treatment and involved snakes different from those used in treatment.

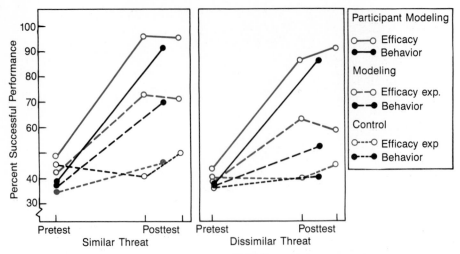

FIGURE 8.4 Level of self-efficacy and approach behavior displayed by subjects toward different threats after receiving vicarious or performance-based treatments or no treatment. (In the posttest phase, level of self-efficacy was measured prior to and after the behavioral avoidance tests with the two snakes.) From "Cognitive Processes Mediating Behavioral Change" by A. Bandura, N. E. Adams, and J. Beyer, 1977, *Journal of Personality and Social Psychology, 35*, p. 131.

The results of the experiment are displayed in Figure 8.4. As can be seen in the figure, the mastery-based participant-modeling treatment produced stronger and more generalized self-efficacy expectations and approach behaviors than the modeling treatment that relied entirely upon vicarious extinction. Both were superior to no treatment. A very important additional finding was that self-efficacy expectations predicted how willing a subject would be to interact with a snake regardless of which treatment group he or she was in. As shown in Figure 8.5, it did not matter whether changes in self-efficacy were produced through participant modeling or vicarious modeling. Compared to their pretreatment behavior, individuals with the largest self-efficacy scores were most willing to approach snakes after treatment. This finding shows strong support for the hypothesized relationship between self-efficacy and behavioral change.

A number of comments can be made about this program of treatment and research. It is clear that Bandura and his colleagues have developed impressively effective intervention techniques that, in many cases, achieve clinical goals in remarkably brief periods of time. Are these techniques limited, however, to the animal phobias treated in the studies described above? No. A number of clinical researchers have found modeling therapies, either used alone or together with other forms of therapy, to be of benefit with such varied problems as examination anxiety, compulsive rituals, sexual underresponsiveness, social anxieties, subassertiveness, autistic behavior, social withdrawal, marital and dating skill deficits, interpersonal skill deficits, and dental and medical stress, among others. Furthermore, this technique has positive effects with individuals in all age groups

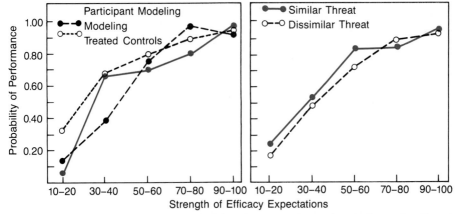

FIGURE 8.5 Probability of successful performance of any given task as a function of strength of self-efficacy. (The left panel shows the relationship for vicarious and performance-based treatments; the right panel shows the relationship between strength of self-efficacy and successful approach responses toward similar and dissimilar threats combined across treatments.) From "Cognitive Processes Mediating Behavioral Change" By A. Bandura, N. E. Adams, and J. Beyer, 1977, *Journal of Personality and Social Psychology, 35,* p. 133.

(see reviews by Rosenthal & Bandura, 1978, and Thelen, Fry, Fehrenback, & Frautschi, 1979). A particularly intriguing facet of this line of research is the use of therapeutic videotape and film modeling. This work suggests the possibilities of self-administered treatment, efficient use of professional time, and the extension of treatment services to much larger numbers of patients, perhaps through closed-circuit television or strategically located special-purpose treatment centers.

Still, one may question the applicability of this work to clinical problems that are more diffuse, highly generalized, and multifaceted. How, for example, could one use Bandura's social-learning approach in the treatment of the young woman described in Leventhal's (1968) report? Some guidelines are suggested by self-efficacy theory. As mentioned before, Bandura (1977) proposes that all psychological methods of treatment act upon the patient's perceived self-efficacy and that these expectations in turn determine the strength and persistence of efforts to cope. In this model, therapies like participant modeling, which are based on performance accomplishment, will be more effective because they provide more dependable information about personal experiences. In contrast, procedures like modeling, which are based on vicarious exposure alone, rely on inferences from social comparison and are therefore less dependable sources of information about one's own capabilities. Still more indirect, and therefore weaker in their effects on self-efficacy expectations and psychological change, are what might be termed "verbal persuasion" methods such as client-centered therapy and Freudian psychoanalysis.

It is too soon to tell how useful self-efficacy theory will be in understanding and predicting the complex phenomena of therapy. However, the theory has begun to stimulate a great deal of thought and empirical research both within and beyond the confines of the field, including other applied areas such as sports medicine, physical rehabilitation, remedial education, and behavioral health.

The research efforts described were selected from the treatment literature primarily because of the emphasis on intervention in contemporary clinical psychology. Nevertheless, examples easily could have been drawn from the growing empirical literatures on psychopathology or clinical assessment, both of which also reflect the interplay of the scientific method and clinical application. To many clinical psychologists, the message carried by these advances is clear: progress in the interest of helping people is being made.

Conclusion

This chapter reviewed information about the nature of clinical psychology. Clinical psychologists draw on the base of knowledge of scientific psychology to measure and understand the abilities, deficits, and personal characteristics of individuals. Clinical psychologists also seek to intervene in the lives of individuals and groups to better help solve personal and group problems. The chapter also considered the exceptional range of professional activities open to clinical psychologists. It was noted that clinical psychologists may be involved in assessment of abilities and deficits, treatment, research, teaching, consultation, and administration.

Finally, examples of three types of clinical research were presented: a case study, a single-subject experimental investigation, and several studies using behavorial modeling that were conducted using experimental designs. In the first, the case study, the treatment of a dependent, anxious, 18-year-old female college student was described. The use of client-centered therapy and systematic desensitization was described. The strengths and weaknesses of the case-study approach were assessed. In the single-subject investigation, a depressed borderline psychotic, 20-year-old female was treated in a state mental hospital with an operant conditioning technique. In an initial baseline period, the frequency of smiling and crying behaviors was observed. Baseline observations were followed by a treatment phase in which the patient was rewarded with tokens (redeemable for privileges) for desirable behavior and fined or punished, again by means of tokens, for undesirable behavior. Subsequent study revealed the power of these reinforcers in controlling the patient's behavior. Most exciting, reinforcement relationships, once established, generalized to the point that the patient could be discharged from the hospital into the community.

As an example of research using experimental designs, treatment strategies based on modeling were reviewed by presenting investigations that evaluated the effectiveness of several types of modeling in overcoming phobias. The differential effects of live-participant modeling, using several different models, as well as filmed symbolic models were investigated in several studies. Finally the applicability of this type of approach to the treatment of other mental problems was discussed.

To conclude this investigation of clinical psychology, it seems appropriate to indulge in some predictions about the future of the field. First, it is likely that the trend toward an emphasis on intervention will continue and will include the exploration of many more novel and hybrid techniques, as well as accompanying evaluation research on therapeutic effectiveness. Given the recent marked success of clinical psychologists in extending their professional roles, it seems probable that clinical psychologists will broaden still further the range of their activities and the settings in which these activities are pursued.

Glossary

behavior therapy   Application of principles of learning theory in order to change maladaptive behaviors.

client-centered therapy   A humanistic therapy that is nondirective and emphasizes the client's personal growth and decision making.

contingency-management techniques   Therapeutic techniques based on operant conditioning that seek to increase desirable behavior through rewards and decrease undesirable behavior through punishment.

eclectic orientation in therapy   The use of a number of different theoretical orientations in therapy. Different orientations may be used with different clients or several therapies from different theoretical perspectives may be used with the same client.

insight therapy   A group of treatment methods that focuses on developing a client's self-understanding.

modeling therapies   A group of treatment methods that uses social learning principles and presents clients with positive models. Learning to emulate the models helps overcome the problems they are experiencing.

participant modeling   A modeling therapy in which clients follow models and actually physically participate in activities that are difficult for them (for example, in overcoming a phobia).

self-efficacy   The feeling individuals have of being able to deal effectively with situations and problems.

symbolic modeling   A modeling therapy in which the client is vicariously exposed to a model (by, for example, seeing a video presentation) and learns the modeled behavior through observation.

systematic densensitization   A technique of behavioral therapy that pairs muscle relaxation with thoughts of objects or situations that are feared. The objects or situations are presented in hierarchical order from least to most feared.

token economy   A controlled environment where individuals are given tokens (like poker chips) in exchange for desirable behaviors. Tokens may also be taken away as fines for undesirable behaviors. The tokens may then be exchanged for reinforcers that are valued by participating individuals.

9 Community Psychology

Irwin N. Sandler
Arizona State University

Manuel Barrera
Arizona State University

The preceding chapter on clinical psychology described how psychologists work with individuals who are experiencing some kind of mental problem in their lives. Community psychology also seeks to help individuals, but in a different way. Community psychology looks for reasons for an individual's problems and solutions to those problems in community systems. This chapter is devoted to the community approach, focusing on (1) a definition of community psychology, (2) a survey of what community psychologists do, and (3) a presentation of representative approaches and research in this area.

What Is Community Psychology?

As you will see, community psychology has much in common with other fields of applied psychology. For example, community psychologists function in many of the same settings as do other applied psychologists — schools, mental health centers, work environments, correctional settings, police departments, and so on. Certain features, however, while not completely unique to community psychology, are especially emphasized in this field. It is the perspective of community psychology that distinguishes it from other fields of application. This perspective focuses on prevention of mental health problems and competence development as desirable objectives, and works within the framework of the natural ecology, the values and cultures of natural environments, to accomplish these outcomes.

Outcome Objectives

Community psychologists use the term **outcome objective** to refer to the things they want to accomplish while working within a community system. Two important outcome objectives are prevention of problems and development of competence.

Prevention as an Outcome Objective.   The concept of prevention can apply to a wide range of problems in the areas of physical and mental health, drug and alcohol abuse, and criminal justice. At its simplest level, prevention refers to interventions that change a problem's natural course of development. Caplan (1984) has described three types of prevention: primary, secondary, and tertiary. Primary prevention refers to efforts to prevent the original occurrence of a problem. Immunization against polio or smallpox would constitute primary prevention of those diseases. Secondary prevention refers to intervention in the early stages of the development of a disorder in order to prevent the problem from becoming ingrained and long lasting. Regular care to identify and repair cavities illustrates secondary prevention in dentistry. Tertiary prevention refers to intervention after a disorder is fully developed and is intended to minimize damage and salvage as much as possible of a person's normal functioning. Bypass surgery to improve function in a diseased heart is an example of tertiary prevention. Community psychologists are especially interested in primary and early secondary prevention, particularly in the area of mental health.

The case for prevention as a focus of activities in the mental health field has been well stated by Emory Cowen (1967) and Bernard Bloom (1979), among others. They point out that, historically, no physical illness has been wiped out by advances in treatment techniques, while many diseases have been conquered by prevention (e.g., polio, smallpox, and malaria). Cowen (1967) pointed out that, from a population perspective, prevention rather than treatment is the only strategy that will make a significant dent in the mental health problems of the nation. There simply are too many people with mental health problems (approximately 15% of children and 16%–25% of adults) to be treated by the limited number of expensive, professional, mental health workers. Furthermore, it is argued that a preventive approach involves intervening when problems are embryonic and more susceptible to change. Because interest in prevention is relatively new in the mental health field, techniques to effectively pursue this goal are just now being formulated. Community psychologists are in the forefront of developing such prevention techniques as early identification of problems, stress reduction, social system change to develop more supportive environments, and training of individuals to handle life's problems. Some of these techniques will be explained later in this chapter when action strategies in community psychology are discussed.

Competence Development as an Outcome Objective. A second type of outcome pursued by community psychologists is that of promoting positive human development, including the enhancement of a sense of control over one's life and of feelings of life satisfaction and well-being (Danish & D'Angelli, 1981; Rappaport, 1981; Sanford, 1972; Zautra & Sandler, 1983). An obvious overlap between these goals and those of prevention is that developing competencies in people helps them cope with life's challenges and prevents maladaptive outcomes. (Cowen, 1977). For example, good problem-solving skills usually denote personal competence and few adverse psychological symptoms. Interestingly, Kohlberg, La Crosse and Ricks (1972) found that the characteristic of children that best predicted good adjustment in adulthood was a high degree of personal competence. Thus there is good reason to believe that developing personal competencies is a useful approach to preventing mental health problems.

A second view, derived from the field of life-span developmental psychology, regards enhancing human competencies as a desirable end-goal in and of itself (Danish & D'Angelli, 1981; Sanford, 1972). Within this view people are seen as developing through different stages over the course of their lives. Each stage has its own predictable sources of conflict, its own challenges, and its own satisfactions. Levinson (1978), for example, described the stage of early adulthood as the period of leaving adolescence and entering adulthood, moving away from dependent relationships with parents and exploring adult roles. Positive handling of such developmental tasks results in attaining self-esteem, autonomy, and control over one's own life. Facilitating the development of these positive attributes is a goal of some community psychologists (Danish & D'Angelli, 1981).

A broader approach to competence development is that of empowerment (Rappaport, 1982). This approach attempts to enhance people's control over their lives by helping them cope with social systems that deprive them of their sense of control. For example, Reiff and Reisman (1967) developed neighborhood centers in which the poor could organize to make bureaucratic service organizations responsive to their needs. Newbrough (1980) stated that because modern industrial society is too complex for individuals to cope with directly, people work through smaller social groups (e.g., families, clubs, churches). In addition to addressing the functioning of these smaller groups, community psychologists may also take part in social policy analysis to define the rights of powerless, unrepresented groups.

Ecological Approach to Intervention

Community psychologists are distinguished not only by their objectives but also by the processes they employ in working with the natural community to achieve these objectives. Community psychologists take what Kelly (1972) has called an **ecological view of human functioning,** meaning that problems are seen as faulty adaptation in the natural environment rather than solely as deficiencies of individuals. The ecological view means that, first, community psychologists need to know the communities in which they are working. A community could be any social environment in which people function — school, neighborhood, hospital, workplace, or church.

Kelly (1972) suggested using four principles from biological ecology to guide community psychologists' assessment of natural social environments. These are the principles of interdependence, cycling of resources, adaptation, and succession.

Principle of Interdependence. Because all the components of a community are interrelated, a change in one affects each of the others. For example, changes that make teachers feel more appreciated and more important will affect their behavior toward children in their classes. This in turn will affect how children behave in school, which in turn may further reinforce teachers' positive feelings about their jobs. On the other hand, the interdependence of components of the school may result in negative effects where they are not expected. For example, introducing a new counseling service for aggressive children may lead teachers to believe that these children are the responsibility of that program. Thus teachers may refer difficult children to the special program and not make a serious effort to handle them in the regular classroom. Childen referred to the service may believe they are labeled as "bad" and increase negative behavior in order to live up to the label. Before planning to institute changes, community psychologists must be aware of the interdependencies between components.

Principle of Cycling of Resources. The community has within itself resources that can be used to solve many of its problems. For example, many people in a school may be skilled in helping students who are experiencing personal problems. Teachers, coaches, other students, parents, as well as guidance counselors, may have relevant interpersonal skills. These skills may be seen as resources of the natural school community and used so by a community to solve its own problems. A community psychologist's role is to help the community mobilize its own resources, not to claim that professional skills are more useful.

Principle of Adaptation. Different skills or competencies are necessary to successfully adapt to the demands of each community. Problem behavior is seen as a failure of adaptation to environmental demands, rather than simply as a deficiency of an individual or as mental illness. What appears to be problem behavior may be quite appropriate in a different environment. For example, immigrant children may be adept at verbal expression in their native language, but may mistakenly be seen as lacking in intelligence because they cannot handle the new language at the proficiency level demanded by the schools. A community psychologist interested in helping these children meet school demands would want to build on already existing competencies rather than to dismiss them.

A second implication of this principle of adaptation is that, for some individuals, the natural environment may not provide roles in which they can use their existing adaptive skills. For example, psychiatric patients who have been hospitalized for many years may not have families, jobs, or friendships to which they can return. Their only role has been that of dependent patient with few skills for independent living. In this situation, a community psychologist might try to create a new social environment in which psychiatric patients may use the skills they do have to lead independent and productive lives. Such a program, the Lodge Program (Fairweather, Sanders, Cressler, & Maynard, 1968), will be presented later in this chapter.

Principle of Succession. In the natural course of things, all communities change. They must adapt to change in the external environment. The role of a community psychologist is not simply to help the community mobilize its resources to solve current problems, but to help it prepare for future changes. For example, a school may be affected by changes in the job market and in local economic conditions, technological advances, and new social pressures. A community psychologist takes a long-term perspective and asks how current work in the community will affect its ability to meet future challenges. Asking this question implies a need to foster the development of leaders in the community. After community psychologists have completed their efforts, who will assume the roles they previously played? Long-term success of community interventions requires planning for the succession to leadership.

Historical Context: A Response to Dissatisfaction

Community psychology has developed largely as a response to perceived problems in using other forms of psychological treatment and intervention. In order to fully understand the perspective of community psychology, one must appreciate the problems it seeks to overcome. The brief history of community psychology is the story of response to needs unmet by traditional practices.

There are no dusty, yellow-paged volumes on the history of community psychology. In many ways these are the developmental years of this emerging field. The event that is regarded as marking the birth of community psychology, the Boston (or Swampscott) Conference, was held in May, 1965. Many who have analyzed the brief history of community psychology have noted that much of the impetus for its development can be attributed to skepticism and discontent over the medical model of mental health care that predominated in the early 1950s (Bernstein & Nietzel, 1980; Heller & Monahan, 1977; Zax & Specter, 1974). The community mental health movement, which has been described as the "third revolution in mental health," was a direct result of the disenchantment voiced throughout the 1950s. Community psychology, in turn, emerged from this revolution by extending mental health concepts from an emphasis on sickness and deficits toward community concepts of health prevention and the development of competencies.

Dissatisfaction with the ways that mental health services have traditionally been provided centered on the limited usefulness of psychotherapy and clinical assessment, the lack of availability of mental health care to people in lower social classes, and overcrowding in mental hospitals.

Questionable Efficacy of Psychotherapy.   One source of disenchantment with the medical model of mental health care was a nagging doubt about the effectiveness of psychotherapy, a primary mode of intervention. One prominent psychologist in particular, Hans Eysenck, cast doubt on the usefulness of this modality. In a landmark review of 24 studies that evaluated the effectiveness of psychotherapy, Eysenck (1952) argued that rates of improvement for neurotic patients following pschotherapy were essentially the same as improvement rates for those who did not receive this form of treatment.

Eysenck's highly controversial conclusions were carefully scrutinized by some researchers, who raised numerous objections and counterarguments. In his historical review of psychotherapy research, VandenBos (1980) labeled the period from 1952-1965 "Eysenck's Era," an explicit acknowledgment of the impact of the challenge. As VandenBos noted, Eysenck's arguments were so thoroughly attacked and discredited by numerous writers that they are not seriously considered today. However, in the 1950s and 1960s Eysenck's conclusions had a strong impact. They were frequently cited by those who expressed doubts about the success of traditional methods in mental health care and favored the development of alternative approaches.

Lowered Expectations Concerning Clinical Assessment.   Psychological assessment was the first prominent function of psychologists in delivering mental health care. During World Wars I and II psychologists assessed thousands of recruits to determine their fitness for service in the armed forces. With an explosion in the availability of psychological tests between 1920 and 1945, assessment occupied a prominent place in work and educational settings as well as in mental health care. The pervasive sense was that, with their special skills and training, clinicians could use psychological tests to understand and predict a wide array of behaviors across diverse settings.

However, while Eysenck was attacking psychotherapy, other psychologists were also questioning the overall utility of assessment and the ability of clinicians to make complex judgments about human behavior. In 1954 Paul Meehl published the results of his review of studies comparing the accuracy of predictions made through clinicians' judgments versus those made by the statistical combination of test results. His findings showed that, of the 20 studies he reviewed, only one supported the superiority of clinical inference while 11 provided clear support for statistical predictions. Meehl's subsequent reviews in 1957 and 1965 provided even stronger support for superiority of some type of statistical combination of assessment information over the evaluations of clinicians. In fact, other research published about this same time also suggested that specialized clinical training can actually lead to an impaired ability to make clinical inferences from assessment information (see Wiggins, 1973, for a review of some of these studies).

Unequal Distribution of Mental Health Care across Social Classes.   The recognition that mental health services were inequitably distributed to the various strata of society was another source of dissatisfaction with traditional methods of mental health care. Several influential studies pointed out that access to such care was heavily determined by individuals' socioeconomics status, and not necessarily by their need for services.

In their pioneering study, Hollingshead and Redlich (1958) surveyed individuals in New Haven, Connecticut, who had received mental health services. These researchers were interested in determining if socioeconomic status was related to the likelihood of receiving mental health services and to the type of services rendered. After grouping people in their study into five socioeconomic classes (with Class I being the highest status and Class V being the lowest), Hollingshead and Redlich compared the representation of each class in the population of mental-health-service users. These comparisons showed that individuals from the highest socioeconomic classes tended to be underrepresented in the ranks of mental health patients while individuals from the lowest socioeconomic class (Class V) were markedly overrepresented. After adjustment for the influence of age and sex, the rate of treated mental illness (per 100,000 of the general population) was 1,668 for Class V but only 553 for the combined Classes I and II.

Socioeconomic class also affected the type of care received by mental health patients. Among severely disturbed patients, those from the higher socioeconomic classes were much more likely to receive psychotherapy than were those from lower socioeconomic classes. Evidence suggested that, compared to patients of higher socioeconomic status, patients in the lower strata were more often treated in public facilities where they were likely to receive drug treatment and other physical interventions (such as psychosurgery and electroconvulsive treatment) or custodial care.

A separate group of investigators explored similar questions in a study of Midtown Manhattan residents (Srole, Langner, Michael, Opler, & Rennie, 1962). In contrast to the New Haven study, the Midtown Manhattan survey was not restricted just to those who had obtained mental health services. Information based on extensive interviews with community residents involved in this survey was used to rate the severity of psychiatric disorder, whether or not an individual was actually receiving mental health treatment. Like the New Haven study by Hollingshead and Redlich, this survey showed that the highest rate of mental disorder was in the lower socioeconomic groups and that individuals from lower social classes were least likely to receive mental health services. In other words, those with the greatest need for mental health services appeared to be least likely to receive them.

Overcrowded Psychiatric Hospitals.　The number of individuals who were hospitalized for mental health care reached its peak in 1955 when over 559,000 patients resided in inpatient psychiatric facilities nationwide. These numbers are even more staggering when one considers that caring for these patients cost over $600 million a year and that psychiatric patients occupied two out of every three hospital beds in the country (Heller & Monahan, 1977). This heavy demand on inpatient facilities occurred prior to the advent of effective drug regimens and at a time when public facilities were barely able to provide custodial care be-

At one time more than half a million Americans resided in mental hospitals, some of them as grim as the overcrowded facility pictured. Since 1963 the movement to deinstitutionalize has brought thousands of patients back to their communities and drastically reduced inpatient admissions.

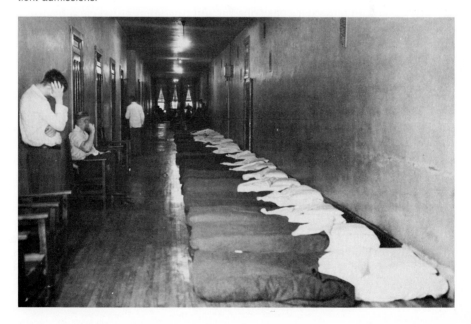

cause of small operating budgets. Thus the argument was made that the traditional mental health system was warehousing hundreds of thousands of patients, without providing a reasonable avenue to recovery or rehabilitation.

New Approaches to Mental Health Care. As discontent mounted, there developed broad agreement among private, government, and professional groups that a thorough analysis of mental health problems was needed, as well as some innovative approaches to solving these problems. Movement toward this goal increased dramatically in 1963 when President John F. Kennedy made history by being the first United States President to deliver a special message to Congress on the topic of mental health. In his message Kennedy highlighted the inadequacies of existing methods of treatment, particularly the overcrowded, expensive, and ineffective state mental hospitals. He proposed an innovative federal initiative designed to lower the population in state mental hospitals and create community mental health centers that would allow individuals to receive services in their own communities rather than in centralized facilities. Treatment was to be provided to the total community, that is, all those in need, rather than just to those who could afford private care. Prevention and community education, touted as approaches holding great promise, were recommended as future areas of emphasis. Following President Kennedy's address to Congress, legislation was proposed to implement the new approaches described in his speech. Controversy surrounded these recommendations, such as the opposition of the American Medical Association (which opposed federal involvement in the provision of mental health care), but Kennedy finally signed the Community Mental Health Centers Act on October 31, 1963, just three weeks before his assassination.

The plan underlying the construction of community mental health centers called for the establishment of nearly 1,500 catchment areas across the nation. Catchment areas were essentially regions consisting of 75,000 to 200,000 residents who would be served by a community mental health center. Centers were to provide five basic services: (1) inpatient hospitalization, (2) outpatient care, (3) emergency treatment, (4) partial hospitalization (such as "day" hospitals), and (5) consultation and education. An important specification of the Act was that services were to be accessible to all residents of the catchment area, including those who could not pay the full cost of the services.

While the Community Mental Health Centers Act was a product of a careful analysis of the nation's mental health needs, its enactment was certainly influenced by the social and political climate of the early 1960s. The civil rights movement focused the nation's attention on the inequities existing in the distribution of services and opportunities for quality education, employment, housing, and other basic resources. The nation was sensitized to the inadequacies of service delivery systems that often failed to reach those in greatest need. Within a year of the signing of the Community Mental Health Centers Act, two other significant pieces of legislation were passed, the Civil Rights Act of 1964 and the Economic Opportunities Act. These acts collectively reflected the federal government's leadership role in remediating inequities through the implementation of the new social policies. It was this era of significant social change that provided the historical context for the birth of community psychology.

In May, 1965, a conference was held in Swampscott, Massachusetts, a suburb of Boston, in order to discuss recent developments in community mental health and the special issues involved in training personnel for this new mental health movement. This conference has been labeled the birthplace of community psychology, since during its five days of discussion many of the basic concepts of community psychology were formulated. Although many psychologists who participated in the conference were converted clinicians, they viewed community psychology as more than just a subspecialty of clinical psychology. Community psychology was portrayed as a field in which broad areas within psychology — such as social, developmental, and organizational psychology — could be integrated. In addition, interdisciplinary approaches to tackling community problems were advocated. This was reflected in the conference's recommendation for the training of community psychologists to include content from fields such as anthropology, sociology, political science, public health, law, and public planning. Many traditional views of clinical psychology, including its terminology and emphasis on sickness and psychological deficits, were rejected in favor of paying greater attention to normal development, well-being, prevention, and societal-level interventions. Perhaps due to their recognition that research was necessary for the survival and growth of the fledgling field, conference participants stressed the importance of the scientific attitude in the evaluation of social interventions and the production of new knowledge.

The years time since the Swampscott Conference have been a time of both growth and continued critical self-examination. Another important training conference, the Austin Conference, was held in 1975 to further clarify the skills involved in community psychology and to describe training models for developing these skills.

Since 1965, the number of psychology departments that offer specialized training in community psychology has grown steadily. The nature of this training and the challenges for the future of community psychology will be discussed later in this chapter.

What Do Community Psychologists Do?

Now that the perspective of community psychology has been defined, it is time to describe what community psychologists actually do. There are in fact several categories of activities in which community psychologists become involved: (1) assessing community needs and services, (2) application of behavioral techniques to social problems, (3) development of human-service programs, (4) planning of changes to solve social problems, and (5) building of competencies in individuals and environments.

Assessing Community Needs and Services

An important skill for community psychologists is the ability to assess a community's mental health needs and the adequacy of existing services for meeting those needs. **Needs assessment** can be characterized as "a research and planning activity designed to determine a community's mental health service needs and utilization patterns, on the basis of which agencies will be able to (1) identify the extent and kinds of needs there are in a community, (2) evaluate systematically their existing programs, and (3) plan new ones in the light of community needs and mental health service patterns" (Warheit, Bell, & Schwab, 1977, p. 4). Oftentimes community planners have the responsibility of identifying specific subpopulations or areas within a community that are at a high risk for the development of disorders and of facilitating the delivery of services to these subgroups or geographic regions. In the medical model of service delivery, needs assessment was not a very important topic. Individuals were viewed as having the responsibility of determining whether they were in need of human services and then obtaining these services through whatever resources were available to them. However, when public planners are responsible for the well-being of the entire community, assessing community needs and facilitating the delivery of services to those in need are critical issues.

Applying Behavioral Techniques to Social Problems

Social-learning theory and behavior therapy generated considerable excitement during the 1960s, just about the same time community psychology was making its appearance. It was predictable that behavioral models would have some impact on the development of the assessment and intervention strategies that are applied to community problems. In community settings — just as in clinical, educational, and criminal-justice settings — behavioral approaches appear to be particularly valuable as a technology for pinpointing skill deficits in individuals, implementing change programs that supply the requisite learning, and carefully assessing the degree to which identified skills are acquired and desired goals met.

Developing Human Service Programs

Community psychologists have been active in developing services for a wide range of human problems including mental health, juvenile delinquency, and physical health. Their approach across specific problem areas is colored by an identifiable perspective. The community approach emphasizes (1) development and utilization of human resources, (2) active delivery of services where and when most useful, and (3) maintaining client integration within the natural environment and minimizing client dependency on, or institutionalization within, the treatment system.

Planning Changes to Solve Social Problems

The activities of community psychologists described up to this point primarily focus on changing individuals. While such activities have often been productive, many community psychologists believe that human problems can be viewed as the consequences of social systems that do not function effectively or within which people do not enjoy access to resources promoting healthy personal development. For example, the mental health problems of some people may be attributed to unemployment, and learning problems of poor and minority children may be due to inadequate school systems. Furthermore, many of the systems society has developed in response to problems (e.g., the juvenile-justice system or psychiatric hospitals) can exacerbate these very problems. Thus many community psychologists work at a societal level to develop and implement new solutions to a wide range of social problems.

Finding new solutions usually requires changes in society's traditional way of handling problems as well as in the responsible organizations themselves. Institutions such as schools, universities, hospitals, correctional facilities, and businesses have developed ways of handling problems over many years. Change in these accustomed ways is viewed as threatening and often resisted. Furthermore, not all new solutions are successful; innovative programs may look promising but in practice may not produce any meaningful improvement. As a result of the context within which change occurs, community psychologists interested in planned social change must be willing to assume the multiple roles of creating, implementing, and evaluating interventions.

Building Competencies in Individuals and Environments

In recent years community psychologists have increasingly focused on building the positive characteristics or competencies of people and on modifying social environments to support positive behavior. This focus is sometimes seen as a path towards **primary prevention,** a way of eliminating the causes of mental health problems (Cowen, 1977). Others suggest that the enhancement of positive qualities of life, such as the ability to control one's own life or to find satisfaction in completing life tasks, is in and of itself an appropriate goal for community psychologists (Danish & D'Angelli, 1981; Zautra & Sandler, 1983). A final role of community psychologists, then, is to develop these competencies in individuals and their environments.

Research and Applications

This section will review in detail some examples of the progress that has been made in applying the approaches of community psychology. Theory and research related to each of the five areas described in the preceding section will be presented.

Assessing Community Needs and Services

Needs assessment actually involves a number of approaches that vary considerably in their complexity, strengths, and weaknesses. Warheit et al. (1977) identified five types of needs assessment approaches: (1) key informant, (2) community forum, (3) rates-under-treatment, (4) social indicators, and (5) field survey.

Key-Informant Approach. In the **key-informant approach** individuals who are extremely knowledgeable about the community are called on to provide relevant information to those who are conducting the needs assessment. These individuals are asked to complete written questionnaires, or are interviewed by telephone or in person to obtain fairly standardized information concerning a set of important issues. Sometimes key informants are brought together in meetings to discuss their views on the community's needs.

Among the advantages of the key-informant approach are simplicity and relatively low cost. Since many of these informants are likely to be community leaders, agency heads, and public officials, a desirable by-product of key-informant surveys is improved communication among influential members of the community. The major disadvantage of this approach is that these informants are not always representative of the community at large. Because they often represent special-interest groups or serve specific populations, their perceptions of the community's needs are likely to be biased.

The community-forum approach to needs assessment can develop a large amount of information, but assessors must be aware that opinions expressed may not be completely representative of community wishes.

Community-Forum Approach.   A second method indentified by Warheit et al. (1977) is the **community-forum approach.** In contrast to the key-informant method, this approach attempts to solicit opinions and information from a broad spectrum of community residents. In order to obtain participants, sponsors announce the open forums in public media such as newspapers, television, and radio, or through social agencies, community organizations, and churches.

Meetings may vary in size, objectives, and the settings in which they take place, but generally the goals are to attract large numbers of community residents, to encourage the open exchange of information from those present, to monitor the discussion so that the desired topics are addressed, and to carefully record the contents of the discussion.

An attractive feature of the forum approach is that it calls for active community participation. Because the forum is largely open-ended, it is useful in developing subjective impressions of a broad range of community needs. A chief limitation of the method is that the needs assessor cannot be confident that the information provided is representative of the entire community. This is particularly the case when attendance at meetings is light or when discussions are dominated by small groups of highly vocal individuals.

Rates-under-Treatment Method.   The **rates-under-treatment method** is an approach that uses information concerning individuals who actually receive treatment from public and/or private treatment facilities. As a needs assessment tool, its basic underlying assumption is that "the needs of the community (population) can be estimated from a sample of persons who have received care or treatment" (Warheit et al., 1977, p. 26). Information regarding the age, employment status, ethnicity, and place of residence of treatment recipients might be evaluated in order to determine the types of people who appear to be in need of services.

In settings that routinely collect these kinds of data, rates-under-treatment studies are relatively easy to conduct. This method also requires few inferences about the demand for services, since the information clearly reflects those individuals who have actually obtained treatment during a specified period of time. Although the rates-under-treatment approach is frequently used for planning services, its value as a needs assessment method has been criticized. It certainly cannot be assumed that all those in need of services actually obtain services. As noted by Bachrach and Zautra (1980): "Possibly the greatest potential misuse of client data lies in the area of needs assessment, when attempts are made to estimate community need based on demand for services. Since the demand for and utilization of services depends upon the availability, acceptability, and accessibility of services along with the public's awareness of these services (Bell et al., 1978), service utilization rates may not accurately reflect need" (p. 368). From a community-psychology perspective, the most relevant question is not, What are the characteristics of those who obtain services? It is, What are the characteristics of those who are in need of services, but who are not receiving them? Making this latter determination is the challenging aspect of needs assessment that cannot be clearly addressed by the rates-under-treatment approach.

Social-Indicators Approach. Some have argued that a community's mental health needs can be inferred from key **social indicators** rather than by direct evaluation of residents' perceptions of those needs. Social indicators are measurable components of community life that are viewed as correlates of needs. For example, divorce rates, family income, residential mobility, housing density, and rates of high school completion might be used as indicators of mental-health-service need. This practice is completely comparable to the use of statistics on unemployment rates, housing starts or new automobiles purchased as indicators of economic vitality.

Information for a social-indicator approach to needs assessment is readily available from census data. The National Institute of Mental Health Demographic Profile System (Rosen, Lawrence, Goldsmith, Windle, & Shambaugh, 1975) provides information on over 100 social-indicator variables for census tracts located within community-mental-health-center catchment areas. The most serious questions concerning social indicators is their validity. Typically such indicators are not obviously measures of mental health need, but they can be predictive of the mental health needs of an area.

Survey Approaches. In survey approaches, data are collected from a sample of community residents in order to characterize the mental health needs of a population. Because individual residents are typically assessed, the kinds of information that can be collected are not restricted to objective sociodemographic characteristics. A survey's contents might include measures of an individual's perceived quality of life, psychological symptomatology, use of community services, extensiveness of social relationships, and satisfaction with human-service delivery systems. Survey methods include mailed questionnaires, telephone interviews, and door-to-door personal interviews. Sophisticated sampling procedures are often used in survey approaches in order to accurately characterize the population interest.

Warheit et al. (1977) regarded the survey approach as the most powerful needs assessment method available and one that avoids many of the shortcomings of the other approaches that have been described. The major disadvantages of the survey modality are cost and the fact that it requires a high rate of cooperation from community residents who are sampled. The cost is high because professional involvement is necessary in designing the survey instrument, training interviewers, and conducting the interviews. The more extensive the interview and the larger the sample, the greater the expense. Sacrifices at any of these steps are likely to deflate the quality of the assessment by decreasing the reliability of the information or by decreasing the generalizability of the findings. Costs can be reduced by using mailed questionnaires rather than personal interviews, but surveys that rely on mailed questionnaires are notorious for their low completion rates. The validity of inferences about the population critically depends on a high degree of cooperation among the sampled population.

Representative Application: Community-Needs Assessment. A study by Bachrach and Zautra (1980) illustrated a needs-assessment approach that used information from the client records of a community mental health center in com-bination with social indicators derived from census data. These researchers took three approaches to analyzing the data. First, they conducted a "geographic" analysis of client and census data. Census tracts that differed in their rates of community mental health center use were compared on a number of social in-dicators that were provided in census data. After dividing the catchment area's census tracts into low-, medium-, and high-use groups, the investigators deter-mined if the groups differed on any of 12 social indicators. Tracts that showed high use rates were distinguished by low income, low education, high marital disruption, and high prevalence of Mexican-American residents.

In a second type of analysis, the demographic characteristics of mental health center clients were compared to those of the general population of the catch-ment area. Among the differences that were revealed, clinic clients showed an unemployment rate of 34% compared to 6% for the catchment area in general. The third set of analyses compared those clinic users who terminated treatment after two sessions with those who remained in therapy for a longer period of time. Widows, the unemployed, the non-college-educated, and non-Caucasians evidenced the highest dropout rates.

Taken together, these analyses allowed for the identification of those charac-teristics of census tracts that contained high numbers of services users, those characteristics of users that distinguished them from the general catchment area population, and those characteristics of early terminators that distinguished them from other clinic users.

As was the case in the Bachrach and Zautra (1980) study, needs assessments often reveal special patterns of psychological symptoms or service utilization for distinct subgroups. When different rates of need are observed, additional studies are sometimes conducted to further understand the factors that appear to account for unusually high or low need. A study by Padilla and his associ-ates exemplified the use of a survey approach to describe the use of mental health services by Mexican-Americans. This survey included a broad assessment of for-mal and informal social supports that may be consulted by Mexican-Americans and others in times of emotional need (Keefe, Padilla, & Carlos, 1979). In numer-ous studies, Mexican-Americans have shown low service-utilization rates (cf. Bar-rera, 1978) but this finding is paradoxical, since they should experience high need on the basis of social indicators that point to this group's low education, low income, poor housing, and so on (Acosta, 1979). One of the explanations that has been offered is that, rather than using formal mental health services, Mexican-Americans more frequently use alternative resources, such as priests and physi-cians, or nonprofessionals, such as friends, family members, and *curanderos* (folk healers).

In order to compare the use of formal and informal mental health services by Mexican-Americans and those of European origin, a study was conducted in three California communities (Keefe et al., 1979). In the first year of the project, 666 Mexican-American and 340 Euro-American residents were interviewed. In this assessment they were asked which helping resources (clinics, physicians, friends, family members, etc.) they had consulted for emotional support during the preceding year. In the second survey, 372 Mexican-American and 165 Euro-American respondents from the first assessment were reinterviewed. This time subjects were asked to indicate which resources they had ever used for emotional support.

The two ethnic groups were similar in age, gender, and marital status, but they differed considerably in education, occupational status, and residential mobility. While 69% of Mexican-Americans had not completed high school, 50% of European-Americans had completed one or more years of college. Most Mexican-Americans (85%) held blue-collar jobs, compared to 55% of European-Americans who were employed in white-collar occupations. Mexican-Americans had lived in the town where they were interviewed an average of 24 years compared to 15 years for European-Americans.

European-Americans were more likely than Mexican-Americans to use mental-health clinics in both the first (5% vs. 2%) and second (10% vs. 7%) interviews. The results for the other sources of emotional support were not so consistent across the two assessment periods. In the first survey, relatively few European-Americans (12%) reported consulting a physician for emotional problems during the year past; 21% of the Mexican-Americans reported doing so. However, in the second survey 34% of Euro-Americans reported the use of physicians for emotional support compared to 25% of Mexican-Americans.

In both surveys, relatives were reported to be important mental health resources for both Mexican- and Euro-Americans, though the exact percentages changed somewhat from the first to the second assessments. In both surveys Euro-Americans more frequently reported friends to be sources of emotional support compared to Mexican-Americans.

Keefe et al. summarized the results of their survey in the following manner. They wrote:

> Anglos appear to have a wider range of mental health resources and more readily recognize a wider range of emotional problems as requiring some type of outside help . . . . In sum, although our research shows that Mexican-Americans rely greatly on familial support, there is no indication that this is a uniquely Mexican-American trait . . . . Therefore, there is little reason to believe that the presence of the extended family can be the reason for an alleged lower incidence of mental illness among Mexican-Americans (Keefe et al., 1979, p. 51).

This study went beyond many needs assessment surveys in that it (a) provided an in-depth analysis of Mexican-Americans, a subgroup that has frequently been shown to underutilize services and (b) assessed the use of a broad range of "alternative" services in order to account for the usage rates of formal mental health services. On the basis of these data, the hypothesis that Mexican-Americans primarily use alternative mental health resources does not appear to be supported and does not account for their underuse of mental health clinics. Planners might interpret these data as evidence that agencies should alter their services in order to make them more attractive to this underserved subgroup. In fact, when agencies have changed their personnel and service-delivery style to accommodate Mexican-American clients, equitable use of services has often resulted (Bloom, 1975; Karno & Morales, 1971; Phillipus, 1971).

Behavioral Approaches to Community Psychology

The technology of behavioral psychology emphasizes the learning of new ideas and skills through some type of reinforcement. The range of techniques used includes positive and negative reinforcement, modeling, and programmed instruction.

Many observers note that the match between community psychology and behavioral approaches is far from perfect, but certain features in the behavioral perspective are compatible with community psychology. Rappaport (1977) cited two areas of compatibility: (1) both behavioral and community perspectives point to environmental factors as keys to understanding individuals' behavior, and (2) both perspectives call for interventions that are broadly applicable and that make efficient use of time and human resources.

Behavioral approaches have been applied to a diversity of community problems. Sections in Nietzel, Winett, MacDonald, & Davidson (1977) are devoted to behavioral applications in problem areas such as criminal justice, employment, education, energy conservation, public transportation, and littering. Examples of the use of behavioral techniques in improving the job skills of individuals are described below.

Representative Application: Development of Underskilled Individuals.   An illustration of one application was provided by Connor and Rappaport (1970), who used behavioral techniques to assist six "hard core," unemployed men in securing a particular job. All the participants in the behavioral intervention had marginal education and histories of long-term unemployment and/or incarceration. To be eligible for the position of childcare aides in publicly funded facilities for the mentally retarded and emotionally disturbed, applicants had to score high on a standardized civil-service examination.

The consultants used a variety of behavioral techniques such as reinforcement, modeling, role playing, and programmed-learning sequences in their efforts to train these men not only in test-taking, but also for engaging in job interviews. Monetary incentives were provided to the participants for attending training sessions, completing in-session tasks, and doing homework assignments. One trainee dropped out of the program and a second man moved out of town, but four of the original six successfully completed this behavioral instruction and obtained the jobs they sought. In light of the subjects' unemployment history and their prior lack of success in academic settings, the authors of the report regarded the behavioral intervention as a real success and a good example of an application of behavioral technology to a significant community problem.

Changing the behavior of individuals can have widespread effects when those individuals occupy key positions in the community and make decisions affecting large numbers of community residents. Another interesting application of behavioral techniques involved the training of the board of directors of a community organization (Briscoe, Hoffman, & Bailey, 1975). The authors of this article noted that social policy changes mandated the inclusion of indigenous community residents in governing bodies of community organizations, but provisions for training members of these boards were never specified in the new policy directives. The purpose of this particular behavioral intervention was to teach members of a community board how to solve problems. Three male and six female board members of a self-help education project were participants in this intervention. These board members ranged in age from 15 to 69, were from low-income households, and had a median education level of eighth grade.

Briscoe et al. were familiar with previous attempts to assist this board in improving their problem-solving abilities. Apparently inadequacy in this area had been noted for a considerable period of time. Prior to the initiation of behavioral procedures, groups of graduate students had worked with individual board members in unsystematic attempts to help them prepare for meetings. These efforts did little to alleviate the board's difficulties in solving problems and initiating constructive actions.

As the initial step in this behavioral approach, problem solving was broken down into three components: (1) identifying the problem, (2) producing and evaluating alternative solutions, and (3) selecting appropriate solutions and making specific plans for implementing them. Prior to training, baseline observations of the board's problem-solving activities were made over the course of seven board meetings. Each of these meetings was videotaped to develop procedures for evaluating the problem-solving behavior of the board members. After training, the board's meetings were again videotaped to evaluate the effectiveness of the interventions.

Training for the board members in each of the problem-solving components was provided in 30-minute segments before each of the board meetings. Behavioral techniques used to train individual board members included prompting of desirable problem-solving behaviors, shaping, and differential social reinforcement for desired behavior. Two of the nine board members who did not receive training served as controls.

The results of this project supported the effectiveness of behavioral procedures in improving problem-solving behaviors. Each of the problem-solving components increased substantially above baseline following the related training phase and showed some evidence of being maintained in subsequent meetings. The two control subjects did not change their problem-solving behavior in any detectible way, even though they participated in the meetings with the other members who had received training.

Limitations of the Behavioral Approach.   Behavioral approaches to community problems have important limitations as well as beneficial effects. Even though behaviorally oriented psychologists look to the environment for the reasons people behave as they do, individuals and their behavior, rather than the environment, are typically targeted for change. A technology aimed at understanding and modifying individual behavior may be of little relevance for understanding a community's behavior (Rappaport, 1977). As Rappaport suggested, "The challenge for community psychology is to apply the individual conceptions useful to person-oriented prevention in conjunction with the social change conceptions of systems-oriented prevention so as to create a psychology of the community rather than one limited to the individual" (p. 80).

A second limitation has to do with the demonstrated effectiveness of behavioral approaches to community problems. Contrary to initial expectations, behavioral approaches have not been effective in creating large and lasting changes (Rappaport, 1977). Following their book-length review of behavioral community psychology applications, Nietzel et al. (1977) commented, "concurrent with the recognition and appreciation of behavioral contributions to the remediation of community problems, one must confront the fact that behavioral strategies for effecting generalized, sustained social change are more a future promise than a present reality" (p. 345).

The marginal effectiveness of behavioral community strategies is partially related to still another of their limitations, that is, the barriers to implementing behavioral interventions in community settings. Even after identifying the reasons why individuals are reinforced to behave as they do, behavioral psychologists may be powerless to alter these factors. "Who controls the reinforcers?" becomes the central question to consider. Many of the issues that Repucci and Saunders (1974) discussed with respect to the implementation of behavioral programs in institutional settings are directly relevant to their implementation in community psychology more generally. These problems included bureaucratic systems that are resistant to change, basic philosophical objections to nonhumanistic elements of behavioral approaches, and resources inadequate to implement effective behavioral programs.

Despite their promise, the contributions of behavioral approaches to community psychology have been modest. Nevertheless, these approaches have their followers who continue to strive to solve community problems through behavioral strategies.

Developing Human-Service Programs

As has been noted, the community approach emphasizes primary prevention — efforts to stop problems from originally occurring — and secondary prevention — efforts to intervene in the early stages of the development of problems. What kinds of human-service programs should be designed to meet these goals? Community psychologists have sought to (a) develop and use human resources already existing within communities, (b) deliver services at the most useful places and time, (c) maintain clients' integration within their natural environments, and (d) minimize client dependency on or institutionalization within the treatment system. Each of these efforts will be treated in more detail.

Development of Existing Helping Resources.   Decades ago it became clear that there was not and never could be a sufficient number of professionals to provide care for the numbers of people in the population who had psychological problems (Albee, 1959). Furthermore, there was little evidence that everyone with mental health problems required the skills of highly trained mental health professionals. It has been argued, for example, that some people, because of their personal characteristics of caring, warmth, enthusiasm, or maturity, may be natural helpers.

Representative Application: Intervention With Paraprofessionals. Poser (1964), for example, found that hospitalized psychiatric patients who attended groups run by undergraduate college students showed more improvement than patients in traditional group therapy conducted by mental health professionals. Similarly, paraprofessionals with relatively little mental health training have been successful in working with adolescents in legal difficulty (Goodman, 1972; Tharp & Wetzel, 1969), preschool children (Specter & Cowen, 1971), people in crisis (McGee, 1974), college students (Tucker, Meginitz, & Vigil, 1970), and school-age children (Cowen, Trost, Lorion, Dorr, Izzo, & Isaacson, 1975). In fact, a recent literature review of 42 studies that compared professional and paraprofessional helpers reported provocative data on the use of paraprofessionals. In 12 of the studies, clients seen by paraprofessionals improve more, in 2 studies clients seen by professionals improved more, and in 28 studies there were no significant differences between clients seen by professionals and paraprofessionals (Durlak, 1979). While it would be incorrect to infer from this evidence that paraprofessionals are necessarily more effective than professionals, it certainly does indicate that relatively untrained persons can be efffectively used in human-service roles.

Active Service Delivery. Some community psychologists have argued that intervention should occur while problems are in their very earliest stages of development, rather than when they are fully developed and ingrained. This is essentially what is termed secondary prevention (Caplan, 1964), based on the idea that later, more serious problems can be prevented by early intervention efforts.

Representative Application: Paraprofessionals in Secondary Prevention. One program that exemplified both the use of paraprofessional mental health workers and early secondary prevention is the Primary Mental Health Project (Cowen et al., 1975). This program will be described in some detail to illustrate elements of the community-psychology approach to human services.

The initial impetus for the Primary Mental Health Project was the observation of school psychologists and social workers that children being seen for mental health problems in the seventh and eighth grades were the same children who had been referred for services in the early primary grades. The initial research target was the scientific validation of this informal observation. Were later child behavior problems predictable from early problems? In order to study this question, psychological screening of all first-grade children was initiated. The screening involved psychological testing of the children, interviews with their parents,

The Primary Mental Health Project was designed to learn if later child behavior problems could be predicted on the basis of early problems. Psychological testing of first-graders was part of the initial screening.

teacher reports, and observations of children in the classroom. A decision of whether a child was currently experiencing mental health problems or was likely to develop such problems in the future (a "red-tag" child) was made by the research team based on all available information. Approximately 30% of the first-grade children were designated as "red-tag." Follow-up evaluation of children at third- and seventh-grade levels found that red-tag children were indeed experiencing more problems than non-red-tag children. Red-tag children had poorer grades, lower scores on standardized achievement tests, and more referrals to the school nurse. They were also rated more negatively by teachers and classmates in both the third and seventh grades. Furthermore, in follow-up studies performed 11 to 13 years subsequent to the assessment, significantly more of the red-tag (19%) than non-red-tag (4.7%) children had received psychiatric services. Thus the very global designation of "red-tag" made early in elementary school did seem to predict later behavior problems, validating the initial observations of project personnel.

What then could be done to head off these later problems? The project experimented with several approaches to intervention, including consultation with teachers to develop plans for working with children in the classroom, after-school activity groups, and parent discussion groups. Its most prominent intervention approach, however, has been to use paraprofessional aides to provide helping relationships with red-tag children. It was reasoned that large numbers of helpers were needed to provide services to the 30% of the school population designated as red-tag. Further, it was believed that this natural helping talent existed in people who had no formal training but whose life experiences equipped them to work well with children, for example, successful mothers. Since the first aides were hired and trained in 1963, the program has expanded to more than 20 schools in Rochester, New York, and to more than 300 schools around the country.

In evaluation, teachers, child aides, and mental health professionals rated children who had gone through the program as significantly improved. This improvement was found to be greater than that of matched control children who were not exposed to the program (Cowen, Gesten, & Wilson, 1979; Weissberg, Cowen, Lotyczewski, & Gesten, 1983). Lorion and Cowen (1976), however, found that the program was more helpful to some children (e.g., those with anxious withdrawal rather than acting-out problems) than to others. Thus, although the program has demonstrated effectiveness in some ways, continual development of an intervention model based on research evidence is needed. The basic Primary Mental Health Project model has been receptive to ongoing modifications; interventions have involved a wide variety of paraprofessional helpers (e.g., retired people, college students), special efforts to work with a range of childhood problems (e.g., acting-out children, children adjusting to parental divorce or parental death), and a variety of techniques (e.g., behavior modification, teacher consultation). Thus the PMHP nicely illustrates community psychology's commitment to long-term program development that is responsive to the continuous feedback of careful program evaluation.

Maintaining Clients in Their Natural Environments. Another goal of community psychology programs is to prevent people from becoming involved in the criminal justice and mental health systems. It has been argued that becoming involved in such systems of deviance control has a negative effect on mental health. For example, patients in psychiatric hospitals are placed in the "role" of patient. They are expected to be dependent and less than competent in making decisions and caring for their own affairs. Rosenhan (1973), for example, conducted a study in which he had eight well-adjusted people admit themselves to psychiatric hospitals with the complaint that they were hearing voices. Once admitted, they acted normally, followed the treatment programs, and sought release from the hospitals. Nevertheless, nearly all were given a diagnosis of schizophrenia and kept in the hospitals for an average of 19 days. During this period their behavior was interpreted by the staffs as being symptomatic of schizophrenic illness. When finally released, they were not judged to be normal, but to be "schizophrenics in remission." The study supported the idea that deviance-control systems tend to label participants as dependent and to perpetuate further involvement in the systems.

The alternative objective of many community programs is to intervene in order to prevent initial involvement in the system. One approach that has successfully been used to prevent psychiatric hospitalization is crisis intervention. Many people come into psychiatric hospitals when they are experiencing extreme distress and feel that they cannot cope with their life situations. If at such times an intensive effort to mobilize their personal resources and the resources of the community can be made, psychiatric hospitalization can often be avoided. Delaney, Seidman, and Willis (1977) found that psychiatric hospital admission could effectively be decreased using this model.

Representative Application: An Alternative to the Juvenile Justice System. The prevention model also applies to adolescents and the juvenile justice system. This system was developed in the early twentieth century to provide supervision, care, and treatment for youths who commit criminal acts or who cannot be effectively controlled by their families. The concept was that these youths should not be punished as adult criminals, but should be provided with corrective experiences to prevent their becoming adult criminals. Treatments offered by the juvenile justice system include supervised probation, referral to various forms of therapy, and placement in state training institutions or small residential facilities. Once a youth has become initially involved in the juvenile justice system, subsequent involvement is highly likely. The high return (recidivism) rates of youth in most juvenile justice programs has led some to argue that the best approach to prevent later involvement in the system is to prevent initial involvement; this has been called "diversion from the system."

Placement in small residential facilities like that shown is one form of treatment offered by the juvenile-justice system. However, diversionary interventions undertaken by various community groups has proven far more effective in reducing juvenile crime and delinquency.

One successful example of such a prevention program is the Community-Based Adolescent Diversion Project (Davidson et al., 1977). The basic goal of the program was to prevent youths from being referred to the juvenile justice system. The authors observed that police already exercised a great deal of discretion in referring children to juvenile court, often simply warning and releasing them (particularly for a first offense or an offense such as truancy or curfew violation). Only when the police were about to file a petition to refer a child to juvenile court did the program become an alternative. The intervention agents were paraprofessional college-student volunteers who developed one-to-one relationships with the juveniles. The goals of the intervention were not so much to change the personalities or other characteristics of the youths but to help them meet their needs in society. Behavioral contracts between the youths and important people in their lives (e.g., parents, teachers) were used to improve their interpersonal relations. Volunteers would also help juveniles gain access to community resources (e.g., vocational, educational) in a process called child advocacy. The juveniles were viewed as competent people who had rights to use these resources, and their delinquency was seen as the result of society's failure to provide them with access to needed resources. Advocacy might involve working with a teacher to make school work more suitable to a youth's needs or helping develop employment for youth.

The evaluation of this experimental program demonstrated an impressive level of effectiveness. Youths referred to the program did better than randomly selected controls who were not assigned to the program. Participants had less involvement with police or the courts from the time they were involved in the program through a two-year follow-up. Interestingly, the data did *not* show that the program influenced the youths' personality characteristics. Its success seemed to be related to maintaining their positive interaction with "normal" social systems and preventing their initial involvement in the justice system.

Three common themes of community psychology's approach to human services thus appear to be (1) using the vast body of helping talent in the community, (2) maintaining integration of people within their natural communities, and (3) developing human services over time, based on careful program evaluation.

Planning Changes to Solve Social Problems

As noted above, many community psychologists believe that human problems can be viewed as the consequences of social systems that do not function effectively or within which people are not given access to the resources that will promote their healthy development. Thus many community psychologists attempt to work at a societal level to solve social problems. Developing innovative solutions for social problems is a complicated task that includes (1) conceptualizing a solution that seems both promising and practical, (2) implementing the solution in the real world, (3) evaluating innovation as an experiment so that its effectiveness is empirically and fairly tested, and (4) disseminating the innovation to other organizations experiencing the problem.

Experimental Social Innovation.   One community psychologist who has devised a model to develop solutions for social problems is George Fairweather. His model, which is called **experimental social innovation** (Fairweather & Tornatzky, 1977), includes each of the four steps outlined in the preceding section. A problem is defined and potential solutions are generated by gathering information from several different sources. First, naturalistic observations of the problem situation are made. For example, the social innovator interested in the problems of ghetto youths spends time with them on their own turf to understand their world as it affects them. Second, the literature pertinent to the problem is studied to try to identify factors that are believed to affect the problem. Third, other professionals with experience in the problem area are consulted. Finally, an experimenter may conduct his or her own research to further clarify the factors that affect a problem. For example, if, based on all available information, the experimenter identifies four variables that affect a problem, a preliminary survey study can be conducted to discover which of these variables are most important.

At this point the experimenter has a good idea of which variables need to be manipulated in order to solve the problem. The next step is to develop solutions that involve changes in these critical variables. Proposed solutions are implemented on an experimental basis and then evaluated to assess their effects. Initially, the experiment is conducted on a small scale. If the program does not work, a different approach is tried. If the program has the intended effect of making a real difference, the next step is to disseminate the results, implementing the program in progressively more settings. Finally, as conditions change and time passes, a program that once worked may no longer be effective. Thus continued program change and experimentation is needed to ensure that programs remain responsive and effective.

Representative Application: Decreasing Rehospitalization of Psychiatric Patients.   The experimental social innovation approach has been applied to problems in a wide range of areas including health, housing, aging, energy utilization, and delinquency. A good illustration is Fairweather's research on the problem of the chronically hospitalized psychiatric patient (Fairweather, Sanders, Cressler, & Maynard, 1969). Early research on this problem found that patients who did not leave the hospital in under one year were in real danger of hospitalization lasting a number of years. A number of characteristics of the patient (e.g., single, severely disturbed at the time of intake, diagnosed as psychotic, judged legally incompetent, not a user of alcohol) were found to be good predictors of chronic hospitalization. Once the problem of chronic hospitalization had been defined, the question was what factors could affect it.

A study was conducted to experimentally compare the effects of three commonly used treatment programs: individual psychotherapy, group psychotherapy, and group living. The effects of these treatment programs were contrasted with a control program where subjects simply worked in the community. Results indicated that none of the three treatment programs was more successful in promoting community adjustment over a long period of time (18 months) than the simple work program was. In addition, some types of patients did poorly regardless of the treatment: chronic psychotic patients with a history of prior hospitalization had a 72.4% rehospitalization rate within 18 months.

Since none of the regularly used treatment programs seemed particularly effective, Fairweather's group developed a new treatment model to prevent re-hospitalization. They had observed that many of the patients who returned to the hospital did so because they had little social contact through which to maintain themselves outside the hospital. They reasoned that if cohesive groups of patients could be developed in the hospital, these social relationships might help support the patients once they went into the community. This reasoning was translated into two questions to be empirically tested: (1) could cohesive groups of mental patients be formed in the hospital? and (2) would these support groups help maintain the patients outside the hospital? Fairweather conducted several experimental studies that involved setting up patient work groups and living groups in the hospital as a means of fostering group cohesiveness, In comparing the effects of these experimental groups to the effects of more traditional hospital treatment, he found that facilitating patient decision-making processes on the ward and in the hospital work setting developed cohesive, supportive groups. Furthermore, patients involved in these groups showed significantly better adjustment and were more likely to be released from the hospital than patients who received traditional treatment. Unfortunately, the benefit of these groups did not carry over outside the hospital. Patients in these groups were no more successful in staying out of the hospital than were traditionally treated patients.

The research team built on these findings to create still another social innovation as a proposed solution to the problem. Perhaps the cohesive small group could be moved outside the hospital as a unit in which patients could continue to support one another. In a new experiment a patient group was moved to its own house in the community (Community Lodge) and developed its own business. The effectiveness of this autonomous ex-patient–run society was compared to the effectiveness of normal postrelease patient follow-up in a community mental health center. The results obtained from a 40-month follow-up study of the program indicate that patients in the lodge spent more time out of the hospital and in the community (80% for lodge, 20% for control) and had full-time employment more of the time (40% lodge, 0% control) than did the control group.

Finally, although Fairweather and his colleagues were able to demonstrate that the lodge program was a successful social innovation that lengthened the amount of time patients spent out of the hospital, they were disappointed to find that the innovation was not widely implemented in other settings. This was true despite the fact that the lodge was also less expensive than alternative treatment programs. Clearly, innovative solutions are not disseminated on the basis of data, logic, or economics alone. How then can a new, improved solution be spread? This question was the focus of still another series of experimental studies that involved almost all of the state mental hospitals in the nation.

In these studies Fairweather sought to identify factors that lead to effective dissemination of an innovation. He found that such factors as developing an effective core of advocates to support the innovation within an organization and provide hands-on consultation were important for disseminating an innovation.

In sum, experimental social innovation is a practical model that allows psychologists to conceptualize, implement, evaluate, and disseminate solutions to social problems. It involves a long-term commitment to solving social problems, cumulatively building on the evidence from prior studies. The process of social innovation is an ongoing one in that solutions are not cast in stone but are modified to adapt to changing social conditions. Thus a major contribution of experimental social innovation is the process of problem solving it involves.

Building Competencies in Individuals and Environments: Prevention and Enhancement

It is interesting to note that historically, while psychologists have obsessively defined, classified, and perfected their assessment of psychopathology, they have paid little attention to systematically identifying the range of human competencies. One relatively simple but appealing approach is to define "competencies" as personal characteristics that enable people to cope effectively with tasks, challenges, and stressful experiences. Over the natural course of life, people marry, divorce, move, lose friends and family, have disappointments and interpersonal problems, and are confronted with the challenges of growing old. Some people cope effectively with these experiences while others develop psychological or physical health problems. Kobasa (1979) has identified a personality characteristic she calls "hardiness," which is found in people who come through such stressful experiences relatively unscathed. Hardiness is described as believing that one has control over one's life, being committed to one's goals and values, and viewing stressors as challenges that one can learn from and overcome. Similarly, other personal characteristics, such as intelligence and the ability to think through and solve interpersonal problems, have been found to predict good mental health. Indeed Kohlberg, LaCrosse, and Ricks (1972) reported that such child competencies as cognitive maturity were the best predictors of adult mental health.

There is also encouraging evidence that systematic efforts to teach competencies can be successful. One model that has received such attention identifies a set of competencies referred to as "interpersonal cognitive problem solving skills" (ICPS), which are useful in solving interpersonal problems. These skills include the ability to generate a range of alternative solutions to a problem and to perceive the possible consequences of one's behavior. In a series of studies, Shure and Spivack (1982) found that ICPS skills can be identified in children as young as four or five, and that youngsters deficient in these skills have more problems of impulsivity, inhibition, and maladjustment than do children high in these skills. Shure and Spivack developed a curriculum to teach ICPS skills to inner-city preschool children and kindergarteners. They found that compared to a control group that did not receive the training, children who were taught the skills became better adjusted and were less likely to have developed behavior problems up to a year after the program ended. An additional study disclosed that inner-city mothers could effectively be taught to teach these skills to their preschool children and that children receiving home training showed more behavioral improvement in school than did controls. While important questions about the long-range preventive impact on this training and its effectiveness with other populations (e.g., older children) remain, progess up to this point does illustrate the potential benefit of teaching personal competencies.

The effect of the social and physical environment on people's health, mental health, and life satisfaction has long been apparent. Bloom (1963), for example, point out that the great advances in public health — the conquest of diseases such as malaria and typhoid — were the consequences of improved sanitation in the physical environment. The challenge to community psychology is to make similar advances in mental health. While few would doubt that such high-impact environments as families, schools, neighborhoods, and workplaces affect mental health, the questions is, how? The challenge for community psychology is to conceptualize and assess the important characteristics of the environment, demonstrate their impact on mental health, develop approaches to change them, and evaluate the effects of these changes.

Representative Application: Social Climate Assessment. Clearly this is an ambitious agenda, but some exciting progress is being made. One approach to assessing the environment is to identify how people within the environment perceive it and feel about it. Moos (1973) calls this the social climate of a setting and has conceptualized three broad dimensions of social climate: (1) relationship, (2) personal growth or goal orientation, and (3) systems maintenance and change. The relationship dimension refers to how well people support each other and are involved with each other and the setting. The personal-growth dimension refers to areas of personal development in the setting, such as academic achievement, independence, and task orientation. The system-maintenace dimension refers to how well organized and orderly the setting is and how it responds to change. These dimensions can be applied in the assessment of a wide range of settings (e.g., families, classrooms, work settings, prisons, college-student living groups, and psychiatric hospitals).

Research on the high-school classroom illustrates some of the findings about the effects of social climates. Moos (1979) summarizes a series of studies to indicate that personal growth, social growth, and student satisfaction are promoted in classrooms where relationships are positive (relationship dimension) and where innovations can occur easily (system-maintenance dimension). Student dissatisfaction and alienation develop in classes that are high on teacher-control scales. High academic achievement occurs in warm, supportive, well-organized classes that emphasize academic tasks.

Although there has been relatively little systematic research in this area, Moos has suggested how social-climate assessment could be used to help develop positive environmental changes. Participants in a setting can use the social-climate scales to describe what the environment currently is and how they would like it to be. The discrepancy between the two suggests the direction of desired changes. When feedback is given to the participants about their social-climate preceptions, they can use it as a tool to evaluate their goals for the setting and how to bring about the desired changes.

Representative Application: Research on Social Support. A second social/environmental concept of intense interest to community psychologists is social support. "Social support" refers to linkages between people; the exchange of information, resources, behaviors, and affection that occurs across these linkages; and the resulting psychological effect of feeling valued, cared for, and belonging. Research over the past 50 years has accumulated evidence that people living in socially disorganized and socially isolated environments have a higher rate of mental health problems (Gottlieb, 1981). Similarly, the loss of important social connections, such as by death of a spouse or divorce, is often followed by physical and mental health problems.

Social support may be particularly important in helping people adapt during times of high stress. For example, Barrera (1981) studied the relationship of stress and social support to adjustment problems in pregnant adolescents. He found that pregnant adolescents who had large social-support networks (more people mentioned as providing support) were less likely to be depressed as a result of stressful experiences. Hirsch (1981) studied the relationship between social support and the adjustment of young widows and mature women who were returning to college. For both groups, an important adaptive task was to develop new social roles that extended beyond their nuclear families. He found

Social workers like the one pictured here are trained to provide support for their clients. Programs to enhance the skills of "natural" helpers in the community can extend and strengthen the support systems of people with problems.

that having friendships that involved several important shared activities (e.g., giving emotional support or receiving career guidance) was positively related to higher self-esteem and more satisfying social relationships for these women. He also found that if these friendships included individuals not associated with their nuclear families, the women experienced better mental health. Hirsch reasoned that both sharing activities with friends and having friends outside of their nuclear families helped women develop their new social roles. Multiple activities with friends tended to validate and support new roles. Few interrelationships between friends and family prevented friendships from focusing only on child- and family-related issues.

The concept of social support is a complex one, and psychologists have only begun to learn how it operates to enhance mental health. Nevertheless, there are already interesting models that suggest how social support can be mobilized to promote effective functioning. One approach is to develop new support groups for people who have recently experienced a stressful life experience such as divorce, death of a spouse, or unemployment. A good example of this is the Widow-to-Widow program, developed by Phyllis Silverman (1976), in which women were invited to participate one month after the death of their husbands. The program involved one-to-one assistance by widows who had successfully resolved their own bereavement and could provide a new widow with a supportive relationship and direct assistance in locating community resources. Participation in small support groups with other recent widows was another component. Evaluation of the effects of the program followed participants over two years and compared their adjustment with that of a control group of widows. The results indicated positive benefits of the program in improving emotional equilibrium (e.g., less depression), social integration (e.g., engaging in more activities), and physical health.

A second approach is to support the natural supporters in the community. Numerous studies have found that in times of distress people naturally seek advice and assistance from such people as clergy, doctors, bartenders, hairdressers, teachers, and lawyers as well as from friends and family. D'Angelli, Vallance, Danish, Young, and Gerdes (1981) developed the Community Helpers Project in rural Pennsylvania to enhance the natural skills of such helpers. They developed a structured series of training sessions to teach basic helping skills, crisis-resolution skills, and life-development skills (e.g., decision making, goal assessment). These skills were taught to people who responded to public notices and advertisements in the community. The program later used people who had been through the training as trainers of other community residents. The project research reported that participants learned these skills and used them in their supportive roles in the community.

The basic point made by the information in this section is that building competencies, both of individuals and of social environments, is an important activity of community psychologists. The approaches mentioned are simply illustrations of this growing direction in community psychology.

Conclusion

It should be apparent that community psychology is not an easily circumscribed and defined specialty area in psychology. Community psychologists work in a wide range of settings: mental health centers, social-planning agencies, corrections facilities, schools, and so on. The outcomes they attempt to accomplish range from preventing mental health problems in young children to social-policy analysis and social-system change. The activities they engage in include training paraprofessionals, needs assessments, program development, and program evaluation. The field has experienced considerable growth and continual critical self-examination since its birth at the Swampscott Conference.

This chapter has reviewed several distinctive features of the community psychology perspective and has shown how this perspective was supported because of dissatisfaction with traditional mental health efforts. The five roles that community psychologists have assumed were described: community-needs assessment, behavoral interventions at the community level, human-services program development, implementation of experimental social changes, and building of personal and environmental competencies. An explanation of theoretical issues involved in these areas was followed by examples of research in each.

The one constant that can be indentified in the development of community psychology is change. The field has steadfastly recognized the need to allow itself the latitude to change and develop as the challenges confronting it have changed and as it has developed new techniques to meet these challenges. Community psychology has consciously avoided prescribing a single fixed model of what a community psychologist should be. Instead, different individuals emphasize one or more of the work roles described above. Over the field's brief history, many of the ideas that were initially advocated by community psychologists have been incorporated within other fields of applied psychology (e.g., the use of paraprofessional mental-health workers, prevention, social/environmental assessment and change). These incorporations should be seen as complements to the field's basic approaches. The future development of this dynamic field will undoubtedly see further changes as community psychologists strive to fill society's needs by working through community systems.

Glossary

community-forum approach to needs assessment   An approach to assessing community mental-health and social service needs that solicits opinions and information from a broad spectrum of community residents.

ecological view of human functioning   The view that problems people experience are caused by faulty adaptation to their environments rather than by deficiencies in the individuals themselves.

experimental social innovation   An applied research approach under which field experiments are carried out in community organizations to answer relevant social-policy questions.

key-informant approach to needs assessment   A method of needs assessment whereby highly knowledgeable members of the community provide information sought in the needs assessment.

needs assessment   A process by which a community's mental-health service needs and use patterns are assessed.

outcome objective   The goals of interventions in community psychology.

primary prevention   As used in this chapter, the prevention of mental health problems before they occur.

rates-under-treatment method of needs assessment   Community needs are estimated from information provided by individuals actually receiving mental health treatment. The method has been criticized since use of services depends on availability, acceptability, and accessibility of services and may not accurately reflect need.

social-indicators approach to needs assessment   An approach to needs assessment that undertakes to measure certain components of community life (termed social indicators) that are viewed as correlates of need for mental health services. Examples of social indicators include divorce rates, family income, housing density, and rates of high-school completion.

10 / Health Psychology

Marc Schaeffer
Uniformed Services University

Andrew Baum
Uniformed Services University

During the last years of the NASA program to put a man on the moon, researchers studied the workers who monitored and controlled the mission from the ground. Not only were these people engaged in exceptionally high-pressure jobs, they also had to deal with a stressful paradox. While their overall occupational goal was to put a man on the moon, the workers realized that accomplishment of this task would result in budget cutbacks and, ultimately, in unemployment. Initially, it appeared that this stressful situation was responsible for increased rates of alcoholism and divorce as pressure to complete the mission increased. More alarming was a spontaneous increase in sudden death among relatively young NASA personnel. These deaths, believed to be caused by heart failure, were almost 50% more frequent than would be expected in the relevant age group. Furthermore, autopsies revealed that heart damage was different from that caused by heart attacks and that the damaged hearts seemed to have been thrown into "overdrive" by heightened physiological activity of the nervous system (Eliot & Buell, 1979).

The NASA example illustrates the influence of psychological factors on physical health. The study of health and the application of behavioral principles to the treatment of illness is a rapidly expanding enterprise. Psychologists interested in the causes of illness, factors that affect disease development, coping with medical exams, surgery, and chronic illness, treatment of illnesses, reduction of stress, improving doctor-patient interactions, and so on, have, within the past decade, made major strides. There is now a recognized field of health psychology that addresses these and an expanding number of topics related to health and behavior.

This chapter will treat a number of issues in health psychology. First it will review information on the nature of health psychology. Then it will analyze stress, a central path by which psychological variables can affect health, and present a number of specific instances of psychological influences on health. Finally, the research and application section will consider conditions that can reduce stress as well as some illnesses that appear to be exacerbated or caused by psychological factors. Also discussed will be health behavior—psychological response to illness or signs of illness, treatment of certain physical conditions, such as pain, and ways people interact with their physicians.

What Is Health Psychology?

Health psychology, a relatively new area of behavioral research and practice, is concerned with the relationships between psychological variables and health. It has been defined as "educational, scientific, and professional contributions of the discipline of psychology to the promotion and maintenance of health, the prevention and treatment of illness, and the identification of etiologic and diagnostic correlates of health, illness, and related dysfunction" (Matarazzo, 1980, p. 815). This definition distinguishes health psychology from interdisciplinary fields such as behavioral medicine or behavioral health, which confront the same issues from a focus combining several behavioral and biological approaches.

However, the work of health psychologists and most of the methods they use are similar to those used in the interdisciplinary fields.

An important function of health psychology is the study of psychobiological processes that may affect health. Rather than rely solely on the traditional medical model that posits direct relationships between pathogens or bodily disturbances and disease, health psychologists assume that behavior can contribute to disease processes, be used to prevent them, and set off complex biological changes. **Stress,** one of the most important concepts in linking behavior and health, is a process that helps "translate" environmental and psychological events into bodily changes.

The most common depiction of stress is as pressure or negative force that explains unusual behaviors and sensations. For example, on the night before her physics final, for which she has studied sufficiently, a hard-working young woman feels compelled to review still more. With a dozen hours remaining until the exam, she begins to feel restless, nervous, and tired, and notes the first signs of a headache. The more the student tries to concentrate on her notes, the more she becomes aware of her pounding heart, aching head, and tense feelings. She has reached a point where she cannot study effectively, nor can she rest. In another scenario, during the evening before a young attorney's first jury trial, he begins to anticipate the impact of his court appearance on the fate of his client. While he is driving home, he tries to convince himself how well prepared he is. Nonetheless he begins to feel feverish, his hands tremble a bit, and his body aches. By the time he reaches home he has lost his voice and cannot even speak to greet his wife.

These two brief examples have common elements. both the student and the attorney are having reactions to their specific environments. It is possible that, in the face of demanding challenge or stress, the student and the attorney have certain anxieties and emotional responses that influence their aches and pains. As you will see, the effects of stress include psychological, behavioral, biochemical, and psychological changes. These changes are often related to environmental events and can affect health.

Stress has been defined in many ways. Some use the term to refer to external forces or events that pressure the human organism or place demands in it. Others define it as a way of responding to threatening or demanding pressures. In fact, stress is probably best defined as a process that includes both the stressor, or the event that elicits pressure, and the stress response, including the many biological and behavioral changes, emotional responses, and coping responses that occur. In short, stress is the process by which people respond to changes in the environment that threaten, harm, or challenge them.

The problem is that many events and environmental changes pose threats or challenges, each different from the others in important ways. Research on stress suggests that one can generalize information about responses to one stressor to the study of responses to a different stressor, but such generalization is limited by the ways in which the stressors differ. Some argue that all stressors cause the same responses, while others claim that each stressor has effects that are unique to it. The degree to which stress response is comparable across events continues to be a topic of debate in the field.

Current knowledge about stress comes from centuries of speculation and decades of research. Hippocrates referred to the stresslike aspects of illness as *ponos,* meaning the struggle involved in resisting disease. In much more recent times, the laboratories of Cannon (e.g., Cannon & de la Paz, 1911) and Selye (1936) have documented physiologic phenomena associated with stressful experiences. The study of stress, however, has evolved from a purely biological stance to one represented by an interaction between physiology and psychology.

Models of Stress

Hans Selye (1956) presented the first comprehensive, influential model of stress, which he called the **General Adaption Syndrome** (GAS). Selye observed that the consequences of many stressors were often manifested in the **endocrine system.** Figure 10.1 presents locations of the various glands in the endocrine sys-

FIGURE 10.1 The human endocrine system.

Human endocrine glands

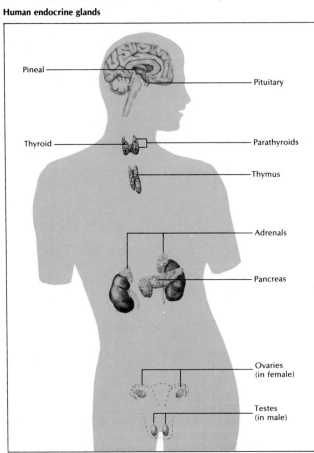

Gland and Function

Pituitary
Regulates ovaries and testes
Stimulates growth

Pineal
Affects activities of the ovaries

Thyroid
Regulates body metabolism
Causes storage of calcium in bones

Parathyroids
Balance calcium level

Thymus
Enables the body to produce antibodies

Adrenals
Regulate blood pressure, salt and water balance in the blood, and metabolism
Prepares the body for action in times of emergency

Ovaries and testes
Influence male and female traits

Pancreas
Regulates blood sugar level

tem responsible for secreting body-regulating hormones, many of which are involved in reactions to stress. Specifically, Selye observed a characteristic response triad that included enlargement of the **adrenal glands,** which are located on top of the kidneys, involution of the thymus gland, which is located under part of the breastbone, and ulceration of the stomach. Selye found that stressors as diverse as heat, cold, exposure to X rays, and exercise also could bring about the same triad of responses. Because a wide variety of stimuli could cause the same consequences, Selye concluded that the stress syndrome was *nonspecific,* that is, all stressors give rise to the same responses in the body. Some studies have supported the notion of nonspecific stress responses, and others have found different responses to different events (Baum, Singer, & Baum, 1981; Frankenhaeuser, 1978; Mason, 1975; Selye, 1976). Whether the stress response is the same for all stressful events remains unclear.

Selye described the GAS as a syndrome occuring in three separate phases, the first two of which are repeatable. The *alarm* reaction is experienced when an organism becomes aware of the stressor and prepares to resist it. Next is *resistance,* during which the organism responds to the stressor and ordinarily, overcomes it. *Exhaustion* occurs when the organism is not successful in overcoming the stressor and depletes its coping reserves.

Several researchers have challenged Selye's model of stress, arguing that stress is *not* nonspecific and that psychological variables are crucial in the nature of bodily responses during stress. John Mason (1975) conducted a number of studies suggesting that the specific changes in bodily responses during stress were different for different stressors. Further support for this comes from a series of studies reported by Marianne Frankenhaeuser (1975). Among other things, they have shown that psychological states have biological correlates or are accompanied by specific bodily changes. By studying hormones that change during stress, including **epinephrine, norepinephrine,** and **cortisol,** both Mason and Frankenhaeuser found that stress responses could be modified if the conditions causing them were altered.

In several studies, for example, Frankenhaeuser and her colleagues found that levels of epinephrine and norepinephrine were related to one's perception of control (e.g., Frankenhaeuser & Rissler, 1980; Frankenhaeuser, 1983). This was true whether the situation was artificial, as when subjects in the laboratory could control electric shocks, or naturalistic, as in the case of workers whose jobs varied in how much control each had over work pace. Thus less controllable events or situations are associated with higher levels of "stress hormones" than are more controllable ones. Other studies found that control and other psychological variables could explain changes in epinephrine and norepinephrine associated with urban commuting, job stress, examination stress, and noise (Collins & Frankenhaeuser, 1978; Johansson, 1977; Lundberg & Frankenhaeuser, 1976; Singer, Lundberg, & Frankenhaeuser, 1978).

While biological factors are important because they are responsible for much of what people feel or do under stress, social and psychological variables determine the overall pattern of responding to stress. Of particular importance in understanding the psychological dimension of the stress concept is the work of

Richard Lazarus (1956) on the role of perception and cognitive appraisal in the stress response. Lazarus argued that the way in which one interprets an event is central to how one reacts. Unless a situation is perceived as threatening, one will not experience stress. If this concept of perception and appraisal is extended to Selye's work, the animals in those experiments must have sensed or been aware of the danger of Selye's stressors in order to respond in the manner of the GAS. Mason found a similar reduction of stress response when awareness of the stress was blocked. Thus two individuals exposed to the same situation may have totally different reactions based upon their subjective appraisal of the ongoing environmental events.

Lazarus's laboratory provided support for this perspective in a series of experiments. Subjects were asked to view "stressful" films, but were not all given the same information about the films. In one study (Speisman, Lazarus, Mordkoff, & Davidson, 1964), subjects were shown a film of primitive initiation rites that involved unanesthetized, painful, and crude genital surgery. One group of subjects was given information emphasizing the pain, danger, and mutilation involved while another group heard a script in which the pain and other consequences were denied and those undergoing the surgery were represented as willing participants. A third group received a detached description of the rites. Results showed that stress responses were less for subjects in the conditions that denied or intellectualized the aversive aspects of the surgery, compared to the responses of those who had been given information that focused on these aspects.

Lazarus's work has gone beyond this demonstration of the effects of different appraisals and has begun to specify the conditions and factors that affect stress (Lazarus & Folkman, 1984). For example, appraisal processes are not the only important factors in deciding whether an event is threatening or not. The amount of demand, one's possible coping options, and a number of other factors are also part of cognitive response during stress. Although some have argued that this kind of approach is unnecessarily mentalistic, it has provided an important view of stress and has helped to explain the fact that different people respond differently to stressors.

Effects of Stress

Space does not permit a detailed catalog of the kinds of effects stress can have. However, some of its general consequences can be described. To a certain extent, these effects are part of stress; sensations such as racing heartbeat, sweating, or a "tense" stomach are often related to the physiological arousal involved in stress.

Physiological Effects. A number of physiological changes accompany stress. One primary mechanism of stress response is through the sympathetic nervous system. Arousal of this system during stress results in increased adrenal gland activity (and the secretion of cortisol, epinephrine and norepinephrine), increased heart rate and blood pressure, faster breathing, sweating, and so on. These effects are part of what Cannon (1929) described as the "fight or flight" response to danger. When danger is recognized, arousal prepares the organism to respond either by resisting or fleeing. Thus stress involves arousal and readying of the organism.

Stress appears to have other biological effects as well. Mason (1974) has described two sets of processes involving these many changes. One set, catabolic processes, is directed towards breaking down stored energy into available forms and readying the individual to respond. This class of changes is similar to that described in Cannon's depiction of response to danger. The other set, anabolic responses, includes changes that are directed towards rebuilding tissue and energy stores. This anabolic response usually follows the catabolic response, and it may reflect the resistance in Selye's model. When anabolic response is no longer possible, exhaustion occurs.

Behavioral Effects.   Some of the many behavioral effects of stress can be classified as **coping behaviors.** Withdrawal from crowding stress, for example, can be either an active coping strategy or an effect of giving up or failing to cope successfully (e.g., Baum & Valins, 1977; Rodin, 1976). Other behavioral effects are consequences of coping. Studies have suggested, for example, that stress can cause people to narrow their attention — to focus on a small part of their surroundings — thereby, reducing sociabilty and ability to detect environmental change (see Cohen, 1978). Research also suggests that stress can interfere with task performance. For example, it has been found that arousal can increase task

Health psychologists have extensively studied the components and effects of stress. The worldwide popularity of "relaxation exercises" like the one pictured here suggests that stress is a phenomenon millions experience.

performance up to a point, but that too much arousal can result in poorer performance (Evans, 1978). To the extent that stress involves arousal, task performance should also be affected.

Researchers have also found that stress can cause aftereffects — effects that show up after the stressor has ended (Cohen, 1980). In one series of studies, subjects were exposed to noise and, in some conditions, such as when the noise was unpredictable, the studies showed effects after the noise had stopped (Glass & Singer, 1972). These effects included reduced tolerance for frustration (giving up quickly on frustrating tasks) as well as poorer performance on a proofreading assignment.

Psychological Effects. It is difficult to separate psychological effects from the processes involved in other consequences of stress. Poor task performance may reflect reductions in ability to concentrate or motivation to succeed. However, it seems clear that stress is related to emotional states; studies have suggested that irritability, apprehensiveness, depression, psychiatric problems, and annoyance are associated with exposure to stress (Baum, Gatchel, & Schaeffer, 1983; Davis, 1975; Frankenhaeuser, 1978; Rose, Jenkins & Hurst, 1978).

Factors That Influence Stress

Clearly, a number of factors are involved in the appraisal of stressors and in the appearance of any of the effects noted. These factors are responsible for the manner in which the organism perceives the stimuli. It is often stated that such variables mediate or govern the stress response. Important variables are social support and perception of control.

Social support, a well-researched mediator of stress, is not merely a matter of how many friends one has but also depends on the perceived adequacy of one's social network to provide emotional or instrumental support. The evidence suggests that having moderate or high levels of social support is beneficial, reducing stress and improving health outcomes (e.g., Cobb, Kasl, French, & Norstebo, 1969; Cohen & Wills, 1985; Gore, 1973).

The reasons why social support has such effects are not known, but several possible explanations have been proposed. One suggestion is that the support of friends and confidantes helps one cope with stress by providing physical assistance (e.g., lending money), emotional aid (e.g., comfort), and/or by affecting how one appraises a stressful situation. If so, differences between people with varying levels of social support should appear only under stress; if support aids coping, it should not make a difference unless stress is present. There is evidence of this buffering effect of social support from studies indicating that those who have greater support exhibit fewer effects under stress that those who do not have much support. However, evidence also suggests that social support is always beneficial, that having more support is better whether one is under stress or not (Cohen & McKay, 1984).

Another possible explanation for social support's effects is related to another mediator of stress, perceived control. It is possible that social support provides one with a heightened sense of control, reducing the aversiveness of stress. Control, referring to the degree to which one is able to predict and manipulate one's surroundings, is generally viewed as being beneficial, although when expectations of control and ability to exercise it are not similar, problems can occur (Wortman & Brehm, 1975). Studies of noise stress in laboratory settings have shown that predictable or controllable noise induced fewer stress-related effects than did unpredictable and uncontrollable noise exposure (Glass & Singer, 1982). This was true even when control was never really used, as none of the subjects in these studies used the control available to them. Studies of stress in naturalistic settings have also suggested that perceptions of control are related to the experience of stress, and that loss of control is stressful (e.g., Baron & Rodin, 1979; Davidson, Baum & Collins, 1982; Singer, Frankenhaeuser, & Lundberg, 1979).

It is clear that social support and perceptions of control affect responses to stress, but the underlying mechanisms remain a mystery. Current speculation involves the relationship between these factors and alterations of the function of the autonomic nervous system. For example, a person who perceives control over a stressful situation, such as driving on ice-slick roads, may be insulated from activation of the autonomic nervous system. Similarly, an individual with a well-developed social support network has several sources of help if a crisis arises. Simply knowing that one has friends who are interested in helping with problems could buffer autonomic responses to stress.

Now that a variety of the prominent features of stress have been reviewed, it is worth asking the question: Why study stress? As with other areas of psychology, the purpose is to understand and predict behavior and its consequences under a wide range of circumstances. Health psychology uses stress as a central concept to help understand connections between events in a person's environment, emotional and cognitive reactions to those events, and psychological disturbances. The precise reasons for the association of stress with illness and disease are not yet known. The following section on illness and behavior will discuss some of the most recent theory and evidence linking stress with disease.

Behavioral Factors in Illness

This section focuses on the relationship between behavior and illness. Everyone has a pretty good idea of what behavior is. Most people sleep, get up, consume food and drink at various times in the day, tackle problems at school or work, celebrate triumphs, and agonize over defeats. However, at some points normal activities and behaviors are disrupted by poor health. Such health disturbances are called disease or illness.

Often when there is a harmful disturbance of the body's equilibrium, the label **disease** is applied. Specifically, disease can be thought of as a morbid process having a characteristic train of symptoms. An illness may affect the whole body or any of its parts, and its origins, development, and prognosis may be known or unknown. Over the past century the study of illness and disease on a mass scale has refined our understanding of the mechanisms by which human beings become ill. In fairly recent times the scope of the disease process has been broadened to include not only the interaction between the body and destructive intruders such as viruses, but also significant interactions of humans with a wide variety of noxious forces in the environment. For example, stress may be caused by annoying, frustrating, or distressing circumstances such as crowding, job pressure, or bereavement. Concepts of disease have also been enlarged. Conditions such as obesity, alchoholism, and drug abuse, which are at least initially the results of voluntary behavior, have been recognized as diseases (see Stunkard & Wolff, 1958; Himwich, 1957).

It has become clear that some diseases unfold over the entire life cycle. For example, there is no known germ that causes either a heart attack or hypertension. Three types of factors have been identified by Krantz, Glass, Contrada, and Miller (1981) that influence illness: direct psychophysiological effects, health-impairing habits, and reactions to illness.

Direct psychophysiological effects are the result of stress and have an identifiable influence on body functioning. For instance, stress can cause both increased heart rate and decreased effectiveness of the immune system. These changes may, in turn, cause or facilitate illnesses. Health-impairing habits such as cigarette smoking, poor diet, lack of exercise, and destructive coping styles, among other aspects of one's lifestyle, have also been clearly linked to increases in disease susceptibility.
Reactions to illness are made up of behavioral factors that affect the treatment of illness. These factors include willingness to seek medical attention, report symptoms, and follow physician advice. If one refuses to go to a doctor, describe symptoms accurately, or comply with recommended treatment, the likelihood of experiencing serious health problems is increased.

While there is now a greater movement to acknowledge behavioral factors in illness, some health professionals still adhere strictly to a biomedical model of disease. They believe that illness is a matter of biology and that sickness is caused by microorganisms or internal malfunction. This is often the case. Although behavior may affect the likelihood of contracting infectious diseases, illnesses such as influenza, smallpox, polio, or AIDS are caused by pathogens that disrupt body functions. In some cases, this view of causation is not adequate and must be supplemented by studying behavior patterns and responses to the environment. Obesity, alcoholism, hypertension, and coronary artery disease appear to develop over a lifetime and are apparently caused by a number of factors including diet, work habits, smoking, and response to stress. Similarly, diseases such as AIDS, which require virological research for finding a cure, can be prevented by altering behavior.

In contrast to the biomedical model is a more comprehensive perspective focusing on the interaction between biological reactions and psychosocial factors. This orientation, known as the diathesis-stress model, suggests that biological vulnerability, although necessary, is not sufficient to explain the onset of many diseases (Levi, 1974). Genetic predispositions are important, but psychological variables and environmental events affect the process as well. While one or more of these factors may be applying negative pressures that induce illness, one or more other factors may be simultaneously supporting good health. This may be illustrated by the following real-world example.

Many health workers, including physicians, come in contact with dozens of sick people in the course of every working day. Interestingly, these overexposed health-care providers appear to have no higher illness rates than normal. Furthermore, health professionals actually show positive blood tests for some illnesses, yet do not manifest even the slightest symptoms. Clearly, factors in addition to exposure to microorganisms are involved in illness. Health psychology includes the study of these additional social and psychological aspects of physical illness.

What Do Health Psychologists Do?

Some combination of teaching, research, and clinical practice describes the jobs of most health psychologists. The exact mix of these activities is determined by the setting where an individual works. Health psychologists may be found teaching in psychology departments at the undergraduate and graduate levels. As is the case for most positions in psychology departments, the balance between teaching and research will depend in large measure on the amount of graduate education a department provides. Health psychologists are also found on the faculties of medical and dental schools where they are involved in the education of health-care professionals.

Health psychologists may hold positions in which their role is primarily research. These individuals most often work in training hospitals associated with university medical schools, in research agencies or in other research organizations. Within these institutions, psychologists have traditionally been affiliated with psychiatric divisions and involved in mental health care. This focus has shown substantial change, and it is now possible to find psychologists assigned to departments as diverse as pediatrics and neurosurgery.

Health psychologists may also be involved in clinical practice, typically within a hospital or clinic setting. They frequently function on interdisciplinary teams and consult with others, often more traditionally "medical" health-care practitioners. Health maintenance organizations (HMOs) are another setting for health psychologists in clinical practice. These organizations are funded by prepaid insurance premiums and emphasize preventive medicine. In their efforts to promote wellness and decrease hospitalization, many HMOs have recognized the importance of psychosocial factors in illness and have turned to health psychologists to help control costs and to promote the well-being of their clients.

Research and Applications

Now that the perspective adopted by most health psychologists has been defined and information about where they perform their work provided, some illustrations of this approach will be presented. First the role of behavioral factors in several specific illnesses will be reviewed, followed by a consideration of health behavior and psychological influences on symptom perception, medical distress, and compliance with physician advice.

Behavior and Heart Disease

The research of Eliot and Buell (1979) underscores the alarming relationship between stress and possible negative health outcomes. Unfortunately their findings are not isolated nor unique. The World Health Organization has predicted that coronary heart disease may result in coming years in the "greatest epidemic mankind has ever faced" (Jenkins, 1971). Heart disease is increasing in frequency and is also afflicting younger and younger individuals.

Coronary heart disease is a generic term referring to diseases of the heart and blood vessels, in which the flow of blood to the heart is reduced. When this happens, the heart muscle cannot be adequately nourished with oxygen and other nutrients carried in the blood. While pain results from temporary insufficiency of oxygen to the heart muscle, more prolonged oxygen deficiency can cause irreversible destruction of the heart muscle (e.g., myocardial infarction) and even death.

But what causes heart disease? Some prominent physical risk factors are high-cholesterol diet, elevated blood pressure, and cigarette smoking. However, in nearly 50% of all new cases of heart disease, these risk factors are not present (Russek & Russek, 1976). In recent years attention has shifted from these more traditional risk factors to psychological risk factors in heart disease. Two cardiologists, Friedman and Rosenman (1974), popularized a specific behavior pattern called **Type A**. According to their thesis, Type A behavior may contribute more to heart disease than all other common physical risk factors combined. It should be pointed out that physicians have suspected the influence of lifestyle factors in the etiology of heart disease for many years (see Osler, 1892).

Type A, or coronary-prone, behavior is characterized by extremes of competitiveness, striving for achievement, aggressiveness, and time urgency (Glass, 1977). In contrast to Type A behavior is **Type B,** which is defined as the relative absence of Type A characteristics. While Friedman and Rosenman first believed that the population was relatively evenly distributed in these two categories, more recent evidence has presented a picture skewed dramatically toward Type A. Recent Type A investigations have also revealed that Type A behavior is not manifested continually, but under special circumstances. For example, Type A individuals show higher levels of arousal when challenged, but not when challenge is absent (see Friedman et al., 1975; Glass et al., 1980). This pattern may represent a coping style geared toward asserting control over potentially uncontrollable situations (Burnam, Pennebaker, & Glass, 1975), and often Type A's respond with accentuated physiological signs relative to Type B's.

Friedman and Rosenman use a clinical interview to determine the presence of Type A characteristics. The interview asks a number of questions about lifestyle; more emphasis is placed on the manner in which questions are answered than on the content of the answer. A second method of determining Type A relies on a paper-and-pencil technique. While the questions on these inventories are similar to the interview, the content of the answer to the questions is all there is to making Type A determinations. This questionnaire method is a weaker predictor of coronary disease than is the interview procedure (Jenkins, Zyzanski, & Rosenman, 1971).

In a study that examined health outcomes of Type A and Type B men, Type A men were found to be more susceptible to heart disease (Rosenman et al., 1966). In this particular study, the influence of such physical risk factors as age, heredity, cigarette smoking, and serum cholesterol levels were controlled statistically so as not affect the results. Thus the argument could not be made that Type A men were older, smoked more, or had higher levels of serum cholesterol than Type B men. The alarming finding was that the incidence of coronary heart disease was twice as frequent in Type A individuals.

Research in this area is now concerned with many issues. For example, is it possible to permanently and effectively change Type A behavior and other coronary risk factors? Are most Type A individuals resistant to elimination of their maladaptive life style? Do specific interventions work better for reducing particular risk factors? The continued pursuit of these questions represents a direction of much needed research.

Behavior and Cancer

The many diseases called cancer together are the second leading cause of death in the United States. In some cases increases in cancers have been linked to specific behaviors or events, as with cigarette smoking or exposure to toxic material. In addition, people are living longer and the over-60 population is larger than at any time in history. Cancer strikes the elderly with higher frequency than it does younger age groups. We are aware of many more *carcinogenic substances* that pollute our environment now, and these may also be responsible for cancer rate increases. Regardless of why, cancer has become a feared and widespread health problem.

Cancer is a disease in which cells lose the ability to perform normally. These altered cells then proceed to multiply wildly out of control, generating tumors. For example, a kidney cell may become transformed into a cancerous cell and discontinue its former physiological function. The cell multiplies and creates a mass of cells that compete with normal, functioning cells for nutrients. This process of proliferation can not only starve normal cells of their nourishment, but also result in organ malfunction and degeneration, and ultimately in death.

Speculation on the reasons for the onset of cancer revolve largely around immune system malfunction. The **immune system** is responsible for determining what is self and what is not self in the body. When the agents of the immune system encounter a foreign invader, they disable the intruder and remove it from the body as a waste product. When a cancerous tumor begins to grow, it should be recognized as "nonself" and attacked as alien matter. For reasons that are not understood, this sometimes does not happen. It remains a puzzle why the immune apparatus allows the invasion of cancerous tumors. It could be that tumor cells are capable of disguising themselves as normal cells and therefore escape being recognized as nonself. Alternatively, or perhaps in addition, tumor cells may secrete some substance into the body to weaken the immune defense.

Several studies have implicated an association of immune deficiencies with behavioral factors. Marked immune system depression was exhibited in males who had just lost their wives (Schleifer, Keller, McKegney, & Stein, 1980). Such reduced immune effectiveness could increase susceptibility to cancer (Tache, Selye, & Day, 1979). In an interesting longitudinal study conducted over a period of 15 years, Thomas and Duszynkin (1974) measured the strength of interpersonal ties among a group of nearly 1,000 medical students. Results indicated that those with weak interpersonal ties were more likely to develop some form of cancer.

Behavior and Arthritis

Rheumatoid arthritis (RA) is classified as an **autoimmune disorder,** yet increasing numbers of researchers agree that this disease has psychosocial aspects. In RA the immune system produces biochemical agents that attack healthy joints, causing them to become stiff, painful, and inflamed. If the process is not arrested, joints can be totally destroyed. As with cancer, RA is thought to be a manifestation of immune-system malfunction. Furthermore, emotional stress has been implicated as an underlying factor in disturbing the immune system.

Some research has associated personality and coping style variables with RA. RA patients have been described, not only by themselves but also by their healthy siblings, as being nervous, tense, worried, depressed, high-strung, moody, and inhibited in expressing anger (Moos & Solomon, 1965). RA patients also have been found to resist major changes (e.g., job changes and moving residences).

Women are the focus of some very interesting aspects of RA. Although about three quarters of RA sufferers are women, research does not disclose differences in the disease process based on hormone actions. Quite interestingly, there are reports of beneficial effects of RA patients under the influence of male hormones (Ahlqvist, 1976) and oral contraceptives (Royal College of General Practioners, 1978). It also is known that many pregnant arthritic women experience temporary relief of symptoms. In most cases, however, symptoms return within a year of delivery. Research in this area also has failed to associate any specific hormone with the amelioration of symptoms during pregnancy.

Because rheumatoid arthritis is classified as an autoimmune disorder, researchers study the diseased victims in hopes of pinpointing the interrelationships between stress and the functioning of the endocrine system.

Selye's development of the General Adaptation Syndrome (1956) included discussion of hormones that increase and reduce inflammation. Both classes of hormones are naturally produced by the cortex of the adrenal glands. Selye speculated that arthritis could be governed by these two classes of hormones, In a series of studies, Selye demonstrated that anti-inflammatory hormones improved the condition of rats with experimentally induced arthritis while pro-inflammatory hormones exacerbated the condition of the animals.

The findings of Selye, in combination with a different literature on the effect of the nervous and endocrine systems on the immune system, have led to some interesting hypotheses. Stress can activate the adrenal glands to produce increased levels of hormones called catecholamines and corticosteroids. These hormones have been implicated in immune-system suppression (Ahlqvist, 1980). Some researchers have considered the possibility of stress causing and/or exacerbating the symptoms of RA through overactive adrenal responding (Kumar, Singh, & Viadya, 1981). It has also been speculated that high levels of these adrenal hormones result from stressful psychosocial states and can be influenced by different coping styles.

The ramifications of this notion are far-reaching and apply to other health problems in addition to RA. The research suggests that elements of behavior could be responsible for altering immune-system functioning and determine susceptibility to a wide range of diseases. If certain behaviors actually suppress immunocompetence, are there other behaviors that can enhance immune response? Using this line of thinking, it could be that behavior is much more important in mediating health than has ever been recognized.

Health Behavior and Treatment

Health behavior may be conceptualized in a number of ways. Some are concerned with healthy people — how they interpret pains or sensations, what makes them seek medical attention, and so on. Others are concerned with sick people and how their behavior affects their treatment. For example, how does a doctor persuade patients to take advice or prescribed medicine or how does hospitalization affect people? Regardless of focus, however, the effect of behavioral factors on health, independent of specific diseases, is of great concern to psychologists. They are interested in perception of symptoms and pain, determinants of medical distress, attitudes toward health care, and compliance with physician advice.

Symptom Perception. An aspect of health behavior that has received a great deal of attention is the area of symptom perception. Everyone experiences bodily sensations — little pains, the feeling of the heart beating, queasiness in the stomach. An individual's interpretation of such sensations determines response and behavior. If pain is thought to be serious, a person will call a doctor or go to an emergency room, but if the pain is interpreted as nothing special, it is quickly forgotten.

Symptoms in this sense are bodily sensations, such as headaches, nausea, or backaches, that may reflect a medical problem. If you have a headache, you may consider how bad it is, what it might have been caused by, and so on. If there is loud music playing in the room next door or if upstairs neighbors are dancing and shaking the ceiling, you may decide that the headache was caused by these external events. Then you would decide whether you should take something for it, see a doctor, or just let it run its course. You could take some aspirin, or you could leave your room to get away from the noise.

Some symptoms are not so easy to identify. Sometimes they occur in clusters. Reporting of symptoms is often used as an index of stress — the presence of stress is inferred from the presence of increasing symptom perception (e.g., Baum et al., 1980).

The perception and interpretation of symptoms is affected by many things. An accumulating body of data shows that people experience the bodily sensations that may constitute symptoms most of the time (cf. Mechanic, 1972; Krantz et al., 1980; Zola, 1966). What is important is the degree to which people attend to these sensations, interpret them as symptoms of a disease, and report symptoms to their health-care provider. If an event occurs that could cause health problems, such as the nuclear accident at Three Mile Island, symptoms that people normally might not report may be brought to the attention of doctors just in case there might be something wrong.

Boredom or social withdrawal, due to a lack of competing stimuli or other things to pay attention to, may increase attention to symptoms, and cultural influences may be important as well (Baum, Aiello, & Davis, 1979; Pennebaker, 1979, 1982). Women may be more likely than men to report symptoms or seek help (Mechanic, 1972), and lower socioeconomic status is associated with a higher frequency of reporting symptoms and seeking medical attention (Koos, 1954).

Though obviously related, symptom perception is not the only determinant of the decision to seek medical attention. Even when people believe that a sensation is an indication of something seriously wrong, they may not seek help. The Health Belief Model (Rosenstock, 1966) is very useful in understanding help-seeking and its relationship to symptoms. Briefly, this model argues that the decision to seek medical attention because of symptoms experienced depends on several factors. People might consider whether the action would increase their concerns about their health or reduce them. They may avoid seeking medical attention out of fear of what they will learn. Factors such as the severity of the symptoms and their possible consequences exert an influence. If symptoms do not suggest severe problems or if there are reasons (such as possible embarrassment) not to report them, people are less likely to look for medical attention.

Perception of Pain.   One of the primary components of symptom perception, and one of the most common medical complaints, is pain. Most persons believe that pain is a physiological event, and, indeed, there is a great deal of research indicating a neural basis of pain perception (Melzack, 1973). However, pain has a large psychological component; as one would expect, it is subjective in nature (Melzack, 1973; Weisenberg, 1977). Pain is not always caused by real tissue damage or dysfunction and may exist without any apparent cause (Fordyce, 1976; Loeser, 1977). Furthermore, surgical interventions aimed at cutting the neural pathways that transmit pain sensations do not always effectively relieve pain (Weisenberg, 1975).

As a result, more complex perspectives on pain have evolved. As Beecher (1959, 1975) has suggested, pain has a sensory component—the actual physical sensations—and a reaction component—the psychological appraisal and interpretation of those sensations. The reaction component is susceptible to such influences as cultural heritage, anxiety about illness, and beliefs about the causes of pain (Sternbach & Tursky, 1965; Zbrowski, 1952; Spear, 1967; Sternbach, 1968).

Beecher's ideas came from a study examining different reactions to pain evidenced by wounded soldiers and by civilians with comparable injuries (1956). Soldiers wounded during the battle at Anzio in World War II were less likely to request medication for pain than were the civilians, 80% of whom asked for painkillers. Interestingly, most of the soldiers either denied experiencing pain or indicated that it was not bad enough to require medication. Beecher concluded that one's emotional state and situation can affect the experience of pain.

Other studies showed the same thing: anxiety increased the pain experienced in some studies while cultural background was found to affect pain in other studies (Christopherson, 1966; Hill, Kornetsky, Flanary, & Wilder, 1952; Sternbach, 1966). Ethnic differences in response to pain have been widely noted but are difficult to explain. For example, "Yankees" (Protestants of English descent) assumed a matter-of-fact, present-oriented attitude towards pain while observations suggested that Irish subjects inhibited expression of pain, Jewish subjects focused on its future implications, and Italian subjects focused on the present and on receiving relief quickly (Tursky & Sternbach, 1967; Sternbach & Tursky, 1965).

Research also shows that responses to pain can be learned (Fordyce & Steger, 1979). Pavlov (1927) demonstrated that by pairing presentation of food with a painful stimulus, the pain came to elicit positive responses associated with the food. More recently, Weisenberg (1977) found that children having teeth pulled showed more distress if their mothers were highly anxious than if not. This suggests that modeling may affect response to pain.

This kind of study has suggested ways to reduce pain without painkilling drugs. Biofeedback—training people to relax muscles—has had some success in reducing pain, but does not appear to be better than other, less expensive methods (Turk, Meichenbaum, & Berman, 1979). Hypnosis, on the other hand, has proven more useful. By inducing a hypnotic state and providing a suggestion that the pained area was no longer sensitive, researchers and clinicians have been able to reduce pain and suffering (Chaves & Barber, 1974; Hilgard, 1975).

Another method of pain reduction, **acupuncture,** has also received attention. By inserting needles into specific places in the body, pain is relieved. It

Once largely a feature of mentalists' stage performances, hypnosis is now recognized as a clinically proven analgesic.

has been noted that the psychological state of the patient is important in determining how well acupuncture works (Katz, Kao, Spiegel, & Katz, 1974; Taub, 1976). In one study, a drug that blocked the effects of analgesic drugs also blocked the relief brought by acupuncture. The results indicated that acupuncture works much like narcotic drugs in reducing pain (Mayer, Price, Barber, & Rafii, 1976).

A number of other methods of treating pain have also been tried. The use of imagery — having subjects imagine different scenes — has met with some success. Horan, Layng, and Pursell (1976) found that by training people to think about positive things, they were able to reduce pain during dental treatment. Barber and Cooper (1972) also found that imagery that distracted people could reduce pain, and Meichenbaum and Turk (1976) have reported success with a program that teaches patients a variety of pain control strategies emphasizing cognitive activity.

The focus on a psychological component of pain has also allowed a better understanding of the **placebo response.** A placebo is a treatment that the subject or patient believes will be effective, but which has no known properties that could make it effective. Sugar pills taken in the belief that they are aspirin may cure a headache. The act of taking a medication or undergoing a treatment may be effective even if the treatment itself has no therapeutic value.

Research has suggested that placebos can effectively reduce pain or relieve other symptoms in more than a third of the population. The pervasiveness of the placebo effect is suggested by the fact that drug companies must experimentally control for the effect when testing new remedies. In order to assure that the drug is responsible for observed effects, one group of patients is also given a substance they think is a new drug. If these people show the same effects as those receiving the real thing, it is unlikely that the remedy is effective in its own right. Responses to placebos are both psychological and physiological — placebo treatments have, for example, been shown to reduce blood pressure (e.g., Shapiro, 1983). A precise understanding of how and why such effects occur awaits further research.

Reducing Medical Distress

Psychological interventions directed toward reducing distress, pain, and anxiety before and after surgery or aversive medical exams have been successful. Surgery can be terrifying, but it is clear that reactions to it are based on appraisal of threat or danger. Thus this distress seems to be readily amenable to the types of reappraisal strategies noted by Lazarus (1966). Most studies of surgical stress reduction have sought to examine the role of fear and appraisal of threat on pre- and postoperative distress.

Janis (1958) studied college studnets who had recently undergone surgery and found that the amount of fear before the operation was an important determinant of recovery from surgery. Those who had reported low preoperative fear reported the most postoperative difficulty. That is, those who said they were not very fearful or apprehensive before surgery ended up being more angry and upset during their recoveries. The students who reported moderate levels of fear before surgery experienced the smoothest recoveries, and those who were extremely fearful before surgery fell somewhere between the other two groups. Fear appeared to contribute both to distress and recovery. Some fear facilitated recovery, but too much fear had a negative effect.

Janis suggests that anticipatory fear and the **work of worrying** were important in response to surgery. Expectations of what might happen during and after surgery caused students to worry about the event. Without this anticipatory fear, patients did not mentally rehearse the dangers confronting them. The absence of fear may have led to helplessness or anger when these dangers or discomforts materialized.

The importance of fear and information has been confirmed in a number of subsequent studies. This research has shown that preoperative information is beneficial for a number of reasons. First, it serves as a warning signal that arouses anticipatory fear and rehearsal of possible consequences of surgery. Second, it serves to make patients aware of ways of coping with the dangers of sur-

The investigations of health psychologists have shown that patients receiving full preoperative information about their procedures require lesser amounts of painkillers following surgery than do those not so informed.

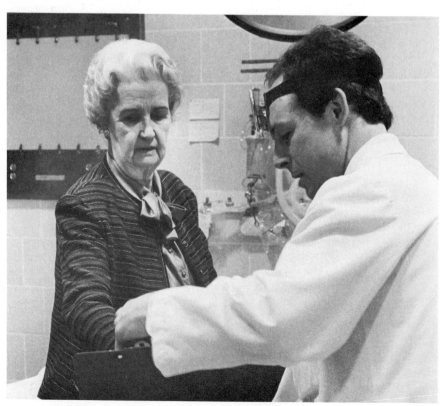

gery so that they are better prepared to deal with such dangers when they do materialize. Third, preparatory information provides patients with realistic expectations of what will hapen to them so that events in the process are recognized and viewed as "normal." For example, Egbert, Battit, Welch, and Bartlett (1964) compared patients exposed to routine hospital messages (very little specific information) with a group who had been given information about the specific pain they would experience after surgery and about specific ways to cope with this pain. The informed group required fewer painkilling drugs following surgery than did the uninformed group. Similarly, research suggests that providing information about unpleasant sensations that will occur during medical examinations can reduce their aversiveness and improve outcomes (e.g., Johnson & Leventhal, 1974).

Attitudes toward Health Care

Studies indicate that different people have different feelings about health care. Some would like information before going into surgery, while others would just as soon know nothing about it until it is over (Andrew, 1970). Some people go to their doctor at the drop of a hat while others refuse to visit a physician even when seriously ill. Some people want doctors to be friendly and others prefer a businesslike aproach. These preferences are associated with attitudes about health care that have been systematically investigated.

An example of this work is that performed with the **Health Locus of Control Scale** (Wallston, Maides, & Wallston, 1976). Some individuals may benefit more than others from an active and informed role in their health care. In order to tap some of these individual differences, Wallston et al. have developed a locus of control scale designed to measure health beliefs. Individuals with high control are classed as internals while those who score low are classed as externals. Internal control conveys the idea that people are to some extent reponsible for their health. External control reflects the belief that other people or environmental factors are the chief determinant of health. Locus of control is only one of a number of variables that may affect preference for different medical approaches.

Another attempt to measure health-care preference is Krantz, Baum, and Wideman's (1980) **Health Opinion Survey** (HOS). This scale taps two dimensions of preference for health-care involvement: participation and information. Individuals who score high on the participation subscale of the HOS want to be involved in making decisions about their health and prefer to care for themselves as much as possible. Individuals who score high on the information subscale want to be given information about their health. Research with the HOS has indicated that, among students, those using the campus infirmary score lower on the participation subscale and suggests that people who participate actively in self-care by treating themselves do not ordinarily seek professional medical attention. The study also found that students in a medical self-help course scored higher on both subscales (Krantz et al., 1980).

Compliance with Physican Advice

Psychological research and behavioral principles have also been applied to health-related issues in the area of compliance. Simply defined, compliance refers to the degree to which patients do what their physicians recommend, advise, or prescribe. A common reference is medication; a prescription will not help unless a patient takes it, and many people fail to do so. On other levels, compliance involves preventive recommendations (getting vaccinated, having check-ups) and advice about changes in diet, lifestyle, and so on. You may have assumed that once a doctor diagnoses a condition or illness, the rest is easy. The fact is that getting people to take their medicine or follow advice is more difficult than you would suppose.

Estimates of noncompliance vary, but all suggest that the problem is fairly widespread, both in regard to prescriptive treatment and preventive advice. It is even a problem getting people to show up for medical appointments — in clinic settings, for example, up to half of those who make appointments for preventive visits fail to appear and up to 60% of patients with illnesses or painful symptoms do not keep their appointments (Hardy, 1956; Burnip, Erickson, Barr, Shinefield, & Schoen, 1976).

Without going into great detail, it is clear that many people are not compliant. Why is this such a problem? Of course, there are times when not doing what a doctor advises will not cause serious problems. However, in general, people who do not follow physician advice are handcuffing health-care providers. Treatment of an illness may or may not be effective. One way that physicians evaluate the effectiveness of treatment is whether or not the illness has abated. If patients *do not follow* the treatment prescribed but *say that they do* and their condition has not improved, the physician may conclude that the diagnosis or treatment prescribed for it was wrong. If the original diagnosis was actually correct, failure to comply may lead to a new, erroneous diagnosis and potential complications.

Why don't people comply? Research has focused on a number of explanations for this seemingly self-destructive behavior. One answer to this question may lie in personal experience. Often, the doctor prescribes enough medicine to take for a week or more, and the typical admonition is to take it all — if the prescription is for ten days, the patient is told to take it for all ten days. By the fifth day, however, symptoms have disappeared. There is no longer any pain, and the person may feel "as good as new." Without considering that the infection might still be present, the person thinks, Why am I still taking medicine if I'm feeling fine? Continued compliance depends on a number of factors, including how much information the doctor has conveyed about the treatment and how well the patient understands this information. Satisfaction with the doctor, including estimates of his or her credibility, can also affect acceptance of advice. If the prescribed regimen is complex or disruptive, people will also be less likely to comply.

Three basic approaches have been taken in studying these issues. One emphasizes characteristics of the patient, physician, or illness, including personal-

of time and do not fit neatly into biomedical models incorporating pathogens. Instead, heart disease, cancer, arthritis, and other diseases appear to have behavioral causes as well as biological ones, and the joint study of these causes has advanced knowledge and understanding of a number of illnesses. The origins and treatment of these psychophysiological disorders were also discussed.

The final section of this chapter dealt with health behavior and treatment. The ways in which people react to illness or to signs of illness, how they cope with health-related situations, and how well they follow medical instructions affect overall health. Symptom perception was related to help-seeking and other aspects of health behavior. Pain was described as having a biologically based component and a psychologically based reaction component, and methods of reducing the stress associated with surgery were described. Finally, the issue of compliance was examined. The factors that cause people to disregard their doctors' advice were analyzed. Failure to follow medical regimens is a widespread problem, and some approaches to reversing it were discussed.

Glossary

acupuncture   A Chinese method of piercing peripheral nerves for pain relief and promotion of healing.

adrenal glands   The adrenal gland is made up of two parts, the adrenal cortex and the adrenal medulla. The cortex is the outer layer of the adrenal gland that makes up the larger part of the gland. It secretes corticosteroids. The adrenal medulla is the core of the adrenal gland that secretes epinephrine and norepinephrine.

autoimmune disorder   Disorder of the immune system.

catecholamine   Epinephrine and norepinephrine (also known as adrenaline and noradrenaline) are described as catecholamines. They are secreted by the adrenal medulla as well as select neurons throughout the nervous system.

coping behaviors   An adaptive process of dealing with stress or threats.

coronary heart disease   Disease of the heart and blood vessels.

cortisol   A corticosteroid secreted by the adrenal cortex that is often used as an index of nonspecific arousal of stress.

disease   A process within the body to combat some problem that may be externally or internally caused.

endocrine system   A system of ductless glands throughout the body that secretes hormones as their products directly into the blood stream. This system is often referred to as the "hormonal system."

epinephrine (or adrenaline)   See catecholamine.

general adaptation syndrome   Selye's model of stress named the General Adaptation Syndrome involves the same pattern of responding to a number of physical and chemical stressors. The hallmarks of the pattern are adrenal enlargement, thymus involution, and stomach ulceration.

Health Locus of Control Scale A scale that measures the degree to which individuals feel able to control their health.

Health Opinion Survey A scale that measures two factors related to health care preferences — degree of active participation in health care and amount of information given in this process.

immune system The system within the body responsible for fighting pathogens.

norepinephrine (or noradrenaline) See catecholamine.

placebo response A response indicative of relief of symptoms or pain from a substance that has no known therapeutic value.

social support Material, instrumental, or emotional aid from networks of individuals which a given person is in close contact.

stress Stress is a process by which environmental events threaten or challenge an organism's well being and by which that organism responds to this threat.

Type A behavior A coping style characterized by time urgent, competitive, aggressive behaviors. This coping style has been studied as a risk factor for cardiovascular disease.

Type B behavior A pattern of behavior characterized by an absence of Type A characteristics.

work of worrying An adaptive response to stressful medical procedures. Worrying allows for rehearsal of dangers and discomforts and if these materialize those who have worried are more prepared for them.

11 / Applied Social Psychology

Steven G. West
Arizona State University

John W. Reich
Arizona State University

Michael A. McCall
Xerox Corporation, Rochester

Arthur Dantchik
First Options, Philadelphia

The development of the science of social psychology from its early beginnings to the present represents an interesting but complicated interplay of "pure theory" and "applied" orientations. The relative importance of these two orientations has changed over time in response to developments in the discipline and in society at large. At present, both orientations include a number of active and important areas of research, some of which have begun to develop intriguing integrations of the two orientations. This chapter will review the applied side of social psychology, highlighting basic characteristics, historical development, and major areas of current activity, particularly those that have begun to marry the theoretical and applied orientations.

A single chapter cannot encompass the great scope and complexity of social psychology; the choice has been to present a generalized overview followed by more detailed analyses of four representative areas of research. Within each area, basic conceptual approaches and methods of the specific studies receive the most attention. It is hoped that the review of these practices and activities conveys the essence of this exciting new social science. Readers interested in additional coverage of the field can gain much by reference to more extended treatments, such as those of Varela (1971), Deutsch and Hornstein (1975), Saxe and Fine (1981), and Oskamp (1984).

Applied activities in social psychology often have historically played a lesser role than more theoretical/laboratory activities. However, since the early to mid-1970s there has been a broad-based expansion of interest and activity in applied concerns. New journals, books and edited series, and even new graduate training programs have appeared in the last ten years. Applied social psychology now has a distinct, although complex and multifaceted, character and appears to be moving toward a more central role in social psychology.

What Is Applied Social Psychology?

Because methods of inquiry and topics of investigation in the field of applied social psychology are so diverse, no strict definition or single-dimension characterization of the science would be very useful. Some themes are common to many subareas of the field, however, a main one being strong concern for relating the science of social psychology to the analysis and amelioration of significant social problems.

Lead by Kurt Lewin's innovative research (e.g., 1947a, 1947b), investigators focused on such problems as prejudice, stereotyping, and intergroup tensions in the earlier formative years of the field. Considerable diversification has occurred since then as researchers have worked on problems ranging from health promotion to energy conservation. Lewin's particular approach focused on **action research** (Bickman, 1980), which emphasized social change somewhat more than theoretical analysis. In contrast, other researchers such as the Sherifs (Sherif

& Sherif, 1953; Sherif, Harvey, White, Hood, & Sherif, 1961) were more explicitly concerned with experimental manipulation of theory-based variables operating in natural settings.

These two types of activities help define the fuzzy outer boundaries of what can now be considered the "field" of applied social psychology. Diversity within that range is the norm. Other approaches such as field studies, evaluation of social programs, and analysis of basic behavioral processes in natural settings have become prominent. If any one theme dominates, it is an abiding concern on the part of researchers to understand social phenomena without the distortion that may be present in laboratory experimentation. Growing concern over **external validity** (see Chapter 2) led to an increasing number of tests of social-psychological principles in real-world settings as diverse as hospitals, classrooms, and apartment buildings. Paralleling this trend, new developments in methodology (see Cook & Campbell, 1979; Judd & Kenny, 1981; West, 1985, for reviews) have greatly strengthened the validity of the conclusions that can be drawn from research in more naturalistic settings. The stage has been set for increasing interplay between basic laboratory and applied research.

Full-Cycle Model

Bob Cialdini (1980) proposed a useful model of how applied research can be integrated with basic research in social psychology. As described in Chapter 1, his **full-cycle model** calls for initial analysis of a social event in a natural setting: social psychologists should first be keen observers of behavior and its situational context. A tentative analysis and explanation of the phenomenon is then developed. This tentative explanation is initially tested in rigorously controlled laboratory analysis and refined if necessary. If the explanation survives to this point, it is tested again in the natural setting. Information from the field may then be used, if necessary, to modify the initial explanation or to suggest potential boundary conditions for the hypothesized relationships. The revised explanation can then be tested further in subsequent labortory research or in other naturalistic settings. Such an interplay between laboratory and field research provides a powerful method of winnowing out explanations that are incomplete, or incorrect, or that are irrelevant to or inconsequential in the real world.

The treatment of applied social psychology in this chapter is restricted to research devoted to (a) testing theoretical/conceptual analyses of social behavior, (b) working with experimental/manipulational models, and (c) studies in natural, nonlaboratory settings. The discussion is limited to research that has taken a more Lewinian approach, focusing on the development and testing of interventions designed to ameliorate significant social problems. Such a focus produces a coherent, concise, integrated analysis of a major area of the field. This chapter demonstrates that the most powerful form of psychology integrates theory with natural or real-world settings. By effectively concentrating on action research, it is possible to demonstrate the nature and uses of the basic science.

Historical Context

The importance of achieveing some degree of integration between basic and applied orientations to the field is illustrated by contrasting two diverse historical periods. The first is the 1940s (the decade of World War II) when the war effort led to a strong focus on applied work, particularly on issues that were relevant to military concerns. The second is the 1960s when the response to the successful launching of Sputnik by the Soviet Union was unprecedented public and financial support for education and basic research in all areas of science. Consistent with this trend, there developed in social psychology a very strong focus on basic laboratory research and a corresponding neglect of applied issues. Both periods led to considerable malaise among social psychologists and to a subsequent correction in the balance between basic and applied concerns.

During the period of World War II, social psychologists were recruited into armed forces activities, and applied concerns became established and accepted (Allport & Veltfort, 1943; Murphy, 1965; Schmeidler & Allport, 1944). Propaganda, attitudes, intergroup relations, industrial and management issues, racial prejudice, and other issues related to the war effort were high on the agenda for social psychologists working in both military and civilian settings. Theory and pure science were set aside.

Writings from the immediate postwar period indicate a considerable sense of discontent with the strong applied orientation being demanded of the field during this time. Cartwright (1948) noted that investigators during that period were forced to drop interesting lines of research in order to meet wartime needs. A number of researchers called for a return to laboratory/theoretical work (Krech & Crutchfield, 1948; Stouffer et al., 1949) and even Lewin, one of the early advocates of applied social psychology, called for more attention to theoretical development (1947a, 1947b).

In contrast to the 1940s, the decade of the 1960s was a period of unprecedented support for basic research, marked by accelerated growth of the theoretical side of social psychology that had been developing in the 1950s. In 1965 the *Journal of Personality and Social Psychology* split off from the more clinically applied *Journal of Abnormal Psychology*. The *Journal of Experimental Social Psychology* that began publication in the same year had a distinct theoretical focus. Indeed, Hendrick (1977) has noted that the laboratory/experimental approach was so dominant during this period that it was "vaguely disrespectful" to use or even to consider using any other approach.

However, during the late 1960s and early 1970s, increasing numbers of social psychologists began to become discontented with basic laboratory research. Numerous methodological issues were raised about the interpretation of standard laboratory experiments (e.g. Rosenthal & Rosnow, 1969). Ethical concerns were raised about the use of deception in many experiments of the time (Kelman, 1967). Traditional models and standard empirical technologies were coming up short: well-known experimental results could not be repeated even under slightly different experimental conditions. Reinterpretations and complicating qualifications were required to account for these results, and even failures to replicate under identical experimental circumstances were becoming increasingly common. The classical models of attitudes, perception, and group processes were falling out of favor. Demands for social relevance, particularly in the social sciences, came from the public, from funding sources, and from students. The impact of these combined forces caused basic laboratory research to begin losing its position as the only approach to true science.

The Current State

The applied orientation, which offers promise of maintaining a scientific approach while meeting the demands for relevance, has become more widely understood and accepted. A number of investigators have even suggested that the applied side will help reinvigorate the traditional field (e.g., Bickman, 1976; Ryckman, 1976; Sherif, 1977; Weissberg, 1976). New developments in methodology (e.g., Cook & Campbell, 1979) now permit very high quality research to be conducted in applied field settings. Certainly the beginnings of a viable and influential integration of basic and applied social psychology have been established; there is little question about the viability of the separate strands. Very likely the melding is a permanent one and future generations of social psychologists will have solid grounding in both applications and theory. The review of the field in this chapter, along with its detailed discussion of several applied topics, support this optimistic view.

What Do Applied Social Psychologists Do?

One way of conceptualizing the roles of applied social psychologists has been suggested by Hornstein (1975). He suggests three categories of activities: research, dissemination, and social technology. Each of these roles is considered in the following section.

Job Activities

Studies conducted in the 1940s show how research activities can function as interventions that result in social change. By understanding how various theoretically relevant variables operate in applied settings, social psychologists can more effectively "translate" the large body of research that has been generated into applications that are socially important. In addition, as the full-cycle model suggests, applications can enrich theory.

Social psychologists functioning in the dissemination role put decision makers in contact with relevant social science information. In this way, administrators in both the public and private sectors are equipped to make informed decisions. Social psychology can offer an alternative and unique knowledge base that allows predictions about probable attitudes and social behaviors in various social situations. Such information can be very valuable to those who must design ways to implement policies and anticipate the impacts of their decisions.

Finally, in the role of social technologist, applied social psychologists work as active change agents involved in facilitating social interaction and in making interactions more effective. This role of the applied social psychologist overlaps in many ways with that of individuals involved in organizational development (see Chapter 5). Like specialists in that field, applied social psychologists may use various techniques such as conflict resolution, survey feedback, and team building to improve the functioning of organizations. Details of these techniques are presented in Chapter 5; it is useful to note that these methods rely on social-psychological principles for their effectiveness.

Work Settings

Because the field of applied social psychology is so diverse, practitioners work in a wide variety of settings. A major employment setting for applied social psychologists is as faculty members in academic departments at universities. These individuals teach courses, conduct research that will be published in professional journals, and often do consulting so that they can apply their knowledge to practical problems. They may also be involved in graduate education by supervising internships and the original research performed by students for master's theses and doctoral dissertations. Further, most faculty members serve on committees involved in the governance of their departments and colleges.

A second employment setting for applied social psychologists is in the market-research, personnel, and statistical analysis departments of both public- and private-sector organizations. Several examples from marketing will serve to illustrate the diversity of these settings. One individual with training in applied social psychology was hired to serve as research director for a state lottery. This person applied knowledge of social-psychological principles and data analytic skills to the marketing of lottery tickets. Another individual worked as director of research for a public television station. In this setting, statistical information on program ratings was collected and analyzed and various fundraising strategies designed and tested. A third individual worked for a large food-manufacturing corporation, tracking and predicting the performance of various products and evaluating consumer preferences for proposed new products. As you can see, such employment settings are very diverse. What they have in common is the use of social-psychological principles to market goods and services and high-level methodological and statistical techniques for understanding complex human social behavior.

A third employment setting for applied social psychologists is as consultants to organizations involved in some type of social change. Again you may refer to Chapter 5 on organizational development for details. The exact roles that consultants assume in the change process range from assisting management of established corporations to fulfill its goals to functioning as participant activists in social advocacy in order to empower disadvantaged groups of people.

Research and Applications

As you have seen, the range of applied social psychological research is very wide. Four representative areas will be reviewed: improving health outcomes by enhancing perceived control; attributional retraining as a means of improving educational performance; reducing prejudice through cooperative (jigsaw) classrooms; and evaluating antismoking and antidrug programs designed to increase children's resistance to peer and adult influences.

Research on Perceived Control and Health

For orientation purposes several distinctions should first be made. Since the purpose of this review is to present representative research methodology and the nature of applied social-psychological approaches, it is more efficient to bypass a conceptual discussion of the notion of control. More thorough discussions of the concept appear in such reviews as those of Averill (1973), Harvey, Harris, and Lightner (1979), Lacey (1979), Thompson (1981), and Rothbaum, Weisz, and Snyder (1982). Here it is appropriate to define **perceived control** as referring to a person's understanding of the degree of relationship between his or her purposeful behavior and what subsequently happens. A continuum is intended, ranging from complete certainty that outcomes are in no way influenced by purposeful behavior to absolute certainty of a complete and invariant connection. Individuals who perceive a strong relationship between their behavior and the outcomes it brings are said to be high in personal control. Those who feel that the relationship is weak or nonexistent are low in control. The greater the degree of control people have over outcomes, the less stress they feel, and hence the less likely they are to display negative emotional reactions to an event. In some cases, enhanced control over outcomes may be expected to lead to better adjustment to stressful situations.

Preparation for Stressful Medical Procedures.   The body of research on psychological factors in health behavior has become quite extensive, and the subarea dealing with cognitive control is now fully developed and growing. One general approach taken by researchers in this area is to select subjects either preparing to undergo, or who are actually undergoing, some form of stressful medical experience such as a physically invasive examination or surgery, and to present them with control-enhancing manipulations designed to improve adaptation and health.

In an early investigation, Langer, Janis, and Wolfer (1975) conducted their reseach in a hospital setting with a set of adult patients awaiting elective surgery. Control-inducing instructions were delivered in written form. These statements concerned how people typically react to stress and how they can learn to cut down their reactivity by appropriate thoughts and emotion-controlling behaviors. Imagery and examples of successful coping strategies were included to strengthen the impact of the instructions. A comparison condition presented preparatory information — basic facts about the surgery and postoperative experiences — but did not include the cognitive-control instructions. Other conditions included a combination of coping and preparatory information and a final control condition where no information concerning stress, reactions to surgery, or coping processes was presented. Dependent measures assessed both presurgery and postsurgery reactions, including felt anxiety, blood pressure and pulse rate, medication needed in the postsurgery phase, and nurses' ratings of the patients' adjustment. The results of the experiment were complex, but across most of the various measures it appeared that information by itself was insufficient to reduce stress; the combination of suggestions for increasing perceived control with preparatory information was the most effective condition.

Johnson and Leventhal (1974) and Johnson, Morrissey, and Leventhal (1973) had applied a similar set of procedures to patients undergoing endoscopic examinations. In this procedure, patients swallow a flexible, light-conducting rod that permits examination of the interior wall of the stomach. One group of patients received behavioral-control instructions on how best to respond to the physical procedures in the examination. A second group received sensory instructions (with photographs) specifically describing the activities and sensations that would be experienced. A third group received both sets of instructions, and a fourth was not told of these variables. During the examination, dependent variables assessed the amount of medication taken, heart rate, and other measures indicative of tension and arousal.

Although the results of the study were again fairly complex, in general the evidence indicated favorable impact of the preparatory, the sensory, and the combined conditions in lowering emotional reactions and decreasing medication needs. All of these results readily lead to the conclusion that giving patients a sense of control is helpful in treating medical conditions, a conclusion confirmed in a recent review by Mumford, Schlesinger, and Glass (1982).

Less intrusive and hence less threatening situations, such as giving blood, also have been shown to be influenced by control manipulations. For instance, Mills and Krantz (1979) were able to show that simply allowing patients to signify which arm to use in taking their blood significantly improves adaptation to the experience. Thus the available studies suggest that enhancing patients' control enhances adjustment to medical procedures. Additional research is needed to identify the possible limitations of this effect; for example, is it possible that under some conditions it may be more helpful for the patient to give over control completely to a very competent outside source (Thompson, 1981)? Nonetheless, the existing literature is relatively consistent and has a number of implications for medical practice and the design of medical institutions (e.g., hospitals), particularly those that tend to minimize patients' perceived control over all areas of their functioning (Taylor, 1979).

Institutionalized Elderly Population. Another at-risk population that has been studied from a control perspective is the elderly. Such a population is particularly interesting because both behavioral and cognitive control are likely to undergo reduction as a function of natural aging and externally imposed events. At some point the aging process makes it more difficult for individuals to cope with the problems of living. Consequently the elderly come to feel that they have less control in their lives. In addition, loss of control is often imposed in the form of institutionalization, forced relocation, reduced income, and so on.

Control theory predicts that such conditions will result in lessened adaptation. At the same time, of course, family, friends, and social institutions are concerned with the problems of the elderly and are mobilized to aid them. Ironically, however, control theory argues that the helping/supporting environments provided for the elderly may inadvertently undermine health and adaptation by the very presence of these well-intentioned but external experiences. If the causation of experiences moves outside the individual, it is likely that individual responsibility and sense of control would be reduced. This possibility was explored by Langer and Rodin (1976; Rodin & Langer, 1977).

The investigators carried out a manipulation of perceived control in the setting of a residential home for the aged. All of the residents who served as subjects were over 65 years old. The manipulation involved two conditions. In the first, control- and responsibility-enhancing instructions were delivered by the home administrator to one floor of the home. In the second, on another floor, the normal procedures of the home were carried out. Normal procedures tended to make residents dependent and to reduce the responsibility they would take for their lives. In the first condition, the director of the home emphasized how much the residents were responsible for caring for themselves, how they could manage their own living arrangements, and how their social and personal experiences were to be guided by their own wishes. In the second (low-control) condition, instructions emphasized how much the staff of the home did for the individuals and how little they had to worry about. Both groups were given small plants; the high-responsibility group was told that they were to take care of them themselves, while the low-control group were told that the nurses would take care of the plants.

Assessment of the health of the residents involved self-reporting of satisfaction and perceived control, and ratings of such things as alertness, general improvement, and time expended in various activities. The follow-up 18 months later (Rodin & Langer, 1977) additionally included medical records and mortality data.

The high-responsibility group was found to express greater satisfaction and to be rated by nurses and the interviewer as happier, more alert, and more active. This continued to be true 18 months later in the long-term follow-up study. As is predictable from control notions, inducing the elderly to take greater responsibility for their lives and to be given the perception that they have control over what happens to them has a favorable influence on them. Conversely, of course, to induce them to give over control to others was shown to be counterproductive.

Another study using elderly nursing home residents (Schulz, 1976) found similar results. The central manipulation here was the presence of social visits by college undergraduates over a two-month period. Both perceived control and

Studies appear to confirm the theory that old people who are allowed to take responsibility for their own living arrangements enjoy better health and experience greater life satisfaction than do those who are controlled by others.

predictability were manipulated by giving elderly residents of a home choice over both frequency and duration of the visits. Other conditions informed the subjects when the visits would occur (predictability), had the visits occur randomly, or had no visits at all. The results showed that both the predictability and perceived control conditons led to significantly more positive adjustment than in the random-visit or no-visit groups.

Schulz and Hanusa (1978) performed a series of follow-up assessments of the individuals in the first study. At 24, 30, and 43 months after the original study, they obtained ratings of health status and zest for life. Both the control and predictability groups had significantly declined over time in both adjustment and actual health, whereas the no-visit and random groups remained stable. Schulz and Hanusa argued that it was not the loss of social contacts at the end of the formal experiment that led to the declines in the two groups—the random group experienced elimination of contacts and yet did not decline. But the experiment had not provided substitute controllable and predictable experiences; the loss of these was at the heart of the serious decline noted in the two groups.

Everyday Activities. A number of studies have suggested that major stressful events in one's life as well as everyday events may lead to effects on mental and physical health (Holmes & Masuda, 1974; Rabkin & Struening, 1976; Sandler

& Guenther, 1985; Zautra & Dohrenwend, 1983). From the perspective of control theory, people who perceive themselves as being responsible for positive events should tend to have better adjustment outcomes than individuals who perceive positive events as being independent of their efforts. To test this hypothesis, Reich and Zautra (1981) attempted to manipulate the degree of control that students felt they had over positive daily events in their lives. Control of high vs. low degrees was manipulated through instructions to engage in 12 or 2 self-selected infrequent pleasurable activities during a 2-week experimental period; a comparison group received no such instructions. A broad-ranging series of outcome measures was assessed, including physical health, psychological well-being, and positive and negative mood.

The results showed that the 12 vs. 2 conditions did not differ, but both led to more positive adjustment than the no-manipulation control group. However, the investigators also had assessed the subjects' immediate prior histories of negative events, and a breakdown of the data by that variable showed that subjects who engaged in the 12 positive, self-chosen activities had recently experienced fewer negative events than those subjects in the other two groups.

This research dealt with "normal" subjects in their natural environment, and not with a sick or threatened population. That factor expands the range of applicability of the control theory and shows it to be influential in normal daily activities. Application to other populations in their natural settings seems to be a logical next step; of even greater interest would be to apply the control theory experimentally to special or at-risk populations in their natural settings. Some early investigations along these lines are currently being conducted (e.g., Taylor, 1983; Taylor, Lichtman, & Wood, 1984).

Summary and Conclusions.   There now exists a fairly broad sampling of medical and other health-related experiences from which to conclude that the control variable is a significant component in adaptation and well-being. Furthermore, the results of these studies could be used to develop relatively inexpensive programs to help people in a variety of settings. The manipulations are simple and could easily involve medical, hospital, and administrative personnel who could be trained in manipulating control variables in the course of routine practice. As noted, the results of these studies often are complex, the types of variables studied in them vary widely, and many potentially related variables have not yet been investigated. But clearly the area seems ready for implementation and evaluation of pilot programs as well as continuing research exploration.

Interventions in Educational Settings: Retraining of Attributions for Success and Failure

Basic laboratory research has shown that in achievement settings, the reasons that are commonly perceived as the cause of success or failure relate to ability, effort, difficult of the task, and luck (Weiner, Frieze, Kukla, Reed, Rest, & Rosenbaum, 1972). Weiner (1974, 1979) has proposed an **attributional model of achieve-ment motivation** in which these four causal factors are classified in two ways: whether the causes originate internally or externally to the person, and whether the causes are stable or unstable over time (see Figure 11.1). Ability and effort are classified as internal determinants, while task difficulty and luck are classi-fied as external. If you claim the reason you did well in a psychology exam is because you studied hard, you are making an attribution to the internal factor, effort. On the other hand, if you think the reason that you could not answer the teacher's question was because it was too hard, you are making an attribu-tion to the external factor, task difficulty. If a factor remains relatively constant over time, it is considered stable (ability and task difficulty) whereas if the fac-tor can vary, it is seen as unstable (effort and luck). For example, the effort one expends on a task can change each time it is attempted, so effort is unstable; the talent one has with which to handle the task remains about the same each time it is attempted, so ability is a stable factor.

Weiner (1979) cited the results of numerous laboratory investigations show-ing that people's attributions for their successes and failures affect their feel-ings of self-esteem and their expectations for future performance. If success is attributed to a stable cause such as a personality characteristic, expectations for future success will be high; however, if failure is attributed to a stable cause, expectations for future success will be low (Frieze & Weiner, 1971; Weiner & Kukla, 1970). In contrast, attributions to unstable causes (such as having a cold on the day of a test) should have little effect on expectations of future success. Thus attributions can influence expectations for future performance and therefore can affect future achievement-related behavior.

This theoretical analysis provided the framework for an initial diagnostic study comparing the attributions of children who give up vs. those who persist following failure. Dweck and Repucci (1973) asked fifth-grade students to copy block designs, which is one of the subtasks on the Wechsler Intelligence Scale for Children. Some children were given a set of blocks that allowed them to solve the puzzle, whereas others were given an incorrect set that made doing the task impossible. In the face of continued failure, some children persisted while others gave up. Of most interest, those subjects who attributed failure to a lack of ef-fort were those who persisted on the task; those who attributed failure to exter-nal factors or to lack of ability tended to give up. Thus making effort attributions

FIGURE 11.1 Weiner's classification scheme for the causes of achievement behavior.

Stability	Locus of Control	
	Internal	External
Stable	Ability	Task difficulty
Unstable	Effort	Luck

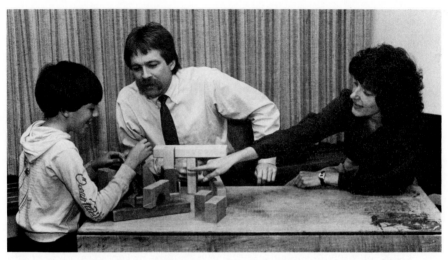

In determining how attributions affect expectations and achievement-related behavior, researchers began with an initial diagnostic study of fifth-graders, some of whom got "easy" puzzle blocks and some of whom worked with "hard" sets.

after failure appears to be associated with continued attempts to succeed at achievement-related tasks.

Based on these findings, Dweck (1975) reasoned that an **attributional retraining** program that taught "helpless" children (those who do not persist in the face of failure) to reattribute their failure to lack of effort would result in increased persistence on the task. The most helpless children within a school were identified and placed into either an attributional retraining program or a success-only condition. Children were given a number of trials in which they were required to solve a certain number of math problems within a limited time period. In the attributional retraining condition, the children were asked on certain trials to solve more problems than was possible in the allotted time. On these failure trials the experimenter who administered the problems attributed the failure to a lack of effort on the child's part. This was the training phase. Dweck reasoned that children could be motivated to persist on future trials by shifting the focus of their attributions from a lack of ability or external factors to effort. The success-only condition was included to test the possibility that higher expectations of success alone may lead to increased persistence (Battle, 1965; Feather, 1966; Tyler, 1958). If the child were only subjected to success trials, then expectations for success should increase and so, therefore, should performance.

After training was over, all the children were tested in a similar way. Subjects in the attribution retraining condition showed more adaptive responses to failure than did subjects in the success-only treatment condition. By the end of training, recipients of attribution retraining showed either marked improvement or no improvement on performance following failure. However, subjects trained using the success-only technique showed significant decreases in the number of problems they were able to solve correctly following a failure trial.

A study by Chapin and Dyck (1976) nicely complements Dweck's findings. Children in grades 5–7 who were experiencing reading difficulties were given a number of sentences to read during the training task. For success subjects, all of the sentences were quite easy. However, for attributional retraining subjects, some sentences were too difficult for their age level so that they inevitably failed. On these trials, subjects were encouraged to attribute their failures to lack of effort. In a later test phase, subjects in the attributional retraining conditions attempted to read a greater number of sentences than subjects in the control conditions. Similar results have been reported by Schunk (1982) and Andrews and Debus (1978), who showed that the effects of attributional retraining transferred across several different achievement-related tasks.

Although the research to date suggests that attributional retraining has considerable promise as a technique for increasing persistence among "helpless" elementary school students, several caveats must be kept in mind. First, although placing students in situations where failure is inevitable may seem unethical, keep in mind the ultimate purpose of the research — to train students to make attributions that will be beneficial to them. Second, all of the research cited above has been conducted with young children whose causal belief structures are dominated by effort (Frieze & Snyder, 1980). Thus attributional retraining involving effort may be less successful for older children and adults for whom ability is perceived as an increasingly important causal factor in success (Nicholls, 1979). Third, all of the research has used highly structured school-related test tasks as the criteria. Whether attributional retraining will generalize to actual school performance remains an open question.

Competitiveness, Achievement, and Race Relations: The Jigsaw Classroom

Applied social psychologists have also explored other facets of the social psychology/education interface. Achievement in the classroom depends upon a variety of social and cognitive factors. Often the structure and composition of the classroom can affect how any one student functions within it. One particular set of classroom variables has been extensively investigated by applied social psychologists.

The Problem. In most traditional classrooms, students are reinforced for being "better" than others. Such competitive classrooms make success and failure highly salient for students. Failure under these conditions leads students to feel more negatively about themselves than does failure in a noncompetitive classroom (Ames, Ames, & Felker, 1977). This is particularly problematic for minority students who do not speak the dominant language and who therefore are at a considerable disadvantage in competitive classrooms. Consistent with this view, Biener and Gerard (1975) have found that black and Mexican-American children showed lower levels of achievement motivation than white students in traditional, competitive classrooms.

In the 1954 Supreme Court case *Brown* v. *Board of Education of Topeka,* it was decided that racially segregated schools could not be equal. The impetus for desegregation resulted in part from Allport's (1954) theory of conflict, proposing that bringing majority and minority children in contact with one another would reduce prejudice. Katz (1968) further believed that through contact minority children would adopt the achievement behaviors displayed by their white counterparts.

In contrast, Stephan and Rosenfield (1978) cite a number of studies that showed desegregation to have negative effects on race relations (e.g., Armor, 1972; Dentler & Elkins, 1967; Williams, Best, & Boswell, 1975). In their own study, Stephan and Rosenfield found that whites and blacks from segregated backgrounds displayed more negative attitudes toward all ethnic groups following desegregation while those from integrated backgrounds did not change their attitudes. Not surprisingly, whites from segregated backgrounds did not change their level of interethnic contact following desegregation. Blacks from segregated and desegregated backgrounds showed no increase in contact with whites, but did show a small increase in contact with Mexican-Americans. Contrary to the early theories, it appears that simple desegregation does not necessarily promote the contact thought useful in increasing the academic performance of minority children. These problems were especially manifest in the Austin, Texas, school system where, following desegregation through busing, a number of racial incidents occurred. A group of social psychologists headed by Elliot Aronson was invited to find ways in which this conflict could be prevented (Aronson, Blaney, Stephan, Sikes, & Snapp, 1978).

The Solution. Upon observing the desegregated classrooms, Aronson and his associates concluded that the competitive environment of the classroom did not encourage the development of friendship; instead, it potentially exacerbated racial tension (Aronson & Osherow, 1980). In searching for potential solutions, Aronson drew upon social-psychological research that showed the benefits of cooperation.

In an early pioneering study, Deutsch (1949) divided members of a psychology class into either competitive or cooperative five-person groups. The students in the cooperative groups were instructed to act as a team to solve the tasks and were told they would be graded as a group. The competitive groups were told that they were going to be graded invidually based upon each person's contribution. Thus in cooperative groups what was good for one was good for all, while in competitive groups what was good for one was deterimental to the others. The cooperative groups were usually more productive and gave better solutions than did competitive groups. Cooperative group members were more receptive to the ideas of others and were rated as more friendly with each other by objective observers. Deutsch showed that in a cooperatively structured laboratory setting, communication and performance were increased.

Sherif (1956) confirmed these results in a field setting, showing that when opposing groups can work for a common goal, they will come to like each other and cooperate more. Boys at a summer camp were divided into two groups that competed in a number of games. Interactions between members of the two groups became unfriendly. A number of cooperative ventures between the two groups were then arranged, leading to increased liking and friendliness between the members of the two groups.

These two studies were quite suggestive, since the initial conditions that existed in the desegregated classrooms closely paralleled the competitive conditions created in the two studies. Therefore, to meet the goals of desegregation (increasing interethnic contact, and increasing achievement levels in minority children), it was thought to be helpful to shift the structure of classrooms from competitive to cooperative. The goal of Aronson and his colleagues was to transform the traditional classroom into a new learning experience where students were mutually dependent upon each other for success. They called their innovative idea the **jigsaw method.**

In the jigsaw classroom students are broken into groups of five or six members. Each member of the group is given a certain portion of the day's lesson and is responsible for teaching that portion to the rest of the group. A student must rely completely on the others in the group in order to learn the whole lesson. Group members will come to realize that each member of the group is equally important, and in fact vital, to the success of the entire group.

A typical jigsaw lesson may operate in the following way: suppose the topic under study was Columbus and the discovery of the New World. One person might be responsible for talking about the motivations for explorations at that time (e.g., search for a better route to Asia), another could deal with the problems of organizing the journey (e.g., getting financial support), a third could relate the perils of the voyage across the ocean, another could tell of the interactions with the Indians, and the last one could be responsible for telling what effects Columbus' voyage had on future explorations. To make sure everyone does a good job, students from different groups with the same topic could meet and discuss the important points. Each person adds some information in order to complete the overall picture. It is analogous to a jigsaw puzzle; no piece can be left out for the puzzle to be complete. Students are then tested individually on the entire lesson. It is always to a student's advantage to listen to members of his or her group and, if need be, to help other members teach their parts of the lesson. The fact that testing is individual ensures that the brighter students are not hindered by slower students.

The teacher plays an important, albeit nontraditional, role in the jigsaw classroom. Rather than being an authority figure, the teacher is a facilitator whose job it is to help group members solve problems. Instead of insisting that someone be more attentive or better behaved, the teacher might ask the group to think

The climate of the jigsaw classroom, in which each student is responsible for teaching a portion of the lesson to the group, appears to enhance both self-esteem and academic performance.

about ways to get people to focus more on the task. The fact that the students play an active role in all aspects of the jigsaw task increases their commitment (Aronson et al., 1978). The teacher also chooses and trains student group leaders whose job it is to keep the jigsaw lesson on track. Leaders are trained in role-playing exercises, from which they develop empathy for others and an understanding of the process. Training sessions are critiqued, and suggestions for appropriate reactions to various situations are made. Before actually participating in groups, student leaders are well prepared for potential problems they may face.

Researchers investigating the effectiveness of the jigsaw method have hypothesized that participation in jigsaw groups would increase liking for groupmates and for school in general, raise self-esteem, and decrease competitiveness (Aronson & Osherow, 1980). These hypotheses were tested in elementary school classrooms over a six-week period by Blaney, Stephan, Rosenfield, Aronson, and Sikes (1977). Seven fifth-grade classes adopted the jigsaw method, while three traditional classrooms served as controls. Students met in jigsaw groups for approximately 45 minutes 3 days a week. Students' attitudes toward school and their liking for others were assessed at the beginning and end of the experiment.

The results generally confirmed all of the hypotheses. Groupmates came to like each other more than the rest of their classmates, although they tended to like other classmates more at the conclusion of the experiment as well. Students in the jigsaw classrooms reported higher self-esteem than did students in traditional classrooms and engaged in fewer competitive behaviors. Interestingly, students in traditional classrooms liked school much less than students in the jigsaw classes, although there were marked differences among ethnic groups. Liking for school increased among whites in jigsaw classes and decreased among whites in traditional classes. Blacks in both conditions disliked school more at the end of the six weeks, although this effect was greater in the traditional classroom. Mexican-American students exhibited the reverse trend; they liked school more in the traditional classroom than in the jigsaw classroom. As an explanation for this unexpected finding, the experimenters speculated that the forced participation required of jigsaw students may have made Mexican-American students uncomfortable because of possible language problems. Consistent with this reasoning, when Geffner (1978) tested the jigsaw method in a California school district where the proportion of Mexican-Americans was much greater than in Austin, he found that jigsaw students liked school more than students in traditional classes. Geffner also showed that in relation to students in traditional classrooms, jigsaw students not only had more positive feelings about their own ethnic group but were also more positive about other groups.

The jigsaw method has been shown to be quite effective for improving relations in the classroom. Further, a preliminary evaluation of its effects on academic performance (Lucker, Rosenfield, Sikes, & Aronson, 1977) showed that jigsaw students improved more on standardized tests than students in traditional classes. These results were primarily due to the enhanced performance of the minority students in the jigsaw classrooms.

The jigsaw method holds considerable promise of improving the self-esteem and performance of minority students in educational settings. The method's design and implementation provide an excellent example of how social-psychological theory and research can be used to produce useful social programs. At this point, more rigorous evaluations of the jigsaw method are needed, ideally through the use of randomized experiments. The optimal educational situations in which the process may be used are at present unknown, as are possible limitations of the technique. For example, certain school topics may be poorly suited to the jigsaw method. Finally, the present promising assessment is based on rather short-term studies; the persistence of the positive effects of the jigsaw method is still to be determined (Aronson et al., 1980).

Summary and Conclusions. It appears that the joining of attribution theory with applied problems has been a productive one in the field of educational theory and practice. Significant improvement in children's cognition and behavior in educational settings is now possible, and programs implementing attribution retraining can be attempted. Additionally, the jigsaw methodology was based on sophisticated conceptual and theoretical analysis of group process derived from laboratory research, showing once again the role of theory in applied work. Jigsaw methodology also appears ready for more widespread adoption in classroom procedures. Both topics are noteworthy examples of social-psychological research in applied settings.

Research on Smoking and Substance Abuse Prevention

In 1974, the first report of the Surgeon General linking cigarette smoking with an increased risk of serious health problems including cancer, heart disease, and respiratory problems was published (U.S. Public Health Service, 1974). Since that time, a number of researchers in psychology and public health have investigated methods of reducing the prevalence of cigarette smoking in the United States.

Much of the early work by psychologists focused on the development of therapeutic techniques that would help adult smokers reduce or eliminate their consumption of cigarettes. As one example, a promising early technique induced aversion in smokers by having them smoke at two-to-three times their normal rate, sometimes in combination with breathing warm, smoky air (Lichtenstein et al., 1973). Some of these techniques achieved high rates of success in quitting or reduced smoking immediately following the completion of therapy. However, later follow-up studies indicated that these techniques were usually only modestly effective in the long term (Lichtenstein & Danaher, 1976; Leventhal & Cleary, 1980), with only 10%–25% of the program participants succeeding in maintaining reduced smoking levels after one year.

Early work by public health researchers, in contrast, emphasized large-scale media campaigns directed primarily toward individuals at high risk for specific illnesses. This approach is illustrated by the Stanford Heart Disease Program (Maccoby & Farquhar, 1975; Farquhar et al., 1977), designed to alter behaviors such as smoking and dietary practices—for example, high intake of fats—associated with high risk of heart disease. An entire community was subjected to two consecutive 9-month media campaigns that included television and radio programs and announcements, newspaper stories and advertisements, billboards, and posters; a separate control community was not exposed to the campaign. Only a slight decrease in smoking rates in the experimental relative to the control community was found in a follow-up two years after the completion of the intensive media campaign. Other large-scale media studies have demonstrated similarly modest results in producing long-term change in adult smokers (see Wallach, 1981).

Given the very modest success of interventions with adult smokers, researchers have begun to explore methods of intervening with children before they try smoking and/or become regular smokers. The early efforts drew heavily on basic social-psychological research and theory in the area of attitude change; more recent efforts take a more general social-influence approach. As will be shown, the attitude-change paradigm has not delivered what program planners had hoped in the area of primary and secondary smoking prevention (Evans, 1976). This comes as no surprise to most social psychologists, who have known for years that simple attitude-change manipulations rarely bring about specific desired behavioral changes (Flay, Johnson, Hansen, Grossman, & Sobel, 1983).

The second area of applied research to be discussed appears quite promising. **Social-influence** models have incorporated many of the most effective social-psychological principles into prevention/treatment packages that, in their preliminary evaluation phases, are producing more positive results than had been expected. In the review of research on smoking and substance-abuse prevention that follows, you will find evaluations of how laboratory-based findings have fared when experimentally tested in the real world. Readers wishing a more comprehensive discussion of this area are referred to reviews by Evans, Smith, and Raines (1984) and Flay (1984) for smoking prevention and Schaps, DiBartolo, Maskowitz, Palley, and Churgin, (1981) and Moskowitz (1983) for drug-abuse prevention.

Attitude and Attitude-Behavior Change Models. There is perhaps no other area in social psychology that has generated more research and scientific inquiry than the study of attitude change and attitude-behavior relationships. In a series of classic papers, McGuire (1969, 1972, 1985) has reviewed the course of attitude-change research since the turn of the century, focusing primarily on what he calls five critical classes of independent variables: source, message, channel, receiver, and destination factors. Underlying the large body of research on these variables is an information-processing model (Hovland, Janis, & Kelley, 1953; Hovland, Lumsdaine, & Sheffield, 1949) based on the assumption that the way new information is processed will depend on the value of each of these variables. Favorable values such as having a highly credible source help incorporate new information into a person's beliefs. Such changes in beliefs or attitudes are assumed to lead naturally to changes in behavior.

Unfortunately, experience in the laboratory has demonstrated that this final assumption does not necessarily follow. Early studies reviewed by Wicker (1969) suggested that attitudes were only weakly related to behavior. More recent investigations have identified a number of conditions under which attitudes do predict behavior (see Sherman & Fazio, 1983), but, in general, attitude change often does not result in behavior change.

The early smoking-prevention programs were based primarily on the information-processing model just described. Information about the negative consequences of smoking was presented in an attempt to change adolescent attitudes towards smoking. For example, in a typical education program, elementary or middle-school children were given information regarding the dangers of smoking or drug use. This information was usually provided in the form of a lecture or series of lectures, supplemented by commercially available filmstrips that presented similar information, often in animated form. Evaluations of the effectiveness of these programs typically have included measures of knowledge about the effects of the substance (for example, tobacco), attitudes toward the substance, and, occasionally, in the better studies, respondents' reports of their actual use of the substance.

Several reviews of the effectiveness of these programs have concluded that school-based smoking education programs have had minimal impact (Flay et al., 1983). Although these programs have differed widely in their means of presenting the information (i.e., pamphlets, lectures, posters, etc.), all have been quite general in nature and have often failed to include the population at highest risk (Evans et al., 1979). These programs have also neglected to define specific measurable outcomes, so that it is not clear whether increased knowledge, decreased substance use, or some combination of the two were the intended effects of the program.

Paralleling the work on smoking prevention, the early work on drug-abuse prevention repeatedly used educational interventions in spite of a lack of empirical support (Moskowitz, 1983) and often in the face of contradicting evidence (Goodstadt, 1980). Similarly, Schaps et al. (1981) presented findings from their review of 127 drug-abuse prevention project evaluations, concluding that the effects of education programs were minimal. Even the most exemplary studies among those using the educational approach reported at best marginally positive effects, with only two of the four studies that used self-report measures of drug usage indicating any positive effects of the program.

Several conclusions can be drawn from the early research on smoking and substance-abuse prevention. Interventions in this area relied primarily on attitude-change models in the form of school-based education programs that provided factual information in the hope of modifying behavior. Most of these programs were poorly designed and suffered from serious methodological flaws that made rigorous scientific evaluations difficult. None of the programs included components that specifically attempted to link changes in attitudes to corresponding changes in behavior. Hence the general lack of success of educational interventions is not surprising.

Social Influence Models. A number of studies have suggested that a variety of social influences are associated with smoking in preteenagers and teenagers. Attitudes and smoking behavior of peers and family, particularly those individuals of the same gender, have been found in numerous studies to be good predictors of adolescent smoking (Allegrante, O'Rourke, and Tuncalp, 1977; Chassin, Presson, Bensenberg, Olshavsky, & Sherman, 1983; Krosnick & Judd, 1982). The great majority of adolescents report smoking their first cigarette with a friend (Bewley, Bland, & Harris, 1974; Palmer, 1970). Hence it would appear that programs that emphasized resisting social influences to smoke should be more successful than simple educational programs. Such programs have now gone through several stages of development, and they continue to be a very promising approach to the prevention of cigarette smoking and possibly substance abuse.

The prototypical social influence program for smoking prevention was developed by Evans and his colleagues at the University of Houston (Evans, 1976;

Evans et al., 1978; Evans et al., 1981). The program was based in large part on basic research by Bandura (1971, 1977) on the effectiveness of modeling in producing behavior change and research by McGuire (1964) on increasing subjects' resistance to persuasive communications. In the program, sixth, seventh, and eighth graders were exposed to a series of films of nonsmoking same-aged peers together with reminder posters. These materials emphasized three areas: (a) social pressures created by friends, parents, and cigarette ads to begin smoking; (b) immediate psychological effects of smoking (e.g., increased carbon monoxide in the breath); and (c) methods of resisting pressures to smoke. Dependent measures included a knowledge test based on the film content, future intentions to smoke, and a self-report of current smoking behavior. The validity of the last measure was enhanced by collecting saliva samples that subjects believed would be analyzed for nicotine (thiocyanate) content, a procedure that encourages more accurate reporting (Evans, Hanson, & Middlemark, 1977; Jones & Sigall, 1971).

The design of the Houston study was quite complex. During the first year, three groups received either the full version or a partial version of the treatment outlined above, whereas three separate control groups received no treatment. The program then continued for three years with students being exposed to one of a variety of treatments ranging from three years of the full program to three years without receiving any treatment. Preliminary results of the study have shown that subjects receiving the treatment have generally reported a lower intention to smoke in the future and less smoking behavior than subjects in the control conditions. For example, 9.5% of subjects receiving the treatment program reported smoking two or more cigarettes per day, whereas 11.1–14.2% of subjects in various control groups reported smoking two or more cigarettes per day at the end of ninth grade.

Following the initial success of this program, a number of investigators attempted to develop a variety of additional components to further strengthen the Houston program. For example, the Robbinsdale Anti-Smoking Project (Hurd et al., 1980) included three new components derived from basic psychological research that were expected to enhance the effectiveness of the program. First, slightly older peer leaders, who have been shown to be highly effective models (Hartup & Loungee, 1975), delivered the program. Second, students made a voluntary public commitment not to smoke (Kiesler, 1971). Finally, students role-played scenarios in which they had to resist pressure to smoke, an experience that should further facilitate their ability to resist social influence (Bandura, 1977). Once again, preliminary evaluations of the program have been encouraging. Of students exposed to the peer-led program in seventh grade, 46% had never tried smoking and only 7% had become regular smokers, whereas 25% had never tried smoking and 25% had become regular smokers in the control group by the end of eighth grade. A subsequent follow-up at the end of ninth grade indicated that the smoking rates in the program group continued to be lower than those in the control group, although the magnitude of the differences had decreased. Similar promising results were obtained in pilot tests of several other programs using augmented versions of the original Houston program (e.g.,Mur-

The object of this role-playing exercise was to act out saying no to a peer offering a cigarette. Programs that emphasize resistance to a social influence are a promising approach to the prevention not only of smoking but of substance abuse in general.

ray, Johnson, Luepker, & Mittelmark, 1984; Perry, Killen, Telch, Slinkard, & Dunaher, 1980; Vartiainen, Pallonen, McAlister, Koskela, & Puska, 1983).

Several researchers have recently begun large-scale tests of enhanced social-influence programs for smoking prevention. One of the most successful studies completed to date was conducted by researchers at the University of Waterloo in Canada (Best et al., 1984; Flay et al., 1985). Using materials patterned after those used in the Houston and Robbinsdale programs, they developed an enhanced social-influence program that was appropriate for their Canadian subjects. All sixth-grade students in 11 schools were initially exposed to the program, with booster sessions being given to these students in grades 7 and 8. Sixth-grade students in 11 other schools served as the control group. The results showed that 5% of the social-influence students were regular smokers at the end of the eighth grade, whereas 13% of the control group had become regular smokers. The program also appeared to be very effective with students who had parents, siblings, or friends who smoked, but who had not yet tried smoking themselves at the beginning of sixth grade. In this "high-risk' group, 67% of those in the program had still never tried smoking at the end of eighth grade, whereas only 22% of the control subjects had still never tried smoking. Such results suggest that programs carefully constructed to help youngsters resist peer and parental pressures to smoke can be very effective in reducing the incidence of teenage smoking.

Given the success of the social-influence programs and research on the development of smoking, extensions of the social-influence approach to substance abuse have recently been undertaken (McAlister, Perry, Killen, Slinkard, & Maccoby, 1980). Some studies (Kandel, Kessler, & Margulies, 1978; O'Donnell & Clayton, 1982) have further suggested that substance usage develops in a fairly invariant sequence. Thus one important extension has been to design and implement more general smoking and substance-abuse prevention programs based on the social-influence model. Johnson, Hansen, Collins, and Graham (1984) have developed a very sophisticated program of this type that is currently being tested in over 100 classrooms in Los Angeles.

Another general extension has developed in part from the observation that programs presented to entire grades or entire schools are typically more successful than programs addressed to isolated classrooms of students (Flay et al., 1985). Presumably, programs that change the norms of the entire peer group to be more actively antismoking also reduce the likelihood of each child being exposed to influence attempts by peers. Extending this reasoning to parent influences, Flay et al. (1983) have recently broadcast televised segments in coordination with a school-based social-influence program in an attempt to change parents' attitudes toward smoking and their actual smoking behavior. Preliminary evaluation has indicated some success: among smoking parents of students who watched the television segments, 40% also watched the program and 30% made an effort to either reduce or quit smoking. Gleaton (1984) has begun to develop programs to organize entire communities and establish strong, antisubstance abuse norms in the community. These programs have considerable potential for significantly reducing the likelihood that adolescents will be exposed to either peer or adult influences to use substances.

Summary and Conclusions.   The area of smoking and substance-abuse prevention has been a very fertile one for the application of social-psychological principles. The early educationally based interventions were poorly grounded in basic research and theory and led to little success. More recent social-influence approaches to smoking prevention, in contrast, provide an excellent example of how basic social-psychological principles can be applied in the design of an important social intervention.

A growing number of scientifically rigorous evaluations of these programs are appearing in the literature. Nearly all of these programs have shown positive results, typically succeeding in deterring substantial numbers of young people from trying smoking and from becoming regular smokers. Yet, as Murray and Perry (1984) point out, there is a need for more research addressing a number of social, developmental, and environmental dimensions that may influence and moderate program effectiveness. More research is also needed to investigate the long-term effectiveness of social influence programs and methods of maintaining their short-term benefits. As this evidence begins to accumulate, social psychological prevention packages are likely to play an important role in the direction of future preventive efforts.

Conclusion

This chapter has described some important developments in the evolution of applied social psychology. This evolution is bringing about a melding of the more theoretical orientations of basic researchers with the social-problem focus of applied researchers. A presentation of Cialdini's (1980) full-cycle model showed how this interplay between theoretical and applied approaches can take place. Two critical periods in the history of social psychology were characterized to show how focusing attention solely on theoretical or applied concerns leaves each deficient in important respects. In contrast, the full-cycle orientation offers promise of maintaining a scientific approach while meeting demands for relevance.

Next, the work activities of applied social psychologists and some of the settings in which they work were described. Three areas of research were then reviewed to demonstrate the usefulness of applied social psychology in understanding and designing interventions to help attack important social problems. These also illustrate the encouraging trend to test applications of basic social psychological principles in naturalistic settings using high-quality methodologies. The research on perceived control and health showed how control-enhancing interventions can prepare individuals more effectively for stressful medical procedures; increase the well-being of elderly individuals who are institutionalized; and facilitate adjustment in everyday activities.

The chapter then treated social-psychological interventions in educational settings, surveying efforts to increase motivation in students through attributional retraining and to increase motivation and cooperation in classrooms through the jigsaw learning technique. A final section described ways in which social-influence models have been applied to help prevent smoking and substance abuse.

You should note that only a few selected examples of this exciting and growing area of research have been presented. Creative applied researchers develop new areas of application each year, drawing on old and important new findings in basic social psychology. This growing diversity has also been fostered by recent graduates of applied social programs who have taken positions in a variety of academic, marketing, and public-health settings, state and federal government agencies, and private industry. Major advances have been made in some areas of research; others have proven to be more difficult and progress has been much slower. Overall, it is clear that applied social psychology has begun to fulfill its long-held promise.

ssary

action research A type of applied research in which researchers cooperate with organizations. A problem is defined and a solution is proposed, data are collected, and changes suggested by the research are implemented in the organization. Evaluations of the effects of the changes may then suggest further research.

attributional model of achievement motivation Weiner's model to describe the causes of success and failure in achievement situations. According to the model, success or failure can be attributed to skill, ability, difficulty of the task, or luck.

attributional retraining A technique whereby individuals experiencing failure due to motivational problems are taught to attribute their failure to lack of effort rather than lack of ability.

external validity The extent to which the results of an experiment can be generalized beyond the conditions represented in the research.

full-cycle model A model of applied research in which a researcher identifies a social phenomenon that exists in everyday experience, and then cycles back and forth between highly controlled laboratory experiments and externally valid field settings to develop a powerful and applicable explanation of social behavior.

jigsaw method of classroom instruction A method of classroom instruction designed to foster cooperation among students by making them dependent on each other for instructional information.

perceived control The perceptions held by individuals that their actions will have an effect on what happens to them.

social influence model of smoking prevention A technique for preventing smoking that is based on peer influence and modeling of nonsmoking behavior.

12 / Psychology and the Law

Valerie P. Hans
University of Delaware

Imagine that you are at home one day and that there is a knock at the door. You answer it, and as soon as the door opens a police officer yells at you, "Freeze." You are stunned, but you comply. After handcuffing you and reading you your rights, the officer explains that she has a warrant for your arrest on charges of armed robbery. You explain that you don't know what she is talking about, as she and her partner lead you to the police car. After arriving at the station, you are booked and jailed.

Time passes, and eventually you meet with your court-appointed lawyer (since you can't afford one) and learn that a series of armed robberies has been committed in your town, that the description of the perpetrator fits you, and that several of your neighbors called the police. You find it all to be very incredible, but it isn't funny when a store clerk who doesn't know you picks you out of a lineup, identifying you as the armed robber.

Since it appears that you will be going to trial, your attorney begins developing a defense for you. A major problem, however, will be discrediting the testimony of the store clerk. Your attorney tells you that she intends to bring in a psychologist as an expert witness. You are surprised and tell your attorney that you don't really want to claim insanity as a defense. She then tells you that the psychologist will testify about the inaccuracy of eyewitnesses. When you remark that you didn't know psychologists could testify about that, she elaborates further, describing a number of different roles that psychologists now play in the legal system.

What roles are played by legal psychologists? Why are they involved with the civil and criminal justice system? What kind of effects do they have on the judicial process? The answers to these and related questions are provided in this chapter. (By the way, with the help of the psychologist, you win the case).

What Is Legal Psychology?

An intriguing debate about the value of applied psychology took place around the turn of the century. At issue was whether psychology had anything at all to offer those who practiced law. The debate summarizes many issues present even today as psychologists apply their knowledge to the practice of law. The issues serve as a starting point for our discussion.

By the early 1900s, psychologists who had begun to study the factors affecting legal testimony were eager to put their findings to use in the courtroom. Psychologist Hugo Munsterberg summarized these studies in his 1908 book, *On the Witness Stand*. In calling upon the legal profession to open its doors to psychologists, Munsterberg wrote:

> The time for such Applied Psychology is surely near . . . the educator will certainly not resist. . . . Even the business world begins to understand. . . . The politician . . . the officer . . . the minister . . . all are ready to see that certain chapters

of Applied Psychology are sources of help and strength for them. The lawyer alone is obdurate. The lawyer and the judge and the juryman are sure that they do not need the experimental psychologists. . . . They go on thinking that their legal instinct and their common sense supplies them with all that is needed, and somewhat more. (Munsterberg, 1908, pp. 9–11)

Munsterberg pointed out that, while the court relied upon modern scientific techniques in assessing the significance of drops of dried blood in murder cases, the court was content with "the most unscientific and haphazard methods of common prejudice and ignorance when a mental product, especially the memory report of a witness, is to be examined" (p. 44). Munsterberg extolled the potential contributions psychological research could make to the law and chastised the legal profession for their reluctance to incorporate the methods and findings of psychology into the law.

Lawyers responded vigorously to Munsterberg's attacks on their open-mindedness and competency. The great legal scholar John Wigmore fashioned a clever rebuttal in the form of a report of an imaginary trial of Hugo Munsterberg on charges of libel (Wigmore, 1909). The judge who decided the case was Judge Solon Wiseman, and the defendant Munsterberg was represented by Mr. R.E. Search, Mr. X. Perry Ment, and Mr. Si Kist. The trial took place on April Fool's Day, in Wundt County. The plaintiffs, members of the Supreme Court, sued Munsterberg for injuring their good name and demanded the grand sum of one dollar as compensation. The plaintiffs argued that, contrary to Munsterberg's claims, psychological methods were not very precise, psychological findings were not generally endorsed as applicable to the American judicial system, and psychological methods had not been shown to be superior to the ones used in the legal system. Therefore lawyers were not closed-minded and stubborn, but instead wisely cautious! In Wigmore's tongue-in-cheek scenario, the case was so clear that the jurors did not even have to retire to deliberate. Instead they whispered together briefly and the foreman announced that the jury had found for the plaintiffs, with damages of one dollar. The lawyers were vindicated, if only in their imaginations.

After initial work by Munsterberg and others in the early part of this century, work in the psychology-law domain was irregular until the 1960s. Since then, however, research in the area has grown tremendously (Monahan & Loftus, 1982). Several factors have prompted this dramatic increase. A desire for relevance led to the expansion of many fields of applied psychology. Worry about the increase in violence and crime in American society stimulated social-science work related to law. Furthermore, the civil rights movement enhanced the concern for the study of legal rights (Anastasi, 1979; Tapp, 1976; Tapp, 1980). While the field of psychology and law has expanded, some of the early tensions revealed in the Munsterberg-Wigmore debate persist. Many psychologists express bewilderment that they are not always welcomed with open arms in the courtroom. Even today, some critics continue to question the value of psychology in the understanding and practice of law.

What Do Legal Psychologists Do?

Today, fulfilling Munsterberg's dream (and Wigmore's nightmare!), legal psychologists are active in a wide variety of work settings. In universities, faculty and students specializing in psychology and law conduct research on legal decision making, the trial process, and eyewitness testimony. They study the psychological impact of crime on victims and factors that lead people to violate the law. Government agencies and private companies employ legal psychologists to analyze the shortcomings of the justice system and to test ways of improving it. Attorneys hire psychologists to testify about a defendant's mental condition, to give expert testimony about key issues in a trial, and to help them in trial strategy and jury selection.

A special category of legal psychology is **forensic psychology,** which concentrates on the evaluation and treatment of criminal defendants. Forensic psychologists often work in mental health agencies, probation and parole divisions, and prisons. In these settings, they conduct psychological evaluations of people charged with or convicted of crimes. They evaluate whether defendants are able to stand trial, whether they are dangerous, and whether or not they could benefit from psychological treatment. Often they testify about their findings in court. Forensic psychologists also provide psychological services for prison inmates.

Research and Applications

To provide an understanding of just what a "legal" psychologist does, this chapter focuses on five specific topics that have captured the interest and participation of psychology-law specialists. First to be considered is the psychologist's traditional role in evaluating the psychological state of individuals, involving predictions of whether or not individuals will be dangerous to themselves or others, how accurate these predictions are, and the manner in which predictions of dangerousness are employed by the courts. The second topic is the controversial insanity defense and the psychologist's role in testifying about a defendant's mental state to help the court decide whether the defendant should be found "Not Guilty by Reason of Insanity."

The third topic is the reliability of eyewitness testimony, which psychologists began to study well before the famous Munsterberg-Wigmore controversy. The fourth topic, jury selection, is of more recent vintage. Psychologists have been helping attorneys pick juries for the last several decades. The last topic, psychologists and criminal behavior, is the variety of ways in which psychologists have attempted to understand and to change criminal behavior, illustrated by their work relating to a specific offense that has engaged a large number of researchers and applied psychologists: the crime of rape. Finally, to give you some exposure to the breadth of involvement of psychologists in the legal and criminal-justice process, the chapter surveys additional roles and topics that have engaged psychologists interested in the psychology-law field and concludes by discussing some of the problems and prospects for legal psychology in the future.

As you review psychologists' contributions to the fields of law and criminal justice, keep two key questions in mind. First of all, how *effective* are psychologists? Are they actually helping to improve the operation of the criminal-justice system? Second, is their involvement *ethical?* In general, are psychologists promoting justice or hindering it? At the end of the review, you may find yourself a modern-day Munsterberg, eager for the expansion of psychology and the law, or a contemporary Wigmore, skeptical of psychology's value to the law.

Predictions of Violent Behavior

One of the most frequent tasks psychologists perform in the criminal-justice system is to judge the likelihood that an individual will be dangerous or violent. Such predictions are required at numerous points in the legal system, as shown in Table 12.1 (Shah, 1978). These points relate to decisions that must be made about bail, sentencing, probation, parole, and involuntary mental hospital commitment of dangerous persons. Researchers have discovered, however, that it is very difficult to predict accurately whether or not a person will be violent. Consider the case of Johnnie Baxstrom.

TABLE 12.1

Points in the Legal System Where Predictions of Violent Behavior Are Required

1. Decisions concerning bail, or release on personal recognizance, for persons accused of crimes, including the level at which bail is to be set.
2. Decisions concerning the waiver to adult courts of juveniles charged with serious crimes.
3. Sentencing decisions following criminal convictions, including decisions about release on conditions of probation.
4. Decisions pertaining to work-release and furlough programs for incarcerated offenders.
5. Parole and other conditional release decisions for offenders.
6. Decisions pertaining to the commitment and release of "sexual psychopaths," "sexually dangerous persons," "defective delinquents," and the like.
7. Determinations of dangerousness for all indicted felony defendants found incompetent to stand trial (e.g., in New York State).
8. Decisions pertaining to the special handling of and transfer to special prisons of offenders who are disruptive in regular prisons.
9. Commitment of drug addicts (because of fears that they will commit violent crimes to support their drug habit).
10. Decisions concerning the emergency and longer term involuntary commitment of mentally ill persons considered to pose a "danger to self or others."
11. Decisions regarding the "conditional" and "unconditional" release of involuntarily confined mental patients.
12. Decisions concerning the hospitalization (on grounds of continued mental disorder and dangerousness) of persons acquitted by reason of insanity.
13. Decisions regarding the transfer to security hospitals of mental patients found to be too difficult or dangerous to be handled in regular civil mental hospitals.
14. Decisions concerning the invocation of special legal proceedings or sentencing provisions for "habitual" and "dangerous" offenders.
15. Decisions concerning the likelihood of continued dangerousness of persons convicted of capital crimes, as a basis for determinations pertaining to the use of the death sentence.

Baxstrom, a black man, was convicted of assault in 1956 and sentenced to Attica State Prison in New York. While he was imprisoned, he was diagnosed as mentally ill and transferred from Attica to New York's Dannemora State Hospital for the criminally insane. In 1961, when his sentence for assault expired, Baxstrom's case was reviewed and he was kept at Dannemora as a civil patient. New York's mental hygiene law allowed such patients to be retained in hospitals for the criminally insane if they were diagnosed as dangerously mentally ill. Baxstrom petitioned state, local, and federal authorities for his release from the correctional hospital. In 1966, the U.S. Supreme Court decided the case of *Baxstrom* v. *Herold,* in which it upheld Baxstrom's petition and required that Baxstrom be given a fuller review under existing civil procedure, including a jury trial on the question of his mental illness. Officials of New York State's Department of Mental Hygiene searched their records and found a total of 966 other individuals in state hospitals for the criminally insane whose cases paralleled Baxstrom's. Instead of providing full and time-consuming reviews for these people, officials transferred all of them from correctional hospitals to civil hospitals.

These "Baxstrom" patients were perceived as highly dangerous. Hospital staff and members of the surrounding communities protested loudly about the wholesale transfers. Yet their fears proved to be largely groundless. By any measure, these patients were not very violent at all. A long-term follow-up study of the Baxstrom patients (Steadman & Cocozza, 1974) showed that only 13 patients had to be returned to the correctional facilities because they were too troublesome in the civil hospitals. Of those patients released to the community, only 11% were subsequently convicted of another crime, and in all but two cases the offenses were relatively minor ones such as public intoxication, disorderly conduct, or vagrancy. Yet these patients had been initially denied release from hospitals for the criminally insane and struck fear in the hearts of the civil hospital staff and community members because of their supposed propensity to violence.

The case of Johnnie Baxstrom is not unique. Throughout the country, people suffer the consequences of being improperly labeled as dangerous or violent. On the other hand, the courts and prisons of our nation are full of individuals who have been wrongly judged to be nondangerous. Why are there so many errors in the prediction of violence? Is there anything that the legal psychologist can do to improve the prediction process? A review of the clinical prediction of violent behavior sheds some light on these concerns.

Clinical Prediction of Violence. A psychologist asked to make a prediction of violence considers two different sets of variables: **predictor variables** and **criterion variables.** *Predictor variables* are the personal and situational factors about an individual that the psychologist uses to infer the person's likelihood of being violent. For example, a psychologist might consider the predictor variables of an individual's age, gender, race, education, previous history of violence, employment record, and family environment.

In contrast, *criterion variables* are the acts one is attempting to predict. It is important to describe criterion variables very specifically. If a psychologist is asked to judge whether an individual will be dangerous in the future, the psychologist should specify exactly what sort of dangerous behavior is likely. For instance, one might use as criterion variables the commission of violent criminal offenses such as robbery, assault, or murder. Specifying the criterion variables for prediction seems a simple enough task, but surprisingly psychologists are often vague about just what it is they are trying to predict! (Bazelon, 1982; Monahan, 1981).

Table 12.2 shows the four outcomes of clinical prediction of violent behavior. Successful predictions include correctly predicting that individuals will be violent (*true positive*) or nonviolent (*true negative*). Errors include predicting that people will be violent when they are nonviolent (*false positive*) or predicting they will be nonviolent when they later engage in violence (*false negative*). No prediction system is perfect. Obviously, conscientious psychologists hope to maximize successful predictions and minimize mistakes. This is especially true when predictions will be used to deprive some people of their liberty and put others at risk of violence.

Because risks associated with some errors are considered worse than risks linked to others, psychologists employ rules to help them decide where to set cutoff points for predicting violence and nonviolence. Such rules are typically called **decision rules,** and they serve as guides in helping interpret the information a psychologist has about a person being evaluated. The more serious the outcome of a false negative (predicting incorrectly that someone will not engage in violence), the more likely that the rule will be stringent. While the choice of a conservative decision rule may decrease the number of false negatives, it has the unhappy consequence of *increasing* the false positives (the number of people incorrectly predicted to be violent).

An example should make this relationship clear. Suppose that you are a clinical psychologist who is asked to assess the dangerousness of 100 boys currently held in a juvenile institution. If you decide that they are not dangerous, they will be released, but if you report that they are dangerous, they will be kept in the institution for another year. The consequences of your decision are of crucial importance to the boys themselves and to the community at large. If you set the cutoff point for the dangerousness label at 10% — individuals who have in your estimation a 1-in-10 chance of committing a violent criminal act — and

TABLE 12.2

Outcomes of Clinical Predictions of Violent Behavior

		ACTUAL OUTCOME	
		Violent	*Not Violent*
Prediction	Violent	true positive	false positive
	Not Violent	false negative	true negative

Testing is one ingredient that goes into predictions of "dangerousness." In developing recommendations for the release of a prisoner, a psychologist employs a set of "decision rules" to interpret information from many sources.

insist on labeling as dangerous and imprisoning all boys at or above that estimate, you will have a relatively low number of false negatives but a high number of false positives. The community has little to fear from the boys who are released, but the majority of boys left in the institution probably do not need to be there.

You ponder this and recall that imprisonment has harmful psychological effects. You consider changing the cutoff point to 50%, where you label as dangerous only those boys who are as likely to commit violence as not. But now, while fewer false positives will be housed in the institution, your false negative rate will increase. The specter of community pressure (even the loss of your job) if a boy you are responsible for releasing commits a serious crime sends you scurrying back to your initial and more conservative decision rule. The visibility and severity of one kind of error — failing to identify a person who later engages in harmful behavior — encourages psychologists to adopt conservative decision rules. A by-product of a conservative rule, however, is the unnecessary detention of individuals like Johnnie Baxstrom.

With this background, let's now take a closer look at research on the process of psychological predictions of violence. What predictor variables do psychologists use in determining dangerousness? Interviews with psychologists reveal how they go about the prediction task. Clinicians report using a range of factors, including an individual's acceptance of guilt for past violent behavior, aggressive fantasies, environmental circumstances and, most importantly and consistently, past history of violent conduct (Dix, 1976; see also Monahan, 1981; Pfohl, 1977; Williams & Miller, 1977).

Two studies (Corcozza & Steadman, 1978; Konecni, Mulcahy & Ebbesen, 1980) looked at the clinical prediction of dangerousness in a somewhat different way. In addition to obtaining clinicians' reports of what they considered in deciding whether a client was dangerous, the researchers also analyzed the statistical relationships between predictor variables and the clinicians' decisions. In both of these studies, clinicians reported a large number of predictor variables they took into account. Yet in one of the studies the only factor significantly related to the prediction of dangerousness was the type of crime (violent or nonviolent) with which the person was charged, while in the other study the past record of the defendant was the major determinant of the prediction of dang usness.

Accuracy of Predictions of Violence. Just how successful are psychologists and psychiatrists when they attempt to predict dangerousness? Psychologist John Monahan (1981) reviewed five different studies in which predictions of violence were made and follow-up data were available. Results indicated that the prediction record is not impressive. Monahan discovered that clinicians were wrong two out of every three times they predicted someone would be violent!

One problem stemmed from the fact that, in these studies, psychologists had to predict whether individuals in institutions would be violent when they were released into the community. Behavior is partly determined by the environment, so correlations between behavior in an institution and in the community will generally be only modest. The fact that psychologists must judge the potential for violence across different types of situations makes prediction quite difficult, yet many judgments of dangerousness are made in this context. In some situations, such as setting bail and civil commitment, where information about a person's behavior in the community is available, predictions may be more accurate (Monahan, 1981).

Can We Improve the Prediction of Violence? Researchers have identified a number of weaknesses in the clinical prediction of dangerousness (Monahan, 1981; Shah, 1978). First of all, many clinicians fail to define precisely their criterion variables—just what it is they are trying to predict. Another problem is relying on often inaccurate stereotypes about psychological and behavioral problems that are linked in the public eye (or psychiatrists' eyes) to violent behavior. Still another difficulty is the documented tendency of decision makers to ignore base rates (Kahneman & Tversky, 1973; Nisbett, Borgida, Crandall, & Reed, 1976).

Statistical base rates of violence for a relevant population constitute the incidence of violent behavior in that population. For example, the base rate of arrests for violent crimes by women is quite low compared to that of men (e.g., 41 violent crime arrests per 100,000 for women, contrasted to 350 violent crime arrests per 100,000 for men in 1977; Monahan, 1981, Table 2). Base rates like these are likely to be the best predictors of the incidence of violence in specific populations. Yet decision makers will often ignore base-rate information in favor of more attention-grabbing facts (Kahneman & Tversky, 1973). For instance, a woman's report that she has aggressive fantasies toward men might overshadow the fact that women have a relatively low rate of violence and might have a disproportionate impact on a clinician's decision to label the woman as dangerous.

A final flaw in the clinical prediction process is ignoring the contribution of situational and environmental variables. Psychological research has demonstrated that both individual and situational variables are important determinants of behavior. Yet psychologists predicting violence have tended to focus on personal characteristics alone (Shah, 1978).

Certain corrections to these weaknesses in the prediction process could increase the ability of psychologists to predict violence. Two important changes would be to incorporate statistical prediction methods into the decision-making process and to consider the role of environmental variables such as employment and social support. A number of studies have established that such variables as past criminal violence, gender, race, age, employment history, income level, and drug and alcohol problems are significantly related to the commission of violence (Monahan, 1981; Pritchard, 1977). A consideration of these statistical correlates of dangerousness may enhance clinical prediction. Monahan (1981) also points out that, although much more research needs to be done on the environmental determinants of violence, considering such factors as family, peers, job situation, and the availability of alcohol, weapons, and victims may also improve the prediction of violence.

Ethical Issues in the Prediction of Violence. Any time psychologists make predictions that will be used to imprison or release individuals, complex ethical issues arise. The American Psychological Association Task Force on the Role of Psychology in the Criminal Justice System has noted:

> By virtue of their scientific and objective image, psychologists unwittingly have usurped or have allowed themselves to be corrupted into making social value decisions, such as how "safe" an offender should be before he or she is released, which more properly should be left to the political and judicial processes. (Monahan, 1980, p. 12)

Judge David Bazelon (1973) has exhorted correctional psychologists to consider to what ends they are being used, noting how much less expensive it is to hire 1000 psychologists than to make even a tiny change in the social and economic structure to redress the causes of crime. For these reasons, the Task Force has recommended that psychologists be extremely cautious when making predictions that will have an impact on individual liberty.

Furthermore, the statement of the Task Force makes the following recommendation:

> If a psychologist decides that it is appropriate in a given case to provide a prediction of criminal behavior, he or she should clearly specify (a) the acts being predicted, (b) the estimated probability that these acts will occur during a given time period, and (c) the factors on which the predictive judgment is based. (Monahan, 1980, pp. 11–12)

While disclosing the bases of one's predictions may resolve some of the ethical dilemmas (Bazelon, 1982), others remain. For example, the statistical base rate for violent behavior for blacks is greater than that for whites. The predictive accuracy of a psychologist using these base rates will probably increase somewhat, but given the errors in violence prediction, a larger proportion of blacks than whites may be unnecessarily detained. Can psychologists justify their involvement in this process, even if they practice "full disclosure"? Finally, Shah (1978) has pointed out a curious shortsightedness on the subject of dangerousness. People focus attention on the violent behavior of individuals while ignoring social conditions and industrial practices that damage the health and safety of millions of Americans, for example, pollution, occupational disease, and disabling injuries. Shah notes that governmental and social responses to these dangers are very different from responses to individual violence, underscoring the need for psychologists to consider the ethical dimensions of their involvement in the prediction of individual violence.

The Insanity Defense

Public debate about the proper relationship among psychology, psychiatry, and the law exploded on June 21, 1982. On that day, a Washington, D.C., jury found John W. Hinckley, Jr., Not Guilty by Reason of Insanity (NGRI) on all charges relating to his attempted assassination of President Reagan. The verdict ended a two-month trial in which defense and prosecution psychiatrists had presented conflicting testimony about the mental state of the defendant.

Hinckley wounded President Reagan and three others as the President was leaving the Washington Hilton Hotel after a speech on March 30, 1981. A camera operator covering Reagan's entourage videotaped the shootings, and television stations broadcast the footage nationwide. Police evidence suggested that Hinckley had been motivated to kill the President in order to impress actress Jodie Foster. Hinckley had been obsessed with Foster since he had seen her in the movie *Taxi Driver.*

With the videotape as evidence, whether or not Hinckley had done the shooting was not an issue at his trial. Hinckley's defense attorney instead argued that Hinckley should be found Not Guilty by Reason of Insanity because of his mental state at the time of the shooting. William Carpenter, a psychiatric expert who testified for the defense, diagnosed Hinckley as suffering from a major depressive disorder and a condition known as process schizophrenia, which is characterized by delusions and breaks with reality. Prosecution psychiatrists countered that while Hinckley did suffer from personality disorders and a condition they labeled depressive neurosis, none of these interfered with Hinckley's ability to control his behavior or to know that shooting the President was wrong.

Heavy media coverage allowed close scrutiny of the trial proceedings, including the psychiatric testimony. As a result, many Americans got their first close look at psychiatry and the law in the Hinckley trial. During the conflicting testimony of the psychiatrists, many people wondered why psychiatrists could not agree on what was wrong with Hinckley. The public began to question both the value of psychiatric testimony in insanity trials and the purpose of the insanity defense itself. Columnist Andy Rooney probably spoke for many Americans when he commented, somewhat humorously, that the only people who looked worse than Hinckley at his trial were the psychiatrists who testified on Hinckley's behalf!

The jury's verdict that Hinckley was Not Guilty by Reason of Insanity sent shock waves through the public and through legal and mental health professions as well. Most people thought that the verdict was unfair and that justice had not been done in the Hinckley case (ABC News, 1982b; Hans & Slater, 1983). In one survey, most respondents said they believed that Hinckley was not insane

Although he has been held in a mental hospital since 1982, controversy over the case of John Hinckley continues unabated. Even psychiatrists' recommendation that he be granted several hours' leave from the facility aroused a storm of protest.

when he shot Reagan. The majority claimed that they would have voted to convict the would-be assassin had they been jurors in the trial. Most respondents had little faith in the psychiatric evidence presented at the trial and only modest confidence that psychiatrists could determine legal insanity. Their negative views were not limited to Hinckley and the psychiatrists. A whopping 87% agreed that the insanity defense was a loophole that allowed too many guilty people to go free (Hans & Slater, 1983).

In the wake of the Hinckley verdict, psychologists and politicians alike called for restriction or elimination of the insanity defense. Legal and mental health organizations responded to public sentiment and made numerous suggestions for reform of the insanity defense and for changes in the legal role of psychologists and psychiatrists. Indeed, the Hinckley verdict has led to an uprecedented amount of change in insanity-defense laws. Since Hinckley was found Not Guilty by Reason of Insanity, the federal government and over half the states have changed their insanity laws (Caplan, 1984).

Controversy surrounding the insanity verdict has brought into sharp focus the justification for the plea and the role of psychologists and psychiatrists who testify in court about defendants' mental states. Although in numerical terms it is a relatively rare occurrence, psychiatric testimony regarding insanity is a very visible example of the psychology used by law. Therefore it has a disproportionate impact on the public's views of the field of psychology and law.

Many questions have been asked in the debates over the Hinckley verdict. Why does our legal system include an insanity plea? Is it a critical element of our legal system, or is it a loophole for criminals? If the public disapproves of the insanity defense, should it be eliminated or curtailed? Have competing psychologists testifying as adversaries about the defendant's mental state made the trial court a "three-ring circus"? Should psychiatrists get out of the courtroom? Answers to these questions require a systematic examination of the insanity plea and its relationship to psychology.

The Purpose of the Insanity Defense.   Just because some defendants suffer from mental illness, why should we relieve them of responsibility for their crimes? The insanity defense is actually a critical part of our legal system. The entire system is structured around the assumption that human beings exercise free will in whatever they do and therefore can be held accountable for it. In a criminal trial, the prosecutor must prove not only that a person engaged in a criminal act but also that he or she *intended* to commit the act. Only then may one be found guilty of the act. The requirement of intent, or a "guilty mind," is a sensible one, as a few examples will illustrate. Suppose you were forced by a man pointing a gun at you to rob an elderly person. Even though you engaged in a criminal act, clearly you should not be held criminally responsible. You were not exercising free will. Rather, you were required to rob the victim by circumstances beyond your control. Similarly, compare the following situations: a reckless driver who deliberately runs down a child playing in the street, and a careful driver who accidentally kills a child darting out in front of the car. The result is the same: Both drivers kill the child. Yet society views the two drivers very differently. The driver who intended to kill the child deserves severe punishment while the careful driver does not.

In the same spirit, it is believed that individuals suffering from mental illness frequently lack a "guilty mind." Mental illness may impair control over one's actions or may reduce the ability to determine that one's actions are wrong. Under carefully defined circumstances, the insanity defense releases some mentally ill defendants from criminal responsibility.

Society attempts to fulfill several purposes by the rule of law: to rehabilitate the criminal, to deter people from committing crime, to protect the public from dangerous persons, and to satisfy desires for retribution (Vidmar & Miller, 1982). Legal scholars maintain that none of these goals is achieved when insane defendants, who lack the ability to control their actions or cannot tell that what they are doing is wrong, are convicted and imprisoned (Kaufman, 1982). The insanity defense, then, is an important and integral part of the system of criminal law.

Is the Insanity Defense a Loophole? The public's negative reaction to the Hinckley trial, while vehement, was not unpredictable. Opinion polls administered over the last two decades have shown consistently that a majority of Americans believe that the insanity defense is a loophole allowing too many guilty people to go free (Bronson, 1970; Fitzgerald & Ellsworth, 1984; Harris, 1971). Other research, however, reveals that people vastly overestimate how many defendants are found Not Guilty by Reason of Insanity. For example, citizens of Wyoming and Delaware estimated that four out of every ten criminals defendants plead NGRI and a third of them are successful (Pasewark, 1981; Hans, 1986). Yet experts estimate that less than 1% of felony defendants are found Not Guilty by Reason of Insanity (ABC News, 1982a; Howell, 1982). Studies of court outcomes in different states show wide variability in the success rate for insanity defenses (from 1% to 25%), but all indicate that only a small proportion of defendants ever use the plea. This minimal use of the insanity defense is clearly in marked contrast to the attention devoted to it by the press and politicians, attention that may contribute to public overestimation of its frequency.

A central concern about the insanity plea is the fear that, once defendants are found Not Guilty by Reason of Insanity, they will be released and repeat their crimes. The widespread belief that NGRI defendants are freed or hospitalized for only brief periods of time is probably mistaken. For example, the majority of Delaware residents estimated in 1982 that Hinckley would spend less than two years in a mental hospital, although experts indicate that Hinckley is likely to undergo a much more lengthy period of confinement. At the time this book went to press in the latter half of 1988, Hinckley was still hospitalized. There is little systematic research on the period of treatment for NGRI defendants. Steadman, Monahan, Hartstone, Davis, and Robbins (1982) have estimated that these defendents are kept in mental institutions in the United States an average of two years, while other researchers have reported longer periods of time in specific jurisdictions. More research on the frequency, success, and consequences of NGRI pleas may go a long way toward improving knowledge and allaying public concern about the insanity defense.

Problems of Defining Legal Insanity.   Setting up rules to determine who is legally insane and therefore not responsible for criminal conduct has never been easy and is the subject of continuing controversy. A completely satisfactory definition is likely to be elusive because it must serve many goals. It must be congruent with the diverse purposes of the criminal law: to rehabilitate the offender, to deter others from committing similar crimes, to protect the public, and to satisfy desires for retribution. Ideally, an adequate definition should also be consistent with ever-changing psychological and psychiatric views of mental abnormality. Finally, it must incorporate public notions of who should and should not be considered responsible for criminal conduct.

One complaint commonly made about definitions of insanity is that they are difficult for juries to understand and to apply. Furthermore, in the United States different jurisdictions operate with various insanity laws. Legal psychologists could help legislators answer these questions by studying the impact of different insanity laws on the percentage of insanity verdicts across jurisdictions with different rules, or within jurisdictions before and after changes in insanity laws. Psychologists could also study how mock juries react to different definitions in laboratory experiments (Finkel, 1982; Simon, 1967).

The Role of Psychiatrists in Insanity Trials.   While the most frequent complaint about the insanity defense is that it is a loophole, the most often voiced criticism of mental health professionals who testify in insanity trials is that they are "hired guns." In one community survey, over half the respondents agreed that if psychiatrists are paid enough, they will say anything about a defendant's sanity. People in the survey had only moderate confidence that psychiatrists could determine legal insanity. Yet for all the flaws the survey respondents saw in psychiatrists, the respondents overwhelmingly agreed that psychiatrists *should* play a role in insanity trials (Hans, 1984).

Many mental health professionals are embarrassed when opposing psychiatrists testifying in a trial vehemently disagree about the mental condition of a defendant. The American Medical Association recommended abolishing the insanity defense partly because it believed that the plea created contempt for the medical and psychiatric professions. Other critics have suggested that the evaluation of the defendant's mental state be removed from adversary presentation and public scrutiny. In one plan, a group of psychologists and psychiatrists would be appointed by the court. They would meet together and develop a joint evaluation and diagnosis of the defendant that would be presented to the court. This plan would reduce public displays of disagreement and presumably would enhance respect for psychiatry. Other critics have recommended less drastic changes. The American Psychiatric Association, for instance, suggested limiting the kind of testimony psychiatrists can give on the stand.

There are also fears about the impact of psychiatric testimony on the jury. Depending on the critic, juries are seen as ignoring psychiatric testimony because they cannot comprehend it, or being so impressed by the authority of the expert that they function merely as a rubber stamp for the psychiatrist. Despite the impassioned rhetoric, little is known about the impact of testimony by mental health professionals on the trial. What evidence there is suggests that juries do not operate as rubber stamps for psychiatrists but rather use their own views of mental illness and the trial record in reaching decisions in insanity trials (Simon, 1967; Simon & Shackelford, 1965). This is a topic that would clearly benefit from systematic investigation by applied psychologists.

Eyewitness Testimony

In 1979, a series of robberies puzzled the police and community in Wilmington, Delaware. According to witnesses, the robberies were committed by a very polite middle-aged white man who often apologized to his victims as he left the scene of the crime. The Delaware press dubbed this considerate robber the "Gentleman Bandit." A composite drawing of the Gentleman Bandit was generated from witnesses' reports and was publicized in the local newspapers. Members of the community reported to the police that the composite bore a striking resemblance to a Roman Catholic priest, Father Bernard Pagano, who was the assistant pastor of St. Mary Refuge of Sinners Church in nearby Cambridge, Maryland. Father Pagano was arrested after some of the robbery victims made tentative identifications that he was the Gentleman Bandit. At his trial, seven witnesses swore that Father Pagano was the robber. Yet, before the case went to the jury, another man, Ronald Clouser, who was very similar to Father Pagano in appearance, came before an astonished court and confessed to the crimes with which Father Pagano was charged. After police had ascertained that Clouser had information about the robberies that only the culprit was likely to possess, and after Clouser pleaded guilty to the robberies, charges against Father Pagano were dropped. To this day, the police, some of the witnesses, and many members of the community still insist that Father Pagano was the Gentleman Bandit (Ellison & Buckhout, 1981).

How could seven different witnesses identify the wrong man? Why is the community reluctant to believe these witnesses were wrong, even though another man confessed to the crime? The case of the Gentleman Bandit is not an isolated one. Legal scholars and others have identified a host of cases in which faulty eyewitness testimony has led to mistaken convictions and even executions (Borchard, 1932; Frankfurter, 1927/1962). Psychologists have been studying the reliability of eyewitness accounts in efforts to explain the phenomenon of mistaken identification and to improve the identification process.

One potential explanation for mistaken convictions is the powerful and lasting impact of an eyewitness identification on the jury. Psychologist Elizabeth Loftus, an expert in memory and eyewitness testimony, conducted a laboratory experiment to explore the impact of such testimony (Loftus, 1974). She had subjects play the role of jurors by listening to evidence in a criminal case of robbery-murder in a grocery store. The mock jurors then decided whether the defendant was guilty or not guilty. Circumstantial evidence, such as the fact that the robber ran into the defendant's apartment building, that money was found in the defendant's room, and that tests revealed there was a slight chance the defendant had fired a gun the day of the robbery-murder, was presented to a group of 50 mock jurors. Only 18% of subjects hearing just this information said the defendant was guilty. Another group of 50 subjects was also given the circumstantial evidence, but another piece of evidence — the store clerk's eyewitness identification of the defendant as the assailant — was added. Of these subjects, 72% convicted the defendant, demonstrating the powerful influence of such eyewitness testimony.

Even more striking, however, were the results of a third condition in Loftus's experiment. It is often claimed that the cross-examination of witnesses, an essential feature of the **adversary system,** is the most effective means of eliciting the truth. To test the potential impact of such cross-examination, Loftus included a third condition. She presented the third group of 50 subjects in her experiment with the circumstantial and eyewitness evidence, and also with information discrediting the eyewitness. During cross-examination the defense attorney showed that the store clerk could not possibly have observed the defendant's face from where he stood at the time of the robbery and murder since he had vision worse than 20/400 and was not wearing his glasses. Nevertheless, the subjects presented with this discrediting information convicted the defendant 60% of the time, about the same rate as those who had not heard the eyewitness discredited! Other researchers have found that mock jurors are sometimes reluctant to discredit eyewitness testimony, but it is not clear how frequently real jurors give too much weight to eyewitnesses (Hans & Vidmar, 1986).

Findings from a research program by psychologist Gary Wells and his colleagues suggest other problems (Wells, Lindsay, & Ferguson, 1979; Wells, Lindsay, & Tousignant, 1980). These researchers were interested in determining whether people could differentiate accurate and inaccurate witnesses to crimes. They staged a "crime" before a number of eyewitnesses. Later, they asked these eyewitnesses to make identification of the "criminal" from a lineup or group of photographs. They also cross-examined these eyewitnesses on videotape about their identifications, how confident they were that they picked the right individual, and so on. In the second stage of their experiment, they had new subjects watch the videotapes of the cross-examinations and rate whether the eyewitnesses had correctly identified the assailant in the staged crime. This, of course, is similar to the task jurors face when confronted with eyewitness testimony. Jurors must make judgments of the veracity of witnesses on the basis of the witnesses' examination and cross-examination in court. The subject-jurors in the Wells et al. experiment, however, had a very difficult time assessing whether a witness had correctly identified the assailant.

The testimony of eyewitnesses is often crucial in building a case. Research shows that jurors rely heavily on eyewitness testimony, a trust that can sometimes be misplaced. What can psychology tell us about factors affecting eyewitness reliability and about ways to improve jurors' abilities to judge eyewitness accounts?

Factors Affecting the Reliability of Eyewitness Testimony.   Traditional notions of the eyewitness held that the witness was akin to a tape recorder. In the courtroom, the witness initially played the tape containing a record of the events in question, while cross-examination revealed gaps in the tape or faults in the recorder. However, a century of research on human perception and memory has clearly demonstrated that these processes do not operate like the mechanical features of a tape recorder. Numerous factors influence what information is processed and remembered. Contemporary research suggests that memory is dynamic and fluid, a fact that poses special problems for a legal system that relies on remembered accounts.

Perception.   During the original event, an individual perceives it and encodes it in memory. Many variables affect the initial perception of the event, such as the length of viewing time, the nature of the viewing conditions, and the degree of attention devoted to the event. While some of this is common sense, other factors affecting perception are not so widely appreciated. For example, people almost always overestimate the amount of time events take. In a typical study of this phenomenon, Robert Buckhout and his colleagues staged an assault on a professor in front of 141 witnesses (Buckhout, Figueroa, & Hoff, 1975). The attack lasted only 34 seconds, but the average estimate of the event's duration by its witnesses was 81 seconds. Other studies have replicated this basic finding.

Elizabeth Loftus points out that time estimates by witnesses may have enormous implications in the courts. In one case she worked on, a young woman claimed self-defense in the killing of her boyfriend. The woman and her boyfriend had an argument and she ran into the bedroom, got a gun, and shot her boyfriend to death. The defense argued that the killing had occurred very suddenly and at a time when the defendant was in great fear for her life. The defendant and her sister both claimed that the event had lasted a matter of seconds. A prosecution witness, however, estimated that the time between getting the gun and firing a shot was closer to five minutes, which would make self-defense less plausible. The jury acquitted the defendant, perhaps because the jurors believed that the prosecution witness overestimated the time (Loftus, 1979). Similar problems arise from people's difficulties in estimating speed and distances, critical issues in many automobile accidents.

The relationship between stress and perception is described by the Yerkes-Dodson Law which states that perception, learning, and performance are best at moderate levels of arousal and worst at very low or very high levels of arousal. Witnessing or being the victim of a criminal act would probably produce high stress, which in turn would hamper the victim/witness's perception and memory of the event. Indeed, research has demonstrated that people's recollection of non-violent events is superior to their memory of violent events (Clifford & Scott,

1978). Stress may impair perception and memory by causing one to pay selective attention to some items. Selective attention may explain the phenomenon of **weapon focus,** in which witnesses are able to describe a weapon in minute detail but have difficulty recognizing the assailant who held the weapon. Additional individual characteristics that may affect perception include witnesses' expectations, personal prejudices, and training (Loftus, 1979).

Courts process a disproportionate number of minority defendants and eyewitness testimony often involves cross-racial identifications. Given the biases against minorities in the criminal-justice system and the consequently greater possibility that members of minorities may be mistakenly charged with crimes, the reliability of cross-racial identification is of paramount importance. Several studies have found that people are better at recognizing members of their own race than members of other races. For example, in one study (Brigham & Barkowitz, 1978), subjects saw photographs of black and white high-school students for brief periods of time. Later, subjects selected those photographs that they had seen before. White subjects were more successful at identifying photographs of whites than those of blacks, while the reverse held true for black subjects. Subjects' attitudes, prejudices, and experiences with the other race did not affect cross-racial identification.

Post-event Information. Some of the most fascinating findings in eyewitness research show how experiences occurring after an event can have an impact on memory of the original event. The effect of post-event information is especially important in the legal system, since every eyewitness who testifies in court will have numerous experiences between the original event and courtroom testimony.

Suppose a woman observes a bank robbery. She will probably talk to the tellers or other customers in the bank. When the police arrive, the witness will give them a statement and may listen to others' statements to the police. She may be called down to headquarters to answer questions and look through photographs. Later she may be asked to attempt to identify the robber in a lineup. If the case goes to trial, the witness will be interviewed by the prosecution team before trial. A preliminary hearing may be held to determine whether there is sufficient evidence to proceed. Finally, at the trial, months or even a year or more after the original event, the witness will provide her recollections of the robbery. Numerous post-event experiences can alter the woman's ability to recall her original perception. Some psychologists claim that, because memory has a dynamic rather than static character, the post-event experiences can transform the original memory itself, not just the ability to recall it (Loftus, 1986; but see McCloskey & Zaragoza, 1985).

Elizabeth Loftus (1979) has demonstrated in a series of experiments that, by manipulating post-event experiences, she can introduce into the memories of her subjects objects that never existed, colors that were never present, changes in speed estimates or sign shapes, and other alterations to the original memory. One of her studies (Loftus & Palmer, 1974) showed that even subtle changes in the wording of a question may affect the original memory. In that study, subjects watched a film of a traffic accident and filled out a questionnaire. Some subjects were asked, "About how fast were the cars going when they hit each other?" while others were asked "About how fast were the cars going when they smashed into each other?" These questions are typical of the sort asked of witnesses to automobile accidents. Loftus and Palmer reasoned that subjects might infer from the wording of the questions that the cars were going at different speeds. Indeed, subjects asked the "smashed" question made significantly greater estimates of the speed of the cars, consistent with the researchers' predictions. One week later, subjects were brought back to answer additional questions about the film. One question was, "Did you see any broken glass?" While there was in fact no broken glass, subjects who the week earlier had been asked the "smashed" question were more likely than the other subjects to respond that they had seen glass (32% versus 14%). Broken glass, of course, would be consistent with an accident involving cars going at high speeds. Loftus and Palmer argued that subjects integrated the original information about the event with the external, post-event information contained in the smashed/hit question. Once such an integration was accomplished, subjects were unable to tell from what source they derived the memory. The result was a false reconstruction of the original event.

Police Procedures. Because memory for original events may be affected by questioning and other post-event information, police procedures in the interrogation of witnesses and identification of suspects must be conducted with ut-

It's happened to many people—one fender-bender followed by four different versions of what happened. With the help of psychologists, some police departments have developed investigative techniques that elicit more accurate information from eyewitnesses.

most care. Psychologists have devoted a good deal of effort to scrutinizing police practices, conducting related research, and developing recommendations for ideal police procedures. In addition to alerting police officers to the dangers of asking leading questions during interviews with witnesses, psychologists have explored ways to make identification procedures, such as the lineup, fairer tests.

Psychologists have defined the elements of a fair identification test. First and most important is that all persons (in a lineup) or faces (in a photospread) should have an equal chance of being selected by someone who is not a witness. Second, the persons or faces should be similar enough to one another and to the original description of the suspect to be confusing to a person who is merely guessing. Finally, the test should be conducted without suggestions or leading questions, ideally by a person who is unaware of the suspect's identity. These qualities of a fair test may be used to determine whether the identification procedures in criminal cases are misleading

A review of the identification practices in the Gentleman Bandit case suggests that police practices may have contributed to the witnesses' mistaken identification of Father Pagano as the culprit. Several witnesses identified Father Pagano in *show-up* rather than *lineup* procedures. In a show-up, a suspect is pointed out or presented to a witness and the witness is asked whether the suspect is the individual he or she saw. The procedure itself suggests to the witness that the police believe they have the correct person. Show-up procedures place pressure on the witness to make a positive identification. Another problem in the Gentleman Bandit case was that police officers in that case provided multiple, successive opportunities for witnesses to identify Father Pagano through photospreads and a lineup. Researchers have pointed out that even witnessess who are merely guessing have a greater chance of picking a police suspect out under these conditions (Levine & Tapp, 1973; Loftus, 1979). Observers of the Gentleman Bandit case also suspected that the lineup identification process was biased (Ellison & Buckhout, 1981)

Psychological research methods can help determine whether lineups are fair. For instance, Anthony Doob and Hershi Kirshenbaum did a psychological study to test whether the lineup was a fair test in the Canadian case of *Regina* v. *Shatford* (Doob & Kirshenbaum, 1973). Shatford's defense attorney contacted them for help because of this concern over Shatford's lineup. Shatford was charged with being one of two men who had robbed a department store of $7,000. The cashier who was robbed reported on the day of the robbery that she wasn't able to remember very much about either of her assailants. In describing the two men, she said only that "they were very neatly dressed, and rather good-looking and they looked enough alike to be brothers." She could not remember any more about them, nor could she contribute to a composite drawing. Nevertheless, she was later able to pick the defendant out of a 12-person lineup. How did she pick him out? Doob and Kirshenbaum speculated that the witness's description of the robbers as "rather good-looking," and a biased lineup, may have helped.

A photograph of the lineup was available, and the researchers showed it to a group of women subjects, who rated Shatford as by far the most attractive

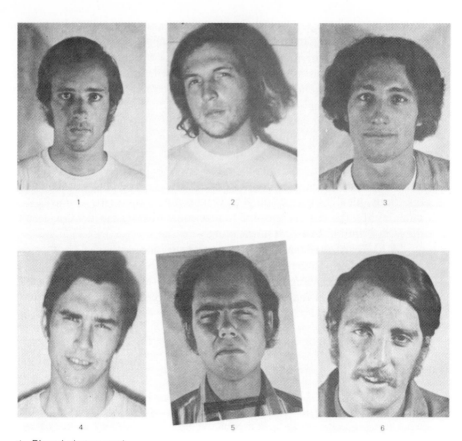

1. Biased photospread

An experiment with the two photospread lineups shown disclosed the influence of suggestion and bias in the identification process. Number 5 was the perpetrator.

man in the lineup. In a second study, Doob and Kirshenbaum presented the lineup photo to a new group of 21 women subjects and told them to imagine that they were witnesses to a crime and that all they could remember about the criminal was that he was rather good-looking. They were asked to do their best to pick out the guilty man from the lineup photo. By chance one would expect 1/12 of the subjects to pick Shatford. This is because there were 12 people in the lineup and if everyone is picking randomly, 1/12 of the subjects, or just 1 or 2 people, should by chance pick Shatford. Yet of the 21 subjects, 11 picked Shatford out of the lineup photo, and 4 more said he was their second choice. This was evidence that the lineup was biased. Similar tests of the fairness of lineups have been done by other psychologists (Wells, Leippe, & Ostrom, 1979).

Expert Testimony. Are jurors aware of the many factors, ranging from speed estimates, to cross-racial identification, to lineup procedures, that affect the reliability of eyewitness testimony? While jurors do a good job discussing some aspects of eyewitness testimony, they fall short in appreciating the effects of selec-

2. Relatively unbiased photospread

tive attention, stress, post-event information, and police procedures (Hastie, 1980). People are not always aware of phenomena such as weapon focus, the influence of post-event information, the inhibiting effects of violence and stress, and the difficulty of cross-racial identification (Loftus, 1979).

To inform jurors about factors affecting eyewitness reliability, psychologists have attempted to testify in trials in which eyewitness identifications are crucial. Sometimes judges have not allowed these experts to testify, ruling that the psychologists were invading the province of the jury or would tell the jury things that were commonly known, although, as you have seen, jurors are likely to be unaware of all the factors influencing eyewitness testimony. In a number of cases, however, judges have decided to allow expert testimony about eyewitness reliability. But increasingly the courts are deciding that, at least in some cases, experts *must* be allowed to testify about eyewitness reliability (*People* v. *McDonald,* 1984; *State* v. *Chapple,* 1983).

How jurors respond to such expert testimony is unknown. Several experimental studies have examined the impact of such expert testimony on simulated juries. The presentation of expert evidence for the defense increased attention to eyewitness accounts and in some instances resulted in fewer guilty verdicts (Loftus,

1980; see also Hosch, 1980; Hosch, Beck & McIntyre, 1980; Wells et al., 1980). Carefully crafted expert evidence may also assist jurors in differentiating among accurate and inaccurate witnesses (Wells, 1986; but see Wells et al., 1980). One important goal for future research is to develop an effective form of presenting information about eyewitnesses to juries. It could not only be introduced by experts in specific cases but also might be incorporated routinely into judges' instructions when eyewitness evidence is present in trials.

Psychologists have vigorously debated the merits of psychological testimony about eyewitness evidence (Loftus, 1983a, 1983b, 1986; McCloskey & Egeth, 1983a, 1983b; McCloskey, Egeth, & McKenna, 1986). Some critics have charged that there is little proof that jurors are gullible when it comes to eyewitnesses. In their view, experimental psychologists have not adequately documented the impact of important factors and the necessity of expert advice. Legal psychologists have responded by conducting additional research to confirm the validity of earlier findings. Hence the debates have served the valuable function of challenging and refining the potential contributions of psychologists in the courtroom.

The Psychology of Jury Selection

Because of a widespread belief that the composition of the jury is a major determinant of its verdict, attorneys have enlisted the aid of psychologists and other social science experts in jury selection over the last several decades. The trial of Joan Little, a black inmate who was charged with the ice-pick murder of her jailer, is an excellent illustration of the varied roles social scientists may play in matters relating to the selection of a jury. In connection with the Joan Little trial, social scientists (1) challenged the composition of the jury panel; (2) conducted a multicounty survey of knowledge about and attitudes toward Joan Little in support of a *change of venue* motion; and (3) assisted in the actual selection of the jury by developing a mathematical model of the ideal juror for the defense and by performing in-court ratings of jurors' authoritarianism and body language. The researchers, John McConahay, Courtney Mullin, and Jeffrey Frederick (1977), wrote about their involvement as social scientists in the Joan Little trial.

The Representative Jury. The crime and trial, which involved a black woman who had allegedly been raped and then had killed a prison guard, evoked the volatile political issues of sexism, racism, and prison reform. Because an individual's race and gender might well affect responses to the trial, the defense attorneys wanted to ensure that the jury pool from which the Joan Little jury would be drawn contained a proportionate share of blacks and women who might be presumed to be more sympathetic to Joan Little. They compared the percentages of blacks and women in the general population (in Beaufort County, the scene of the crime) with their percentages in the jury pool. While the proportions of women in the population and in the jury pool were nearly identical, the defense team found that blacks were significantly underrepresented in the jury pool. While blacks constituted 30.3% of the population of Beaufort County, only 13.5% of the jury pool was black.

The finding that blacks were underrepresented in the jury pool of Beaufort County is similar to the discovery of researchers in other jurisdictions. The way in which the jury pool is selected tends to underrepresent blacks and other minorities as well as women, the poor, and the transient (Alker, Hosticks, & Mitchell, 1976; Van Dyke, 1977). The underrepresentation stems from many sources: the use of voters' lists (which themselves do not accurately reflect the community) as a source for jury pool members, the differential return rate of jury questionnaires on which recipients indicate their eligibility and availability for jury service, and the differential use of disqualifications and exemptions. Discriminatory practices such as the failure to mail jury questionnaires to groups whose members often claim exemptions (for example, women and the elderly) have also been documented.

Why is it important to have a representative jury pool anyway? A series of U.S. Supreme Court decisions has established that the jury pool from which trial juries are selected must constitute a representative cross-section of the community. Legal theorists and Supreme Court justices maintain that such a requirement will maximize the jury's ability to find the facts, since the jury will be drawn from a heterogeneous group of people whose varied experiences, skills, and in-

U.S. Supreme Court decisions have had the result of establishing a requirement that jury pools represent a cross-section of the community. While the assumptions underlying the "representativeness" rule have not been scientifically validated, the legitimacy of verdicts by juries drawn from such pools is less likely to be challenged.

sights will all be brought to bear on the case. A second value of the representativeness requirement is that juries and their verdicts may be seen as more legitimate representations and expressions of the community will. These assumptions underlying the cross-section requirement are psychological in nature but have not really been tested (Hans & Vidmar, 1982).

If the assumptions are correct, a representative jury pool would have enhanced the jury's ability as a fact-finder and also would have increased the legitimacy of the verdict ultimately reached by the jury—very important in a nationally prominent case involving the issues of racism and sexism.

While these are important values, it has been very difficult in individual cases to establish a convincing enough case of nonrepresentativeness before a trial judge so that the judge orders a new panel to be drawn up or overturns decisions reached by juries drawn from a nonrepresentative pool. Indeed, almost all successful appeals concerning the cross-section requirement have involved extraordinarily large disparities between a group's proportion in the population and the jury pool as well as evidence that discrimination occurred during the selection of the panel. The defense motion in the Joan Little case, like so many of its predecessors, failed.

Change of Venue. The defense team was more successful in a change of venue motion, in which they petitioned to move the trial of Joan Little to another location. The legal system recognizes that there may be special circumstances in which the location of a trial must be changed in the interests of fairness. Such circumstances include those in which a large proportion of the community knows or is related directly or indirectly to the parties; has prejudicial knowledge (e.g., information about a criminal record) that will be withheld from the jury; has preconceived attitudes about the defendant's case; or has been influenced by prejudicial pretrial publicity.

In the past, when defense or prosecution attorneys have petitioned to change the place of a trial, they have submitted two different kinds of evidence: (a) local newspaper articles and reports of local television coverage, along with statements pointing out prejudicial pretrial publicity, and (b) affidavits from members of the community, preferably well-known local people, stating that prejudice existed in the community and a fair trial would not be possible. Most psychologists recognize that these indicators of bias are inadequate. The publication of prejudicial news coverage does not constitute proof that the community is biased. Nor are affidavits about public opinion likely to reflect accurately the degree of prejudice in the community (Hans & Vidmar, 1982).

Social scientists working for the defense in the Joan Little case recognized the inadequacies of these traditional means of demonstrating community prejudice. To fill the gap, they decided to conduct a scientific survey of public opinion in Beaufort County and 23 other counties in North Carolina. They conducted random sample telephone surveys in these counties, asking individuals about their exposure and preconceptions about the Joan Little case and more general attitudes. The defense attorneys submitted the results of the survey together with newspaper articles and affidavits.

The defense argued on the basis of this evidence that Joan Little's trial should be moved from Beaufort, not to adjoining Pitt County, as the judge was contemplating, but rather to the more distant, urban Orange County, where prejudice against the defendant was less prevalent. The judge was apparently convinced by all the evidence. Although he did not follow the defense recommendation to move the trial to Orange County, he did order it to be moved to another urban district, Wake County. When he announced his decision in court, the judge mentioned the high level of racism and pretrial publicity as factors in granting the change of venue. McConahay et al. (1977) state: "It is our opinion that the most important thing we did to insure a fair trial [and an acquittal] for Joan Little was to present evidence and testimony that secured a change of venue for her trial." (p. 210).

Picking the Jury. A trial officially begins with the in-court selection of the jury from the jury panel. It is here that psychologists and other social scientists have been most visibly employed in jury selection. It is also in this realm that the greatest controversy over the ethics of their involvement exists. Before discussing how psychologists assisted attorneys in the Joan Little case, a number of psychological issues in the selection process will be reviewed.

First of all, the provision for in-court selection of jurors entails a number of psychological assumptions. It is presumed that people differ in their orientation to a case and that some individuals may be so biased by previous experience, knowledge, or attitudes that they cannot decide a case in a fair and impartial manner on the evidence presented at trial. The legal system has developed mechanisms for identifying and eliminating these biased individuals. There are two ways in which prospective jurors may be eliminated from the jury: **challenges for cause** and **peremptory challenges.** During a pretrial question period called the *voir dire,* potential jurors may be asked by the attorneys and/or the judge about their qualifications for jury service and their familiarity with and attitudes toward the parties or issues in the case. If, as a result of these responses, the trial judge believes that a potential juror is biased, the judge will dismiss the person for cause. Traditionally, if jurors swore under oath that they would judge a case impartially, they were not rejected for cause unless it could be demonstrated that they had a vested interest in the case. Today, partly as a result of psychological research showing the effects of unconscious biases on behavior, the grounds for dismissal are somewhat broader.

The most widely employed method by which prospective jurors are eliminated from the jury is the peremptory challenge. In the United States, both the prosecutor and the defense attorney have a limited number of these challenges, which they may exercise without providing reasons. Thus both sides have some ability to alter the composition of the jury that will hear the case. Over the years, a tremendous amount of folklore has developed about how lawyers can pick favorable juries. A close examination of the folklore, immortalized in lawyer's trial tactics handbooks, shows that attorneys frequently make inferences about the psychological predispositions of individuals with different ethnic origins, race, class, gender, or occupations. For example, Bailey and Rothblatt (1971) recommend that defense attorneys look for artists, actors, writers, and salespeople, since people in these adventurous occupations will not be as easily shocked by crime compared to those with more mundane jobs.

Gender also figures prominently in trial tactics handbooks and the folklore that surrounds jury selection. The famous attorney Clarence Darrow advised defense attorneys to avoid women in all cases (1936). In contrast, others have recommended that women should be preferred because they generally are more sympathetic to defendants (Bailey & Rothblatt, 1971). An article in *The Texas Observer* hinted that "women's intuition" may help the attorney who can't win a case on the facts alone, but observed that older women wearing too much makeup are usually unstable (*The Texas Observer,* 1973).

While this sort of advice to lawyers is alternately entertaining and infuriating, the alert reader may realize that is is based on stereotypes rather than scientific evidence. Psychologists have learned through research about the futility of relying on stereotypes or demographic characteristics in predicting behavior (e.g., Ajzen & Fishbein, 1980; Fishbein & Ajzen, 1975). As a result, psychologists have developed a set of techniques, labeled "scientific" jury selection, that can be employed to help attorneys select jurors in particular trials. These techniques were used in the trial of Joan Little. First and most crucial to the selection process was the *community survey* they conducted to obtain opinions about Joan Little's probable guilt from members of the local community. In the survey, respondents answered a variety of questions relating to perceptions of the trial and Little's guilt, and also provided demographic information such as age, gender, race, education, and political party. The researchers were then able to develop demographic profiles of "good" and "bad" defense jurors based on opinion patterns in the community survey. For example, favorable defense jurors might have been black women, or young Democrats with at least a college education. The researchers then combed the list of jury panel members for people with demographic characteristics matching the prodefense or proprosecution types. They identified in advance of the trial those prospective jurors who were likely to be favorable or unfavorable to the defense.

A second way psychologists helped attorneys select the Joan Little jury was by courtroom observation and rating of the jurors' authoritarianism and body language. According to theory and research on the personality trait of authoritarianism, persons high in the characteristic are likely to be politically conservative, racist, punitive, and prosecution-oriented (Adorno, Frenkel-Brunswick, Levinson, & Sanford, 1950; Christie, 1976). The social scientists working on the Joan Little defense believed that prospective jurors who had high ratings on this personality trait would be undesirable jurors. They employed the social scientist Richard Christie to observe prospective jurors during the *voir dire* and to train others in his techniques for courtroom rating of jurors' authoritarianism. These ratings were then considered as a factor in deciding whether to challenge prospective jurors.

An expert on body language observed prospective jurors during questioning to attempt to determine their truthfulness and anxiety levels. The expert noted body posture and movements, eye contact, vocal intonation, and hesitancy in speech, and rated the jury panel members on a five-point favorability scale. Finally, adding to the social scientists' information were the intuitions of the experienced defense attorneys and a psychic as well as Ms. Little herself. McConahay et al. likened the final decision process of accepting or rejecting jurors to a football huddle. The defense team members huddled together and compared their individual judgments of the desirability of a particular juror. The defense team was nearly unanimous in their support for the jurors finally selected. Their trust was not misplaced: the jury found Joan Little not guilty of all charges at the end of a five-week trial.

The use of scientific jury selection in the Joan Little case as well as in other trials (e.g., Christie, 1976; Tapp & Kenniston, 1976; Zeisel & Diamond, 1976) has been criticized on two main grounds: effectiveness and ethics. Advocates of scientific jury selection have pointed out that in most of the trials where it has been used by the defense, the defendants have been acquitted. But critics note that other factors besides scientific jury selection may have been responsible for the verdicts.

Many early trials in which scientific jury selection has been used were political in nature, involved the difficult-to-prove charge of conspiracy, or were characterized by weak prosecution evidence. For example, the judge presiding at the Joan Little trial described the case against her as one of the weakest he had seen in 20 years on the bench. "Placebo" effects may also result from the use of scientific jury selection. In the Joan Little trial, McConahay et al. speculated that the extensive jury selection process used by the defense may have made the jurors actually selected feel special, indoctrinated jurors to be impartial, raised the spirits of the defense team, and lowered the morale of the prosecution team. These effects, rather than scientists' abilities to pick a sympathetic jury, may have led to Little's Not Guilty verdict. To date, there is no definitive research showing that scientific jury selection is (or is not) more effective than the traditional selection of jurors by unassisted attorneys. There are considerable difficulties in setting up an adequate evaluation of the impact of systematic jury selection. Thus we can expect an ongoing debate about whether or not it works (Vidmar, 1976).

In addition to criticizing its effectiveness, opponents of systematic jury selection have questioned whether it is ethical for social scientists to help attorneys "stack the jury." Amital Etzioni (1974) feels that scientific jury selection tips the scales of justice towards defendants with ample resources, while other critics argue that a trial loses legitimacy when the jury is "stacked" by social scientists. Michael Saks (1976) maintains that psychologists are actually deceptive in their use of systematic jury selection since he believes social scientists are no better and possibly worse than attorneys in picking favorable juries. Proponents argue in response, however, that scientific jury selection is effective and that any imbalance in favor of the defendant is more than offset by the advantages of the state in most criminal prosecutions. There are a number of personal questions that arise for psychologists who are asked to help select juries in specific cases.

Most early cases in which the techniques of scientific jury selection were developed were political trials, and social scientists ideologically committed to the defense cause often donated their own time. Such techniques are now often being used by corporations or wealthy criminal defendants, and psychologists are forced to confront anew the ethical dilemma of their involvement in the adversary system of justice.

Psychologists and Criminal Behavior: A Focus on Rape

One of the most frequent ways in which psychologists are involved in issues relating to the criminal justice system is in their analysis and treatment of criminal behavior. Within this broad area, psychologists have engaged in experimental and applied work exploring the causes of aggression, deviance, and abnormal behavior. They have worked out classification systems for convicted offenders, have developed, staffed, and evaluated treatment programs for offenders, and have counseled victims of crime. To introduce the reader to the wide variety of roles psychologists play in the understanding and treatment of criminal behavior, this section will treat a a particular crime that has gained considerable attention over the past decade: rape.

Few crimes evoke such strong yet ambivalent sentiment as the offense of rape. For example, a recent *London Times* opinion poll of 1056 British men and women (Lipsey, 1982) found that a third of the respondents believed that women who have been raped are usually to blame for it in some way, and a quarter thought that men are often convicted of rape they did not commit. Despite their doubts about victim involvement and trial court justice, 85% of the sample recommended that convicted rapists be executed or incarcerated for seven years or more. In the United States, Blumstein and Cohen (1980) compared the actual time offenders serve in prison with the sentence recommendations of persons surveyed. The public's view of the appropriate length of incarceration for rapists was two to four times the average length of time convicted rapists serve in prison. In contrast to this apparently strong reaction to rapists, Burt (1980) has documented widespread adherence to the notion that rape victims are to blame for their victimization. The search for the causes of rape, then, takes place within a context of strong yet enigmatic public opinion about the crime.

The Psychological Causes of Rape.   Psychologists have conducted a good deal of basic research on the determinants of aggressive and violent behavior. This research ranges from laboratory and naturalistic studies of aggression in animals, to projects in nursery schools that examine the influence of aggressive models or violent television, to social-psychological experiments on arousal, frustration and aggression. This body of research identifies a number of factors that produce aggressive behavior, including social disruption, competition, frustration, social learning, perceived inequity, crowding, and the portrayal of violence in the media (Bandura, 1973). Clinical psychologists have analyzed the life history and demographic variables associated with juvenile delinquents, aggressive individuals, and convicted offenders. Despite the fact that much basic research has been conducted, the causes of rape are not yet clearly identified.

Obtaining a complete picture of the rapist has not been easy. The stumbling block is that only a relatively small proportion of men who rape are ever identified. Estimates are that from one in three to one in ten rapes are reported to the police. Furthermore, a study sponsored by the Law Enforcement Assistance Administration (1978) found that less than 5% of rape complaints resulted in rape convictions. Studies of reported rapes or convicted offenders, typical in this research area, yield a nonrepresentative portrayal of the rapist. Nevertheless, some useful information about the causes of rape has been developed by interviewing offenders. One avenue psychologists have explored to try to understand the rapist's motivation has been to interview rapists, most often convicted offenders who are incarcerated. On the basis of these interviews, typologies or classification systems of criminal behavior are established, and individuals are labeled or classified in some way. Through such classification systems, psychologists' understanding of a specific offender's motivations may be enhanced, and their ability to formulate appropriate treatment programs for individual offenders may be improved (Megargee & Bohn, 1979). Different classification systems for rapists have been developed by other researchers.

One classification scheme has been developed by researchers A. Nicholas Groth, Ann Burgess, and Lynda Holstrom from their work with over 500 sex offenders (Groth, 1979; Groth, Burgess, & Holmstrom, 1977). these researchers identified three distinct patterns of rape: the **anger rape,** the **power rape,** and the **sadistic rape.**

The anger rape occurs when the offender uses the sexual assault to express feelings of pent-up anger. These rapes are characterized by a good deal of physical brutality. More force than necessary is often used to accomplish the rape. The sexual dimension of the attack is relatively unimportant; many rapists experience sexual disfunction during the assault. These features of the anger rape are reflected in one offender's report of his rape:

> I was enraged when I started out. I lost control and struck out with violence. After the assault I felt relieved. I felt I had gotten even. There was no sexual satisfaction; in fact, I felt a little disgusted. I felt relieved of the tension and anger for a while, but then it would start to build up again, little things, but I couldn't shake them off. (Groth, 1979, p. 15)

The offender committing this type of rape typically reports that he was upset and distressed at the time of the attack and did not premeditate it. Victims of the anger rape experience it as a life-threatening event and usually have considerable physical trauma, since the anger rape is often extraordinarily brutal.

In a second pattern of rape, power rather than anger appears to underlie sexual assault. Groth and his colleagues maintain that in the power rape, the goal of the offender is the sexual conquest and possession of the victim. Rape is a means by which the offender attempts to compensate for his own feelings of inadequacy. Rape is a vehicle for control and mastery, as displayed in this offender's report of his motivations:

> All my life I felt I was being controlled, particularly by my parents, that people used me without any regard for my feelings, for my needs, and in my rapes the important

part was not the sexual part but putting someone else in the position in which they were totally helpless. I bound and gagged and tied up my victims and made them do something they didn't want to do, which was exactly the way I felt in my life. (Groth, 1979, p. 30)

The power rapist, perhaps to protect his own sense of virility, frequently denies that the rape was forced and reports that the victim (bound and gagged though she may be) wanted the sexual experience with him. Distortions and misperceptions of the victims's experience appear common. For example, one rapist described how he tricked his way into a woman's apartment and raped her. When he left her apartment for 20 minutes to get something to drink and found her gone upon his return, he stated, "I guess she figured I pulled a fast one on her — that I had just come in for the sex and wasn't going to stick around" (Groth, 1979, p. 39). Following the assault, the power rapist may talk at length to the victim, drive her around, or engage in other efforts to normalize their relations.

Finally, in sadistic rape, sexuality and aggression are combined in a cruel and abusive manner. The sadistic rapist is excited and often sexually aroused by inflicting pain on his victim and witnessing her suffering. Assaults are often premeditated, involve torture, have bizarre, ritualistic features, and may in some instances result in the victim's death. If the victim survives the assault, expert psychiatric care and social support are often necessary to recover from the terror of this category of rape. Groth, Burgess, and Holmstrom estimate that this type of rape is relatively infrequent.

How useful are such typologies in understanding rape? Critics of this sort of classification system are quick to point out that the categories generated by psychologists are developed primarily from interviews or case histories of convicted offenders, who represent only a small proportion of men who rape. However, correctional psychologists maintain that classification systems are useful for planning treatment programs for convicted offenders. The categorization of offenders may highlight their individual problems and may indicate desirable treatment for them. When a classification system is employed in an institution, psychologists are also able to evaluate the effectiveness of different treatment programs for each category of offender.

Growing numbers of psychologists and other social scientists argue that it is nearsighted to focus on individual offenders to understand the causes of rape. In addition to the problem of nonrepresentative samples of rapists available to researchers, many psychologists maintain that the prevalence of rape in our society is a function not just of individual psychopathology but also of cultural attitudes and societal practices that are supportive of rape. In this view, characteristics of our culture create a climate in which rape and other violent attacks on women are tolerated and even encouraged.

Anthropologist Peggy Sanday discovered evidence of sociocultural determinants of rape in a cross-cultural study. She found that the frequency of rape varies markedly in different societies. In "rape-free" cultures, in which rape was reported as rare or absent, women were treated respectfully, prestige was attached to female reproductive and productive roles, nature was revered, and interpersonal violence of all types was low. In contrast, "rape-prone" societies, in which sexual assault was culturally allowable or tolerated, were characterized by violence, antagonism between men as a group and women as a group, and views of women as property (Sanday, 1981). Feminists have pointed to the acceptance of interpersonal violence and the degrading images of women that characterize comtemporary society as causes of the high level of rape in North America (Brownmiller, 1975; Clark & Lewis, 1977).

A growing body of psychological research has explored and tested feminist hypotheses about the causes of rape. For example, Martha Burt (1980) has found that attitudes toward rape are correlated with acceptance of interpersonal violence, sex-role stereotyping, and views that all sexual relationships are basically exploitative. Burt has suggested that beliefs in rape myths (e.g., that women ask for it, or that women who hitchhike deserve what they get) may encourage the commission of rape. Indeed, research has demonstrated that convicted rapists hold more callous attitudes about rape and believe more in rape myths compared to other men (Malamuth, 1981). Other studies have examined the effects of exposure to media containing degrading images and violent treatment of women (Malamuth & Donnerstein, 1982). For example, Neil Malamuth and James Check (1981) had groups of subjects watch either control films or films with violent sexual content. Exposure to films portraying violent sexuality influenced male subjects' attitudes about the acceptability of violence against women. There is a good deal of support, then, for the view that culturally shaped attitudes and societal-level characteristics like level of respect for women and overall amount of interpersonal violence in a society play a causal role in rape. This suggests that to prevent rape the focus must be not only on the understanding and treatment of individual offenders but also on public education about rape and social change.

The Victim of Rape.   During the 1970s, the women's movement, responding to a dramatic increase in reported rapes, focused national attention on the plight of the rape victim. After the terror of the rape itself, many victims faced disbelief, joking, blame, and lack of sympathy when they told friends and family about the experience or decided to report the rape to officials. Rape victims have commented that the ordeal of testifying in a rape trial rivals the criminal episode itself. Psychologists have attemped to ease the situation of rape victims by providing psychological services to them, by studying the range of victim reactions to rape, and by exploring societal attitudes toward rape victims.

Rape-crisis counselors and researchers have identified a common reaction following rape victimization that they have labeled "rape trauma syndrome" (Burgess & Holmstrom, 1974). In the first and acute phase of the rape trauma syndrome, victims experience disruption in their lives and disorganization of behavior. Inital response to rape victimization is intense generalized distress, including anxiety, fear, depression, and low self-esteem (Kilpatrick et al., 1981). The second stage of the rape trauma syndrome involves the long-term adjustment of the victim. Victims may have difficulties resuming their normal activities after a rape. Problems include continuing elevated levels of fear and anxiety (Kilpatrick et al., 1981), nightmares, insomnia, changes in eating habits, curtailing of social activities, and disruption of interpersonal relationships (McCahill, Meyer, & Fischman, 1979). Psychologists have also noted a common reaction of rape victims: blaming themselves for the sexual assault.

Ronnie Janoff-Bulman (1979) has distinguished between two types of self-blame in rape victims: behavioral and characterological. In behavioral self-blame, victims focus on their behavior and what they could have done to prevent the assault. This may serve a positive psychological function for rape victims in that it helps them to regain a sense of control over their lives and to reduce their perceptions of the likelihood that they will be raped again. According to psychologists and other rape-crisis counselors, about two-thirds of all rape victims engage in behavioral self-blame.

Approximately one in five rape victims engages in characterological self-blame. These victims come to believe they were raped not for what they did or did not do (e.g., wear a skirt, walk alone) but rather because of who they are (e.g., worthless, deserving of rape). Characterological self-blame is similar to clinical depression and often has devastating psychological consequences. These and other analyses of rape victims' reactions have aided psychologists in developing adequate treatment programs for the victims of sexual assault.

Psychologists have studied the many aspects of rape—profiling the rapist, analyzing societal and cultural factors contributing to the incidence of the crime, investigating victim reactions. Psychological research aids counselors in the many rape crisis centers that have been established throughout the United States.

Assistance for rape victims has also come from two other sources: procedural and legal changes in rape prosecutions and trials, and public education about the nature of rape. Psychologists have been involved in both these efforts. Observers of rape trials, and the victims themselves, have long noted that in a case of sexual assault, it often seems that it is the victim rather than the defendant who is on trial. In the past, special procedures allowed general questioning about the sexual activities of victims or required the judge to instruct the jury that a rape victim's testimony should be corroborated by other independent evidence in the case before it was safe to convict the accused. As a result, juries have been reluctant to find defendants guilty of rape (Kalven & Zeisel, 1966; McCahill, Meyer, & Fischman, 1979). Researchers in the psychology-law area have demonstrated experimentally the negative impact of these special procedures in rape cases (Borgida, 1981; Borgida & Brekke, 1985, Hans & Brooks, 1977).

Some jurisdictions have instituted special units devoted to rape prosecutions, staffed by people with special training in the psychology of the rape victim. Rape crisis centers have established liaisons with police and prosecutors in efforts to sensitize them to victims' needs. Legal changes eliminatng special procedures in rape cases, redefining criteria for sexual assualt, and revising sentencing practices have occurred in many jurisdictions, although their impact may be mostly symbolic (Chappell, 1982; Loh, 1981).

A final step in easing the trauma experienced by rape victims is in educating the public about the crime of rape and the role of the victim. Public views of the causal role of the victim contribute to the lack of sympathy victims experience from others, and to their own guilt and self-blame. Research by psychologists and other social scientists, as it illuminates the character and causes of rape, will also place the victim in proper perspective.

Treatment of Offenders. To complement their long-term efforts to decrease the prevalence of rape in our society, psychologists have developed treatment programs to rehabilitate rapists. These programs most typically treat convicted offenders housed in correctional facilities. As a consequence, many special issues emerge, including the right to treatment, an inmate's consent to treatment, limits on the types of allowable therapies, the issues of termination of treatment by the offender without penalty, and the lack of adequate personnel and program funding (Brodsky, 1980).

The first step in developing a treatment program is the clinical assessment of an offender. Most offenders entering correctional facilities are given a battery of diagnostic tests that examine their intellectual and job skills, educational needs, dangerousness, escape risk, personality traits, and psychopathology. Groth (1979) describes additional assessment for sex offenders, including the classification of their sexual assault, family background, interpersonal development, and criminal history. For some male offenders, a device called a penile plethysmograph is fitted over the penis and measures sexual arousal to various stimuli. This technique may be employed to identify patterns of deviant sexual arousal associated with viewing children or scenes involving violent sexuality.

The results from clinical assessment are used to develop individualized treatment programs for individual offenders. The diversity of motives and specific circumstances surrounding the crime of rape implies that no one technique will be successful for all rapists. Rather, psychologists must employ diverse rehabilitation methods with different offenders. Common treatments for sex offenders include psychotherapy, training in life-management skills, and behavior modification. Chemotherapy, in which antiandrogen drugs such as Depo-Provera, which reduces sexual drive, are given to offenders, has also been employed.

The advantages of different methods of treatment have been debated (Abel, Blanchard, & Becker, 1976; Groth, 1979; Pacht, 1976). Good evaluation research is conspicuously absent in this area. Indeed, determining whether treatments are successful is quite difficult. One central problem stems from the fact mentioned earlier that only a small proportion of rapists are ever arrested and convicted. This is a serious drawback if the measure of a program's success relies upon rearrest statistics.

Another problem is that few correctional facilities are able to offer a range of treatment options or more than minimal psychological treatment for offenders. This section has described treatment programs for rapists in the ideal. The reality is that limited prison funds go primarily to house and feed offenders and pay guards, rather than to support rehabilitation programs and correctional psychologists. With ever-increasing overcrowding, one can expect even less money to be devoted to treatment programs. Few incarcerated rapists enjoy the luxury of individual treatment programs and frequent, intensive counseling by staff psychologists. The negative psychological impact of imprisonment (Haney, Banks, & Zimbardo, 1973) compounds these problems and creates a poor climate for rehabilitation.

Other Topics in the Psychology-Law Area

The preceding descriptions of the involvement of psychologists in predicting dangerousness, testifying about insanity, studying eyewitness reliability, helping attorneys select jurors, and assessing and treating offenders represent the wide array of methods and topics legal psychologists have explored. It is obviously not an exhaustive review, however. This section will survey a number of additional issues psychology-law researchers have examined.

The legal psychologist's major role revolves around the defendant's mental state. Already discussed have been psychologists' contributions in assessing and treating offenders, in predicting dangerousness, and, most visibly but infrequently, in offering the court information about criminal responsibility. Another function a psychologist serves in this domain is to provide assessment to the court of a defendant's competency to stand trial. A competency evaluation conducted by a psychologist explores a defendant's understanding of the charges against him or her and a defendant's ability to assist the attorney in preparing the defense. Prior to or during legal proceedings, anyone — judge, prosecutor, or defense attorney — may ask to have a defendant's capacity to continue with the trial examined. If a psychological evaluation convinces the judge that a defendant is incompetent to stand trial, proceedings are postponed until the accused person is fit to be tried (Roesch & Golding, 1980; Steadman, 1979). You will recall that an earlier section described how researchers have examined psychologists' predictions of dangerousness. Similarly, researchers have looked at factors psychologists employ in competency evaluations. Ronald Roesch and Steven Golding (1980), in their study of competency evaluations, demonstrated that many psychologists who testify in court about the defendant's competency confuse competency criteria with criteria for psychopathology. Roesch and Golding have worked to improve the evaluation of competency and the psychologist's court report so that both will better meet the court's needs.

Thomas Grisso (1981) has looked at a different aspect of competency: the ability of juveniles to waive their legal rights to silence and counsel. His work challenges the notion that juveniles are generally competent in these areas. For example, over half of the 10–16-year-olds he studied were unable to comprehend at least one of the *Miranda* warnings about a suspect's rights. Other legal psychologists have studied the competency of children to testify in court or to consent to treatment (Goodman, 1984; Melton, 1981).

Psychologists often provide assessment and treatment of juveniles who come into conflict with the law. The juvenile justice system was first developed to divert young offenders from the adult system. The emphasis within juvenile justice traditionally has been on rehabilitation rather than punishment. As a consequence, psychologists have been called upon for help in rehabilitation efforts. Yet the success rate for treatment programs with juveniles is discouragingly low. Over half the young offenders who are placed in juvenile training facilities are ultimately reincarcerated (Rappaport, Lamiell, & Seidman, 1980). The search for effective interventions with juveniles is an important one, since most adult offenders have juvenile criminal records.

Although the more traditional involvement of psychologists working in the criminal justice field has been as experts or providers of treatment for offenders, over the last 15 years many psychology-law researchers have focused on courtroom procedures or legal decision making. Many legal procedures are based in part on psychological assumptions. For instance, those countries that use an adversary system of justice assume that such a system will ensure the most complete development of the facts in a case, will minimize bias in the decisions of judge and jury, and will be most satisfactory to the parties in a dispute. Laboratory research comparing individuals exposed to adversary and nonadversary systems has supported the validity of at least some of these psychological assumptions (Houlden, LaTour, Walker, & Thibaut, 1978; Lind, 1982; Thibaut & Walker, 1975). But research by Blair Sheppard and Neil Vidmar (1980) has demonstrated that under some circumstances an adversary system may produce decidedly biased testimony on the part of witnesses. Psychological assumptions about the superiority of the adversary system are regularly aired in debates about changes in the criminal justice process and in planning alternative dispute resolution mechanisms. Thus these studies are of practical significance in evaluating existing procedures and developing new methods of resolving disputes.

Rules of evidence in the courtroom, which regulate the presentation of facts in cases, are also frequently based on psychological assumptions. One good example is the rule of evidence governing the use of a defendant's criminal record. If a defendant takes the stand during trial, the fact that he or she has a criminal record may be introduced as evidence. However, the judge must instruct the jury to consider the record only in judging the defendant's credibility and not in inferring the defendant's guilt. There are several psychological premises underlying this rule of evidence. One provides the justification for allowing a criminal record to be introduced in the first place. It is assumed that a defendant who has a criminal record is likely to be a less credible witness. It is also presumed that jurors are able to compartmentalize their decision making, and are capable of following judges' instructions about the proper use of criminal-record information.

Jury simulation studies (Doob & Kirshenbaum, 1972; Hans & Doob, 1976) have shown that jurors apparently do not follow judges' instructions to disregard a defendant's criminal record in deciding an accused person's guilt. These studies, along with others exploring the effects of judges' instructions to disregard inadmissible evidence (Sue, Smith, and Caldwell, 1973; Wolf & Montgomery, 1977) indicate that reforms of the rules of evidence are overdue. Other researchers (Sales, Elwork, & Alfini, 1977) have argued that most if not all jury instructions should be changed to make them more comprehensible to jurors. Legal instructions are often difficult for laypeople to follow, yet comprehension can be dramatically improved by fairly simple changes, based on psycholinguistic research, in the jury instructions.

Because of their interest in the social psychology of group dynamics, many psychologists have been drawn to the study of the jury decision-making process. Relying on jurors' personal accounts (Zerman, 1977), jury simulation research, and other methods (e.g., Kalven & Zeisel, 1966), psychologists have studied the stages of the jury decision-making task, participation in deliberations, and factors affecting the jury's decision. One set of studies on the impact of jury size illustrates the potential (and also the problems) of psychology-law research for legal change. In 1970, the U.S. Supreme Court decided the case of *Williams* v. *Florida*. The defendant Williams had been convicted by a 6-person jury after requesting a 12-person jury. He appealed his conviction on the grounds that he had been denied his right to a 12-person jury. The Supreme Court held that juries with fewer than 12 members were not unconstitutional, and mentioned in its decision that the few studies comparing 6- and 12-person juries showed no significant differences due to size.

Psychologists critically analyzed these studies and conducted a number of other research projects that revealed differences in decision making in 6- versus 12-person juries (Davis, Kerr, Atkin, Holt, & Meek, 1975; Saks, 1977). The Supreme Court relied on these studies (somewhat inappropriately, critics have noted: Tanke & Tanke, 1979) when it next considered jury size in *Ballew* v. *Georgia* (1978). In that case, the Court drew the bottom line for jury size at 6. It stated that jury size was important in preserving the functions of the jury and cited as supportive evidence the psychological research studies showing differences between 6- and 12-person groups. Research on jury decision making has also been discussed by appellate courts in cases involving the requirement that juries deliver a unanimous verdict (*Apodaca* v. *Oregon,* 1972; *Johnson* v. *Louisiana,* 1972) and capital punishment (*Lockhart* v. *McCree,* 1986; see also Haney, 1984).

Psychologists have studied another key decision maker: the judge. Champagne and Nagel (1982) review research on psychological explanations for judicial behavior, including attempts to apply psychoanalytic principles to judges' decision making, or to fit judges into personality type categories such as the "intellectual scholar." Researchers have correlated judicial decisions with background variables such as political-party affiliation, religion, age, and class. A judge's political party is most strongly and consistently related to decision making: Democrats tend to vote in a liberal direction while Republicans vote more conservatively. Konecni and Ebbesen (1982) have studied the case factors that influence judges' decisions about bail and sentencing. Psychologists Shari Diamond (1982) has looked at the problem of disparity among judges in the sentences they mete out to defendants. She has explored methods of reducing this disparity, such as sentencing councils or fixed sentences for specific crimes.

Many students of the courts have noted that the prosecutor has enjoyed a tremendous increase in power and scope over the past few decades. Yet psychologists have devoted little attention to prosecutorial decision making. Since most criminal cases are settled by a defendant's guilty plea, it is also surprising that only a few psychologists have investigated the widespread practice of plea bargaining (Gregory, Mowen, & Linder, 1978; Houlden, 1980–1981). Many relevant psychological questions could be addressed through experimentation. For example, Gregory et al. looked at how the number and severity of original charges influenced a defendant's willingness to accept a plea bargain. Studies of this sort may be useful in developing and enhancing procedures for legal negotiations. As John Carroll has shown in his work on parole decision making, such research can be a fruitful source of ideas for improving the criminal justice system (Carroll & Coates, 1980).

The decision making of other participants in the criminal justice system could benefit from additional study by psychologists. June Tapp's intriguing work on what she calls "legal" socialization indicates that a thorough analysis of legal decision making must include not only legal constraints and case factors but also the decision makers' level of legal development (Tapp & Kenniston, 1976).

The focus of this chapter has been on psychologists' work in criminal law, primarily because that is where most of their contributions have been made to date. But there is increasing interest in exploiting psychological insights in the field of civil law. For example, the techniques of scientific jury selection pioneered in criminal cases are now being used in civil trials (Hunt, 1982). The same statistical techniques used to show discrimination in jury panels have also been employed to document racial and gender inequities in employment discrimination cases. Family courts, accident compensation, and tax reform are just a few of the topics ripe for exploration. As psychologists become more familiar with the general field of law, we can expect an increase in their work in the civil area.

Finally, while we have reviewed research on the legal and correctional systems, it should be mentioned that psychologists have also worked with the police. Their traditional contributions have been in the areas of personnel selection, training, and treatment for psychological stresses on the job. More recently, they have applied social psychological principles to crowd control and hostage incidents (Mann, 1980).

Conclusion

This chapter has revealed the wide range of roles and issues legal psychologists have adopted. Yet amid the diversity there are several common threads. Two chief concerns of applied psychologists working in the legal system involve *effectiveness* and *ethics*. The aims of individual psychologists vary, yet like the pioneer Hugo Munsterberg most hope their involvement will be effective in increasing the justice and fairness of the legal system. The topics focused on in this chapter have highlighted instances in which psychologists' contributions fall short of their aims. If John Wigmore were alive today, he would have much to talk about. You will recall the problems in predicting dangerous behavior, in determining when defendants are legally insane, and the almost universal failure of treatment programs for offenders. You will remember that researchers have also questioned whether psychological experts can pick favorable juries or noticeably enhance jurors' abilities to differentiate between reliable and unreliable eyewitnesses. Legal scholars have also berated psychologists for their naiveté about the legal system, charging that psychological research on the law is more often than not irrelevant or tangential to central legal concerns.

Others have wondered whether the standard psychological research technique of laboratory simulation is an effective tool for studying the legal system. On this issue psychologists have been their own sternest critics (Konecni & Ebbesen, 1979; Vidmar, 1979; Weiten & Diamond, 1979). Among the criticisms are (1) that experiments and simulations tell little about actual courtroom behavior; (2) that typical experiments are legally naive, worthless, or misleading; and (3) that laboratory experiments are simply inappropriate for the study of applied questions (Bray & Kerr, 1982). Some psychologists maintain that because of these and other shortcomings, simulation research should not be done:

> . . . Erroneous information obtained by scientific methods (and therefore having an aura of truth) is more harmful than no information at all . . . especially when issues as sensitive as legal ones are being dealt with, and people's futures are quite literally at stake. (Konecni & Ebbesen, 1979, p. 668)

But others have responded that laboratory simulation is a reasonable strategy that has already made significant contributions to the understanding of the legal process. While many past simulation studies have been characterized by legal naivete, and only modest generalizability, well-designed simulation research can be useful in evaluating legal policies (Vidmar (1979); see also Bray & Kerr, 1982).

The controversy about simulation as a research tool for studying the legal system will no doubt continue for some time. One desirable side effect of the debate has been a steady improvement in the quality and realism of simulation research. Psychologists' increasing familiarity with law, and the popularity of joint psychology-law degree programs, will help to eliminate the naiveté psychologists have displayed in past work on the legal system.

Other questions about legal psychologists' effectiveness concern not their research methods but rather their assessment and treatment abilities. Consider the involvement of psychologists in assessing and treating convicted offenders. As was reported, there is little or no evidence that treatment programs developed and administered by psychologists work to decrease criminal behavior. A major problem, however, is that there have been very few well-designed studies evaluating the effectiveness of different techniques with different types of offenders. The results of such studies could be incorporated into the planning and design of additional treatment efforts to maximize effectiveness. Rigorous training in evaluation methodology is an important first step in the improvement of psychologists' contributions.

The second theme that has echoed throughout this chapter involves the ethical questions confronting psychologists who work in or study the criminal justice process. One aspect of ethics is linked to effectiveness. If psychologists are ineffective in selecting juries or predicting violence, is their involvement in these practices fraudulent and therefore unethical? Other ethical issues arise from the multiple responsibilities psychologists have — to their patients, to the institution that employs them, and to the public. Psychologists are often left wondering just who their client is. One psychologist's response to a national survey of ethical issues for psychologists working in criminal justice reveals the dilemma:

> One particular problem emerges all the time. . . .In my position I am responsible for making recommendations to a parole board on men I have in psychotherapy. Naturally, I know more about my patients than the official record reflects, and I know that the things I tell the parole board will largely determine whether or not the man is granted parole. The philosophy of the board is conservative; I'm a liberal humanist. Where do my responsibilities lie? To the patients I'm treating or to the board that employs me? Most often I decide in favor of the patient and keep from the board information which I feel would hurt the patient. Implied in this also is my responsibility for the protection of society. There are simply no easy answers. (Clingempeel, Mulvey, and Repucci, 1980, p. 130

There are few simple responses to the multitude of ethical dilemmas confronting applied psychologists working in the criminal justice system. Yet if legal psychologists hope to advance justice rather than thwart it, they must ensure that their contributions are both effective and ethical.

Glossary

adversary system   A system of justice under which defendants are allowed to confront and question their accusers.

anger rape   A type of rape in which the offender uses the sexual assault to express feelings of pent-up anger.

challenge for cause   In jury selection, if pretrial questioning reveals that a potential juror is biased, the juror may be dismissed by the judge for cause.

criterion variable   A variable that represents what a researcher is trying to predict.

decision rules   As used in this chapter, a set of rules used by psychologists to help predict violent behavior.

forensic psychology   A branch of legal psychology that concentrates on the evaluation and treatment of criminal defendants.

peremptory challenge   In jury selection, either the defense or prosecution can have a potential juror dismissed without giving a reason. Both sides are given a limited number of peremptory challenges.

power rape   A type of rape in which the goal of the offender is sexual conquest and possession of the victim.

predictor variable   A variable that is used to predict some criterion variable. Usually used in multiple-regression research designs

sadistic rape   A type of rape in which sexuality and aggression are combined in a cruel and abusive manner.

weapon focus   A memory phenomenon by means of which witnesses can typically describe a weapon in great detail but are unable to recognize the assailant who held the weapon.

Applied Environmental Psychology

13

W. Jeffrey Burroughs
Clemson University

What is the psychological impact of stressors like air pollution and noise? What can or should be done about such problems? Since individuals often must function in crowded environments, what physical and social changes can be implemented to increase satisfaction in these settings? How can architects and urban planners design environments for users that they do not know and with whom they share few cultural ties? When individuals select neighborhoods to live in, what attributes are most important? Are some people just naturally sensitive to the environment, or are such feelings learned and therefore modifiable? How should office buildings and universities be designed so that people can find their way around easily?

The above questions are a sampler of issues environmental psychologists are concerned about. The field of environmental psychology has been defined in many different ways (see texts by Bell, Fisher, & Baum, 1983; Gifford, 1987; Holahan, 1982); for this chapter an appropriate working definition is: Environmental psychology is the study of the interrelationships between the physical environment and human behavior.

This consideration of applied environmental psychology will take several directions. First, some generalizations will be provided about the nature of the field as a whole, to give an overall feeling for the approach individuals in this discipline see as most productive. Second, some of the work activities of environmental psychologists will be investigated and information provided about the organizations they work for. Finally, some representative examples of research and application in this dynamic area will be presented.

What Is Environmental Psychology?

As you can see from the questions above, the range of interests among people who call themselves environmental psychologists is very great. How can a field that is concerned with so many content areas still maintain coherence? The answer is in the unique perspective that environmental psychologists adopt to do their work. Briefly, the field can be characterized as highly applied, as interdisciplinary, as viewing environment and behavior as interrelated, and as using what may be termed a molar level of analysis. Each of these characteristics will be considered in detail.

Applied Orientation

In 1947 Kurt Lewin, one of the founding fathers of experimental social psychology, suggested that academic institutions develop cooperative, interdependent relationships with the communities of which they are a part. The institutions would furnish expertise while the communities would provide applied experience and settings for student training and research. A number of environmental psychologists (Holahan, 1982; Proshansky, 1972; Sommer, 1977) have cited Lewin's

(1947) notion of action research as a model for the field. In such a conception, theory and application go hand in hand. Research is performed to yield solutions to real-world questions, but theory may then evolve from the results of the problem solving.

Interdisciplinary Nature of the Field

Any discipline, at its inception, will draw individuals who wish to identify themselves with the new way of pursuing knowledge. For example, early psychologists were drawn from the fields of philosophy, religion, physics, medicine, and mathematics, among others. The same has been true of environmental psychology. Among those who call themselves environmental psychologists are former social psychologists, urban planners, architects, anthropologists, and social geographers.

Although it is difficult to predict future trends, the highly applied focus of environmental psychology has to date tended to cause individuals to retain some of their original disciplinary orientation. As a result, environmental psychology remains highly interdisciplinary. This characteristic has had both positive and negative effects. Positively, the field is enriched by many diverse viewpoints and applications across different research areas (Stokols, 1981). Theories and methods that have been developed to solve problems in some areas may be applied to others with fruitful results. Further, the field of potential "consumers" of research results is broad because information from environmental psychology reaches practitioners in many disciplines.

Conversely, the interdisciplinary nature of environmental psychology has had a negative impact because to date comprehensive theories of person-environment relations have not been forthcoming. The field is so diverse that few individuals have had the interest or the expertise to propose comprehensive theory.

Interrelationship of Environment and Behavior

A third general characteristic of environmental psychology as a field is the conception of environment-behavior relationships as interrelationships. Behavior is influenced by the environment in which it occurs, while at the same time the environment is altered by the behaviors that occur in it. Traditionally, experimental psychologists have sought to define the nature of stimuli, or the environment, and of responses, or behaviors, independently of each other. By so doing, highly deterministic statements could be made about the effects of independent stimuli on behavior. While this approach has the advantage of allowing us to construct very precise statements of cause and effect, environmental psychologists feel a complete account of behavior is more complex. To an environmental psychologist, a more fruitful approach is one in which people are seen as goal-directed agents who modify their environments and are in turn influenced by them.

From this general viewpoint, several theoretical and methodological distinctions follow. First, it is possible to isolate behavior in the laboratory by controlling the environment in which behavior occurs. Alternatively, one could analyze behavior in its naturally occurring environmental context. So, for example, a researcher might attempt to study littering behavior in the laboratory by asking subjects their opinions about different littered landscapes or by giving them handouts that could later be thrown away inappropriately. In contrast, a researcher could go to a public park, introduce some intervention like a talking trash can, and observe effects on littering behavior by counting the number of pieces of litter on the ground. The former method allows behavior to be broken down and analyzed into very fine components. The latter retains the context of the behavior in question.

Environmental psychologists argue that behaviors and the settings where they occur form naturally occurring units that must be respected if reciprocal environmental-behavior relationships are to be understood (Ittelson, Proshansky, Rivlin, & Winkel, 1974). This is not to say that laboratory research has no place in environmental psychology. Irwin Altman (1976) has proposed a compromise position, suggesting that conclusions drawn from analytical laboratory research must be qualified and supplemented by a knowledge of intact environment-behavior units. The concern for the integrity of environment-behavior units leads environmental psychologists to field studies (more completely discussed in the section on the work activities of environmental psychologists).

A second distinction that follows from environmental-behavior interrelationships is the treatment of behavior actively or passively. William Ittelson and his associates (1974) have characterized the reciprocal impact of environment and behavior as a continuous, dynamic interchange between people and their settings. This means that the influence that people have on their environments is constantly occurring and that environments in turn are continually influencing human behavior. Exchanges between people and their environments occur over time. For example, the physical attributes of a deserted building that may "trigger" vandalism to that structure might only become evident over time as the building deteriorates and as destructive activities start. To get a complete account of the influence of environment on behavior, studies need to be conducted so that behavior can be sampled at different times.

Finally, a third distinction that follows from environment-behavior interrelationships is a univariate versus a multivariate approach. Many areas of psychology have traditionally relied on statistical methods where the impact of a small number of independent variables on a single dependent variable is assessed. Using such methods, the interrelationships among these variables may be precisely determined, but the effects of additional contextual variables are not examined. Environmental psychology seeks to understand the relationships between groups or systems of variables that make up environment-behavior units. Such a systems approach again allows a more complete understanding of the causes and effects of behavior within an environmental context.

It should be noted that despite the goal of understanding systems of variables, not all studies in environmental psychology are multivariate in nature. Univariate studies are frequently conducted but generally with the intention of expanding and synthesizing the results of individual studies into descriptions of systems of relationships.

An example can highlight the ways that environment and behavior are interdependent. In central Pennsylvania where the writer has lived, a large number of people have converted to wood heating because that fuel is plentiful and inexpensive. The use of this type of heat affects behavior because of the effort that must be made to initially procure the wood, to split and stack it, and finally to feed it into a hungry fire all winter long.

These energy-consuming behaviors in turn have an influence on the environment. For example, timber has been marketed on private property, and downed wood in state and national woodlands has now become scarce. As a result, the types of energy sources available in the Pennsylvania environment have influenced the types of energy-consuming behavior that occur. Further demonstrating the continuing interaction between behavior and environment is the amount and type of air pollution in the area just described. On a calm winter day the fires in wood stoves all over the area cause a dense bluish smoke to hover over the town—an attribute of rural living that would not normally be expected.

Level of Analysis

In a seminal definition of environmental psychology, Kenneth Craik (1970) stated that the unifying theme of the area is the way that human behavior relates to everyday physical environment. A distinctive feature of environmental psychology, then, is the level of analysis applied. Just what does the phrase, "everyday physical environment," mean? To answer, one must first realize that psychologists can analyze behavior-influencing stimuli at many different levels. Traditionally, however, highly impoverished stimulus environments have been used in experiments. In order to study a specific aspect of human experience, psychologists have often eliminated everything that is potentially distracting in the materials they present to the people in their experiments. For example, many experiments in perception have presented subjects with extremely simple stimuli, such as line drawings or letters, rather than with the complex stimuli of everyday experience.

In contrast, environmental psychologists are interested in studying the environment as it is normally experienced in people's lives. Such an approach is known as using a **molar level of analysis.** For example, rather than studying the ability to represent space internally by doing studies that use microspaces like tabletop models or single objects as has been done by some experimental psychologists (e.g., Piaget, Inhelder, & Szeminska, 1960), environmental psychologists have placed subjects in large-scale environments that surround individuals and include them as one of the objects in the space (e.g., Acredolo, 1976; 1977).

What Do Applied Environmental Psychologists Do?

At the outset you should realize that environmental psychology is an emerging area and that activities and work settings are still being defined. In many respects, each person who chooses to work in this area of psychology defines his or her own job — especially in applied settings. Still, some generalizations are possible. The sections that follow will describe some of the activities that environmental psychologists pursue and look at some of the settings where they are employed.

Job Activities

As you read about typical activities that environmental psychologists engage in, remember that environmental psychology is an emerging field and that many different work activities are performed. But those reviewed in this section are distinctive — they are representative of the work environmental psychologists do that sets them apart from other psychologists. The four activities are field studies, behavioral programming in architecture, postoccupancy evaluation, and participatory planning.

Field Studies. One of the characteristics of environmental psychology is a concern for the interlocking relationship between environment and behavior. Given this basic orientation, research is conducted in a wide variety of settings. Some of these settings will be sampled in the final section of the chapter, but you should realize that at some point in the research process, almost all environmental psychologists feel compelled to go outside of their laboratories and perform studies in real-life situations.

Behavioral Programming in Architecture. An **architectural program** is a document designed to specify what a building is supposed to do. Programs may consider a wide variety of factors in articulating client desires and user needs. Areas of concern might include (but certainly are not limited to) economic, cultural, behavioral, structural, and psychological factors. Some "technical" programs quantify aspects of the proposed building by specifying such things as amount of floor space, specific materials and hardware, or maximum cost estimates for the structure. In this type of program the performance of specified elements is implicit. For example, a particular brand and model of light fixture might be designated for illumination over outside doors. In such a situation, the program might not specify a certain durability or ease of maintenance for the fixture because those attributes are expected.

In contrast, the requirements of a building could be expressed in a "performance" program. This type of document specifies the attributes a building should have in terms of its ultimate performance. For example, rather than specifying a particular brand and model of light fixture to illuminate outside doors, the program could specify that the light meet certain durability and illumination standards. The concept of building performance has been extended to include the ability to engage in various behaviors in the building in question. The physical form of schools should encourage learning, and the physical form of medical facilities should encourage healing. More specifically, the program for a home for the elderly might include the criterion that residents be able to easily interact with visiting families. A program for an elementary school might specify that students be able to carry on their work without being distracted by noise from other classrooms. Behavioral performance programs require architects to consider behaviors facilitated or discouraged by buildings.

Research in architectural programming facilitates design work in two ways. First, it can help in writing behavioral programs. What are the critical behaviors that should be facilitated in a home for the elderly? By identifying these requirements, performance programs can be written that will satisfy relevant user needs. Second, once it is clear that a relevant need exists, programming research can help a designer determine if various design decisions will satisfy the need in question. Answers to these questions must come from research in environmental psychology.

Postoccupancy Evaluation.   Once a building has been constructed and users have moved in, they will begin to adapt to their new environment. Most people have had the experience of moving into a new house and needing time to get adjusted to new features — or the lack of them. The same thing holds true for users of any building. Once this adaptation period has taken place, it is useful to ask, Does the building function as it was intended to?

Since millions of environments are built each year, what places should be evaluated? Zube (1980) has pointed out that environments requiring major investment of public funds and affecting large numbers of people should be scrutinized. Examples are locations such as parks, subways, universities, and state and federal administrative buildings. Furthermore, the design of environments that will be duplicated over again such as libraries, post offices, and public housing could be improved if information about user experience with prototypes is available. Don't you wish that someone had evaluated user satisfaction with your dormitory design after they had built one or two, before building more of them? Finally, users are very dependent upon some environments for satisfaction and even life. Environments for young, elderly, or disabled individuals, or for those working in extreme circumstances such as outer space or ocean depths, all impact upon users to a great extent and should be evaluated.

In order to evaluate a structure some criterion for success of the building must be established — basically, what constitutes good performance in a building. One way to specify this is to identify the original intentions of the designers and owners of the structure. This might be done through reference to a behavioral program, if one has been developed, or through direct interviews with the design team to ask about their original goals for the design. In addition, archival materials such as publicity and promotional documents or records of the meetings of administrative bodies (such as school boards or boards of directors), may provide information on the intents of those responsible for the construction of the building. Finally, accepted standards of design practice can serve as an evaluation standard, formally through regulations and statutes and informally from research that has identified design principles functional in various settings.

Once criterion measures have been established, hypotheses can be derived and tested. Such evaluation might be from direct observations, archival use data, or interviews with users of the structure. The data must then be compiled, analyzed, and presented in a form that designers will find understandable and useful. Postoccupancy evaluation of a building allows for an assessment of the good and bad qualities of that particular structure, but perhaps more importantly furnishes information about how similar buildings should be constructed in the future.

Participatory Planning. As designers and planners do their work, they are often called upon to formulate design solutions for potential users they do not know. Under such conditions, design decisions benefit greatly if users are consulted. The purpose of **participatory planning** is to systematically obtain input from actual users or individuals who resemble those users. For example, in obtaining user input for the design of a cancer clinic in a metropolitan area, future users of the clinic were not available. As a representative substitute user group, users of four large, urban, cancer therapy clinics were interviewed.

As environmental psychologists have sought user input into design decisions, another fact has emerged—individuals *like* to have an influence on the nature of their environments. In a series of studies of energy-efficient commercial buildings, Min Kantrowitz (1985) has shown that individuals like to set their own thermostats and adjust their own window shades. When such opportunities do not exist, individuals often act to regain that control even if it means breaking into locked electrical controls, hiding keys, or sabotaging computer controls. In order to satisfy the people who will use buildings, the opportunity to control environments needs to be provided to individuals. The challenge to environmental psychologists is to find ways of allowing meaningful user participation that fits appropriately into the design process.

Work Settings

After reviewing the distinctive work activities of environmental psychologists, you may wonder where they work. By far the greatest number of psychologists with environmental interests work in university settings. Their jobs are a combination of research, teaching, and consulting, with the exact mix of these activities being determined by the requirements of the particular school and the inclinations of the individual. Some schools emphasize teaching, with research being only a peripheral part of an individual's work. In contrast, in other schools the pattern is reduced teaching loads and increased research expectations. University professors working in psychology departments spend their time writing and delivering lectures, speaking with students, designing and conducting experiments, and writing results in scholarly articles. In departments that offer graduate education, professors may be called on to be major advisors to graduate students as they pursue their advanced degrees and to sit on committees supervising the original research required for a student to earn a master's or doctoral degree. University professors are also typically involved in the governance of their departments and universities and in professional services such as manuscript reviewing and organizing conferences.

University professors with environmental interests also may work in architecture, urban planning, or environmental design departments. Their work is similar to that performed in psychology departments but will typically not include designing and running experiments. Most individuals working in architecture, planning, and design departments also spend considerable time participating in or listening to juries or group critiques of the work of students or peers. It is also highly likely that these university professors will engage in some form of consulting for clients outside the university. Examples of this work might include architectural programming and design work, or postoccupancy evaluations of buildings that have already been constructed.

A second group of environmental psychologists work for consulting firms that provide services to industrial and governmental clients. The most marketable services that these organizations have to offer are the planning, programming, and evaluation activities described above, but environmental consulting organizations also undertake a wide variety of research projects. Some consulting firms are large, but most are small — one person or a partnership between two or three persons. Independent consultants are in business for themselves and face all of the entrepreneurial challenges that any other small business must deal with. In addition to research that is performed, a consulting environmental psychologist must raise capital for offices and equipment, promote and market services, and perform accounting for the firm's financial assets.

Finally, some environmental psychologists work for governmental agencies. Although this represents a small percentage of the jobs available to environmental psychologists, these individuals potentially make large contributions by providing information to federal and state regulatory bodies. In addition, some environmental psychologists are employed by the military. For example, research conducted in part by environmental psychologists at the Army's Construction Research Laboratory contributes to an understanding of humane housing in severe weather conditions.

Research and Applications

The material presented in the chapter so far has given you an idea of what environmental psychology is like and, generally, what environmental psychologists do. But what kinds of problems do they work on? As has been noted, the problems are diverse. What follows is a sampling — selected to illustrate the range of topics studied with examples chosen to be representative and interesting.

Interpreting the Environment: The Problem of Wayfinding

A basic activity that all individuals must engage in is that of orienting them-selves and navigating in the environment. We all must move from place to place in order to accomplish our goals. Consider the simple problem of obtaining a loaf of bread at the supermarket. One must first locate one's car, navigate the car through a series of potentially confusing paths to a supermarket, find the location of the bread in the market, relocate one's car in the parking lot, and return home. Such spatial-problem solving is so efficiently handled by most in-dividuals that they are unaware of the degree of skill required to perform these operations.

Although spatial-problem solving can be accomplished cartographically, that is, with reference to some explicit map, the everyday navigational problems of most people are solved through reference to internalized cognitive or mental representations often termed **cognitive maps.** When environmental psychologists study cognitive mapping, they are interested in the processes by which a person acquires, organizes, stores, recalls, and manipulates information about the lo-cations and attributes of places.

A cognitive map is an internal representation – not a little graphic map in your head, but a personalized, idiosyncratic version of your spatial experience. As a result of this personalization, your "map" might not match a cartographic one; your actions are typically based on your representation rather than on a cartographic map (Downs & Stea, 1973). Most applications of environmental perception and cognition research have taken advantage of this fact and have tapped internal representations of individuals in trying to predict and explain behavior.

Representative Application: Designing for Perceptual Clarity.   Our knowledge of the way that people perceive the environment is useful in structuring build-ings so that individuals can find their way around them efficiently and easily. Being able to clearly identify where one is in a building obviously facilitates such wayfinding. An example of great need for this kind of perceptual clarity may be found in psychiatric institutions. For example, Osmund (1966) and Spivack (1967) have noted that design features present in many institutions may cause perceptual distortions similar to those experienced by individuals who are men-tally disturbed. Long corridors that are devoid of visual features may lead to decrements in cognitive and sensory feedback. Without such feedback, time and distance may become distorted – a problem for all but especially disturbing to psychiatric patients. Frequently the walls, ceilings, and floors of such passage-ways are finished with glossy surfaces for easy maintenance. Such settings com-bined with harsh institutional lighting can lead to shimmering distortions in the images of peope and their shadows. Again this problem is frustrating to all but may be disturbing to patients.

Spivack (1967) has documented a ramp that caused perceptual distortions similar to an Ames room (cf. Ittleson & Kilpack, 1952). In an Ames room, in-dividuals are seen to change size as they pass from one side of the room to the

Two women of average height were photographed in an Ames room, a structure that demonstrates the ways architectural features, such as a ramp, influence perceptual cues.

other. Of course the people remain the same size, but the perceptual cues are such that change seems to take place. Because of particular perceptual cues, as one views the ramp in question, individuals seem to shrink as they descend and seem to grow larger as they ascend. Although spaces where visual cues are contradictory are extremely interesting to psychologists, they are clearly inappropriate for therapeutic settings. After all, seeing people apparently changing sizes could not be beneficial to someone hospitalized for experiencing hallucinations. If architects understand the behavioral impact of settings that lack perceptual clarity, such design mistakes may be avoided in the future.

Another example of the desirability of perceptual clarity in design is Weisman's (1981) study of wayfinding in academic buildings. He proposed that the ease with which people can find their way around was related to features of the building that either promoted or hindered perceptual clarity. One of these features he termed **perceptual access,** defined as the degree to which users can actually see intermediate or final destinations as they move through a building. Structures with high perceptual access can reduce the possibility of people getting lost. A second design feature is a composite variable Weisman termed **visual differentiation.** This variable is an index of the distinctiveness of the attributes of a building. Attributes that were visually distinct and significant were highly differentiated, resulting in high clarity and easy wayfinding. Finally, Weisman noted that the presence of linguistic signs aided orientation and wayfinding.

Representative Application: Cognitive Maps and Shopping Behavior.   An additional application of cognitive maps has been in predicting the spatial behavior of consumers. David Mackay and his associates (Mackay, Olshavsky, & Sentil, 1977) assessed the cognitive maps of supermarket shoppers. These cognitive maps were then used to predict the supermarket a person would choose to shop in.

In their experiment, these investigators used a computer program to produce a composite cognitive map based on the responses of their subjects and cognitive maps for each individual. The composite map was closely associated with physical maps, but substantial variation was present between the maps of individuals and the composite. These personal variations were related to consumer behavior; when an individual's cognitive map departed from the norm, so did that person's choice of supermarkets. Further, cognitive distances were shown to be better predictors of shopping behavior than were actual physical distances.

Interpreting the Environment: Differences Between People

Research in environmental perception and cognition emphasizes the way that people generally *remember* the environment. In contrast, research in personality and the environment investigates differences between individuals in the way they *interpret* the environment. Two major efforts have been made in applying personality research to environmental psychology. First, a number of existing personality scales have been used to predict individuals' behavior in the physical environment. Second, several new scales have been used to assess individual differences in enduring styles of relating to the environment that have been termed **environmental dispositions.**

Craik and McKechnie (1977) have suggested several applications of personality variables to environmental problems. They point out the value of providing summary descriptions of groups and of comparing groups that play important roles in environmental policy formation. At present, little is known about the personal characteristics of environmental decision makers such as architects and urban planners and how they may differ from other people. Second, personality variables may be used in predicting who will engage in important environmental behaviors. Behaviors such as use of recycling centers, housing choice, and outdoor recreational activities have all been forecast by means of personality variables.

Representative Application: The Environmental Response Inventory and Migration Behavior.   The Environmental Response Inventory (ERI), developed by George McKechnie (1974), is an instrument for assessing environmental dispositions. This personality scale summarizes behavioral and experiential differences found among persons as they relate to their environments. The ERI is a paper-and-pencil test consisting of 184 statements that an individual rates as either self-descriptive or not self-descriptive. Eight ways of relating to the environment are measured by the ERI. These are *pastoralism* — preservation of natural environments; *urbanism* — enjoyment of cities; *environmental adaptation* — willingness to modify the environment to satisfy needs and desires; *stimulus seeking* — exploration of unusual places; *environmental trust* — confidence in potentially dangerous environments; *antiquarianism* — enjoyment of antiques and historical places; *need for privacy* — isolation from stimuli; and *mechanical orientation* — interest in technological processes. Each of these dimensions are subscales on the ERI that together paint an overall picture of the way individuals relate to their environments.

The scale has been used to study migration behavior in order to understand psychological motivations for locating in certain places. In one study, Kegel-Flom (1976) studied the locational preferences of 59 graduates of the University of California at Berkeley School of Optometry. Of these individuals, 27 chose to practice in urban areas and 32 in rural areas. The urban optometrists were found to score significantly higher on the urban subscale of the ERI than the rural group. Further, in assessments of optometrists in various parts of the nation, urban-rural differences have continued to show up on the ERI. These personality differences may assist in planning health-service delivery systems in specialties (like optometry) where rural practitioners are in short supply.

A second application of the ERI is in the assessment of architectural clients. Often architects are required to design for diverse client groups whom they may not know and with whom they share little in common. McKechnie has pointed out that "the ERI and other measures of environmental dispositions provide standardized yardsticks by which the environmental preferences and values of user groups may be systematically assessed" (1977, p. 266). By having a systematic understanding of their clients, architects are able to tailor designs to better fit diverse user groups.

Acting in the Environment: Reinforcement of Environmentally Relevant Behavior

Subsequent to interpretation of our environments comes active modification of the environment. Taking an operant point of view, psychologists working in this area of environmental psychology apply behavior modification techniques to the understanding and control of environmental problems and behaviors. John Cone and Steven Hays (1980) have pointed out that the vast majority of research in environmental psychology is reactive in nature. That is, the reactions of individuals (either cognitive, affective, or behavioral) to various environmental stimuli were considered. Cone and Hays assert that while this approach may lead to a better understanding of environmental problems and to eventual solutions, it is possible and desirable to attack these problems more directly with the principles of operant conditioning and behavior modification.

A useful model for conceptualizing research in this area is Platt's (1973) **social trap** analysis. Using the reinforcement language of operant conditioning

(Skinner, 1953), a particular behavior is preceded by some event termed a *discriminative stimulus* (S^D). The S^D sets the environmental context for behaviors and alerts the individual that particular behaviors are called for. For example, an empty soda-pop can in a person's hand might be a discriminative stimulus for the behavior of littering. The particular behaviors of interest in this context are termed responses in reinforcement language. Responses (R) are followed by consequences that may be either positive or negative. Positive consequences are termed *positively reinforcing stimuli* (S^{R+}) while negative consequences are termed *aversive stimuli* (S^A). According to reinforcement theory, responses followed by positive stimuli will increase in frequency, while responses followed by aversive stimuli will decrease in frequency. The two basic systems can be illustrated like this:

$$S^D \rightarrow R \rightarrow S^{R+} \quad \text{or} \quad S^D \rightarrow R \rightarrow S^A$$

Platt goes on to note that in environmental contexts rewards and punishments often have a time element attached to them. Frequently, particular responses are followed by stimuli that are reinforcing in the short term but are punishing in the long run. For example, a warm house might serve as a discriminative stimulus (S^D) for the behavior (R) of turning down the air conditioning thermostat to 68 degrees. The short-term consequences would be a cooler house and increased comfort (S^{R+}). The long-term effect, however, would be a higher electricity bill and an increased draw on the electrical generating capacity of the public utility from which power is purchased (S^A). Since behavior tends to be controlled by those consequences that follow responses most closely in time, short-term reinforcements often obscure long-term punishments.

An additional aspect of social traps involves reinforcements and punishments to individuals and to groups. Frequently, short-term reinforcements benefit individuals while long-term punishments harm groups. In the example mentioned, the behavior of turning down the thermostat benefits the individual but punishes the group. If many individuals turn down their air conditioning, the generating capacity of the public utility will be exceeded, additional generating capacity will need to be purchased, and rates will typically rise—a group punishment. Because the short-term, individual rewards are more attention getting than the potential long-term group punishments, individuals continue to engage in behaviors that are environmentally destructive.

The social-trap analysis has been applied to a wide variety of environmental problems including the whaling industry, recycling, litter control, transportation, energy conservation, and residential water conservation. Considered here will be examples of research in the area of energy conservation.

Representative Application: Behavioral Control of Energy Use. A number of different strategies have been implemented to attempt to behaviorally reduce home energy consumption. They may be viewed as attempts to narrow the gap between short-term individual rewards and long-term group punishments. Two problem areas have been addressed: patterns of energy consumption and overall levels of energy consumption.

The problem of patterns of consumption is also known as *peaking*. This means that during certain times of the day, energy use dramatically increases and community-wide power requirements become very high. Although the total amount of energy consumed over the course of a day may not exceed the total generating capacity available to a utility, problems arise during peak hours when demands temporarily exceed capacity and cause brownouts. This pattern of energy consumption requires utilities to build expensive generating equipment to meet demand at peak times, rather than to meet overall demand. If patterns of consumption can be changed so that peaking is reduced, generating plants can be smaller, resulting in savings for both utilities and consumers.

Little research has been performed in the area of reducing peaks in power consumption. One interesting approach (Zarling & Lloyd, 1978) provided immediate feedback if energy consumption exceeded predetermined criterion for 15 minutes. The criterion was set by considering baseline usage during all waking hours. Results indicated that this manipulation reduced peaking and the total amount of power consumed. In addition, many public utilities have introduced what is termed "off-peak metering" to provide financial incentives in the form of less expensive power during evenings and weekends. Under this type of metering, individuals are reinforced by paying inexpensive rates for using power during off peak times, like between 8:00 P.M. and 8:00 A.M., and are punished with higher rates for using power during peak hours.

A second problem in energy conservation is the reduction of overall levels of consumption. Four approaches to the problem will be considered: information appeals, feedback, rate structures, and incentives.

One way to encourage people to conserve is to inform them of the need for conservation and to provide information about how to do it. In general, such information has not been effective in reducing power consumption. For example, Heberlein (1975) assessed power consumption in 84 apartment units before and after the 1974 Arab oil embargo. During that time, the government and conservation groups filled the media with energy conservation appeals. The millions of dollars spent during this time on conservation messages had little effect in promoting changed behaviors. Results indicated no significant differences in oil consumption before and after the embargo.

Although broad information appeals seem ineffective in changing behavior, situation-specific messages or reminders have been shown to be useful. Such messages are termed "prompts" and serve as discriminative stimuli for specific behaviors. Probably the most commonly used prompts are "please turn out the lights" messages placed directly above light switches in many organizations. Such prompts have been shown to be quite effective in reducing use of the appliances to which they are attached.

A second way of increasing conservation, feedback, allows power users to see the effects of their behaviors more clearly. The more frequent the feedback, the less delay there is between a behavior and its effects. Power consumption feedback allows individuals to see the costs of their consuming behaviors more immediately, either through special meters or through bills mailed or delivered more frequently than a typical monthly bill. Feedback studies have most commonly yielded reductions in power consumption of 10% – 20% (Hays & Cone, 1977; Seligman & Darley, 1977; Seligman, Becker, & Darley, 1981).

A third way conservation has been attempted is through the revision of rate structures. Often, power is sold on a sliding scale so that the more an individual or organization purchases, the less is paid per kilowatt hour. Alternatives are flat rates (everyone would pay the same rate regardless of consumption) or so-called inverted rates, (progressively more power would cost progressively more per kilowatt). Little experimentation has been done in this area, in part because of the hesitation of power companies to alter their rate structures. In one of the few studies in this area, Kohlenberg and his associates (Kohlenberg, Phillips & Proctor, 1976) found no independent effects of rate structure.

A fourth way of curbing energy use has been through financial incentives. In this plan, direct reinforcements have been applied for reductions in power consumption. Either decreases in rates or direct monetary rebates have been provided. Such manipulations have led to reductions in power use of up to 30% (Kohlenberg et al., 1976; Winett, Kagel, Battalio, & Winkler, 1978).

All power conservation strategies cost money—conservation information messages must be produced and distributed, feedback information must be provided at some cost, changes in rate structures will typically lose utilities some revenue, and direct financial incentives are obviously costly. Before leaving this topic, it must be noted that power conservation must be cost-effective. If a particular conservation program costs a utility more money than it saves, the program will not be implemented on a long-term basis. For example, even though it is possible to dramatically decrease power consumption through financial incentives, the money spent on those incentives typically exceeds the savings to the utility that the power conserved would bring. Such market considerations provide especially challenging circumstances for environmental psychologists and are also representative of the conditions under which applied psychologists often work.

Acting in the Environment: Proxemics

The operant formulation just described is very broad and can be applied to nearly any behavior. A more restricted topic is *proxemics,* the use of space. Although somewhat narrower in scope, aspects of proxemics have been very thoroughly studied with considerable success. The way that individuals use space to regulate social interaction is the major concern of research in this area (Stokols, 1978). Influence of space on social interaction can be illustrated by examining research in the areas of territoriality, privacy, and crowding.

Territoriality. Researchers studying **territoriality** are interested in the psychological effects of the control and ownership of space and resources. The concept of territoriality has both ethological and sociocultural roots. Early conceptuali-

Oscar Newman's research found that the arrangement of buildings in public housing projects like this one could foster territoriality and increase feelings of community and responsibility among groups of residents.

zations (see Edney, 1974, for a review) were based on studies of the use of space by animals. These definitions emphasized the reproductive and survival-related functions of territoriality. Viewed in this way, animal territories are primarily the province of males and function to communicate information about reproductive fitness to potential mates. A reproductively fit animal is one that will contribute high-quality genetic material to offspring. Animals that can maintain and defend large, high-quality territories will be physically strong and more likely to be reproductively fit. Territoriality thus functions as a medium of social communication in the reproductive process.

Most studies of territoriality in animals have been concerned with occupation and defense of geographical areas. Analyses of territoriality in humans have broadened the concept and have emphasized control of and access to resources in general. As you sit in your dorm room, you control and maintain a spatial territory, but the knowledge you have gained by reading this chapter might also be considered a resource that you control and even defend (for example, during a course examination that covers this material). The functions of territoriality in controlling social interaction have also been explored (Edney, 1976).

Representative Application: Defensible Space.   Probably the clearest application of territorial principles is in Oscar Newman's (1972) defensible space model. Newman analyzed patterns of crime in public housing projects and related them to the design of the buildings and grounds in the projects. He concluded that those settings that, by virtue of their design, generate territorial behavior in their occupants were the most crime-free. Newman identified design features that fostered territoriality. Among these were the placement of buildings on sites in order to define zones of influence for particular buildings. When it is clear to residents that the areas around their buildings "belong" to them, more responsibility is taken for activities that occur there. Strangers are challenged and a sense of community emerges among residents.

A second mechanism for promoting territorial behavior is the use of symbolic barriers to alert residents and intruders to the fact that the space into which they are passing is private and that their presence there requires justification. Design features such as low fences, open gateways, entrance stoops, or changes in the texture of the walking surface may serve as symbolic barriers. The implementation of such barriers allows the creation of a hierarchy of increasingly private zones — from public streets to a person's own residence. When such a hierarchy is present, residents assert their territorial rights, a statement which in turn may lead to reduction in criminal behavior.

Privacy. **Privacy** deals with the regulation and pacing of social interaction with others. Investigators in the field of privacy have sought to (a) conceptualize precisely what privacy is, (b) understand what psychological functions privacy serves, and (c) understand the mechanisms used by individuals to establish and control their privacy. Proposals have been made in all areas, but little consensus exists, and empirical work that tests different conceptualizations against one another has been sparse, relative to work in other areas of proxemics.

Probably the most influential model of privacy is Altman's (1975) boundary regulation model. In this model, privacy is viewed as the point of balance between desires for social contact and desires for seclusion. At any given time, individuals have a *desired* level of privacy and an *achieved* level of privacy. If these levels match, individuals will desire the same level of interaction they are currently experiencing. In contrast, if the levels are not equal, individuals will attempt to adjust their achieved level of privacy up or down. Altman argues that territoriality, personal space, and verbal/nonverbal behaviors are used to regulate the degree of achieved privacy. In this way, privacy becomes an organizing concept for other proxemics constructs and assumes a leading theoretical role. Although Altman's ideas are useful in linking together a wide range of social behaviors, empirical research and applications have been slow in coming.

Representative Application: Privacy in the Workplace. A useful application of privacy research is Sundstrom, Burt, and Kamp's (1980) analysis of privacy in office settings. In this study, two types of privacy were defined: architectural privacy, defined as visual and acoustic isolation provided by the environment, and psychological privacy, defined as a sense of control over access to information about oneself by others. Architectural privacy was assessed by measuring objective features of workspaces such as distances to coworkers and visibility to supervisors. Psychological privacy was assessed with self-report measures.

Architectural privacy, whether achieved by partitions, walls, or space, appears to be significantly correlated with job satisfaction in general.

Results showed a number of correlations between architectural and psychological privacy. In a survey of administrative heads and their assistants in the state of Tennessee, workers felt most private when their workspace was surrounded by partitions or walls, when coworkers were not visible, and when they had a door on their workspace. In another sample of clerical employees in a hospital who worked in an open-plan office, feelings of privacy were correlated with greater distances between workers, being far from corridors, and having few visible neighbors. In a final study of staff members at the University of Tennessee at Knoxville, workers felt more private when they had few neighbors and when they were not visible to their supervisors. Sundstrom and his associates also found that feelings of privacy were significantly correlated with the satisfaction employees felt with their workspace and with job satisfaction in general. In the context of efforts to improve the quality of work life for employees, these results have direct implications for management.

Crowding. Psychologists who study **crowding** are interested in the impact of high density on behavior. An initial distinction has been made between density (or the number of persons per unit of space) and crowding, a psychological reaction to high density. One of the variables may be assessed objectively by physical measurement, while the other is an internal state. Further, different ways of measuring density will result in different psychological experiences. For example, spatial density refers to the amount of space present around a consistent number of people. An experiment using a spatial-density manipulation would keep the number of people constant while varying the amount of space they are in. In contrast, social density refers to the number of people present in a consistent amount of space. An experiment using a social-density manipulation

Psychologists have proposed three major models to account for the effects of crowding on human behavior: arousal, density-intensity, and constraint. Most people say they just don't like the feeling.

would vary the number of people present while keeping the amount of physical space constant. It is highly likely that the experience of changes in social versus spatial density are very different psychologically.

Three major groups of models have been proposed to account for the effects of density on human behavior. The arousal hypothesis (Evans, 1978) states that, as density increases, the lack of space causes physiological arousal as individuals try to cope with the stress. If high-density conditions continue, an individual's resources can become depleted with the accompanying effect of stress. According to this model, crowding effects are a specialized case of a general stress reaction. A second hypothesis is known as the density-intensity model (Freedman, 1975). According to this view, density has the effect of intensifying whatever affective or behavioral response would otherwise occur. The third conceptualization is the behavior-constraint hypothesis (Baron & Rodin, 1978). High-density situations cause people's behavior to be physically constrained. This reduction in control in turn interferes with one's freedom of choice. When freedom of choice is restricted, people experience psychological reactance—they feel hemmed in and try to reassert their freedom to choose. These feelings are the experience of crowding.

Representative Application: Relieving Crowding in a College Dormitory. While each of the above theories has been the subject of considerable empirical investigation, much of this work has centered on the development and refinement of theory. A noteworthy exception is Baum and Davis's (1980) effort to relieve crowding in a college dormitory by means of architectural manipulation. These researchers assessed perceived crowding, patterns of social interaction, and use of space in three settings. The settings investigated were a student dorm with

FIGURE 13.1 Floor plans of the dormitories investigated by Baum and Davis. The top plan is a long corridor design, middle is a short corridor design, and bottom a long corridor design modified for the study. From "Reducing the Stress of High-Density Living" by A. Baum and G. E. Davis, 1980, *Journal of Personality and Social Psychology, 38:* 475.

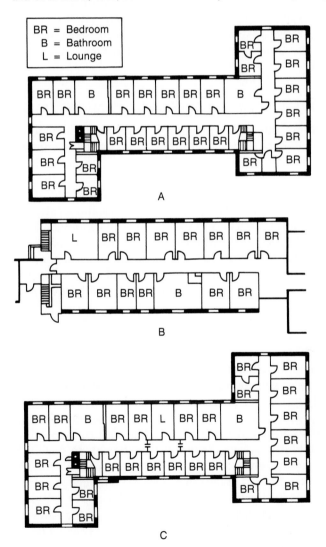

a long corridor (40 residents sharing space), a student dorm with a short corridor (20 residents sharing space), and a student dorm with a long corridor that had been modified by creating a three-room lounge that bisected the living space (two groups of 20 residents sharing space).

Results indicated that the architectural manipulation (adding the lounge) was effective in reducing perceived crowding and residential social problems. The major conceptual predictions in the study were based on a behavior-constraint and perceived-control model of crowding. The data collected showed that frequency of social interaction, formation of informal social groups, and regulation of privacy all influenced the degree of control subjects felt in their dorms. Finally, the research is an excellent example of the twin theoretical/applied goals of action research as they were described in the first section of this chapter. In conducting the study, two goals were accomplished: a cost-effective method of dealing with dormitory crowding was developed and a theoretical model of crowding was explicated.

Responding to the Environment: Impact of the Physical Environment

The focus now moves from action upon the environment to human responses to environmental stimuli. First to be considered is the physical environment. Environmental psychologists have basically investigated the impact of the physical environment on behavior by looking at the effects of stressors such as air, heat, and sonic pollution. As Russell and Ward (1982) have pointed out, the concept of stressors is far from clear. Stress is the internal mediator of the effects of adverse external conditions in a family of theoretical formulations (Stokols, 1979). These explanations of the effect of stress range from highly internal models that view the effects of stress in physiological terms to sociological conceptualizations that consider responses of society at large. Psychological investigations of stress have concentrated on the cognitive, emotional, and behavioral impacts of external stimuli.

An early stimulus to psychological research on environmental stressors was a series of studies conducted by Glass, Singer, and their colleagues (cf. Glass, Reim, & Singer, 1971; Glass, Singer & Pennebaker, 1977). As noted in Chapter 10 on health psychology, subjects in these studies were exposed to predictable and unpredictable noise and controllable and uncontrollable noise in a variety of circumstances. In one interesting study, some subjects were exposed to bursts of noise but were given a control button to terminate the sounds if they became intolerable. Subjects were asked not to use the button if they could possibily avoid it, but were told it was there if needed. Even though no one pushed the button, this group presumably had increased feelings of control. Other subjects had no button but were exposed to the same noise. Even though the actual noise exposure was the same for the two groups, the performance of the group with control over the noise was much less impaired in a series of problem-solving tasks.

Glass and Singer concluded that uncontrollable noise is much more costly psychologically than is noise that is controllable and predictable. Further, these investigators interpreted their results in terms of a stress model. They posited that the aversive external stimuli caused an internal stressful condition, which in turn caused behavioral effects such as poor performance on cognitive tasks and reduced tolerance for frustration. Perhaps most interesting, these problems generally were aftereffects that were detected after the noise was terminated.

The relationship between personal control and response to stressors has become a dominant theme in research on the psychological effects of physical stimulation. Several theories have been proposed to account for this relationship. Cohen (1978, 1980) has proposed a model based on attentional capacity. He theorizes that uncontrollable events are potentially threatening and therefore require more extensive monitoring because of their complexity and novelty. Because these events require monitoring, less attentional capacity is available for task performance and the performance is therefore impaired.

An alternative conceptualization is based on research in learned helplessness (Seligman, 1975). According to this model, helplessness is learned when people are repeatedly exposed to stimuli that they cannot influence (as is often the case with environmental stressors) and an expectation is formed that personal behavior will not change one's own circumstances. This expectation results in decreased motivation and, in turn, decreased performance.

Although a detailed review of research on specific environmental stressors is beyond the scope of this chapter, environmental psychologists have investigated a wide variety of stressors. The impact of adverse environmental conditions including noise, temperature, and atmospheric conditions such as odor, air pollution, atmospheric radiation, and wind have all been investigated. Much of the research in this area has looked at various stressors in isolation, an approach that is overly simple. A major need in the area is the development of models that incorporate various stressors and their internal mediators.

Representative Application: Effects of Aircraft Noise on the Performance of School Children.   An important series of studies performed by Sheldon Cohen and his associates (Cohen, Evans, Krantz, & Stokols, 1980) has investigated the effects of aircraft noise on children's performance in school. In this research 142 children from schools located under the air corridor of the Los Angeles International Airport were compared with 120 children from quiet schools. The schools were matched on factors such as grade level, ethnic composition, occupational and educational levels of parents, and percentage of children whose families were receiving governmental assistance. This was done so that if any differences were obtained in performance between children attending schools, the results could not be attributed to differences in the subjects' backgrounds.

Compared to students from the quiet schools, children from the noisy schools were less proficient at solving a difficult puzzle and gave up more easily. Specifically, 53% of the children from the noisy schools were unable to solve the puzzle within a time limit of 4 minutes. In contrast, only 36% of the students from the quiet schools were unable to complete the task. Even more striking, 31% of the children from noisy schools who failed to complete the task totally gave up trying to solve the puzzle before time was called. In contrast, only 7% of the failing students from the quiet schools quit before the allotted time ran out. These results suggest that persistence and cognitive ability decrements may be attributable to routine noise exposure. The lack of persistence on the tasks exhibited by the children from the noisy schools supports the notion of learned helpessness advanced earlier and indicates that the effects of noise in learning environments are especially serious.

Responding to the Environment: Ecological Psychology

As noted above, most research on environmental stress considers the impact of aspects of the environment in isolation. In contrast, ecological psychology is the most comprehensive attempt to document the effects of the environment on human behavior. Primary to the ecological viewpoint is the concept of **behavior settings** — the social/physical situations in which behavior occurs. Such settings are thought to direct behavior by encouraging and sometimes requiring certain actions and by discouraging or prohibiting others.

Roger Barker and his associates (see Wicker, 1979 for a review) identified the basic components of behavior settings in field research conducted in the 1950s. Such settings are defined by the interaction between standing patterns of behavior and a physical milieu. Standing patterns of behavior are those that are repeated over and over by different individuals as they enter and leave behavior settings. For example, the behavior setting of a post office window is associated with a series of behaviors that may include waiting in line, interacting with a clerk, purchasing stamps, mailing letters, or receiving packages. Individuals who come into this setting tend to engage in a similar range of behaviors. Notice that the personnel are substitutable — the same pattern of behavior "stands" no matter who is in the setting.

Equally important are the physical components of the behavior setting — the physical milieu. The milieu provides the boundaries in space and time within which standing patterns of behavior occur. Ecological psychologists see behavior as closely linked with the physical attributes of places. For example, a lifeguard stand at a swimming pool is near the water and elevated. This physical placement is linked to the behaviors that lifeguards engage in — observing swimmers and, if necessary, diving in to save someone. The linkage described is rather small scale. Ecological psychologists argue that most behaviors are influenced by physical surroundings. Such coordination between behavior patterns and objects nearby is termed *synomorphy* — the fit between human and nonhuman components of behavior settings.

An additional characteristic of behavior settings is their personnel requirements. Wicker, McGrath, and Armstrong (1972) have identified the "maintenance minimum" and "setting capacity" of different behavior settings. The former refers to some minimum number of people required to make a setting run smoothly. The latter refers to the maximum number of people a setting can accommodate. Using these concepts as criteria, it has been possible to determine if any given setting is under-, adequately, or overstaffed independent of the actual number of people in the setting. Thus any behavior setting can be considered to have an optimum level of individuals to staff it. Significant deviations above or below the optimum level will cause changes in the satisfaction and motivation people feel in the setting.

In summary, Barker argues that the environment is composed of lawfully ordered behavior settings. Commenting further, he says the environment "is not a chaotic jumble of independent odds and ends, and it has more than statistical regularity. It consists of bounded and internally patterned units that are frequently arranged in precisely ordered arrays and sequences" (Barker, 1968, pp. 154). The major goal of ecological psychology is the understanding of these behavior setting units and the way their components influence and are influenced by human behavior.

Representative Application: Relieving Congestion at a Bus Stop.   Wicker and Kirmeyer (1976) studied the behavior setting of a bus stop in Yosemite National Park and introduced a queuing device that affected behavior in the setting and measured its effects. To provide some background on the problem, Yosemite is one of the nation's most heavily used national parks. Most of the congestion is concentrated in the 7-square-mile area that is Yosemite Valley. In order to relieve some of the congestion, the Park Service in the early 1970s prohibited automobiles in the valley and established a shuttle-bus system. Using mass transit has created a new set of problems associated with inadequate bus space. In their investigation, Wicker and Kirmeyer frequently observed these behaviors: pushing other visitors, boarding and exiting buses through open windows, running alongside buses as they stopped in order to position oneself in front of a door, and cutting in front of others waiting to board the bus.

To these investigators the behavior setting was clearly overstaffed. Since reducing the number of people in the setting was not possible, they desired to provide an intervention that would alter the standing pattern of behavior in the setting to increase safety, make boarding the shuttle buses more efficient, and ensure equity in boarding. They observed behavior at two bus stops with equivalent traffic for three weeks and then introduced a queuing device made of iron pipes and chain at one of the stops. They then evaluated the effectiveness of the device during a subsequent three weeks of observation.

Results indicated that pushing at the experimental stop decreased slightly and that running next to the bus for position decreased markedly—both contributing to greater safety. Observation also indicated that the speed of boarding increased when bus users were queued. Finally, observations indicated that boarding the buses was substantially more equitable with the queuing device. Less than 8% of the users were found to violate the queuing order when the device was in effect.

To summarize, imposing an additional physical feature in the behavior setting of a bus stop changed behavior at the stop considerably for the better. Ironically, the Park Service judged the device unsightly and removed it before Wicker and Kirmeyer's results were presented.

Evaluating the Environment: Environmental Attitudes

The preceding section gave accounts of the impact of the environment on behavior. The focus in this section is reversed, as it considers people's attitudes toward the environment and environmental assessment. It is clear that the two are highly intertwined. When one evaluates a particular place, attitudes will be formed. In the same way, a general attitude about the environment will often have some specific referent that was considered when the attitude was formed. For purposes of this analysis, **environmental attitudes** will refer to broad feelings about the environment in general. A question such as, "What is your feeling about air pollution?" would fall into this category. In contrast, **environmental assessments** will refer to evaluations of specific places. A question such as, "What is your feeling about the air pollution over Los Angeles today?" would fall into this category.

One way of distinguishing the two areas is to consider how broadly one could apply information obtained from attitude measures versus assessment techniques. For example, an attitude against pollution could be expected to apply in a wide variety of circumstances, from a child's littering behavior to a manufacturer's release of waste water into a river. In contrast, the results of the assessment of a specific place would have a much narrower range of application. For example, the evaluation of an extended care facility for the elderly would be of value in the design of other similar facilities, but not in the construction of banking institutions.

Now that the domains of attitudes and assessment have been distinguished, research on environmental attitudes will be considered. Measurement of environmental attitudes is just like measurement of attitudes toward anything. Self-report techniques that social psychologists have used for decades are the most common way of determining attitudes. Research into environmental attitudes falls into two categories. First, research has been conducted to assess the degree of concern and knowledge of environmental problems (e.g., depletion of resources). Second, general environmental preferences (e.g., what type of forest view is beautiful) have been assessed.

Often survey research techniques have been used to identify personal characteristics associated with environmental concern. For example, a series of studies has indicated that liberal social views are associated with positive attitudes toward conservation (Buttel & Flinn, 1978b; Dunlap, 1975; Koenig, 1975). Further research indicates that these views are held by individuals of different educational and economic levels (Buttel & Flinn, 1978a; Wohlwill, 1979). In addition, several scales that measure attitudes toward conversation have been developed and validated (Maloney, Ward, & Braucht, 1975; Weigel & Weigel, 1978).

A second area of exploration has been the development of scales measuring general attitudes about scenic beauty. For example, recent research in this area has investigated preference for landscapes (Kaplan, 1977), urban places (Herzog, Kaplan, & Kaplan, 1976), forest vistas (Daniel & Boster, 1976), and roadside rights-of-way (Evans & Wood, 1980).

An additional area of research in the measurement of environmental attitudes is the development of Perceived Environmental Quality Indices (PEQIs). PEQIs are really at the interface between measurement of broad environmental attitudes and assessment of specific locations. Early research in the area sought to create a standard index with which to assess all environments. However, as Bechtel (1976) has pointed out, so many situational variations exist between environments that no one scale can capture the richness present and be applied universally. What has arisen instead are PEQIs for various environmental domains. PEQIs currently exist for assessing air, water, sonic, and residential quality, as well as transportation, institutional, and work environments (Craik & Zube, 1976).

Representative Application: Using an Attitude Measure to Predict Environmentally Relevant Behavior.   An interesting application of an attitude scale is Weigel and Newman's (1976) prediction of several environmentally relevant behaviors with a scale measuring environmental concern (Weigel & Weigel, 1978). These investigators administered the environmental concern scale to a group of 44 respondents. Three months after these initial data were collected, a confederate of the experimenters approached the subjects seeking signatures on three ecology petitions. One and one-half months later, a different confederate approached the same group of subjects with a request to participate in a litter collection project. Finally, after another interval of two months, a third confederate requested subjects' participation in a recycling program.

Results indicated that significant correlations existed between each of these behavioral measures of environmental concern and the paper-and-pencil scale developed to assess the attitude. Individuals who scored high on the environmental concern scale were more likely to engage in the behaviors the investigators measured. The results indicate that it is possible to predict environmentally relevant behavior with an attitude scale over an extended period of time.

Evaluating the Environment: Environmental Assessment

Researchers who are interested in environmental assessment are basically concerned about the question of environmental quality. Specifically, the quality of an environment is defined in terms of the perceptions and experiences of users of that place. This type of quality evaluation has direct application in two areas: first, in the establishment of laws and policies produced by legislative bodies and executive regulatory agencies in government, and, second, in planning and design activities.

In 1969, the federal government passed the National Policy Act requiring that ecological, cultural, historic, and aesthetic values as well as economic concerns be considered in decisions that impact environmental policy. Further, input from specialized groups and from the general public was identified as primary to establishment of policy. Regardless of the legal requirements for consideration of social and citizen inputs, Zube (1980) has pointed out that considerable gaps often exist between policy and practice. For example, environmental impact statements should, by federal mandate, contain significant sections on social impacts. This is generally not the case since greater weight is frequently given to physical elements such as air, water, and land. Further, most decision makers share a belief that social scientists are politically naive and therefore do not produce information that is useful in decision making (Caplan, Morrison, & Stambaugh, 1975). Finally, the definition of what social impact assessment should entail is not agreed upon. To some, a description of community and population characteristics is sufficient, while others have argued for a finer-grained psychological level of analysis.

Although difficult to solve, the policy-practice gap in the use of behavioral science inputs in formulating environmental policy can be bridged. Zube (1980) points out that communication between researchers and decision makers can be improved, that some governmental organizations do use large amounts of social-science data, that research interests are being coordinated with policy-relevant issues, and that decision makers are being involved in the formulation of research questions.

A second area of application of environmental evaluation research is in planning and design activities. As environmental psychology has expanded, these applications have become more and more central to the daily activities of applied researchers in this area . As was noted earlier in the chapter, the functions of evaluation of existing environments, evaluation of alternative future environments, and postconstruction evaluation of buildings are all extremely important and distinctive parts of the role of environmental psychologists.

Representative Application: Postconstruction Evaluation of Easter Hill Village. Easter Hill Village is a public housing project in Richmond, Virginia. Completed in 1954, the project was hailed by architects and planners as an important and innovative contribution to public housing. User opinion, however, was not clear. In 1964, Clare Cooper (1975) undertook what was to become a classic study of user satisfaction in built environments. The evaluation attempted to establish the design goals of the planners and ascertain to what extent those goals had been met. Among the design goals for the project were avoiding the institutional image often associated with public housing and providing each family a house of its own with private outdoor space attached. On a social level, the planners desired to foster neighborliness and to create subgroups within the community by arranging clusters of dwellings. Furthermore, the needs of children to have play areas and places for field sports were considered. Finally, the costs of construction and maintenance were to be kept to a minimum.

The design solution to the housing goals was to build row-house units, each with back and front yards. The facades of the houses were varied with different porch designs, window and door arrangements, and colors in order to provide greater individuality. The street pattern within the project was curvilinear with many cul-de-sacs. Large boulders found during construction were used in landscaping and in play areas.

Cooper (1975) interviewed a random sample of 52 of the 300 households in the project. In general, those surveyed felt that the design goals were important to them as well as to the planners. For example, people in the project valued separate houses and private yards. However, actual perceptions of the project and specifically of the housing units did not bear out the design goals in many cases. Although respondents liked Easter Hill Village better than other public housing, they still saw the row houses as institutional and impersonal. Moreover, altering the facades of the houses did not create a sense of individuality as the architects had hoped. A lack of soundproofing in the adjoining walls of the units further reduced the feeling that residents lived in separate houses. Keeping costs to a minimum led to other design compromises that the residents felt were detrimental. For example, to save money, interior space of the units was reduced and storage space was not provided. Exterior spaces received mixed evaluations. Although retention of the large boulders was seen by residents as an excellent idea, they complained of the noise generated by small play areas located around the project. Further, a central play field for group sports was used only by the subgroup of children who lived near it (an interesting instance of territoriality).

In spite of these problems, respondents generally held a favorable impression of Easter Hill Village. When asked what they liked best about the project, they mentioned their neighbors; when asked what they liked least, they mentioned physical facilities. Cooper suggested that designers need to to give greater attention to the behavioral impact of the features they create. In particular, she pointed to the spaces in between buildings in public housing as important but neglected sources of satisfaction.

Conclusion

This chapter has reviewed some of the basic characteristics of the approach of environmental psychologists to psychology. In addition, it has considered examples of major content areas of the discipline and has reviewed representative applied research that has been conducted in each area. It seems appropriate to conclude with some ideas about the current status and future of environmental psychology.

In the decade of the 1960s, social scientists who held a vision of applying their disciplines to improve the quality of everyday life began investigations into person-environment relationships. The discipline of environmental psychology came into its own in the early 1970s with the publication of several seminal articles, a book of readings, and a new journal (*Environment and Behavior*). Nearly all of the original proponents of environmental psychology shared the common vision that the field would have applied and academic interests and that these interests would go hand in hand. Now, two decades later, it seems that this promise has only been partially realized.

The academic branch of the discipline is well established and recognized. Numerous graduate programs, textbooks, and journals have been introduced and researchers from other, more established areas of psychology have taken an interest in environmental issues. Further, as Robert Sommer (1980) has pointed out, the assumptions and methods of environmental psychology are no longer considered radical. Statements concerning the influence of the physical environment on behavior and the effects of the physical presence of other people are no longer unexpected by psychologists.

It is in applications that the difficulties arise. Often the problem has been referred to as the "applicability gap." It basically has to do with conflicting goals that practitioners and researchers hold. Practitioners such as architects and planners are in need of behavioral data. However, they need to have the answers to their questions in concise, decisive, and financially realistic terms. A designer is typically under constraints that do not allow for the painstaking investigations and attention to minutiae of which psychologists are so fond. Research results that are so qualified that courses of action are unclear are of little value.

In contrast, researchers often have difficulty providing answers that practitioners desire because they feel that the total picture is not conveyed and that, in the absence of understanding underlying processes, critical gaps in knowledge may later become evident. Further, psychologists involved in research are not often sensitive to the financial constraints of the real world. Such constraints require that answers be generated quickly and efficiently if anyone will be willing to pay for them. In summary, practitioners are saying, "What's the answer?" and "Now!" while researchers reply, "Hold on, let me study it."

Obviously, much applied work has been done. What is the remedy for the applicability gap? One major solution seems to be in the training of both practitioners and researchers. New interdisciplinary programs are increasing the sensitivity of researchers to the problems that must be overcome to deliver research answers to practitioners in understandable and financially realistic terms. The goal of creating applications that are successful supplants a concept of theoretical purity and brings real-world information into the development of theory. On the other hand, practitioners have been trained in the research methods of the behavioral sciences, and communication problems between the two groups have been eased. These designers are more likely to be receptive to the input that researchers can provide.

Finally, it should be reiterated that environmental psychology is a new discipline. The data are still being gathered to develop the research base from which authoritative answers to applied questions can be derived. For example, a researcher who knew almost everything that had been written about the behavioral aspects of office buildings should have available a backlog of information to legitimize his or her claimed expertise. Under those circumstances, a consulting environmental psychologist could make a significant contribution to the solution of applied problems within the cost and information constraints imposed by a client. The problem is that much of the research upon which a hypothetical expert would rely is only starting to be conducted. The call then is for more relevant research focused on applied settings. From this perspective, the future of applied environmental psychology rests with researchers and their desire to solve relevant problems.

Glossary

architectural program   A document prepared before a building is designed to define the physical and sometimes the behavioral specifications of a building.

behavior settings   Barker's name for the sociospatial units of the environment that influence behavior. Behavior settings consist of a standing pattern of behavior and a milieu—the time and place where behavior takes place.

cognitive map   The internal or cognitive representation of large-scale physical space.

crowding   The negative psychological experience associated with high physical density.

environmental attitudes   As used in this chapter, broad feelings and cognitions about the environment in general

environmental assessments   As used in this chapter, feelings and cognitions about specific locations within the environment.

environmental dispositions   Individual differences in enduring styles of relating to the environment.

molar level of analysis   As used in this chapter, the analysis of the environment as it is experienced in everyday life.

participatory planning   Soliciting of information about satisfaction for existing facilities and preferences for proposed facilities from users or prospective users of those facilities.

perceptual access   An attribute of perceptual clarity, the degree to which users can see intermediate or final destinations as they move through a building.

privacy   A process by which individuals regulate the amount of social interaction they have with others.

social trap   A social problem where the long-term costs of a behavior to a group of people are obscured by the short-term rewards that behavior provides to an individual.

territoriality   The psychological effects of the control and ownership of space and resources.

visual differentiation   An attribute of perceptual clarity, the degree to which the attributes of a building are visually distinct and significant.

Part 4

Psychology and Human Development

14 Applied Psychology in Education

Timothy J. Pettibone
University of Tennessee

Hal W. Jernigan
University of Tennessee

This chapter deals with psychology and psychologists in educational settings. By now, you probably have a pretty good idea of what psychology is all about. You may not, however, understand education, even though you have experienced a great deal of it to get where you are. Just what is education?

Since education is so closely related to learning, it might be a good idea to deal with the concepts together. A popular definition is that **learning** is the act of changing behavior through experience. While learning is certainly the objective of education, **education** is the systematic effort designed to cause learning to take place. Many times the term *education* is associated with the formal system established to transmit accumulated knowledge (and knowledge skills), as well as culture and values to the youth in our society. This is the kind of education provided by public and private schools, universities, and colleges.

In a simpler fashion, the concept of education is sometimes related to the "learning" of a set of skills. Take typing, for example. The objective of typing education is to have students gain typing skills (change their behavior). How is this accomplished? For one thing, someone develops learning objectives, structures a learning environment containing, in this case, the necessary equipment and materials (typewriters and typing paper), and tries to teach someone something by means of a variety of activities. Effective education also involves the assessment of learning (behavior changes) that can provide a "feedback loop" to improve the process or just to assign grades.

This example of typing education can be extended to any subject matter, simple or not. Take "citizenship" as another example. As long as there are learning objectives, a sequence of instruction, a learning environment, materials (and equipment, if necessary), activities, and assessment, then education is probably taking place. So, in this case, if a teacher (1) has the objective of teaching students to identify their state's representatives in Congress; (2) conducts activities directed toward accomplishing this objective, such as lectures, discussion groups, guest speakers, and reading and paper assignments; (3) provides an environment and materials supportive of the stated ojective (bulletin board, handouts, up-to-date textbooks, and films as examples); and (4) assesses the accomplishment of the objective (through tests, paper grading, interviews, and discussion sessions), one probably can conclude that citizenship education is taking place (at least as far as the single objective would indicate).

It is clear that education is an applied field. However, some would say that it is an applied science, while others consider it to be an art. Similar situations exist for engineering and medicine. In the applied-science sense, engineering rests on a strong foundation of the hard sciences (for example physics, chemistry, and mathematics). Medicine also relies heavily on the sciences, especially biology. Both medicine and engineering, however, also require intuition and insight. In a similar manner, education depends greatly on sociology and psychology for its scientific basis. It also has an "art" component because it allows for (and in some cases demands) human judgment. While the "art" portion of education is important and interesting, the focus of this chapter is on the scientific arm of applied psychology in education.

Teacher preparation generally includes a significant amount of psychological training. Principles of learning, human growth and development, and measurement and testing are some of the important components of teacher-training programs. In addition, those who teach in public schools are usually required to continue their studies in order to maintain certification. Often this continuing education includes additional psychological coursework at the graduate level. Thus the practice of education is dependent upon psychology both during and after initial training. Although teachers are not generally considered to be applied psychologists, the most successful among them are usually those who understand the application of psychological principles.

There are two major categories of applied psychologists in education: (1) school psychologist, and (2) educational psychologist. Sometimes social and community psychologists work in educational settings (see Chapters 9 and 11), but this discussion will be limited to school and educational psychologists.

What Is School Psychology?

In her award-winning story, *A Wrinkle in Time,* Madeleine l'Engle describes the problems that her heroine Meg faced in school. Meg's parents were both brilliant physicists but she did poorly in her studies. Her performance frustrated her, and she became antagonistic toward school staff members who might have helped her. Was Meg just not a bright student? Or, was she so bright that the work she was given bored her? What about her home environment? Did it support the educational process or create a series of expectations that only made the situation worse? These are questions that could be addressed by a school psychologist. In this case, Meg *was* a brilliant student, and her problems could have been helped through assessment, consultation with parents and teachers, and possibly therapy. This section of the chapter will consider the work roles of school psychologists and learn about how they could help in situations like the one described above.

In the chapter introduction, we noted that education is often associated with the formal system established to transmit knowledge and skills, as well as culture and values, to youth in any society. In the modern world, the institutions most often responsible for this process are schools of various types. School psychologists apply psychological knowledge to prevent or solve problems students may encounter and to help schools achieve the knowledge, skills, and acculturation goals that are intrinsic to education.

A national survey conducted during the 1983–84 school year resulted in some interesting statistics. Fagan (1986) reports that the National Association of School Psychologists found that there were approximately 20,000 school psychologists. According to Fisher, Jenkins, and Crumbley (1986), their 1983–84 survey found a 1:2209 psychologist-to-child ratio. This, of course, is not a caseload — the majority of children successfully pass through school without the need of the direct services of a school psychologist. But a ratio this high clearly means that many children who need the services of school psychologists are not receiving them. As high as this ratio sounds, when compared to the results of an earlier study (Meacham & Peckham, 1978), the 1983–84 figure is significantly lower and indicates a trend toward somewhat more adequate delivery of school psychologist services to students. For persons considering entering the field, it should be clear that there is a substantial demand for school psychologists.

What Do School Psychologists Do?

Typically, school psychologists are involved in a number of activities. Fisher et al. (1986) identified six roles in a survey of several hundred school psychologists. The respondents rank-ordered these roles in terms of time spent on each in their present jobs. In addition, respondents rank-ordered their roles in terms of their preferences for each role. The ranked actual and preferred roles are shown in Table 14.1. Obviously, they would not necessarily be involved in all of these activities at the same time.

Historical Perspective

As you will see, the current work activities of school psychologists have emerged over a number of years. In order to deal with the question of work activities, a small amount of history is in order. First of all, school psychology grew out of a changing philosophy of education. Around the turn of the century democratic societies everywhere decided that all children had rights of educational opportunity. "All children" covers a wide array of abilities. Teachers of

TABLE 14.1

Actual and Preferred Rank Orders of Various Work Activities of School Psychologists

Actual
1. Assessing student abilities by giving interviews and tests
2. Interpreting test and interview results
3. Consulting with parents or teachers
4. Performing therapy with students
5. Acting as change agent in organization
6. Performing research in some aspect of school performance

Preferred
1. Consulting with parents or teachers
2. Assessing student abilities by giving interviews and tests
3. Interpreting test and interview results
4. Acting as change agent in organization
5. Performing therapy with students
6. Performing research in some aspect of school performance

From "A Replication of a Survey of School Psychologists: Congruence between Training, Practice, Preferred Role, and Competence" by G. L. Fisher, S. J. Jenkins, and J. D. Crumbley, 1986, Psychology in the Schools, 23, pp. 276–277.

the day would have preferred to have poor learners removed from their classrooms. As mentioned in Chapter 1, in 1915 the State of Connecticut hired Arnold Gesell (who was trained both as a psychologist and as a medical physician) to identify and test mentally backward children, and to help school districts accommodate the educational needs of these students. In fact, Gesell may have been the first person to have been called "school psychologist" (Fagan, 1987).

About the same time as this changing educational philosophy was emerging, the *testing movement* was developing. The intelligence scale developed by Alfred Binet in France was converted to usage in English and stimulated a rapid incorporation of testing in American education (Glover, Bruning, & Filbeck, 1983).

Two additional events have been identified as having helped to launch the school-psychology movement. These were the work of Lighter Witmer at the University of Pennsylvania and the early effort of the public schools of Chicago. Witmer, the founder of the Universtiy of Pennsylvania Psychological Laboratory (which has the distinction of being called the first psychological clinic), began to recognize the need for a new field. In 1896 Witmer stated:

> In fact, we must look forward to the training of men to a new profession which will be exercised more particularly in connection with education problems but for which the training of the psychologist will be prerequisite. (Cutts, 1955, p. 18).

The other event was the formation of the Department of Child Study and Pedagogic Investigation in the Chicago public schools by Walter Christopher in 1889. Extensive testing was conducted at the laboratory, along with studies of educational problems and individual problem children. (Wallin & Ferguson, 1967).

Around 1915 the guidance movement initiated by Brewer greatly affected school psychology because of the heavy individual-counseling component in guidance. In fact, the common role of school psychologists in the diagnosis and remediation of students' problems probably developed in the context of guidance (Tindall, 1964). Another movement, that of mental health (founded in the same decade), influenced the development of school psychology. Because of the emphasis on prevention, mental health became attentive to those in an early stage of life—school children. These two movements contributed heavily to a clinical view of school psychology (Tindall, 1964).

More recently, the formation of professional associations (and divisions of existing associations) have contributed to the development of school psychology as a unique field. Division 16 (school psychology) of the American Psychological Association, established in 1947, has played a major role in establishing school psychology as a legitimate field. In 1969, the National Association of School Psychologists (NASP) was founded, partially in response to what were considered overly conservative attitudes on the part of Division 16 leadership and policy. More will be said about this controversy later in this chapter. Some 44 state school-psychology associations are affiliated with NASP (Fagan, 1986).

Other associations involved in school psychology include American Personnel and Guidance Association (established in 1952) and the Council for Exceptional Children (established in 1941). These two organizations, while not exclusively involved in school psychology, have made important contributions toward establishing school psychology as a profession.

While there have been literally hundreds of court cases that are relevant to the school psychology movement, one case, *Brown* v. *Board of Education of Topeka,* stands out in general importance. This Supreme Court decision of 1954 ruled against the "separate but equal" doctrine used to support racial segregation in the schools. While segregation in fact (*de facto*), as contrasted with segregation by law (*de jure*), may still exist, schools in the United States have generally bcome more integrated. Not only are integrated schools racially mixed, they also tend be more economically heterogeneous as well. An impact of this diversity on school psychologists has been a general increase in the range of student abilities in schools. More diverse student bodies have resulted in the need for more complex assessment and placement decisions.

Two cases have had a specific impact on the practices of school psychologists. One case is the 1968 ruling of the unconstitutionality of tracking lower-ability students (*Mobson* v. *Hanson,* 1967). This means that it is no longer legal

Laws require that students of less than normal physical or mental ability be included in regular classes. "Mainstreaming" these students has increased the need for school psychologists to design diagnostic and remedial services.

to consistently place low-ability students in special classes where they are offered little educational opportunity. Instead, these students are placed in classes with students of normal ability and given the same educational experiences. A second important legal decision is the continuing case of *P.* v. *Riles* (1974, 1979) in California, which has raised serious questions about the use of intelligence tests in the labeling of children who may require special educational experiences. The argument of the plaintiff has been that the labels applied to children who score low on intelligence tests tend to stick with them — in school and beyond — and that this labeling process produces an additional (and illegal) handicap.

In addition to court cases, legislation also had a great impact. Probably the most important piece of legislation affecting school psychology has been Public Law 94-142. This law requires that all children, regardless of handicapping condition, receive a free and appropriate education. The ages of students is specified as 0–21 years unless otherwise specified by state law. Section 504 of the Rehabilitation Amendments of 1973 protects the rights (including educational rights) of the handicapped. The effect of these laws has been to greatly increase the need for diagnostic and remediation services, with resulting increased numbers of school psychologists being trained and subsequently employed.

Recognizing the abbreviated nature of this "history," what can be concluded? First of all, until fairly recently, the term *school psychologist* only meant that the psychologist worked in the schools. There was no unifying single description of school psychology (nor is there yet, but it may be coming). Until the formation of professional associations that dealt exclusively with school psychology, the term only indicated the place of employment. Two early influences remain in school psychology: (1) assessment and (2) clinical practice. The degree of emphasis attributed to each of these influences depends on the individual and the setting. Some people prefer the clinical role, while others are more comfortable in the assessment role. Of course, job requirements sometimes dictate the acceptable role or roles, and most individuals fill both. Lastly, litigation and legislation have been extremely important in defining and refining the role of school psychology and the demands on the field.

Job Activities

It should be obvious from the previous discussions of the roles and historical development that school psychologists do a lot of different things, including individual psychoeducational assessment, individual and group counseling, and consulting with teachers, administrators, and parents. However, school psychologists are probably best known for the *assessment role*. One finds school psychologists deeply involved with evaluating a number of characteristics of children who are referred to them by teachers, administrators, other professionals in education, and parents. Intelligence, aptitude, personality, psychomotor, and perception are only a few of the types of tests administered. School psychologists are also involved in the prescription of remediation for whatever difficulty may be detected. Some people call this an example of the application of the "medical" model: Refer students who have a problem, assess to diagnose the problem, then treat the problem. This last step may require referral to other professionals or agencies.

In the *clinical role,* school psychologists concentrate on the treatment of problems once they have been identified, and may also be involved in directly treating students with some form of therapeutic intervention. Individual and group counseling can also be involved. Sometimes school psychologists will cooperatively work with psychologists in private practice or psychiatrists (who hold degrees in medicine) on specific cases.

Are school psychologists the same as counselors? People sometimes confuse the two roles. This is understandable as the distinction is a bit hazy at times. Counselors are involved in career guidance, scheduling and advisement, standardized-test interpretation, teacher consultation, and, sometimes, helping students with personal problems. On occasion counselors find themselves responsible for discipline, a role felt to be in conflict with the psychologist's helping role. Counselors have usually received specialized training in what is known as student personnel work. Typically counselors hold at least the master's degree and have generally come through the ranks of teachers. School psychologists are trained as psychologists, not educators, although a number of training programs combine the two fields very effectively.

Are school psychologists the same as educational diagnosticians? No, not really, but the two groups do sometimes work closely together. Because of the fairly recent growth in the field of special education, another assessment-related field has emerged, that of educational diagnostics. Educational diagnosticians typically are trained in colleges of education and specialize in the testing and

In dealing with her young clients, a school guidance counselor, though not herself a psychologist, draws heavily on the principles and research findings of school psychology.

diagnostic aspects of special education. The training of diagnosticians normally includes a number of psychology courses, but the bulk of their training involves education and special-education courses.

Work Settings

Obviously, most school psychologists are found in school systems and schools. However, not all school psychologists work in schools. As Ramage (1979) reports, 79% are employed by school systems and 7% by colleges and universities. The remaining 14% are employed by state governments, mental health institutions, or are self-employed.

Issues in School Psychology

School psychology is a relatively new phenomenon. The discipline is maturing, but a large number of controversies remain. For example, there is currently no universal definition of school psychology. Different professional and licensing organizations have varying opinions as to activities properly in the domain of school psychology. Developing agreement on what activities are appropriate for individuals who are licensed as school psychologists is critical. Also, what educational credential is appropriate for a school psychologist? Can individuals function in this role with master's degrees, or should more education be required? Furthermore, if a doctoral degree is required, should it be an Ed.D. (an educational doctorate) or the more research-oriented Ph.D.? The issue of doctoral versus subdoctoral degree is a complex and controversial one. There are those, including Division 16 of APA, who insist that the doctoral degree be made a requirement for becoming a school psychologist. More generally, APA does not recognize the title "psychologist" in any form unless the person holds a doctoral degree. Consistent with this policy, "regular" membership in Division 16 of APA requires the doctorate, while only "associate" memberships are available to those who lack the degree. Others, including members of NASP, feel that the requirement of the doctorate is neither necessary nor practical for school psychology at present. Approximately three quarters of all present school psychologists hold nondoctoral degrees (Brown, Horn & Lindstrom, 1980). However, many of these individuals would have substantial educational credits beyond the master's degree.

Psychological testing has also been the subject of controversy and has come under considerable attack in terms of negative public opinion and in legal cases. Yet school psychologists rely on test results for many of the decisions they make in evaluating students. The future of psychological testing in school settings is not clear at this point.

Other questions of concern to school psychologists relate to budget cutbacks that have become common both at the federal and local levels. The legal requirements to provide school psychological services have remained the same despite reductions in fundings. How will school psychology manage in an era of austerity? Will future legislation and court cases enhance or detract from the practice of school psychology?

Careers in School Psychology

Persons wishing to become school psychologists need at least a master's degree, more probably an educational specialist degree, and possibly a doctorate. The specialist's degree is now the minimum entry-level degree recommended by NASP. Brown and Minke (1986) report that almost 40% of the students training to be school psychologists are in doctoral programs. While it is not an absolute necessity, a student is probably better off going to an institution that has a special program in school psychology. Be aware that all programs are not alike. The title may be the same, but the training may be different (different content, different emphases). As of 1984 there were 79 doctoral and 254 nondoctoral school psychology training programs in the United States with an enrollment of approximately 7,000 students (Brown & Minke, 1986). The results of an earlier survey of school psychology programs indicated that about 44% were found in departments of psychology, 16% in departments of educational psychology, 12% in education departments, and the rest (28%) in either interdisciplinary or in differently titled human-services departments (Goh, 1977).

The three levels of training may lead to three different types of jobs. Individuals holding master's degrees in school psychology may function in schools as school psychologists under the direction of doctoral-level school psychologists. Many practicing school psychologists hold the educational specialist degree. In most states this degree requires around 30 graduate credits beyond the master's degree. While the APA does not recognize this degree, as was noted above many certified school psychologists working today hold this degree. Finally, individuals may hold some form of doctoral degree—the Ph.D., the Ed.D., or the Psy.D. a practitioner's doctorate in psychology. Persons with any of these doctoral degrees may work in university settings as professors or in school systems as school psychologists.

What Is Applied Educational Psychology?

In 1984 the State of Tennessee began to implement a new program to pay teachers based on their performance in the classroom. Superior teachers would receive substantial salary increases. But how could the state differentiate between the many good teachers and the truly outstanding few? Such a problem in educational evaluation is the domain of educational psychologists. The State of Tennessee devised an evaluation method based on classroom visits, lesson-plan review, teacher interviews, and questionnaire responses from a teacher's principal, students, and peers. The program is now a trend-setter nationwide, and student achievement scores in Tennessee are increasing. This example illustrates one way that educational psychologists can apply their expertise to improve the educational process.

Like school psychology, educational psychology is an applied branch of the parent discipline of psychology. Also like school psychology, educational psychology has a long history that initially parallelled that of its parent discipline.

Educational psychology began to emerge as a unique discipline as early in the history of psychology as the 1880s. In Europe, Wilhelm Wundt established the first psychological laboratory in Wurzburg, Germany, in 1878. The German scholar Hermann Ebbinghaus was the first to see that Wundt's methods were directly useful to education. Ebbinghaus applied these techniques to the study of memory and retention.

During the same period in the United States, William James had also started a laboratory for the scientific study of psychological ideas at Harvard University. As a well-established scientist in 1899, James published his classic book *Talks to Teachers*, in which he discussed the relationship between the science of psychology and the art of teaching. James saw limited initial benefits for education from the new science of psychology. He wrote:

> I say, moreover, that you make a great, a very great mistake, if you think that psychology, being the science of the mind's law, is something from which you can deduce definite programmes and schemes and methods of instruction for immediate schoolroom use (James, 1962, pp. 5–6).

The title of "father of educational psychology" is usually reserved for a student of James's, Edward L. Thorndike. Thorndike exerted the strongest influence on the direction of educational psychology's early development. In 1903, he published the first text that bore the title *Educational Psychology*, setting the direction of the new discipline, emphasizing strict scientific studies of educational programs and deemphasizing those studies that might view education as simply an "art." In *Educational Psychology*, Thorndike stated the following:

> This book attempts to apply to a number of educational problems the methods of exact science. I have therefore paid no attention to speculative opinions and very little attention to the conclusions of students who present data in so rough and incomplete a form that accurate quantitative treatment is impossible (Mitzel, 1982, p. 1495).

Unlike James, Thorndike saw unlimited benefits for people by applying what was learned through psychology to educational practices. He emphasized the belief that people could change, and for the better. In 1910, the *Journal of Educational Psychology* was founded, and the first article in the first issue was written by Thorndike (Mitzel, 1982). He remained highly influential in the field throughout his long career.

It is through the efforts of early writers such as Thorndike that the field of educational psychology was founded. They shared a strong conviction that through the rigorous application of scientific research methods, educational psychology could be established as a true scientific discipline.

What areas have been explored in the literature since these early studies, and just how is the field positioned at present? One attempt to answer this question was made by analyzing the articles published in the *Journal of Educational Psychology* during its first 75 years, 1910–1985 (Ball, 1984). What was found was "that educational psychology involved such a mixture of topics that it would do justice to an academic version of mulligan stew" (Ball, 1984, p. 993). The emphasis of research topics has changed over the years, with the early writings directly related to practical issues of teaching and school curriculum, and later studies less directly related to the classroom and more interested in the theoretical issues that surround teaching and learning. The field is seen to be "like a chameleon, changing its emphasis perhaps to conform to its environment" (Ball, 1984, p. 998).

There has also been a continuing debate concerning whether educational psychology is truly a discipline or simply an interest area. As late as 1969, D.P. Ausubel felt it necessary to argue that although many educational psychology textbooks regrettably contained little more than a "watered-down miscellany of general psychology" (Ausubel, 1969, p. 232), educational psychology was a unique discipline in its own right and, furthermore, should be viewed as "that special branch of psychology concerned with the nature, condition, outcomes, and evaluation of school learning and retention" (Ausubel, 1969, p. 232).

Whether truly a discipline or not, educational psychology continues to have a widespread effect on educational practices. The field is now expected to provide leadership within the educational community. Its traditional research base truly validates the practices of education and teaching.

What Do Applied Educational Psychologists Do?

Educational psychologists are deeply involved with psychological principles of learning and their application (potential and actual) to educational settings. Some of these specialists are trying to discover new principles and further refine what is known about the learning process. This section will review some of the roles educational psychologists play in the process of education.

Job Activities

To start with a few examples, an applied educational psychologist might be found developing materials and procedures for the training division of a business or industrial firm, evaluating training materials, or reviewing training procedures. Educational psychologists may develop (or evaluate) computer-aided instructional software, serve as consultants to the personnel divisions of organizations, carry out validation studies for test-development organizations, or teach teachers how to teach.

Educational psychologists work in universities and in research and development laboratories. However, the unique qualities of their role can best be seen in settings away from the university. Several examples will convey the special functions of these individuals.

Test-development firms often hire educational psychologists. Educational Testing Service (the company that produces and administers the Scholastic Aptitude Test, or SAT) and American College Testing, as examples, need their assistance in designing fair and reliable tests. A number of publishing companies

Developers of standardized tests and instructional materials for all grade levels rely heavily on the expertise of educational psychologists in the design and evaluation of their products.

and software producers use educational psychologists to help develop and evaluate educational materials for students at a wide range of levels. In industry, training directorships are often filled by people with educational psychology backgrounds who can develop and carry out training programs for their employers. Some educational psychologists do this type of work as external consultants rather than as employees. Schools, governmental organizations, and military facilities also have a need for outside evaluators to assess various instructional programs. Not only is this process helpful to programs in terms of improvement, but, many times, it is required by law or regulation. (See Appendix A for a more detailed discussion of evaluation.)

The federal government has set up a number of research and development (R&D) laboratories around the country. These labs often hire educational psychologists for a variety of tasks. As an example, the Northwest Regional Educational Laboratory in Portland, Oregon, has several hundred employees, a number of whom are educational psychologists. Projects range from providing training services to school districts, to material development, to applied research efforts on a state-wide basis.

Work Settings

Most of the time, educational psychologists are not found in the public schools, but rather in universities and in research and development laboratories (both private and governmental). In universities, educational psychologists generally are involved in teacher training. Courses such as human growth and development, educational psychology, and tests and measurements are typically taught by educational psychologists. Further specialized courses help prospective teachers understand the diversity of people with thom they will be dealing in different school settings. Educational psychologists in universities are usually involved in research as well as in teaching. Some examples of current research performed by educational psychologists will be covered in a subsequent section. As referred to earlier, educational psychologists are also employed by R&D laboratories in both government and industry. A number of educational psychologists also work as independent consultants. Many of these individuals are associated with universities as their primary place of employment, while others either have their own consultant firms or work for other such firms.

Research and Applications

This section reviews some specific areas of research application as examples of what has been done by educational psychologists, first considering research into effective teaching and then looking at research in learning.

What Is Known about Effective Teaching

Surprisingly, although a great deal is known about teaching, the method of "knowing" has not been rigorously addressed. Unlike research in much of experimental psychology, most of the educational psychology research investigating effective teaching has been *correlational*—that is, no variables are manipulated. Instead, existing educational conditions are analyzed, and correlations between those conditions and the results obtained under various instructional conditions are assessed. To do otherwise would either be unethical or impractical in light of the real-world situation of education. Nevertheless, some true experiments where variables are manipulated have been conducted in this area. Unfortunately, according to Gage (1978b), the number of subjects in many of the studies (correlational as well as experimental) has been so small as to require unrealistically high correlations or differences to be found significant. Therefore much of the reported research has not been very helpful in increasing understanding of effective teaching. In addition to the sample-size problem, many studies have been of the "single shot" variety and have not investigated factors that might influence learning over a period of time.

Gage (1978a) used a statistical technique that allowed him to analyze the results of a number of studies regarding several hundred teacher-behavior and classroom-activity variables. The studies he analyzed all investigated the reading achievement of third-graders. The analysis was one of sifting through the variables, looking at the definitions of the variables, and studying their correlations with reading achievement.

The eternal question, What is a good teacher? The research suggests that effective teaching depends on a complex of conditions in four categories: preinstructional decisions, the instruction itself, the educational climate, and postinstructional factors.

While Gage reached a number of conclusions, his basic finding was that third-grade teachers could expect higher student achievement in reading if they organized or managed what they called their classes' "time on task." Rosenshine and Berliner (1978) reported a similar summary study and called the effect "academic engaged time ." Others have termed time spent on learning tasks as **academic learning time (ALT).** Whatever the name, the finding is fairly straightforward. If you want students to learn a body of material, make sure that they spend time studying that material. However, the same techniques of organizing and managing do not necessarily work for all students all the time. In fact, Medley (1977) discovered that several teaching techniques found to be successful with low socioeconomic status (SES) students failed with high-SES students. Nevertheless, the results of all these studies provide a basic understanding of what factors promote classroom learning.

Gage used the phrase ALT to describe the time-on-task concept. He felt that ALT would be correlated with achievement, yet this was only weakly and inconsistently supported in the research he reviewed. He mentions the possibility that "these results indicate that differences in ALT alone will probably be far from adequate to account for differences in achievement" (1979b, p. 75). He then proposed that researchers need to study how the ALT is filled. What goes on during the academic learning time is probably as important as ALT duration.

In an interview conducted by Schneider (1979), Charles Fisher of the Far West Laboratory was asked what the model classroom would look like. Fisher stated:

Our study suggests several interrelated factors. An ideal classroom has a clear focus on learning. The students expect to work and are held responsible for doing so. Adults and students interact comfortably and frequently on work activities. That is, the teacher demonstrates that the school's purpose is learning and that everyone is there to work together to reach that goal. (p. 5).

More recently, Berliner (1984) summarized the research on teaching. He noted that this research has been conducted for only about 20 years. Four groups of critical factors to be considered by educational psychologists appear in this literature. First are the preinstructional factors, which include (1) content decisions (what gets taught); (2) time-allocation decisions (how much time is assigned to each subject); (3) pacing decisions (the more material covered in a time period, the more material learned); (4) grouping decisions (the size and composition of the instructional group); and (5) decisions about what learning activities should be used (recitation, small group, individualized, etc.). Even before instruction takes place, the teacher's decisions in these matters may make a difference in student achievement.

The next set of factors are those directly dealing with instruction. These include (1) engaged time, (2) time management, (3) monitoring success rate, (4) academic learning time, (5) structuring of materials, and (6) questioning of students.

Another set of factors relates to educational climate. These factors are (1) communicating academic expectations for achievement; (2) developing a safe, orderly, and academically focused environment for work; (3) sensible management of deviancy; and (4) developing cooperative learning environments.

Not surprisingly, the last set of factors is called "postinstructional" and includes things that occur after instruction that seem to make a difference in student achievement. These are (1) tests (the match of standardized tests to course content and the use of test results for diagnosis); (2) grades (grades do motivate students); and (3) feedback (reinforcement for correct or proper behavior, ignoring of inappropriate behavior, and lack of sarcasm and personal attacks).

Another author (Westbrook, 1982) synthesized the findings of over 100 studies in his attempt to identify characteristics related to effective schools. Westbrook cautions the reader that his conclusions must be viewed in light of the following qualifications:

1. School effectiveness is defined only in terms of scores on standardized tests. Effective and ineffective schools are identified in terms of relatively low versus high scores.
2. Much of the research was done in urban environments, limiting its generalizability.
3. Most studies are "snapshots" rather than longitudinal in nature.
4. Few attempts have been made to look at the process of becoming effective. Factors associated with maintaining effectiveness are not well known.

The factors identified in Westbrook's synthesis are presented in Table 14.2:

TABLE 14.2

Variables That Influence Effectiveness of Classroom Instruction

1. **Time on Task.** The more time, the more effective.
2. **Expectations of High Performance.** The higher the expectations for student performance, the higher that performance.
3. **Success Rate.** The higher the success rate (percentage of correct responses per unit time), the higher the performance. However, there also seems to be a balance between success rate and challenging work—if work becomes too challenging, the success rate will drop.
4. **Curriculum Alignment.** The closer the match between objectives, instructional activities, and evaluation, the higher the achievement.
5. **Staff Task Orientation.** Closely linked with time on task, efficient use of available class time for instruction. Ending class early was found to be negatively correlated with achievement.
6. **Behavior Management.** While fair, appropriate, and consistent application of discipline is found in the more effective schools, a high level of corporal or physical punishment is not found in such schools.
7. **School Environment.** The effective school typically has a pleasant atmosphere. Interestingly, the effective school is usually in better physical condition than the less effective school.
8. **Cooperation.** Effective schools have a high degree of cooperation among staff members.
9. **Instructional Leadership.** Principals (or other instructional leaders) with a strong viewpoint regarding instruction who are actively involved in teaching activities with teachers and students.
10. **Parent Participation.** Effective schools have more parental participation.
11. **Instruction Practice.** Effective schools have teachers who interact more often with students; monitor student progress more often; provide students with frequent and quality feedback; and use direct instructional techniques. It should be noted that while higher achievement is associated with the use of direct instruction, there is some evidence to indicate that creativity, problem-solving ability, positive attitudes, independence, and curiosity are not related to achievement.

From Considering the Research: What Makes an Effective School, *(pp. 15–25) by J. D. Westbrook, 1982, Austin, Texas: Southwest Educational Development Lab.*

As in all areas of applied psychology, answers to specific questions in the area of instructional effectiveness are not as clear as one would like. In reading the research literature in this area, one often finds comments like the statement of Anderson and Faust (1973):

> Unfortunately, research attempting to answer the practical questions — e.g., whether small classes [lead to superior instruction], whether the discovery method is better than the expository method, whether televised lectures are superior to live lectures, etc. — has been almost uniformly inconclusive. (p. 4).

Such statements are really a call for further applied research. The studies that seem to make a difference are those that systematically synthesize the results of many similar studies; long-term studies seem to yield more valid results than single-shot studies.

The foregoing look at research regarding effective teaching and schooling has only scratched the surface. Obviously, there have been thousands of studies that could have been mentioned; the review highlighted the most promising research relative to making a difference in the practice of education.

How Human Beings Learn

There is no simple answer to the question of how learning takes place. Obviously, it is an important question for educational psychologists, and there are many plausible and acceptable answers. First of all, the importance of theory in the discussion must be accepted. As opposed to the popular view that "theoretical" stuff is impractical and of little interest, theory is critical to an understanding of learning.

Just what is theory? A theory is simply an explanation of a number of facts. In one sense, a theory is the hatrack upon which to hang a set of observed phenomena. It helps one organize and understand experience. Generally a theory is thought to have been tested and supported, in contrast to a hypothesis, which is a plausible explanation, but untested. A good theory can explain, predict, and control behavior, with at least some probability of success.

There is no single agreed-upon learning theory. In fact, there are many such theories. Generally, these theories can be organized into two groups, behavioral and cognitive. Actually, there may be at least one other group of theories, those that have a physiological basis, but much of the current work in this area remains in the realm of basic research.

Behavioral theories are based on experiments in **classical** and **operant conditioning.** Classical conditioning is anchored in the work of Pavlov (1934) and operant conditioning in the work of Skinner (1953). Pavlov worked with behaviors that occur as reflex responses to stimuli. For example, people are startled in response to a loud noise, blink their eyes when air is suddenly blown in them, and salivate at the sight and smell of delicious food. Pavlov initially worked with the stimulus of food and the response of salivation in dogs. During conditioning he presented food with an additional stimulus that was unrelated to the food—in his early work he sounded a tone when the food was presented. After conditioning had occurred, the dogs would salivate to the tone alone. They had learned an association between a naturally occurring stimulus for salivation (the food) and the stimulus previously unrelated to the food and salivation (the tone). Although classical conditioning helps one understand how learning occurs in many important situations, it is not extremely applicable in classroom settings.

A second behavioral theory is based on Skinner's work in operant conditioning. A stimulus is presented after a particular behavior occurs. In the simplest case, if one wishes to increase the frequency of a particular behavior, the behavior is followed by a desirable consequence. For example, after studying hard for a test, a student is rewarded with a good grade. A relationship between a response (in this case studying) and a reinforcer (the good grade) is what is learned. Because many different things can serve as reinforcers to many different responses, this is a very flexible type of learning with clear applications in classroom settings.

The operant approach to learning has been applied in schools in behavior-modification programs. These programs may be classified into three groups: (1) programs designed to maintain order in the classroom, (2) programs designed to reward or punish students based on the amount or correctness of their classroom work, or (3) programs designed to modify teacher behavior to improve children's learning of academic material and skills (Ruggles & LeBlanc, 1982). Representative of the general approach is the application of a **token economy** in maintaining order in the classroom. The use of a token system to modify behavior was previously described in Chapter 8 on clinical psychology. In the research reported there, investigators used tokens to either reward (give tokens to) or fine (take tokens away from) a depressed, borderline psychotic individual who could in turn exchange the tokens for privileges. Token economy systems used in classrooms operate on similar principles—tokens are given when behavior is desirable and taken away when it is not. These tokens can then be exchanged for things the students find desirable, such as candy, toys, or the chance to participate in some enjoyable event.

In applying a token economy in the classroom, the student behaviors thought to be desirable and undesirable are first identified. Typically, disruptive behaviors like getting out of one's seat without permission, talking out of turn, rattling papers, laughing, or banging chairs are designated as undesirable. Behaviors like reading one's textbook, working on workbook pages, or raising one's hand are typically designated as desirable. Notice that designating these behaviors as desirable and undesirable involves value judgments about what activities are most educationally useful. Certainly, to some teachers, the quiet, docile classroom described above would not be seen as optimal for learning (see for example, Winett & Winkler, 1972).

Once the target behaviors that are to be increased and decreased in frequency have been identified and described to the class, tokens are given or taken away when students engage in the designated desirable or undesirable behaviors. They then get the opportunity to exchange their tokens for what is termed the backup reinforcers—those things they really want. It is necessary to establish *exchange rules* so that teachers and students know what a token will "buy." Research with token economies shows that they are powerful tools for controlling the behavior of children. Issues related to the educational value of such control are less clear-cut and are the subject of continuing debate (for a discussion of the issue of values in behavior modification, see Goldstein & Krasner, 1987).

In contrast to the operant approach, cognitive theorists believe that stimulus-response approaches do not account for complex situations such as learning concepts and ideas. The cognitive approaches emphasize the thinking process. **Gestalt theory,** one form of cognitive theory, maintains that what is happening in the whole cannot be deduced from the separate pieces (Wertheimer, 1944). Learning by insight (Kohler, 1959) is another form of cognitive theory, which views mental reorganization as the learning process, rather than establishing associations between stimuli and responses.

One application of the cognitive approach to learning has been in investigations into the ways human beings solve problems. Imagine that you are playing tick-tack-toe and it is your move. The game may be thought of as a problem that you need to solve, and you consider every possible move you might make, your opponent's possible responses, your next possible moves, and so forth. You are exploring what cognitive psychologists have called your **problem space** — the range of possible solutions for a particular problem. Because this problem is relatively simple, you can consider every possible solution — that is, every move you might make. In most situations, though, the problem space is not so well defined and a large part of solving the problem is to search for the various solutions. Cognitive psychologists have identified two basic methods that may be used to search the problem space — **algorithms** and **heuristics.** An algorithm is a precise set of steps that may be followed to allow a complete search (if necessary) of the problem space. When you apply a method to review all the possible moves you might make in playing tick-tack-toe, you are using an algorithm. In contrast, when the problem space is very large or not well defined, it may be very impractical to search for each solution. For example, it would be very difficult to consider every possible reason why your car won't start. Instead, you use heuristics to solve the problem. A heuristic is a rule of thumb that guides your search through the problem space. Heuristics give you a set of general principles that allow you to solve a problem more rapidly and easily. In the example of starting your car, if the engine will not even turn over, you can use a heuristic that says, "Check the electrical system connections, especially around the battery," and save yourself a great deal of potentially wasted effort.

Psychologists using a cognitive approach to learning have tried to identify how algorithms and heuristics are used by individuals as they attempt to solve complex problems. For example, what cognitive strategies are used by students who are successful in solving physics problems? By understanding the approaches used by individuals who are successful problem solvers, psychologists hope to teach these strategies to others and help them to improve their performance.

"So", you ask, "which approach to learning is right?" Neither and both! The behaviorist believes the cognitive theorist to be enamored of psychological constructs such as "thinking," "insight," and "problem solving." The cognitive theorist, on the other hand, sees the behaviorist as being shallow and is upset by the behaviorist's lack of consideration of internal processes. These two, unfortunately, don't talk with each other very often. The fact is that both theoretical viewpoints have something to offer and that in some learning situations behavioral theories are most applicable, while other situations are best described by cognitive theories.

Careers in Educational Psychology

Students interested in careers in educational psychology should be aware of several facts. First, education. While exceptions exist, the typical educational psychologist has a doctoral degree (either an Ed.D. or Ph.D.). In university or college settings, the doctoral degree has become almost mandatory. The doctoral degree also seems to give industrial or governmental-agency educational psychologists more credibility. Regardless of the setting in which educational psychologists work, more opportunities seem to exist for those individuals who hold a doctoral degree.

Conclusion

This chapter has reviewed ways in which psychology is applied in educational settings. Two job specializations, school psychologist and educational psychologist, have been considered. Both fields offer interesting opportunities. School psychology is a fascinating field, combining psychology with education in a very practical way. The chapter surveyed historical influences on school psychology and examined the roles of school psychologists, a primary one being the assessment of pupils referred for a variety of academic, emotional, and behavioral reasons. An important secondary role is that of consultation—working with those who need diagnostic information and helping to develop remediation strategies. Sometimes these consultations are directly with parents, and sometimes with other professionals (teachers, administrators, nurses, counselors, and so on). Depending on the employment circumstances and personal preferences, individual or group counseling or therapy may also be involved in a school psychologist's duties.

The second field, applied educational psychology, aids the educational process by bringing knowledge from the discipline of psychology to bear on teaching and learning. Again, historical influences on educational psychology were summarized in order to provide a definition of the area. It was pointed out that educational psychologists can be found working in university classrooms or laboratories, training divisions of corporations, research and development laboratories (government and private), and for book and computer software publishers. Finally, the chapter reviewed research related to making teaching effective and learning efficient.

Glossary

academic learning time (ALT)   The amount of time spent in the classroom that is devoted to instructional activities.

algorithm   A systematic rule for solving problems that allows for a search of every possible solution.

classical conditioning   The repeated association of a neutral stimulus with a second stimulus that elicits some nonvoluntary response (for example, pain). After conditioning, the previously neutral stimulus will elicit the same response as the second response did originally.

education   A systematic effort designed to cause learning to take place.

Gestalt theory   An approach to psychology that emphasizes the importance of complete units or wholes. For example, the whole that emerges from the pieces of perception is greater than the sum of the parts.

heuristics   A rule-of-thumb that allows for an efficient search for the solution to a problem.

learning   The act of changing one's behavior through experience.

operant conditioning   The presentation of a stimulus after a certain response. In the case of reinforcement, a stimulus that increases the probability that the response will reoccur is administered. In the case of punishment, a stimulus that decreases the probability of the response is presented.

problem space   The range of possible solutions to a problem.

token economy   A controlled environment where individuals are given tokens (like poker chips) in exchange for desirable behaviors. Tokens may also be taken away as fines for undesirable behaviors. The tokens may then be exchanged for reinforcers that are valued by participating individuals.

15 / Applied Sport Psychology

Mark Anshel
University of Wollongong
Wollongong, New South Wales, Australia

Debi Thomas, U.S. figure skating champion, was leading her opponents going into the finals of the 1988 Winter Olympic figure skating competition in Calgary, Alberta, Canada. According to media reports, she was expected to win a gold medal. So was Dan Jansen, a world class speed-skating champion, who learned that his sister had died of leukemia the day of his first race. Sadly, Debi slipped (but still received a bronze medal) and Dan fell so badly that he was eliminated from competition. Both of these highly skilled or **elite athletes** had competed hundreds of times and had an extensive history of success. Yet this was not the case in the 1988 Winter Olympic Games. Why had they not performed according to their own and the world's high expectations? Certainly both athletes were highly motivated and comfortable with the pressures of competitive sport. Although no one knows for sure, the difficulties in each athlete's performance might be explained by psychological factors.

It is possible that the personal tragedy in Dan's life affected his mental state, which in turn reduced his concentration and proper arousal level. Furthermore, his attentional focus to the task at hand may have been misdirected. This is a common malady for athletes whose thoughts distract and interfere with the execution of complex motor skills. Debi may have suffered from a condition called "warm-up decrement." In this phenomenon, skilled athletes tend to perform less well after a rest as compared to their prerest level. Debi was the last competitor in the ladies' event and, as such, waited almost an hour between warming up and performing. Then, again, maybe she was just unlucky or more nervous than usual.

Of course without information from the two athletes, these explanations are conjecture; however, they are compatible with the findings of research conducted with other sport performers. Perhaps Debi's and Dan's performances would have been improved if their coaches had been able to anticipate certain psychological problems and suggest that the competitors use mental strategies to help prevent or overcome their difficulties.

These examples serve to illustrate just a small part of an emerging and exciting discipline called sport psychology. This chapter will discuss (1) the areas in which sport psychology is studied; (2) how the results of research in this area apply to coaching and performing sports skills, especially in competitive situations; and (3) the role of sport psychologists in studying sport behavior and the competitive environment and in applying this information in actual sport settings.

What Is Sport Psychology?

Although sport psychology was studied and practiced in the United States — albeit rarely — as early as 1925, it is only in recent years that the field has received national recognition. In 1977, the U.S. Olympic Committee (USOC) appointed Jerry R. May, Ph.D., a clinical psychologist from the University of Nevada at Reno, as its first part-time sport psychologist. In 1983, the USOC convened a panel of experts to establish guidelines for the competent practice of sport psychology. The first full-time resident sport psychologist, Shane Murphy, Ph.D., also trained in clinical psychology, was hired in 1986 to work with athletes and coaches at the U.S. Olympic Training Center in Colorado Springs. In recognition of the scholarly research in this field, both the American Psychological Association and the Americal College of Sports Medicine have integrated sport psychology into their organizations since 1982. It is clear that the importance of psychological factors in sport is becoming more and more recognized.

Sport psychology is a science that deals with the psychological and emotional aspects of physical performance. In the context of competitive sport, it is the ability to describe, explain, and predict behavior in the environment of competitive athletics. This is done by applying principles of psychology in a sport setting.

For example, in describing factors that affect group cohesion—the "sticking together" of group members—research has shown that members of sport teams that tend to win are more friendly toward each other than are players on teams that consistently lose. However, it is important to note that this finding is based on correlational relationships between player attitudes toward teammates and the team's record. It does not necessarily mean that losing actually causes teammates to dislike each other, nor that winning has the opposite effect—at least the available research does not suggest this. Examples of explaining sport behavior were given earlier in the cases of the two Olympic athletes. Predicting sport behavior is a more difficult task given the variety of interacting factors in the sport environment and the uniqueness of each athlete's personality. It may be achieved by determining which athletes will exhibit heightened anxiety in competition. Perhaps no single psychological factor contributes more to inhibiting quality sport performance than athlete anxiety, an issue that will be discussed later in this chapter.

Sport Psychology and Athletic Performance

Three principal factors studied in sport psychology contribute to athletic performance: athlete, coach (team leader), and environment in which these individuals—and others—interact (see Figure 15.1).

The athlete's performance is, of course, the primary concern in sport psychology. By studying the attitudes, feelings, and other mental processes of skilled competitors, one can begin to identify their psychological characteristics and the strategies they use before, during, and after an event. Researchers can also better understand the factors that separate successful athletes from their less successful counterparts. Why, for instance, does one performer consistently win while another one frequently loses, given virtually equal ability? What are the unique psychological needs of skilled players? What should coaches do to meet these needs? Why do athletes, especially at younger ages, drop out of sport? What can sport leaders—coaches and parents—do to promote participation in sport and make the competitive experience more satisfying for important populations such as children, minorities, females, older adults, and the economically disadvantaged?

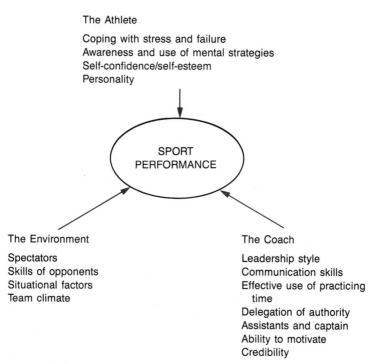

The Athlete

Coping with stress and failure
Awareness and use of mental strategies
Self-confidence/self-esteem
Personality

SPORT
PERFORMANCE

The Environment

Spectators
Skills of opponents
Situational factors
Team climate

The Coach

Leadership style
Communication skills
Effective use of practicing
    time
Delegation of authority
Assistants and captain
Ability to motivate
Credibility

FIGURE 15.1 Examples of the three interacting factors that contribute to the quality of sport performance.

Coaching behaviors are studied extensively in sport psychology. Clearly, they have the most significant impact on the athlete's performance. A participant's success is often tied to a coach's ability to teach sport skills and strategies. Good coaches are good teachers. But successful coaches are also able to promote an athlete's desire to excel over an extended time period. This skill is developing the individual's intrinsic motivation. Intrinsic motivation refers to the internal satisfaction individuals feel when they succeed. As the novelist Henry Miller wrote, "The real leader has no need to lead—he is content to point the way" (*The Wisdom of the Heart,* 1941). Because coaches tend to learn their trade by observing the habits and techniques of other coaches, perhaps the sport psychologist has no greater challenge than to convince these sport leaders that psychology offers an untapped source of knowledge that can contribute to their success. Unfortunately, there are numerous myths associated with coaching practices and habits. It is a sport psychologist's job to reduce or eliminate as many of these false beliefs about coaching as possible. Several of these myths will be discussed later in the section on research and application.

The sport environment forms the final component of the sport psychology triad. Competition does not occur in a vacumn. The performer is exposed to a multitude of factors that contribute, directly and indirectly, to the final outcome. One factor that appears to markedly affect performance is the presence of spectators. Researchers have studied the effect of different types, sizes, and

How does the roar of the crowd affect athletes? What happens when the contest takes place before empty seats? Sport psychology investigates the effects of environment on performance.

behaviors of audiences on performance. Characteristics of the performer that may further influence this audience effect have also received attention. For example, a player who has not mastered a complex sport skill will tend to feel more anxious and less confident in the presence of spectators than a highly skilled competitor will. Furthermore, the performance of players might be adversely affected if they perceived some members of the audience as threatening. For example, the presence of college recruiters or professional scouts might cause performers to be overly anxious and not perform their best. Other environmental issues in sport psychology include the following questions. Does cheering or booing by the crowd really influence performance for all sports and situations? Is a gymnast, who will compete when the arena is quiet, correctly preparing for the meet by practicing in a noisy environment? Is an athlete capable of listening to and remembering information when it is presented by the coach in an angry manner? Should skill instruction be attempted during the contest in contrast to learning and mastering the skill during practice? In an area of recent interest called social loafing, scientists have found that athletes who perform skills simultaneously as a team — for example, in football blocking, rope pulling, or rowing — tend to exert less strength and effort than if they performed the skill individually. It appears that performers become somewhat dependent on others to reach the goal and, perhaps, take less responsibility for the outcome when the same task is performed by others at the same time. How can the effects of social loafing be counteracted?

Historical Context

A brief look at the background of sport psychology will also help you understand what it is today. Surprisingly, sport psychology began as early as 1897 when Norman Triplett, a psychologist at Indiana University, published what can be identified as the first sport psychology experiment in the *American Journal of Psychology*. He investigated a phenomenon now called **social facilitation** — in this case referring to the effect of observers on sport skill performance. Triplett noticed that cyclists pedaled faster when competing against other cyclists, and speed increased on a tandem bicycle, when cyclists acted in conjunction with a teammate as opposed to bicycling alone. E. W. Scripture, a psychologist at Yale University, concluded in *Popular Science Monthly* (1899) that participating in sport could lead to desirable personality traits. The contemporary view (albeit one not yet proven in research) that participating in athletic competition builds character is rooted in Scripture's conclusion.

Like most academic disciplines, sport psychology has a pioneer. Dr. Coleman Roberts Griffith, referred to as "the father of sport psychology in America," is acknowledged to have been the first person to carry out systematic and frequent sport psychology experimentation over a number of years (Wiggins, 1984). In 1925 at the University of Illinois, he developed the first sport psychology laboratory, in which he measured muscular coordination, muscular tension, and relaxation, mental alertness, reaction time to light, sound, and pressure, and learning ability. Based on his interview with football's Red Grange, it appears that Griffith was the first to acknowledge that better athletes perform sports skills automatically. That is, after making a decision for action, they respond in the virtual absence of conscious thought. This phenomenon is recognized today. As both media reporters and researchers have indicated, when an elite athlete is asked to explain how he or she "does it," the likely response is, "I don't know, I just do it."

Griffith taught the first sport psychology college course at Illinois in 1923 and wrote the first sport psychology texts in 1926 (*Psychology of Coaching*) and 1928 (*Psychology of Athletics*). In addition, working in a setting that today's sport psychologists would envy, Griffith was hired by the Chicago Cubs baseball club to be a consulting sport psychologist for the 1938 season. He administered various motor and psychological inventories to determine each player's current psychological status, ability, and potential as competitive athlete from spring training to the season's end.

The 1960s was an enigmatic period for the field. On the plus side, textbooks, research, and college courses in sport psychology began to proliferate. Books such as *Problem Athletes and How to Handle Them* (1966) by clinical psychologists Bruce Ogilvie and Thomas Tutko, *Movement Behavior and Motor Learning*

(1966) by Bryant Cratty, and Joseph Oxendine's *Psychology and Motor Behavior* (1967) generated considerable interest in the psychological aspects of sport performance. More and more research in this area was also conducted and published, most notably in the *Research Quarterly* (called *Research Quarterly for Exercise and Sport* since 1981). The 1960s also saw the establishment of professional organizations in sport psychology. Annual meetings of the North American Society for the Psychology of Sport and Physical Activity (NASPSPA), its Canadian counterpart, the Canadian Society for Psychomotor Learning and Sport Psychology (CSPLSP), and the International Society for Sport Psychology (ISSP) all began in the 1960s. Their collective purpose was to enhance professional standards and expand the directions of sport psychology through research, teaching, and consultation to athletes, coaches, and sport organizations. On the minus side, during the 1960s sport psychology took a few bumps and bruises in nonacademic settings. This was mostly due to individuals who called themselves "sport psychologists" and who promised more than they could deliver. More will be said about this in the next section.

More recently (1986) the Association for the Advancement of Applied Sport Psychology (AAASP), including perhaps the largest groups of students, faculty, and clinicians in psychology and sport education, was formed to bridge the gap between research and practice. The AAASP includes three areas of interest: health psychology, intervention/performance enhancement, and social psychology. Together with the sport psychology divisions in the American College of Sports Medicine, and the American Psychological Association, the AAASP has had a significant impact on the field. All of these organizations have annual conferences in which to exchange ideas and expose new areas of research and practice, and they all make memberships available to students (undergraduate and graduate), university faculty, and other interested parties. Becoming a member is the best way to be in touch with new developments in the field and to become aware of the locations and dates of annual conferences.

In the 1970s and 1980s sport psychology has become well established. More journals, professional organizations, and academic programs have come into existence, and individuals working in the field are increasingly able to make contributions in applied settings.

What Do Sport Psychologists Do?

A sport psychologist is someone who practices the discipline of sport psychology. Simple enough? Not quite, because "sport psychology" means different things to different people. Some persons who call themselves sport psychologists may be viewed by others as lacking expertise or even as misrepresenting the profession. According to Dr. Bruce Ogilvie, a trained clinical psychologist and pioneer of applied sport psychology, "The problem has been that we've had too many charlatans, too many cons, and too many people promising too many things." Examples of unprofessional conduct abound. A psychiatrist in California who worked with the San Diego Chargers football team was found guilty of distributing illegal drugs to the players. Somewhat less serious but still harmful to the profession of sport psychology was his claim, quite false it turned out, that the personality characteristics of players determine the positions for which they are best suited. According to this person, the personality of quarterbacks is different from that of linemen, linebackers different from halfbacks, and so on. His research was faulty, relying on opinion rather than on valid scientific analyses. In this same direction, a widely distributed and recognized personality instrument called the Athletic Motivation Inventory (AMI) was constructed in the 1960s to, according to its authors, detect the presence or absence of sport-related personality characteristics and predict athletic success. One must wonder about the number of athletes whose careers were wiped out by "poor" scores on this inventory. Subsequent data in sport personality research have indicated that personality scores are very poor predictors of a player's skills, extent or frequency of success, preferred sport in which to engage, or the type of position on a team. The rate of successfully predicting sport behavior is a mere 10% (Fisher, 1977).

Another issue that stunted the growth of sport psychology concerned the claims of a few psychologists and other entrepreneurs that they could help players reach their performance potential through some device or mental technique. For instance, a story reported in the national print media was an optometrist's claim that an athlete's reaction time—the period between observing a stimulus and initiating a response to it—could be hastened if the person engaged in a series of reaction-time tasks in the doctor's laboratory. This claim was never tested and validated in a research experiment, but a hockey team in the National Hockey League paid the optometrist considerable money to help its players. Although the team's goalie claimed the "training" helped him to some degree, researchers have not found that laboratory reaction-time tasks benefit performance in actual competitive situations.

Job Activities

A person can be safely called a doctor or lawyer after earning an academic degree, and passing a certification exam; identifying a sport psychologist is less certain. One way to ensure the proper use of techniques and reduce fraud in the profession is to monitor self-claims of expertise through some type of regulation or certification. Clinical sport psychologist Robert Nideffer, Ph.D., (1981) suggests that "it is important to define the roles a sport psychologist fills, and to identify the educational experiences that should be prerequisites" (p. iii). This was the mission of a meeting of the United States Olympic Committee (USOC) held in August, 1982. Among the meeting's objectives was to define the scope of sport psychology and to state the minimum credentials that a sport psychologist should have. The committee identified three broad activities engaged in by, and, therefore, three "missions" or different roles of, sport psychologists: clinical, educational, and research.

Clinical Sport Psychologists. The activities and education of individuals wishing to become clinically oriented sport psychologists will differ depending on the way the individual wants to practice the profession. Some may choose to become university educators who teach sport psychology classes and/or conduct sport psychology research. Others may function strictly as clinicians in nonacademic settings where they counsel athletes, coaches, and sports teams. If the latter type of career is preferred, then it makes sense to be trained as a clinical psychologist in a reputable university psychology program while completing at least one or two elective courses in sport psychology. Ideally, the university that is chosen should have a sport psychology program; many do not. However, if an individual would like to teach and/or conduct research in sport psychology and work part-time as a sport psychology consultant to some team or program, completing a Ph.D. program with an emphasis in sport psychology in a physical education department is recommended. Departments of psychology do not tend to offer sport psychology programs, nor do their graduate students usually complete their thesis or dissertations in this area. Physical education departments are more likely to offer the specific courses, full programs, trained faculty, and opportunities for research (particularly for thesis and dissertation studies) in sport psychology.

According to the standards established by the USOC, individuals wishing to become sport psychologists should meet the standards required for full membership in the American Psychological or Psychiatric Associations (this means they would hold the Ph.D. or M.D. degree) and demonstrate competence in applying psychological principles to sports as athletes, coaches, or practitioners.

Educational Sport Psychologists. University physical education departments employ educational sport psychologists, usually to teach courses in sport psychology. However, the USOC has recommended that the educational sport psychologist have a doctorate in psychology or psychiatry, or in a related field with background in psychology. Also required by the USOC is at least three years of demonstrated postdoctoral experience as an athlete or coach, or practitioner in the application of psychological principles to sports, as well as reference letters from institutions or organizations about the applicant's teaching skills. In reality, educational sport psychologists are more likely to be familiar with the professional literature because they teach from it and contribute their own research to it. In theory, however, clinical sport psychologists should also be familiar with the research journals because they also need to understand the psychological factors that affect performance. In the 1970s and early 1980s, sport psychologists were typically trained in the educational and research areas with less familiarity in the clinical area. Today all graduate students with a sport psychology emphasis are required to have taken at least one graduate course in clinical or counseling psychology.

Research Sport Psychologists. Of course, clinical and educational sport psychologists have the opportunity to perform research and sometimes to publish or report their findings at conferences. But in defining a separate category of research sport psychologist, the USOC is attempting to regulate the quality of research. The committee recommends that researchers possess a doctorate in psychology or psychiatry or in a related field with a background in psychology that would meet the standards required for full membership in APA. Also required is evidence of scholarly research contributions to the field of sport psychology and reference letters from recognized institutions/organizations that comment on the quality of research conducted by the applicant.

It is important to point out that a lack of credentials recommended by the USOC does not mean a person is unable to practice sport psychology in whatever way he or she chooses. For example, as reported at recent meetings, the two main sport psychology professional organizations, AAASP and NASPSPA, most of their members have their primary training in departments of physical education rather than in psychology and therefore are not licensed psychologists. In addition, a perusal of journals in sport psychology and related textbooks clearly indicates that most authors of the material are employed in physical education rather than in psychology. No policy or law yet exists that mandates a specific set of qualifications for licensing or certification as a sport psychologist. The USOC has simply established guidelines or recommended credentialing standards for practicing sport psychology.

So, to summarize, who are, and what are the roles of, sport psychologists? Unlike most other practioners of subdisciplines of psychology who have matriculated in standardized academic programs that usually (though not always) ensure certification, sport psychologists have no clear-cut answers to these questions. Members of the sport psychology profession, in and out of academic settings, are concerned about the lack of quality control and the potential for abuse and poor, even fraudulent, service in practicing sport psychology. Still, sport psychologists, through their research, their development of professional organizations, academic programs, and journals, and their direct work with coaches and athletes—including those at the Olympic and professional levels—have gained increasing acceptance in recent years.

Work Settings

The preceding discussion has focused on the different jobs of sport psychologists. But where do they work? First, contrary to the dreams and fantasies of many interested students, sport psychologists are almost never hired as full-time consultants to sports teams. This is for several reasons. First, coaches and, to a lesser extent, athletes, often do not believe in the value of sport psychology consulting. The feeling is, "I made it this far without it, why start now?" or "I don't want anyone 'playing' with my head." Some coaches tend to be ill at ease with another person—a "noncoach"—interacting directly with "their" athletes. Hence when sport psychologists are team consultants, they are asked to offer specific services to specific athletes, not to have full-time coaching responsibilities and interact with every team member. Because there are relatively few individuals who desire input from sport psychologists, their role, as it is usually defined on sports teams, is simply not a full-time job.

Second, coaches and athletes are talented in what they do and work very hard to perfect their skills. Therefore it is equally important that they, not some other individual, take full responsibility for their success. A successful sport psychologist keeps a low profile on a team, attending practices, making and recording observations of behaviors, meeting privately with individual players, and occasionally conducting team sessions. But sport psychologists always do two things: they keep all information obtained from players strictly confidential, and they never credit themselves for successful sport performance but instead congratulate the players and coaches. The sport psychologist who speaks publicly of his or her role on a given team, especially with reference to specific players, or takes even partial credit for the success of a team or athlete, is engaging in unethical practice. Furthermore, the career of such a person with the team will typically be shortened. Finally, most sports teams simply cannot afford, or choose not to expend funds for, a full-time team psychologist.

So where *do* sport psychologists work? Typically sport psychologists are employed as full-time or adjunct university or college faculty and/or as practicing clinical/counseling psychologists. Very few clinicians can earn an adequate income working only with athletes, so most of their clientele is from the general public—nonathletes. But a number of university faculty, each of whom has established a reputation through publishing and presenting papers at conferences, combine teaching, research, counseling, and consulting careers. Examples include working with a team in their university's athletic department (often as a volunteer rather than as a paid consultant); as a paid part-time consultant for a team at another university or with one of the U.S. Olympic teams (there is only one full-time position at the U.S. Olympic Training Center); or as an advisor to a youth sports program helping coaches to develop communication and teaching skills. Other sport psychologists seek clients by advertising in the print media as clinical psychologists with a specialization in sport psychology and sport performance enhancement. Still others might originate and direct youth summer sports camps that are based on sport skill development while not stressing competition.

The best way for a student who is contemplating a career in sport psychology to begin is to attend annual professional conferences where hundreds of practicing sport psychologists gather or to correspond directly with university faculty who teach in this area. It is likely that this dynamic field will offer more, not fewer, opportunities for employment on university faculties and as consultants in future years.

Research and Applications

Just as sport psychologists have different roles and job descriptions, the field of sport psychology includes several components, each within a different discipline of psychology. As illustrated in Figure 15.2, these areas include educational psychology, social psychology, developmental psychology, experimental psychology, health/exercise psychology, psychophysiology, and personality psychology. Examples of research from each of these areas will be presented.

SPORT
PSYCHOLOGY

Educational
Psychology

Experimental
Psychology

Social
Psychology

Clinical
Psychology

Sport
and
Physical
Activity

Developmental
Psychology

Health/Exercise
Psychology

Psychophysiology

Personality
Psychology

FIGURE 15.2 Components of the discipline of applied sport psychology.

Educational Psychology

Good coaching is good teaching. Performance improvement can occur only when sport skills are properly taught and mastered by the competitor. Principles of psychology are inherent in the areas of skill instruction, acquisition, and retention. Ironically, the ability to teach sport skills is the one area in which most coaches have received the least training and tend to exhibit minimal expertise. Yet highly successful coaches have superb teaching skills, essential if athletes are to absorb the coach's expert advice and transfer it to the competitive arena.

Sport psychology consultants must be able to detect poor communication and instructional skills and assist coaches in changing at least some of their teaching habits. To do this, they should understand the psychological processes that underlie learning, remembering, and performing sports skills. In this way, they can better understand the external factors that affect an athlete's performance and, perhaps, help coaches improve their instructional and communication techniques.

A few examples of the questions consultants address include: Is the coach presenting too much information to the players and/or at too rapid a pace for mastery? Is the coach making the wrong assumptions about what the athlete knows or is able to do before presenting new material or teaching a new skill? Is informative feedback being offered and, if so, is it communicated so that the athlete can use it? Or, is the feedback too general and abstract? Is the sequence of a skill being presented in the proper order? Can the competitor master earlier

Sport psychology consultants can demonstrate to coaches the psychological processes that figure in learning and practicing athletic skills. Perhaps even more important, consultants can help coaches develop effective communication techniques.

subskills prior to attaining subsequent skill mastery? A few suggestions that researchers have made to instructors of sports skills are presented in Table 15.1.

One popular area of applied research in educational sport psychology has been the effect of mental practice on learning and performing sport skills. Mental practice involves going over a particular sport activity mentally rather than physically. Mental practice is important to athletes for getting "psyched up" before a contest, reducing stress, coping with anxiety, and rehabilitation from injuries when physical practice is not feasible. Investigators—and coaches—have asked whether a given amount of mental practice prior to performing a motor skill will enhance one's subsequent performance. According to Feltz and Landers (1983), there have been over 100 research studies on this topic since the 1930s and many more since the publication of their review in 1983.

Most of these studies have compared the performance of subjects who had previous mental practice with a no-practice (control) group, a physical practice group, and a group that received both physical and mental practice. In typical experiments, subjects were pretested on some task of interest. Then, after using either physical or mental practice strategy, subjects except the controls practiced the skill daily. After this practice period, the subjects' skills were examined under standard conditions that differed from the practice situation but were identical to the pretest. Would their performance scores be affected by the practice condition they experienced? If the mental-practice group's scores were superior to the no-practice group, then it could be said that mental practice was effective in improving performance. This was precisely the finding in many of the studies

TABLE 15.1

Suggestions For Instructors of Sport Skills

1. *Talk less, show more.* Coaches tend to be too verbal when teaching a skill. Learners do not process verbal information as effectively as visual information. It has been found that within a minute of talking, no one is listening.
2. *State the goal of the instructional session.* Learners should be told what they are expected to do after instruction.
3. *Use first names.* This tends to motivate and raise the alertness of learners. Instruction becomes more meaningful, and the coach "knows my name."
4. *Slow down.* New information is processed more slowly than familiar, previously learned input.
5. *Attach new to old.* Athletes should be reminded of how the new skill or strategy is related to something they already know. This greatly improves retention.
6. *Simulate game conditions in practice.* Practice sessions should include the rehearsal of skills and techniques that competitors will experience in the actual event. Practicing a skill in an unrealistic environment will decrease the probability that it will be replicated in the contest.

reviewed by Feltz and Landers, although physical practice was usually found to be superior to mental practice. The combination of physical and mental practice usually elicited the best performance of any group.

To determine the extent to which mental practice influences motor performance and the underlying reasons for this effect, Feltz and Landers (1983) used a statistical technique called meta-analysis that analyzes the combined effect of many different studies. In summary, they found that (1) mental practice is more beneficial to tasks with a relatively higher cognitive component — extensive planning, internal rehearsing, or decision making, for example — as opposed to highly motoric tasks with which physical responses are more "automatic" or performed in rapid sequence: (2) mental practice affects performance for both novices (in the early learning stages) and skilled performers (at later stages), but more experienced performers appeared to benefit to a greater degree than did beginners; (3) the effects of mental practice tend to be greater when the posttest is given later rather than immediately after the mental-practice session. The authors surmise that this posttest delay "may give subjects a greater opportunity to mentally practice and perhaps perfect additional cognitive strategies that are advantageous in preparing for action on motor/strength tasks" (p. 50).

Educational sport psychology focuses on the interaction between external factors that affect learning and performing motor skills. Much research is still needed to understand this relationship more clearly, particularly in field settings where these processes are being experienced.

Social Psychology

Whereas educational sport psychology is often directed to understanding internal factors that affect performance, the social psychology of sport is focused almost strictly on the environmental factors that influence athletic performance. Examples of areas of scientific inquiry that are also of interest to coaches and

Feltz and Landers found that, in preparing to perform, mental practice was superior to no practice, but that a combination of physical and mental practice got the best results.

athletes include (1) the role of group dynamics and team cohesion in group and individual performance; (2) identification and effectiveness of various leadership styles in coaching and the conditions under which each style is most appropriate; (3) techniques to improve team climate and facilitate player leadership and interaction among group members; (4) effects of different types and sizes of audiences on player performance; and (5) a study of aggression in sport.

A topic that is of great concern to sport psychologists, coaches, and athletes is the effects of coaching behavior—often referred to in the literature as leadership style—on an athlete's feelings, attitudes, and performance. There exists marked disagreement in this area between the suggestions of sport psychologists and the actual practices of coaches. Whereas coaches tend to be relatively autocratic, that is, to be the primary decision makers and expect athletes to respond to their commands without question, sport psychologists recommend a more sensitive, relationship-oriented approach that is somewhat more humanistic in relating to the participants. What does the research indicate? Interestingly, the data support both points of view. Chelladurai and Carron (1983) report that athletes with increasing experience show a correspondingly increased preference for autocratic coaching behavior. However, child athletes and competitors with relatively low skills prefer a more humanistic, relationship-oriented coaching style.

Developmental Sport Psychology

What are the effects of early sport experiences on sport performance later in life? Should parents be concerned with exposing their children to competitive sport so that they develop strong character, become self-sufficient and responsible, stay physically active, and develop healthy attitudes about physical activity? Are youth sport leagues beneficial to child athletes? If so, why do so many kids — up to 80% in some studies — drop out of sport? The special needs of the child athlete, an area referred to as youth sports in the sport literature, has become an extensive field of research and forms the primary area of inquiry in developmental sport psychology. The other increasingly popular subject for contem-

Will sports be a happy and fulfilling strand in this Little Leaguer's life, or will she drop out? Increasingly, sport psychologists are investigating children's responses to their athletic experiences, especially in the competitive category.

porary research is a better understanding of the characteristics and needs of female athletes, especially in comparison to their male counterparts, across all age groups.

Child Athletes.   The research literature is filled with testimony that the youth sport leagues are not doing the job for which they were intended. For example in a study of 822 Canadian children, ages 7 to 14 years, Wankel and Kreisel (1985) found that "getting rewards" and "pleasing others" ranked very low in importance as reasons for participating in sport. "Having fun," "improvement of skills," and "personal accomplishment" were rated very high. The primary reason that children drop out of sport, according to research surveys, is because "it isn't fun" (Gould, 1984). Why isn't it fun? Gould found it was because of the overemphasis on winning. Lack of success, not playing, and "other interest" were also rated highly as reasons for leaving.

Stress in competitive sport is difficult even for adults. For child athletes, it can be unbearable. Sport psychologists Tara Scanlon and Michael Passer (1978) have concluded, based on their extensive research in this area, that competitive stress is based on the child's perceptions of inadequacy in meeting performance demands successfully and their perceptions of the consequences of failure. If children predict that not scoring a goal will result in negative consequences, stress is heightened. But if children feel that doing their best, regardless of the consequences, is all that is needed to be successful or gain the approval of others, the perception of threat is reduced or removed. Coaches and parents of children in youth sports should be primarily concerned with skill instruction and performance improvement. Their reactions to the young participants should be similar whether a team wins or loses—as long as children made their best effort.

In 1979, the Youth Sports Task Force from the National Association for Sport and Physical Education prepared a set of guidelines that they called "The Bill of Rights for Young Athletes" (edited by Drs. Rainer Martens and Vern Seefeldt and available from AAHPERD Publications, 1900 Association Drive, Reston, VA 22091). Its purpose was to help parents, coaches, and administrators of youth sport leagues provide a quality, fulfilling program for their young participants. The 10-item "Bill of Rights" is presented in Table 15.2.

TABLE 15.2

The Bill of Rights for Young Athletes

1. Right to participate in sports
2. Right to participate at a level commensurate with each child's maturity and ability.
3. Right to have qualified adult leadership
4. Right to play as a child and not as an adult
5. Right of children to share in the leadership and decision making of the sport participation
6. Right to participate in safe and healthy environments
7. Right to proper preparation for participation in sports
8. Right to an equal opportunity to strive for success
9. Right to be treated with dignity
10. Right to have fun in sports

Female Athletes.   Researchers have traditionally focused relatively little attention on the unique needs and psychological characteristics of female sport competitors. Relevant research questions in this area include (a) a better understanding
of the ways in which female athletes are socialized into sport in contrast to male
athletes; (b) how the female competitor is psychologically affected by her sport
experience; (c) the effects of using mental techniques on skill acquisition, undesirable pregame emotions such as anxiety and arousal, and sport performance;
(d) sex differences in personality traits of athletes and nonathletes; and (e) a
comparison of the manner in which male and female athletes explain the causes
of their performance.

Only recently has research on female athletes gained wider recognition in
the literature. Why only recently? Pemberton and Petlichkoff (1988) argue that
"many sport psychologists have assumed that if an intervention strategy works
for the elite male athlete, then the intervention strategy should be applied to
the elite female athlete in the same way, with the results assumed to be similar.
Instead of making these assumptions, sport psychologists should include gender
as a variable when developing a research line" (p. 58).

Experimental Sport Psychology

Research sport psychologists are primarily concerned with the effects of certain
treatments, environmental conditions, or cognitive (internal) factors that influence
athletic performance. Perhaps the most encompassing topic of investigation in
recent years in this area has been that of the many factors associated with motivation.

Sport psychologist Richard Alderman (1974) defines motivation as "the tendency for . . . behavior to be controlled by its connections to consequences, and
the tendency of this behavior to persist until a goal is achieved" (p. 186). Taking
Alderman's definition literally means that coaches must be aware of what provides an incentive for the athlete—and what does not. Furthermore, coaches
must ask if athletes perceive a relationship between athletic performance and
desirable (or undesirable) consequences. It is also important to know if the coach's
use of a motivational technique will foster persistence of the performer's behavior "until a goal is achieved" or if it will have only a short-term effect. Could
the coach's strategy actually heighten frustration, thereby reducing the competitor's efforts? Often it does.

Coaching and Motivation.   Certainly motivating athletes is one of the most
challenging tasks for a coach. No matter how talented performers may be, unless they desire to make the necessary effort to perform at an optimum level,
it is unlikely that they will succeed consistently. Unfortunately, less sophisticated
coaches attempt to motivate their players in a negative manner. Threats, intimi-
dation, criticism, sarcasm, guilt, and sometimes even physical abuse have been
used to increase or prolong the athlete's incentive to compete. Ironically, although
these techniques often—though not always—increase a performer's arousal and

effort in the short term, rarely do these strategies have long-term benefits. Sport psychologists contend that a coach's frequent use of words and actions perceived by athletes as having negative consequences are a much less effective motivating strategy than is the expectation of positive consequences for desirable athlete behaviors (Martin & Hrycaiko, 1983). For example, it is more effective to stress the benefits of getting and staying in top physical condition rather than to use physical exercise as punishment. In the latter scenario, athletes (like students in physical education classes) associate physical activity with unpleasant feelings and situations they would like to avoid ("You're five minutes late to practice/class; take two laps around the field").

Martin and Hrycaiko (p. 16) suggest that coaches can alert themselves to the benefits of positive coaching by considering the following questions:

1. Have I encouraged my athletes to set individual goals?
2. Do I praise my athletes in every practice for progress shown?
3. Do I regularly assess the correct components of the skills of individual athletes and do I provide them with formal evaluations?
4. Do I dispense a higher ratio of reward and praise than reprimands to my athletes at practices and during games?
5. Do I provide intermittent rewards for effective and correct execution during competitions, even though my athlete(s) may be losing?

Attributions and Motivation.   An area of research that has received considerable attention in the sport science literature—an area that is also familiar to social and experimental psychologists—is attribution theory. A cognitive approach to motivation, the theory is based on the assumption that people attempt to explain, understand, and predict the causes of their behavior. Attribution theory provides the basis for considering motivation in another setting, school achievement, that was discussed earlier in the book in Chapter 11 on applied social psychology. According to the theory's originator, Fritz Heider (1958), individuals perceive four major causes of success or failure: their ability, their effort, the level of task difficulty, and luck. A detailed explanation of the model goes beyond the scope of this section. However, the theory has gained widespread support in sport psychology to help explain the effect of making certain attributions (about the causes of performance) on an individual's motivation to persist at a task, especially if the attributions are not accurate.

For instance, Roberts (1984) concluded that the primary reason that children drop out of sport, particularly during the preadolescent years, is that they begin to define "poor performance" as failure—a 9-year-old is happy just to finish a race, whereas a 12-year-old receives messages that he or she failed by not winning the race. Morever, beginning at about age 11 or 12, participants often attribute their "failure" to a lack of ability. At this time, social approval from others also becomes more important. Thus the lack of approval after "losing" reinforces a child's perception of low ability. Good-bye sport, hello computer games and comic books. This cycle of (1) perceiving a performance outcome in sport as "failure," (2) explaining the undesirable outcome, especially if it occurs consistently, as due to low ability, and (3) dropping out and not making new attempts to learn and perform the skills is common, even through the adult years. This is why an individual's perceived ability and explanations of the causes for his or her performance outcomes should be accurate — and should begin in childhood.

What can coaches and parents do about it? Perhaps the most cogent approach is suggested by Dweck (1975) and is described in Chapter 11. Her attributional training program helps children to overcome feelings of "learned helplessness" — the feeling that success is beyond one's control. In sport, a similar program can help participants overcome feelings that no matter what they do, they are destined for failure. The key to Dweck's program is to develop the performer's feelings that effort — a factor that can be controlled — is linked to success. She found that low-achieving children identified as exhibiting learned helplessness could be attributionally retrained to associate failure with a lack of effort. What coaches and parents say to children who are experiencing learned helplessness in a sport context, then, may significantly influence players' interpretation of their performance. Given the absence of physical limitations in the child, the important goal here is to help sport participants attribute effort as the causal determinant of success and failure. Furthermore, making attributions to effort may foster feelings of competence and intrinsic motivation, the latter of which is another popular area of sport psychology research.

Intrinsic Motivation.   If you have ever wanted to do something just for the fun or pleasure of it, then you realize that you could persist in such an activity, even without some tangible reward or outcome. Athletes are good examples of people who typically engage in an activity because it is desirable and gives them gratification, chances to become successful, achieve goals, and have fun. (After all, a person usually becomes an athlete by choice.) Individuals who participate in sport for these reasons are said to be **intrinsically motivated.** Too often, however, what should be an enjoyable, self-determining venture turns into an unpleasant, stressful one. The reasons for participating change. Satisfaction in sport becomes a matter of winning, trophies, and other external rewards. Intrinsic interest is undermined as the rewards for participation become externalized; the individual perceives sport as a vehicle to acquire the expected reward. No reward means less enjoyment from the activity. Even more important is that extrinsic motivation, because it depends on external, less controllable agents for satisfaction, is usually of shorter duration than intrinsic motivation, which is internally controlled and less dependent on external factors. Greene and Lepper (1974) refer to the misuse of rewards as "turning play into work."

Intrinsic motivation has its roots in Edward Deci's (1975) **cognitive evaluation theory** and has received considerable attention by sport psychologists. According to Deci, rewards have two primary functions: (1) controlling the person's behavior, and (2) giving informational feedback to the performer. Figure 15.3 shows Deci's pattern of motivation. Competitors who engage in sport primarily

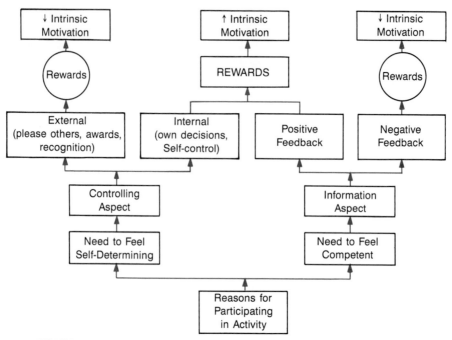

FIGURE 15.3 The effect of rewards on intrinsic motivation according to Deci's Cognitive Evaluation Theory.

to receive rewards such as trophies, applause, compliments, and attention—factors that are external to themselves and not under their own control—are said to be extrinsically motivated. But when they participate because they enjoy the activity and want to feel competent at it, their reasons for involvement are internal. This is why the rewards, if used at all in sport, should be offered to all participants in recognition for something they did well, something observable such as performance improvement, making a good effort, or good attendance at practices, for example, In other words, rewards should have a message, one that offers positive feedback about performance, and every participant should receive this message. Vallerand's (1983) results supported cognitive evaluation theory. Ice-hockey players, ages 13 to 16 years, who received positive verbal feedback on a hockey-related task showed more intrinsic motivation and higher feelings of competence, regardless of how often they received the information, than did subjects in a control (no feedback) group.

Experimental sport psychology usually follows the protocol of theoretically based, valid, and reliable research paradigms, what Martens (1987) calls "orthodox science." Martens refers to this "traditional" approach as academic sport psychology. He recognizes the emergence of another approach to the field, what he terms practicing sport psychology, as a very necessary alternative to study and understand human and sport behavior. The area in which this latter category has gained significant popularity in recent years is counseling sport psychology, as reflected by published articles, conference presentations, membership in professional sport psychology organizations, and the expertise of conference atttendees.

Counseling Sport Psychology

The common adage, "What you see is what you get," is not necessarily true in sport. Sport performance is a function of a competitor's abilities and previously learned skills and strategies. But, sometimes, thoughts and feelings get in the way of performing up to one's capability. Athletes who are unable to transfer their performance potential into achievement may need the help of a person who can offer guidance and counsel to help identify the underlying issues and develop mental skills to overcome the psychological problem. This is one role of the counseling sport psychologist. Counseling is advised for athletes who:

1. Demonstrate superb skills in practice sessions but cannot replicate this quality during the contest.
2. Consistently lose or perform poorly in important contests, even though their skills may be superior to opponents.
3. Are chronically injured.
4. Are not concentrating during games.
5. Do not, or appear unable to, follow the directions of the coach.
6. Are not doing well in school.
7. Have not made any friends on the team.
8. Drink alcohol excessively or ingest illegal drugs.
9. Cannot cope with failure.
10. React to the comments of coaches, teammates, or others in a defensive or negative manner.
11. Feel very anxious or "uptight" before the contest
12. Are bored and unexcited before the contest.
13. Are suffering from athletic burnout, are unmotivated to give 100% effort, or are thinking about quitting the team.

Samples from the sport psychology literature describe some counseling situations.

Burnout.   Dr. Ronald Smith (1986), a clinical sport psychologist at the University of Washington in Seattle, has developed a model that shows the interaction between situational, cognitive, physiological, and behavioral components of stress and **burnout.** The first stage of the model, the situation, is a function of an imbalance between demands and resources. Demands can be external, such as confronting a strong opponent in an important contest, or internal, such as desired goals or personal standards. When these demands are not met, the result can be heightened anxiety, guilt, anger, and self-derogation. Subsequent negative self-evaluations can lower self-esteem and self-confidence. Athletes might ask themselves, What am I doing here? as an expression of these feelings.

In the second stage, athletes cognitively appraise the situation to understand the nature and intensity of their stress. Do they feel overloaded? Do they feel helpless to alter the situation or to feel differently? Do they perceive their participation on the team as meaningless with few past or present accomplishments? To Smith (1986), a key issue that contributes to burnout is the source of the athlete's self-worth. " . . . An athlete who believes that his or her self-worth depends on success will attach a different meaning to athletic outcomes than will an athlete who can divorce self-worth from success or failure" (p. 41). These unpleasant feelings may be manifest in stress-induced physiological responses, the model's third stage. Physiological arousal can mobilize the athlete's resources to confront or cope with competitive situations. In a less constructive direction, symptoms of burnout can include insomnia, tension, anger, fatigue, and susceptibility to physical illness.

The final stage concerns the individual's behavioral reactions to the stressors. Will performance suffer? Will relationships with coaches, teammates, and others deteriorate? Will a player withdraw psychologically from competitive sport through inattentiveness, daydreaming, and a lack of effort? Or will an athlete quit the team? The objective at this point is to teach athletes to use coping behaviors that will allow them to interpret (appraise) the personal situation in a meaningful way and then to enact cognitive and behavioral strategies to reduce the feelings of burnout. Cognitive techniques include, but are not limited to, the following: mental imagery to create positive feelings and ideas about competition; thought-stopping techniques to inhibit negative feelings; progressive relaxation to help cope with too high a level of competitive arousal; and cognitive reappraisal to find a new perspective on the entire athletic situation. All these techniques serve to reduce tension and engender a sense of renewed purpose toward athletic participation. Behavioral strategies might include setting realistic, performance-based (as opposed to outcome-based) goals, communicating feelings to coaches and others whose views are considered meaningful, staying away from the sport environment for a few days or longer (with the coach's permission), ensuring proper nutrition, and working out concerns that are not directly related to the sport situation but might be a contributing factor to feelings of stress and burnout.

The Injured Athlete.   Sadly, injuries in sport competition are inevitable. In fact, quality athletes regularly engage in risk-taking behaviors that increase the possibility of injuries. Fortunately, advances in sports medicine have decreased the frequency of athletic injuries and the time needed to recover from them. But why then do so many athletes who sustain an injury that requires rehabilitation fail to perform at levels commensurate with their pre-injury skills? Even with a physician's clearance, why do some players "come back" after an injury while others eventually quit or resist returning to competition? More strangely, why do some players seem to become injured very frequently and be rehabilitated at a relatively slow pace? Sport psychologists now recognize that **psychological rehabilitation of injuries,** although not acknowledged by most coaches and athletes, is a critical factor in the athlete's ability to compete after sustaining a serious injury.

Although lacking in empirical evaluations, literature reviews from Wiese and Weiss (1987) and Rotella and Heyman (1986) have concluded that getting injured is related to certain psychological factors such as need for recognition, fear of failure ("If I'm hurt, I can't play, and that means I can't fail"), fear of

Psychological rehabilitation is recognized as a critical factor in an athlete's ability to "come back" after an injury.

success ("If I do well, there will be pressure to continue my success"), low ability to cope with stress, stress in other parts of the player's life, and need to induce guilt in others ("I'll show the coach how wrong he was to take me out of the game" or "My teammates/parents/coach will feel sorry for me"). They also conclude that injuries occur more frequently with athletes whose pain threshold (the point at which pain is first detected) and pain tolerance (the maximum amount of pain with which a person can continue to function) is relatively low in contrast to participants with high pain threshold and tolerance. Research findings indicate that, in general, athletes of contact sports, for example, football or hockey, have a higher pain threshold and tolerance than noncontact sport players, for example, baseball or golf.

There are at least two psychological explanations for an athlete's failure to "come back" after an injury. First, the injured player tends to be psychologically preoccupied with the rehabilitated area, a condition referred to as having a narrow **internal focus of attention,** instead of shifting attention internally and externally, narrowly and broadly, as task demands require. For example, skilled performers scan the sport environment to detect cues to which they will physically respond. Athletes who are not psychologically rehabilitated tend to be internally focused on the previously injured area and less cognizant of environmental cues such as the position of opponents or handling the ball. Consequently, performance demands such as turning sharply ("cutting") in football to avoid a tackle or using one's natural motion when throwing a baseball or running may not be met successfully.

To remedy the situation, the authors cited above recommend (a) counseling to identify and begin resolving underlying issues related to the occurrence of injuries or slow physical and psychological rehabilitation, and (b) practicing mental imagery and other cognitive strategies to improve concentration and anticipation of events, heighten arousal, reduce discomfort, gain self-confidence, and direct attention toward the appropriate cues.

Coping.   Like injuries, stress and failure are inherent in sport. Losing, pregame anxiety (nervousness), and making physical and mental errors are among the most common stressors. Other typical stressors in sport include being a substitute (especially when the athlete feels that he or she has the necessary skills to play or start), physical fatigue, giving too much time to the team and not enough to academic studies and social life, boredom, little communication or poor relationships with the coach and/or teammates, and being reprimanded by the coach. Of course, sport psychologists can only help athletes who seek assistance and communicate their concerns. It is generally acknowledged that female athletes are more open in disclosing personal information, particularly to female rather than male coaches, than are male competitors (Officer & Rosenfeld, 1985).

One very important role of a counseling psychologist working with athletes is to understand the issues, related and unrelated to being a sport participant, that often intrude into the competitor's life both on and off the field or court and affect sport performance. The skilled athlete brings to the session unique needs and experiences. For this reason counseling psychologists who work with athletes should be familiar with the sport psychology literature, especially with respect to the psychological issues and cognitive strategies that influence performance outcomes. One more important issue: the ability to gain the respect and trust of athletes is a time-consuming endeavor. Counseling/clinical psychologists who are team consultants must take the time to observe and interact with each player in a warm, sensitive, and nonthreatening manner. Based on interviews with 75 Canadian Olympic athletes regarding their experiences with sport psychology consultants, Canadian sport psychologists Terry Orlick and John Partington (1987) found that the best consultants not only were well liked as individuals but had the knowledge and the ability to teach mental skills that the athletes could use. But to properly take advantage of the consultant's skills requires time. The athletes expressed dissatisfaction with consultants with whom they did not have adequate contact time, particularly for individual follow-up and feedback. Successful consultants interacted with the athletes individually as well as in group settings.

Other factors that contributed to favorable attitudes toward consulting sport psychologists were having an approachable coach who supported the consultant's presence (athletes of unapproachable coaches were hesitant to disclose personal information, fearing a lack of confidentiality) and meeting times that did not consume the athletes' free time, which was often needed for rest. Effectiveness of sports psychologists was also increased if athletes understood the reasons for completing confidential personality inventories and were convinced that a coach would not use the scores to diminish their status on the team. Sport psychologists were more effective if they were consistent and reliable during the practice sessions and present prior to and during the competition. Finally, conducting research during the consulting period was seen as lowering a consultant's credibility in terms of serving athletes' best interests.

The athletes reported that sport psychology consultants made a significant contribution to their performance. They expressed a desire to interact with sport psychologists in the future; 98% requested greater availability of high-quality psychological services. Yet Orlick and Partington report that "there are very few consultants with the right kind of personal characteristics and applied knowledge to fill that need" (p. 9). The authors, critical of the highly academic content of most graduate sport-psychology courses, call for more opportunities to train clinical consultants in existing graduate programs.

Health and Exercise Psychology

The contributions of this area to sport psychology are based on the relationships between physical activity and health and the factors that distinguish active lifestyles from sedentary ones. Health psychology is an integral component of the primary professional organization of sport psychologists, AAASP. You have already been introduced to health psychology in Chapter 10. Sport psychologists with an emphasis in health psychology are interested in how sport and exercise relate to disease development, remediation, and prevention. A primary concern of the field, then, is with the close relationship between mental health and physical health. Recent years have seen the sport psychology literature reflect considerable interest in the relatively new area of health and exercise psychology. One primary evidence of this new thrust is a title change of the *Journal of Sport Psychology* to the *Journal of Sport and Exercise Psychology*. An increasing number of research articles and books attest to the increasing popularity of exercise habits and programs in corporate fitness, disease prevention, wellness, aging, and rehabilitative health programs, and also to the attention given to the psychological aspects of such programs. The sections that follow will take a brief look at some of the research published in this area.

Perceived Exertion.   Referred to in the literature as **ratings of perceived exertion** (RPE), this area of research is concerned with one's ability to judge and moderate physical effort by subjectively assessing the intensity of one's effort. RPE enables a person to perform efficient, safe, and productive training/exercise sessions while avoiding overexertion or injury. This is particularly important, for example, for injured participants, cardiac patients, and pregnant women. Researchers have examined RPE with respect to sex differences, the effects of cognitive strategies, personality, differences in physical attributes and physical fitness, and task demands (see Regeski, 1981, for a review).

Type A Behavior.   As noted in Chapter 10 on health psychology, Type A and Type B reflect typical behaviors individuals may exhibit in stressful situations. One such stressful situation is found in competitive sports. Persons with Type

Out of the relatively new area of health and exercise psychology has come the rating of perceived exertion (RPE), which helps people judge and moderate physical effort. This is especially important for those with medical problems.

A behavioral patterns are said to be competitive, have a high need to achieve, be aggressive, suppress attention to fatigue, have high self-expectations for success, feel more frustrated, and exhibit more hostility than Type B individuals, who usually exhibit opposite characteristics. Exercise psychologists are examining the effectiveness of cognitive strategies, (mental imagery, thought stopping, and various approaches to relaxation) and behavioral techniques (time management, goal setting, or involvement in recreational activities) in an attempt to reduce the negative effects of Type A behaviors. In a sport context, Carver, Degregorio, and Gillis (1981) found that Type A intercollegiate football athletes exerted themselves closer to their limits and ignored injuries in order to perform at optimal levels, in contrast to Type B players.

Exercise Adherence. In their review of related literature, Martin and Dubbert (1985) concluded that adherence to exercise programs may be markedly increased — as high as 80–85% — if the program includes (1) tangible rewards for class attendance or adherence, (2) flexible self-set goals, (3) social support with personal feedback, praise, and group exercising, (4) exercising at moderate intensity, and (5) a convenient type and location of exercise.

Physical Activity and Depression, Anxiety, and Stress. Common findings suggest that people with high life-stress tend to have psychological and physical health problems. These maladies are compounded, often being accompanied by depression in sedentary people, in contrast to their physically active counterparts. Typically researchers have found that engaging in a physical exercise program, usually of 6 to 10 weeks duration, significantly reduces tension and other unpleasant psychological conditions while fostering the ability to cope with unavoidable life stress (Roth & Holmes, 1985). A review of literature by Weinstein and Meyers (1983) indicated that running significantly reduces depression and improves mood.

Drugs and Athletic Competition. Drug abuse by athletes has received widespread media attention, probably because of the apparent epidemic nature of the problem. Scientists in health sport psychology (e.g., Cook, Tricker, & McGuire, 1987), psychiatry (e.g., Chappel, 1987), and sports medicine (e.g., Collins, Pippenger, & Janesz, 1984) have concluded that the reasons for sport's "drug problem" — most notably the use of cocaine, marijuana, heroin, and steroids — has likely been due to (1) the "status" associated with exposure to certain drugs and high income ("Cocaine, with its phenomenal expense, glamorous allure, and severe legal penalties, is an attractive vehicle for demonstrating wealth, status, and power" [Collins et al., 1984, p. 487]); (2) the availability of drugs, especially to well-known athletes; (3) boredom due to excessive free time and unstructured lifestyles; (4) a belief that drugs will improve performance; (5) the fear of failing, of being injured, or of an opponent; (6) weight control; (7) low self-esteem, which often comes across as fulfilling a macho image; (8) lack of team identity and little loyalty to the team and coach, particularly among substitute players; (9) personality characteristics related to risk taking or stimulus seeking; (10) peer pressure ("everyone's doing it") or peer acceptance ("join the party"); (11) feelings of depression, tension, anxiety, or low life satisfaction; (12) physical and/or mental fatigue; (13) family problems; (14) curiosity (although this rarely leads to a habit of drug abuse); and (15) the "Superman Complex," in which athletes feel impervious to the effects of drugs.

Because many coaches do not look for or acknowledge a drug problem on their teams, attempts are being made by sport and health psychologists to work with coaches in looking for signs of drug use by players and to invoke strategies to help prevent it. The thought of dismissing a player, of receiving negative team publicity, and possibly of their own guilt as occasional drug-users during their own playing days has prevented some coaches from reacting to the problem with greater urgency. Widespread media reports of abuse by professional athletes and the deaths of well-known players have demonstrated a need for team and individual counseling programs.

Psychophysiology. Psychophysiology has been defined as "a body of knowledge concerned with the inference of psychological processes and emotional states from an examination of physiological measures" (Hatfield & Landers, 1983, p. 244). These physiological measures are recorded from the body surface; for example, an electroencephalogram (EEG) records brain waves, an electrocardiogram (EKG) reflects contractions of the heart muscle, and an electromyogram (EMG) records muscle activity. In a typical EEG procedure, for example, small electrodes are attached to various areas of the scalp. The electrodes are sensitive to tiny electrical currents emitted by the brain that are then amplified and recorded. Patterns of electrical activity are analyzed in order to infer underlying psychological processes.

Psychophysiological research in sport psychology is process-oriented. This means that researchers attempt to identify the underlying causes of performance rather than to simply examine electrophysiological responses to different treatments. For instance, sport researchers have acknowledged for years that anxiety is highly related to performance. Why is this so? Weinberg and Hunt (1976) attempted to answer this question. Not only did the throwing accuracy of baseball pitchers decrease with higher levels of anxiety, but continuous EMG recordings indicated that the coordination between the muscle groups required for throwing was affected during higher stress levels. This effect in turn may have decreased the accuracy and steadiness of the throwing motion. The authors identified a possible locus of the problem (lack of coordination between muscle groups) rather than reporting only the result of different experimental conditions (high versus low anxiety). Perhaps this is why various relaxation and imagery procedures are effective in reducing stress and anxiety, emotions that underlie muscular tension.

Other sport-related psychophysiological research was concerned with analyzing the heart rate of expert air-rifle shooters. Landers, Christina, Hatfield, Daniels, and Doyle (1980) found that, invariably, the shooters fired the shot between successive heart contractions. Shots that were fired during the contraction resulted in significantly lower accuracy, up to a full point lower. They also found that expert shooters hold their breath just prior to pulling the trigger, but that the optimal heart rate (when their best scores are achieved) during this breath-holding period differs for each athlete. This means that all expert shooters should not have the same goals in meeting a predetermined heart rate.

This issue of individual differences is pervasive in the psychophysiology research literature. Performers differ widely in their physiological responses to different thoughts, emotions, and attitudes. Hatfield and Landers (1983) cite other literature in which the averaging of psychophysiological responses across a group of subjects does not reveal the effects of treatments on performance nor give a true measure of a person's physiological reponses to psychological processes. Instead, it is suggested that the responses of individuals be compared over time and in different situations. By so doing it is possible to detect changes in psychophysiological responses that would otherwise be obscured by individual differences.

Examples of future research in sport psychology that uses a psychophysiological approach include (a) processes of attention and emotion and how they affect or are related to different levels of sport performance, (b) underlying causes of mental imagery, and (c) psychophysiological effects of exercise on depression, anxiety, and the "runner's high."

Personality Psychology

Can one actually predict who will and who will not be a successful athlete by using a psychological inventory? Do expert athletes have different personality characteristics from those of their less skilled counterparts or of nonathletes? Do the personality profiles of athletes in various sports differ from each other? For example, do participants in contact sports have different personalities than participants in noncontact sports? Does participating in sports influence the performer's personality, perhaps by enhancing cooperation, building leadership, acting as a catharsis for aggression, building character, and other desirable outcomes as is commonly thought?

In the 1960s and early 1970s, personality research in sport settings was quite popular. It was contended (by less informed "scientists," it was later found) that completing a particular personality profile would elicit scores on a series of traits that supposedly could predict athletic success. This was especially true of the Athletic Motivation Inventory (AMI), which "assesses" 11 personality traits such as drive, aggressiveness, determination, self-confidence, and mental toughness. The AMI was widely acclaimed by coaches everywhere. But a critical review of the AMI by Martens (1975) indicated that the AMI lacked validity—it wasn't measuring what it was purported to measure. Its authors failed to supply data indicating its reliability—how consistent the responses of individuals would be on repeated administrations of the test. Data were also missing in terms of the AMI's ability to predict athletic success from the 11 traits that it measured. Nor was proof forthcoming about the test's purported ability to offer remediation for "problem athletes."

The AMI was not the only personality inventory that underwent a critical examination in sport research. Other common tests that have been used to try to predict sports-related behavior include the Minnesota Multiphasic Personality Inventory (MMPI), the California Personality Inventory (CPI), the Cattell Sixteen Personality Factor Questionnaire (16 PF), the Eysenck Personality Inventory (EPI), and the Edwards Personal Preference Schedule (EPPS). None of these inventories were developed for sport participants. Thus it is not surprising that the amount of variance accounted for in sport personality research (that is, the ability to explain, understand, or predict behavior) is less than 10%. This means that 90% of the time, personality test scores are not related to how one competes in a sport situation (Fisher, 1977). The answer to the above questions, then, is no.

Fisher (1977) and Morgan (1980) have listed the following concerns about personality testing in sport:

1. There is low generalizablity from nonsport to sport situations; individuals may be predisposed to act in a certain way under many, but not necessarily all, circumstances. Fisher (1977) asserts it is wrong to assume that assessments related to nonsport situations could be generalized to various sport situations.

2. Many of the inventories used in sports were developed for nonsport populations. For instance, the MMPI was created to examine persons with various mental illnesses, schizophrenia, for example. Using the MMPI with athletes, then, is inappropriate. No wonder such tests in sport have low predictability, as indicated earlier.

3. The terms and factors being measured have not been universally defined. For example, "athlete" to one researcher might be a participant in a collegiate intramural program, whereas another investigator might define athlete as intercollegiate competitor. In addition, such traits as sociability, ego strength, shrewdness, dominance, and others are defined differently in various tests.

4. Finally, Morgan (1980) warns that it is wrong to assume that all respondents answer each question with full candor and honesty. He contends that athletes "fake good" (called motivation distortion), "fake bad," and answer randomly rather than pondering each question thoughtfully and responding appropriately.

Despite these problems in the literature, sport psychologists have identified certain characteristics of elite athletes of both sexes. The use of different inventories and sport teams notwithstanding, athletes tend to be intelligent, achievement-oriented, dominant, tough-minded, stable, aggressive, sociable, group-dependent, and adventurous. But given the low predictability of performance from these traits and the low generalizability of these profiles to sport situations, a sport researcher (and coach) has a right to ask, "so what?"

Contemporary sport research in this area is more likely to examine specific unique characteristics of athletes, such as anxiety or need for achievement. These characteristics seem to have direct implications for competition. For example, athletes high in anxiety might use certain cognitive strategies in mental preparation to reduce tension because of their greater susceptibility to it. Coaches could be made aware of these unique individual characteristics and work with players to capitalize on strengths while diminishing the effects of weaknesses.

Conclusion

An article appearing in the *Journal of Sport Psychology* (Dishman, 1983) was entitled "Identity Crises in Sport Psychology: Academics in Professional Issues." More recently, *The Physician and Sportmedicine* published an article entitled "Sport Psychology: A Crisis of Identity?" (Monahan, 1987). What's the problem?

It's called growing pains, and the field of sport psychology is having its share of them. What is the field's focus? How is sport psychology defined? How should it be practiced and who should practice it? These issues are currently being debated at professional conferences and in the literature.

The fears of academicians and established researchers is that, as the field expands, controlling the quality of practice and research in sport psychology might diminish or, worse, border on unethical practices such as persons purporting to be "sport psychologists" despite the lack of proper training or making promises that cannot be kept. Even sport psychologists themselves cannot agree on what constitutes a sport psychologist or on the direction the field should go. As Professor Mary Ann Roberton from the University of Wisconsin said in a conference paper (1984), "What do sport psychologists not do?"

Still, the need for the practice of sport psychology exists. Athletes and coaches are beginning to realize the importance of the role of emotion, attitudes, and the efficacy of clinical and performance intervention techniques in maximizing performance outcomes. In practice, the objective of the field is to help athletes reach their full potential. Few athletes claim that they are the best performers they can be. They know something is missing or that they have yet to reach their potential. More and more of them believe, as shown by the inclusion of a sport psychologist with each Olympic team, that often the difference between success and failure, winning and losing, first place and second place, is possessing the mental edge over opponents. This is what practicing or applied sport psychologists try to teach participants and what research sport psychologists are attempting to further examine.

In this chapter, the primary components of sport psychology were reviewed from research and applied perspectives. An attempt was made to explore virtually all aspects of the field, both its content and the roles of researchers, educators, clinicians, and consultants who work directly with the coaches and athletes.

Sport psychology is gaining widespread acceptance from older, well-established disciplines such as psychology and sports medicine. This recognition is due in no small part to evidence of quality research, the ability to present this information at professional conferences in a sophisticated manner, the inclusion of topic areas such as exercise and health psychology, and psychophysiology (which is compatible with the sports medicine field), the establishment of research journals to disseminate information, and the growing popularity of sport psychology among researchers and practitioners in several fields of endeavor.

Working in sport psychology can be a very rewarding and pleasant experience. When one understands the factors that influence athletic performance, one can assist individuals in reaching their full potential. Especially interesting is the ability of skilled athletes to be able to handle failure in a constructive manner. For example, even the outbursts of tennis professional John McEnroe are part of his own strategy to cope with frustration and failure. It is also highly rewarding to see that an understanding of psychological principles can help coaches be more effective at their jobs by using correct motivation and productive communication.

Despite what is known about sport-related behavior, applied sport psychology has been called by some psychologists, "a lot of moving around in the dark" (Monahan, 1987, p. 205). There is still much to investigate and understand. Not unlike medical researchers, sport psychologists often feel that they have discovered a new and effective remedy, but don't quite know how to apply it in a specific case. But the real joy of practicing sport psychology, in any form — research, consultant, or educator — is the opportunity to promote a mentally healthy and pleasant environment in which sport participants of all ages and skill levels can succeed, perform at their best, and have fun.

Glossary

burnout A syndrome that may be experienced by individuals in high-stress jobs. It is characterized by apathy, decrease in self-esteem, rationalizations of failure, irritability, and resistance to change.

cognitive evaluation theory Deci's theory to describe the psychological functions of rewards. According to the theory, rewards function primarily to control behavior and provide informational feedback about performance quality.

elite athletes Athletes who are able to perform at high skill levels.

internal focus of attention During recovery from an injury, an athlete may focus internally on the injured body part rather than shifting attention internally and externally as required by an athletic activity.

intrinsic motivation The internal satisfaction that comes from competent performance.

psychological rehabilitation of injuries In addition to physical healing of injuries, athletes must recover psychologically in order to reach their full performance capabilities.

ratings of perceived exertion (RPE) Subjective judgments of how much physical exertion an individual is expending at a given time.

social facilitation Improved performance on well-learned tasks in the presence of others.

16 Applied Developmental Psychology

Nancy Eisenberg
Arizona State University

Jerry Harris
Arizona State University

Karlsson Roth
Arizona State University

Developmental psychology is one of the newest branches of psychology. In fact, 20 years ago there were relatively few university programs that provided degrees or extensive training in developmental psychology. Even today, many large universities do not offer programs specifically in this area of psychology, even though they have programs in clinical, experimental, and social psychology. Consequently, it is not surprising that many students are unsure of what developmental psychology is and of the topics that are examined by developmental psychologists.

What Is Applied Developmental Psychology?

Developmental psychology is the study of change in any aspect of development typically examined by psychologists. Thus developmental psychologists study the development of language, cognition, social behavior, perception, and personality characteristics. However, unlike experimental or social psychologists, who usually examine a given process or behavior at only one age (usually during early adulthood because college students are readily accessible for research), developmental psychologists tend to study how a process or behavior changes as people age.

Many people think that developmental psychology is synonymous with child psychology. It is true that developmental psychologists, especially in the past, have tended to focus primarily on changes during chidhood. This is probably due to two factors. First, as anyone who has spent much time with a young child will know, change is very rapid and observable during childhood. Consequently, psychologists interested in changes may naturally focus on childhood. A second reason for the focus on childhood is that influential theorists such as Sigmund Freud have emphasized the significance of early childhood experiences, and have promoted the idea that an individual's personality is shaped early in life and changes relatively little with age. Based on this perspective, many psychologists have assumed that they can best understand an individual's personality and behavior by studying their formation during childhood.

More recently, developmental psychologists have realized that change does not stop at adolescence but occurs throughout life. Consequently, many developmental psychologists are now examining change during adulthood and old age. In fact, there is now an area of study called "life-span developmental psychology," an area that is rapidly expanding.

The history and scope of academic (nonapplied) developmental psychology has direct relevance to applied developmental psychology. Because developmental psychologists can apply concepts and information only in areas they have studied, the domain examined by developmental psychologists directly influences the potential areas of application. Moreover, innovations or changes in the field of developmental psychology will be reflected in the types of applications that are possible. For example, although developmental psychologists are now applying their knowledge and skills to real-world problems concerning adults and the aged (as well as children), in the recent past developmental psychologists had little competence in these areas.

What Do Applied Developmental Psychologists Do?

In reality, developmental psychology is not yet very applied. Evidence for this assertion is the fact that the first journal of applied development psychology (the *Journal of Applied Developmental Psychology*) was established as recently as 1981. Most developmental psychologists still work at academic institutions, and much of their research has not yet been applied to real-world issues and problems. However, this state of affairs is beginning to change. More and more developmental psychologists are now beginning to work in nonacademic settings such as hospitals, schools, and counseling facilities. Moreover, as the field has developed, some of the research has progressed past the conceptual level to the point of potential application. Consequently, a number of developmental psychologists who are employed by academic institutions are now out in the community applying their knowledge to real-life problems.

Historical Context

It was not always the case that developmental psychologists were primarily academicians employed at universities and colleges. The study of child development first arose from the need to better understand and deal with issues contributing to the welfare of children. In fact, many of the people who were involved in research and theorizing concerning child development in the early 1900s were practitioners, especially social workers, teachers, and doctors, (Sears, 1975). However, as the study of children increasingly became dominated by psychologists, much of the research on children moved into the laboratory. Indeed, by the 1950s, most of the best-known developmental psychologists were studying children primarily in the laboratory rather than in applied, real-life settings.

The recent trend toward a more applied approach among developmental psychologists has been stimulated by an least three factors. First, developmental psychologists, like other psychologists, recently have become quite concerned with the issue of "ecological validity," that is, with the degree to which research findings reflect what is really going on in the world outside the laboratory. More specifically, psychologists have become concerned that their methods of study not be too contrived or artificial, and that their data and theorizing reflect, as nearly as possible, the multitude of interacting influences that actually affect behaviors, cognitions, and personalities (see Bronfenbrenner, 1979; Mussen, 1977). Due to this recent interest in ecological validity, developmental psychologists have begun to conduct a number of studies in natural settings, a practice that was common in the early study of child development.

A second probable reason for the renewed interest in applied aspects of developmental psychology has to do with changes in the social climate of the United States. During the 1960s, public concern regarding social problems such as racism and poverty began to mount. This concern was reflected in President Johnson's policies, policies purportedly designed to promote the development of a fair and prosperous "great society." Moreover, due perhaps to the realities of poverty, prejudice, and the Vietnam War, the public, including academicians, became more concerned with the "relevance" or real-life practicality of ideas and policies. Consequently, a number of developmental psychologists began to focus on issues of social concern and to study methods of dealing with social problems.

Although public interest in education, welfare, and other social issues has apparently waned somewhat in the 1970s and 1980s, a third, quite recent factor has stimulated developmental psychologists' interest in applied issues. This factor is economic. Because college budgets have decreased and because there has been an increase in the number of psychologists trained, it is more difficult for developmental psychologists to obtain jobs in academic institutions than it was in the past. Consequently, more and more developmental psychologists have been seeking careers in nonacademic environments such as in community settings. Slowly but surely, developmental psychologists, as well as psychologists in a number of other fields, are creating niches for themselves outside the ivory tower of the university.

Job Activities and Work Settings

Because applied developmental psychology is such a new field, the job activities and settings where those jobs are performed vary greatly from person to person. In some respects, applied developmental psychologists must create their own work settings. Perhaps most have started from a teaching and research position in a university and then have broadened the scope of their activities to include work in applied settings. Because the field is so new, this chapter will describe job activities and settings through a series of examples to illustrate both the types of settings in which applied developmental psychologists work and the range of issues they are currently studying. Of course, it is impossible to discuss in one chapter all the issues developmental psychologists examine and all the settings where they work. Nonetheless, it is hoped that admittedly selective discussion will provide the reader with an overview of the reality and potential of applied developmental psychology.

Research and Applications

The remainder of this chapter will be organized chronologically. Topics relating to infancy will be reviewed first, followed by discussion of issues relevant to early childhood, middle childhood, and adulthood.

Infant Development

One of the areas in which developmental psychology is most often applied is in the domain of infant development. Obviously, findings concerning the development of healthy, happy infants are of considerable relevance both to parents and professionals who deal with children (for example, pediatricians, nurses, and social workers), and can be used to enhance infant development. Moreover, information regarding optimal infant development can be used as the basis for implementing new policies in institutions such as hospitals and schools, as well as in counseling parents.

Today there are quite a few developmental psychologists employed by hospitals, primarily in pediatric and psychiatric departments. In a number of large hospitals, developmental psychologists and other professionals are conducting ongoing research concerning the development of both normal infants and high-risk infants (infants who are likely to have physical, mental, or psychological problems). Their findings are already influencing the lives of many individuals.

Research on Bonding.   Psychologists have long recognized that a child's behavior, mental functioning, and emotional development are profoundly influenced by the quality of the parent-child relationship. For this reason, psychologists, social workers, and doctors are greatly concerned with methods of improving parent-child interactions.

In the past decade, doctors and psychologists have been investigating one potential influence on parents' attitudes and behaviors — the process of the **bonding** of mother (and/or father) to an infant in the early days of the infant's life. Several researchers have found that mothers are more likely to establish an optimal relationship with their newborns if they have access to their infants during the "critical" or "sensitive" period soon after birth, for example, the first hours of life (Klaus & Kennell, 1976; see Lamb & Hwang, 1982, for a review). It is assumed that during this period, mothers may be hormonally primed to be specially sensitive and responsive to characteristics of their infants. In addition, because infants themselves appear to be especially responsive and alert immediately after labor and delivery, interaction with the infant in the first hour of life is believed to be very reinforcing and pleasurable for the parent. Thus some researchers assume that during this period the groundwork is laid for the mother's future relationship with her child, and that she will be more responsive and concerned with her infant if she has contact with it during this interval of time. The absence of such interaction during the sensitive period after birth is associated with an increased probability of subsequent child abuse and neglect (Klaus & Kennell, 1976).

Published research on human bonding began to appear at a time when existing obstetrical practices were being criticized by parents as well as by some members of the medical profession. Mothers in the United States participated as little as possible in the birthing process (they were often drugged and sometimes unconscious), babies were whisked away from the parents immediately after delivery, and fathers were not allowed in the delivery room. These procedures were viewed by many as being sterile and dehumanizing. Furthermore, parents resented the enforced separations from each other and from their infants that were standard procedure in most hospitals, and some doctors and nurses questioned the advisability of these policies. Thus research that was consistent with the view that separations are not good for either parents or infants provided the needed impetus for the revamping of hospital procedures relating to child-birth. In fact, due in large part to the research on bonding, in many hospitals fathers are now encouraged to attend the delivery of their infants, mothers are encouraged to be active participants in giving birth, and infants "room" with their mothers (that is, they stay in their mothers' rooms rather than in the nurs-ery; Lamb, 1982). Even parents of critically ill newborns usually are encouraged to visit, hold, and assist in the care of their infants as soon as possible after birth.

Although many health-care professionals strongly support the change in hospital practices described above, the critical role of postbirth parent-child in-teraction in the bonding process has recently been questioned. Specifically, the research on bonding has been criticized for two reasons. First the argument in support of a sensitive period for mother-infant bonding was based, in part, on research conducted with nonhuman species (see Klaus & Kennell, 1976). In this research, it was demonstrated that (a) changes in the hormonal levels of rats affected maternal responsiveness to their pups (Rosenblatt, 1967, 1970); (b) sepa-

Although it is widely believed that parent-child interaction in the first hours of an infant's life—bonding—is critical to successful parenting, critics have found methodological flaws in the research supporting the theory.

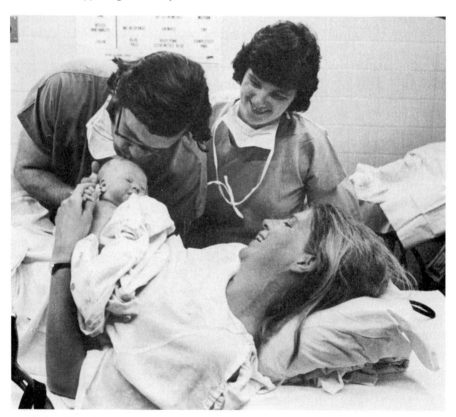

ration of domestic sheep and goats from their young soon after birth resulted in maternal rejection of the infant when mother and infant were reunited only hours later (Collias, 1956); and (c) in some species, especially birds, newborns form bonds with adults during a "critical" period of time soon after birth (Lorenz, 1935/1970). Although the animal research on bonding is interesting, its relevance for an understanding of human infant development is questionable. Sensitive periods for the formation of maternal behavior seem to exist only for species whose "social organization, reproductive patterns, and infant characteristics are substantially different from our own" (Lamb & Hwang, 1982, p. 51). Thus it is probably inappropriate to draw a parallel between other species and humans regarding the establishment of a bond between parents and infants.

A second line of criticism of the bonding research is based upon methodological flaws in the research itself (see Goldberg, 1983; Lamb & Hwang, 1982). The finding that parent-child interaction in the first hours of an infant's life is associated with better parenting (such as increased attentiveness to the child's needs) has been difficult to replicate, even when researchers have used measures similar to those in the initial research. Moreover, in the few instances in which apparently sound evidence in favor of bonding has been obtained, it is quite possible that these findings occurred because the mothers in the research who were allowed to interact with their infants immediately after birth were also given special treatment by the nursing and medical staff (the staff knew which mothers were receiving special treatment).

Finally, in several of the early studies on bonding, researchers failed to distinguish between the effects of "early contact" (contact soon after birth) and "extended contact" (more hours of contact). While early mother-infant contact soon after birth is the variable popularly believed to influence the development of a parent-infant bond, in the early research on bonding, mothers who were provided with early contact also received extended contact with their newborns. Thus the findings in these studies may have been due to more hours of mother-child contact, to contact immediately after delivery, or to a combination of these two factors. Moreover, in the few studies in which the effects of timing and amount of contact were differentiated, there are consistent reports of the short-term effects of early contact, but no consensus on the nature of these effects. For example, the effects of mother-child contact seem to be different in different social classes, but the research has not provided explanations for this inconsistency in findings (Goldberg, 1983).

Despite theoretical and methodological flaws in the research on bonding, it has resulted in what many would consider to be a postive outcome. The humanization of birthing and obstetrical practices that were associated with the popularization of the research in bonding has continued. Consequently, parents and infants now have more opportunities to get to know each other than in the past. Nonetheless, reservations concerning the theoretical basis for these policies contine to be voiced, with the weight of recent evidence proving only minimal support for positive short-term effects of early contact and no empirical basis for Klaus and Kennell's more extreme assertions.

Individual Differences in Infants. Another area of developmental research that has applied implications is the research relating to individual differences in infants. Sigmund Freud (1950) and a few pioneer workers in the field of child development (Gesell, 1937; Shirley, 1933) recognized that there were significant differences in the behavior of infants. However, until recently few researchers examined the role of early behavioral differences in psychological development.

Today most developmental psychologists believe that development is a function of the interaction between nature (the innate biological characteristics of the child) and nurture (the individual's environment). Consequently, they are concerned with the issue of differences among people. Moreover, because environmental influences increasingly affect the child's development soon after birth, a great deal of research is being conducted with newborn infants. By studying newborns, researchers hope to detect individual differences in behavior while minimizing the effects of environmental influences such as language and parent interaction.

Another reason for the recent interest in the individuality of very young infants is that professionals dealing with infants and their families have recognized the need to develop a better understanding of early variations in infant behavior. These professionals have realized that the characteristics of an infant — especially deviations from the normal — affect how that baby interacts with others. Consequently, although the majority of the studies on individual differences in infants have been conducted with normal babies, investigators have also studied infants who are physically, mentally, or psychologically abnormal.

A study by T. Berry Brazelton (1961) is a good illustration of the ways in which the characteristics of an infant can affect his or her caregiver. Brazelton described an infant whose unusual states of arousal were so difficult for his mother that she became depressed and ineffectual. The mother was a young professional who had been excited at the prospect of becoming a parent and whose pregnancy had been without complications. However, the infant she delivered was difficult from birth: he was capable of only two extreme states. In one state, the infant appeared to be in a deep sleep during which his muscle tone was poor, he was difficult to arouse, and he was oblivious to any external stimuli. In the other state, the infant screamed continuously, and was hyperactive and extremely sensitive to any stimulation. The only action that calmed him when he was in this aroused state was the restraint of his movements by wrapping him securely. Unfortunately, however, this intervention had the effect of inducing the state of deep sleep. Furthermore, the subsequent development of the child was uneven, although neurologists found no abnormalities. Even at age 3 the boy frequently screamed or withdrew into a trance-like state in which he appeared to neither see nor hear. From the time of the baby's birth, the mother felt rebuffed by her child and overwhelmed by the task of mothering an infant on whom she had little effect; she was unable to comfort him when he was upset or to reach him when he withdrew.

The extreme difference in infants is highlighted by another study. Prechtl (1963) followed the development of eight infants who had medical complications prior to and at birth, and who all exhibited a syndrome Prechtl called "hyperkinesis." These eight babies cried more than normal babies and showed sudden shifts in their state of awareness—from being drowsy and difficult to arouse to being wide awake and difficult to pacify. He noted that nearly all the infants' responses were exaggerated and that they had a remarkably low threshold to stimuli (that is, they reacted to environmental stimuli very easily). Prechtl reported that although none of the mothers of the eight infants were aware that their infants showed identifiable signs of brain dysfunction, seven of the eight mothers either rejected their infants to some degree or were overanxious about them. In contrast, for a control group of 10 normal babies, Prechtl found that only one mother was troubled or overanxious. Interestingly, in spite of the hyperkinetic infants' obvious deviance, almost invariably the mothers of these abnormal babies blamed themselves for problems with their children and felt that they had mishandled their baby in some way. However, Prechtl reported that during neurological examinations of the babies, he and his colleagues were often "annoyed" with these infants because of their exaggerated reactions and their sudden changes in states. The different perceptions of mothers and researchers highlight the extreme responsibility most parents feel for their children—a topic that will be continued later in the chapter.

Asssessing Individuality in Newborns.　Because individual differences in infants play an important role in development, psychologists and physicians have had to develop ways to detect these differences. To fill this need, Brazelton (1973) developed what is perhaps the best-known systematic approach to assessing individual differences in newborns. Although several other researchers had been successful in developing methods for describing the physical and neurological status of the neonate (Apgar, 1966; Parmelee & Haber, 1973; Prechtl & Beintema, 1964), Brazelton sought to design a system for evaluation that would be useful for detecting some of the more subtle differences in the functioning of newborns. Moreover, because the way in which an infant acts is likely to have some effect on those who care for him or her (Bell & Harper, 1977), Brazelton attempted to measure aspects of an infant's individuality that might influence future interactions at home with the infant's parents.

With the **Brazelton Neonatal Behavioral Assessment Scale** (called the **NBAS;** Brazelton, 1973), individuality in the newborn is measured in several ways. The initial 20 reflex items are designed to assess an infant's neurological state by eliciting reflexes such as sucking and the startle response. Each reflex is rated on a four-point scale (0–3) with the average full-term newborn receiving a rating of 2. The infant is also evaluated on two overall behavioral dimensions, *attractiveness* and *need-for-stimulation. Attractiveness* refers to the newborn's social attractiveness as perceived by the Brazelton tester and is interpreted as a measure of how much the infant contributed to the interaction during testing. The attractiveness rating is an attempt to perceive the infant as he or she might be perceived by the parents, and to describe the strengths and weaknesess that each individual infant may contribute to the overall caregiving system. In contrast, the *need-for-stimulation* rating refers to a baby's utilization of, and apparent need for, external stimulation to facilitate his or her own functioning. For instance, some newborns benefit from handling and seem able to adapt better when being held—somehow this stimulation allows the infant to function more smoothly. Other infants appear to pay little attention to outside stimulation and seem better able to control their behavior when left alone.

The majority of the Brazelton items are used to assess the baby's capacity to interact with people and objects. The 25 items on the NBAS have been grouped together or "clustered" into four behavioral dimensions that reflect the organization of the newborn's interactive abilities. The cluster that is called *interactive capacities* refers to the infants' ability to pay attention to and understand their environment. More specifically, this cluster of items is used to assess attention and social responsiveness and is composed of items related to the type of attention an infant pays to the tester's face and voice, and an infant's cuddliness (for example, does the baby snuggle close to the body or push away?). The second behavioral dimension is called *motor and tonic capabilities* and refers to an infant's ability to control his or her movements and to coordinate these movements into acts such as putting a thumb or fingers into the mouth for comfort. This dimension also includes items relating to muscle tone and activity level. The third cluster of behavioral items is called *organizational capacities with respect to state control.* In it are items relating to a baby's ability to maintain some measure of self-control despite increasing environmental stimulation from items such as bells, lights, and rattles. The final cluster is named *organizational capacities with respect to physiologic responses to stress* and is used to assess how well an infant has recovered from the demands of labor and delivery. This cluster is composed of items relating to an infant's skin tone, and to startle responses and tremors.

Representative Application: Parental Involvement in Infant Assessment. To investigate individual differences in the behavior of an average group of randomly selected newborns, Brazelton and his colleagues studied the development of 54 healthy, full-term infants delivered at a hospital in Boston (Tronick, Wise, Als, Adamson, Scanlon, & Brazelton, 1976). These newborns were medically and neurologically normal after delivery, and their mothers had uncomplicated prenatal histories and deliveries. Seven repeated Brazelton NBAS evaluations were made for each infant, with the first four administered in the hospital prior to discharge and the remaining three at home. The result of this research was a description of the changes in behavior exhibited by this select group of newborns over the first 10 days of life. Specifically, Brazelton found that healthy full-term newborns become more mature and better organized behaviorally over that 10-day period. Research such as this has shown that babies are demonstrably different from each other.

The early research on individual differences in the behavior of newborn infants has had several positive consequences. Most notably, based on the data resulting from this research, an increasingly differentiated and individualized view of babies has developed. Brazelton (1981) and others have recognized the

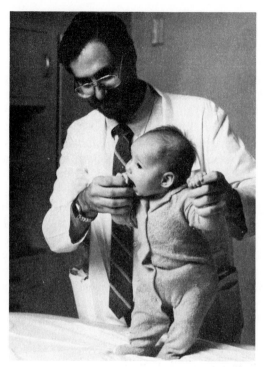

A number of instruments designed by developmental psychologists help pediatricians assess infant temperament, enabling them to provide appropriate guidance to parents.

importance of assessments of individual characteristics not only for research purposes, but also as a means of identifying for parents some of the strengths and capabilities of their own infants. Indeed, according to Brazelton:

> . . . Each assessment in which parents participate does automatically become an intervention. By participating *with* parents in the identification of the child's strengths and weaknesses, and by sharing with parents the information we gain, we can help them distinguish stimuli that are appropriate and can be utilized, from stimuli likely to overwhelm them. We can share with parents our working understanding of the child's internal organization and response systems and try to channel their energy and understanding of the child toward optimization of function. We can certainly enhance the power of a nurturing environment to provide opportunities for plasticity (change). Perhaps most important of all, we can reinforce their self-image as parents so that they in turn can nurture their child's. (p. xix)

Researchers have demonstrated that parental participation in an assessment of their infant's strengths and weaknesses can enhance parents' abilities to provide appropriate stimulation for their infants, and that, over time, infants of these parents seem to progress better developmentally. For example, Widmayer and Field (1981) investigated the effectiveness of using the Brazelton scale to teach mothers of healthy premature infants about their newborn's behavior. In their study, one group of mothers was invited to watch a trained tester administer the scale to their infants at birth and to complete a similar scale for their own babies (the Mother's Assessment of the Behavior of Her Infant, MABI) once a week for four weeks after the baby's discharge from the hospital. A second group of mothers did not view the Brazelton test administration, but were asked to complete the MABI shortly after their infants' births and once a week for the first month of the infants' lives. A third group of mothers did not view the Brazelton administration or complete the MABI; however, they were asked to complete questionnaires about the development of their infants. All infants were then studied in their homes at 1, 4, and 12 months of age corrected for prematurity (that is, 1, 4, and 12 months after the expected date of birth had the infant not been premature).

At 1 month, the two groups of infants whose mothers completed the MABI did better on Brazelton scale items assessing the infant's interactive capabilities and interacted more positively with their mothers. At 4 months of age, these same infants exhibited superior fine-motor abilities on a developmental-milestones screening device and superior face-to-face parent-child interactions. At 12 months, the infants whose mothers had been involved in testing received significantly higher scores on a test of mental functioning. There were few significant differences between the two groups of mothers who completed the MABI at home. Widmayer and Field concluded that mothers who are made aware of their infants' skills and abilities may actually interact in more optimal ways with their babies and that these interactions can enhance the infants' early development.

Research of this type has led more and more hospitals to employ professionals and paraprofessionals trained in the administration of the Brazelton. The goal is to prevent problems between parents and their infants by helping parents to become more aware of the individual characteristics of their babies. Evaluations of newborns with the parents present are sometimes done by a developmental psychologist who functions as part of an interdisciplinary team that provides services to hospital units responsible for the care of infants. Increasingly, nurses and physical and occupational therapists in newborn units also are being trained to use the Brazelton test to encourage parental appreciation of infants' capabilities. Because the Brazelton was designed for use with infants 38 to 44 weeks gestational age (babies are born on the average at a gestational age of 40 weeks), the majority of testing is done in the hospital prior to the infant's discharge home. Not only is this the most convenient time to see both parents and their infant together, but it is a time when parental interest in the newborn is extremely high. Moreover, parents frequently want to learn as much as possible about their infant before finding themselves alone with the baby at home.

Individual Differences in Later Infancy. Although the Brazelton assessment appears to be of value in furthering understanding of the newborn period, its usefulness is limited by the fact that it may be used only with infants less than one month old. Because infancy is characterized by rapid changes, it has become necessary to develop methods to document changes beyond the earliest stages of life.

There are several questionnaire assessment instruments currently being used to measure individuality past early infancy. The majority of these are believed to assess individual differences in "temperament." Temperament is a term used by Harold Thomas and Stella Chess (1977) to refer to a child's specific style of behavioral individuality or "personality." In Chess and Thomas's (1973) view, psychological development is the result of how each child's specific individual characteristics interact with people, things, and events in the child's environment. Thomas, Chess, and Birch (1968) set out to document the nature of the interaction between individual differences and the child's environment by identifying initial personal characteristics in infancy and studying their stability and change over time.

To study the development of temperament, Thomas, Chess, and Birch (1968) followed the development of 141 children from 3 months of age to 20 years. The researchers had frequent contact with these children, their parents and families, and eventually their teachers. Nine basic behavioral variables thought to represent the fundamental ways in which these children varied temperamentally were identified. These nine variables were activity level, rhythmicity, approach/withdrawal, adaptability, threshold of responsiveness, intensity of reaction, quality of mood, distractability, and attention span or persistence.

Although Thomas and his colleagues stressed that each child is a unique individual, they were able to identify three common types of youngster, each with its own style of relating to the world. One type of child, the *difficult* child, reacts in a predominantly intense and negative manner to new situations, is very slow to adapt to changes in his or her schedule or environment, and is considered irregular in sleeping and eating habits. On the other hand, the *easy* child, who accounted for the overwhelming majority of the children in the study, is regular and predictable, generally positive in mood, and readily adapts to new situations and people. Thomas, Chess, and Birch also identified an intermediate type of youngster who, although initially quite hesitant and withdrawing, will eventually adapt quite well to stress and environmental change if not approached too rapidly or pressured. This temperamental type is called the *slow-to-warm* child. By following all three types of youngsters over time, the researchers discovered that classification into one category or another did not guarantee or reliably predict whether or not a child would develop a behavioral disturbance. Interestingly, those children who did develop serious enough problems to warrant outside intervention came from all three categories, and behavior problems were most characteristic of children whose parents were unable to adapt their parenting styles to the unique behavioral characteristics of their own children.

Based on the work of Thomas and Chess, other, more easily administered measures of temperament have been developed. For example, the Carey Infant Temperament Questionnaire (Carey, 1970) was developed exclusively for use in clinical settings such as hospitals and clinics. This questionnaire is a multiple-choice version of the interview used in Thomas, Chess, and Birch's research. The same nine temperament dimensions are assessed in infants aged 4 to 8 months, and, based on this scale, children are grouped into the same three temperamental types discussed by Thomas, Chess, and Birch. Although this particular instrument is used to assess individual differences in infants under 1 year of age, other questionnaires have been developed to assess differences in youngsters from 1 to 12 years old (Fullard, McDevitt, & Carey, 1978; McDevitt and Carey, 1975). These instruments are now readily available to psychologists and doctors.

The major problem with some of the measures of children's temperament is that they are based on parental reports of children's behaviors. It is possible that parents' perceptions of their children are not always accurate. Indeed, it appears that parental ratings of temperament reflect both characteristics of the parent (e.g., maternal personality and family background) and real differences in children's responses (Bates & Bayles, 1984). In brief, it is important to recognize that indices of temperament may reflect adults' perceptions of children as well as actual individual differences in children.

Representative Application: Assessment of Infant Temperament. Researchers who have used temperament questionnaires in pediatric settings have found that individual differences in infant behaviors are related to various concerns of parents. For instance, one aspect of temperament, the tendency to respond quickly and easily to environmental stimuli, has been associated with incidents of nightwaking in infants 4 to 8 months old (Carey, 1974). Also, infants rated as "difficult" have been found to experience episodes of colic during the early months and are more likely to receive injuries requiring medical intervention than infants rated "easy" (Cary, 1972).

In many private medical practices where infants are seen for "well-child" care, the Carey Infant Temperament Questionnaire is routinely administered to the parents of all infants at least once during the first year of life. Information gained from this report may be used by the pediatrician or pediatric nurse practitioner to alert parents to the specific behavioral style exhibited by their infant. In this way, parents are able to acquire knowledge about infant variability and to adjust their caretaking practices to their own child's individual style. Many parents report that the simple act of completing the questionnaire has helped them to see their children as individuals and has focused their attention on specific ways in which their children react to various situations and people. Appreciation of such differences can, no doubt, assist parents in perceiving and interacting with their youngsters in ways that are more productive and pleasurable for both parent and child.

Group health-care practices are becoming more commonplace, and many such organizations feel the need (and have the resources) to employ a person specifically trained in child development. Such child-development specialists are usually well aware that infants differ in "personality" or temperament, as well as in the rate of physical growth, number of infectious illnesses, and motor development. Typically, in such settings, parents of "difficult" infants will be referred by the physician to the psychologist for assistance in understanding and working with their children. In these situations, disordered parent-infant interactions sometimes can be improved by specifying for the parent the infant's unique contribution to the caregiving situation.

Because parents often feel totally responsible for the way in which an infant or child "turns out," guilt concerning malfunctioning parent-child relationships is common. Recall the young mother cited in the Brazelton study (1961) who felt that she had somehow erred in her caretaking of, and relationship with, her young son with the deviant states of arousal. She was overwhelmed by the thought that somehow she was responsible for the problem. Similarly, the eight mothers in the Prechtl investigation (1963) of brain-damaged infants felt that their children's aberrant behavior was due, in some way, to their mishandling of the children. Perhaps the most important application or outcome of research on early individuality has been to help parents like these realize that an infant's or child's behavioral "difficultness" is not necessarily the direct result of poor parenting. To know that some of the difficulties parents have encountered with an infant might well be due to characteristics of the infant can do much to prevent the deep feelings of guilt and inadequacy that many parents experience regarding their child's problems. Moreover, by providing parents with insight into their children's unique characteristics, psychologists can help parents to find means of coping with their children. For example, psychologists can recommend that the parents seek additional support from relatives, friends, and professionals; such support has been related to irritable infants' positive social development (Crockenberg, 1981)

High-Risk Infants.   The issue of neonatal risk status is another area in which the research of developmental psychologists has had great practical impact. As medical care has become increasingly sophisticated in recent decades, more and more premature and other infants considered at "high risk" for future developmental difficulties are now surviving. Since an estimated 7% to 10% of all live births fall into the category of infants who would have died in the past, reliable information pertaining to the growth and development of these special infants is of increasing importance. In recent years, developmental psychologists have been conducting more and better research concerning the mental and motor development, the behavioral organization, and the interactive idiosyncrasies of these infants. As more is learned about these topics, the better adapted early caregiving practices will be to the particular needs and demands of these very small and immature babies.

Prematurity is one type of medical risk about which much has been learned. According to recent research, how well a premature child develops is strongly related to the home environment the infant experiences (Sameroff & Chandler, 1975). In fact, the quality of parent-infant interactions appears to be one of the best predictors of development for high-risk infants, as well as for normal infants (Beckwith & Cohen, 1978). Since infant characteristics affect their interactions with caregivers, knowledge about the ways in which preterm infants differ from their full-term counterparts can be useful to parents and professionals dealing with high risk children.

Development of Premature Infants. In early studies on the effects of prematurity on development, psychologists were most often concerned with the mental and physical development of these infants. In general, they found that prematurity per se was not a good predictor of later development, but that some infants born prematurely were at greater risk for developmental retardation than were others. For instance, there appears to be a greater likelihood of developmental problems in infants experiencing medical complications at birth and in the newborn period. Thus an infant born prematurely with low birthweight but who otherwise requires no specific medical intervention is more likely to develop normally than a low-birthweight premature infant who has a breathing problem or cardiac complications. Moreover, premature infants who experience central nervous system complications (e.g., hemorrhages or seizures) alone or in combination with other illness are more likely to exhibit poor mental and motor development at 1 year of age than either healthy prematures or prematures who are merely sick (Roth, Eisenberg, & Sells, 1984). However, even within subgroups of premature infants, there is wide variability in functioning; consequently, neonatal medical status is a less-than-adequate means of identifying infants at highest risk for future problems.

Behavior of Premature Infants. In early work with premature infants, researchers clearly demonstrated that premature infants differ in their behavior from full-term infants. In comparison to other babies, premature infants have been found to be more irritable, to have more frequent bouts of crying (Elmer & Gregg, 1967) and sleep disturbances (Dreyfus-Brisac, 1974), and to be characterized by periods of prolonged sleep and drowsiness with few episodes of alert attentiveness (Klaus & Kennell, 1976). Moreover, with the development of instruments such as the Brazelton Neonatal Behavioral Assessment Scale (Brazelton, 1973) and other systems for observation of neonatal behaviors, much has been learned about how high-risk newborns, particularly infants born prematurely, differ from normal, full-term infants.

Frequently, preterm infants' ability to organize behavior and to respond appropriately to stimulation from the environment appears to be impaired as a result of coming into the world with immature systems. Their neurological functioning, reflexes, and states of arousal are often impaired or deviant, probably due to uneven maturation of the nervous system or delayed development of the infants' ability to coordinate their psychological systems when responding to stimulation (Parmalee, 1974). For example, Groski, Davison, and Brazelton (1979), using a form of the Brazelton Neonatal Behavior Assessment Scale (1973) especially adapted for use with a preterm population, found that premature infants may have difficulty in maintaining prolonged states of alertness. Conse-

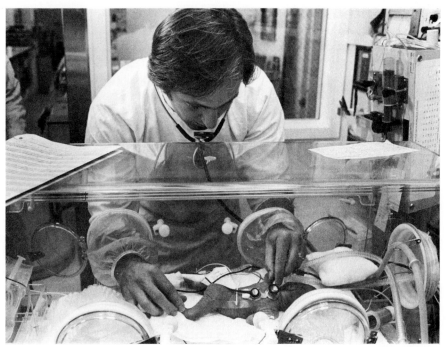

Psychologists observe and evaluate high-risk newborns both in intensive-care nurseries and after discharge. The data gathered are used in formulating predictions of developmental problems.

quently, the infant's readiness to respond may be lower than that of a normal full-term infant, who can and does become alert without much difficulty. Preterm high-risk infants also fatigue easily, and the periods of alert attentiveness they display may easily overtax their immature psychological capacities, producing variations in breathing patterns. Due to immature and weak musculature, coupled with the infant's diminished ability to shut out potentially disturbing stimulation (e.g., bright lights, loud noises, or handling), a premature infant's response to stimuli frequently is either absent or sluggish, or overexaggerated and jerky.

Representative Application: Improved Care of High-Risk Infants.   Observations of infant behavior can provide clues to the responses of which they are capable and to those responses an infant may need help in regulating. Consequently, detailed evaluations of high-risk newborns are routinely being conducted in intensive-care nurseries across the country.

Because the first weeks and sometimes months of a premature infant's life are spent in the hospital, it is especially important that hospital personnel (e.g., physicians, nurses, and therapists) have access to information concerning individual differences in high-risk infants' capacities and reactions. Based on this information, hospital staff can tailor their caretaking practices to the needs of the individual child. Although some infants respond positively to regular patterns of hospital care with respect to feeding, sleep, and handling, other infants may not be able to tolerate such intrusions except on a schedule that is highly individualized and sensitive to the baby's own needs and demands. Moreover, once high-risk infants are discharged from the hospital, it is important that their parents know which caretaking techniques are most effective for their specific children.

Because infants who have received intensive care at birth are more likely than other infants to require special psychological or medical assistance during childhood, most neonatal intensive-care nurseries provide a system of follow-up evaluations. Generally, these are conducted at specified intervals beginning soon after the infant is discharged and goes home, and are intended to detect problems with development as soon as possible in order to provide early intervention.

The majority of infants considered at risk for future development problems do not in fact manifest such problems; thus it is not economically feasible for newborn programs to continue to follow up on all high-risk infants. Consequently, psychologists have attempted to develop assessment instruments that will accurately identify those infants who are likely to experience problems after the initial period of hospitalization (e.g., Parmelee, Sigman, Kopp, & Haber, 1976). For example, in one study, a developmental psychologist, Tiffany Field, and her colleagues (Field, Hallock, Ting, Dempsey, Dabiri, & Shuman, 1978) studied three groups of infants for the first 12 months of their lives. Included in the study was a group of high-risk infants born prematurely who experienced respiratory distress, a group of high-risk infants born late who suffered from postmaturity syndrome, and a group of normal infants. The infants' development was evaluated every 4 months with a variey of developmental instruments (e.g., the Brazelton, Carey Infant Temperament Questionnaire and the Infant Bayley Scales of Mental and Motor Development). Field found that the sickest infants at birth (those suffering from respiratory distress) were still exhibiting both mental and motor delays at 12 months of age, and that the postmature infants were behind in mental development at 12 months. Most important, she found that the possibility of developmental problems could be more accurately predicted from information gathered over the entire first year of life than from the infant's medical status at birth alone. Such refinements in the developmental concept of "risk" can be used to make reasonable decisions regarding follow-up procedures. For example, based on Field and her colleagues' findings, one might choose to limit follow-up visits for infants who overcome their initial "risk" conditions, and to increase monitoring procedure for infants with minimal or greater risk at birth who fail to progress on schedule.

In summary, developmental issues are of considerable importance to practitioners working with infants and young children. Consequently, developmental psychologists are making significant contributions to the understanding of healthy development and are important members of the health-care team in numerous pediatric units.

Day Care and Intervention Programs in the Preschool Years

Another applied issue of concern to developmental psychologists is the effect of various types of preschool or day-care programs on young children's development. Due to increasing rates of both maternal employment and single parenthood in recent years, many preschool children spend large portions of their days in day-care centers or other alternative systems of child care (*Child Care Data and Materials,* 1974). Moreover, in the past two decades, the government, universities, and other groups or institutions have sponsored a variety of special programs that are designed to stimulate the cognitive development of young children, especially those from culturally diverse backgrounds. Because of the numbers of children involved in alternative-care programs and the potential benefit or harm that could result from both day-care and special intervention programs, developmental psychologists have been active in the attempt to evaluate the effects of these programs on children's emotional, social, and cognitive development.

Day Care.   Many developmental psychologists first became concerned with the potential effects of day care because of theory and research in the 1960s and early 1970s concerning children's relationships with their parents. At that time, John Bowlby, an influential theorist, suggested that most young children develop close relationships with only a few people (usually parents, among others), and that separations of children from those they are attached to frequently have negative consequences for the parent-child relationship (Bowlby, 1973). Moreover, at the time that Bowlby's theory was gaining wide acceptance, results of research on the development of children's attachments were consistent with the view that separation of mother and child could have a negative effect on children's development (see Ainsworth, 1973; Ainsworth, Blehar, Waters & Wall, 1978).

More specifically, Mary Ainsworth (a prominent developmental psychologist) and other researchers have found that children with sensitive mothers (mothers who are attuned to their children's needs, respond promptly and appropriately to the children's cues, are accepting and warm, and who consider the children's wants and needs as well as their own) have more **securely attached children** (Ainsworth, 1973). Being securely attached to one's caretaker (usually the mother or father) apparently has numerous positive consequences for the child. For example, securely attached children, in comparison to insecurely attached children, are more curious, flexible and resilient, obedient, positive towards others, and self-regulated; further, securely attached children appear to be more competent in both peer interactions and in their attempts to accomplish frustrating tasks (Arend, Gove, & Stroufe, 1979; Lieberman, 1977; Londerville & Main, 1981; Matas, Arend, & Stroufe, 1978; Pastor, 1981; Stayton, Hogan, & Ainsworth, 1971; Waters, Wippman, & Stroufe, 1979). Because it was assumed that long separations between parent and child during the day would prevent sensitive mothering and consequently would result in less secure attachments, psychologists feared that the day-care experience would have long-term negative consequences such as poor parent-child relationships, increased anxiety and emotional problems, impaired social competence, and, possibly, lower cognitive functioning (Ainsworth, 1973; Blehar, 1974; Bowlby, 1973).

Limitations of the Research on Day-Care Environments. Today, due primarily to the efforts of developmental psychologists, there is a considerable amount of research concerning the effects of day care on the emotional, social, and cognitive development of children. Consequently, it is now possible to begin to assess the effects of day care on children. However, it is clear that we do not yet know nearly enough about the potential influences of child care outside the home. This is true for at least four reasons (Belsky & Steinberg, 1978).

One of the reasons that we do not know enough about the effects of day care is that there is not yet sufficient quality research on the effects of various methods of child care. The first empirical day-care study was published in 1970 (Caldwell, Wright, Honig, & Tannenbaum, 1970), and much of the existing research is methodologically flawed. A second reason is that nearly all of the existing research has been conducted in day-care centers. This is problematic because most preschoolers who are not cared for by their parents during the day are not enrolled in day-care centers or nurseries — they are cared for by babysitters in their own home or in someone else's home. Indeed, only 11% of children six years of age or younger who receive substitute care are in nurseries, preschools, or day-care centers (*National Childcare Consumer Study,* 1975). Thus while the results of most of the research on alternative child care are informative regarding the effects of placement in day-care centers, this research should not be interpreted as pertaining to other types of child-care arrangements (e.g., a babysitter in the home) used by many parents

A third problem with the existing research on the effects of day care is that nearly all of this research has been conducted in high-quality centers. Unfortunately, the majority of day-care centers, expecially those that are proprietary (for-profit) rather than nonprofit centers, do not provide high-quality care (Keyserling, 1972). Hence, the findings of research conducted in high-quality centers may not be generalizable to the quality of care available to most families.

Two other problems with the research on the effects of day care are methodological in a nature. First, few researchers have examined the long-term effects of day care beyond the preschool years. Thus it is quite possible that any effects of day care that have been reported disappear with time as children age, or that some effects have not yet been noted because they are not observable until a later age. Second, in most studies on the effects of day care, children in day-care centers are compared with children who are not in day-care centers and whose parents chose not to enroll them in a center. Thus the two groups of children differ not only in day-care experience, but also in their parents' attitudes toward day care and the parental role. Because parental attitudes and values influence child-rearing practices (Kohn, 1963), which in turn affect the child's development, any finding of a difference between home-care and day-care groups in many studies could be due to differences in parental values, and not to day care itself.

One way of dealing with the problem of comparability or similarity of samples is to select children for the sample of non-day-care children from those on waiting lists to get into day care. Then the researcher can be somewhat more confident that the parents of the two samples of children are equivalent in their attitudes toward day care. This has been done in only a few studies (e.g., Cochran, 1977; Cummings, 1980). However, as researchers have become aware of this problem, they have begun to change their methods of studying the effects of day care.

Now that the shortcomings of the existing research on the effects of day care have been outlined, the results of this research will be summarized and the effect of day care on emotional, cognitive, and social development will be considered.

Emotional Development. As was mentioned previously, many psychologists concerned with the attachment process have suggested that the separation of the child from his or her mother that results from day care impairs the development of a strong mother-child relationship. Overall, however, the research is not consistent with this view. True, a few researchers have noted that day-care children exhibit more negative reactions (considered a sign of an insecure attachment) than do home-reared children during or after separation from the mother (Blehar, 1974; Cochran, 1977; Regozin, 1980). Only a few differences however, have typically been found in these studies (Cochran, 1977; Ragozin, 1980), and other researchers have found that home-reared children, not day-care children, exhibit more distress when separated from their mothers (e.g., Moskowitz, Schwarz, & Corsini, 1977). More important, most researchers have found no differences in the behavior of home-reared and day-care children toward their mothers (e.g., Belsky & Steinberg, 1978; Brookhart & Hock, 1976; Caldwell, Wright, Honig & Tannenbaum, 1970; Clarke-Stewart & Fein 1983; Portnoy & Simmons, 1978; Roopnarine & Lamb, 1978). Moreover, the child's relationship with an alternative caretaker (e.g., a day-care teacher) does not seem to interfere with or replace the child's emotional attachment to his or her own mother (Cummings, 1980; Farran & Ramey, 1977; Ricciuti, 1974).

There does seem to be one important exception to the conclusion that day care does not have any consistent negative effects on children's emotional development. It is possible that there are negative effects for children who enter day care prior to 12 months of age. In studies in which children have entered day care in the first year of life, researchers generally have found higher levels of avoidance of the mother in day-care than in stay-at-home children (Hock, 1980; Vaughn, Gove, and Egeland, 1980; Schwartz, 1983). More research is needed to clarify the significance and prevalence of this avoidance behavior by infants in day care.

In summary, according to the research on the effects of day care, there is little reason to believe that high-quality day care had a negative effect on the bond between child and mother, at least if the child enters day care after 12 months of age. However, older day-care children may act slightly more distant than home-reared children, and day care may have negative effects on very young children's attachments. It is important that researchers start to examine the long-term effects of day care so that it is possible to determine whether or not the early avoidant or distant behaviors sometimes associated with day care are of real significance.

Cognitive Development. Another issue that concerns developmental psychologists is the effect of day care on preschoolers' cognitive development. However, although there is a considerable amount of research concerning the effects of special programs designed to enrich a preschooler's environment, there is much less research on the effects of regular day care on cognitive development.

In general, researchers have examined the effects of day care on cognitive development by administering standardized tests of intelligence to day-care and home-reared children. According to the limited data collected in this manner, there appear to be no long-term effects of day care on the cognitive development of low-risk — that is, nondisadvantaged — children (e.g., Caldwell et al., 1970; Cochran, 1977; Moore, 1974; see Belsky and Steinberg, 1978). In contrast, in an important study involving 31 different day-care programs in New York City, a group of researchers (Golden, Rosenbluth, Crossi, Policare, Freeman, & Brownlee, 1978) found that normal day care has a positive influence on the cognitive development of high-risk children from disadvantaged homes. More specifically, the researchers found that at 18 months of age, children who had been enrolled in day care outside the home between the ages of 2 and 14 months scored higher on a test of cognitive ability than did children reared at home. By 36 months of age, the day-care center children scored higher than both children reared at home and those receiving care in another family's home. Enrollment in day care did not raise the disadvantaged children's IQs, but it did seem to prevent the decline in IQ with age that is frequently found for high-risk children.

The reason why day care may improve the intellectual functioning of some children is not clear. It is likely, however, that children in day care receive more direct teaching than do children at home and that the style of the instruction given is more conducive to learning intellectual tasks. This style is bolstered by the availability of a variety of equipment and structured activities (Clarke-Stewart & Fein, 1983). More research is needed, however, to pinpoint both the degree of cognitive advance that is associated with day care and the mechanisms that facilitate any advance.

Social Development. One reason that parents may send their children to day care is that they expect the day-care program to help their children get along socially with other children. Another reason is that parents hope the day-care providers will teach their children adult-like behaviors such as cooperation and self-control. In recent years, developmental psychologists have attempted to determine if these are valid expectations, that is, if the day-care experience has a positive effect on preschoolers' social development.

Although the research is not entirely consistent, it appears that day-care children are more likely to approach their peers than are home-reared children (Belsky

Day care: major national concern, political issue, economic factor. Applied developmental psychologists are addressing a number of key questions, for example, how to identify characteristics of centers associated with superior child development.

& Steinberg, 1978; Clarke-Stewart & Fein, 1983; Ricciuti, 1974.) Indeed, the amount of day-care experience is related to the amount of positive interaction with peers; children who are enrolled in day care for the full day exhibit a higher rate of positive peer interactions at their center than children enrolled for only half-days (Vlietstra, 1981). Moreover, day-care or preschool experience appears to have effects on the development of social competence. For example, children in early-childhood programs appear to be more self-confident, outgoing, self-regulated, self-assured, independent, friendly, and assertive than home-reared children (Clarke-Stewart, in press; Clarke-Stewart & Fein, 1983; Howes & Olenick, 1986; Moore, 1975; Rubenstein, Howes, & Boyle, 1981). In addition, day-care children, when they go to school, are better adjusted, more task-oriented, and more often leaders than are other children (Clarke-Stewart & Fein, 1983; Fowler & Khan, 1974).

In this country, the day-care experience is not only associated with sociability toward peers, but also with childlike rather than adultlike behavior. More specifically, day-care children seem to be somewhat more aggressive, less cooperative, and less conforming than their home-reared peers (Moore, 1964; Raph, Thomas, Chess, & Korn, 1964; Schwarz, Strickland & Krolick, 1974; see Belsky and Steinberg, 1978). The day-care experience also seems to lead to a decrease in the amount of interaction with adults (McCutcheon & Calhoun, 1976), and to more negative interactions with teachers when in first grade (Raph et al., 1964).

Although day care in America is associated with peer-orientation and more childlike behaviors, this does not seem to be the case in some other cultures. When the goals of day care are to promote an adult orientation and conformity (as in the U.S.S.R., Bronfenbrenner, 1970), day care is usually associated with these outcomes. In brief, with regard to social behaviors, children in day care seem to learn the social behaviors that children in their culture are allowed or expected to exhibit.

Representative Application: Identifying Characteristics of Centers Associated with Optimal Development.   Developmental psychologists are interested not only in the effects of day care, but also in the characteristics that determine if a specific center has a positive or negative influence on children's development.

With regard to the relationship between the staff of a day-care center and the children, children seem to feel more positive toward their caretakers if their caretakers have been at the center for a relatively long period of time, that is, if they are stable (Cummings, 1980), and if the center is of high quality (in terms of facilities, program, and equipment) (Anderson, Nagle, Roberts, & Smith, 1981). Moreover, as might be expected, children tend to show more attachment behaviors toward caretakers who spend relatively large amounts of time involved in positive interactions with the children at a close range (Anderson et al., 1981).

In a large government-sponsored study of day-care centers, researchers found that several other aspects of the day-care environment influence the quality of care (*Final Report of the National Day Care Study: Children at the Center,* 1979). For preschool children, quality of care was related to the size of the group, the education of the teacher, and the ratio of teachers to children. For example, in smaller groups, as contrasted to larger ones, teachers of preschoolers engaged in more social interaction with children. Further, the children were more cooperative, less hostile, more innovative, more likely to express their opinions and preferences, and made greater gains on tests of cognitive skills. For infants and toddlers, small group size and a high ratio of caretakers to children were associated with an absence of distress and apathy among the children, a low incidence of potentially harmful behavior among the children, and a high proportion of time spent by caretakers directing activities likely to promote optimal development. Moreover, the number of years a teacher had attended school was found to be related to quality day care for infants and toddlers, while the amount of education in child development a teacher had received was associated with better day care for preschoolers.

In summary, by interviewing parents and teachers, and by observing children in day care, psychologists and educators have been able to determine some of the factors that contribute to the quality of day care. Surely, given the increasing role of day care in today's society, developmental psychologists are likely to remain interested in this issue for some time.

Cognitive-Enrichment Preschool Programs.   It has been clear for some time that children from economically disadvantaged backgrounds tend to perform more poorly in school and on tests of cognitive ability than do children from middle-class or upper-class families (Hess, 1970). In the 1960s, due in part to the social and political atmosphere of the time (this was the era of President Johnson's War on Poverty, which involved considerable social reform), psychologists, educators, legislators, and the general public became concerned with the discrepancy between the cognitive performance of economically disadvantaged and more advantaged children. Consequently, the government started to fund programs designed to enhance the cognitive development of the nation's poor children (for example, Head Start), and researchers became involved in the effort to develop and evaluate cognitive-enrichment projects.

Most of the Head Start enrichment programs funded by the government were haphazardly conducted and were not evaluated for effectiveness. In contrast, a number of psychologists in the 1960s initiated and implemented research-based, early education programs — programs that not only provided services for young children and/or their families, but also were used as a basis for empirically evaluating the effectiveness of various procedures for stimulating cognitive development during infancy and the preschool years. Developmental psychologists designed and spearheaded many of these programs.

Early intervention programs designed to promote cognitive enrichment can be divided into four types: home-based, parent-oriented programs; center-based, parent-oriented programs; home-based, child-oriented programs; and center-based, child-oriented programs. In home-based programs, the intervention process is conducted in the home, while in center-based programs, the program is based in a place outside the home. In parent-oriented programs, parents, not children, are the ones who directly participate in the program. The philosophy underlying this approach is that a parent is a child's primary socializer; consequently, the best way to produce significant, lasting change in children is to modify their parents' child-rearing practices, teaching techniques, use of language with the child, and so forth. In child-oriented programs, the interventions are administered directly to the children, not to the parents; thus the children participate in activities designed to stimulate language and cognitive development. Examples of these activities are "games" involving numbers, the use of language, or concepts such as color and shape.

The effects of enrichment intervention programs have been evaluated with a variety of measures, In general, evaluation measures have been administered to the target children some time after the program has been initiated and, frequently, a year or more after the child (or his/her parent) is no longer participating in the intervention program. With these measures, the researchers can evaluate both the immediate and long-term effects of the interventions. Measures that have been used for these purposes include intelligence tests, school grades, tests of language ability, and interview questions concerning the child's achievement-orientation and self-concept. Moreover, in some studies, variables such as maternal satisfaction with the child's performance in school and mothers' aspirations for their children are assessed.

The early reports concerning the effectiveness of early intervention programs (especially the government-sponsored Head Start programs) were discouraging.

The early research indicated that pioneer cognitive-enrichment programs, such as the Head Start class pictured, were not effective. Later programs, especially those that were research-based, appeared to prevent the decline in cognitive functioning experienced by some disadvantaged children as they grew older.

For example, in one nationwide study of Head Start programs, researchers found that these programs had relatively little effect on children's achievement and personal adequacy (Cicirella, 1969). These initial findings fueled a heated debate regarding both the effectiveness of intervention programs and the relative role of enivronmental factors (such as stimulation and type of schooling) and hereditary factors in cognitive development (Jensen, 1969; Hunt, 1969; Scarr-Salapatek, 1971). Later research findings, however, especially those concerning research-based intervention programs (those developed and evaluated by researchers) rather than Head Start programs, were more encouraging. In general, according to the more recent research, there appear to be immediate positive effects within the first three years of life for lower-class, economically disadvantaged children enrolled in these programs (Beller, 1979). The longer the length of the intervention, the stronger the effect seems to be (Beller, 1979). More specifically, enrichment programs seem to prevent the decline in cognitive functioning that usually occurs as the children age (Beller, 1979; Lazar & Darlington, 1982; Smith & Bissell, 1970).

Some of the most exciting research findings concerning the effects of early cognitive enrichment programs are the result of collaborative efforts by a number of psychologists (primarily developmental psychologists). In 1974, in response to public statements that early intervention programs were ineffective for economically disadvantaged children, Irving Lazar and Edith Grotberg developed the idea of conducting a follow-up of the children who were participants in the intervention programs begun in the 1960s. As a result, in 1975, the investigators who had conducted 11 different independent studies decided to pool their original data and conduct a joint follow-up study. This unusual collaboration was coordinated by Irving Lazar and Richard Darlington.

In 1976, this consortium (collaborative group) located and studied many of the children who had been involved in intervention programs when they were preschoolers (in the 1960s). Some of these children had graduated from high school by 1976; the range of ages of the children was approximately 8 to 18 years. As part of the follow-up, the children were given achievement and IQ tests, and the children and their mothers were questioned regarding their attitudes. Also, information concerning the children's academic performance was obtained from their schools.

The results of the follow-up were quite interesting. The researchers found that the early-intervention programs had long-lasting effects in four areas: school competence, cognitive abilities, children's attitudes and values, and impact on the family. Children who had attended the programs were less likely than children who had not attended similar programs to be assigned to special-education classes or to be held back a grade in school (this was true for all the children regardless of sex, ethnic background, initial ability level, or early family background). Moreover, the children who had attended the intervention programs scored higher than comparable children on IQ tests for several years after the programs had ended, and performed somewhat better on some tests of achievement. Furthermore, in 1976, 4 to 12 years after the various programs had ended, the children who had attended the early-education programs were more likely than comparable children to give achievement-related reasons (such as work or school accomplishments) for being proud of themselves. Similarly, in 1976, mothers of the program children were more satisfied with their children's school performance and had relatively high occupational aspirations for their children (higher than those of the children themselves).

In summary, it is now clear that the early-education programs instituted by psychologists did have positive effects on children's academic performance, test scores, and achievement-related attitudes. Findings such as these have important conceptual and practical implications. The fact that early-education programs are associated with higher cognitive performance is consistent with the argument that intelligence is not a relatively unchangeable, inherited ability, but is significantly influenced by early experiences. Moreover, it is clear that children can obtain the types of experience that enhance cognitive development in quality early-education programs.

Due to both the initial negative reports concerning the success of early intervention programs and the government's current socioeconomic policies, relatively few intervention programs are now being initiated or funded. However, because recent research has demonstrated the positive consequences of these programs, it is possible that there will be renewed interest in the issue of enhancing early cognitive development. If this is true, developmental psychologists will certainly play an important role in developing future intervention techniques and programs.

Assessment and Training of Social Skills in Children

As developmental psychologists have become more applied in their interests, the areas of inquiry that they pursue have come to overlap to a greater extent with topics of interest to practitioners in other psychological specialities, the helping professions, and education. The assessment and training of **social skills** is one such area of research and practice in which developmental psychologists are part of a larger set of contributors.

Definition of Social Skills.   Most people recognize, among their friends and acquaintances, individuals who are very socially skilled and others who are socially inept. What factors differentiate these groups—what kinds of behaviors or cognitions distinguish the two? A variety of answers to questions such as these have been offered by investigators and practitioners in their attempts to define social skills. Not surprisingly, in a field as diverse as social-skills assessment and training, no universally accepted definitions have emerged (Beller, 1979). Indeed, a major contributor to the field has identified the problem of definition as the major issue within the entire social-skills arena (Curran, 1979).

One of the earliest attempts to define social skills stressed assertiveness (Chittenden, 1942) or modes of interpersonal interaction that influence others without causing them harm. Emphasis on appropriate assertion is evident as well in some contemporary conceptions of social skills (Rotheram, 1980). From this perspective, socially skilled individuals are well aware of their own needs and represent those needs clearly and appropriately in dealing with others.

Another frequently cited definition focuses on the consequences associated with one's behavior in a social context. Socially skilled people behave so that they maximize their reinforcements and minimize their punishments (Libet & Lewinsohn, 1973).

Some definitions of social skills are so broad that they include self-help skills such as personal grooming. Others are much narrower and limit the term *social skills* to behaviors that can be directly observed (Curran, 1979).

Definitions sometimes reflect theoretical orientations. Many recent definitions from behaviorally oriented psychologists include one or more of the following elements:

1. Social skills are best conceived of as a discrete set of verbal and nonverbal behavior.
2. Social skills are situation-specific.
3. Social skills are learned.

Regarding the discrete set of verbal and nonverbal behaviors included in the behavioral definition of social skills, there is some agreement that, in the abstract, such a set exists, but its composition is subject to debate. Those who attempt to construct such a list face a number of difficulties, not the least of which is **situational specificity.** As used here *situational specificity* means that behaviors may be socially sanctioned in one setting or set of circumstances and considered inappropriate under other conditions. For example, in many cultures a socially competent individual may smile when greeted by a friend but not when the friend tells of a death in the family. Because socially skilled behavior depends on the situation a person is in, the lists of skills proposed by various behaviorally oriented researchers and trainers must be different in different situations. In short, there is no single set of behaviors that socially skilled individuals consistently engage in.

Investigators and practitioners who are more cognitive in orientation tend to view social skills not as a set of behaviors but rather as a set of cognitive abilities that help a person to act appropriately (Rotheram, 1980). Several of these abiliteis are covert problem-solving processes — the ability to interpret and solve social problems; social inferential ability — the ability to predict what will happen next in social situations; and perspective taking — the ability to see another's point of view (D'Zurilla & Goldfried, 1971; Spivack & Shure, 1974). Socially skillful behavior occurs when certain cognitive processes are brought to bear in an interpersonal context. From this viewpoint, one would not identify a specific list of behaviors in a definition of social skills, but might provide examples of the range of behaviors that can reflect important cognitive or emotional processes underlying social skills.

Assessment of Social Skills. Another perspective from which to examine conceptions of social skills is that of assessment. What social-skills trainers assess, and how they conduct their assessment, tells us much about their thinking.

Sociometric Procedures. One of the more commonly used methods for assessing social skills in children is the sociometric procedure or device. Sociometric measures are usually administered to groups of children — most often to all children within a classroom or some other natural grouping. When using the sociometric approach, researchers ask children questions about their relationships with other children in their group in order to measure who is and who is not socially skilled. Children are asked to nominate or rate peers in the group with reference to some particular criterion. When the **nomination procedure** is used, they are asked to identify or select a specified number of peers. For example, pupils might be asked to name the five classmates with whom they would like to work on a special project. Or, they might receive the instruction, "Name the three classmates you don't especially like or like least." In contrast to nomination procedures, with the **peer rating procedure,** children are given a list of names for all those in their class and are asked to rate each on some scale. For example, they might be asked to rate on a 5-point scale how much they would like to play with each classmate, and an average rating is then computed for each child. Usually, ratings from opposite-sex peers are excluded in determining the average because there is often a sex bias in children's sociometric ratings (Singleton & Asher, 1977).

Of the two sociometric procedures, the peer rating method rather than the peer nomination procedure seems to be more reliable (Oden & Asher, 1977). In addition, peer rating can facilitate identification of behavioral deficits and excesses that may become the target of further study or intervention. Peer nomination procedures seem to be better suited to identification of children who are accepted or rejected (Gresham & Elliott, 1984). Especially when used for these respective purposes, both varieties of sociometric procedures appear to give reliable results and correctly measure who in a group is the most socially skilled (Asher & Renshaw, 1981; Busk, Ford, & Schulman, 1973; MacMillan & Morrison, 1980; Roff, Sells, & Golden, 1972) except perhaps among preschool children (Hymel, 1983).

Observational Procedures.   Observing a child's behavior in natural settings is another of the more common methods used to assess social skills. Relatively unstructured, narrative descriptions of social interactions have been used on occasion to identify children in need of training or to evaluate the effects of an intervention. More often, however, structured, precoded observational systems are employed. With these systems, information may be recorded regarding the frequency, duration, or magnitude of various social behaviors or behavior classes. That is, one may record how often a social behavior occurs, or for how long, or the strength of the behavior. For example, in one representative study, Combs and Lahey (1981) observed, among other behaviors, eye contact (i.e., facial orientation and gaze directed at another person's face) and verbal initiation (i.e., starting a conversation). In another study, Allen, Hart, Buell, Harris, and Wolf (1964)

Unlike the human information-processing system, a video camera can record reactions and behavior simultaneously. A developmental researcher can then screen and separate responses for accurate assessment.

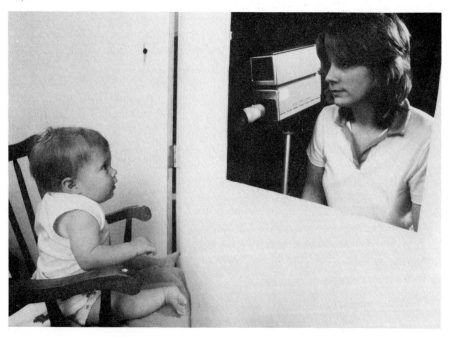

recorded proximity (i.e., closeness to another child or adult) and interaction (i.e., smiling, looking at, touching, helping, or talking with another person) in their study of a socially isolated preschooler. In other studies, researchers have examined strategies that children use in achieving goals (Krasnor & Rubin, 1983) or entering a social group (Dodge, 1983; Putallaz & Gottman, 1981).

When used by trained observers, precoded observational systems that have been carefully developed can lead to reliable information concerning patterns of behavior. Selection of the aspects of behavior to be recorded is of particular importance when judgments are to be made regarding social competence. It has been noted, for example, that the observed rate or frequency of social interaction does not correlate with peer acceptance as measured by sociometric procedures (Gottman, 1977). On the other hand, when qualitative aspects of behavior are the focus of observation (i.e., the nature of interactions), positive correlations with sociometric acceptance do occur (Gresham, 1979). An example of a coding system, adapted and simplified from a system used by Dodge (1983), is presented in Figure 16.1. Dodge's system was designed for use in play groups made up of 7- and 8-year-old boys. The original, more complex system has been used to identify behavioral correlates of peer social status.

As is true with several assessment procedures, **reactivity** may be a problem in the use of observational systems. Measures are said to be reactive when they influence that which is being measured. Children are likely to behave differently when a strange adult appears in the room and intently watches all that they do. Fortunately, reactive effects to observation tend to decrease as the nonparticipant observer spends more time in the setting. As contrasted with sociometrics, observational procedures can be used on a daily basis. Consequently they are generally better suited to monitoring the ongoing effects of social-skills training programs than are sociometric devices or most other methods of social-skill assessment.

Analogue Measures.   Analogue measures usually involve the use of observation systems, but behavior is not observed and recorded in naturally occurring settings or situations. Rather the child is instructed to role-play in a simulation of some real-world interaction or event. In other words the child pretends to be in some situation that the assessor describes, and is asked to respond as she or he normally would or as one "should." The role-play situation usually involves interaction with another person.

An example of an analogue procedure is that used by Rinn, Mahla, Markle, and Barnhart (cited in Rinn & Markle, 1979) in a study of social skills among pupils in grades 3 through 6. Videotapes of 17 social situations calling for a variety of responses were presented. Children's reactions to the various scenarios were recorded on videotapes and subsequently coded for acceptance of compliments, appropriate affect, praising others, and numerous other self-expressive and assertive behaviors.

The Behavioral Assertiveness Test for Children, or BAT-C (Bornstein, Bellack, & Hersen, 1977), another analogue measure, is administered by two per-

OBSERVATION SYSTEM FOR USE IN PLAY GROUPS

Directions for Observers

Observe child number one for 6 minutes, then move on to child number two. Record each occurrence of a behavior by placing the code for that behavior in the proper cell. Each cell represents a 10-second interval of time. Begin in the upper left-hand cell and work horizontally across the form.

Behaviors to be Recorded and Coded

S—Target child engages in a solitary activity such as playing alone, watching peers play, or sitting alone.

I—Target child engages in interactive play such as playing cooperatively in games or turn-taking activities, engaging in rough and tumble play or aggressive play.

V—Target child verbalizes such as engaging in social conversation with peers, giving directives to peers, or making hostile or supportive statements to peers.

P—Target child makes physical contact with peer such as hitting a peer, grabbing an object from a peer, or holding hands with or hugging a peer.

L—Target child converses with or is reprimanded by the group leader.

Form:

Child _____ Observer _____ Date _____

Time _____

FIGURE 16.1 Precoded observation system for use in play groups. Adapted and simplified from "Behavioral Antecedents of Peer Social Status" by K. Dodge, 1983, *Child Development, 54,* pp. 1386–1399.

sons. One person describes a situation or scene, and the second takes the part of an individual in the scene. For example, the second person might take the part of a child who is returning a borrowed pencil and confesses that she has broken the point. The child being tested assumes the role of the lender.

Research with analogue measures suggests that these techniques hold some promise for assessment of social skills, but that caution should be exercised in their use. Factors such as the gender and familiarity of role models (Eisler, Hersen, Miller, & Blanchard, 1975) and the elaborateness of the scenario (Bellack, 1979) appear to influence how subjects respond. Also, it is not clear how well children's behavior in these contrived situations reflects sociometric status or patterns of behavior in natural settings (Matson, Esveldt-Dawson, & Kazdin, 1983; Van Hasselt, Hersen, & Bellack, 1981).

Other Procedures.   At least three other procedures are used to assess various aspects of social functioning in children: interviews, rating scales or inventories, and tests of social cognition and affect.

Eisler (1976) has suggested a list of interpersonal behaviors that can be explored via the interview, and Cartledge and Milburn (1980) have adapted the list for use with children. An interview with a child provides an opportunity to collect informal observational data as well as the child's perceptions concerning his or her social competence and interpersonal history. Interviews with parents, teachers, or others are another potential source of information concerning a child's social functioning. Interviews are most likely to be used in a clinical setting in which remediation or therapy is being considered for some children.

Rating scales that are completed by a teacher or parent are another procedure for assessing children's social skills. Practitioners or researchers may construct their own scales or use previously developed, standardized scales. One such scale is the Social Behavior Assessment (SBA) measure (Stephens, 1979; 1980). The scale consists of 136 items, for which the teacher indicates that a child's behavior is acceptable or unacceptable, or that the behavior never occurs. The items are organized into four categories (environmental, interpersonal, self-related, and task related) and the completed scale provides a profile for the individual child across the four areas. Scales such as the SBA quickly and easily lead to quantified information, and there is some evidence that teacher ratings on the SBA and similar measures are reasonably reliable and valid (Gresham, 1981; Stumme, Gresham, & Scott, 1982).

Self-report inventories are often similar to analogue measures in that a scene is described to which the child responds. However, the response takes the form of choosing from written alternatives the one that indicated how the child thinks he or she would react in the situation. For example, with the Self-Report Assertiveness Test for Boys, children are presented with 20 scenarios. In a typical item children are asked to pretend that they are watching television with a friend and that the friend turns the channel to a program the child does not like. Children are then presented with various alternatives and asked how they would respond. Some self-report inventories measure a broader range of social behaviors. However, based on available research, the technical adequacy of these self-report measures for assessing children's social skills has yet to be established (Gresham & Elliott, 1984).

Cognitive theorists who study social skills in children sometimes employ tests of social cognition and emotion. These theorists believe that our thoughts about external events give rise to feelings and then to behavior. Consequently, in their view, assessment of social competence must involve attention to how children think about social events and to developmental changes in these capabilities (Eisenberg & Harris, 1984).

One of the many cognitive factors that appear to be associated with social behavior is role-taking ability. This is the ability to consider one's own point of view and that of another at the same time (Shantz, 1983). A typical procedure for assessing role-taking involves stories that a child makes up about a series of pictures. After a story is completed, the child is asked to retell it from the point of view of some character in the story. Other tests of social cognition are similar to the previously discussed analogue and self-report measures. The child identifies appropriate behaviors and gives reasons for them after reading about a social situation.

Representative Application: Social-Skills Training. As one might expect on the basis of the varied definitions of social skills, approaches to social-skills training with children are quite diverse. All training programs are aimed at improving interpersonal behavior, and nearly all involve the use of several "means of influence" or methods for inducing change. The particular combination of methods varies across programs, however, as do the length or intensity of the program, the specific aspects of interpersonal functioning that are the focus of intervention, and the populations for whom the program is intended.

With respect to the last point, a trainig program may be designed for a "clinical" population or for children who show no particular signs of inter- or intrapersonal difficulty. Among the clinical populations of children with whom social-skills training has been undertaken are the behavior disordered (Strain & Timm, 1974), the socially isolated (Oden & Asher, 1977) or withdrawn (Gresham & Nagle, 1980), the autistic (Strain, Kerr & Ragland, 1979), the mentally retarded (Matson, Kazdin, & Esveldt-Dawson, 1980), and the learning disabled (Cooke & Apolloni, 1976). Aggressive hospitalized children have also received social-skills training (Bornstein, Bellack, & Hersen, 1980). When used with "normal" populations, the goal of social-skills training may be the prevention of later mental-health problems or the fostering of the full development of an individual's potential.

Regarding the specific behavioral targets of interventions, some attempts at social-skills training are of limited scope and focus on just a few select behaviors. For example, in an intervention designed to enhance the social skills of an unpopular girl in a summer-camp setting, Blom and Zimmerman (1981) identified two goals. The first was increasing the amount of time that the girl remained in the bunkhouse during periods normally devoted to conversation. The second goal was to increase the proportion of the girl's verbalizations that could be viewed as positive comments and that did not involve interrupting another speaker.

In a social-skills training program with a much broader focus, Goldstein, Sprafkin, Gerhaw, and Klein (1980) employed procedures to identify deficiencies in and provide training for 50 social skills. Included in the 50 were beginning social skills (e.g., starting a conversation or giving a compliment), advanced social skills (e.g., asking for help or apologizing), skills for dealing with feelings (e.g., expressing affection or dealing with someone else's anger), skills for alterntives to aggression (e.g., negotiating or responding to teasing), skills for dealing with stress (e.g., dealing with embarrassment or with an accusation), and planning skills (e.g., deciding what caused a problem or setting a goal).

As mentioned earlier, most social-skills training programs incorporate a combination of techniques. Specific goals of the program, theoretical orientation of trainers, characteristics of a client population, and practical considerations are only some of the factors that influence the choice of methods.

Social-skills interventions designed by trainers with a strong behavioral orientation often emphasize the use of reinforcement. For example, in the previously cited study by Blom and Zimmerman (1981), camp counselors used positive reinforcement to influence the amount and the quality of verbal interactions for Renee, an 11-year-old girl.

Specifically, during phase 1 of the study, counselors recorded how much time Renee spent with peers in the bunkhouse during discussion periods. In addition, they used a precoded system to record the qualitative aspects (i.e., whether a verbalization was positive or negative) of her first 12 statements during each period. In phase 2, positive reinforcement was given for spending more time in the bunkhouse during discussion times. That is, if she remained with her group during four of the six contact periods, Renee was allowed to sort the mail, an activity valued in the camp. During phase 3, increases in positive, noninterruptive comments were reinforced by free access to the camp canteen. Phase 4 involved elimination of the outside reinforcers.

Renee's group contact time increased from 23% during phase 1 to 83% in phase 4. The proportion of her statements to peers that were positive and noninterruptive increased by more than 200% over the same period. Two sociometric measures were also administered to Renee's group before and after treatment. Following the intervention, her rating as one who could be helpful in a time of need increased significantly.

As noted earlier, most social-skills training programs involve a combination of methods for promoting improvement. In one such intervention, LaGreca and Santogrossi (1980) used modeling, coaching, and behavior rehearsal with feedback for groups of children who were poorly accepted by peers. Skill areas identified for trained were smiling, greeting, joining, inviting, conversing, sharing and cooperating, complimenting, and grooming. The modeling component consisted of a videotape of a peer model demonstrating the skill, followed by group discussion. A group leader coached or provided verbal instruction in how to pay a compliment, greet an acquaintance, and so forth. Next, children were given opportunities to rehearse the skills in role-play situations, and, as homework, were instructed to use the skills with peers outside the group meeting. LaGreca and Santogrossi used an analogue measure, a self-report inventory, behavioral observations in a natural setting, and sociometric measures to evaluate the effectiveness of the treatment. On all outcome measures except the sociometric rating, children in the training group evidenced gains beyond those found in a control group.

The focus of some studies has been the relative contributions of various forms of treatment. For example, Bierman and Furman (1984) compared the relative effects of coaching in conversation skills, a group experience in which children worked together to achieve a common goal, a combination of the two treatments, and a control condition. They found that coaching and group-experience conditions had strong but different effects. Children who received coaching in conversational skills improved in this regard, and peer acceptance improved for those in the group-experience condition. However, significant and sustained improvement in both conversational skills and peer acceptance occurred only for children in the combined treatment group. Similar results occurred in a subsequent study (Bierman, 1986).

More and more, procedures such as those described above are being used to foster development of social skills in the general population of "normal" children. Frequently, these programs are aimed, in part, at influencing cognitive and affective factors that are thought to contribute to socially skilled functioning. One of the more ambitious programs of this kind, the Child Development Project (Battistich, Watson, Solomon, & Solomon, 1982; Schaps, Cooper, Ritchey, & Tuck, 1982; Solomon, Watson, Battistich, Solomon, & Schaps, 1981) was implemented in three schools in the greater San Francisco/Oakland area in the fall of 1982.

The Child Development Project was a five-year program to foster the development of prosocial behavior in children—that is, to promote interpersonal behavior responsive to the legitimate needs of others and to oneself. The varied components of the training program reflect the belief of the project staff that, in addition to specific behavioral competencies, positive social functioning involves a number of identifiable cognitive, affective/motivational, and personality factors. This belief is based upon a large body of research conducted, in large part, by developmental psychologists (see Eisenberg, 1986; Harris, Eisenberg, & Carroll, 1982; Mussen & Eisenberg-Berg, 1977; Staub, 1979).

To promote the desired cognitive, affective/motivational, personality, and behavioral functioning, five program components were developed. In *cooperative activities,* groups of children share responsibility for achieving a common group goal. For example, students might work cooperatively to prepare a group report. Or, parents might be encouraged to hold family meetings, devise cooperative procedures for completion of household chores, or participate in cooperative as opposed to competitive games (Orlick, 1981).

Helping activities such as peer tutoring, assigned responsibilities around the home such as doing dishes, and community service activities are included in the program. Modeling, or *setting positive examples,* is another important component. Deliberate modeling activities are undertaken by teachers and parents, and films, TV programs, and curricular materials are selected or developed to provide positive models. To *enhance the understanding of others,* activities such as role-playing or perspective-taking games and exposure to selected plays and stories are included in the program. The fifth major component, *positive discipline,* focuses on aspects of adult-child relationships and consists of numerous elements. Teachers and parents are instructed in ways to communicate positive social norms and expectations, to involve children in setting rules, and to articulate rules clearly.

Although somewhat mixed, findings after the first three years of the project include a number of positive effects. For example, pupils in treatment schools evidenced better interpersonal problem-solving approaches and conflict resolution than did pupils in comparison schools (Solomon et al., 1986).

The Child Development Project is a more ambitious and long-term intervention than is typically implemented. However, in several respects it is representative of the contributions being made in the area of social-skills assessment and training by developmental psychologists. Knowledge derived from research concerning social-skills development in the general population of children — research undertaken largely by developmental psychologists — serves as the basis for the design of many change strategies. Not surprisingly, the population for which the intervention is intended is normal children, and the goals are more preventive than remedial. That is, programs of this type are intended to foster the development of positive social behaviors in all children, rather than to eliminate deficits in the socially maladjusted. The Child Development Project is also representative of the work of developmental psychologists in that considerable attention has been given to refinement of the techniques used in the assessment of social skills.

Stimulation of Cognitive Performance in Old Age

As was discussed earlier in this chapter, developmental psychologists now frequently study adult development as well as child development. Consequently, they are now beginning to apply their findings to real-word problems of adults.

One issue of practical importance is that of cognitive problem-solving skills in the elderly. Although there is debate concerning the degree to which there is a decline of intellectual functioning during the aging process (Baltes & Schaie, 1976; Botwinick, 1977; Horn & Donaldson, 1976, 1977; Schaie & Baltes, 1977), most psychologists recognize that there is at least some intellectual decline associated with aging. Today the emphasis is more on specifying which abilities decline, and under what conditions, than on the issue of whether or not decline occurs.

In general, researchers have found that fluid intelligence (problem-solving in tasks dealing with complex relations and novel materials) declines with age, while crystalized intelligence (processes that reflect the mental abilities that depend on experience, including formal education and informal learning experiences) is relatively stable throughout most of adulthood (Horn, 1970). Some psychologists have argued that the decline in fluid intelligence is not inevitable and that many older persons are capable of performing at a higher level than they exhibit (Baltes & Willis, 1982; Denney, 1979). Research supporting this perspective has great practical significance; if the decline in fluid intelligence noted for many aging individuals frequently is *not* inevitable, the cognitive functions of the aged could be enhanced by interventions designed to prevent or reverse this decline.

A substantial amount of research now supports the idea that simple intervention procedures, such as direct instruction, practice, and feedback, can enhance cognitive functioning in older adults.

A group of developmental psychologists, including Paul Baltes and Sherri Willis, have been conducting a research project at Pennsylvania State University aimed at examining the range of plasticity or flexibility in the intellectual performance of older persons. This project, labeled the Adult Development and Enrichment Project (or ADEPT), has involved both identifying some of the factors relating to the decline of fluid intelligence in adulthood, and the development of intervention procedures that enhance cognitive functioning among older adults.

In one of their first studies, the project researchers examined the effects of practice on the elderly's performance on tests of fluid intelligence (Hofland, Willis, & Baltes, 1981). As part of this study, 30 older subjects (with an average age of 69 years) participated in 8 one-hour practice sessions distributed over approximately one month. During each of these sessions, the subjects performed the same two tests of intelligence. They were given no feedback, however, concerning their performance on the tests; they merely practiced the tests themselves.

The researchers found that the test performance of the elderly subjects increased steadily over the practice sessions. In other words, the subjects' scores on tests of fluid intelligence were improved merely by the opportunity to practice taking the tests. These findings suggest that the elderly sometimes perform relatively poorly on tests of intelligence merely because they have had little experience with such tests.

While it is true that not all reseachers have found that practice improves elderly persons' problem-solving abilities (see Denney, 1979, for a review), few researchers have examined the effects of multiple practice sessions. Certainly it is logical to assume that repeated practice sessions would have a greater positive effect on performance than one or a few practice sessions.

In an effort to examine other methods of enhancing the cognitive functioning of the elderly, the researchers on the ADEPT project have conducted a series of studies concerning the effects of training specific cognitive skills. In these studies, the researchers have instructed older individuals in the use of the cognitive skills required for successful performance on tests of fluid intelligence, generally over a number of one-hour training sessions. They have found that these training sessions are associated with significant increases in performance on several different tests of fluid intelligence. Moreover, the training sessions resulted not only in improvement in the specific aspect of fluid intelligence for which the elderly people received training, but also in the enhancement of other related aspects of cognitive performance (Baltes & Willis, 1982; Plemons, Willis, & Baltes, 1978; Willis, Blieszner, & Baltes, 1981). Although there is relatively little other research on the effects of direct training on the elderly's cognitive performance (Denney, 1979), the researchers on the ADEPT project have obtained strong support for the idea that older people often perform better on cognitive tasks after receiving instructions regarding the concepts involved in the task.

Other intervention procedures besides practice and direct training have been shown to enhance elderly persons' performance on problem-solving tasks. For example, the elderly are more likely to use efficient problem-solving strategies (on tasks such as sorting objects by color, shape, and size or for playing a game similar to 20 Questions) if they view another person (a model) using an effective strategy (Denney, 1974; Denney & Denney, 1973, 1974). Similarly, providing feedback to older people regarding the correctness of their performance on a task appears to have a beneficial effect on their problem-solving behaviors (Hornblum & Overton, 1976). Finally, a combination of intervention techniques such as direct instruction and feedback can be an effective means of facilitating the elderly's performance on cognitive tasks.

To summarize, researchers have found that the decline in cognitive performance associated with aging frequently can be reversed or eliminated by means of relatively simple intervention procedures. Although these intervention procedures have not yet been used on a large-scale basis to enhance older persons' intelligence, the potential for practical application of this knowledge is obvious. Most important, the research on cognitive interventions has been instrumental in heightening awareness of the plasticity of cognitive performance during old age. Now that researchers have demonstrated that the aged can be helped to function more effectively, it is likely that more professionals dealing with older people will institute appropriate intervention procedures.

Conclusion

As was previously discussed, although most developmental psychologists still work primarily in academic settings, they have become somewhat more applied in orientation than in the recent past. Moreover, as developmental psychologists have started to tackle applied issues, their interests frequently have overlapped with those of practitioners in the field, for example, educators, school psychologists, and clinical psychologists. This overlap generally has proved to be productive; developmental psychologists tend to bring new perspectives to the issues and tasks they address and frequently are more highly trained in methodological (research) skills than are many practitioners. Thus developmental psychologists have much to contribute to applied psychology, especially with regard to issues concerning human development.

Glossary

bonding Close association between mothers (and/or fathers) to an infant in the first days of the infant's life. Such associations are assumed to lay the groundwork for future relationships.

Brazelton Neonatal Behavioral Assessment Scale (NBAS) An instrument designed to assess individuality in newborn infants. Assessment is made of neurological functioning and the capacity to interact with people and objects.

nomination procedure A sociometric procedure to assess social skills. Members of a group are asked to name some number of individuals who best exhibit a characteristic of interest. For example, children in a first-grade class might be asked to name the five children in the class that they would most like to play with.

peer rating procedure A sociometric procedure to assess social skills. Members of a group are presented with the names of all members of the group and asked to rate them on some scale of interest. For example, children in a first-grade class might be presented with the name of each child in the class and asked to rate how much they would like to play with each child on a 5-point scale.

reactivity As used in this chapter, changes in behavior that occur when a person is being observed.

securely attached children Children who have formed secure attachments with their caregivers. Secure attachments are characterized by expectations that the caregiver will be available, warm, and responsive to the child's needs.

situation specificity As used in the chapter, a problem encountered when trying to identify specific lists of social skills. Social skills that may be appropriate in one situation may not be so in another.

social skills Abilities to engage in appropriate social interaction in various situations. See chapter for a discussion of the difficulty in defining social skills.

Appendix

A

An Introduction to Program Evaluation

W. Larry Gregory
New Mexico State University

Imagine that you are the chief administrator of a large metropolitan hospital. The past year has not been a good one from a financial perspective, and the board of directors has ordered you to cut costs by cutting back on some of the hospital's outpatient programs. Your hospital offers many different programs, so which ones should you cut? How will you decide?

One reasonable approach would be to drop programs that are not being used by very many people. After all, if you have to hurt people by cutting back on services or eliminating some altogether, you personally would prefer to hurt the least number. Another possibility would be to cancel programs that really aren't needed; maybe some duplicate services offered by other departments in the hospital or are offered by other nearby hospitals. Or, you could eliminate programs that aren't accomplishing their goals, without hurting the public at all. Finally, you might be able to change a program so that it does about the same amount of good, but for less money.

But how can you be sure that you do not cut the most used, most needed, or most successful of the programs? How can you determine if a cheaper program can do the same job as a more expensive program? The answers to these and other similar questions posed by administrators, bureaucrats, legislators, and concerned scientists can frequently be answered through program evaluation.

What Is Program Evaluation?

Program evaluation is usually concerned with the outcome of a program, that is, it attempts to determine the final effects of a social program on its intended clients and society in general. Another, broader definition states that program evaluation is concerned with "determining the degree to which a program is meeting its objectives, the problems it is encountering and the side effects it is creating" (Definitions and Classifications Committee, 1973, p. 75). Thus a program evaluation can be concerned with observing, assessing, or measuring a number of variables. These can include such information as where funds for a program come from, a program's staff, how clients are brought into a program and a description of clients on intake, a description of services, what clients are like after completing a program, what clients are like many months later, and perhaps certain effects on the community as a whole.

Purposes of Program Evaluation

Robert Coursey (1977) has summarized four major purposes that program evaluation can serve. First, it can be a means of *accounting*. The costs of a particular program can be weighed against its benefits, and the program's administrators or a legislature can then decide whether a program is worth continuing. Second, program evaluation can serve as a means of *feedback* to an organization so that the staff can improve or change services to make them better, or emphasize the existing strengths of a program. Third, a very thorough evaluation can be used to gather *information for dissemination.* That is, a clear description of the workings of a program, along with its benefits and costs, can be documented so that other agencies or organizations can duplicate successful programs and avoid programs that fail to fulfill their purpose. Fourth, program evaluation occasionally serves as a *means of theory-building.* This occurs when an evaluation is designed that serves to uncover how a program does what it does. The question that is answered is, "What parts of a program cause the observed effects?"

Summative and Formative Evaluations. Another way of conceptualizing the purpose of evaluations is to examine two general categories of evaluation research, summative and formative evaluations. Summative research is concerned with the outcomes produced by a program and so represents the type of evaluation fulfilling the first two purposes above. These evaluations are concerned with such questions as "Is the program working?" and "What are its effects?" Formative research is oriented toward understanding the processes of a program and so represents the third and fourth purposes above. These evaluations are concerned with questions such as, What is it? or What makes it work?

Formative evaluations are useful for providing feedback to administrators on how to revise programs to improve them. They are often used during the early stages of a program when there exists a greater opportunity for modification. Summative evaluations are usually done after a program has been in place for some time and can reasonably be expected to have produced its intended effects. These evaluations are usedful in determining whether to maintain funding for a program at existing levels, or expand or cut the program.

Program Evaluation as a Profession

A person who does program evaluations is known as a program evaluator. Many program evaluators hold doctorates or master's degrees in disciplines such as social or community psychology, political science, social work, sociology, or business. These people, in the course of their training in the body of information pertaining to their field, are also trained in various research methodologies, some of which were reviewed in Chapter 2. In addition, they may learn certain methodologies that are more useful in evaluation research, some of which will be reviewed in this Appendix. Because of the increased demand for evaluation research through the 1960s and 1970s, there now exist a few graduate programs that offer advanced degrees in program evaluation. Today, large organizations (e.g., community mental health centers, medical schools, management consulting firms) that sponsor or provide services to many different ongoing programs have program evaluators on staff. Smaller organizations will hire consulting firms to perform program evaluations for them. Many state governments employ program evaluators who spend their time examining the various programs offered by different state agencies. The federal government often contracts with private evaluation consulting firms or universities to perform evaluations of large ongoing federally sponsored programs.

In fact, prior to the cutbacks in human-service programs imposed by the Reagan administration, much of the state and federal legislation that funds programs carried the stipulation that a certain percentage of the budget be spent on evaluation. Mandatory evaluations ensured the detection of effective and ineffective programs, with the result that unsucessful programs were not funded again. The knowledge that programs that do not meet announced objectives may be closed down leads to certain pressures on administrators: they may decide to fund less-than-optimal evaluations in order to guarantee that their program will look good. This has led to the development of a subspecialty within program evaluation: evaluators who evaluate the quality of program evaluations. These individuals, who usually work for higher funding sources such as the state or federal governments or for large private foundations, spend their time reviewing evaluation reports prepared by others in order to determine if the methodology employed in an evaluation was adequate.

Program evaluators who work within an agency are known as in-house evaluators. In-house evaluators have a special kind of pressure placed on them. They must perform evaluations of the various programs offered by their own agency. If they find that a particular program is unsuccessful, it may mean that a friend with whom they have worked for years will be out of a job. On the other hand, an administrator's pet program may be found to be inadequate and the evaluators themselves may be out of a job. Program evaluators must keep these factors in mind and attempt to build in safeguards to keep their own biases from influencing the results of an evaluation. Because of these kinds of pressures, some agencies insist on employing outside consultants, or independent evaluators, to do their evaluations, since they are presumed to be more objective than in-house evaluatiors. (Independent evaluators prefer not to be called "out-house evaluators.") But, in-house evaluators sometimes have advantages over consultants. Because evaluators working within an agency can have a better feel for what is going on, they are more apt to ask the right questions when it comes to doing a tough evaluation. Also, they may be more trusted than some stranger brought in to do an evaluation, with the result that they obtain more complete and reliable information from other staff members concerning a particular program's operations. Further, since they are on the premises full time, they are more able to see the program as it really operates (Posavac & Carey, 1980).

Strategies in Evaluation

The purpose for performing an evaluation, who the client group is, what methodology is used, and how extensive the evaluation is will all have effects on the outcomes of the evaluation. This section presents information on different ways evaluation research can be performed in order to meet the varying requirements of evaluation situations.

Factors to Consider in Planning Evaluations

A careful program evaluator will consider many factors involved in the evaluation process. A first step is to determine for whom the evaluation is to be performed. On first thought, this seems like a simple question to answer. But in reality there are three different groups for whom an evaluation can be done. The obvious one is the agency or administrator requesting an evaluation. In the hospital example at the beginning of this Appendix, you were the administrator. In that situation, an evaluator would need to consider your motives in requesting an evaluation, both stated reasons and less obvious ones. As a stated motive, you may wish to obtain information that will aid you in making decisions about which programs to cut back on or cut altogether, or about how to continue service through more economical means. An unstated motive might be that you want the evaluator to be a scapegoat to be blamed for any decisions that adversely affect your personnel. A less obvious group for whom an evaluation is performed is the funding source, or the board of directors of an agency or program. In the hospital example, you, as chief administrator, are responsible to the board of directors, who are responsible to the stockholders in the hospital corporation. Thus your evaluation is also done for them and must bear up under their scrutiny. A third group that must be considered in designing an evaluation is the client population. If services are deleted or improved as the result of an evaluation, the clients are surely affected.

The types of clients served must also be considered. Suppose your hospital were administering a nutrition program for preschool children. In designing your research you could not include questionnaires that had to be completed by the clients, since they can't read. For another example, suppose one of your programs was a hospice, a home-like environment provided for terminally ill patients. You would want to be careful in designing an evaluation so that it did not intrude on the patients and their families.

In planning an evaluation, the evaluator would meet with relevant administrators and personnel to obtain preliminary information on the issues just outlined. Additional information would be gleaned from these meetings. For example, two very important questions are related to time and money. How much is to be spent on the evaluation? When is it to be completed? Yet another matter of concern is staff cooperation. Will the staff of a program be available for interviews, and will any of them be assigned to assist with data collection (e.g, recording information from client records, interviewing clients)?

The evaluator would also ascertain, in general, how the program to be evaluated works and what its intended effects are to be. This is useful in an obvious way, since an evaluation design cannot be determined without this information. But two other, more subtle issues can be examined through obtaining this information. The first concerns the expectations of the administrators. Sometimes, especially when a program involves the application of some innovative concept, administrators have unrealistic optimism concerning what the program can accomplish.

For example, as chief administrator, you may have been integrally involved in the development of a new out-patient youthful drug offender program that you believe will stop all drug abuse in your community, motivate all the participants to obtain part-time jobs, make straight A's in school, go to church on Saturday and Sunday, and prevent dental cavities. An evaluator might wish to ease your head out of the clouds so that you aren't disappointed when the results come in, or worse, so that you don't throw the evaluation in the trash can while muttering about how one can't find good help these days.

A second issue concerns the underlying values implied by the stated goals of a program or through the way it is actually operated. In the drug offender program example, an obvious value that the program designers hold is that drug use by young people is harmful, wrong, or bad. But suppose that you sponsored a program that treated battered women and their husbands in an attempt to stop the abuse. A nonobvious value implicit in such a program is that you consider the family an important unit that should not be broken up: The woman and her husband should attempt to work their problems through and stay together. If you had different values, you might have developed a battered wives program that focused on convincing the wives to take their children (if they have any), leave their husbands, divorce them, and begin new lives. A battered wife who seeks outside help may have in mind only the goal of not being abused. Thus the type of program she encounters, with its own goals influenced by the underlying values of its designers, will ultimately affect the solution she chooses. An evaluator must consider such underlying values in deciding what success in a particular program actually is. For example, in the battered wife programs described above, the first program may define success as a preserved, well-functioning family while the latter may see success as a battered wife living independently. The definition of success used by an evaluator will affect the design and outcome of an evaluation. It is also critical that the client and the evaluator share the definition of success. An outside consultant would consider such information along with everything else in deciding whether to undertake the evaluation. (It is unusual for an in-house evaluator to be able to decide whether an evaluation should be undertaken.)

Program evaluators are not expected to be experts in every given field that they are called upon to evaluate. When they are called upon to evaluate an area unfamiliar to them, most evaluators will do a review of relevant literature on the topic. Sometimes a literature review can be accomplished with a single visit to a university library. Occasionally, a meeting with a few colleagues will turn up all the relevant literature needed. Also many of the abstracting indexes or services, such as Psychological Abstracts or the Educational Resource and Information Center (ERIC), have placed their listings into computerized databases. There is even a service exclusively designed for evaluation research, Data on Program Evaluation (DOPE). Most major university libraries have personnel trained in operating computers that can access these databases. Researchers can have relatively inexpensive (around $35) computerized searches done using key words relevant to the problem area they wish to know about. A literature search will usually come up with the title and location of references containing information on the types of measures and methodologies that have proven useful (or not useful) in assessing programs in the area of interest.

A literature review can be useful in selecting a methodological strategy appropriate for the evaluation. Then the final step of this initial phase can be undertaken: a concise written proposal is prepared for consideration by the administrator or board of directors. Such a document can prevent misunderstandings that might not be discovered until after an evaluation has been completed. The evaluator and the person(s) who have requested the evaluation will have agreed on the goals of the study, what kind of cooperation will be required of the staff, what kind of information will be obtained, when the evaluation will be complete, and how much it will cost. You can see that it is expecially useful for an outside consultant to prepare a written proposal.

Methodologies for Evaluation Research

Evaluation methodologies can be divided into three main categories: experimental, nonexperimental, and quasi-experimental.

The Experimental Method. The experimental method described in Chapter 2 is the same experimental method used in evaluation research; that is, there is some type of control group and an experimental group, or there are several experimental groups. These groups are compared to one another using a preselected dependent variable or variables. Since research participants are assigned randomly to the various experimental conditions, any final differences on the dependent variable are presumably due to the treatments they received.

Often, however, in evaluation research the consultants or program evaluators do not have the rigorous control over extraneous variables that experimenters prefer. For example, in the mid-1970s, this author was involved with a national program funded by the U.S. Department of Transportation (DOT). The program was designed to evaluate the effectiveness of different programs to keep persons who were arrested for drunken driving from repeating this offense. A number of large metropolitan cities were selected to participate in the study. Funding was provided by DOT to each city to set up a program to offer persons charged with driving-while-intoxicated (DWI) a plea bargain: if the accused agreed to participate in the special rehabilitation program, he or she would be allowed to plead guilty to a less severe traffic violation. In each city, several different programs were tried, including group therapy, power motivation training, traditional educational films, and scary traffic-accident movies. A control group was to receive no treatment. Participants were indeed randomly assigned to the conditions. However, in one of the cities, the municipal judges felt that it would be irresponsible on their part to allow persons charged with DWI to "get off" without any kind of treatment. Since all plea bargains had to be approved by the judges, the program evaluators had to compromise with the judges. The result was that no true control group, that is, a group that received no treatment, was employed. The closest thing was a group that received a home-study course made up of some educational readings concerning the effects of alcohol on the body and fill-in-the-blank questions that had to be returned to the program staff. Thus the final results of the study were qualified by this one change that had to be made to accommodate the judges.

Yet another example of the problems associated with evaluators' use of the experimental method comes from a study of the number of police assigned to a patrol car in San Diego (Boydstun, Sherry, & Moelter, 1977). Many police who patrol in vehicles feel that they are safer and much less likely to be injured if two officers are assigned to each patrol car. Since it is more economical to have only one officer in a car, it seemed appropriate for an evaluation study to compare injury rates for officers working alone in patrol cars to those of officers working in pairs in patrol cars. This is a very simple experimental design, one that should be hard to mess up. The data that were obtained in the study revealed that police assigned to single-officer patrol cars were *less* likely to be assaulted or injured than police assigned to two-officer patrol cars. On the surface, these results would support the cost-saving conclusion that that it is acceptable to send out single-officer patrol cars. However, when the program evaluators delved further into the procedures followed by the police during the course of the evaluation, they found that the dispatchers at police headquarters had knowingly assigned two-officer patrols to respond to calls that sounded more dangerous, probably hoping to protect what they felt to be the less secure single-officer patrols. This practice renders the reasons for the results of the evaluation quite ambiguous. Are single-officer patrols really safer than two-officer patrols, or did it just appear that way because they were assigned to respond to safer calls?

Still, use of the experimental method can lead to very successful evaluations, with meaningful results. The Los Angeles County Sheriff's Department Police Academy allowed a consultant to compare the effects of two different training programs on the performance of police trainees (Earle, 1973). Traditionally, police training programs are very military-like. The administrators who run them apparently assume that the stress and discipline of this kind of environment leads to superior performance when officers are on the job. A secondary purpose of such programs may be to weed out persons not capable of dealing with stress in effective ways. In the evaluation study, police recruits were assigned randomly to either a military-environment training program or to a less stressful program that resembled a college atmosphere. Both subjective and objective dependent variables were employed, including the recruits' self-ratings of their work quality, supervisors' ratings of the recruits' work, and the number of complaints and commendations received by the recruits during their first two years on the job. The evaluators found that the trainees who had gone through the less stressful training had more knowledge of their job, seemed more adaptable, exhibited greater responsibility, got along better with other officers, and were even better on the firing range. The study was replicated several times, and, as a result, the Police Academy made some permanent changes in its training program.

The Nonexperimental method.   As an example of a nonexperimental approach, consider the following: Your fictitious hospital has a smoking treatment clinic. The goal is to get participants to stop smoking and to stay stopped. In this case, you are really comparing the participants to themselves. If 100% of them are smoking when they come in for help, and only 20% of them are smoking at the end of the program, and only 35% are smoking six months later, you might conclude that you have a reasonably effective program. Or suppose you have a heroin addiction treatment program. The goal is not only to get your clients off heroin but to help them get jobs and keep those jobs. If only 5% of your clients have jobs at the beginning of the program, and 65% have jobs at the end, and 45% still have jobs eight months later, you might conclude that your program is effective in this area. Of course, you would also have to look at the percentages of clients still using heroin. And, if you were really sophisticated, you might even cross-tabulate your results to see what percentage of those with jobs use heroin and what percentage of those without jobs use heroin. If you found that every single person of the 45% who had jobs after eight months were not on heroin, while a large percentage of those without jobs was still using it, you might revise your program to emphasize job finding and job keeping even more than it presently does. This kind of nonexperimental approach involves what is termed a *pretest-posttest single-group design.*

There are many problems associated with nonexperimental designs. For example, suppose 45 of 50 people dropped out of your smoking treatment program before completing it. Of the 5 that remained, all stopped smoking by the time they completed the program. Thus if you said, "One hundred percent of those who complete our smoking treatment program are able to stop smoking," it would be an accurate statement, but you really have a very unsuccessful program since 90% of the people leave before completing it. This problem is referred to as *subject mortality.* No one has necessarily died, but they aren't around for you to measure them on the dependent variable.

Another problem is selection. Suppose you changed your single-group design into an experimental design and randomly assigned half the people who had signed up to participate in your smoking treatment program to wait at home for six months, while the other half got the treatment. You also locate a group of smokers who haven't signed up for your program. At the end of six months, you determine what percentage in each group is smoking. Suppose about 20% of those who went through your program are smoking, about 20% of those who signed up for but didn't go through your program are smoking, and 100% of those who never were interested in your program are smoking. You might conclude that people who sign up for smoking treatment programs are motivated to stop smoking, and many will stop even without treatment. People who wanted to stop smoking selected themselves into the program. You would also conclude that your program is not very effective, since its results are no better than those of the no-treatment group who wanted to be in the program. You could never have reached this conclusion with a single-group design, which does not address this problem of *subject selection* (or in this case, self-selection).

Although there are other problems with nonexperimental designs, only one more will be described: *history*. With single-group designs, you can never be quite sure whether it was your program or something else that was happening in the participants' lives that caused the observed effects. Consider the heroin program example again. Remember that a larger percentage of the participants was employed after the program than before. What if a large clothing manufacturer had just begun operations in your city at about the time you started your program and employed primarily unskilled workers? Although only some of your participants were working there, the clothing manufacturer undoubtedly pulled away workers from other, lower-paying jobs, leaving those jobs open for your participants. How could you then conclude, with confidence, that you had a successful program? Perhaps your program participants would have gotten the jobs anyway, since there were suddenly a lot of job openings in the community. Usually, however, you don't know about most of the things going on that could affect the history of your participants.

Quasi-experimental Designs.   Of the several types of quasi-experimental designs, one increasingly used is the *time-series design*. In this approach, some unit of analysis (another name for a dependent variable) is selected. For example, one recent report that employed a time-series design (Hennigan et al., 1982) examined different categories of crime, such as burglary, auto theft, violent crime, and larceny. Quantitative observations were made on this variable over a number of time intervals. In this study, the "observations" were made by going to the police archives and tabulating the number of each type of crime that occurred each year between 1933 and 1976. Finally, the part that makes the design quasi-experimental is that the time intervals observed both precede and follow some important event (sort of an independent variable) that the researchers are interested in. In the Hennigan et al. study, the researchers were interested in the effects (if any) of the introduction of television into the American home. They were able to plot on a chart the number of larcenies each year for several years prior to the introduction of television, and the number of larcenies each year following the introduction of television. Using a statistical technique that accommodates the random fluctuations that sometimes occur, these researchers were able to conclude that the introduction of television significantly increased the number of theft-related crimes in the cities and states included in their study.

Another type of quasi-experimental design involves the use of the *nonequivalent control group*. This involves sampling a group of people in a program and of a comparable group of people not in the program. This second group is not a true control group since you have not randomly assigned any of the people to the experimental or control conditions. Going back to the heroin program example, you could have controlled for the effects of history by collecting information from an equal number of persons not addicted to heroin who were similar in age, education, and marital and employment status. Thus, if their employment did not increase over time as it did for the heroin addicts who went through your program, even though the clothing factory opened, you could rule out history as an alternative explanation for the effects of the study. Nonequivalent control groups are used especially when it is unethical to require some of your participants to receive no treatment and when there are too few participants to divide them into experimental groups.

Although other types of designs are employed by program evaluators, the ones presented here should provide you with some idea of the creative lengths evaluators must go to in order to ensure that an evaluation will give meaningful answers to the questions asked. Evaluation methodologies have improved markedly over the last two decades as persons performing them have become more familiar with the types of problems encountered in doing research in societal settings.

Medical and Tailored Models of Evaluation

Thomas Cook (1973) has distinguished between two major approaches to doing an evaluation. One he has termed the medical model, while the other is referred to as the tailored model.

Medical-Model Evaluations.   The medical-model approach to evaluations is based on a tradition in medical research that involves the assessment of treatment effects in four areas. When determining the effects of a potential cure, a first question to ask is whether the symptoms to which the cure is addressed are indeed completely removed, alleviated, or are left unchanged. The parallel with program evaluation is obvious: Does a treatment program affect the treatment population in the intended way? However, the second question asked in medical evaluations is not so easily anticipated by social scientists who have been concerned principally with documenting the positive effects of a social intervention. This second question is whether the cure has undesirable side effects or unanticipated negative consequences. In certain heroin-addiction treatment programs, an unanticipated negative consequence has indeed been found: the addicts become addicted to methadone, the drug being used to keep them off heroin. The third area of concern in medical evaluations is the assessment of unanticipated positive consequences. For example, if addicts participating in a program that was intended only to break their habits were found to have a high employment rate, that would be a very positive unanticipated consequence. Finally, medical evaluations seek to determine the time interval over which a treatment remains effective. For example, suppose one compared two different heroin-addiction treatment programs and found that 40% of the addicts quit using heroin in one program while only 30% quit in the other. Based on that finding only, sponsors would certainly prefer refunding or expanding the first program. However, suppose that one year later almost all the successful graduates of the first program had resumed their heroin use and none of those from the second program has regressed. The inclusion of the time element shows that the second program is the better of the two.

There are several advantages to medical-model evaluations. First, they provide a variety of measures of a program's effects. This can (1) allow greater comparability between different programs, including programs assessed in other places at different times; (2) provide more information about how a program's effects might be generalized to different phenomena; and (3) provide very useful information on both positive and negative side effects, and on the temporal duration of a program's effects. Second, medical-model evaluations reinforce the ideas that programs exist to solve or prevent programs and cannot be justified in their own right.

Among the disadvantages is the implication that one can expect relatively insignificant and short-term treatments to have lasting effects. This factor can serve to make program administrators wary of medical-model evaluations. They may fear that, if it is found that their program has few positive side effects or does not produce eternal changes in the intended area, it will be shut down or suffer reduced funding. Another disadvantage of medical-model evaluations is the difficulty involved in implementing them: they cost a great deal of money and take a lot of time to organize and implement.

Tailored-Model Evaluations. If a program evaluation is uniquely developed to measure specific behavioral objectives of a program, the evaluation is referred to as a tailored evaluation. Tailored evaluations use measures that closely reflect what goes on in a program and test for effectiveness in areas where a program is most likely to show effects. In the heroin program example, suppose the aim was to elevate the self-esteem of addicts, assuming that enhanced self-esteem would help them quit. A tailored evaluation would measure the self-esteem of the addicts after they had been through the program and compare it either to the self-esteem of the addicts before they entered the program or to the self-esteem of addicts not in the program. That way, if it were found that the program was not successful in getting and keeping addicts off heroin, the developers might have some ideas about what to do about it. For example, if the program was successful in enhancing self-esteem and unsuccessful in breaking the habits of addicts, the conclusion might be that enhancing self-esteem does not help addicts quit, suggesting the need for a whole new approach. Conversely, if a tailored evaluation disclosed that self-esteem was not increased, the failure to get addicts to quit might be due to that factor. The program could be redesigned to make it more effective in enhancing self-esteem.

Tailored evaluations have the advantage of evaluating programs for what they are, rather than for what someone might hope them to be. Program directors are not as likely to be defensive, as they might be if an evaluator wanted to measure a lot of other variables that a program is not especially designed to affect. Furthermore, tailored evaluations can help in understanding which parts of a program are effective. Lastly, tailored-model program evaluations are usually much less expensive than medical-model evaluations.

The disadvantages of tailored-model program evaluations are the opposite of the advantages of medical-model evaluations. For example, tailored evaluations restrict comparisons of different programs. When measures that are idiosyncratic to a particular program's objectives are used in an evaluation, it is impossible to compare the outcome of the evaluation to other evaluations since they have different measures. Similarly, it is difficult to draw generalizations from the results of tailored evaluations, and they do not provide information about positive and negative side effects and about the temporal duration of any effects measured.

Issues in Program Evaluation

A number of issues exist in program evaluation, some of which are of an ethical nature, while others are political or philosophical. Program evaluators must be sensitive to these issues or risk offending the service providers they are evaluating, the administrators who hire them, government officials who may fund them, or the political constituency in the locales where they work.

Withholding Treatment

One ethical issue in program evaluation was touched upon earlier—the withholding of treatment from persons needing it. Recall that in the DWI prevention program described earlier, program evaluators had wanted some offenders to receive no treatment in order to satisfy the methodological need for a control group. The judges who had to approve the plea bargains (which were used to induce participation in the program) would not allow a no-treatment group, possibly for political reasons (since the judges could look bad if they let some drunk drivers off with a light penalty and no treatment). However, there may have been some concern that was of an ethical nature. If it is really believed that these prevention programs are effective, can treatment ethically be withheld from persons who could benefit from it?

In 1987, work was stopped years ahead of schedule on a large-scale study of the effectiveness of taking an aspirin every other day in reducing the risk of heart attack (Edwards, 1988). Preliminary data analyses suggested that there was indeed a beneficial effect. A judgment was made that it would be unethical to ask the control condition participants not to take aspirin if its use could save lives. Although the decision to stop the study may seem to have obvious positive consequences without any negative ones, the issue is not that simple. It may never be known if there are unanticipated negative consequences of regular aspirin use, an effect considered possible by some scientists.

Bureaucratic Resistance to Program Evaluations

A colleague of the author once did a program evaluation of a private mental hospital's juvenile substance-abuse program when the colleague was in graduate school. The evaluation was considered part of his graduate training. As such, he was supervised by a faculty member and collaborated with several professors in designing, implementing, and analyzing the results of the evaluation. The graduate student's evaluation revealed that the hospital's very expensive (to parents) program was ineffective in keeping juveniles off drugs. When the hospital's administrators were presented with these results, they discounted the evaluation as the poor-quality work of a student who had not yet acquired a Ph.D. The much distressed student sought counsel from a supervising faculty member; his work for the hospital was supposed to teach him how to do high-quality evaluations and yet they didn't believe the results. His professor gave assurances that the evaluation was of a very high quality and that the results were probably accurate. The professor went on to say a very important thing: the student's involvement with the evaluation was not to learn how to do it. The young man was already trained in doing evaluations or the faculty would not have let him do the work for the hospital. Instead, the real reason for his receiving the assignment was to teach him how bureaucracy works.

The lesson is an invaluable one in the field of program evaluation. Sometimes when administrators are disappointed in the results of an evaluation, they disparage its quality in order to retain their belief that the program is effective. Michael Patton (1978) attempts to deal with this problem by advocating *utilization-focused evaluation*. Prior to the adoption of program evaluation as a means to make funding decisions about various social programs, Patton argues that two models of evaluation were popular: the charity model and the pork-barrel model.

The charity model of evaluation uses as its criterion for determining whether a program is good or not the sincerity of the funders and the program staff. As long as all involved with the program care enough to do their best and help the less fortunate, it must be a good program.

The pork-barrel approach to evaluation examines the strength and leverage of the program's political constituency. If political, parochial, and partisan interests are served by the creation and continued existence of a program, then it must be a good program.

In contrast, utilization-focused evaluation emphasizes that what happens during an evaluation determines its eventual impact long before a final report is produced. The ways in which an evaluator interacts with administrators and program personnel—the ways in which an evaluator involves them in planning and implementing the evaluation process—play a large role in whether the results of the evaluation will be used by the administrators. Thus, by the time a study is over, the potential for utilization has been largely determined. Patton does not describe utilization-focused evaluation as a formal model for how to conduct evaluations. Instead, it is an orientation with many options. Patton suggests that evaluators be sensitive and adaptable to the people who are the potential information users, and to those persons who will make decisions about the program (if they are different from the information users). He believes that the first step an evaluator should make is to identify the relevant decision makers and information users, and to organize them in a way that enhances communication between them. The critical task of the evaluator is then to "work actively, reactively, and adaptively with these identified decision-makers and information users to make all other decisions about the evaluation—decisions about research focus, design, methods, analysis, interpretation, and dissemination" (Patton, 1978, p. 284). By drawing these others into the evaluation process and making them in part responsible for the research methods and conclusions drawn, it becomes less likely that these administrators, funders, and other individuals can easily dismiss the results of an evaluation.

Cost-Benefit Analysis

Once a program evaluation has been completed, many administrators or decision makers want more information to help them make program decisions. They want to know the values of different program effects and how those differently valued effects can be combined to assist with their decision making. These decisions can include (1) comparing all the good effects of programs with all the bad effects to assist in determining whether to continue a program; (2) determining which of several versions of a program are best; and (3) deciding which programs might be the best investment within a given budget. These are the challenges for cost-benefit analysis to meet.

With the enactment of the River and Harbor Act of 1902 and the Flood Control Act of 1936, the use of cost-benefit analysis as one tool in the decision-making process for projects was established (Thompson, 1980). This legislation mandated that individual water projects were to be justified by comparing their benefits with their costs. Benefits could include such things as cheaper electricity from the hydroelectric power produced by a dam, lake recreational activities, and flood control. Costs could include the money spent in building the dam, the scenic beauty destroyed by the resultant reservoir, and the increased number of drownings. Ideally, sponsors want to implement or retain only those programs in which the benefits outweigh the costs.

Some of the above costs and benefits are not easily quantified for purposes of comparison. This same problem occurs when examining the costs and benefits of various social or psychological interventions. It is easy to understand, then, that the task of a cost-benefit analyst is not easy. Anytime there are nonmonetary attributes on which a program can be judged, it becomes more difficult for the evaluator to come up with a commensurate standard by which the nonmonetary attributes can be compared to one another and to monetary attributes. Many different complex techniques for deriving commensurate standards have been developed.

Sometimes when the effects of a program are too intangible or abstract, evaluators may resort to performing a cost-effectiveness analysis. For example, suppose a heroin-addiction treatment program cost $750,000 a year to administer. Each year, approximately 100 addicts are rehabilitated and remain drug-free. If one ignores the fact that some of them get jobs (a benefit) and that burglaries may go down in one's city because fewer heroin addicts are stealing to support their habit (another benefit), one can calculate a simple cost-effectiveness ratio by dividing $750,000 by 100 addicts. The result, $7,500, is how much it costs to successfully rehabilitate one addict. If the funding source for the program decides that the cost is not worthwhile, the program would be discontinued. Although the evaluator has sidestepped the issue of attaching a value to saving one heroin addict, the decision maker who cancels the program has attached a value, and in this case has decided that rehabilitating one heroin addict is not worth $7,500.

The Experimenting Society

To close the discussion of program evaluation, it is fitting to reflect on a lecture originally delivered in 1971 by Donald Campbell, a past president of the American Psychological Association, a prolific scientist, and an evaluation researcher. In his speech, titled "The Experimenting Society," Campbell (1981) discussed two aspects of evaluation research that led him to speculate about what an experimenting society would be like. First, as evaluators attempt to implement high-quality program evaluations, they experience frustrations with the existing political system and are compelled to think about alternative political systems. Second, in recommending to government ways to implement programs so that their impact can be evaluated, evaluators often propose novel procedures for political decision making. They are in fact designing alternative political systems.

From these concepts, Campbell develops a profile of what an experimenting society, or a scientific society, would be like. First, it would be *nondogmatic*. While its agenda would state ideal goals and methods for reaching them, there would be no attempt to defend either against disconfirming evidence. Second, an experimenting society would be *honest*. It would be committed to reality testing through experimentation, openness to self-criticism, and avoidance of self-deception. Third, the society would be *accountable*. The public would have access to the information used to make social decisions and could challenge those decisions. Fourth, the society would embrace a *means-idealism/ends-idealism* philosophy. It would indefinitely experiment and attempt to improve itself, never assuming that perfection had been achieved. Accordingly an experimenting society would not only be seeking an ideal end-state, but would be in a continual state of transition so that the means to the end would also have to be an ideal.

The experimenting society would have several methodological problems to solve. One of them concerns the ethics of randomized experiments. Several years ago the U.S. Government conducted a negative income tax experiment in New Jersey (Rossi & Lyall, 1976). The participants knew they were in a study, and they knew what was happening to them. Some impoverished individuals received a guaranteed annual income at 50% of the established poverty level. But these people did not know that there were other individuals receiving 100% of the established poverty level—a substantially greater income. Had they known, it might have affected the outcome of the experiment. But, in terms of the ethics of the evaluation, should they have been told?

A second methodological problem concerns the use of opinion surveys. These surveys are important in the political decision-making process. In the experimenting society, survey participants would need to be told who paid for the survey research and how the information would be used. They would need to have access to the results and be able to use them in political debate. In a sense, they would be co-owners of the opinions expressed. As a consequences of this, surveys would have less validity as people might distort their opinions in an attempt to influence the political process. In the early stages of the 1988 Republican presidential primaries, campaign workers of the former television evangelist, Pat Robertson, told his political constituents to lie to pollsters about their political preferences. This was done so that the final, larger percentage of the vote that his staff expected him to receive would be a surprise to the news media and public and therefore have a greater impact.

A third methodological problem needing resolution would be the misuse of social indicators to determine the success of programs. Campbell speculates that "the more any social indicator is used for social decision-making, the greater the corruption pressures upon it" (Campbell, 1981, p. 17). As an example, Campbell cites a case from the Soviet Union. When the managers of a nail factory were judged on the basis of how many tons of nails were produced, the factory overproduced large spikes. Then, when the standard was changed to how many nails were produced (in an attempt to overcome this problem), the factory's output was primarily very small nails, which were overproduced. How can this problem be resolved?

A fourth methodological problem is raised by the potential answer to the previous problem: the use of multiple indicators to determine the state of some phenomenon. With many different measures, each susceptible to different distortions, one would probably have a better idea of the actual state of affairs. But the different measures would undoubtedly produce a variety of estimates of the benefits and costs of various programs. Which ones to use? How will legislative bodies and administrators know which are the more reliable measures? Campbell believes that it will be difficult resolving the need for complete information with the democratic decision-making process, since many of the decision makers will not be sophisticated in understanding the various measures produced by differing research methods. He believes that it will be necessary to create new institutions such as an "auxiliary legislature of quantitative social scientists." These scientists could help elected legislators make decisions on the basis of scientific evidence, rather than on the recommendations of lobbyists who stand to gain finincially from certain legislation.

Wouldn't that be an interesting world?

Resources for Additional Information on Applied Psychology

W. Jeffrey Burroughs
Clemson University

W. Larry Gregory
New Mexico State University

Although the chapters in the text give you a feeling for what work in the various applied fields is like, they do not provide a great deal of information about the training experiences needed to work in those areas. The omission of such data was intentional, since information about undergraduate and graduate training in psychology and related applied fields is readily available elsewhere. The purpose of Appendix B is to draw your attention to some of these resources and to indicate where they may be obtained. The following books and pamphlets will increase your knowledge of training opportunities in applied psychology. Entries indicate title, cost, where the information may be obtained, and include a short annotation to describe the resource. It should be noted that some psychology departments maintain libraries that include these resources.

1. *Careers in Psychology,* no charge, available from the American Psychological Association, 1200 Seventeenth Street N.W., Washington, DC 20036, request the pamphlet by name.

    This is an informative, brief description of psychology's fields and careers.

2. *Is Psychology the Major for You? Planning for Your Undergraduate Years,* cost is currently $9.95, available from Order Department, American Psychological Association, P.O. Box 2710, Hyattsville, MD 20784, Order No. 4300020.

    This book provides an in-depth look at the undergraduate major in psychology. Questions such as what type of courses will you typically take, what can you do with the degree after you earn it, and what types of graduate training are available are considered. This book will help you decide if psychology is a field you should pursue and will prepare you to approach your education in psychology much more systematically.

3. *Graduate Study in Psychology and Associated Fields* (book is updated yearly), cost is currently $18.50, available from Order Department, American Psychological Association, P.O. Box 2710 Hyattsville, MD 20784, Order No. 4270011.

    This book is the single most important resource for those seeking graduate education in psychology. It contains a comprehensive listing of graduate programs in psychology and related areas, organized alphabetically by state and by college or university within each state. There are separate sections for doctoral programs in psychology, doctoral programs in related areas, master's level programs in psychology, and master's level programs in related areas. The book also provides an excellent index that makes it possible to review all the graduate programs offering courses of study in particular content areas. For example, it reviews all the graduate programs in industrial/organizational, clinical, and environmental psychology. Each entry presents data on admission standards, academic achievement of students admitted in the last year, financial support, and a summary of the programs offered by the department. This book is a very valuable aid in selecting a graduate school or in just learning about opportunities in various applied fields.

4. *Directory of Graduate Programs in Applied Sport Psychology,* for information write: Dr. Michael Sachs, P.O. Box 4005, Timonium MD 21093.

    This directory published by the Association for the Advancement of Applied Sport Psychology (AAASP) contains a comprehensive listing of graduate programs in the area. Because sport psychology programs are often found outside of psychology departments, some programs will not be represented in the APA guide described above.

References

Sources cited by authors in the individual chapters are fully recorded in the listings that follow.

Chapter 1

Baddeley, A. (1981). The cognitive psychology of everyday life. *British Journal of Psychology, 72,* 257–269.

Connecticut Special Education Association (1936). *History of special education for mentally deficient children in Connecticut.* New Haven, CT: The Association.

Cialdini, R. B. (1980). Full cycle social psychology. In L. Bickman (Ed.), *Applied Social Psychology Annual,* Vol 1. Beverly Hills, CA: Sage.

Goldstein, A. P., & Krasner, L. (1987). *Modern applied psychology.* New York: Pergamon.

Lewin, K. (1951). *Field theory in social science.* New York: Harper.

Munsterberg, H. (1908). *On the witness stand.* New York: Clark, Boardman.

Munsterberg, H. (1915). *Psychology: General and applied.* New York: Appleton.

Scott, W. D. (1903). *The theory of advertising.* Boston: Small and Maynard.

Scott, W. D. (1908). *Psychology of advertising.* Boston: Small and Maynard.

Thorndike, E. K. (1903). *Educational psychology.* New York: Lemcke and Buechmen.

Chapter 2

Agras, W. S., Barlow, D. H., Chapin, H. N., Abel, G. G., & Leitenberg, H. (1974). Behavior modification of anorexia nervosa. *Archives of General Psychiatry, 30,* 279-286.

Fitts, P. M., & Jones, R. E. (1947). Analysis of factors contributing to 460 "pilot-error" experiences in operating aircraft controls (Report No. TSEAA-694-12). Wright-Patterson Air Force Base, OH: Army Air Forces Air Material Command, Engineering Division, Aero Medical Laboratory.

Fitts, P. M., & Jones, R. E. (1947). Psychological aspects of instrument display. I. Analysis of 270 "pilot-error" experiences in reading and interpreting aircraft instruments (Report No. TSEAA-694-12A). Wright-Patterson Air Force Base, OH:

U.S. Air Forces Air Material Command, Engineering Division, Aero Medical Laboratory.

Fitts, P. M., Jones, R. E., & Milton, J. L. (1950). Eye movements of aircraft pilots during instrument-landing approaches. *Aeronautical Engineering Review, 9,* 24–29.

Herman, J. A., de Montes, A. I., Dominguez, B., Montes, F., & Hopkins, B. L. (1973). Effects of bonuses for punctuality on the tardiness of industrial workers. *Journal of Applied Behavioral Analysis, 6,* 563–570.

Chapter 3

Benotat, R., & Hunt, D. P. (1977). *University curricula in ergonomics.* Meckenheim, Germany: Forschungs-institut für Anthropotechnik.

Caplan, S. H. (1982). Designing new cameras for improved holdability. In *Proceedings of the 26th Annual Meeting of the Human Factors Society.* Santa Monica, CA: Human Factors Society, 195–198.

Chapanis, A. (1965). *Man-machine engineering.* Belmont, CA: Wadsworth.

Chapanis, A., & Kincade, R. G. (1972). Design of controls. Chapter 8 in H. P. Van Cott & R. G. Kincade, (Eds.), *Human engineering guide to equipment design.* U.S. Government Printing Office.

Daniels, G. S. (1952). The "average man?" (Technical note WCRD 53-7) Wright-Patterson Air Force Base, OH: Wright Air Development Center, USAF (AD-10203).

Farrell, R. J., & Booth, J. M. (1975). *Design handbook for imagery interpretation equipment.* Seattle, WA: Boeing Aerospace Co. (D180-19063-1).

Faulkner, T. W., & Rice, T. M. (1982). Human factors, photographic space, and disc photography. In *Proceedings of the 26th Annual Meeting of the Human Factors Society.* Santa Monica, CA: Human Factors Society.

Faulkner, T. W., Rice, T. M., & Heron, W. K. (1983). The influence of camera configuration on preference. *Human Factors, 25,* 127–141.

Hunt, D. P., & Craig, D. R. (1954). The relative discriminability of thirty-one differently shaped knobs. Report WADC-TR-54-108, Wright-Patterson Air Force Base, OH: Wright Air Development Center, USAF.

Mackett-Stout, J., & Dewar, R. (1981). Evaluation of symbolic public information signs. *Human Factors, 23,* 129–151.

Roebuck, J. A., Jr., Kroemer, H. E. & Thomson, W. G. (1975). *Engineering anthropometry methods.* New York: Wiley.

Chapter 4

Aldefer, C. P. (1987). The design of work teams. In J. W. Lorsch (Ed.), *Handbook of organizational behavior.* Englewood Cliffs, NJ: Prentice-Hall.

Arvey, R. D. (1979). *Fairness in selecting employees.* Reading, MA: Addison-Wesley.

Arvey, R. D., & Campion, J. E. (1982). The employment interview: A summary and review of recent research. *Personnel Psychology, 35,* 281–322.

Arvey, R. D., Miller, H. E., Gould, R. & Burch, P. (1987). Interview validity for selecting sales clerks. *Personnel Psychology, 40,* 1-12.

Asher, J. J., & Sciarrino, J. A. (1974). Realistic work sample tests: A review. *Personnel Psychology, 27,* 519-533.

Barrick, M. R., & Alexander, R. A. (1987). A review of quality circle efficacy and the existence of positive-finding bias. *Personnel Psychology, 40,* 579-592.

Bass, B. M. (1985). *Leadership and performance beyond expectations.* New York: Free Press.

Bass, B. M. (1981). *Stodgill's handbook of leadership: A survey of theory and research* (rev. and exp. ed.). New York: Free Press.

Bureau of Labor Statistics. (1980). Recent trends in labor force participation rates: A chartbook. U.S. Department of Labor, September 1980, Report 609. Washington, DC: Superintendent of Documents, U.S. Government Printing Office.

Business Week. (1987). Corporate women: They're about to break through to the top. June 22, 1987, 72-77.

Cascio, W. F. (1987a). *Applied psychology in personnel management* (3rd ed.). Reston, VA: Reston.

Cascio, W. F. (1987b). *Costing human resources.* Boston: Kent Publishing.

Cascio, W. F. (1986). *Managing human resources.* New York: McGraw-Hill.

Collins, B., & Goetzkown, H. A. (1964). *A social psychology of group processses for decision-making.* New York: Wiley.

Cotton, J. L., & Tuttle, J. M. (1986). Employee turnover: A meta-analysis and review with implications for research. *Academy of Management Review, 11,* 55-70.

Decker, P. J., & Cornelius, E. T. (1979). A note on recruiting sources and job survival rates. *Journal of Applied Psychology, 64,* 463-464.

Deitch, C. R., & Dilts, D. A. (1981). Getting absent workers back on the job: The case of General Motors. *Business Horizons,* pp. 52-58.

Dougherty, T. W., Ebert, R. J., & Callender, J. (1986). Policy capturing in the employment interview. *Journal of Applied Psychology, 71,* 9-15.

Doverspike, D., Barrett, G. V., & Alexander, R. (1985). The feasibility of traditional validation procedures for demonstrating job relatedness. *Law Psychological Review, 9,* 35-44.

Eurich, N. P. (1985). *Corporate classrooms.* Princeton, NJ: Carnegie Foundation.

Fiedler, F. E., & Garcia, J. E. (1987). *New approaches to leadership: Cognitive resources and organizational performance.* New York: Wiley.

Flamholtz, E. (1974). *Human resources accounting.* Encino, CA: Dickenson Publishing.

Friedlander, F. (1987). The ecology of work groups. In J. W. Lorsch (Ed.), *Handbook of organizational behavior.* Englewood Cliffs, NJ: Prentice-Hall.

Gannon, M. J. (1971). Sources of referral and employee turnover. *Journal of Applied Psychology, 55,* 226-228.

Ghiselli, E. E. (1973). The validity of aptitude tests in personnel selection. *Personnel Psychology, 26,* 461-477.

Goldstein, I. L. (1986). *Training in organizations: Needs assessment, development, and evaluation* (2nd ed.). Monterey, CA: Brooks/Cole.

Grant, D. L. (1980). Issues in personnel selection. *Professional Psychology, 11,* 369-384.

Griggs v. *Duke Power Company*, 401 U.S. 424 (1971).

Guion, R. M., & Gibson, W. M. (1988). Personnel selection and placement. In M. R. Rosenzweig and L. W. Porter (Eds.), *Annual Review of Psychology*, Vol. 39, Palo Alto, CA: Annual Reviews, Inc.

Hackman, J. R. (1981). Work redesign for organization development. In H. Meltzer & W. Nord (Eds.), *Making organizations humane and productive: A handbook for practitioners*. New York: Wiley.

Hackman, J. R., & Morris, C. G. (1975). Group tasks, group interaction process, and group performance effectiveness: A review and proposed integration. In L. Berkowitz (Ed.), *Advances in experimental social psychology*, Vol. 8. New York: Academic Press.

Hackman, J. R. (1987). The design of work teams. In J. W. Lorsch (Ed.), *Handbook of organizational behavior*. Englewood Cliffs, NJ: Prentice-Hall.

Hakel, M. D. (1982). Employment interviewing. In K. M. Rowland & G. R. Ferris (Eds.) *Personnel management*. Boston: Allyn and Bacon.

Hinrichs, J. R. (1980). *Controlling absenteeism and turnover*. Scarsdale, NY: Work in America Institute, Inc.

House, R. J. (1985). *Research contrasting the behavior and effect of reputed charismatic versus reputed non-charismatic U.S. presidents*. Presented at Annual Meeting of the Administrative Science Association, Montreal.

House, R. J., & Singh, J. V. (1987). Organizational behavior: Some new directions for I/O psychology. In M. R. Rosenzweig and L. W. Porter (Eds.), *Annual Review of Psychology*, 38. Palo Alto, CA: Annual Reviews, Inc.

Howell, W. C., & Dipboye, R. L. (1982). *Essentials of industrial & organizational psychology* (rev. ed.). Homewood, IL: The Dorsey Press.

Hunter, J. E., & Hunter, R. F. (1984). Validity and the utility of alternative predictors of job performance. *Psychological Bulletin, 96,* 72–95.

Imada, A. S., & Hakel, M. D. (1977). Influence of nonverbal communication and rater proximity on impressions and decisions in simulated employment interviews. *Journal of Applied Psychology, 62,* 295–300.

Janis, I. L. (1972). *Victims of groupthink*. Boston: Houghton Mifflin.

Johnson, D. P. (1974). Social organization of an industrial work group: Emergence and adaptation to environmental change. *The Sociological Quarterly, 15,* 109–126.

Jurgensen, C. E. (1978). Job preferences (what makes a job good or bad?). *Journal of Applied Psychology, 63,* 267–276.

Kandy, F. J. (1976). The validity of the interview in police officer selection. *Journal of Applied Psychology, 61,* 193–198.

Karlins, M. (1981). *The human use of human resources*. New York: McGraw-Hill.

Katz, D., & Kahn, R. L. (1978). *The social psychology of organizations* (2nd ed.). New York: Wiley.

Katzell, R. A., & Guzzo, R. A. (1983). Psychological approaches to productivity improvement. *American Psychologist, 38,* 468–473.

Kerr, C., & Rosnow, J. M. (Eds.). (1979). *Work in America: The decade ahead*. New York: Van Nostrand.

Klimosky, R., & Brickner, M. (1987). Why do assessment centers work? The puzzle of assessment center validity, *Personnel Psychology, 40,* 243–260.

Latane, B., Williams, K., & Harkins, S. (1979). Social loafing. *Psychology Today,* October.

Latham, G. P., Saari, L. M., Pursell, E. D., and Campion, M. A. (1980). The situational interview. *Journal of Applied Psychology, 65,* 427–442.

Lawler, E. E. III (1982). Strategies for improving the quality of work life. *American Psychologist, 37,* 486–493.

Levine, E. L. (1983). *Everything you always wanted to know about job analysis.* Tampa, FL: Mariner.

Lyman, H. B. (1963). *Test scores and what they mean.* Englewood Cliffs, NJ: Prentice-Hall.

Mangum, S. L. (1982). Recruitment and job search: The recruitment tactics of employers. *Personnel Administrator, 27,* 96–104.

McCormick, E. J. (1979). *Job analysis: Methods and applications.* New York: AMACOM.

McEvoy, G. M., & Cascio, W. F. (1985). Strategies for reducing employee turnover: A meta-analysis. *Journal of Applied Psychology, 70,* 342–353.

Miner, J. B. (1978). Twenty years of research on role motivation theory of managerial effectiveness. *Personnel Psychology, 31,* 739–760.

Mitchell, T. R. (1982). People in organizations (2nd ed.). New York: McGraw-Hill.

Mobley, W. H. (1982). *Employee turnover: Causes, consequences, and control.* Reading, MA: Addison-Wesley.

Muchinsky, P. M. (1987). *Psychology applied to work: An introduction to industrial and organizational psychology.* Chicago: Dorsey Press.

Navy worried about growing jet losses. (1986, March 23). *Honolulu Star Bulletin & Advisor,* pp. A-1, A-4.

Owens, W. A., & Schoenfeldt, L. F. (1979). Toward a classification of persons. *Journal of Applied Psychology, 46,* 329–332.

Pearce, J. A., & David, F. R. (1983). A social network approach to organizational design-performance. *Academy of Management Review, 18,* 436-444.

Pearce, J. L. (1981). Bringing some clarity to role ambiguity research. *Academy of Management Review, 6,* 665–674.

Peters, L. H., & Terborg, J. R. (1975). The effects of temporal placement of unfavorable information and of attitude similarity on personnel selection decisions. *Organizational Behavior and Human Performance, 13,* 279–293.

Peters, T. J., & Waterman, R. H. (1982). *In search of excellence, lessons from America's best-run companies.* New York: Harper & Row.

Reilly, R. R., & Chao, G. T. (1982). Validity and fairness of some alternative employee selection procedures. *Personnel Psychology, 35,* 1–62.

Roethlisberger, F. J., & Dickson, W. J. (1939). *Management and the worker.* Cambridge, MA: Harvard University Press.

Rowland, K. M., & Ferris, G. R. (1982). *Personnel management.* Boston, MA: Allyn and Bacon.

Roy, D. F. (1960). Banana time: Job satisfaction and information integration. *Human Organizations, 18,* 158–168.

Sasser, W. E., Jr., & Leonard, F. S. (1980). Let first-level supervisors do their job. *Harvard Business Review,* March–April, 113–121.

Schmidt, F. L., Hunter, J. E., & Outerbridge, A. (1986). Impact of job experience and ability on job knowledge, work sample performance, and supervisory ratings of job performance. *Journal of Applied Psychology, 71,* 432–439.

Schmitt, N., and DeGregorio, M. B. (1986). Results of society survey. *The Industrial/Organizational Psychologist, 23,* 27–34.

Schneider, B. (1976). *Staffing organizations.* Pacific Palisades, CA: Goodyear.

Schneider, B., & Schmitt, N. W. (1986). *Staffing organizations.* Glenview, IL: Scott, Foresman.

Shaw, M. E. (1976). *Group dynamics.* New York: McGraw-Hill.

Steers, R. M., & Rhodes, S. R. (1978). Major influences on employee attendance: A process model. *Journal of Applied Psychology, 63,* 391–407.

Stodgill, R. M. (1950). Leadership, membership and organization. *Psychological Bulletin, 47,* 1–14.

Taylor, M. S., & Schmidt, D. W. (1983). A process-oriented investigation of recruitment source effectiveness. *Personnel Psychology, 36,* 343–354.

Tenopyr, M. L. (1981). The realities of employment testing. *American Psychologist, 36,* 1120–1127.

Vroom, V. H., & Jago, A. G. (1988). *The new leadership: Managing participation in organizations.* Englewood Cliffs, NJ: Prentice-Hall.

Walton, R. E. (1977). Work innovations at Topeka: After six years. *Journal of Applied Behavioral Science, 13,* 422–433.

Wanous, J. P. (1980). *Organizational entry: Recruitment, selection and socialization of newcomers.* Reading, MA: Addison-Wesley.

Webster, E. C. (1964). *Decision making in the employment interview.* Montreal: Eagle.

Webster, E. C. (1982). *The employment interview: A social judgment process.* Schomberg, Ontario, Canada: S.I.P. Publications.

Yukl, G. A., & Van Fleet, D. D. (1982). Cross-situational and multi-method research on military leader effectiveness. *Organizational Behavior and Human Performance, 30,* 87–108.

Zwerdling, D. (1978). *Democracy at work.* Washington, DC: Association for Self-management.

Chapter 5

Beckard, R. (1969). *Organization development: Strategies and models.* Reading, MA: Addison-Wesley.

French, W. L., & Bell, C. H. (1972). A brief history of organization development. *Journal of Contemporary Business,* Summer, 1–8.

French, W. L., Bell, C. H., & Zawacki, R. A. (1983). OD interventions: An overview. In W. L. French, C. H. Bell, & R. A. Zawacki (Eds.), *Organization Development.* Plano, TX: Business Publications.

Goad, T. (1979). Needed: A new OD model. *Training and Development Journal, 33,* 46–48.

Lewin, K. (1951). *Field theory in social science.* New York: Harper & Row.

McGregor, D. (1960). *The human side of enterprise.* New York: McGraw-Hill.

McLagen, P. A., & Bedrick, D. (1983). Models for excellence: The results of the

ASTD training and development competency study. *Training and Development Journal, 37,* 10–20.

Roethlisberger, F. J., & Dickson, W. J. (1939). *Management and the worker.* Cambridge, MA: Harvard University Press.

Schein, V. E. (1985). Organizational realities: The politics of change. *Training and Development Journal, 39,* 37–41.

Warrick, D. D., & Donovan, T. (1979). Surveying organization development skills. *Training and Development Journal, 33,* 22–25.

Chapter 6

Baddeley, A. (1981). The cognitive psychology of everyday life. *British Journal of Psychology, 72,* 257–269.

Biederman, I. (1981). On the semantics of a glance at a scene. In M. Kubovy & J. R. Pomerantz (Eds.), *Perceptual organization* (pp. 213–254). Hillsdale, NJ: Erlbaum.

Biederman, I., Mezzanotte, R. J., & Rabinowitz, J. C. (1981). Scene perception: Detecting and judging objects undergoing relational violations. *Cognitive Psychology, 14,* 143–177.

Biederman, I., Mezzanotte, R. J., Rabinowitz, J. C., Francolini, C. M., & Plude, D. (1981). Detecting the unexpected in Photointerpretation. *Human Factors, 23,* 153–164.

Chomsky, N. (1980). *Rules and representations.* New York: Columbia University Press.

Gibson, J. J. (1979). *The ecological approach to visual perception.* Boston: Houghton Mifflin.

Johnston, V., Partridge, D., & Lopez, P. (1983). A neural theory of cognitive development. *Journal of Theoretical Biology, 100,* 485–509.

Loftus, G. R., & Mackworth, N. H. (1978). Cognitive determinants of fixation location during picture viewing. *Journal of Experimental Psychology: Human Perception and Performance, 4,* 565–576.

Mandler, G. (1967). Organization and memory. In K. W. Spence & J. T. Spence (Eds.), *The psychology of learning and motivation: Advances in research and theory.* New York: Academic Press.

Massaro, D. W. (1975). *Experimental psychology and information processing.* Chicago: Rand-McNally.

Miller, G. (1956). The magical number seven, plus or minus two: Some limits on our capacity for processing information. *Psychological Review, 63,* 81–97.

Neisser, U. (1967). *Cognitive psychology.* New York: Appleton-Century-Crofts.

Norman, D. A. (1976). *Memory & attention: An introduction to human information processing* (2nd ed.). New York: Wiley.

Norman, D. A. (1981a). The trouble with UNIX. *Datamation, 27,* 139–150. (a)

Norman, D. A. (1981b). Categorization of action slips. *Psychological Review, 88,* 1–15.

Norman, D. A. (1981c). A psychologist views human processing: Human errors and other phenomena suggest processing mechanism. Paper presented at IJCAI, Vancouver, British Columbia.

Norman, D. A. (1982). Steps toward a cognitive engineering: Design rules based on analyses of human error. *Proceedings of the Conference on Human Factors in Computer Systems,* March, Gaithersburg, Maryland.

Perlman, G. (1981). *Two papers in cognitive engineering: The design of an interface to a programming system and MENUNIX:* A menu-based interface to UNIX. Center for Human Information Processing Report No. 8105. La Jolla, California.

Piaget, J. (1977). *Biology and knowledge.* Chicago, IL: University of Chicago Press.

Premack, D., & Woodruff, G. (1978). Does the chimpanzee have a theory of mind? *Behavioral and Brain Sciences, 1,* 515–526.

Shebilske, W. L., & Fisher, D. F. (1983). Understanding extended discourse through the eyes: How and why. In R. Groner, D. F. Fisher, & R. A. Monty (Eds.), *Eye-movements and psychological functions: International views.* Hillsdale, NJ: Erlbaum.

Yarbus, A. L. (1967). *Eye movements and vision.* New York: Plenum.

Chapter 7

Action for Children's Television, Newton, MA. (1977). Petition to promulgate a rule prohibiting the advertising of candy to children on television, submitted to the Federal Trade Commission.

Armstrong, G. M., Gurol, M. N., & Russ, F. A. (1979). Detecting and correcting deceptive advertising. *Journal of Consumer Research, 6,* 237–246.

Asch, S. E. (1956). Studies of independence and conformity: A minority of one against a unanimous majority. *Psychological Monographs, 70,* No. 9 (Whole No. 416).

Atkin, C., & Miller, M. (1975). The effects of TV advertising on children: Experimental evidence. Paper presented to the Mass Communication Division, International Communication Association, Chicago.

Bettman, J. R. (1979). *An information processing theory of consumer choice.* Reading, MA: Addison-Wesley.

Bogen, J. E. (1977). Some educational implications of hemispheric specialization. In M. C. Wittrock (Ed.), *The human brain.* New York: Prentice-Hall.

Broadbent, D. E. (1977). The two processes of attention. *American Psychologist, 32,* 109–118.

Cialdini, R. B., & Ascani, D. K. (1976). Test of a concession procedure for inducing verbal, behavioral, and further compliance with a request to give blood. *Journal of Applied Psychology, 61,* 295–300.

Deglin, V. L. (1976). Journey through the brain, *UNESCO Courier,* January, 4–14.

Donohue, T. R., Henke, L. L., & Donohue, W. A. (1980). Do kids know what TV commercials intend? *Journal of Advertising Research, 20,* 51–57.

Freedman, J. L., & Fraser, S. (1966). Compliance without pressure: The foot-in-the-door technique. *Journal of Personality and Social Psychology, 4,* 195–202.

Goldberg, M. E., & Gorn, G. J. (1978). Some unintended consequences of TV advertising to children. *Journal of Consumer Research, 5,* 22–29.

Goldberg, M. E., Gorn, G. J., & Gibon, W. (1978). TV messages for snack and breakfast foods: Do they influence children's preferences? *Journal of Consumer Research, 5,* 73–81.

Hansen, F. (1981). Hemispheral lateralization: Implications for understanding consumer behavior. *Journal of Consumer Research, 8,* 23–36.

Kassarjian, H. H. (1982). Consumer psychology. *Annual Review of Psychology, Vol. 33,* 619–649. Palo Alto, CA: Annual Reviews, Inc.

Katona, G. (1975). *Psychological economics.* Amsterdam: Elsevier.

Kimura, D. (1973). The asymmetry of the human brain—recent progress in perception. *Scientific American, 232,* 246–254.

Krugman, H. E. (1965). The impact of television advertising: Learning without involvement. *Public Opinion Quarterly, 29,* 349–356.

Krugman, H. E. (1977). Memory without recall, exposure without recognition. *Journal of Advertising Research, 17,* 7–12.

Lindzay, P. H., & Norman, D. A. (1977). *Human information processing.* New York: Academic Press.

McClelland, D. C. (1986). Personality: An integrative view. In J. L. McCary, (Ed.), *Psychology of personality.* New York: Grove Press.

McNeal, J. U. (1964). *Children as consumers.* Austin: Bureau of Business Research, University of Texas.

Olshavsky, R. W., & Granbois, D. (1979). Consumer decision making—fact or fiction? *Journal of Consumer Research, 6,* 93–100.

Ornstein, R. E. (1973). *The nature of human consciousness.* San Francisco: Viking.

Poulos, R. W. (1975). *Unintended negative effects of good commercials on children: A case study.* San Francisco: Media Action Research Center.

Robertson, T., & Rossiter, J. R. (1976). Children's consumer satisfaction. Working paper, Center for Research in Media and Children, University of Pennsylvania.

Robertson, T., Rossiter, J. R., & Gleason, T. C. (1979). Children's receptivity to proprietary medicine advertising. *Journal of Consumer Research, 6,* 247–255.

Roedder, D. L. (1981). Age differences in children's responses to television advertising: An information processing approach. *Journal of Consumer Research, 1981, 8,* 144–153.

Sadalla, E., & Burroughs, J. (1981). Profiles in eating: Sexy vegetarians and other diet-based social stereotypes. *Psychology Today, 15,* 51–57.

Sawyer, A. G. (1974). The effects of repetition: Conclusions and suggestions about experimental laboratory research. In G. P. Hughes & M. L. Ray (Eds.), *Buyer/consumer information processing.* Chapel Hill: University of North Carolina Press.

Shimp, T. A., Dyer, R. F., & Divita, S. (1976). An experimental test of the harmful effects of premium oriented commercials on children. *Journal of Consumer Research, 3,* 1–11.

Venkatesan, M. (1966). Experimental study of consumer behavior, conformity, and independence. *Journal of Marketing Research, 3,* 384–387.

Winn, M. (1977). *The plug-in drug.* San Francisco: Viking.

Wright, P. (1975). Consumer choice strategies: Simplifying vs. optimizing. *Journal of Marketing Research 12,* 60–67.

Zajonc, R. R. (1980). Time and functions of mind. *ISR Newsletter,* Spring, 3–5. Ann Arbor: University of Michigan.

Chapter 8

Bandura, A. (1969). *Principles of behavior modification.* New York: Holt, Rinehart, and Winston.

Bandura, A. (1971). Psychotherapy based upon modeling principles. In A. E. Bergin & S. L. Garfield (Eds.), *Handbook of psychotherapy and behavior change.* New York: Wiley.

Bandura, A. (1977). Self-efficacy: Toward a unifying theory of behavior change. *Psychological Review, 84,* 191–215.

Bandura, A., Adams, N. E., & Beyer, J. (1977). Cognitive processes mediating behavioral change. *Journal of Personality and Social Psychology, 35,* 125–139.

Bandura, A., Blanchard, E. B., & Ritter, B. (1969). The relative efficacy of desensitization and modeling approaches for inducing behavioral, affective, and attitudinal changes. *Journal of Personality and Social Psychology, 13,* 173–199.

Bandura, A., Grusec, J. R., & Menlove, F. L. (1967). Vicarious extinction of avoidance behavior, *Journal of Personality and Social Psychology, 5,* 16–23.

Bandura, A., & Menlove, F. L. (1968). Factors determining vicarious extinction of avoidance behavior through symbolic modeling, *Journal of Personality and Social Psychology, 8,* 99–108.

Beers, C. W. (1921, originally published 1908). *A mind that found itself* (5th ed.). New York: Doubleday.

Bernstein, D. A., & Nietzel, M. T. (1980). *Introduction to clinical psychology.* New York: McGraw-Hill.

Boring, E. G. (1950). *A history of experimental psychology* (2nd ed.). New York: Appleton-Century-Crofts.

Ellis, A. (1982). *Reason and emotion in psychotherapy.* New York: Lyle Stuart.

Fulcher, R., & Stapp, J. (1981). *Preliminary report: 1980 doctorate employment survey.* Washington, DC: American Psychological Association.

Garfield, S. (1974). *Clinical psychology: The study of personality and behavior.* Chicago: Aldine.

Garfield, S., & Kurtz, R. (1976). Clinical psychologists in the 1970s. *American Psychologist, 31,* 1–9.

Goldenberg, H. (1973). *Contemporary clinical psychology.* Monterey, CA: Brooks/Cole.

Hilgard, E. R. (Ed.). (1977). *American psychology in historical perspective, 1892–1977.* Washington, DC: American Psychological Association.

Howard, A., Pion, G. M. Gottfredson, P. E., Oskamp, S., Pfafflin, S. M., Bray, D. W., & Burstein, A. G. (1986). The changing face of American psychology. *American Psychologist, 41,* 1311–1327.

Joint Commission on Mental Illness and Health. (1961). *Action for mental health.* New York: Basic Books.

Kanfer, F. H. (1975). Self-management methods. In F. H. Kanfer & A. P. Goldstein (Eds.), *Helping people change: A textbook of methods.* New York: Pergamon.

Korchin, S. J. (1976). *Modern clinical psychology.* New York: Basic Books.

Korman, M. (Ed.). (1976). *Levels and patterns of professional training in psychology.* Washington, DC: American Psychological Association.

Leitenberg, H. (1973). The use of single case methodology in psychotherapy research. *Journal of Abnormal Psychology, 82,* 87–101.

Leventhal, A. M. (1968). Use of a behavioral approach within a traditional psychotherapeutic context: A case study. *Journal of Abnormal Psychology, 73,* 178–182.

Lewinsohn, P. M., Weinstein, M. S., & Shaw, D. A. (1969). Depression: A clinical-research approach. In R. D. Rubin & C. W. Franks (Eds.), *Advances in behavioral therapy, 1968.* New York: Academic Press.

O'Leary, K. D., & Wilson, G. T. (1975). *Behavior therapy: Application and outcome.* Englewood Cliffs, NJ: Prentice-Hall.

Reisinger, J. J. (1972). The treatment of "anxiety-depression" via positive reinforcement and response cost. *Journal of Applied Behavior Analysis, 5,* 125–130.

Reisman, J. M. (1966). *The development of clinical psychology.* New York: Appleton-Century-Crofts.

Rogers, C. R. (1951). *Client-centered therapy.* Boston: Houghton Mifflin.

Rosenthal, T., & Bandura, A. (1978). Psychological modeling: Theory and practice. In S. L. Garfield & A. E. Bergin (Eds.), *Handbook of psychotherapy and behavior change.* New York: Wiley.

Smith, D. (1982). Trends in counseling and psychotherapy. *American Psychologist, 37,* 802–809.

Stapp, J., & Fulcher, R. (1981). The employment of APA members. *American Psychologist, 36,* 1263–1314.

Stapp, J., Tucker, A. M., & VandenBos, G. R. (1985). Census of psychological personnel: 1983. *American Psychologist, 39,* 1317–1351.

Sundberg, N. D., & Tyler, L. E. (1962). *Clinical psychology: An introduction to research and practice.* New York: Appleton-Century-Crofts.

Sundberg, N. D., & Tyler, L. E., Taplin, J. R. (1973). *Clinical psychology: Expanding horizons.* Englewood Cliffs, NJ: Prentice-Hall.

Thelen, M. H., Fry, R. A., Fehrenbach, P. A., & Frautschi, N. M. (1979). Therapeutic videotape and film modeling: A review. *Psychological Bulletin, 86,* 701–720.

Watson, J. B., & Rayner, R. (1920). Conditioned emotional reactions. *Journal of Experimental Psychology, 3,* 1–14.

Wolpe, J. (1958). *Psychotherapy by reciprocal inhibition.* Stanford, CA: Stanford University Press.

Chapter 9

Acosta, F. X. (1979). Barriers between mental health services and Mexican-Americans: An examination of a paradox. *American Journal of Community Psychology, 7,* 503–520.

Albee, G. W. (1959). *Mental health manpower trends.* New York: Basic Books.

Bachrach, K. M., & Zautra, A. (1980). Some uses of client and census records in community mental health planning. *American Journal of Community Psychology, 8,* 365–378.

Barrera, M., Jr. (1978). Mexican-American mental health utilization: A critical examination of some proposed variables. *Community Mental Health Journal, 14,* 35–45.

Barrera, M., Jr. (1981). Social support in the adjustment of pregnant adolescents: Assessment issues. In B. H. Gottlieb (Ed.), *Social networks and social support.* Beverly Hills, CA: Sage Publications.

Barton, A. K., Andrulis, D. P., Grove, W. P., & Aponte, J. F. (1976). A look at community psychology training programs in the seventies. *American Journal of Community Psychology, 4,* 1–13.

Bell, R. A., Nguyen, T. D., Warheit, G. J. & Buhl, J. M. (1978). Service utilization, social indicator, and citizen survey approaches to human service need assessment. In C. C. Attkisson, W. A. Hargraves, M. J. Horowitz, & J. E. Sorenson (Eds.), *Evaluation of human service programs.* New York: Academic Press.

Bennett, C. C. (1965). Community psychology: Impressions of the Boston conference on the education of psychologists for community mental health. *American Psychologist, 20,* 832–835.

Bernstein, D. A., & Nietzel, M. T. (1980). *Introduction to clinical psychology.* New York: McGraw-Hill.

Bloom, B. L. (1965). The "medical model," miasma theory, and community mental health. *Community Mental Health Journal, 1,* 333–338.

Bloom, B. L. (1975). *Changing patterns of psychiatric care.* New York: Human Sciences Press.

Bloom, B. L. (1977). *Community mental health: A general introduction.* Monterey, CA: Brooks/Cole.

Bloom, B. L. (1979). Prevention of mental disorders: Recent advances in theory and practice. *Community Mental Health Journal, 15,* 179–191.

Briscoe, N., Hoffman, D., & Bailey, J. (1975). Behavioral community psychology: Training a community board to problem solve. *Journal of Applied Behavior Analysis, 8,* 157–168.

Caplan, G. (1964). *Principles of preventive psychiatry.* New York: Basic Books.

Cowen, E. L. (1967). Emergent approaches to mental health problems: An overview and directions for future work. In E. L. Cowen, E. A. Gardner, & M. Zax (Eds.), *Emergent approaches to mental health problems.* New York: Appleton-Century-Crofts.

Cowen, E. L. (1973). Social and community interventions. *Annual Review of Psychology, Vol. 24,* 423–472. Palo Alto, CA: Annual Reviews. Inc.

Cowen, E. L. (1977). Baby-steps toward primary prevention. *American Journal of Community Psychology, 5,* 1–23.

Cowen, E. L., Gesten, E. L., & Wilson, A. B. (1979). The Primary Mental Health Project (PMHP): Evaluation of current program effectiveness. *American Journal of Community Psychology, 7,* 293–303.

Cowen, E. L., Trost, M. A., Lorion, R. P., Dorr, D., Izzo, L. D., & Isaacson, R. V. (1975). New ways in school mental health: Early detection and prevention of school maladaptation. New York: Human Sciences, Inc.

Danish, S. J., & D'Angelli, A. R. (1980). Promoting competence and enhancing development through life development intervention. In L. A. Bond & J. C. Rosen (Eds.), *Primary prevention of psychopathology (Vol. 4).* Hanover, NH: University Press of New England.

D'Angelli, A. R., Vallance, T. R., Danish, S. J., Young, C. E., & Gerdes, J. L.

(1981). The Community Helpers Project: A description of a prevention strategy for rural communities. *Journal of Prevention, 1,* 209–224.

Davidson, W. S., Rappaport, J., Seidman, E., Berck, P., Rapp, C., Rhodes, W., & Herring, J. (1977). A diversion program for juvenile offenders. *Social Work Research and Abstracts, 1,* 47–56.

Delaney, J. A., Seidman, E., & Wills, G. (1978). Crisis intervention and the prevention of institutionalization: An interrupted time series analysis. *American Journal of Community Psychology, 6,* 33–47.

Durlak, J. A. (1979). Comparative effectiveness of paraprofessional and professional helpers. *Psychological Bulletin, 86,* 80–93.

Eysenck, H. J. (1952). The effects of psychotherapy: An evaluation. *Journal of Consulting Psychology, 16,* 319–324.

Fairweather, G. W., Sanders, D. H., Cressler, D. L., & Maynard, H. (1969). *Community life for the mentally ill: An alternative to institutional care.* Chicago: Aldine.

Fairweather, G. W., & Tornatzky, L. G. (1977). *Experimental methods for social policy research.* New York: Pergamon Press.

Golann, S. E. (1970). Community psychology and mental health: An analysis of strategies and a survey of training. In I. Iscoe & C. D. Spielberger (Eds.), *Community psychology: Perspectives in training and research.* New York: Appleton-Century-Crofts.

Goodman, G. (1972). *Companionship therapy: Studies of structural intimacy.* San Francisco: Jossey-Bass.

Gottlieb, B. H. (1981). Social networks and social support in community mental health. In B. H. Gottlieb (Ed.), *Social networks and social support.* Beverly Hills, CA: Sage Publications.

Gurin, G., Veroff, J., & Feld, S. (1960). *Americans view their mental health: A nationwide interview survey.* New York: Basic Books.

Heller, K., & Monahan, J. (1977). *Psychology and community change.* Homewood, IL: Dorsey Press.

Hirsch, B. J. (1980). Natural support systems and coping with major life changes. *American Journal of Community Psychology, 8,* 159–173.

Hollingshead, A. G., & Redlich, F. C. (1958). *Social class and mental illness: A community study.* New York: Basic Books.

Iscoe, I., Bloom, B. L., & Spielberger, C. D. (Eds.). (1977). *Community psychology in transition.* Washington, DC: Hemisphere.

Iscoe, I., & Spielberger, C. D. (Eds.). (1970). *Community psychology: Perspectives in training and research.* New York: Appleton-Century-Crofts.

Jahoda, M. (1958). *Current concepts of positive mental health.* New York: Basic Books.

Joint Commission on Mental Illness and Health. (1961). *Action for mental health.* New York: Basic Books.

Karno, M., & Morales, A. (1971). A community mental health service for Mexican-Americans in a metropolis. In N. N. Wagner & J. Hang (Eds.), *Chicanos: Social and psychological perspectives.* St. Louis: C. V. Mosby.

Keefe, S. E., Padilla, A. M., & Carlos, M. L. (1979). The Mexican-American extended family as an emotional support system. *Human Organization, 38,* 144–152.

Kelly, J. G. (1970). Antidotes for arrogance: Training for a community psychology. *American Psychologist, 25,* 524–531.

Kelly, J. G., Snowden, L. R., & Munoz, R. F. (1977). Social and community interventions. *Annual Review of Psychology, Vol. 28,* 323–361. Palo Alto, CA: Annual Reviews, Inc.

Kobasa, S. C. (1979). Stressful life events, personality, and health: An inquiry into hardiness. *Journal of Personality and Social Psychology, 37,* 1–11.

Kohlberg, L., La Crosse, J., & Ricks, D. (1972). The predictability of adult mental health from childhood behavior. In B. B. Wolman (Ed.), *Manual of child psychopathology.* New York: McGraw-Hill.

Levinson, D. J. (1978). *The seasons of a man's life.* New York: Knopf.

Lorion, R. P., & Cowen, E. L. (1976). Comparison of two outcome groups in a school based mental health project. *American Journal of Community Psychology, 4,* 65–73.

McGee, R. K. (1974). *Crisis intervention in the community.* Baltimore, MD: University Park Press.

Meehl, P. E. (1954). *Clinical versus statistical prediction: A theoretical analysis and a review of the evidence.* Minneapolis: University of Minnesota Press.

Meehl, P. E. (1965). Seer over sign: The first good example. *Journal of Experimental Research in Personality, 1,* 27–32.

Meehl, P. E. (1957). When shall we use our heads instead of the formula? *Journal of Counseling Psychology, 4,* 268–273.

Meyer, M. L., & Gerrard, M. Graduate training in community psychology. *American Journal of Community Psychology, 5,* 155–164.

Moos, R. H. (1973). Conceptualization of human environments. *American Psychologist, 28,* 652–665.

Moos, R. H. (1979). *Evaluating educational environments.* San Francisco: Jossey-Bass.

Newbrough, J. R. (1980). Community psychology and the public interest. *American Journal of Community Psychology, 8,* 1–19.

Nietzel, M. T., Winett, R. A., MacDonald, M. L., & Davidson, W. S. (1977). *Behavioral approaches to community psychology.* New York: Pergamon.

O'Connor, R. D., & Rappaport, J. (1970). Application of social learning principles to the training of ghetto blacks. *American Psychologist, 25,* 659–661.

Phillipus, M. J. (1971). Successful and unsuccessful approaches to mental health services for an urban Hispano-American population. *Journal of Public Health, 60,* 820–830.

Poser, E. G. (1966). The effect of therapist training on group therapeutic outcome. *Journal of Consulting and Clinical Psychology, 30,* 283–289.

Rappaport, J. (1981). In praise of paradox: A social policy of empowerment over prevention. *American Journal of Community Psychology, 9,* 1–25.

Rappaport, J., & Chinskey, J. M. (1974). Models for delivery of service from a historical and conceptual perspective. *Professional Psychology, 5,* 42–50.

Repucci, N. D., & Saunders, T. J. (1974). Social psychology of behavior modification: Problems of implementation in natural settings. *American Psychologist, 29,* 649–660.

Riessman, F. (1967). A neighborhood-based mental health approach. In E. L. Cowen, E. A. Gardner, & M. Zax (Eds.), *Emergent approaches to mental health problems.* New York: Appleton-Century-Crofts.

Rosen, B. M., Lawrence, L., Goldsmith, H. F., Windle, C. D., & Shambaugh, J. P. (1975). Mental health demographic profile system description: Purpose, contents, and samples of uses. Series C, No. 11, DHEW Publication No. (ADM)

76–263. Washington, DC: Superintendent of Documents, U.S. Government Printing Office.

Rosenhan, D. (1973). On being sane in insane places. *Science, 179,* 250–258.

Sandler, I. N., & Keller, P. A. (1984). Trends observed in community psychology training descriptions. *American Journal of Community Psychology, 12,* 157–164.

Sanford, N. (1972). Is the concept of prevention necessary or useful? In S. E. Golann & C. Eisdorfer (Eds.), *Handbook of community mental health.* New York: Appleton-Century-Crofts.

Shure, M., & Spivack, G. (1982). Interpersonal problem solving in young children: A cognitive approach to prevention. *American Journal of Community Psychology, 10,* 341–356.

Silverman, P. R. (1976). *If you will lift the load, I will lift it too: A guide to developing widow-to-widow programs.* New York: Jewish Funeral Directors of America.

Specter, G., & Cowen, E. L. (1971). A pilot study in stimulation of culturally deprived infants. *Child Psychiatry and Human Development, 1,* 168–177.

Srole, L., Langner, T. S., Michael, S. T., Opler, M. K., & Rennie, T. A. C. (1962). *Mental health in the metropolis.* New York: McGraw-Hill.

Tharp, R. G., & Wetzel, R. J. (1969). Behavior modification in the natural environment. New York: Academic Press.

Tucker, B. J., Megenitz, D., & Vigil, L. (1970). Anatomy of a campus crisis center. *Personnel and Guidance Journal, 48,* 343–348.

VandenBos, G. R. (Ed.). (1980). *Psychotherapy: Practice, research, policy.* Beverly Hills, CA: Sage.

Warheit, G. J., Bell, R. A., & Schwab, J. J. (1977). *Needs assessment approaches: Concepts and methods.* DHEW Publication No. (ADM) 79-472. Washington, DC: Superintendent of Documents, U.S. Government Printing Office.

Weissberg, R. P., Cowen, E. L., Lotyczewski, B. S. & Gesten, E. L. (1983). The Primary Mental Health Project: Seven consecutive years of program outcome research. *Journal of Consulting and Clinical Psychology, 51,* 100–108.

Wiggins, J. S. (1973). *Personality and prediction: Principles of personality assessment.* Reading, MA: Addison-Wesley.

Zautra, A., & Sandler, I. (1983). Life event needs assessments: Two models for measuring preventable mental health problems. *Journal of Prevention in Human Services, 2,* 35–58.

Zax, M., & Specter, G. A. (1974). *An introduction to community psychology.* New York: Wiley.

Chapter 10

Alexander, F. (1950). *Psychosomatic medicine: Its principles and applications.* New York: Norton.

Andrew, J. M. (1970). Recovery from surgery, with and without preparatory instruction, for three coping styles. *Journal of Personality and Social Psychology, 15,* 223–226.

Ax, A. F. (1953). The physiological differentiation between fear and anger in humans. *Psychosomatic Medicine, 1953, 15,* 433–442.

Ahlqvist, J. (1976). Endocrine influence on lymphatic organs, immune response, inflammation, and autoimmunity. *Acta Endocrinologica (Copenhagen), Supplement,* 206.

Ahlqvist, J. (1981). Hormonal influences on immunologic and related phenomena. In R. Ader (Ed.), *Psychoneuroimmunology* (pp. 355–403). New York: Academic Press.

Balint, M. (1964). *The doctor, the patient, and his illness.* London: Pitman.

Barber, T. X., & Cooper, B. J. (1972). The effects on pain of experimentally induced and spontaneous distraction. *Psychological Reports, 31,* 647–651.

Bartrop, R. W., Luckhurst, E., Lazarus, L., Kiloh, L. G., & Penny, R. (1977, April). Depressed lymphocyte function after bereavement. *The Lancet,* 834–836.

Baron, R., & Rodin, J. (1978). Personal control as a mediator of crowding. In A. Baum, J. E. Singer, and S. Valins (Eds.), *Advances in environmental psychology,* Vol. 2. Hillsdale, NJ: Erlbaum.

Baum, A., Aiello, J., & Davis, G. (1979). Neighborhood determinants of stress symptom perception. Paper presented at the Meeting of the American Psychological Association, New York City.

Baum, A., Gatchel, R. J., & Schaeffer, M. A. (1983). Emotional, behavioral and physiological effects of chronic stress at Three Mile Island. *Journal of Consulting and Clinical Psychology, 51,* 565–572.

Baum, A., Gatchel, R., Streufert, S., Baum, C. S., Fleming, R., & Singer, J. E. (1980). Psychological stress for alternatives of decontamination of TMI-2 reactor building atmosphere. U.S. Nuclear Regulatory Commission (Nureg/CR-1584).

Baum, A., Singer, J. E., & Baum, C. S. (1981). Stress and the environment. *Journal of Social Issues, 37,* 4–34.

Baum, A., & Valins, S. (1977). *Architecture and social behavior: Psychological studies in social density.* Hillsdale, NJ: Erlbaum.

Becker, M. H. (1976). Sociobehavioral determinants of compliance with health and medical care recommendations. In D. L. Sackett and R. B. Haynes (Eds.), *Compliance with therapeutic regimens.* Baltimore: Johns Hopkins University Press.

Becker, M. H., & Maiman, L. A. (1975). Sociobehavioral determinants of compliance with health and medical care recommendations. *Medical Care, 13,* 10–24.

Beecher, H. K. (1959). *Measurement of subjective responses: Quantitative effects of drugs.* New York: Oxford University Press.

Beecher, H. K. (1956). Relationship of significance of wound to the pain experienced. *Journal of the American Medical Association, 161,* 1609–1613.

Beecher, H. K. (1975). Quantification of the subjective pain experience. In M. Weisenberg (Ed.), *Pain: Clinical and experimental perspectives.* St. Louis: Mosby.

Benson, H. (1975). *The relaxation response.* New York: William Morrow.

Blum, L. H. (1972). *Reading between the lines: Doctor patient communication.* New York: International Universities Press.

Boyle, C. M. (1970). Differences between doctors' and patients' interpretation of some common medical terms. *British Medical Journal, 2,* 286–289.

Burch, J. (1972). Recent bereavement in relation to suicide. *Journal of Psychosomatic Research, 16,* 361–366.

Burnam, M. A., Pennebaker, J. W., & Glass, D. C. (1975). Time consciousness, achievement striving, and the Type A coronary-prone behavior pattern. *Journal of Abnormal Psychology, 84,* 76–79.

Burnip, R., Erickson, R., Barr, G. D., Shinefield, H., & Schoen, E. J. (1976). Well-child care by pediatric nurse practitioners in a large group practice. *American Journal of Disease of Children, 130,* 51–55.

Buss, A. H. (1966). *Psychopathology.* New York: Wiley.

Cannon, W. B. (1929). *Bodily changes in pain, hunger, fear, and rage.* Boston: Branford.

Cannon, W. B., & de la Paz, D. (1911). Emotional stimulation of adrenal secretion. *American Journal of Physiology, 27,* 64–70.

Chaves, J. F., & Barber, T. X. (1974). Cognitive strategies, experimenter modeling, and expectation in the attenuation of pain. *Journal of Abnormal Psychology, 83,* 356–363.

Chen, E., & Cobb, S. (1960). Family structure in relation to health and disease. *Journal of Chronic Disease, 12,* 544–567.

Christopherson, V. (1966). Socio-cultural correlates of pain response. Final report of project #1390, Vocational Rehabilitation Administration. Washington, DC: U.S. Department of Health, Education and Welfare.

Cobb, S. (1976). Social support as a moderator of life stress. *Psychosomatic Medicine, 38,* 300–314.

Cobb, S., Kasl, S. V., French, J. R. P., & Norstebo, G. (1969). The intrafamilial transmission of rheumatoid arthritis. VI: Why do wives with rheumatoid arthritis have husbands with peptic ulcer? *Journal of Chronic Diseases, 22,* 279–293.

Cohen, S. (1978). Environmental load and the allocation of attention. In A. Baum, J. E. Singer, & S. Valins (Eds.), *Advances in environmental psychology,* Vol. 1. Hillsdale, NJ: Erlbaum.

Cohen, S. (1980). Aftereffects of stress on human performance and social behavior: A review of research and theory. *Psychological Bulletin, 88,* 82–108.

Cohen, S., & Wills, T. A. (1985). Stress, social support, and the buffering hypothesis. *Psychological Bulletin, 98,* 310–357.

Cohen, S., & Hoberman, H. M. (1983). Positive events and social supports as buffers of life change stress. *Journal of Applied Social Psychology, 13,* 99–125.

Cohen, S., & McKay, G. (1984). Social support, stress and the buffering hypothesis. In A. Baum, S. Taylor, & J. E. Singer (Eds.), *Handbook of psychology and health,* Vol IV. Hillsdale, NJ: Erlbaum.

Collins, A. & Frankenhaeuser, M. (1978). Stress response in male and female engineering students. *Journal of Human Stress, 4,* 43–48.

Dalessio, D. J. (1972). *Wolff's headache and other head pain.* New York: Oxford University Press.

Davidson, L. M., Baum, A., & Collins, D. L. (1982). Stress and control-related problems at Three Mile Island. *Journal of Applied Social Psychology, 12,* 349–359.

Davis, G. E. (1975). Attitudinal mediation of annoyance to transportation noise. Unpublished manuscript.

Davis, M. S. (1968). Variations in patients' compliance with doctors' advice: An empirical analysis of patterns of communication. *American Journal of Public Health, 58,* 274–288.

Dimatteo, M., & Dinicola, D. D. (1982). *Achieving patient compliance.* New York: Pergamon.

Dunbar, F. *Psychosomatic diagnosis*. (1943). New York: Harper & Row.

Egbert, L. D., Battit, G. E., Welch C. E., & Bartlett, M. K. (1964). Reduction of postoperative pain by encouragement and instruction of patients. *New England Journal of Medicine, 270,* 825–827.

Eliot, R., & Buell, J. (1979). Environmental and behavioral influences in the major cardiovascular disorders. Presented at the annual meeting of the Academy of Behavioral Medicine Research. Snowbird, UT.

Evans, G. W. (1978). Human spatial behavior: the arousal model. In A. Baum & Y. M. Epstein (Eds.), *Human response to crowding*. Hillsdale, NJ: Erlbaum.

Fordyce, W. E. (1976). *Behavioral methods for chronic pain and illness*. St. Louis: Mosby.

Fordyce, W. E., & Steger, J. C. (1979). Chronic pain. In O. F. Pomerleau & J. P. Brady (Eds.), *Behavioral medicine: theory and practice*. Baltimore: Williams and Wilkins.

Francis, V., Korsch, B. M., & Morris, M. J. (1969). Gaps in doctor-patient communication. *New England Journal of Medicine, 280,* 535–540.

Frankenhaeuser, M. (1972). Biochemical events, stress, and adjustment. *Reports from the Psychological Laboratories,* University of Stockholm, (368).

Frankenhaeuser, M. (1975). Sympathetic-adrenomedullary activity, behavior and the psychosocial environment. In P. H. Venables and M. J. Christie (Eds.), *Research in Psychophysiology*. New York: Wiley.

Frankenhaeuser, M. (1977). Quality of life: Criteria for behavioral adjustment. *International Journal of Psychology, 12,* 99–110.

Frankenhaeuser, M. (1978). Coping with job stress: A psychobiological approach. *Reports from the Department of Psychology,* University of Stockholm, (532).

Frankenhaeuser, M. (1983). The sympathetic-adrenal and pituitary-adrenal response to challenge: Comparison between the sexes. In T. M. Dembroski, T. H. Schmidt, and G. Blumchen (Eds.), *Biobehavioral bases of coronary heart disease*. Basel: S. Karger.

Frankenhaeuser, M., Nordheden, B., Myrsten, A. L., & Post, B. (1971). Psychophysiological reactions to understimulation and overstimulation. *Acta Psychologia, 35,* 298–308.

Frankenhaeuser, M., & Rissler, A. (1970). Effects of punishment on catecholamine release and efficiency of performance. *Psychopharmacologia, 17,* 378–390.

Friedman, M., Byers, S. O., Diamanti, J., & Rosenman, R. H. (1975). Plasma catecholamine response of coronary-prone subjects (Type A) to specific challenge. *Metabolism, 4,* 205–210.

Friedman, M., & Rosenman, R. H. (1974). *Type A behavior and your heart*. New York: Knopf.

Glass, D. C. (1977). *Behavior patterns, stress, and coronary disease*. Hillsdale, NJ: Erlbaum.

Glass, D. C., Krakoff, L. R., Finkelman, J., Snow, B., Contrada, R., Kehoe, K., Mannucci, E. G., Isecke, W., Collins, C., Hilton, W. F., & Elting, E. (1980). Effect of task overload upon cardiovascular and plasma catecholamine responses in Type A and B individuals. *Basic and Applied Social Psychology, 1,* 199–218.

Glass, D. C., & Singer, J. E. (1972). *Urban stress: Experiments on noise and social stressors*. New York: Academic Press.

Glass, D. C., & Singer, J. E. (1977). Environmental stress and the adaptive process. In A. Monat & R. S. Lazarus (Eds.), *Stress and coping*. New York: Columbia University Press.

Gore, S. (1973). The influence of social support and related variables in ameliorating the consequences of job loss. Unpublished doctoral dissertation, University of Pennsylvania.

Grace, W. J., & Graham, D. J. (1952). Relationship of specific attitudes and emotions to certain bodily diseases. *Psychosomatic Medicine, 14,* 242–251.

Graham, D. T. (1977). Psychosomatic medicine. In N. S. Greenfield & R. A. Sternback (Eds.), *Handbook of psychophysiology.* New York: Holt, Rinehart, & Winston.

Graham, D. T., Kabler, J. D., & Graham, F. K. (1962). Psychological responses to the suggestion of attitudes specific for hives and hypertension. *Psychosomatic Medicine, 24,* 159–169.

Graham, D. T., Stern, J. A., & Winokur, G. (1958). Experimental investigation of the specificity hypothesis in psychosomatic disease. *Psychosomatic Medicine, 20,* 446–457.

Greer, S., & Morris, T. (1975). Psychological attributes of women who develop breast cancer: A controlled study. *Journal of Psychosomatic Research, 19,* 147–153.

Hardy, M. (1956). Patient resistance to need for remedial and preventive services. *Journal of Pediatrics, 48,* 104–114.

Healy, K. M. (1968). Does preoperative instruction make a difference? *American Journal of Nursing, 68,* 62–67.

Henry, J. P., & Stephens, P. M. (1977). *Stress, health, and the social environment,* New York: Springer-Verlag.

Hieb, E., & Want, R. (1974). Compliance: The patient's role in drug therapy. *Wisconsin Journal of Medicine, 73,* 152–174.

Hilgard, E. R. (1975). The alleviation of pain by hypnosis. *Pain, 1,* 213–231.

Hill, H. E., Kornetsky, C. G., Flanary, H. G., Wilder, A. (1952). Effects of anxiety and morphine on the discrimination of intensities of pain. *Journal of Clinical Investigation, 31,* 473–480.

Himwich, H. E. (Ed.). (1957). *Alcoholism, basic aspects and treatment,* Washington, DC: American Association for the Advancement of Science.

Horan, J. J., Layng, F. C., & Pursell, C. H. (1976). Preliminary study of effects of "in vivo" emotive imagery on dental discomfort. *Perceptual and Motor Skills, 42,* 105–106.

Janis, I. L. (1958). *Psychological stress: Psychoanalytic and behavioral studies of surgical patients.* New York: Wiley.

Jenkins, C. D. (1971). Psychologic and social precursors of coronary disease. *New England Journal of Medicine, 284,* 307–317.

Jenkins, C. D., Zyzanski, S. J., & Rosenman, R. H. (1976). Risk of new myocardial infarction in middle-aged men with manifest coronary heart disease. *Circulation, 53,* 342–347.

Johansson, G. (1977). Case report on female catecholamine excretion in response to examination stress. *Reports from the Department of Psychology,* University of Stockholm, (515).

Johnson, J. E. (1973). Effects of accurate expectations about sensations on the sensory and distress components of pain. *Journal of Personality and Social Psychology, 27,* 261–275.

Johnson, J. E., & Leventhal, H. (1974). Effects of accurate expectations and behavioral instructions on reactions during a noxious medical examination. *Journal of Personality and Social Psychology, 29,* 710–718.

Kasl, S. V., & Cobb, S. (1966). Health behavior, illness behavior, and sick role behavior. *Archives of Environmental Health, 12,* 531–541.

Kates, R. W. (1962). Hazard and choice perception in flood plain management. Research Paper 78. Chicago: Department of Geography, University of Chicago.

Katz, R. L., Kao, C. U., Spiegel, H., & Katz, G. J. (1974). Pain, acupuncture, hypnosis. In J. J. Bonica (Ed.), *Advances in neurology, Vol. 4, International symposium on pain.* New York: Raven.

Koos, E. (1954). *The health of regionville.* New York: Columbia University Press.

Korsch, B., Freeman, B., & Negrete, V. (1971). Practical implications of doctor-patient interactions: Analysis for pediatric practice. *American Journal of Disease of Children, 121,* 110–114.

Korsch, B. M., Gozzi, E. K., & Francis, V. (1968). Gaps in doctor-patient interaction and patient satisfaction. *Pediatrics, 42,* 855–871.

Korsch, B. M., & Negrete, V. F. (1972). Doctor-patient communication. *Scientific American, 277,* 66–74.

Krantz, D. S., Baum, A., & Wideman, M. (1980). Assessment of preferences for self-treatment and information in health care. *Journal of Personality and Social Psychology, 39,* 977–990.

Krantz, D. S., Glass, D. C., Contrada, R., & Miller, N. E. (1981). *Behavior and Health. National Science Foundation's second five year outlook on science and technology.* U.S. Government Printing Office, Washington, DC.

Kumar, R., Singh, L. M., & Viadya, M. P. (1981). Immunoregulatory role of stress mediation in rheumatoid arthritis. *Zeitschrift fur Rheumatologie, 40,* 122–125.

Lacey, J. I. (1966). Somatic response patterning and stress: Some revisions of activation theory. In M. H. Appley and R. Trumbull (Eds.), *Psychological stress.* New York: McGraw-Hill.

Lazarus, R. S. (1966). *Psychological stress and the coping process.* New York: McGraw-Hill.

Lazarus, R. S., & Launier, R. (1978). Stress related transactions between person and environment. In L. A. Pervin & M. Lewis (Eds.), *Perspectives in interactional psychology.* New York: Plenum.

Lazarus, R. S., Opton, C. M., Jr., Nomikos, M., & Rankin, N. (1965). The principle of short-circuiting of threat: Further evidence. *Journal of Personality, 33,* 622–635.

Lazarus, R. S., & Folkman, S. (1984). *Stress, appraisal, and coping.* New York: Springer.

Levi, L. (1974). Psychosocial stress and disease: A conceptual model. In E. K. Gunderson & R. H. Rahe (Eds.), *Life stress and illness.* Springfield, IL: Thomas.

Ley, P., Bradshaw, P. W., Kincey, J., & Atherton, S. T. (1976). Increasing patients' satisfaction with communication. *British Journal of Social and Clinical Psychology, 15,* 403–413.

Ley, P., & Spelman, M. S. (1967). *Communicating with the patient.* London: Staples Press.

Lichtenstien, S., Slovic, P., Fischhoff, B., Layman, M., & Combs, B. (1978). Judged frequency of lethal events. *Journal of Experimental Psychology: Human Learning and Memory, 4,* 551–578.

Lindeman, C., & Van Aernam, B. (1971). Nursing intervention with the presurgical patient—the effects of structured and unstructured preoperative teaching. *Nursing Research, 20,* 319–331.

Loeser, J. D. (1977). Mechanisms of central pain. In W. Weisenberg (Ed.), *The Control of Pain.* New York: Psychological Dimensions.

Lundberg, U., & Frankenhaeuser, M. (1976). Adjustment to noise stress. *Reports from the department of psychology,* University of Stockholm, (484).

Malmo, R. B., & Shagass, C. (1949). Physiologic study of symptom mechanisms in psychiatric patients under stress. *Psychosomatic Medicine, 11,* 25–29.

Maranon, G. (1924). Contribution à létude de l'action émotive de l'adrénaline. *Revue Française Endocrinologique, 2,* 301–325.

Matarazzo, J. D. (1982). Behavioral health and behavioral medicine: Frontiers for a new health psychology. *American Psychologist, 35,* 807–817.

Mason, J. W. (1974). Specificity in the organization of neuroendocrine response profiles. In P. Seeman & G. M. Brown (Eds.), *Frontiers in neurology and neuroscience research. First International Symposium of the Neuroscience Institute.* Toronto, Ontario: University of Toronto.

Mason, J. W. (1975). Emotions as reflected in patterns of endocrine integration. In L. Levi (Ed.), *Emotions: Their parameters and measurement.* New York: Raven.

Mayer, D. J., Price, D. D., Barber, J., and Rafii, A. (1976). Acupuncture analgesia: Evidence for activation of a pain inhibitor system as a mechanism of action. In J. J. Bonica and D. Albe-Fessard (Eds.), *Advances in pain research and therapy,* Vol. 1. New York: Raven.

McKenney, J. M., Slining, J. M., Henderson, H. R., Deuins, D., & Barr, M. (1973). The effect of clinical pharmacy services on patients with essential hypertension. *Circulation, 48,* 1104–1111.

Mechanic, D. (1972). Social psychological factors affecting the presentation of bodily complaints. *New England Journal of Medicine, 286,* 1132–1139.

Meichenbaum, D., & Turk, D. (1976). The cognitive-behavioral management of anxiety, anger, and pain. In P. O. Davidson (Ed.), *The behavioral management of anxiety, depression and pain.* New York: Brunner/Mazel.

Melzack, R. (1973). *The puzzle of pain.* Harmondsworth, England: Penguin.

Moos, R. H., & Soloman, G. F. (1965). Psychologic comparison between women with rheumatoid arthritis and their non-arthritic sisters. *Psychosomatic Medicine, 22,* 135–149.

Osler, W. (1892). *Lectures on angina pectoris and allied states.* New York: Appleton.

Parkes, C. M. (1972). *Bereavement: Studies of grief in adult life.* New York: International Universities Press.

Pavlov, I. P. (1927). *Conditioned reflexes.* New York: Dover.

Pennebaker. J. (1979). Environmental determinants of symptom perception. Paper presented at the meeting of the American Psychological Association, New York City.

Pennebaker, J., & Brittingham, G. (1982). Environmental and sensory cues affecting the perception of physical symptoms. In A. Baum & J. E. Singer (Eds.), *Advances in environmental psychology: Environment and Health,* Vol. 4. Hillsdale, NJ: Erlbaum.

Peters, J. E., & Stern, R. M. (1971). Specificity of attitude hypothesis in psychosomatic medicine: A reexamination. *Journal of Psychosomatic Research, 15,* 129–135.

Reynolds, R. C. (1974). Community and occupational influences in stress at Cape Kennedy. In R. S. Eliot (Ed.), *Stress and the Heart,* Mt. Kisco, NY: Futura.

Riley, C. S. (1966). Patients' understanding of doctors instruction. *Medical Care, 4,* 34–37.

Rodin, J. (1976). Density, perceived choice and response to controllable and uncontrollable outcomes. *Journal of Experimental Social Psychology, 12,* 564–578.

Rodin, J., Solomon, S., & Metcalf, J. (1978). Role of control in mediating perceptions of density, *Journal of Personality and Social Psychology, 36,* 988–999.

Rose, R., Jenkins, C., & Hurst, M. (1978). *Air traffic controller health change study.* Boston: Boston University School of Medicine.

Rosenstock,. I. M. (1966). Why do people use health services? *Milbank Fund Quarterly, 44,* 94–127.

Rosenman, R. H., Friedman, M., Straus, R., Jenkins, C. D., Zyzanski, S. I., & Wurm, M. (1966). Coronary heart disease in the western collaborative study group: A follow-up experience of two years. *Journal of American Medical Association, 195,* 86–92.

Royal College of General Practitioners. (1978). Reduction in the incidence of rheumatoid arthritis with oral contraceptives. *Lancet, 1,* 569–571.

Russek, H. I., & Russek, L. G. (1976). Is emotional stress an etiologic factor in coronary heart disease? *Psychosomatics, 17,* 63–67.

Sackett, D. I., & Haynes, R. B. (1976). *Compliance with therapeutic regimens.* Baltimore: Johns Hopkins University Press.

Schachter, J. (1957). Pain, fear, and anger in hypertensives and normotensives: A psychophysiologic study. *Psychosomatic Medicine, 19,* 17–29.

Schachter, S., & Singer, J. E. (1962). Cognitive, social and physiological determinants of emotional state. *Psychological Review, 69,* 379–399.

Schleifer, S., Keller, S., McKegney, F., & Stein, M. (1980). Bereavement and lymphocyte function. Paper presented to the American Psychiatric Association, Montreal.

Selye, H. (1936). A syndrome produced by diverse noxious agents. *Nature, 138,* 32.

Selye, H. (1956). *The stress of life.* New York: McGraw-Hill.

Shapiro, A. P. (1983). The non-pharmacologic treatment of hypertension. In D. Krantz, A. Baum, & J. E. Singer (Eds.), *Handbook of Psychology & Health, Vol. III.* Hillsdale, NJ: Erlbaum.

Sherrod, D. R. (1974). Crowding, perceived control and behavioral aftereffects. *Journal of Applied Social Psychology, 4,* 171–186.

Singer, J. E., Lundberg, U., & Frankenhaeuser, M. (1978). Stress on the train: A study of urban commuting. In A. Baum, J. E. Singer, & S. Valins (Eds.), *Advances in Environmental Psychology,* Vol. I. Hillsdale, NJ: Erlbaum.

Spear, F. G. (1967). Pain in psychiatric patients. *Journal of Psychosomatic Research, 11,* 187–193.

Speisman, J. C., Lazarus, R. S., Mordkoff, A., & Davidson, L. (1964). Experimental reduction of stress based on ego defense theory. *Journal of Abnormal and Social Psychology, 68,* 367–380.

Sternbach, R. A. (1968). *Pain: A psychophysiological analysis.* New York: Academic.

Sternbach, R. A. (1966). *Principles of psychophysiology.* New York: Academic.

Sternbach, R. A., and Tursky, B. (1965). Ethnic differences among housewives in psychophysical and skin potential responses to electric shock. *Psychophysiology,* 241–246.

Strain, J. J. (1978). Noncompliance: Its origins, manifestations, and management. *The Pharos of Alpha Omega Alpha, 41,* 27–32.

Stunkard, A. J., & Wolff, H. G. (1958). Pathogenesis in human obesity. Function and disorder of a mechanism of satiety. *Psychosomatic Medicine, 20,* 17–29.

Symington, T., Currie, A. R., Curan, R. S., & Davidson, J. N. (1955). The reaction of the adrenal cortex in conditions of stress. In *Ciba Foundation Colloquia on Endocrinology. Vol 8. The Human Adrenal Cortex.* Boston, MA: Little, Brown, 70–91.

Tache, J., Selye, H., & Day, S. B. (1979). *Cancer, Stress, and Death.* New York: Plenum, 1979.

Taub, A. (1976). Acupuncture "anesthesia": A critical view. In J. J. Bonica & D. Albe-Fessard (Eds.), *Advances in pain research and therapy,* Vol. 1. New York: Raven.

Taylor, D. W., Sachett, D. L., Haynes, R. B., Johnson, A. L., Gibson, E. S., & Roberts, R. S. (1978). Compliance with antihypertensive drug therapy. *Annals of the New York Academy of Science,* 390–403.

Taylor, V. (1976). *Delivery of mental health services in disasters.* Columbus: Disaster Research Center, Ohio State University.

Thomas, C. B., & Dusznski, K. R. (1974). Closeness to parents and the family constellation in a prospective study of five disease states: Suicide, mental illness, malignant tumor, hypertension, and coronary heart disease, *Johns Hopkins Medical Journal, 134,* 251–270.

Turk, D. C., Mechenbaum, D. H., & Berman, W. H. (1979). Application of biofeedback for the regulation of pain: A critical review. *Psychological Bulletin, 86,* 1322–1338.

Tursky, B., & Sternbach, R. A. (1967). Further physiological correlates of ethnic differences in response to shock. *Psychophysiology, 4,* 67–74.

Wallston, K. A., Maides, S., & Wallston, B.S. (1976). Health-related information seeking as a function of health-related locus of control and health value. *Journal of Research in Personality, 10,* 215–222.

Warheit, G. F. (1974). Occupation: A key factor in stress at the manned space center. In R. S. Elliot (Ed.), *Stress and the heart,* Mt. Kisco, NY: Futura.

Weisenberg, M. (1975). *Pain: Clinical and experimental perspectives.* St. Louis: Mosby.

Weisenberg, M. (1977). Pain and pain control. *Psychological Bulletin, 84,* 1004–1008.

Wilbur, J. A., & Barrow, J. G. (1969). Reducing elevated blood pressure. *Minnesota Medical, 52,* 1303.

Wittkower, E. D., & Dudek, S. E. (1973). Psychosomatic medicine: The mind body-society interaction. In B. Wolman (Ed.), *Handbook of general psychology.* Englewood Cliffs, NJ: Prentice-Hall.

Wolf, S. (1965). *The stomach.* New York: Oxford University Press.

Wolf, S., & Goodell, H. (Eds.). (1968). *Stress and disease (2nd ed.),* Springfield, IL: Thomas.

Wolf, S., & Wolff, H. G. (1947). *Human gastric function.* New York: Oxford.

Wortman, C. B., & Brehm, J. W. (1975). Responses to uncontrollable outcomes. An integration of reactance theory and the learned helplessness model. In L. Berkowitz (Ed.), *Advances in experimental social psychology,* Vol 8. New York: Academic Press.

Zbrowski, M. (1952). Cultural components in response to pain. *Journal of Social Issues, 8,* 16–30.

Zola, I. K. (1963). Socio-cultural factors in the seeking of medical care. *Transcultural Psychiatric Research, 14,* 62–65.

Zola, I. K. (1966). Culture and symptoms: An analysis of patient's presenting complaints. *American Sociological Review, 31,* 615–630.

Chapter 11

Allegrante, J. P., O'Rourke, T. W., & Tuncalp, S. (1977). A multivariate analysis of selected psychosocial variables in the development of subsequent youth smoking behavior. *Journal of Drug Education, 1,* 237–248.

Allport, G. W. (1954). *The nature of prejudice.* Cambridge, MA: Addison-Wesley.

Allport, G. W., & Veltfort, H. W. (1943). Social psychology and the civilian war effort. *Journal of Social Psychology, SPSSI Bulletin, 1,* 165–233.

Ames, C., Ames, R., & Felker, D. W. (1977). Effects of competitive reward structure and valence of outcome on children's achievement attributions. *Journal of Educational Psychology, 69,* 1–8

Andrews, G. R., & Debus, R. L. (1978). Persistence and the causal perception of failure. Modifying cognitive attributions. *Journal of Educational Psychology, 70,* 154–166

Armor, D. J. (1972). The evidence on busing. *The Public Interest, 28,* 90–126.

Aronson, E., Blaney, N., Stephan, C., Sikes, J., & Snapp, M. (1978). *The jigsaw classroom.* Beverly Hills, CA: Sage.

Aronson, E., & Osherow, N. (1980). Cooperation, prosocial behavior and academic performance: Experiments in the desegregated classroom. In L. Bickman (Ed.), *Applied Social Psychology Annual,* Vol. 1. Beverly Hills, CA: Sage.

Averill, J. R. (1973). Personal control over aversive stimuli and its relationship to stress. *Psychological Bulletin, 80,* 286–303.

Bandura, A. (1977). *Social learning theory.* Englewood Cliffs, NJ: Prentice-Hall.

Battle, E. (1965). Motivational determinants of academic task persistence. *Journal of Personality and Social Psychology, 2,* 209–218.

Best, J. A., Flay, B. R., Towson, S. M. J., Ryan, K. B., Perry, C. L., Brown, K. S., Kersell, M. W., & d'Avernas, J. R. (1984). Smoking prevention and the concept of risk. *Journal of Applied Social Psychology, 14,* 257–273.

Bewley, B. R., Bland, J. M., & Harris, R. (1974). Factors associated with the starting of cigarette smoking by primary school children. *British Journal of Preventive Social Medicine, 28,* 37–44.

Bickman, L. (1976). Fulfilling the promise: A response to Helmreich. *Personality and Social Psychology Bulletin, 2,* 131–133.

Bickman, L. (1980). Introduction: Applied social psychology, SPSSI, and Kurt Lewin. In L. Bickman (Ed.), *Applied Social Psychology Annual,* Vol. 1. Beverly Hills, CA: Sage.

Biener, L., & Gerard, H. B. (1975). Effects of desegregation on achievement-relevant motivation. In H. B. Gerard & N. Miller (Eds.), *School desegregation.* New York: Plenum Press.

Blaney, N. T., Stephan, C., Rosenfield, D., Aronson, E., & Sikes, J. (1977). Interdependence in the classroom: A field study. *Journal of Educational Psychology, 69,* 139–146.

Cartwright, D. (1948). Social psychology in the United States during the Second World War. *Human Relations, 1,* 333–352.

Chapin, M., & Dyck, D. G. (1976). Persistence in children's reading behavior as a function of N length and attribution retraining. *Journal of Abnormal Psychology, 85,* 511–515.

Chassin, L., Presson, C. C., Bensenberg, M., Olshavsky, R. W., & Sherman, S. J. (1981). Predicting adolescents' intentions to smoke cigarettes. *Journal of Health and Social Behavior, 22,* 445–455.

Cialdini, R. B. (1980). Full cycle social psychology. In L. Bickman (Ed.), *Applied Social Psychology Annual,* Vol. 1. Beverly Hills, CA: Sage.

Cohen, E., & Roper, S. (1972). Modification of interracial interaction disability on application of status characteristics theory. *American Sociological Review, 6,* 643–657.

Cook, T. D., & Campbell, D. T., (1979). *Quasi-experimentation: Design and analysis issues for field settings.* Boston: Houghton Mifflin.

Dentler, R. A., & Elkins, C. (1967). Intergroup attitudes, academic performance, and racial composition. In R. A. Dentler & C. Elkins (Eds.), *The urban r's: Race relations as the problem in urban education.* New York: Praeger.

Deutsch, M. (1949). An experimental study of the effects of cooperation and competition upon group process. *Human Relations, 2,* 29–40.

Deutsch, M., & Horstein, H. A. (1975). *Applying social psychology: Implications for research, practice, and training.* Hillsdale, NJ: Erlbaum.

Dweck, C. S. (1975). The role of expectations and attributions of the alleviation of learned helplessness. *Journal of Personality and Social Psychology, 31,* 674–685.

Dweck, C. S., & Repucci, N. D. (1973). Learned helplessness and reinforcement responsibility in children. *Journal of Personality and Social Psychology, 25,* 109–116.

Evans, R. I. (1976). Smoking in children: Developing a social psychological strategy of deterrence. *Journal of Preventive Medicine, 5,* 122–127.

Evans, R. I., Hanson, W. B., & Mittelmark, M. B. (1977). Increasing the validity of self-reports of smoking behavior in children. *Journal of Applied Psychology, 62,* 521–523.

Evans, R., Henderson, A., Hill, P., & Raines, B. (1979). Smoking in children and adolescents: Psychosocial determinants and prevention strategies. In *Smoking and health: A report of the Surgeon General* (Public Health Service, DHEW Pub. No. [PHS] 79-5006). Washington, DC: U.S. Government Printing Office.

Evans, R., Rozelle, R., Maxwell, S., Raines, B., Dill, C., Guthrie, T., Henderson, A., & Hill, P. (1981). Social modeling films to deter smoking in adolescents: Results of a three-year field investigation. *Journal of Applied Psychology, 66,* 339–414.

Evans, R. I., Rozelle, R. M., Mittelmark, M. B., Hansen, W. B., Bane, A. L., & Havis, J. (1978). Deterring the onset of smoking in children: Knowledge of immediate physiological effects and coping with peer pressure, media pressure and parent modeling. *Journal of Applied Social Psychology, 8,* 126–135.

Evans, R. I., Smith, C. K., & Raines, B. E. (1984). Deterring cigarette smoking in adolescents: A psycho-social-behavioral analysis of an intervention strategy. In A. Baum, S. E. Taylor, & J. E. Singer (Eds.), *Handbook of psychology and health,* Vol. 4: *Social psychological aspects of health.* Hillsdale, NJ: Erlbaum.

Farquhar, J. W., Maccoby, N., Wood, P. O., Alexander, J. K., Breitrose, H., Brown, B. W., Jr., Haskell, W. L., McAlister, A. L., Meyer, A. J., Nash, J. D., & Stern, M. P. (1978). Community education for cardiovascular health. In T. D. Cook & Associates (Eds.), *Evaluation studies review annual,* Vol. 3. Beverly Hills, CA: Sage.

Feather, N. T. (1966). Effects of prior success and failure on expectations of success and subsequent performance. *Journal of Personality and Social Psychology, 3,* 287–298.

Flay, B. R. (1984). What do we know about the social influences approach to smoking prevention?: Review and recommendations. In C. Bell et al. (Eds.), *Prevention research: Deterring drug abuse among children and adolescents* (pp. 67–112). Washington, DC.: National Institute on Drug Abuse Research Monograph, Series #63.

Flay, B. R., d'Avernas, J. R., Best, J. A., Kersell, M. W., & Ryan, K. B. (1983). Cigarette smoking: Why young people do it and ways of preventing it. In P. Firestone & P. McGrath (Eds.) *Pediatric and adolescent behavioral medicine.* New York: Springer-Verlag.

Flay, B. R., Johnson, C. A., Hansen, W. B., Grossman, L. M., Sobel, J. L., (1983). Evaluation of a school-based, family-oriented, television-enhanced smoking prevention and cessation program: The importance of implementation evaluation. Paper presented at the meeting of the Evaluation Research Society, Chicago, IL.

Flay, B. R., Ryan, K. B., Best, J. A., Brown, K. S., Kersell, M. W., d'Avernas, J. R., & Zanna, M. P. (1985). Are social psychological smoking prevention programs effective?: The Waterloo study. *Journal of Behavioral Medicine, 8,* 37–59.

Frieze, I. M., & Snyder, H. N. (1980). Children's beliefs about the causes of success and failure in school settings. *Journal of Educational Psychology, 72,* 186–196.

Geffner, R. (1978). The effects of interdependent learning on self-esteem, inter-ethnic relations, and intro-ethnic attitudes of elementary school children: A field experiment. Unpublished doctoral dissertation, University of California, Santa Cruz.

Gleaton, T. J. (1984). Community prevention research in alcohol and drug abuse. Unpublished manuscript, Georgia State University, College of Education, Atlanta.

Goodstadt, M. (1980). Drug education: A turn off or a turn on? *Journal of Drug Education, 10,* 89–99.

Hartup, W. W., & Lougee, M. D. (1975). Peers as models. *School Psychology Digest, 4,* 11–21.

Harvey, J. H., Harris, B., & Lightner, J. M. (1979). Perceived freedom as a central concept in psychological theory and research. In L. C. Perlmuter & R. A. Monty (Eds.), *Choice and perceived control.* Hillsdale, NJ: Erlbaum.

Hendrick, C. (1977). Social psychology as an experimental science. In C. Hendrick (Ed.), *Perspectives on social psychology.* Hillsdale, NJ: Erlbaum.

Holmes, T. H., & Masuda, M. (1974). Life changes and illness susceptibility. In B. S. Dohrenwend & B. P. Dohrenwend (Eds.), *Stressful life events: Their nature and effects.* New York: Wiley.

Hovland, C. I., Janis, I. L., & Kelley, H. H. (1953). *Communication and persuasion.* New Haven: Yale University Press.

Hovland, C. I., Lumsdaine, A. A., & Sheffield, F. D. (1949). *Experiments on mass communication.* Princeton: Princeton University Press.

Hurd, P., Johnson, C., Pechacek, T., Bast, C., Jacobs, D., & Luepker, R. (1980). prevention of cigarette smoking in seventh grade students. *Journal of Behavioral Medicine, 3,* 15–28.

Johnson, C. A., Hansen, W. B., Collins, L. M., & Graham, J. W. (1984). Final report to National Institute on Drug Abuse: The high school anti-smoking project. Health Behavior Research Institute, University of Southern California.

Johnson, J. E., & Leventhal, H. (1974). Effects of accurate expectations and behavioral instructions on reactions during a noxious medical exam. *Journal of Personality and Social Psychology, 29,* 710–718.

Johnson, J. E., Morrissey, J. F., & Leventhal, H. (1973). Psychological preparation for an endoscopic examination. *Gastrointestinal Endoscopy, 19,* 180–182.

Jones, E. E., & Sigall, H. (1971). The bogus pipeline: A new paradigm for measuring affect and attitude. *Psychological Bulletin, 76,* 349–364.

Judd, C. M., & Kenny, D. A. (1981). *Estimating the effects of social intervention.* New York: Cambridge University Press.

Kandel, D. B., Kessler, R. C., & Margulies, R. Z. (1978). Antecedents of adolescent drug initiation into stages of drug use: A development analysis. In D. B. Kandel (Ed.), *Longitudinal research on drug use: Finding and methodological issues.* Washington, DC: Hemisphere.

Kelman, H. C. (1967). Human use of human subjects: The problem of deception in social psychological experiments. *Psychological Bulletin, 67,* 1–11.

Kiesler, C. A. (1971). *The psychology of commitment: Experiments linking behavior to belief.* New York: Academic Press.

Krech, D., & Crutchfield, R. S. (1948). *Theory and problems of social psychology.* New York: McGraw-Hill.

Krosnick, J. A., & Judd, C. M. (1982). Transitions in social influence at adolescence: Who induces cigarette smoking? *Developmental Psychology, 18,* 359–368.

Lacey, H. M. (1979). Control, perceived control and the methodological role of cognitive constructs. In L. C. Perlmuter, & R. A. Monty (Eds.), *Choice and perceived control.* Hillsdale, NJ: Erlbaum.

Langer, E. J., Janis, I. L., & Wolfer, J. A. (1975). Reduction of psychological stress in surgical patients. *Journal of Experimental Social Psychology, 11,* 155–165.

Langer, E. J., & Rodin, J. (1976). The effects of choice and enhanced personal responsibility for the aged: A field experiment in an institutional setting. *Journal of Personality and Social Psychology, 34,* 191–198.

Leventhal, H., & Cleary, P. D. (1980). The smoking problem: A review of the research and theory in behavioral risk modification. *Psychological Bulletin, 88,* 370–405.

Lewin, K. (1947a). Frontiers in group dynamics: Concept, method and reality in social science; social equilibria and social change. *Human Relations, 1,* 5–41.

Lewin, K. (1947b). Frontiers in group dynamics. II. Channels of group life; social planning and action research. *Human Relations, 1,* 143–153.

Lichtenstein, E., & Danaher, B. G. (1975). Modification of smoking behavior: A critical analysis of theory, research, and practice. In M. Hersen, R. M. Eisler, & P. M. Miller (Eds.), *Progress in behavior modification,* Vol. 3. New York: Academic Press.

Lichtenstein, E., Harris, D. E., Birchler, G. R., Wahl, J. M., & Schmahl, D. P. (1973). Comparison of rapid smoking, warm, smoky air, and attention placebo in the modification of smoking behavior. *Journal of Consulting and Clinical Psychology, 40,* 92–98.

Lucker, G., Rosenfield, D., Sikes, J., & Aronson, E. (1977). Performance in the interdependent classroom: A field study. *American Educational Research Journal, 13,* 115–123.

Maccoby, N., & Farquhar, J. W. (1975). Communication for health: Unselling heart disease. *Journal of Communication, 25,* 114–126.

McAllister, A. M., Perry, C., Killen, J., Slinkard, L. A., & Maccoby, N. (1980). Pilot study of smoking, alcohol and drug abuse prevention. *American Journal of Public Health, 70,* 719–721.

McGuire, W. J. (1964). Inducing resistance to persuasion. In L. Berkowitz (Ed.), *Advances in experimental social psychology,* Vol. 1. New York: Academic Press.

McGuire, W. J. (1969). The nature of attitudes and attitude change. In G. Lindzey & E. Aronson (Eds.), *Handbook of social psychology* (2nd ed.; Vol. 3). Reading, MA: Addison-Wesley.

McGuire, W. J. (1972). Attitude change: An information processing paradigm. In C. G. McClintock (Ed.), *Experimental social psychology.* New York: Holt, Rinehart, & Winston.

McGuire, W. J. (1985). Attitudes and attitude change. In G. Lindzey & E. Aronson (Eds.), *Handbook of social psychology* (3rd ed., Vol. 2). Reading, MA: Addison-Wesley.

Mills, R. T., & Krantz, D. S. (1979). Information, choice, and reactions to stress: A field experiment in a blood bank with laboratory analogue. *Journal of Personality and Social Psychology, 37,* 608–620.

Moskowitz, J. M. (1983). Preventing adolescent substance abuse through drug education. In Glynn, T. J., Leukefeld, C. G., & Ludford, J. P. (Eds.), *Preventing adolescent drug abuse: Intervention strategies.* Rockville, MD: National Institute on Drug Abuse Research Monograph 47.

Mumford, E., Schlesinger, H. J., & Glass, G. V. (1982). The effects of psychological intervention on recovery from surgery and heart attacks: An analysis of the literature. *American Journal of Public Health, 72,* 141–151.

Murphy, G. (1965). The future of social psychology in historical perspective. In O. Klineberg & R. Christie (Eds.), *Perspectives in social psychology* (rev. ed.). New York: Harper & Row.

Murray, D. M., Johnson, C. A., Luepker, R. V., & Mittelmark, M. B. (1984). The prevention of cigarette smoking in children: A comparison of four strategies. *Journal of Applied Social Psychology, 14,* 274–288.

Murray, D. M., & Perry, C. L. (1984, April). The prevention of adolescent drug abuse: Implications from etiological development, behavioral and environmental models. Paper presented at Research, Analysis, and Utilization System meeting, National Institute on Drug Abuse, Bethesda, MD.

Nicholls, J. G. (1979). Development of perception of own attainment and causal attribution for success and failure in reading. *Journal of Educational Psychology, 71,* 94–99.

O'Donnell, J. A., & Clayton, R. R. (1982). The stepping-stone hypothesis— marijuana, heroin, and causality. *Chemical Dependencies: Behavioral and Biomedical Issues, 4,* 229–241.

Oskamp, S. (1984). *Applied social psychology.* Englewood Cliffs, NJ: Prentice-Hall.

Palmer, A. B. (1970). Some variables contributing to the onset of cigarette smoking in junior high school students. *Social Science and Medicine, 4,* 359–366.

Perry, C., Killen, J., Telch, M., Slinkard, L. A., & Dunaher, B. G. (1980). Modifying smoking behavior of teenagers: A school-based intervention. *American Journal of Public Health, 70,* 722–725.

Rabkin, J. G., & Struening, E. I. (1976). Life events, stress, and illness. *Science, 154,* 1013–1020.

Reich, J. W., & Zautra, A. (1981). Life events and personal causation: Some relationships with satisfaction and distress. *Journal of Personality and Social Psychology, 41,* 1002–1012.

Rodin, J., & Langer, E. J. (1977). Long-term effects of a control-relevant intervention with the institutionalized aged. *Journal of Personality and Social Psychology, 35,* 897–903.

Rosenthal, R., & Rosnow, R. L. (1969). *Artifact in behavorial research.* New York: Academic Press.

Rothbaum, F., Weisz, J. R., & Snyder, S. S. (1982). Changing the world and changing the self: A two-process model of perceived control. *Journal of Personality and Social Psychology, 42,* 5–37.

Ryckman, R. M. (1976). Applied social psychology—a haven for the comfortable radical pussycat: A response to Helmreich. *Personality and Social Psychology Bulletin, 2,* 127–130.

Sandler, I. & Guenther, R. (1985). Assessment of stress events. In P. Karoly (Ed.), *Measurement strategies in health psychology.* New York: Wiley.

Saxe, L., & Fine, M. (1981). *Social experiments: Methods for design and evaluation.* Beverly Hills, CA: Sage.

Schaps, E., DiBartolo, R., Moskowitz, J., Palley, C. S., & Churgin, S. (1981). A review of 127 drug abuse prevention program evaluations. *Journal of Drug Issues, 11,* 17–44.

Schmeidler, G. R., & Allport, G. W. (1944). Social psychology and the civilian war effort: May, 1943–May, 1944. *Journal of Social Psychology, SPSSI Bulletin, 20,* 145–180.

Schulz, R. (1976). Effects of control and predictability on the physical and psychological well-being of the institutionalized aged. *Journal of Personality and Social Psychology, 33,* 563–573.

Schulz, R., & Hanusa, B. H. (1978). Long-term effects of control and predictability-enhancing interventions: Findings and ethical issues. *Journal of Personality and Social Psychology, 36,* 1194–1201.

Schunk, D. H. (1982). Effects of effort attributional feedback on children's perceived self-efficacy and achievement. *Journal of Educational Psychology, 74,* 548–556.

Sherif, M. (1956). Experiments in group conflict, *Scientific American, 195,* 53–58.

Sherif, M. (1977). Crisis in social psychology: Some remarks toward breaking through the crisis. *Personality and Social Psychology Bulletin, 3,* 368–382.

Sherif, M., Harvey, O. J., White, B. J., Hood, W. R., & Sherif, C. W. (1961). *Intergroup conflict and cooperation: The Robbers Cave experiment.* Norman, OK: Institute of Group Relations, University of Oklahoma.

Sherif, M., & Sherif, C. W. (1953). *Groups in harmony and tension.* New York: Harper & Row.

Sherman, S. J., & Fazio, R. H. (1983). Parallels between attitudes and traits as predictors of behavior. *Journal of Personality, 51,* 308–345.

Stephan, W. G., & Rosenfield, D. (1978). Effects of desegregation on race relations and self-esteem. *Journal of Educational Psychology, 70,* 670–679.

Stouffer, S. A., Lumsdaine, A. A., Lumsdaine, M. H., Williams, R. N., Smith, M. B., Janis, I. L., Star, S., & Cottrell, L. S. (1949). *Studies in social psychology in World War II: Adjustment during army life,* Vol. I. Princeton, NJ: Princeton University Press.

Taylor, S. E. (1979). Hospital patient behavior: Reactance, helplessness, or control? *Journal of Social Issues, 35,* 156–184.

Taylor, S. E. (1983). Adjustment to threatening events: A theory of cognitive adaptation. *American Psychologist, 38,* 1161–1173.

Taylor, S. E., Lichtman, R. R., & Wood, J. V. (1984). Atrributions, beliefs about control, and adjustment to breast cancer. *Journal of Personality and Social Psychology, 46,* 489–502.

Thompson, S. C. (1981). Will it hurt less if I can control it? A complex answer to a simple question. *Psychological Bulletin, 90,* 89–101.

Tyler, B. B. (1958). Expectancy for eventual success as a factor in problem solving behavior. *Journal of Educational Psychology, 49,* 166–172.

U.S. Public Health Service (1964). *Smoking and Health: Report of the Advisory Committee to the Surgeon General.* Department of Health, Education, and Welfare.

Varela, J. (1971). *Psychological solutions to social problems.* New York: Academic Press.

Vartiainen, E., Pallonen, U., McAllister, A., Koskela, A., & Puska, P. (1983). Effect of two years of educational intervention in adolescent smoking (The North Karelia Youth Project). *Bulletin of the World Health Organization, 61,* 529–532.

Wallach, L. M. (1981). Mass media campaigns: The odds against finding behavior change. *Health Education Quarterly, 8,* 209–260.

Weiner, B. (1974). *Achievement motivation and attribution theory.* Morristown, NJ: General Learning Press.

Weiner, B. (1979). A theory of motivation for some classroom experiences. *Journal of Educational Psychology, 71,* 3–25.

Weiner, B., Frieze, I., Kukla, A., Reed, L., Rest, S., & Rosenbaum, R. M. (1972). Perceiving the causes of success and failure. In E. E. Jones, D. Kanouse, H. H. Kelley, R. E. Nisbett, S. Valins & B. Weiner (Eds.), *Attribution: Perceiving the causes of behavior.* Morristown, NJ: General Learning Press.

Weiner, B., & Kukla, A. (1970). An attributional analysis of achievement motivation. *Journal of Personality and Social Psychology, 15,* 1–20.

Weissberg, N. (1976). Methodology or substance: A response to Helmreich. *Personality and Social Psychology Bulletin, 2,* 119–121.

West, S. G. (1985). Beyond the laboratory experiment: Experimental and quasi-experimental designs for interventions in naturalistic settings. In P. Karoly (Ed.), *Measurement strategies in health psychology.* New York: Wiley.

Wicker, A. W. (1969). Attitudes vs. actions: The relationship of verbal and overt behavioral responses to attitude objects. *Journal of Social Issues, 25,* 41–78.

Williams, J. E., Best, D. L., & Boswell, D. A. (1975). The measurement of children's racial attitudes in the early school years. *Child Development, 46,* 494–500.

Zautra, A., & Dohrenwend, B. P. (1983). The measurement of small events. In B. P. Dohrenwend (Chair), Measurement innovations in the study of life stress processes. Symposium conducted at the meeting of the American Psychological Association, Anaheim, CA.

Chapter 12

ABC News. (1982a, June 21). Hinckley—Insane. *Nightline.*

ABC News. (1982b, June 22). Insanity plea on trial. *Nightline.*

Abel, G. G., Blanchard, E. B., & Becker, J. V. (1976). Psychological treatment of rapists. In M. J. Walker & S. L. Brodsky (Eds.). *Sexual assault.* Lexington, MA: Lexington Books.

Adorno, T., Frenkel-Brunswick, E., Levinson, D., & Sanford, R. (1950). *The authoritarian personality.* New York: Harper.

Ajzen, I., & Fishbein, M. (1980). *Understanding attitudes and predicting social behavior.* Englewood Cliffs, NJ: Prentice-Hall.

Alker, H. R., Hosticks, C., & Mitchell, M. (1976). Jury selection as a biased social process. *Law and Society Review, 11,* 9–41.

Anastasi, A. (1979). *Fields of applied psychology* (2nd ed.). New York: McGraw-Hill.

Bailey, F. L., & Rothblatt, H. B. (1971). *Successful techniques for criminal trials.* New York: Lawyers Cooperative.

Bandura, A. (1973). *Aggression: A social learning analysis.* Englewood Cliffs, NJ: Prentice-Hall.

Bazelon, D. (1973). Psychologists in corrections—are they doing good for the offender or well for themselves? In S. L. Brodsky (Ed.), *Psychologists in the criminal justice system.* Urbana: University of Illinois Press.

Bazelon, D. (1982). Veils, values, and social responsibility. *American Psychologist, 37,* 115–121.

Bermant, G. (1975, May). Juries and justice: The notion of conspiracy is not tasty to Americans. *Psychology Today,* pp. 13–15.

Blumstein, A., & Cohen, J. (1980). Sentencing of convicted offenders: An analysis of the public's view. *Law and Society Review, 14,* 223–261.

Borchard, E. M. (1932). *Convicting the innocent: Errors of criminal justice.* New Haven: Yale University Press.

Borgida, E. (1981). Legal reform of rape laws. In L. Bickman (Ed.), *Applied Social Psychology Annual,* Vol. 2. Beverly Hills, CA: Sage.

Borgida, E., & Brekke, N. (1985). Psychological research on rape trials. In A. Burgess (Ed.), *Research handbook on rape and sexual assault.* Garland Publishing Company.

Bray, R. M., & Kerr, N. L. (1982). Methodological considerations in the study of the psychology of the courtroom. In N. L. Kerr & R. M. Bray (Eds.), *The psychology of the courtroom.* New York: Academic Press.

Brigham, J. C., & Barkowitz, P. (1978). Do "they all look alike?" The effect of race, sex, experience, and attitudes on the ability to recognize faces. *Journal of Applied Psychology, 8,* 306–318.

Brodsky, S. L. (1980). Ethical issues for psychologists in corrections. In J. Monahan (Ed.), *Who is the client?* Washington, DC: American Psychological Association.

Bronson, E. J. (1970). On the conviction-proneness and representativeness of the death-qualified jury: An empirical study of Colorado veniremen. *University of Colorado Law Review, 42,* 1–32.

Brownmiller, S. (1975). *Against our will: Men, women, and rape.* New York: Simon & Schuster.

Buckhout, R., Figueroa, D., & Hoff, E. (1975). Eyewitness identification: Effects of suggestion and bias in identification from photographs. *Bulletin of the Psychonomic Society, 6,* 71-74.

Burgess, A. W., & Holmstrom, L. L. (1974). Rape trauma syndrome. *American Journal of Psychiatry, 131,* 981-986.

Burt, M. R. (1980). Cultural myths and supports for rape. *Journal of Personality and Social Psychology, 38,* 217-230.

Caplan, L. (1984, July 2). Annals of law: The insanity defense. *The New Yorker,* pp. 45-46, 48-52, 54-78.

Carroll, J. S., & Coates, D. (1980). Parole decisions: Social psychological research in applied settings. In L. Bickman (Ed.), *Applied social psychology annual,* Vol. 1. Beverly Hills, CA: Sage.

Champagne, A., & Nagel, S. (1982). The psychology of judging. In N. L. Kerr & R. M. Bray (Eds.), *The psychology of the courtroom.* New York: Academic Press.

Chappell, D. (1982, November). The impact of rape reform legislation: Some comparative trends. Paper presented at the annual meeting of the American Society of Criminology, Toronto.

Christie, R. (1976). Probability v. precedence: The social psychology of jury selection. In G. Bermant, C. Nemeth, & N. Vidmar (Eds.), *Psychology and the Law.* Lexington, MA: Lexington.

Clark, L., & Lewis, D. (1977). *Rape: The price of coercive sexuality.* Toronto: The Women's Press.

Clifford, B. R., & Scott, J. (1978). Individual and situational factors in eyewitness testimony. *Journal of Applied Psychology, 63,* 352-359.

Clingempeel, W. G., Mulvey, E., & Reppucci, N. D. (1980). A national study of ethical dilemmas of psychologists in the criminal justice system. In J. Monahan (Ed.), *Who is the client?* Washington, DC: American Psychological Association.

Cocozza, J., & Steadman, H. (1978). Prediction in psychiatry: An example of misplaced confidence in experts. *Social Problems, 25,* 265-276.

Darrow, C. (1936, May). Attorney for the defense. *Esquire,* pp. 36-37; 211-213.

Davis, J. H., Kerr, N. L., Atkin, R. S., Holt, R., & Meek, D. (1975). The decision processes of 6- and 12-person mock juries assigned unanimous and two-thirds majority rules. *Journal of Personality and Social Psychology, 32,* 1-14.

Diamond, S. S. (1982). Order in the court: Consistency in criminal court decisions. In C. J. Scheirer & B. L. Hammonds (Eds.), *The Master Lecture Series,* Vol. 2: *Psychology and the law.* Washington, DC: American Psychological Association.

Dix, G. (1976). "Civil" commitment of the mentally ill and the need for data on the prediction of dangerousness. *American Behavioral Scientist, 19,* 318-334.

Doob, A. N., & Kirshenbaum, H. M. (1972). Some empirical evidence on the effect of Section 12 of the Canada Evidence Act upon the accused. *Criminal Law Quarterly, 15,* 88-96.

Doob, A. N., & Kirshenbaum, H. M. (1973). Bias in police line-ups — partial remembering. *Journal of Police Science and Administration, 1,* 287-293.

Ellison, K. W., & Buckhout, R. (1981). *Psychology and criminal justice.* New York: Harper & Row.

Etzioni, A. (1974, November/December). Creating an imbalance. *Trial, 10,* pp. 28-30.

Finkel, N. J. (1982). *Insanity defenses: Jurors' assessments of mental disease, respon-*

sibility, and culpability. Paper presented at the meeting of the American Psychological Association, Washington, DC.

Fishbein, M., & Ajzen, I. (1975). *Belief, attitude, intention, and behavior: An introduction to theory and research.* Reading, MA: Addison-Wesley.

Fitzgerald, R., & Ellsworth, P. C. (1984). Due process vs. crime control: Death qualification and jury attitudes. *Law and Human Behavior, 8,* 31–51.

Frankfurter, F. (1927/1962). *The case of Sacco and Vanzetti.* New York: Little Brown.

Goodman, G. S. (1984). The child witness: An introduction. *Journal of Social Issues, 40,* 1–7.

Gregory, W. L., Mowen, J. C., & Linder, D. E. (1978). Social psychology and plea bargaining: Applications, methodology, and theory. *Journal of Personality and Social Psychology, 36,* 1521–1530.

Grisso, T. (1981). *Juveniles' waiver of rights: Legal and psychological competence.* New York: Plenum.

Groth, A. N. (1979). *Men who rape: The psychology of the offender.* New York: Plenum.

Groth, A. N., Burgess, A. W., & Holmstrom, L. L. (1977). Rape: Power, anger, and sexuality. *American Journal of Psychiatry, 134,* 1239–1243.

Haney, C. (1979). Social psychology and the criminal law. In P. Middlebrook, *Social psychology and modern life.* New York: Random House.

Haney, C. (Ed.). (1984). Death qualification [Special issue]. *Law and Human Behavior, 8,* Nos. 1 & 2.

Haney, C., Banks, C., & Zimbardo, P. (1973). Interpersonal dynamics in a simulated prison. *International Journal of Criminology and Penology, 1,* 69–97.

Hans, V. P. (1986). An analysis of public attitudes toward the insanity defense. *Criminology, 24,* 393–414.

Hans, V. P., & Brooks, N. (1977). Effects of corroboration instructions in a rape case on experimental juries. *Osgoode Hall Law Journal, 15,* 701–716.

Hans, V. P., & Doob, A. N. (1976). Section 12 of the Canada Evidence Act and the deliberations of simulated juries. *Criminal Law Quarterly, 18,* 235–253.

Hans, V. P., & Slater, D. (1983). John Hinckley, Jr., and the insanity defense: The public's verdict. *Public Opinion Quarterly, 141,* 202–212.

Hans, V. P., & Vidmar, N. (1982). Jury selection. In N. L. Kerr & R. M. Bray (Eds.), *The psychology of the courtroom.* New York: Academic Press.

Hans, V. P., and Vidmar, N. (1986). *Judging the jury.* New York: Plenum.

Harris, L., and Associates. (1971). Study No. 2016 (on file at NAACP Legal Defense Fund, 10 Columbus Circle, New York, NY 10019).

Hastie, R. (1980, June). *From eyewitness accuracy to beyond reasonable doubt.* Paper presented at the meeting of the Law and Society Association, Madison.

Hosch, H. M. (1980). A comparison of three studies of the influence of expert testimony on jurors. *Law and Human Behavior, 4,* 297–302.

Hosch, H. M., Beck, E. L., & McIntyre, P. (1980). Influence of expert testimony regarding eyewitness accuracy on jury decisions. *Law and Human Behavior, 4,* 287–296.

Houlden, P. (1980–1981). Impact of procedural modifications on evaluations of plea bargaining. *Law and Society Review, 15,* 267–291.

Houlden, P., LaTour, S., Walker, L., & Thibaut, J. (1978). Preference for modes of dispute resolution as a function of process and decision control. *Journal of Experimental Social Psychology, 14,* 13–30.

Howell, R. J. (1982). In defense of the insanity plea. *Bulletin of the American Academy of Forensic Psychologists, 3,* 1–2.

Hunt, M. (1982, November 28). Putting jurors on the couch. *The New York Times Magazine,* pp. 70–72; 78; 82; 85–86; 88.

Janoff-Bulman, R. (1979). Characterological versus behavioral self-blame: Inquiries into depression and rape. *Journal of Personality and Social Psychology, 37,* 1798–1809.

Kahneman, D., & Tversky, A. (1973). On the psychology of prediction. *Psychological Review, 81,* 237–251.

Kalven, H., & Zeisel, H. (1966). *The American jury.* Boston: Little Brown.

Kaufman, I. K. (1982, August 8). The insanity plea on trial. *The New York Times Magazine,* pp. 16–20.

Kilpatrick, D. G., Resnick, P. A., & Veronen, L. J. (1981). Effects of a rape experience: A longitudinal study. *Journal of Social Issues, 37,* 105–122.

Konecni, V. J., & Ebbesen, E. B. (1979). External validity of research in legal psychology. *Law and Human Behavior, 3,* 39–70.

Konecni, V. J., & Ebbesen, E. B. (Eds.). (1982). *The criminal justice system: A social-psychological analysis.* San Francisco: W. H. Freeman.

Konecni, V. J., Mulcahy, E., & Ebbesen, E. B. (1980). Prison or mental hospital: Factors affecting the processing of persons suspected of being "mentally disordered sex offenders." In P. Lipsett & B. Sales (Eds.), *New directions in psycholegal research.* New York: Van Nostrand Reinhold.

Law Enforcement Assistance Administration. (1978). *Forcible rape: Final project report.* Washington, DC: U.S. Government Printing Office.

Levine, F. J., & Tapp, J. L. (1973). The psychology of criminal identification: The gap from *Wade* to *Kirby. University of Pennsylvania Law Review, 121,* 1079–1131.

Lind, E. A. (1982). The psychology of courtroom procedure. In N. L. Kerr & R. M. Bray (Eds.), *The psychology of the courtroom.* New York: Academic Press.

Lipsey, D. (1982). Send rapists to jail—the public's verdict. *The Sunday Times.*

Loftus, E. F. (1974). Reconstructing memory: The incredible eyewitness. *Psychology Today, 8,* 116–119.

Loftus, E. F. (1979) *Eyewitness testimony.* Cambridge, MA: Harvard University Press.

Loftus, E. F. (1980). Impact of expert psychological testimony on the unreliability of eyewitness identification. *Journal of Applied Psychology, 65,* 9–15.

Loftus, E. F. (1983a). Silence is not golden. *American Psychologist, 38,* 564–572.

Loftus, E. F. (1983b). Whose shadow is crooked? *American Psychologist, 38,* 576–577.

Loftus, E. F. (1986). Ten years in the life of an expert witness. *Law and Human Behavior, 10,* 241–263.

Loftus, E. F., & Palmer, J. C. (1974). Reconstruction of automobile destruction: An example of the interaction between language and memory. *Journal of Verbal Learning and Verbal Behavior, 13,* 585–589.

Loh, W. D. (1981). Q: What has reform of rape legislation wrought? A: Truth in criminal labelling. *Journal of Social Issues, 37,* 28–52.

Malamuth, N. M. (1981). Rape proclivity among males. *Journal of Social Issues, 37,* 138–157.

Malamuth, N. M., & Check, J. V. (1981). The effects of mass media exposure on acceptance of violence against women: A field experiment. *Journal of Research in Personality, 15,* 436–446.

Malamuth, N. M., & Donnerstein, E. (1982). The effects of aggressive-pornographic mass media stimuli. In L. Berkowitz (Ed.), *Advances in experimental social psychology,* Vol. 15. New York: Academic Press.

Mann, P. A. (1980). Ethical issues for psychologists in police agencies. In J. Monahan (Ed.), *Who is the client?* Washington, DC: American Psychological Association.

McCahill, T. W., Meyer, L. C., & Fischman, A. M. (1979). *The aftermath of rape.* Lexington, MA: Lexington Books.

McCloskey, M., & Egeth, H. E. (1983a). Eyewitness identification: What can a psychologist tell a jury? *American Psychologist, 38,* 550–563.

McCloskey, M., & Egeth, H. E. (1983b). A time to speak, or a time to keep silence? *American Psychologist, 38,* 573–575.

McCloskey, M., & Egeth, H., & McKenna, J. (Eds.) (1986). The ethics of expert testimony [Special issue]. *Law and Human Behavior, 10,* Nos. 1 and 2.

McCloskey, M., & Zaragoza, M. (1985). Misleading postevent information and memory for events: Arguments and evidence against memory impairment hypotheses. *Journal of Experimental Psychology: General, 114,* 1–16.

McConahay, J., Mullin, C., & Frederick, J. (1977). The uses of social science in trials with political and racial overtones: The trial of Joan Little. *Law and Contemporary Problems, 41,* 205–229.

Megargee, E. I., & Bohn, M. J., Jr. (1979). *Classifying criminal offenders.* Beverly Hills, CA: Sage.

Melton, G. B. (1981). Children's competency to testify. *Law and Human Behavior, 5,* 73–85.

Monahan, J. (Ed.). (1980). *Who is the client?* Washington, DC: American Psychological Association.

Monahan, J. (1981). *The clinical prediction of violent behavior.* Rockville, MD: U.S. Department of Health and Human Services.

Monahan, J., & Loftus, E. F. (1982). The psychology of law. *Annual Review of Psychology, 33,* 441–475.

Munsterberg, H. (1908). *On the witness stand.* New York: Doubleday, Page.

Nisbett, R., Borgida, E., Crandall, R., & Reed, H. (1976). Popular induction: Information is not necessarily informative. In J. Carroll & J. Payne (Eds.), *Cognition and social behavior.* Hillside, NJ: Erlbaum.

Pacht, A. R. (1976). The rapist in treatment: Professional myths and psychological realities. In M. J. Walker & S. L. Brodsky (Eds.), *Sexual assault.* Lexington, MA: Lexington Books.

Pasewark, R. A. (1981). Insanity plea: A review of the research literature. *Journal of Psychiatry and Law, 9,* 357–401.

Pfohl, S. (1977). The psychiatric assessment of dangerousness: Practical problems and political implications. In J. Conrad & S. Dinitz (Eds.), *In fear of each other.* Lexington, MA: Lexington Books.

Pritchard, D. (1977). Stable predictors of recidivism. *Journal Supplement Abstract Service, 7,* 72.

Rappaport, J., Lamiell, J. T., & Seidman, E. (1980). Ethical issues for psychologists in the juvenile justice system: Know and tell. In J. Monahan (Ed.), *Who is the client?* Washington, DC: American Psychological Association.

Roesch, R., & Golding, S. L. (1980). *Competency to stand trial.* Urbana, IL: University of Illinois Press.

Ryan, W. (1971). *Blaming the victim.* New York: Random House.

Saks, M. J. (1976). The limits of scientific jury selection: Ethical and empirical. *Jurimetrics Journal, 17,* 3–22.

Sakes, M. J. (1977). *Jury verdicts.* Lexington, MA: Lexington Books.

Sales, B. D., Elwork, A., & Alfini, J. J. (1977). Improving comprehension for jury instructions. In B. D. Sales (Ed.), *Perspectives in law and psychology,* Vol. 1. *The criminal justice system.* New York: Plenum.

Sanday, P. R. (1981). The sociocultural context of rape: A crosscultural study. *Journal of Social Issues, 37,* 5–27.

Shah, S. (1978). Dangerousness: A paradigm for exploring some issues in law and psychology. *American Psychologist, 33,* 224–238.

Sheppard, B. H., & Vidmar, N. (1980). Adversary pretrial procedures and testimonial evidence: Effects of lawyer's role and Machiavellianism. *Journal of Personality and Social Psychology, 39,* 320–332.

Simon, R. J. (1967). *The jury and the defense of insanity.* Boston: Little, Brown.

Simon, R. J., & Shackelford, W. (1965). The defense of insanity: A survey of legal and psychiatric opinion. *Public Opinion Quarterly, 29,* 411–424.

Sinclair, U. (1928). *Boston,* Vol. 1. New York: Albert and Charles Boni.

Steadman, H. J. (1979). *Beating a rap? Defendants found incompetent to stand trial.* Chicago: University of Chicago Press.

Steadman, H. J., & Cocozza, J. (1974). *Careers of the criminally insane.* Lexington, MA: Lexington Books.

Steadman, H. J., Monahan, J., Hartstone, E., Davis, S. K., & Robbins, P. C. (1982). Mentally disordered offenders: A national survey of patients and facilities. *Law and Human Behavior, 6,* 31–38.

Sue, S., Smith, R. E., & Caldwell, C. (1973). Effects of inadmissible evidence on the decisions of simulated jurors: A moral dilemna. *Journal of Applied Social Psychology, 3,* 344–353.

Tanke, E. T., & Tanke, T. J. (1979). Getting off a slippery slope: Social science in the judicial process. *American Psychologist, 34,* 1130–1138.

Tapp, J. L. (1976). Psychology and the law: An overture. *Annual Review of Psychology, 27.* Palo Alto, CA: Annual Reviews, Inc.

Tapp, J. L. (1980). Psychological and policy perspectives on the law: Reflections on a decade. *Journal of Social Issues, 36,* 165–192.

Tapp, J. L., & Kenniston, A. (1976, August). *Wounded Knee—Advocate or expert.* Paper presented at the meeting of the American Psychological Association, Washington, DC (update).

The Texas Observer. (1973, May 11). Jury selection in a criminal case. *The Texas Observer,* p. 9.

Thibaut, J., & Walker, L. (1975). *Procedural justice: A psychological analysis.* New York: Erlbaum/Halstead.

Van Dyke, J. (1977). *Jury selection procedures.* Cambridge, MA: Ballinger.

Vidmar, N. (1979). The other issues in jury simulation research: A commentary with particular reference to defendant character studies. *Law and Human Behavior, 3,* 95–106.

Vidmar, N., & Miller, D. T. (1982). Social psychological processes underlying attitudes toward legal punishment. *Law & Society Review, 14,* 565–602.

Weiten, W., & Diamond, S. S. (1979). A critical review of the jury simulation paradigm: The case of defendant characteristics. *Law and Human Behavior, 3,* 71–93.

Weithorn, L. A., & Campbell, S. B. (1982). The competency of children and adolescents to make informed treatment decisions. *Child Development, 53,* 1589–1598.

Wells, G. L. (1986). Expert psychological testimony: Empirical and conceptual analyses or effects. *Law and Human Behavior, 10,* 83–95.

Wells, G. L., Leippe, M. R., & Ostrom, R. M. (1979). Guidelines for empirically assessing the fairness of a lineup. *Law and Human Behavior, 3,* 285–293.

Wells, G. L., Lindsay, R. C. L., & Ferguson, T. J. (1979). Accuracy, confidence, and juror perceptions in eyewitness identification. *Journal of Applied Psychology, 64,* 440–448.

Wells, G. L., Lindsay, R. C. L., & Tousignant, J. P. (1980). Effects of expert psychological advice on human performance in judging the validity of eyewitness testimony. *Law and Human Behavior, 4,* 275–285.

Wigmore, J. H. (1909). Professor Munsterberg and the psychology of evidence. *Illinois Law Review, 3,* 399–445.

Williams, W., & Miller, K. (1977). The role of personal characteristics in perceptions of dangerousness. *Criminal Justice and Behavior, 4,* 421.

Wissler, R. & Saks, M. J. (1985). In the inefficacy of limiting instruction: When jurors use prior conviction evidence to decide guilt. *Law and Human Behavior, 9,* 37–48.

Wolf, S., & Montgomery, M. (1977). Effects of inadmissible evidence and level of judicial admonishment to disregard on the judgments of mock jurors. *Journal of Applied Social Psychology, 7,* 205–219.

Zeisel, H., & Diamond, S. S. (1976). The jury selection in the Mitchell-Stans conspiracy trial. *American Bar Foundation Research Journal, 1,* 151–174.

Zerman, M. B. (1977). *Call the final witness.* New York: Harper & Row.

Cases cited:

Apodaca v. *Oregon,* 406 U.S. 404 (1972).

Ballew v. *Georgia,* 435 U.S. 223 (1978).

Baxstrom v. *Herold,* 383 U.S. 107 (1966).

Johnson v. *Louisiana,* 406 U.S. 356 (1972).

Lockhart v. *McCree,* 106 S. Ct. 1758 (1986).

People v. *McDonald,* 37 Cal.3d. 351 (1984).

State v. *Chapple,* 135 Ariz. 281, 660 P.2d. 1208 (1983).

Williams v. *Florida,* 399 U.S. 78 (1970).

Chapter 13

Acredolo, L. P. (1976). Frames of reference used by children for orientation in unfamiliar spaces. In G. Moore & R. Golledge (Eds.), *Environmental knowing,* Stroudsburg, PA: Dowden, Huchinson & Ross.

Acredolo, L. P. (1977). Developmental changes in the ability to coordinate perspectives of a largescale environment. *Developmental Psychology, 13,* 1–8.

Altman, I. (1975). *The environment and social behavior.* Monterey, CA: Brooks/Cole.

Altman, I. (1976). Privacy: A conceptual analysis. *Environment and Behavior, 8,* 7–31.

Barker, R. G. (1968). *Ecological psychology: Concepts and methods for studying the environment of human behavior.* Stanford, CA: Stanford University Press.

Baron, R. M. & Rodin, J. (1978). Perceived control and crowding stress. In A. Baum, J. Singer, & S. Valins (Eds.) *Advances in environmental psychology.* Vol. 1. Hillsdale, NJ: Erlbaum.

Baum, A. & Davis, G. E. (1980). Reducing the stress of high-density living: An architectural intervention. *Journal of Personality and Social Psychology, 38,* 471–481.

Bechtel, R. B. (1976). Perceived quality of residential environment: Some methodological issues. In K. E. Craik & E. H. Zube (Eds.), *Perceiving environmental quality: Research and application.* New York: Plenum.

Bell, P. A., Fisher, J. D., & Baum, A. (1983). *Environmental psychology* (2nd ed.). Philadelphia, Saunders.

Buttel, F. H. & Flinn, W. L. (1978a). Social class and mass environmental beliefs: A reconsideration. *Environment and Behavior, 10,* 433–450.

Buttel, F. H., & Flinn, W. L. (1978b). The politics of environmental concern: The impacts of party identification and political ideology on environmental attitudes. *Environment and Behavior, 10,* 17–36.

Caplan, N., Morrison, A., & Staumbaugh, R. J. (1975). *The use of social science knowledge in policy decisions at the national level.* Ann Arbor: Institute for Social Research, University of Michigan.

Cohen, S. (1978). Environmental load and the allocation of attention. In A. Baum, J. E. Singer, & S. Valins (Eds.), *Advances in environmental psychology,* Vol. 1. Hillsdale, NJ: Erlbaum.

Cohen, S. (1980). After effects of stress on human performance and social behavior: A review of research and theory. *Psychological Bulletin, 88,* 82–108.

Cohen, S., Evans, G. W., Krantz, D. S., Stokels, D., & Kelly, S. (1981). Aircraft noise and children: Longitudinal and cross-sectional evidence on adaptation to noise and the effectiveness of noise abatement. *Journal of Personality and Social Psychology, 40,* 331–345.

Cone, J. D., & Hayes, S. C. (1980). *Environmental problem/behavioral solutions.* Monterey, CA: Brooks/Cole.

Cooper, C. C. (1975). *Easter Hill village.* New York: The Free Press.

Craik, K. H. (1970). Environmental psychology. In *New directions in psychology,* Vol. 4. New York: Holt.

Craik, K. H., & McKechnie, G. E. (1977). Personality and the environment. *Environment and Behavior, 9,* 155–168.

Craik, K. H., & Zube E. H. (1976). The development of perceived environmental quality indices. In K. H. Craik & E. H. Zube (Eds.), *Perceiving environmental quality: Research and applications.* New York: Plenum.

Daniel, T. C., & Boster, R. S. (1976). *Measuring landscape esthetics: The Scenic Beauty Estimation method.* (Paper RM-167.) USDA Forest Service, Rocky Mountain Forest and Range Experiment Station.

Downs, R. M., & Stea, D. (1973). Cognitive maps and spatial behavior: Process and products. In R. M. Downs & D. Stea (Eds.), *Image and environment: Cognitive mapping and spatial behavior.* Chicago: Aldine.

Downs, R. M., & Stea, D. (1977). *Maps in minds: Reflections on cognitive mapping.* New York: Harper & Row.

Dunlap, R. E. (1975). The impact of political orientation on environmental attitudes and actions. *Environment and Behavior, 7,* 428–455.

Edney, J. J. (1974). Human territoriality. *Psychological Bulletin, 81,* 959–975.

Edney, J. J. (1976). Human territories: Comment on functional properties. *Environment and Behavior, 8,* 31–49.

Evans, G. W. (1978). Human spatial behavior: The arousal model. In A. Baum & Y. Epstein (Eds.), *Human response to crowding.* Hillsdale: NJ: Erlbaum.

Evans, G. W., & Wood, K. W. (1980). Assessment of environmental aesthetics in scenic highway corridors. *Environment and Behavior, 12,* 255–273.

Freedman, J. L. (1975). *Crowding and behavior.* San Francisco: Freeman.

Glass, D. C., Reim, B., & Singer, J. E. (1971). Behaviorial consequences of adaptation to controllable and uncontrollable noise. *Journal of Experimental Social Psychology, 7,* 244–257.

Glass, D. C., Singer, J. E., & Pennebaker, J. W. (1977). Behavioral and physiological effects of uncontrollable environmental events. In D. Stokols (Ed.), *Perspectives on environment and behavior: Theory, research, and applications.* New York: Plenum.

Hayes, S. C., & Cone, J. D. (1977). Reducing residential electrial energy use: Payments, information, and feedback. *Journal of Applied Behavior Analysis, 10,* 425–435.

Heberlein, T. A. (1975). Conservation information: The energy crisis and electricity consumption in an apartment complex. *Energy Systems and Policy, 1,* 105–117.

Herzog, T. R., Kaplan, S., & Kaplan, R. (1976). The prediction of preference for familiar urban places. *Environment and Behavior, 8,* 627–647.

Holahan, C. J. (1982). *Environmental psychology.* New York: Random House.

Ittelson, W. H., Proshansky, H. M., Rivlin, L. G., & Winkel, G. H. (1974). *An introduction to environmental psychology.* New York: Holt.

Ittelson, W. H., & Kilpatrick, F. P. (1952). Experiments in perception. *Scientific American, 185,* 50–55.

Kantrowitz, M. (1985). Has environment and behavior research "made a difference." *Environment and Behavior, 17,* 25–46.

Kaplan, R. (1977). Preference and everyday nature: Method and application. In D. Stokols (Ed.), *Perspective on environment and behavior: Theory, research, and applications.* New York: Plenum.

Kegel-Flom, P. (1976). Identifying the potential rural optometrist. *American Journal of Optometry and Physiological Optics, 53,* 479–482.

Koenig, D. J. (1975). Additional research on environmental activism. *Environment and Behavior, 7,* 472–485.

Kohlenberg, R., Phillips, T., & Proctor, W. (1976). A behavioral analysis of peaking in residential electrical energy consumers. *Journal of Applied Behavior Analysis, 9,* 13–18.

Lewin, K. (1947). Group decision and social change. In T. M. Newcomb & E. L. Hartley (Eds.), *Readings in social psychology.* New York: Holt.

MacKay, D. B., Olshansky, R. W., & Sentill, G. (1975). Cognitive maps and spatial behavior of consumers. *Geographical Analysis, 7,* 532–547.

Newman, O. (1972). Defensible space: *Crime prevention through urban design.* New York: Macmillan.

Osmond, H. (1966). Design must meet patients' human needs. *The Modern Hospital, 106,* 98–170.

Piaget, J., Inhelder, B., & Szeminska, A. (1960). *The child's conception of geometry.* New York: Basic Books.

Platt, J. (1973). Social traps. *American Psychologist, 28,* 641–651.

Proshansky, H. M. (1972). For what are we training our graduate students? *American Psychologist, 27,* 205–212.

Russell, J. A., & Ward, L. M. Environmental psychology. *Annual Review of Psychology, 33.* Palo Alto, CA: Annual Reviews, Inc.

Seligman, C. & Darley, J. M. (1977). Feedback as a means of decreasing residential energy consumption. *Journal of Applied Psychology, 62,* 363–368.

Seligman, C., Becker, L. J., & Darley, J. M. (1981). Behavioral approaches to residential energy conservation. In A. Baum and J. E. Singer (Eds.), *Advances in environmental psychology:* Vol. 3. *Energy conservation: Psychological perspectives.* Hillsdale, NJ: Erlbaum.

Seligman, M. E. P. (1975). *Helplessness.* San Francisco: Freeman.

Skinner, B. F. (1953). *Science and human behavior.* New York: MacMillan.

Sommer, R. (1977). Action research. In D. Stokols (Ed.), *Perspectives on environment and behavior: Theory, research, and application.* New York: Plenum.

Sommer, R. (1980). Architecture, psychology: The passion has passed. *American Institute of Architects Journal,* April, 1980.

Spivack, M. (1967). Sensory distortions in tunnels and corridors. *Hospital and Community Psychiatry,* January, 1967, 24–30.

Stokols, D. (1978). Environmental psychology. *Annual Review of Psychology, 29.* Palo Alto, CA: Annual Reviews, Inc.

Stokols, D. (1979). A congruence analysis of human stress. In I. G. Sarason & C. D. Spielberger (Eds.), *Stress and anxiety,* Vol. 6. Washington, DC: Hemisphere.

Stokols, D. (1981). The environmental context of behavior and well-being. In D. Perlman & C. Cozby, *Social Psychology.* New York: Holt.

Sundstrom, E., Burt, R. E., & Kamp, D. (1980). Privacy at work: Architectural correlates of job satisfaction and job performance. *Academy of Management Journal, 23,* 101–117.

Weigel, R. H., & Newman, L. S. (1976). Increasing attitude-behavior correspondence by broadening the scope of the behavioral measure. *Journal of Personality and Social Psychology, 33,* 793–802.

Weigel, R. H., & Weigel, J. (1978). Environmental concern: The development of a measure. *Environment and Behavior, 10,* 3–16.

Weisman, J. (1981). Evaluating architectural legibility. *Environment and Behavior, 13,* 189–204.

Wicker, A. W. (1979). *An introduction to ecological psychology.* Monterey, CA: Brooks/Cole.

Wicker, A. W., & Kirmeyer, S. L. (1976). From church to laboratory to national park. In S. Wapner, S. B. Cohen, and B. Kaplan (Eds.), *Experiencing the environment.* New York: Plenum.

Wicker, A. W., McGrath, J. E., & Armstrong, G. E. (1972). Organization size and behavior setting capacity as determinants of member participation. *Behavioral Science, 17,* 499–513.

Winett, R. A., Kagel, J. H., Battalio, R. C., & Winkler, R. C. (1978). Effects of monetary rebates, feedback, and information on residential electricity conservation. *Journal of Applied Psychology, 63,* 73–80.

Wohlwill, J. F. (1979). The social and political matrix of environmental attitudes:

An analysis of the vote on the California coastal zone regulation act. *Environment and Behavior, 11*, 71–86.

Zarling, L. H. & Lloyd, K. E. (1980). A behavioral analysis of feedback to electrical consumers. Cited in J. Cone & S. Hayes, *Environmental problems/behavioral solutions.* Monterey, CA: Brooks/Cole.

Zube, E. H. (1980). *Environmental evaluation: Perception and public policy.* Monterey, CA: Brooks/Cole.

Chapter 14

Anderson, R. C., & Faust, G. W. (1973). *Educational psychology: The science of instruction and learning.* New York: Dodd, Mead & Co.

Ausubel, D. P. (1969). Is there a discipline of educational psychology? *Psychology in the Schools, 6,* 232–244.

Ball, S. (1984). Educational psychology as an academic chameleon: An editorial assessment after 75 years. *Journal of Educational Psychology, 76,* 993–999.

Berliner, D. C. (1984). The half-full glass: A review of research on teaching. In P. Hosford (Ed.), *Using what we know about teaching.* Alexandria: Association for Supervision and Curriculum.

Brown, D. T., & Minke, K. M. (1986). School psychology graduate training: A comprehensive analysis. *American Psychologist, 41,* 1328–1338.

Brown, D. T., Horn, A. J., & Lindstrom, J. P. (1980). *The handbook of certification/licensure requirements for school psychologists.* Washington, DC: National Association of School Psychologists.

Brown v. Board of Ed., 347V. S493 (1954).

Charles, D. (1976). A historical overview of educational psychology. *Contemporary Educational Psychology, 1,* 76–88.

Corsini, R. (Ed.). (1987). *Concise encyclopedia of psychology.* New York: Wiley.

Cutts, N. E. (1955). *School psychologists at mid-century: A report of the Thayer Conference on the training of school psychologists.* Washington. DC: American Psychological Association.

Fagan, T. K. (1986) School psychology's dilemma: Reappraising solutions and directing attention to the future. *American Psychologist, 41,* 851–861.

Fagan, T. K. (1987). Gesell: The first school psychologist. Part II. Practice and significance. *School Psychology Review, 16,* 399–409.

Fagan, T. K., Hensley, L. T., & Delugach, F. J. (1986). The evolution of organizations for school psychologists in the United States. *School Psychology Review, 15,* 127–135.

Fisher, G. L., Jenkins, S. J., & Crumbley, J. D. (1986). A replication of a survey of school psychologists: Congruence between training, practice, preferred role, and competence. *Psychology in the Schools, 23,* 271–279.

Gage, N. L. (1978a). The yield of research on teaching. *Phi Delta Kappan,* November 1978, 229–235.

Gage, N. L. (1978b). *The scientific basis of the art of teaching.* New York: Teachers College Press.

Glover, J., Bruning, R., & Filbeck, R. (1983). *Educational Psychology: Principles and applications.* Boston: Little, Brown.

Goh, D. S. (1977). Graduate training in school psychology. *Journal of School Psychology, 15,* 207–218.

Goldstein, A. P., & Krasner, L. (1987). *Modern Applied Psychology,* New York: Pergamon Press.

Hobson v. Hansen, 269 F. Supp. 401 (D.D.C. 1967).

James, W. (1962). *Talks to teachers on psychology.* New York: Dover.

Kohler, W. (1959). Gestalt psychology today. *American Psychologist, 14,* 727–734.

Lewin, K. (1936). *Principals of topological psychology.* New York: McGraw-Hill.

Meacham, M. L., & Peckham, P. D. (1978). School psychologists at three-quarters century: Congruence between training, practice, preferred role and competence. *Journal of Psychology, 16,* 195–206.

Medley, D. M. (1977). *Teacher competence and teacher effectiveness: A review of process-product research.* Washington, DC: American Association of Colleges for Teacher Education.

Mitzel, H. (Ed.) (1982). *Encyclopedia of Educational Research, Vol. 3.* New York: The Free Press.

P. v. Riles, 343 F. Suppl. 1306 (N.D. Cal. 1972) aff'd 502 F.2d. 963 (9th Cir. 1974) (preliminary injunction); No. C-71-2270 RFP slip. op. (Oct. 15, 1979) (decision on merits).

Pavlov, I. P. (1934). A contribution to the physiology of the hypnotic state of dogs. *Character and Personality, 2,* 189–200.

Ramage, J. C. (1979). National survey of school psychologists: Update. *School Psychology Review, 8,* 153–161.

Ramage, J. C. (1987). Larry P. decision continues impact. *NASP Communique, 16,* 1–16.

Rosenshine, B. V., & Berliner, D. C. (1978). Academic engaged time. *British Journal of Teaching Education, 4,* 3–16.

Ruggles, T. R., & LeBlanc, J. M. (1982). Behavior analysis procedures in classroom teaching. In A. S. Bellack, M. Hersen, & A. E. Kazdin (Eds.), *International handbook of behavior modification and therapy.* New York: Plenum.

Schneider, E. J. (1979). Researchers discover formula for success in student learning. *Educational R&D Report, 2,* 1–6.

Skinner, B. F. (1953). *Science and human behavior.* New York: Macmillan.

Tindall, R. H. (1964). Trends in development of psychological services in the school. *Journal of School Psychology, 3,* 1–12.

Wallin, J. E., & Ferguson, D. G. (1967). The development of school psychological services. In J. F. Magary (Ed.), *School Psychological Services.* Englewood Cliffs, NJ: Prentice-Hall.

Wertheimier, M. (1944). Gestalt theory. *Social Resources, 11,* 78–99.

Westbrook, J. D. (1982). *Considering the research: What makes an effective school.* Austin, TX: Southwest Educational Development Lab.

Winkler, R. C., & Winett, R. A. (1982). Behavioral interventions in resource conservation: A systems approach based on behavioral economics. *American Psychologist, 38,* 421–435.

Wise, P. S. (1985). School psychologist's rankings of stressful events. *Journal of Psychology, 23,* 31–41.

Wright, J. W. (1987). *American almanac of jobs and salaries.* New York: Avon.

Chapter 15

Alderman, R. (1974). *Psychological behavior in sport.* Philadelphia: Saunders.

Carver, C. S., Degregorio, E., & Gillis, R. (1981). Challenge and type A behavior among intercollegiate football players. *Journal of Sport Psychology, 3,* 140–148.

Chappel, J. N. (1987). Drug use and abuse in the athlete. In J. R. May and M. J. Asken (Eds.), *Sport psychology: The psychological health of the athlete.* New York: PMA Publishing.

Chelladurai, P., & Carron, A. V. (1983). Athletic maturity and preferred leadership. *Journal of Sport Psychology, 5,* 371–380.

Collins, G. B., Pippenger, C. E., & Janesz, J. W. (Fall, 1984). Links in the chain: an approach to the treatment of drug abuse on a professional football team. *Cleveland Clinic Quarterly, 51,* 485–492.

Cook, D. L., Tricker, R. & McGuire, R. (October, 1987). The issues of drugs in sport: Athletes at risk, drugs of choice and a prevention/intervention model. Presented at the Association for the Advancement of Applied Sport Psychology conference at Newport Beach, CA.

Deci, E. L. (1975). *Intrinsic motivation.* New York: Plenum.

Dishman, R. K. (1983). Identity crises in North American sport psychology: Academics in professional issues. *Journal of Sport Psychology, 5,* 123–134.

Dweck, C. S. (1975). The role of expectations and attributions in the alleviation of learned helplessness. *Journal of Personality and Social Psychology, 31,* 74–685.

Feltz, D., & Landers, D. M. (1983). The effects of mental practice on motor skill learning and performance: A meta-analysis. *Journal of Sport Psychology, 5,* 25–57.

Fisher, A. C. (1977). Sport personality assessment: Facts, fallacies, and perspectives. *Motor Skills: Theory Into Research, 1,* 87–97.

Gould, D. (1984). Psychosocial development and children's sport. In J. R. Thomas (Ed.), *Motor development during childhood and adolescence.* Minneapolis: Burgess.

Greene, D., & Lepper, M. R. (1974). Effects of extrinsic rewards on children's subsequent intrinsic interest. *Child Development, 45,* 1141–1145.

Hardy, C. J., Hall, E. G., & Prestholdt, P. H. (1986). The mediational role of social influence in the perception of exertion. *Journal of Sport Psychology, 8,* 88–104.

Hatfield, B. D., & Landers, D. M. (1983). Psychophysiology—A new direction for sport psychology. *Journal of Sport Psychology, 5,* 243–259.

Landers, D. M., Christina, R. W., Hatfield, B. D., Daniels, F. S., & Doyle, L. A. (1980). Moving competitive shooting into the scientists's lab. *American Rifleman, 128,* 36–37; 76–77.

Long, B. C., & Haney, C. J. (1986). Enhancing physical activity in sedentary women: Information locus of control, and attitudes. *Journal of Sport Psychology, 8,* 8–24.

Martens, R. (1975). *Social psychology & physical activity.* New York: Harper & Row.

Martens, R. (1987). Science, knowledge, and sport psychology. *The Sport Psychologist, 1,* 29–55.

Martin, J. E., & Dubbert, P. M. (1985). Adherence to exercise. In R. L. Terjung (Ed.), *Exercise and Sport Sciences Reviews.* New York: Macmillan.

Martin, G., & Hrycaiko, D. (1983). Effective behavioral coaching: What's it all about? *Journal of Sport Psychology, 5,* 8–20.

Monahan, T. (September, 1987). Sport psychology: A crisis of identity? *The Physician and Sportsmedicine, 15,* 203–205; 208–209; 212.

Morgan, W. P. (1980). Sport personology: The credulous-skeptical argument in perspective. In W. F. Straub (Ed.), *Sport psychology: An analysis of athlete behavior.* Ithaca, NY: Mouvement.

Nideffer, R. M. (1981). *The ethics and practice of applied sport psychology.* Ithaca, NY: Mouvement Publications.

Officer, S., & Rosenfeld, L. B. (1985). Self-disclosure to male and female coaches by female high school athletes. *Journal of Sport Psychology, 7,* 360–370.

Orlick, T., & Partington, J. (1987). The sport psychology consultant: Analysis of critical components as viewed by Canadian Olympic athletes. *The Sport Psychologist, 1,* 4–17.

Pemberton, C. L., & Petlichkoff, L. (1988). Sport psychology and the female Olympic athlete: An uncharted frontier. *Journal of Physical Education, Recreation, & Dance, 59,* 55–58.

Regeski, W. J. (1981). The perception of exertion: A social psychophysiological integration. *Journal of Sport Psychology, 3,* 305–320.

Roberts, G. C. (1984). Children's achievement motivation in sport. In J. Nicholls (Ed.). *The development of achievement motivation.* Greenwich, CT: JAI Press.

Rotella, R. J., & Heyman, S. R. (1986). Stress, injury, and the psychological rehabilitation of athletes. In J. M. Williams (Ed.), *Applied sport psychology: Personal growth to peak performance.* Palo Alto, CA: Mayfield.

Roth, D. L., & Holmes, D. S. (1985). Influence of physical fitness in determining the impact of stressful life events on physical and physiologic health. *Psychosomatic Medicine, 47,* 164–173.

Scanlan, T. K., & Passer, M. W. (1978). Anxiety-inducing factors in competitive youth sport. In F. L. Small & R. E. Smith (Eds.), *Psychological perspectives in youth sports.* Washington, DC: Hemisphere.

Smith, R. E. (1986). Toward a cognitive-affective model of athletic burnout. *Journal of Sport Psychology, 8,* 36–50.

Vallerand, R. J. (1983). The effect of differential amounts of positive verbal feedback on the intrinsic motivation of male hockey players. *Journal of Sport Psychology, 5,* 100–107.

Wankel, L. M., & Kreisal, P. S. J. (1985). Factors underlying enjoyment of youth sports: Sport and age group comparisons. *Journal of Sport Psychology, 7,* 51–64.

Weinberg, R. S., & Hunt, V. V. (1976). The interrelationships between anxiety, motor performance, and electromyography. *Journal of Motor Behavior, 9,* 219–224.

Weinstein, W. S., & Meyers, A. W. (1983). Running as treatment for depression: Is it worth it? *Journal of Sport Psychology, 5,* 288–301.

Wiese, D. M., & Weiss, M. R. (1987). Psychological rehabilitation and physical injury: Implications for the sportsmedicine team. *The Sport Psychologist, 1,* 318–330.

Wiggins, D. K. (1984). The history of sport psychology in North America. In J. M. Silva & R. S. Weinberg (Eds.), *Psychological foundations of sport.* Champaign, IL: Human Kinetics.

Chapter 16

Ainsworth, M. D. S. (1973). The development of infant-mother attachment. In B. M. Caldwell & H. N. Ricciuti (Eds.), *Review of child development research* (Vol. 3). Chicago: University of Chicago Press.

Ainsworth, M. D., Blehar, M. C., Waters, E., & Wall, S. (1978). *Patterns of attachment: A psychological study of the strange situation.* Hillsdale, NJ: Erlbaum.

Allen, K. E., Hart, B., Buell, J. S., Harris, F. R., & Wolf, M. M. (1964). Effects of social reinforcement on isolate behavior of a nursery school child. *Child Development, 35,* 511–518.

Als, H., Tonick, E., Lester, B. M., & Brazelton, T. B. (1981). Specific neonatal measures; The Brazelton Neonatal Behavioral Assessment Scale. In J. D. Osofsky (Ed.), *Handbook of infant development.* New York: Wiley.

Als, H., Tronick, E., & Adamson, L. (1976). The behavior of the full-term yet under-weight newborn infant. *Developmental Medicine and Child Neurology, 18,* 590–602.

Anderson, C. W., Nagle, R. J., Roberts, W. A., & Smith, J. W. (1981). Attachment to substitute caregivers as a function of center quality and caregiver involvement. *Child Development, 52,* 53–61.

Apgar, V. (1966). The newborn (Apgar) scoring system. *Pediatric Clinics of North America, 13,* 645–650.

Arend, R., Gove, F. L., & Sroufe, L. A. (1979). Continuity of individual adaption from infancy to kindergarten: A predictive study of ego-resiliency and curiosity in preschoolers. *Child Development, 50,* 950–959.

Asher, S., & Renshaw, P. (1981). Children without friends: Social knowledge and social skill training. In S. Asher & J. Gottman (Eds.), *The development of children's friendships.* Cambridge: University of Cambridge Press.

Baltes, P. B., & Schaie, K. W. (1976). On the plasticity of intelligence in adulthood and old age: Where Horn and Donaldson fail. *American Psychologist, 31,* 720–725.

Baltes, P. B., & Willis, S. L. (1982). Enhancement: Plasticity of intellectual functioning of old age: Penn State's adult development and enrichment program. In F. I. M. Craik & S. E. Trehub (Eds.), *Aging and the cognitive processes.* New York: Plenum Press.

Bates, J. E., & Bayles, K. (1984). Objective and subjective components in mothers' perceptions of their children from age 6 months to 3 years. *Merrill-Palmer Quarterly, 30,* 111–130.

Bates, J. E., Maslin, C. A., & Frankel, K. A. (1985). Attachment security, mother-child interaction, and temperament as predictors of behavior-problem ratings at age three years. *Monographs of the Society for Research in Child Dvelopment, 50,* 167–193.

Battistich, V., Watson, M., Solomon, D., & Solomon, J. (1982, July). *Procedures for assessing prosocial values, motives, and behaviors.* Presented at meetings of International Association for the Study of Cooperation in Education, Provo, UT.

Beckwith, L., & Cohen, S. (1978). Preterm birth: Hazardous obstetrical and postnatal events as related to caregiver-infant behavior. *Infant Behavior and Development, 1,* 403–411.

Bell, R. Q., & Harper, L. V. (1977). *Child effects on adults.* Lincoln: University of Nebraska Press.

Bellack, A. (1979). Behavioral assessment of social skills. In A. Bellack & M. Hersen (Eds.), *Research and practice in social skills training.* New York: Plenum Press.

Beller, E. K. (1979). Early intervention programs. In J. D. Osofsky (Ed.), *Handbook of infant development.* New York: Wiley.

Belsky, J., & Steinberg, L. D. (1978). The effects of daycare: A critical review. *Child Development, 49,* 929–949.

Bierman, K. L. (1986). Process of change during social skills training with preadolescents and its relation to treatment outcome. *Child Development, 57,* 230–240.

Bierman, K., & Furman, W. (1984). The effects of social skills training and peer involvement on the social adjustment of preadolescents. *Child Development, 55* 151–162.

Blehar, M. (1974). Anxious attachment and defensive reactions associated with day care. *Child Development, 45,* 683–692.

Blom, D., & Zimmerman, B. (1981). Enhancing the social skills of an unpopular girl: A social learning intervention. *Journal of School Psychology, 19,* 295–303.

Bornstein, M. R., Bellack, A. S., & Hersen, M. (1977). Social skills training for unassertive children: A multiple baseline analysis. *Journal of Applied Behavioral Analysis, 10,* 183–195.

Bornstein, M., Bellack, A. S., & Hersen, M. (1980). Social skills training for highly aggressive children. *Behavior Modification, 4,* 173–186.

Botwinick, J. (1977). Aging and intelligence. In J. E. Birren & K. W. Schaie (Eds.), *Handbook of the psychology of aging.* New York: Van Nostrand Reinhold.

Bowlby, J. (1973). *Attachment and loss: Separation.* New York: Basic Books.

Brazelton, T. B. (1961). Psychophysiological reactions in the neonate. I. The value of observation of the neonate. *Journal of Pediatrics, 58,* 508–512.

Brazelton, T. B. (1973). Neonatal Behavior Assessment Scale. *National Spastics Monograph.* No. 50. Philadelphia: Lippincott.

Brazelton, T. B. (1981). Introduction. In C. C. Brown (Ed.), *Infants at risk: Assessment and intervention, an update for health care professionals and parents.* Johnson & Johnson Pediatric Round Table, No. 5. Johnson & Johnson.

Bronfenbrenner, U. (1970). *Two worlds of childhood: U.S. and U.S.S.R.* New York: Russell Sage Foundation.

Bronfenbrenner, U. (1979). *The ecology of human development: Experiments by nature and design.* Cambridge, MA: Harvard University Press.

Brookhart, J., & Hock, E. (1976). The effects of experiential background on infants' behavior toward their mothers and a stranger. *Child Development, 47,* 333–340.

Busk, P., Ford, R., & Schulman, J. (1973). Stability of sociometric responses in classrooms. *Journal of Genetic Psychology, 123,* 69–84.

Caldwell, B. M., Wright, C. M., Honig, A. S., & Tannenbaum, J. (1970). Infant care and attachment. *American Journal of Orthopsychiatry, 40,* 397–412.

Carey, W. B. (1970). A simplified method for measuring infant temperament. *Journal of Pediatrics, 77,* 188–194.

Carey, W. B. (1972). Clinical applications of infant temperament measurements. *Journal of Pediatrics, 81,* 823–828.

Carey, W. B. (1974). Night walking and temperament in infancy. *Journal of Pediatrics, 84,* 756–758.

Carey, W. B., & McDevitt, S. C. (1978). Revision of the infant temperament questionnaire. *Pediatrics, 61,* 735–739.

Cartledge, G., & Milburn, J. (1980). Steps in teaching social skills. In G. Cartledge & G. Milburn (Eds.), *Teaching social skills to children.* New York: Pergamon.

Chess, S., & Thomas, A. (1973). Temperament in the normal infant. In J. C. Westman (Ed.), *Individual differences in children.* New York: Wiley.

Child Care Data and Materials. (1974). Committee on Finance, United States Senate. Washington, DC: U.S. Government Printing Office.

Chittenden, G. (1942). An experimental study in measuring and modifying assertive behavior in young children. *Monographs of the Society for Research in Child Development, 7*(1, Serial No. 31).

Cicirelli, V., et al. (1969, June). *The impact of Head Start: An evaluation of Head Start on children's cognitive and affective development.* Office of Economic Opportunity (Contract #B89-4536). Westinghouse Learning Corporation for Federal Scientific and Technical Information: U.S. Institute for Applied Technology.

Clarke-Stewart, A. (in press). The social ecology of early childhood. In N. Eisenberg (Ed.), *Contemporary topics in developmental psychology.* New York: Wiley.

Clarke-Stewart, A., & Fein, G. G. (1983). Early childhood programs. In P. Mussen (Ed.), *Handbook of child psychology. Vol. 2. Infancy and developmental psychology* (edited by M. M. Harth & J. J. Campos). New York: Wiley.

Cochran, M. (1977). A comparison of group day and family child-rearing patterns in Sweden. *Child Development, 48,* 702–707.

Collias, N. E. (1956). The analysis of socialization in sheep and goats. *Ecology, 37,* 226–239.

Combs, M., & Lahey, B. (1981). A cognitive social skills training program. *Behavior Modification, 5,* 39–60.

Cooke, T., & Apolloni, T. (1976). Developing positive social-economic behaviors: A study of training and generalization effects. *Journal of Applied Behavior Analysis, 9,* 65–78.

Crockenberg, S. (1981). Infant irritability, mother responsiveness and social support influences on the security of infant-mother attachment. *Child Development, 52,* 857–865.

Cummings, E. M. (1980). Caregivers stability and day care. *Developmental Psychology, 16,* 31–37.

Curran, J. (1979). Social skills: Methodological issues and future directions. In A. Bellack & M. Hersen (Eds.), *Research and practice in social skills training.* New York: Plenum Press.

Daniels, D., Plomin, R., & Greenhalgh, J. (1984). Correlates of difficult temperament in infancy. *Child Development, 55,* 1184–1194.

Denney, N. W. (1974). Classification abilities in the elderly. *Journal of Gerontology, 29,* 309-314.

Denney, N. W. (1979). Problem solving in later adulthood: Intervention research. In P. B. Baltes & O. G. Brim, Jr. (Eds.), *Life-span development and behavior* (Vol. 2). New York: Academic Press.

Denney, D. R., & Denney, N. W. (1973). The use of classification for problem solving: A comparison of middle and old age. *Developmental Psychology, 9,* 275-278.

Denney, N. W., & Denney, D. R. (1974). Modeling effects on the questioning strategies of the elderly. *Developmental Psychology, 10,* 458.

Dodge, K. (1983). Behavioral antecedents of peer social status. *Child Development, 54,* 1386–1399.

Dreyfus-Brisac, C. (1974). Organization of sleep in prematures: Implications for caretaking. In M. Lewis & L. Rosenblum (Eds.), *The effect of the infant on its caregiver.* New York: Wiley.

D'Zurilla, T., & Goldfried, M. (1971). Problem-solving and behavior modification. *Journal of Abnormal Psychology, 78,* 107–126.

Eisenberg, N. (1986). *Altruistic emotion, cognition and behavior.* Hillsdale, NJ: Erlbaum.

Eisenberg, N., & Harris, J. D. (1984). Social competence: A developmental perspective. *School Psychology Review, XIII,* 267–277.

Eisler, R. (1976). Behavioral assessment of social skills. In M. Hersen & A. Bellack (Eds.), *Behavioral Assessment: A practical handbook.* Elmsford, NY: Pergamon.

Eisler, R., Hersen, M., Miller, P., & Blanchard, E. (1975). Situational determinants of assertive behaviors. *Journal of Consulting and Clinical Psychology,* 1975, 43, 330–340.

Elmer, E., & Gregg, G. S. (1967). Developmental characteristics of abused children. *Pedriatrics, 40,* 596–602.

Farran, D., & Ramey, C. (1977). Infant day care and attachment behaviors toward others and teachers. *Child Development, 48,* 1112-1116.

Field, T. M., Hallock, N., Ting, G., Dempsey, J., Dabiri, C., & Shuman, H. H. (1978). A first-year follow-up of high-risk infants: Formulating a cumulative risk index. *Child Development, 49,* 119–131.

Final Report of the National Day Care Study: Child at the Center. Day Care Division. (1979, June). Administration for Children, Youth, and Families. Office of Human Development Services. U.S. Department of Health, Education, and Welfare (Contract No. 105–74–1100). Abt Associates.

Fowler, W., & Khan, N. (1974). *The later effects of infant group care: A followup study.* Toronto: Institute for Studies in Education.

Freud, S. (1950). *Analysis, terminable and interminable.* In Collected Papers, Vol. 5. London: Hogarth Press.

Fullard, W., McDevitt, S. C., & Carey, W. B. (1978). *The Toddler Temperament Scale (1–3 year old children).* Unpublished manuscript.

Gesell, A. (1937). Early evidence of individuality in the human infant. *Journal of Genetic Psychology, 45,* 217–225.

Goldberg, S. (1983). Parent-infant bonding: Another look. *Child Development, 54,* 1355–1382.

Golden, M., & Birns, B. (1976). Social class and infant intelligence. In M. Lewis (Ed.), *Origins of intelligence.* New York: Plenum.

Golden, M., Rosenbluth, L., Grossi, M., Policare, H., Freeman, H., & Brownlee, E. (1978). *The New York City Infant Day Care Study.* New York: Medical and Health Research Association of New York City.

Goldstein, A., & Pentz, M. (1984). Psychological skill training and the aggressive adolescent. *School Psychology Review, 13,* 311–324.

Goldstein, A., Sprafkin, R., Gershaw, N., & Klein, P. (1980). The adolescent: Social skills training through structural learning. In G. Cartledge & G. Milburn (Eds.), *Teaching social skills to children.* New York: Pergamon.

Gorski, P. A., Davison, M. F., & Brazelton, T. B. (1979). Stages of behavioral organization in the high-risk neonate: Theoretical and clinical considerations. *Seminars in Perinatology, 3,* 61–72.

Gottman, J. M. (1977). Toward a definition of social isolation in children. *Child Development, 48,* 513–517.

Gresham, F. M. (1979). Comparison of response cost and timeout in a special education setting. *Journal of Special Education, 13,* 199–208.

Gresham, F. (1981). Social skills training with handicapped children: A review. *Review of Educational Research, 51,* 139–176.

Gresham, F., & Elliott, S. (1984). Assessment and classification of children's social skills: A review of methods and issues. *School Psychology Review, 13,* 292–301.

Gresham, F. M., & Nagle, R. J. (1980). Social skills training with children: Responses to modeling and coaching as a function of peer orientation. *Journal of Consulting and Clinical Psychology, 48,* 718–729.

Harris, J. D., Eisenberg, N., & Carroll, J. L. (1982). Facilitating prosocial behavior in children. In T. Kratochwill (Ed.), *Advances in school psychology.* Vol. 2. Hillsdale, NJ: Erlbaum.

Haskins, R. (1985). Public school aggression among children with varying day-care experience. *Child Development, 56,* 689–703.

Hertzig, M. E., & Mittleman, M. (1984). Temperament in low birth weight children. *Merrill-Palmer Quarterly, 30,* 201–211.

Hess, R. D. (1970). Social class and ethnic influences on socialization. In P. H. Mussen (Ed.), *Carmichael's manual of child psychology.* Vol. 2. New York: Wiley.

Hock, E. (1980). Working and nonworking mothers and their infants: A comparative study of maternal caregiving characteristics and infant social behavior. *Merrill-Palmer Quarterly, 26,* 79–102.

Hofland, B. F., Willis, S. L., & Baltes, P. B. (1981). Fluid intelligence performance in the elderly: Intraindividual variability and conditions of assessment. *Journal of Educational Psychology, 73,* 573–586.

Horn, J. L. (1970). Organization of data on life-span development of human abilities. In L. R. Goulet & P. B. Baltes (Eds.), *Life-span developmental psychology: Research and theory.* New York: Academic Press.

Horn, J. L., & Donaldson, G. (1976). On the myth of intellectual decline in adulthood. *American Psychologist, 31,* 701–719.

Horn, J. L., & Donaldson, G. (1977). Faith is not enough: A response to the Baltes-Schare claim that intelligence does not wane. *American Psychologist, 32,* 369–373.

Hornblum, N. J., & Overton, W. F. (1976). Area and volume conservation among the elderly: Assessment and training. *Developmental Psychologist, 12,* 68–74.

Howes, C., & Olenick, M. (1986). Family and child care influences on toddler's compliance. *Child Development, 57,* 202–216.

Hunt, J. McV. (1969). Has compensatory education failed? Has it been attempted? *Harvard Educational Review, 39,* 278–300.

Hymel, S. (1983). Preschool children's peer relations: Issues in sociometric assessment. *Merrill-Palmer Quarterly, 29,* 237–260.

Jensen, A. R. (1969). How much can we boost IQ and scholastic achievement? *Harvard Educational Review, 39,* 1–123.

Keyserling, M. D. (1972). *Windows on day care.* New York: National Council of Jewish Women.

Klaus, M., & Kennell, J. (1976). *Maternal-infant bonding.* St. Louis: Mosby.

Kohn, M. (1963). Social class and parent-child relationships: An interpretation. *American Journal of Sociology, 68,* 471–480.

Krasnor, L., & Rubin, K. (1983). Preschool social problem solving: Attempts and outcomes in naturalistic interaction. *Child Development, 54,* 1545–1558.

Ladd, G., & Mize, J. (1983). A cognitive-social learning model of social-skill training. *Psychological Review, 90,* 127–157.

LaGreca, A. M., & Santogrossi, D. A. (1980). Social skills training with elementary school students: A behavioral group approach. *Journal of Consulting and Clinical Psychology, 48,* 220–227.

Lamb, M. E. (1982). Early contact and maternal infant bonding: One decade later. *Pediatrics, 70,* 763–768.

Lamb, M. E. & Hwang, C. P. (1982). Maternal attachment and mother-neonate bonding: A critical review. In M. E. Lamb & A. L. Brown (Eds.), *Advances in developmental psychology.* (Vol. 2). Hillsdale, NJ: Erlbaum.

Lazar, I., & Darlington, R. (1982). Lasting effects of early education: A report from the consortium for longitudinal studies. *Monographs of the Society for Research in Child Development, 47,* Serial No. 195, 1–151.

Lee, C. L., & Bates, J. E. (1985). Mother-child interaction at age two years and perceived difficult temperament. *Child Development, 56,* 1314–1325.

Lester, B. M., Hoffman, J., & Brazelton, T. B. (1985). The rhythmic structure of mother-infant interaction in term and preterm infants. *Child Development, 56,* 15–27.

Libet, J. M., & Lewinsohn, P. M. (1973). Concept of social skills with specific reference to the behavior of depressed persons. *Journal of Consulting and Clinical Psychology, 40,* 304–312.

Lieberman, A. F. (1977). Preschoolers' competence with a peer: Relations with attachment and peer experience. *Child Development, 48,* 1277–1287.

Londerville, S., & Main, M. (1981). Security of attachment, compliance, and maternal training methods in the second year of life. *Developmental Psychology, 17,* 289–299.

Lorenz, K. (1935/1970). Companions as factors in the bird's environment. In K. Lorenz (Ed.), *Studies in animal and human behavior* (Vol. 1). Cambridge, MA: Harvard University Press.

Lütkenhaus, P., Grossman, K. E., & Grossman, K. (1985). Infant-mother attachment at twelve months and style of interaction with a stranger at the age of three years. *Child Development, 56,* 1538–1542.

MacMillan, D. L., & Morrison, G. M. (1980). Correlates of social status among mildly handicapped learners in self-contained special classes. *Journal of Educational Psychology, 72,* 437–444.

Matas, L., Arend, R. A., & Stroufe, L. A. (1978). Continuity in adoption: Quality of attachment and later competence. *Child Development, 49,* 547–556.

Matson, J., Esveldt-Dawson, K., & Kazdin, A. E. (1983). Validation of methods for assessing social skills in children. *Journal of Clinical Child Psychology, 12,* 174–180.

Matson, J. L., Kazdin, A. E., & Esveldt-Dawson, K. (1980). Training interpersonal skills among mentally retarded and socially dysfunctional children. *Behaviour Research and Therapy, 18,* 419–427.

McCutcheon, B., & Calhoun, K. (1976). Social and emotional adjustment of infants and toddlers to a day care setting. *American Journal of Orthopsychiatry, 46,* 104–108.

McDevitt, S. C., & Carey, W. B. (1978). The measurement of temperament in 3–7 year old children. *Journal of Child Psychology and Psychiatry, 19,* 242–253.

Moore, T. (1964). Children of full-time and part-time mothers. *International Journal of Social Psychiatry,* Special Congress Issue 2, 1–10.

Moore, T. (1975). Exclusive early mothering and its alternatives: The outcome to adolescence. *Scandinavian Journal of Psychiatry, 16,* 255–272.

Moskowitz, D., Schwarz, J., & Corsini, D. (1977). Initiating day care at three years of age: Effects on attachment. *Child Development, 48,* 1271–1276.

Mussen, P. (1977, August). *Choices, regrets, and lousy models (with reference to prosocial development).* Presidential address, Division 7, Annual meeting of the American Psychological Association, San Francisco.

Mussen, P., & Eisenberg-Berg, N. (1977). *Roots of caring, sharing, and helping: The development of prosocial behavior in children.* San Francisco: W. H. Freeman.

National Childcare Consumer Study. (1975). Washington, DC: Office of Child Development, Department of Health, Education, and Welfare.

Oden, S., & Asher, S. R. (1977). Coaching children in social skills for friendship making. *Child Development, 48,* 495–506.

Orlick, T. (1981). Positive socialization via cooperative games. *Developmental Psychology, 17,* 426–429.

Parmelee, A. H. (1974). *Newborn neurological examination, UCLA.* Unpublished manuscript.

Parmelee, A. H., & Haber, A. (1973). Who is the risk infant? *Clinical Obstetrics and Gynecology, 16,* 376–387.

Parmelee, A. H., Sigman, M., Kopp, C. B., & Haber, A. (1976). Diagnosis of the infant at high risk for mental, motor, and sensory handicaps. In T. D. Tjossem (Ed.), *Intervention strategies for high-risk infants and young children.* Baltimore: University Park Press.

Pastor, D. L. (1981). The quality of mother-infant attachment and its relationship to toddlers' initial sociability with peers. *Developmental Psychology, 17,* 326–335.

Pellegrini, D. (1985). Social cognition and competence in middle childhood. *Child Development, 56,* 253–264.

Plemons, J. K., Willis, S. L., & Baltes, P. B. (1978). Modifiability of fluid intelligence in aging: A short-term longitudinal training approach. *Journal of Gerontology, 33,* 224–231.

Portnoy, F., & Simmons, C. (1978). Daycare and attachment. *Child Development, 49,* 239–242.

Prechtl, H. F. R. (1963). The mother-child interaction in babies with minimal brain damage. In B. M. Foss (Ed.), *Determinants of infant behavior.* Vol. II. London: Methuen.

Prechtl, H. F. R., & Beintema, D. (1964). The neurological examination of the newborn infant. *Clinics Developmental Medicine* (Vol. 12). London: Heinmann.

Putallaz, M., & Gottman, J. (1981). An international model of children's entry into peer groups. *Child Development, 52,* 986–994.

Ragozin, A. S. (1980). Attachment behavior of day-care children: Naturalistic and laboratory observations. *Child Development, 51,* 409–415.

Raph, J. B., Thomas, A., Chess, S., & Korn, S. J. (1964). The influence of nursery school on social interactions. *Journal of Orthopsychiatry, 38,* 144–152.

Renshaw, P., & Asher, S. (1983). Children's goals and strategies for social interaction. *Merrill-Palmer Quarterly, 29,* 353–374.

Ricciuti, H. (1974). Fear and development of social attachments in the first year of life. In M. Lewis & L. A. Rosenblum (Eds.), *The origins of human behavior: Fear.* New York: Wiley.

Rinn, R., & Markle, A. (1979). Modification of social skills deficits in children. In A. Bellack & M. Hersen (Eds.), *Research and practice in social skills training.* New York: Plenum Press.

Roff, M., Sells, S., & Golden, M. (1972). *Social adjustment and personality development in children.* Minneapolis: University of Minnesota Press.

Roopnarine, J., & Lamb, M. (1978). The effects of day care on attachment and exploratory behavior in a strange situation. *Merrill-Palmer Quarterly, 24,* 85–95.

Rosenblatt, J. S. (1967). Nonhormonal basis of maternal responsiveness in the rat. *Science, 156,* 1512–1515.

Rosenblatt, J. S. (1970). Views on the onset and maintenance of maternal behavior in the rat. In L. R. Aronson, J. S. Rosenblatt, & D. S. Lehrman (Eds.), *Development and evolution of behavior.* Vol. 1. San Francisco: Freeman.

Roth, K., Eisenberg, N., & Sell, E. R. (1984). The relation of preterm and full-term infants' temperament to test-taking behaviors and developmental status. *Infant Behavior and Development, 7,* 495–505.

Rothbaum, R., Zigler, E., & Hyson, M. C. (1981). Modeling, praising, and collaborating: Effects of adult behavior on children of same sex and opposite sex. *Journal of Experimental Child Psychology, 31,* 403–423.

Rotheram, M. (1980). Social skills training programs in elementary and high school classrooms. In D. Rathjen & J. Foreyt (Eds.), *Social competence: Interventions for children and adults.* New York: Pergamon.

Rubenstein, J. L., Howes, C., & Boyle, P. (1981). A two-year follow-up of infants in community based infant day care. *Journal of Child Psychology and Psychiatry, 22,* 209–218.

Sameroff, A. J., & Chandler, M. (1975). Reproductive risks and the continuum of care-taking causality. In F. D. Horowitz (Ed.), *Review of Child Development Research* (Vol. 4). Chicago: University of Chicago Press.

Scarr-Salapatek, S. (1971). Unknowns in the IQ equation. *Science, 174,* 1223–1228.

Schaie, K. E., & Baltes, P. B. (1977). Some faith helps to see the forest: A final comment on the Horn and Donaldson myth of the Baltes-Schaie position on adult intelligence. *American Psychologist, 32,* 1118–1120.

Schaps, E., Cooper, C., Ritchey, W., & Tuck, P. (1982, July). *The Child Development Project: A school and home based program for promoting prosocial development.* Presented at meetings of International Association for the Study of Cooperation in Education, Provo, Utah.

Schwarz, J. C., Strickland, R. B., & Krolick, G. (1974). Infant day care: Behavioral effects at preschool age. *Developmental Psychology, 10,* 502–506.

Schwartz, P. M. (1983). Length of daily separation due to child care and attachment behaviors of 18-month-old infants. *Child Development,* 1073–1078.

Sears, R. R. (1975). Your ancients revisited: A history of child development. In E. M. Hetherington (Ed.), *Review of child development research,* Vol. 5. Chicago: University of Chicago Press.

Shantz, C. U. (1983). Social cognition. In P. H. Mussen (Ed.), *Handbook of child psychology: Cognitive Development,* Vol. 3. New York: Wiley.

Shirley, M. M. (1933). *The first two years: A study of 25 babies.* Minneapolis: University of Minnesota Press.

Singleton, L. C., & Asher, S. R. (1977). Peer preferences and social interaction among third-grade children in an integrated school district. *Journal of Educational Psychology, 69,* 330–336.

Smith, M. S., & Bissel, J. S. (1970). The impact of Head Start: The Westinghouse-Ohio Head Start Evaluation. *Harvard Educational Review, 40,* 51–104.

Solomon, D., Watson, M., Battistich, V., & Schaps, E. (1986, April). *Promoting behavior in schools: An interim report on a five-year longitudinal intervention program.* Paper presented at the meeting of the American Educational Research Association, San Francisco, CA.

Spivack, G., & Shure, M. (1974). *Social adjustment of young children: A cognitive approach to solving real-life problems.* San Francisco: Jossey-Bass.

Sprigle, J. E., & Schaefer, L. (1985). Longitudinal evaluation of the effects of two compensatory preschool programs on fourth- through sixth-grade students. *Developmental Psychology, 21,* 702–708.

Staub, E. (1979). *Positive social behavior and morality. Vol. 2. Socialization and development.* New York: Academic Press.

Stayton, D. J., Hogan, R., & Ainsworth, M. D. S. (1971). Infant obedience and maternal behavior: The origins of socialization reconsidered. *Child Development, 42,* 1057–1069.

Stephens, T. M. (1979). *Social behavior assessment.* Columbus, OH: Cedars Press.

Stephens, T. M. (1980). *Technical information: Social behavioral assessment.* Columbus, OH: Cedars Press.

Strain, P. S., Kerr, M. M., & Ragland, E. U. (1979). Effects of peer-mediated social initiations and prompting/reinforcement procedures on the social behavior of autistic children. *Journal of Autism and Developmental Disorders, 9,* 41–54.

Strain, P., & Timm, M. (1974). An experimental analysis of "spillover" effects on the social interaction of behaviorally handicapped preschool children. *Journal of Applied Behavior Analysis, 7,* 583–590.

Stumme, V. A., Gresham, F. M., & Scott, N. A. (1982). Validity of Social Behavior Assessment in discriminating emotionally disabled from nonhandicapped students. *Journal of Behavioral Assessment, 4, 327*–342.

Thomas, A., & Chess, S. (1977). *Temperament and development.* New York: Brunner/Mazel.

Thomas, A., Chess, S., & Birch, H. G. (1968). *Temperament and behavior disorders in children.* New York: New York University Press.

Tolan, K., & Krantz, M. (1981). Reward allocation and friendship in preschool children. *Journal of Genetic Psychology, 138,* 207–217.

Tronick, E., Wise, S., Als, H., Adamson, L., Scanlon, J., & Brazelton, T. B. (1976). Regional obstetric anesthesia and newborn behavior: Effect over the first ten days of life. *Journal of Pediatrics, 58,* 94–100.

Van Hassselt, V. B., Hersen, M., & Bellack, A. S. (1981). The validity of role play tests for assessing social skills in children. *Behavior Therapy, 12,* 202–216.

Vaughn, B. E., Gove, F. L., & Egeland, B. (1980). The relationship between out-of-home care and the quality of infant-mother attachment in an economically disadvantaged population. *Child Development, 51,* 1203–1214.

Vlietstra, A. G. (1981). Full versus half-day preschool attendance: Effect in young children as assessed by teacher ratings and behavioral observations. *Child Development, 52,* 603–610.

Walker, H. M. (1970). *The Walker problem behavior identification checklist. Test and manual.* Los Angeles: Western Psychological Services.

Waters, E., Wippman, J., & Sroufe, L. A. (1979). Attachment, positive affect, and competence in peer group: Two studies in construct validation. *Child Development, 50,* 821–829.

Wasserman, G. A., Allen, R., & Solomon, C. R. (1985). At-risk toddlers and their mothers: The special case of physical handicap. *Child Development, 56,* 73–83.

Widmayer, S., & Field, T. (1981). Effects of Brazelton demonstrations for mothers in the development of preterm infants. *Pediatrics, 67,* 711–714.

Willis, S. L., Blieszner, R., & Baltes, P. B. (1981). Intellectual training research in aging: Modification of performance on the fluid ability of figural relations. *Journal of Educational Psychology, 73,* 41–50.

Wynn, R. L. (1979, March). *The effect of playmates on day care and home-reared toddlers in a strange situation.* Paper presented at the biennial meeting of the Society for Research in Child Development, San Francisco.

Appendix A

Boydstun, J. E., Sherry, M. E., & Moelter, N. P. (1977). Patrol staffing in San Diego: One or two-officer units. Washington, DC: Police Foundation.

Campbell, D. T. (1981). Introduction: Getting ready for the experimenting society. In L. Saxe and M. Fine, *Social experiments: Methods for design and evaluation.* Beverly Hills, CA: Sage.

Cook, T. D. (1973). "Sesame Street" and the medical and tailored models of summative evaluation research. In J. G. Abert & M. Kamrass (Eds.), Social experiments and social program evaluation. Cambridge, MA: Ballinger.

Coursey, R. D. (1977). Basic questions and tasks. In R. D. Coursey (Ed.), *Program evaluation for mental health: Methods, strategies, participants.* New York: Grune & Stratton.

Definitions and Classification Committee. (1973). Mental health statistics series #8: Definition of terms in mental health, alcohol abuse, drug abuse, and mental retardation. Washington, DC: National Institute of Mental Health.

Earle, H. H. (1973). Police recruit training: Stress vs. nonstress. Springfield, IL: Charles C. Thomas.

Edwards, D. D. (1988). Aspirin cuts risk of heart attack. *Science News, 133,* 68.

Hennigan, K. M., DelRosario, M. L., Heath, L., Cook, T. D., Wharton, J. D., & Calder, B. J. (1982). Impact of the introduction of television on crime in the United States: Empirical findings and theoretical implications. *Journal of Personality and Social Psychology, 42,* 461–477.

Posavac, E. J., & Carey, R. G. (1980). *Program evaluation: Methods and case studies.* Englewood Cliffs, NJ: Prentice-Hall.

Rossi, P., & Lyall, K. C. (1976). *Reforming public welfare: A critique of the negative income tax experiment.* New York: Russell Sage Foundation.

Thompson, M. S. (1980). *Benefit-cost analysis for program evaluation.* Beverly Hills, CA: Sage.

Acknowledgments

Credits for photographs, illustrations, and quoted material not given on the page where they appear are listed below.

PHOTO CREDITS
Unless otherwise acknowledged, all photos are the property of Scott, Foresman and Company.

Part 1 1 Reprinted from *Psychology Today* magazine, Copyright © 1987 American Psychological Association

Chapter 1
3 Bohdan Hrnewych/ Stock Boston
5 Walter P. Reuther Library/The Archives of Labor and Urban Affairs, Wayne State Univ.
7 Courtesy U.S. Coast Guard

Chapter 2
25 Hazel Hankin, Stock Boston
27 Reprinted from *Psychology Today* magazine, Copyright © 1986 American Psychological Association
34 David R. Frazier Photolibrary
38 Courtesy United States Air Force

Part 2 41 Ellis Herwig/ The Picture Cube

Chapter 3
43 Craig Hammell/ The Stock Market
50 Joe McNally/General Electric/RCA/Wheeler Pictures
52 Photri, Inc.
59 Peter Menzel/Stock Boston

Chapter 4
77 Peter Menzel/Stock Boston
84 Peter Menzel/Stock Boston
97 Donald Dietz, Stock Boston
100 Jon Feingersh/ The Stock Market
106 Peter Menzel/Stock Boston
114 Brian Seed/Click/ Chicago Ltd.
117 David R. Frazier Photolibrary
121 Ellis Herwig/Stock Boston

Chapter 5
128 Darryl Baird, Lightwave
138 Jacques Charlas/Stock Boston

142 Jon Feingersh/The Stock Market
144 Lynn Johnson/Black Star
149 Suzanne Szasz/Photo Researchers

Chapter 6
156 Courtesy of Pre-college Program, Gallaudet College, Kendall Green, Washington, DC
159 Mike Penney/David R. Frazier Photolibrary
170 George Kufrin/Click, Chicago Ltd.
175 John Coletti/Stock Boston

Chapter 7
185 Gabor Demjen/Stock Boston
189 Paul Solomon/Wheeler Pictures
194 Nancy D'Antonio/Photo Researchers
198 H. Armstrong Roberts
206 R. Solomon/Monkmeyer Press Photo Service
207 Owen Franken/Stock Boston

Part 3 211 Mimi Forsyth/ Monkmeyer Press Photo Service

Chapter 8
215 Sybil Shelton/Peter Arnold, Inc.
229 Allan Grant
232 Don Hogan Charles/NYT Pictures

Chapter 9
263 George Bellerose/Stock Boston
265 Mimi Forsyth/ Monkmeyer Press Photo Service
271 Ellis Herwig/Stock Boston

Chapter 10
281 Ed Kashi
289 Ed Kashi
292 Randy Duchaine/The Stock Market
294 Richard Pasley/Stock Boston
298 Elizabeth Crews/Stock Boston

Chapter 11
310 MacDonald Photography/ The Picture Cube
313 Judy S. Gelles/Stock Boston

Chapter 12
334 UPI/Bettmann Newsphotos
338 Ferry/Gamma-Liaison
346 Ellis Herwig/Stock Boston
348–349 Photos reproduced from R. Buckhout, D. Figueroa, and E. Hoff. Eyewitness identification from

photographs. *Bulletin of the Psychonomic Society,* 1975, 6(1), 71–74. Photographs copyright Robert Buckhout, 1973.
351 Camerique
360 Rhoda Sidney/Southern Light

Chapter 13
379 Bob Berger/Science Digest
385 Peter Southwick/Stock Boston
387 Ellis Herwig/Stock Boston
388 Jean-Claude Lejeune/Stock Boston

Part 4 401 Pete Saloutos/ The Stock Market

Chapter 14
407 Peter Vandermark/Stock Boston
409 Mike Penney/David R. Frazier Photolibrary
414 Arthur Grace/Stock Boston
416 Paul Conklin/Monkmeyer Press Photo Service

Chapter 15
428 David Madison
436 David Madison
438 David Madison
439 David Madison
447 David Madison
450 David Madison

Chapter 16
462 Suzanne Szasz/Photo Researchers
467 J. T. Miller/The Stock Market
473 Peter Menzel/Stock Boston
479 Laimute E. Druskis/Stock Boston
482 Christopher Vail
486 Joe McNally/Wheeler Pictures
494 Dean Abramson/Stock Boston

FIGURES AND TABLES
Chapter 3
57 Fig. 3.4 From *Man-Machine Engineering* by A. Chapanis. Copyright © 1965 by Wadsworth Publishing Company, Inc. Reprinted by permission of Brooks/Cole Publishing Company, Pacific Grove, California.
58 Fig. 3.5 From *Man-Machine Engineering* by A. Chapanis. Copyright © 1965 by Wadsworth Publishing Company, Inc. Reprinted by permission of Brooks/Cole Publishing Company, Pacific Grove, California.
Fig. 3.6 From "Evaluation of Sym-

bolic Public Information Signs" by J. Mackett-Stout and R. Dewar. From *Human Factors,* 1981, Vol. 23 (2), p. 142. Copyright 1981 by the Human Factors Society, Inc., and reproduced by permission.
67 Fig. 3.12 "Human Factors, Photographic Space, and Disc Photography," by T. W. Faulkner and T. M. Rice, from Proceedings of the Human Factors Society 26th Annual Meeting 1982, Figure 1. Copyright 1982 by the Human Factors Society, Inc., and reproduced by permission.
68 Fig. 3.13 "Human Factors, Photographic Space, and Disc Photography," by T. W. Faulkner and T. M. Rice, from Proceedings of the Human Factors Society 26th Annual Meeting 1982, Figure 2. Copyright 1982 by the Human Factors Society, Inc., and reproduced by permission.
69 Fig. 3.14 From "The Influence of Camera Configuration on Preference" by T. W. Faulkner, T. M. Rice, and W. K. Heron, from *Human Factors* Vol. 25 (2) 1983. Copyright 1982 by the Human Factors Society, Inc., and reproduced by permission.
70 Fig. 3.15 From "The Influence of Camera Configuration on Preference" by T.W. Faulkner, T.M. Rice, and W.K. Heron, from *Human Factors* Vol. 25 (2) 1983. Copyright by the Human Factors Society, Inc., and reproduced by permission.

Chapter 4
82 Table 4.1 Reprinted with permission of Macmillan Publishing Company from *Psychology and Industry Today* by Duane P. Schultz and Sydney Ellen Schultz. Copyright © 1986 by Duane P. Schultz.

98 Fig. 4.3 From Ernest J. McCormick/Daniel Ilgen, *Industrial Psychology,* 7e, © 1980, p. 137. Adapted by permission of Prentice Hall, Inc., Englewood Cliffs, New Jersey.
109 Table 4.3 From Janis, Irving L., *Groupthink,* Second Edition, Copyright © 1982 by Houghton Mifflin Company. Used with permission.
110 Fig. 4.5 From J. Richard Hackman, "The Design of Work Teams," in *Handbook of Organizational Behavior,* Lorsch, ed., © 1987, p. 325. Reprinted by permission of Prentice-Hall, Inc., Englewood Cliffs, New Jersey.
224 Table 8.2 Adaptation of Table 5 from "The Employment of APA Members" by J. Stapp and R. Fulcher, 1981, *American Psychologist, 36,* p. 1285. Copyright 1981 by the American Psychological Association.

Chapter 8
233 Fig. 8.1 From "Factors Determining Vicarious Extinction of Avoidance Behavior" by A. Bandura, J. R. Grusec, and F. L. Menlove, 1967, *Journal of Personality and Social Psychology, 8,* p. 21. Copyright 1967 by the American Psychological Association. Reprinted by permission of the author.
234 Fig. 8.2 From "Factors Determining Vicarious Extinction of Avoidance Behavior through Symbolic Modeling" by A. Bandura and F. L. Menlove, 1968. *Journal of Personality and Social Psychology, 8,* p. 102. Copyright 1968 by the American Psychological Association. Reprinted by permission of the author.
236 Fig. 8.3 From "The Relative Efficacy of Desensitization and Modeling Approaches for Inducing

Behavioral, Affective, and Attitudinal Changes" by A. Bandura, E. B. Blanchard, and B. Ritter, 1969, *Journal of Personality and Social Psychology, 5,* p. 183. Copyright 1969 by the American Psychological Association. Reprinted by permission of the author.
238 Fig. 8.4 From "Cognitive Processes Mediating Behavioral Change" by A. Bandura, N. E. Adams, and J. Beyer, 1977, *Journal of Personality and Social Psychology, 35,* p. 131. Copyright 1977 by the American Psychological Association. Reprinted by permission of the author.
239 Fig. 8.5 From "Cognitive Processes Mediating Behavioral Change" by A. Bandura, N. E. Adams, and J. Beyer, 1977, *Journal of Personality and Social Psychology, 35,* p. 133. Copyright 1977 by the American Psychological Association. Reprinted by permission of the author.

Chapter 13
389 Fig. 13.1 From "Reducing the Stress of High-Density Living" by A. Baum and G. E. Davis, 1980, *Journal of Personality and Social Psychology, 38,* p. 475. Copyright 1980 by the American Psychological Association. Adapted by permission of the author.

Chapter 15
440 Table 15.2 Reprinted by permission of the American Alliance for Health, Physical Education, Recreation, and Dance, 1900 Association Drive, Reston, VA 22091.

Chapter 16
488 Fig. 16.1 Copyright © 1983 by the Society for Research in Child Development, Inc.

Index